Greenhill Books

CROMWELL'S
ARMY

CROMWELL'S ARMY

A HISTORY OF THE ENGLISH
SOLDIER DURING THE CIVIL WARS,
THE COMMONWEALTH
AND THE PROTECTORATE

C H FIRTH, MA

with a new introduction
by JOHN ADAIR

Greenhill Books, London
Presidio Press, California

This edition of *Cromwell's Army* first published 1992
by Greenhill Books, Lionel Leventhal Limited, Park House,
1 Russell Gardens, London NW11 9NN
and
Presidio Press,
P.O. Box 1764, Novato, Ca.94948, U.S.A.

British Library Cataloguing in Publication Data
Firth, Sir Charles Harding
Cromwell's Army: History of the English Soldier During the
Civil Wars, the Commonwealth and the Protectorate. – New ed
I. Title   355.00941

ISBN 1–85367–120–7

Library of Congress Cataloging-in-Publication Data available

Publishing History
*Cromwell's Army: A History of the English Soldier during the Civil
Wars, the Commonwealth and the Protectorate* by C. H. Firth, M.A.,
was first published in 1902 (Methuen). A second edition was
published in 1912 and a third, revised edition, on which this reprint
is based, in 1921. This 1992 edition reproduces the entire text,
complete and unabridged, from the third and last edition, and has
had added to it a New Introduction by John Adair.

Printed and bound in Great Britain by
Biddles Limited, Guildford and King's Lynn

Contents

THE COUNCIL OF THE ARMY
From a woodcut prefixed to the collection of the Army's
Declarations published by Matthew Simmons in September, 1647.

Introduction

UNTIL THE PUBLICATION of *Cromwell's Army* in 1902, the New Model Army was one of the puzzles of history. What was the secret of its string of military successes? How did it differ from its predecessors? When and why did it become involved in politics? These are the questions that Sir Charles Firth set out to answer in his pioneer book.

Firth subtitled his study *A History of the English Soldier during the Civil Wars, the Commonwealth and the Protectorate*. During the First Civil War, as most people know, Oliver Cromwell did not actually command any of the three main Parliamentarian armies, serving no higher than a second-in-command as Lieutenant General of Horse in the Earl of Manchester's Army and also to Sir William Waller in 1645. Nor did he replace Fairfax as Commander-in-Chief of the New Model Army until the latter's resignation in June 1650. And so *Cromwell's Army* must not be taken too literally as a title: the scope of the book is much wider than that. But then local historians of the Civil War are wearily accustomed to having Cromwell's name attached to every battlefield, siegework, battery or burial mound!

On re-reading *Cromwell's Army* one is constantly surprised at how little Firth's account has dated. That is because Firth, as a true scholar, kept close to his primary sources, which cannot date. For later historians of the English Parliamentarian armies of the period, Firth was a hard act to follow, which probably explains why there has been no similar reconstruction on such a large scale of the operational capabilities and daily life of the New Model Army. However much one knows about the period it is impossible not to learn more about the English soldier and his art by quarrying again in this veritable mine of information.

Like all large canvasses, however, that are approaching a century in age, Firth's panorama does need some restorative work. Historical study has not stood still. Although *Cromwell's Army* is still an excellent introduction to the subject, students today can supplement and correct Firth by recourse to other more specialised books. An obvious example is the companion study that Firth himself compiled with the assistance of Godfrey Davies, an almost encyclopaedic history of the various units of the New Model Army published in two volumes in 1940 and entitled *The Regimental History of Cromwell's Army*.

When new editions of *Cromwell's Army* appeared in 1912 and 1921, Firth added two more prefaces to his original one (reproduced below) in which he listed books then recently published on his subject or some aspect of it. These later prefaces have been omitted here, not least because some of the books that Firth mentioned have not stood the tests of time as well as his own books have done. But Firth set a useful precedent which I shall try to follow here. Imagining myself as Firth, I have listed here the supplementary or complementary books or studies which I feel sure Firth himself would have selected had we been fortunate enough to have had him writing this introduction. In doing so I have been greatly helped by Dr Ian Roy of King's College London, one of our leading scholars of this period of military history.

In his opening sentence Firth identifies his main theme: 'The history of the Civil War is the history of the evolution of an efficient army out of a chaos.' This judgement does now have to be tempered. Reading the two magisterial studies on Tudor armies by C. G. Cruikshank, *Elizabeth's Army* (second edition 1966) and *Army Royal: Henry VIII's Invasion of France 1513* (1969), gives one a much more accurate picture of the army before the Civil War than the one that meets the eye in Firth's opening chapter. The army that Henry VIII assembled and led with indifferent skill was far from being 'a chaos'. Responding to Firth's charge in this book that the military system which the Tudors bequeathed to the Stuarts was completely inefficient, Cruikshank comments: 'While this is entirely true as far as it goes, it leaves on one side the effort by Elizabeth and her Privy Council to make the system more efficient.'

Again, Firth tended to overemphasise the differences of quality between the New Model Army and its immediate predecessors: the armies of Essex, Waller and Manchester. My own studies of Waller's Army in *Roundhead General: The Life of Sir William Waller* (1969) and *Cheriton 1644: The Campaign and the Battle* (1973) are relevant in this respect. For example, in the latter I published for the first time the court martial papers of Waller's Army in 1644, which at least shows us a care for discipline not inferior to that in the New Model Army, in which many of Waller's better officers were to serve. Clive Holmes in his *The Eastern Association and the English Civil War* (1974), equally enlightens us about Manchester's Army but we still lack a comparable study of Essex's army.

Such local confederations as the Eastern Association were made up, of course, of counties – the bricks of civil and military administration. Firth mentioned some of the early county studies but a great deal more work has been done in this area in the last thirty years. Among the best are the pioneering study of Kent by A. M. Everitt, *The Community of Kent and the Great Rebellion* (1966), A. Fletcher, *A County Community in Peace and War; Sussex, 1600–1660* (1975), D. Underdown, *Somerset in the Civil War and Interregnum* (1973) and J. Morrill, *Cheshire, 1630–1660* (1974). A new model of the politics of the 'county community' in the period is offered by Ann Hughes in her *Politics, Society and Civil War in Warwickshire, 1620–1660* (1987), and much recent work in the administrative history of the war is summarised brilliantly in J. Morrill, *The Revolt of the Provinces* (1976). Also useful are the various contributions by different hands in the volume he edited, *Reactions to the English Civil War* (1982). Very up-to-date and readable are the short essays on different aspects of the war in his most recent volume *The Impact of the English Civil War* (1991).

Despite his subtitle, Firth does not have a great deal to say about the Royalist armies in the Civil War, except to contrast them with the Parliamentarian ones in certain respects. This is hardly surprising because the Cavalier army had received virtually no attention from historians during his lifetime. That want has now been largely remedied by Brigadier Peter Young, who graduated from the study of military history in Firth's Oxford in 1938. He became in a sense the C. H. Firth of the Royalist Army, with his *Edgehill 1642: The Campaign and the Battle* (1967) providing much the same sort of function as this book and his monumental unpublished card index of Royalist officers rivalling Firth and Davies on the regimental lists of the New Model (now lodged in the National Army Museum).

Later books such as Peter Young and Wilfred Emberton, *The Cavalier Army: Its Organisation and Everyday Life* (1974), Ronald Hutton, *The Royalist War Effort 1642–6* (1982), Joyce Lee Malcolm, *Caesar's Due: Loyalty and King Charles 1642–6* (1983) and Peter Young, *Naseby 1645: The Campaign and the Battle* (1985) have filled much of the picture. Ian Roy has also edited *The Royalist Ordnance Papers 1642–6* (2 vols, Oxfordshire Record Series, 1964, 1975). There is much more valuable research on the pay and organisation of the Royalist armies which is still buried in unpublished dissertations, notably Ian Roy, *The Royalist Army in the First Civil War* (Oxford D. Phil, 1963).

For the reader seeking further or complementary information on the typical arms, armour and artillery of the period – how they were used, who made them, what they looked like and what were their distinctive features – there is an excellent, well-illustrated Royal Armouries' publication by David Blackmore, entitled *Arms and Armour of the English Civil War* (1990). Blackmore makes much use of the outstanding collection at Littlecote House in Wiltshire, part of the equipment of Colonel Alexander Popham's troop of horse and company of foot in Waller's abortive 'new modelled' army of 1643. David Blackmore has also edited an important seventeenth-century military manual, Jacob de Gheyn's *The Exercise of Armes* (1986).

Yet Firth is still unsurpassed on the tactics of infantry, cavalry and dragoons in the battlefield. All that later military historians – both national and local – have done is to supply fresh shot and powder in the form of examples to what Firth describes so comprehensively. A possible exception relates to sieges, that most technical aspect of seventeenth-century warfare where studies such as Young and Embleton, *Sieges of the Great Civil War 1642–1646* (1978) and Christopher Duffy, *Siege Warfare: The Fortress in the Early Modern*

World 1494–1660 (1979) do add much more to Firth's brief chapter on that subject.

Firth's chapters on religion and politics in the Army should likewise be taken as no more than introductory. Those subjects are of course interwoven with the social composition of the New Model, both as far as officers and soldiers are concerned. Firth throws more light upon their backgrounds, political opinions and religious beliefs in the companion regimental history already mentioned. Some significant work has been done in this area by Mark Kishlansky in *The Rise of the New Model Army* (1979); it is especially valuable for the Army's politics in 1646–8. In brief, Kishlansky argues that the Army only became a politically and religiously radical force in the course of 1647. A further contribution recently published is Ian Gentles' *The New Model Army in England, Ireland and Scotland, 1645–1653* (1991). It reveals the importance of Londoners among the officers of the army, and also demonstrates that a high proportion of them, in relative terms, were Cromwell's own kin. On the much-debated question of the officers' social origins, Gentles' painstaking investigation demonstrates that, where known, most were of gentry or professional status.

Less easy to obtain are two studies concerned with the important topic of the machinery, and especially the financing, of the war on the Parliamentarian side, a matter on which Firth's generation of historians had too little to say. The introduction of D. Pennington and I. Roots to their edition of the order book of Parliament's county committee for Staffordshire, *The Committee of Stafford* (1957), is a classic of its kind: and an American doctoral thesis, J. S. Wheeler's *English Army Finance and Logistics, 1642–1660* (1980), deals competently with the 'sinews of war', without which the army's endeavours would scarcely have been possible.

As Firth explained in the introduction to *Cromwell's Army*, it would not normally be necessary, in a study of an army, to discuss its politics and its religion; but this was an unusual army, which the rank and file of, not just the officers, were quite prepared to formulate strongly held, if often diverse, political and religious views, and to use their muscle to influence decisions on these matters. Firth was the first to make available the classic text for any discussion of the army's opinions in 1647, the notes of William Clarke, Fairfax's secretary, on the Putney Debates. Nowadays the most popular edition is A. S. P. Woodhouse's *Puritanism and Liberty*, first published in 1938, but still in print (and in paperback). There have been differing interpretations of this and other sources, and the Levellers' influence on the soldiery, by Gentles, and by Mark Kishlansky; but for the moment the matter has been put largely beyond dispute by a superb piece of historical detective work, combined with masterly judgment, in A. Woolrych's *Soldiers and Statesmen: the General Council of the Army and its Debates, 1647–48* (1987). In Firth's day and later it was thought that a crucial influence in the radicalisation of the army was the fiery preaching of chaplains such as Hugh Peter and William Dell. But a new study by Anne Laurence, *Parliamentary Army Chaplains, 1642–1651* (1990), has shown that most were mainstream Puritans, who served for short periods only, and whose views reflected those of their commanders.

The presence, for the first time, of a standing army in the British Isles, and its role in the politics and government of the 1650s, is an important topic which Firth discussed in works other than *Cromwell's Army*. In particular his edition of the Clarke Papers threw light on the military government of Scotland, for Fairfax's secretary had gone on to occupy the same post under George Monck, the effective ruler of Protectoral Scotland. F. Dow, in *Cromwellian Scotland* (1979), newly appraised English military rule in the sister republic; and the third nation of the Interregnum union, where the impact of the Cromwellian conquest was most lasting, was the subject of T. Barnard's *Cromwellian Ireland* (1975).

General Edmund Ludlow was the military governor of Ireland until his dismissal by Cromwell for his hard-line republicanism, but it is less for this phase of his career than for the light shed on his character and beliefs that the discovery and publication of part of his memoir, *A Voyce from the Watch Tower*, edited by A. B. Worden for the Royal Historical Society's Camden series in 1978, was such a notable event.

Regardless of the political or religious views of its members a standing national army in peacetime was enough to arouse deep hostility in many an English breast. Lois Schwoerer's *No Standing Armies! Anti-Army Ideology in Seventeenth Century England* (1975) is another welcome American contribution to our understanding of seventeenth-century constitutional conflicts. Memories of marauding soldiers in the 1640s and of the major-generals in 1655–56 were proof enough to the natural critics that a standing army meant central interference, with over-mighty officers and their commissioners purging local administration and levying punitive taxes.

While Cromwell ruled, however, such critics made little headway. Sir William Waller, for example, who attempted with former generals to raise regiments so that Parliament could oppose the continued existence of the New Model Army, found himself in prison without trial for three years. When Cromwell interviewed him later he showed no signs of having known him previously. It had indeed become Cromwell's Army. Hence an understandable focus of interest on the man who made it his lengthened shadow. For Cromwell's career and the campaigns he conducted in all three nations, and some of the momentoes by which he is, occasionally erroneously, commemorated, are conveniently set out, along with much else of interest to the student of wars, in P. Gaunt's *The Cromwellian Gazetteer. An Illustrated Guide to Britain in the Civil War and Commonwealth* (1987). This volume is well supplied with maps of Cromwell's itineraries.

For an excellent recent collection of essays on different aspects of the man himself, the product of much new research, one can equally recommend *Oliver Cromwell and the English Revolution* (1990), edited by John Morrill.

Cromwell did not survive, but his army did. For the purely military sequel to *Cromwell's Army* you can do no better than to read about the establishment of the regular army, the direct ancestor or the British Army, in John Childs' *The Army of Charles II* (1976).

But it is not necessary to plough your way through these later works in order to understand what it was like to be a pikeman, or fire your musket or charge with the Ironsides, or to while away those long boring hours in camp or garrison. Firth was such a good historian and such a good writer that an extraordinarily accurate and vivid picture of that military life – not least its more mundane or humdrum aspects – leaps from his pages. Who can forget his account of the long and festering quarrel between Captain Francis Freeman and his colonel John Okey? Ostensibly it was over theology but it owed much more to what we would now diagnose as a personality clash. When Cromwell held an informal hearing of their mutual grievances Okey soon shifted his ground away from religion. He complained that Freeman, while riding at the head of his company on the journey to Scotland, had been heard to sing songs that were 'a grief to all godly Christians'.

Freeman protested that *New Oysters*, which he taught to some of his dragoons, and the other six or seven songs he sang himself, were not bawdy. (By consulting the words and music of *New Oysters* and *Here Dwells a Pretty Maid* – another of Freeman's songs – in Lewis Weinstock's *Songs and Marches of the Roundheads and Cavaliers* (1971), we can not only see that Freeman was right, but also sing or play in tune with Freeman ourselves). Cromwell wisely refrained from giving an opinion on the songs, but gravely told Freeman that since he and Okey could not work together it was best that he should immediately leave the regiment, promising him the court martial he desired to clear his name once the Scottish campaign was over. Whether he ever had that doubtful privilege or not, history – or at least Firth's history – does not relate.

It is for such glimpses of human nature, as well as for its wealth of facts and figures about the management of the New Model Army, that Sir Charles Firth's *Cromwell's Army* is to be valued today. The words of John Milton (who, incidentally, applied to become adjutant-general in Waller's Army in 1644), are here entirely apt: 'A good book is the precious life-blood of a master spirit, embalmed and treasured up on purpose to a life beyond life.'

JOHN ADAIR, 1992

Preface to the First Edition

IT IS NECESSARY to begin this book with an apology. A civilian who undertakes to write the history of an army courts many perils, and cannot hope to escape them all. The subject is full of pitfalls, which a little technical knowledge would enable a writer to avoid, and abounds with questions which it requires both technical knowledge and military experience to treat adequately. But though fully aware of the difficulty of the task and of the defects in my own equipment for it, I felt obliged to make the attempt. In studying the history of the Great Rebellion it became necessary for me to study every side of it, the military history as much as the political or the religious history. It was not enough to try to understand the characters of the leaders, and the beliefs and ideals of their parties. A civil war is not only the conflict of opposing principles, but the shock of material forces. It was necessary, therefore, to ask what the purely military causes were which led to the triumph of one cause, and the downfall of the other. How was it that the Parliament succeeded in creating an efficient army, while the King could not do so, and what was the secret of the efficiency of the New Model? When I began to seek the answers to these questions it became necessary to go farther than I had at first intended. The political histories of the period and the standard histories of the English army left many things unexplained, and there were many parts of the subject on which they gave me no light. It was necessary, therefore, to try to get to the bottom of the whole matter; and to endeavour to find out all the details of the organization of the army, even if those details appeared at first sight to have little bearing on the general result of the war. Because it was only by learning to understand the little things that it was possible to understand the important things, and to make certain of appreciating their significance. Chance threw into my way some papers which other inquirers into the military history of the seventeenth century had never seen, and by piecing together this new information with that which earlier writers had collected, it became possible to form a clear conception of the character and the organization of the army which fought under Fairfax and Cromwell.

A brief account of some of the authorities used in this compilation will show the chief sources of information accessible, and may be of use to future inquirers into the same subject. Four general histories of the army are of special value to any student of the Cromwellian Army. Francis Grose's *Military Antiquities Respecting the History of the English Army* (two volumes, ed. 1801) contains a collection of facts and evidence relating to every side of its subject. Sir Sibbald

Scott's *The British Army, Its Origin, Progress and Equipment* (three volumes, 1868–80) supplements and completes Grose on most points, and fills up the gaps in his treatise. Grose, for instance, says next to nothing on the subject of the Civil War, while Sir Sibbald Scott brings together a considerable amount of information relating to the armies of that period, although that particular portion of his book is still, in many respects, very defective. The best summary of the military development of England during the years between 1640 and 1660 is contained in the hundred pages devoted to that time by the Hon. J. W. Fortescue in his *History of the British Army* (two volumes, 1899). Colonel Clifford Walton's *History of the British Standing Army from 1660 to 1700* is a work of great and permanent value, founded on an exhaustive study of official records. Though dealing primarily with a later period, it throws much light upon the equipment and organization of the Cromwellian Army, for the army of Charles the Second followed in most points the system which had existed in the army disbanded in 1660, at all events whilst Monck was commander-in-chief.

A very large number of books on the art of war were published in England during the sixteenth and seventeenth centuries, many of which are of considerable historical value. Captain Cockle's *Bibliography of English Military Books up to 1642, and of Contemporary Foreign Works*, published in 1900, is an indispensable guide to this literature. These books, however, need to be used with great caution by anyone who is studying the organization and tactics of English armies during the Civil War. For the most part their authors describe the military systems which existed in foreign armies, and set forth the results of their experiences and observations in continental wars. Ward and Hexham, for instance, studied war in the Netherlands; Monro and Turner in the Swedish, Danish and German service. The Cromwellian Army borrowed more from the Swedish than from any other military system, but it followed no foreign model exactly, and had many peculiarities of its own. In its organization, and in many details of its tactics and equipment, it was essentially original and national. Hence the information which these books on the art of war afford requires to be sifted and tested before it is accepted as evidence about the English army. The most useful of all these books is Elton's *Complete Body of the Art Military* (1650 and 1659), for Elton's service was entirely in the armies of the Parliament, the Commonwealth and the Protectorate. Unfortunately, his title promises more than he performs, for he confines himself entirely to the subject of infantry, and devotes his attention chiefly to drill.

A mass of miscellaneous evidence relating to the history of the army is contained in pamphlets, newspapers, narratives of battles, and in the memoirs and correspondence of the different actors in the Civil War. The Journals of the two Houses of Parliament frequently contain not only records of important votes on military questions, but reports and other documents of great value. The *Calendars of the Domestic State Papers* supply details of every kind as to pay, equipment, and matters of administration in general. The collection of uncalendared papers in the Record Office, called *Exchequer Papers, Interregnum,* consists of about 300 bundles of papers, which include army accounts, warrants for the payment of officers and soldiers, bills for the purchase of stores and arms, muster-rolls, and other matter of the same kind. Much has been gathered from this source to explain and illustrate the practical working of the military system which existed during the period. Another source of information of great value is the collection of papers made by William Clarke, one of the secretaries attached to Fairfax's army from 1647 to 1649, and secretary to successive commanders in Scotland from 1651 to the Restoration. This collection, now in the Library of Worcester College, Oxford, contains the order-books of General Monck from 1654 to 1660. Monck was probably the best military administrator of the time, and his orders show what the ordinary routine was in all matters connected with the internal government of the army of occupation. Letters and papers from the same source concerning the military government of Scotland are also included in the two volumes entitled *Scotland and the Commonwealth,* and *Scotland and the Protectorate,* edited for the Scottish History Society by the present writer. The four volumes of *Clarke Papers,* published by the Camden Society and the Royal Historical Society, between 1891 and 1901, are also full of materials for the political, religious and administrative history of the Cromwellian Army.

From these various printed and manuscript sources the following chapters have been put together. There are many points in the military history of the period which, from the lack of the necessary evidence, still remain obscure. There are other points of interest which considerations of space have prevented me from discussing as fully as I should have desired. The volume does not aim at being an exhaustive treatise on the military history of the Civil War: it is an attempt to describe as clearly and as accurately as possible the salient features of Cromwell's military system and the character of the army which he organized.

C. H. FIRTH

THE
SOULDIERS
Pocket Bible :

Containing the most(if not all)those
places contained in holy Scripture,
which doe shew the qualifications of his
inner man, that is a fit Souldier to fight
the Lords Battels, both before he fight,
in the fight, and after the fight ;

Which Scriptures are reduced to severall heads, and fitly applyed to the
Souldiers severall occasions, and so may
supply the want of the whole Bible;
which a Souldier cannot conveniently
carry about him :

And may bee also usefull for any
Christian to meditate upon, now in
this miserable time of Warre.

Imprimatur, *Edm. Calamy:*

Jos.18. This Book of the Law shall not depart out
of thy mouth,but thou shalt meditate therein day
and night, that thou maist observe te doe according to all that is written therein, for then thou
shalt make thy way prosperous, and have good
successe.

Printed at *London* by *G.B.* and *R.W.* for
Aug:3ᵈ *G.C.* 1643.

CHAPTER I

The Army Before the Civil War

THE HISTORY OF the Civil War is the history of the evolution of an efficient army out of a chaos. The military system which the Tudors bequeathed to the Stuarts was completely inefficient. It had broken down long before the Tudor period ended. The defensive value of the Elizabethan army was never really tested, for the fleet alone succeeded in repelling every attempted invasion. But for offensive purposes a fleet by itself was insufficient, as the last years of Queen Elizabeth's reign proved. Without an army organized for service beyond seas it was impossible to bring the war with Spain to a conclusion, or to utilize the successes of the navy. The lack of such an army made the attack upon Lisbon in 1589 a failure, and the capture of Cadiz in 1596 a fruitless victory.[1]

It is difficult to realize the military impotence of England under the rule of James the First and his successor. But for its fleet the alliance of England would have been of little value to any continental power, and its hostility lightly regarded. The intervention of James and Charles in the European struggles of their time was feeble and futile, not only because there was no consistency in their policy and no skill in their diplomacy, but because the material force at their disposal was insufficient to strike an effective blow. As a recruiting ground, however, England was a valuable field for its allies, and James preferred to act as an auxiliary rather than as a principal. In 1620 the King's military advisers – a council of national defence which met irregularly and had no real authority – estimated that an army of 25,000 foot and 5,000 horse would be required for the defence of the Palatinate.[2] James decided to remain ostensibly

[1] Cf. Corbett, *The Successors of Drake,* pp. vii, 408–10; *Drake and the Tudor Navy,* ii, 320, 350

[2] Grose, *Military Antiquities,* i, 241.

neutral, and to leave the dominions of his son-in-law to be defended by English volunteers, equipped by a national subscription. The 2,200 men who sailed for Germany under the command of Sir Horace Vere were excellent fighting material and they were well officered. 'This regiment,' said a contemporary, 'was the gallantest for the persons and outward presence of men that in many ages hath appeared, either at home or abroad.' They proved their courage in the defence of Heidelberg, and Mannheim, and Frankenthal, but, too few for effective resistance, they could only make a useless sacrifice of their lives.[1] Then came an open breach with Spain, and in the summer of 1624 6,000 more volunteers were sent to Holland to assist the Dutch against the Spaniards. It would be difficult, thought an observer, to raise so many men without pressing, 'for our people do apprehend too much the hardships and miseries of soldiers in these times'.[2] So it proved, and in the autumn, when 12,000 men were to be raised to serve under Count Mansfield in Lower Germany, it was necessary to resort to impressment. 'Such a rabble of raw and poor rascals have not lightly been seen,' said one who saw them embark, 'and they go so unwillingly that they must rather be driven than led.'[3] They had good reason to be unwilling. They sailed in January 1625, so ill provided that 4,000 died before they landed in Holland, and by the following April scarce 1,200 of the 12,000 were left. Hardships and disease killed them without fighting. 'They die as fast,' said an English officer, 'as if God were not well pleased that a stranger should command our nation.'[4]

Charles was a bolder man than his father, and he intervened in the European conflict as a principal with English armies under native generals. In 1625 took place the expedition to Cadiz, in 1627 that to the Isle of Rhé, and each of them ended in disaster. The history of the expedition to Cadiz shows why. It was commanded by Sir Edward Cecil, an officer who had served long and with much distinction in the Dutch army.[5] Clarendon says that

---

[1] Markham, *Lives of Sir Francis and Sir Horace Vere*, pp. 397–419; Gardiner, *History of England*, iii, 364.

[2] Dalton, *Life of Sir Edward Cecil*, ii, 62, 81.

[3] Ibid., ii, 74–79.   [4] Ibid., ii, 86, 111.

[5] See Mr. C. Dalton's elaborate life of Cecil, which narrates and vindicates his military career; Clarendon, *Rebellion*, i, 85.

he 'had in truth little more of a Holland officer than the pride and formality', but it is not true. Cecil was not without capacity, and with trained soldiers he might have captured Cadiz as easily as Essex had done in 1596. His soldiers, however, were the pressed men of whom regiments meant for foreign service were usually composed under the later Tudors, and pressed men of the usual material.[1] 'In England,' wrote Barnaby Rich in 1587, 'when service happeneth we disburthen the prisons of thieves, we rob the taverns and alehouses of tosspots and ruffians, we scour both town and country of rogues and vagabonds.'[2] Men of substance and respectability paid to escape from impressment. For many press-masters, like Sir John Falstaff, 'misused the King's press damnably'.

'I press me none but good householders, yeomens sons,' said Sir John, 'I enquire me out contracted bachelors, such as had been asked twice in the banns, such a commodity of warm slaves as would as soon hear the devil as a drum.' Falstaff ransomed these unwilling recruits for £300, and filled up the room of his 150 yeomen's sons with 150 odd prodigals lately come from swine keeping. So lusty young men like Bullcalf went free, and Shadow and Feeble went to the wars.[3]

Many of Sir Edward Cecil's soldiers were of this kind. 'The number of lame, impotent, and unable men, unfit for actual service, is very great,' wrote one of his subordinates.[4] When the general took command of his army at Plymouth in September 1625, he found them undrilled, undisciplined and unarmed, though they had been idly waiting there for three months; and, moreover, though there were many old soldiers amongst these officers, most were inexperienced courtiers recommended by

[1] Dalton, ii, 112, 133.

[2] Rich, *A Pathway to Military Practice*, 1587, 4to. In another pamphlet called a *Dialogue between Mercury and an English Soldier*, written in 1574, Rich says: 'The pety constable, when he perceyveth the wars are in hand, foreseeing the toyles, the infinite perills, and troublesome travayles that is incident to souldyers, is loth that anye honest man, through his procurement should hazard himselfe amongst so many daungers; wherefore if within his office there hap to remayne any idle fellow, some dronkerd, or seditiouse quariler, a privy picker, or such a one as hath some skill in stealing of a goose, these shall be presented to the servyce of the Prince' (Quoted in the *Lancashire Lieutenancy*, I, xxii).

[3] *Henry VI*, pt. I, act iv, sc. 2; pt. II, act ii, sc. 2.

[4] Dalton, ii, 114.

Buckingham. Cecil worked hard, and in a month, armed, regimented and embarked his troops.[1] Then his troubles really began. As soon as they were on board it was discovered that many of their muskets were defective – some muskets had no touch-holes – the bullets were often too large for the barrels, and no one knew in what ship the bullet-moulds were to be found. They were put on short allowance of victuals at starting, and died by hundreds from bad food as they returned. They had no discipline, and even when sober they were ungovernable. When they reached Cadiz they were landed without any provisions in their knapsacks, and at the end of the first day's march they came across a storehouse full of Spanish wine, and all obedience was at an end.[2] 'What with their emptiness and the heat,' said a colonel, 'they became so drunk that in my life I never saw such beastliness; they knew not what they did or said, so that all the chiefs were in hazard to have their throats cut.'[3]

A few days later they embarked again, and as they marched off, 300 Spanish musketeers fell hotly upon their rear. 'We found the want of the use of their arms in our men,' continues the colonel, 'they made few or no shot to any purpose, blew up their powder, fled out of their order, and would hardly be persuaded to stand from a shameful flight.' The sailors fought well, but 'the landmen', asserted Cecil himself, 'were so ill exercised that when we came to employ them, they proved rather a danger to us than a strength, killing more of our own men than they did of the enemy'.[4]

Two years later took place Buckingham's expedition to the Isle of Rhé. The thin ranks of the Cadiz regiments were recruited by fresh supplies of pressed men, and this time the material both in men and arms was better than it had been in 1625. But the result was no better. Buckingham spent four months in besieging a third-rate fortress. As he drew off his diminished army, and abandoned the siege, the French fell upon him and cut his rearguard in pieces. The best of his officers died fighting,

[1] Ibid., ii, 130–2, 143.

[2] Ibid., ii, 154, 156, 179, 193, 195.

[3] Ibid., ii, 200, Sir William St. Leger to the Duke of Buckingham.

[4] Ibid., ii, 201, 213, 218, 221.

deserted by their soldiers, and out of 8,000 men who landed in the island not much more than 3,000 returned to England.[1]

Let us consider now the provision made for the defence of the nation. For home defence the military system was based on the duty of every man to serve when the country was invaded. As in Elizabeth's time men who held estates of a certain value, or by a certain tenure, were bound to provide armed horsemen, while every other man above sixteen who was capable of bearing arms could be called upon to serve as a foot soldier. Elizabeth had ordered that in every county from the general mass 'a convenient number of able men' should be selected – men 'meet to be sorted in bands, and to be trained and exercised in such sort as may reasonably be borne by a common charge of the whole county'.[2] This was the origin of the trained bands, who bore that name rather because they were selected for training than because they were actually trained. From these sources, when the Spanish Armada came, Elizabeth calculated that a force of 130,000 men could be got together, and by 1623 the number of men who could be collected was said to be 160,000.[3]

Yet so untrained was this militia that all experienced captains shrank from the prospect of meeting a French or a Spanish invasion with such forces. In 1588 when Sir John Norris saw the raw levies who were to be pitted against Parma's veterans he wondered, he said, that he could see no man in the kingdom afeared but himself.[4] In 1628 when there was some prospect of a French invasion, Sir Edward Cecil echoed Norris's words, 'The danger of all is that a people not used to war believeth no enemy dare venture upon them.' Since Elizabeth's time the nation had grown unwarlike. 'This kingdom hath been too long in peace – our old commanders both by sea and by land are worn out, and

[1] Lord Herbert of Cherbury, *The Expedition to the Isle of Rhé*, Philobiblion Society, 1860, pp. 46, 182, 226, 260, 283. Buckingham landed with about 6,100 or 6,200 men and received 2,400 more during the siege (*Court and Times of Charles I*, i, 245, 248, 262, 271, 274, 282; *Cal. State Papers, Dom.*, 1627–8, pp. 383, 396, 419, 438, 450, 454). Dr Gardiner omits to reckon the reinforcements in his calculation of Buckingham's losses (*England under the Duke of Buckingham and Charles I*, i, 163).

[2] Grose, *Military Antiquities*, i, 87, Instructions for the execution of the Commission directed to the Justices of the Peace, etc., Feb., 1572–3; cf. Scott, *British Army*, i, 344.

[3] Scott, *British Army*, i, 374, 387.

[4] Dalton, *Life of Cecil*, ii, 402.

few men are bred in their places, for the knowledge of war and
almost the thought of war is extinguished.' 'Peace hath so besotted us, that as we are altogether ignorant, so are we so much
the more not sensible of that defect, for we think if we have men
and ships our kingdom is safe, as if men were born soldiers.'[1]
The difference, he concludes, between those that are soldiers and
those that are not is, that the one prepares beforehand, the other
too late.[2]

Very little had been done since the reign of Elizabeth to improve the organization of the forces upon which the kingdom
depended for its defence. In one respect things were worse than
they had been in that reign, for the cavalry of the militia was
admittedly less efficient in the reign of Charles the First than
it had been then. There are repeated complaints of the decrease
of horsemen and the decay of the breed of horses. 'As for horse,'
wrote a famous soldier of the time, Sir Edward Harwood, 'this
kingdom is so deficient that it is a question whether or not the
whole kingdom could make 2,000 good horse that might equal
2,000 French.'[3] In 1632 Cecil complained that service in the
cavalry was out of fashion in England. English soldiers who
served in the Dutch army preferred to serve on foot, and the
English troops of horse in that army had disappeared for lack of
English recruits. He called on the King to apply a remedy for
this neglect. Let Charles, he urged, 'recommend the brave exercise of horsemanship' to the two Universities. Then the young
gentry and nobility would be able to practise horsemanship for

[1] Ibid., ii, 395, 399.   [2] Ibid., ii, 402.

[3] *Harleian Miscellany*, iv, 273, ed. Park. The letter of the Privy Council to
the Duke of Buckingham, in January 1628, confesses the decay of the
mounted forces of the nation: 'His majestie, out of his princely care and
wisdome, foreseeing how necessary it is in these hostile and dangerous
tymes to haue the trayned bandes within this kingdome to bee kept in such
a warlyke preparacion that they may be readie upon all occasions of present
seruice; and beeing informed that at this present tyme they are generally
soe ill provided and furnished that they are noe wayes soe fitt as they
ought to be, if there should bee suddayne occasion to performe the service
for which they are ordayned, and that not onely the defectes are great in
those that doe show their horses and armes, but that many for saving of
charges doe borrowe their horses and armes to showe as their owne, and
many doe presume not to finde the horses and armes with which they are
charged; his majestie, therefore, thinkes fitt to take a muster and viewe of
the horse of very many of the sheires in his owne person, because the
frequent direcions of this table haue not hitherto preyvayled to reforme the
neglects and to supply the defects' (*Verney Papers*, p. 129).

military purposes at home, instead of being obliged to abandon other kinds of learning and to go into foreign countries 'to learn this dexterity'. For, he argued, 'Who may better do it than the Universities, which are ordained for the learning of all manner of virtues?'

Charles did not make the suggested addition to the curriculum of the Universities. All he did was to impose upon the nobility and high officers of State, in the year 1635, the duty of keeping a certain number of horses fit for military purposes. The Secretaries of State were ordered to keep two war-horses apiece, and the Archbishop of Canterbury eight.[1]

The infantry of the militia was as badly drilled as it had been in Elizabeth's days, but it was better armed. In 1588 an English regiment of foot – or band, as it was then termed – contained men armed with five different kinds of weapons.[2] There were pikemen and billmen – the latter armed with long-handled battle-axes, intended to guard the standards and do execution upon a broken enemy.[3] Then there were three kinds of 'shot', as the phrase was – first the musketeers, secondly the calivermen, whose weapon may be roughly defined as a sort of short, light musket, and, lastly, the archers. The ballad of Lord Willoughby illustrates this. Describing how with 1,500 fighting men he defeated 14,000 Spaniards in Flanders, it represents him as exhorting his 1,500 thus:

[1] Dalton, *Life of Sir E. Cecil*, ii, 329–32.
[2] Sir John Smythe in his *Instructions, Observations and Orders Military*, 1595, p. 11, speaks of 'our English bands' as 'chiefly consisting of five different weapons; that is of piques, battleaxes, musquetiers, harquebuziers, and archers'. In 1590 the Essex foot bands, in all 3,600 men, were composed of 882 pikemen, 442 musketeers, 1,076 calivers, 840 archers, 333 billmen (Bruce's *Report on the arrangements made for the defence of England against the Spanish Armada*, p. cccxxviii).
[3] About 1588 Lord Gray, Sir Francis Knollys, and other experienced soldiers made the following recommendations: 'Alsoe for th' encrease of armed pikemen, in this time of scarcity of armor we thinke good that all the armed bill men bee armed pikemen, and that able bill men unarmed should bee levied and chosen in theire places, because the ranckes of bill-men in battaile are invironed with pikes, for the billmen serve especially for execution of the ennemie in battaile overthrowne, but here is to be noted there must be reserved a fewe armed billmen, or halbards, to garde ther rancks wherin the ensignes and drommes &c. are placed in battaile....
'We thinke it alsoe necessary that throughout all the counties of the Realme this proportion, as well amongst the armed and trained as the unarmed, of Pikes and Bills bee observed. that is to say that of every hundred there bee 80 Pikes and 20 Bills' (*Fifteenth Rep. Hist. MSS. Comm.*, ii, p. 268).

Stand to it, noble pikemen,
And look well round about,
And shoot you right, you bowmen,
And we will keep them out:
You musket and caliver men
Do you prove true to me,
I'll be the foremost man in fight,
Says brave Lord Willoughby.[1]

Before the end of Elizabeth's reign the bill and the bow were definitely abandoned. In 1596 the government issued instructions that in all the local forces throughout England the billmen were to be converted into pikemen and the bowmen into musketeers.[2] A generation later the calivermen had disappeared also, so that by the time of Charles the First the English trained bands were composed exclusively of musketeers and pikemen. The government of Charles the First also fixed a pattern to which the armament of the trained bands was to conform, and a price for repairing their arms, which all armourers were ordered to observe.[3] On the other hand, the trained bands were still as untrained as they had been in Elizabeth's reign. They met to drill once a month during the summer for the space of one day, but as Colonel Ward complained in 1639, these meetings were treated as 'matters of disport and things of no moment'.[4] 'As trainings are now used,' he added, ' we shall, I am sure, never be able to make one good soldier; for

---

[1] *Roxburghe Ballads*, iv, 9. The ballad was probably written about 1626, but is supposed to describe the battle of Nieuport which took place in 1600. See *Transactions of the Royal Historical Society*, third series, vol. iii, p. 110.

[2] The process began in 1588. 'We cannot greatly yet increase the number of our forces,' wrote the Deputy-Lieutenants of Kent to the Lord High Treasurer on 12th July 1588; 'but we in this sort have very much amended and strengthened the same, for we have procured the greatest number of all of our trained archers, to provide muskets, or at least calivers, which we judge far more serviceable' (Bruce, p. cxvii). By 1596 the government was ordering the local authorities to 'change your bowmen into muskets and your billmen into pikes according to our former directions not yet accomplished' (Scott, *British Army*, ii, 96). In 1588 an order for raising 4,000 men in Devonshire specified that 1,600 should be 'shot', 800 bows, 800 pikes, and 800 bills. In the directions for raising men in the same county in 1598 neither billmen nor bowmen are mentioned (*Fifteenth Rep. Hist. MSS. Comm.*, pt. vii, pp. 5, 24, 37).

[3] In 1629. Grose, ii, 323–37; cf. Dalton, *Life of Sir E. Cecil*, i, 46; ii, 319.

[4] Ward, *Animadversions of War*, p. 30.

our custom and use is, nowadays, to cause our companies to meet on a certain day, and by that time the arms be all viewed, and the muster master hath had his pay (which is the chiefest thing many times he looks after) it draws towards dinner time; and, indeed, officers love their bellies so well as that they are loath to take too much pains about disciplining of their soldiers. Wherefore, after a little careless hurrying over of their postures, with which the companies are nothing bettered, they make them charge their muskets, and so prepare to give their captain a brave volley of shot at his entrance into his inn: where after having solaced themselves for a while after this brave service every man repairs home, and that which is not so well taught them is easily forgotten before the next training.'[1]

According to Ward the chief thing the trained bands learnt was to drink. Whenever they met near a great town, many of the soldiers would slip away and stay 'in the inns and taverns tippling when they should be exercising in the field'. The God they worshipped in their trainings, as another writer put it, was not Mars but Bacchus.[2]

Nor did the soldiers of the trained bands compensate for their lack of drill by making themselves good shots. There was very little shooting practice. At first the men were simply taught how to handle their muskets – the postures of the musket, as the

[1] Ward goes on to make the following suggestions: 'If we trained but twice in the year, and at each time kept the Companies together, but three or foure dayes at the most; they would be better acquainted with their Armes and the use of them: so often practising of them at one time, would make them remember what is shewed, better than seven yeares practice as now we goe to worke.

'But, peradventure some will thinke, that to keepe souldiers so long together at once, would damnifie the Country by reason of neglect of husbandry: But as farre as I conceive, it would rather be beneficial to the Country; for now every Moneth in the Summer, they lose a day by reason of the Training, and the greater part of the Souldiers use to fall a drinking after the Training and happily lose the next day also; and so in the Moneths of June, July and August, which are busie times for Hay, and Harvest, they lose three days or more: which is more damage to them, than eight days in May and September, for these are the two times in the yeare, wherein husbandmen have more leisure, than in any other of the Summer-Moneths; in May, because all their seed is then in the ground, and no Hay or Corne ready; the latter end of September, because Harvest and Hoptime, for the most part is over, and wheat-seed not fully come; wherefore I thinke, with lesse damage, they might spare foure dayes together in May, and so many also in September, than to spare in every of the Summer moneths but one.'

[2] Thomas Venn, *Military and Martial Discipline*, 1672, p. 6.

phrase was. Then they were for some time 'exercised with false
fires', that is to say, taught to put a pinch of powder in the pan
of the musket and to pop it off, that so they might inure their
eyes to the flash, and learn not to shut them when they fired.[1]
The last stage in their education was shooting at a mark, but
that was a perfection which few attained to, because their
counties grudged supplying them with the necessary ammunition.[2]

London was the only part of the kingdom in which any
attempt was made really to drill and exercise the trained bands.
The trained bands of the City, whose number was fixed in 1614
at 6,000, were long the butt of contemporary satirists. Beaumont and Fletcher had ridiculed them in the *Knight of the*

[1] 'Nevertheless, it is not held necessary, until the Souldiers be perfect in
their Postures, and ready managing of the Pike when they are armed, and
the Musket together with the Rest, that there should be any expence of
Powder at all: And then for some time to be exercised with some false fires,
which is only a little Powder in the Pan: Nor at any time to blow away their
Powder in vain; but that Powder which should be allowed by the Country
for training, be bestowed only at Marks: In which case it is to be wished,
that little small Prizes might be provided at the cost of the Country, to be
shot for at the Marks, which would give an ambition to men to carry them
away, and would save the Country more in Powder than their value: And a
desire in men to render themselves perfect, would make them to find themselves Powder with that money, which on those days, and in those times,
would be worse spent in an Alehouse' (Instructions for Musters, 1639,'
Rushworth, iii, Appendix 139; cf. Sir Francis Walsingham's 'Instructions'
issued about 1585, printed in Harland's *Lancashire Lieutenancy under the
Tudors and Stuarts*, 1859, p. xliv).

[2] Here is a letter from a landowner declining to supply powder for the use
of the trained bands:—

'MR. CONSTABLE GILL,—I hear by my tenant, that you are commanded by
your captain to bring to this muster one pound of powder for every musket,
which to me seemeth strange, seeing our captains here in our division command no powder at all. Only they bestow upon their musketeers one shot,
or such like, but at their own costs, not at the charge of the country, and so
did Captain Pole Thursday last, at Honyton, where I was. Its said the
captains have now no authority to command powder. I conceive we are all
governed by one rule and authority, and I know no reason but it should be
all alike, save only the musters with you are commonly far greater than with
us, which I conceive is especially by reason of the great store of powder you
spend at general and petty musters more than we do. You know I must pay
the most of any one in your parish, (and yet I find for all my estate three
men's arms, here where I dwell,) and you also know with what abundance of
rates and taxes we are continually charged, therefore I tell you plain,
seeing your command for a pound of powder for every musket is contrary to
the command of other captains, I will not pay to that charge of one pound
of powder for every musket, (if it be true your command be such), except it
shall please the Deputy-Lieutenants to command me to pay the same,
whose command I must and will obey' (John Chase to John Gill, 17th
May 1637, *Trevelyan Papers*, pt. iii, 190).

Burning Pestle. The play pictures Ralph the prentice reviewing what the dramatist calls a company of pewterers and poulterers. One has a musket with a foul touch-hole, another brings his powder in a paper instead of a horn, a third has no nozzle to his flask. After the pompous march out to Mile End comes a sham fight, and before it the captain makes a speech to his soldiers. 'Gentlemen, countrymen, friends, and my fellow-soldiers. I have brought you this day from the shops of security and the counters of content, to measure out honour by the ell and prowess by the pound,

> '*Remember then whose cause you have in hand,*
> *And like a set of true-born scavengers,*
> *Scour me this famous realm of enemies*'.[1]

The wits of the court laughed at the citizen soldiers, but a small band of enthusiasts rescued them from ridicule by teaching them at least their drill. There were little societies of citizens meeting at the Artillery Garden in Bishopsgate and the Military Garden in St. Martin's Fields to practise their drill, under expert soldiers whom they hired to instruct them. Between 1630 and 1640 these societies flourished greatly, and they became, as a military writer called them, 'two great nurseries or academies of military discipline'.[2] Men taught in them came in time to officer the trained bands, and did good service during the Civil War. But the comparative efficiency attained by the London regiments was never reached by the trained bands of the rest of England.

To sum up, the military system which the Stuarts had inherited from the Tudors produced armies for foreign service incapable of striking an effective blow in a continental war, and a militia for home defence incapable of resisting a small number of trained soldiers. James made no attempt to reform the system, but at least he laboured to avoid war. Charles plunged

---

[1] *Knight of the Burning Pestle*, act v, sc. i, ii; cf. Jonson, *Every Man in His Humour*, act iii, sc. ii; Underwoods, lxii.

[2] Elton, *Complete Body of the Art Military*, pp. 67, 68. The growth of the trained bands of London may be traced in Sharpe's *London and the Kingdom*, ii, 64–68, 120, 126, 161, 165, 171, and Masson, *Life of Milton*, ii, 446; see also Lord Dillon's *MS. List of the Officers of the London Trained Bands in 1643, Archæologia*, vol. lii.

rashly into war with France and Spain, but he made no serious attempt to reorganize the military forces of the nation. It was fortunate for England that he blundered into peace again.

For the ten years which followed these wars England enjoyed profound peace. But all Europe was fighting, and the arts of war made rapid progress. 'We see,' wrote a soldier, 'the face of war and the forms of weapons alter almost daily; every nation striving to outwit each other in excellency of weapons.'[1] In England alone there was no progress. English volunteers were fighting under almost every flag in Europe. In Holland, France, Spain, Sweden, Denmark, Austria, and even in Russia, there were regiments of English and Scottish soldiers, but it was in the Swedish and Dutch armies that they served with most frequency. A soldier who served the King of Sweden could flatter himself as Colonel Robert Monro did, that he was fighting for the distressed Queen of Bohemia and for his oppressed brethren in Christ, the German Protestants, as well as to instruct himself in the profession of arms. A soldier who served the States-General could boast like Captain Dalgetty that he served the most punctual paymasters in the world.[2]

In all these different fields the English soldiers who had reaped nothing but disgrace under their own flag, gained honour. 'If they be well ordered and kept in by the rules of good discipline,' wrote one of their officers, 'they fear not the face or the force of the stoutest foe, and have one singular virtue beyond any other nation, for they are always willing to go on; and though at first they be stoutly resisted, yet will they as resolutely undertake the action the second time, though it is to meet death itself in the face.'[3]

Evidently the disasters of the English arms were due to the military system, and not to the decay of the breed of men. In 1639 came the rebellion in Scotland, and there was another exhibition of the defects of the system. It broke down once more, and dragged the monarchy of the Stuarts down with it. For it was not merely the emptiness of the treasury and the disaffection of the people which obliged Charles to give way to his

[1] Lupton, *Warlike Treatise of the Pike*, 1642, p. 131.
[2] *Monro His Expedition*, ii, 62, 70; Scott, *Legend of Montrose*.
[3] Lupton, p. 36.

rebellious subjects. In spite of both he could put into the field
an army as numerous as that which was led by Leslie. But thanks
to his neglect to organize the military resources of his kingdom
in time of peace, the army he collected was never an efficient
fighting body. In the first of the two Scottish wars Charles
raised in all about 20,000 men. He sent a fleet with 5,000 men
under the Marquis of Hamilton to threaten the Scottish coasts,
and to keep Leslie's army at home. Hamilton reported that his
men were good, well clothed, and well armed, but so little exercised that out of the 5,000 there were not 200 that could fire a
musket.[1] Meanwhile Charles himself gathered upon the Border
about 15,000 men, mostly consisting of the trained bands of the
northern counties, but they too left much for a general to desire.
'Our men,' wrote Sir Edmund Verney from the King's camp in
May 1639, 'are very raw, our arms of all sorts naught, our
victuals scarce, and provisions for horses worse. . . .' 'I daresay
there was never so raw, so unskilful, and so unwilling an army,
brought to fight.'[2] All the King could do was to entrench himself
and stand firmly upon the defensive, and a month later he concluded the treaty of Berwick, and yielded to the demands of
the Covenanters.

Next year, in the second Scottish war, the King got together
about 25,000 men. This time the bulk of the army was composed of pressed men drawn from the shires south of the Hum-
ber. The northern trained bands, commanded by officers who
were their landlords or their neighbours, had been tolerably
well-behaved, and in the end they were by no means reluctant
to strike a blow at their old enemies the Scots. But the pressed
men from the southern counties were commanded by inexperienced courtiers or officers from foreign parts of whom their followers knew nothing, and so they plundered and mutinied as
they pleased. When the Dorsetshire men reached Faringdon

[1] 'These men were good bodies, well clothed and well armed, but so little
exercised that out of the 5,000 there were not 200 that could fire a musket.
The occasion of this was a clause in the council's letter to the lieutenants of
the counties in which they were levied, that if other good men could be had,
the trained men should be spared; and the deputy lieutenants upon this
ordered it so, that not so much as the sergeants and corporals were trained'
(Burnet, *Lives of the Hamiltons*, p. 154).

[2] *Verney Papers*, pp. 228, 233.

they murdered the lieutenant who conducted them, and threatened to put the rest of their commanders to the sword, 'insomuch that they all fled'. The Devonshire men were zealous
Protestants; and murdered their lieutenant because they suspected him of being a Papist. The Essex men, who were Protestants of a milder mood, signalized their march by breaking
into churches and making bonfires of surplices and communion
rails.[1]

With an army composed of such materials defeat was a fore-
gone conclusion. The rout at Newburn in August 1640, merely
precipitated the inevitable end which was bound to follow from a
collision between the King's forces and the Scots. For Leslie's
men, though they were raw soldiers, were fairly drilled, fairly
disciplined, and eager to fight. In short, they were an army and
not an armed mob.

[1] See the passages collected in Mr John Bruce's Introduction to *Notes of
the Treaty at Ripon.*

CHAPTER II

The First Years of the Civil War

TWO YEARS AFTER the battle of Newburn came the Civil War. As soon as the appeal to arms took place each party had the same problem to face: it had to improvise an army out of masses of untrained men with no trained soldiers to serve as its nucleus. In the French Revolution the Convention was able to make head against a European coalition because it possessed in the remains of the army of the Bourbons a sufficient number of veteran regiments to stiffen its battalions of volunteers. Neither the King nor the Parliament had this advantage, but each had at their disposal a large number of expert officers who had learnt their trade in every army in Christendom. Of the Royalist commanders Astley had fought under Gustavus, Hopton under the King of Bohemia, Goring under the Dutch flag, Gage under the Spanish. On the Parliament side Skippon and Balfour had long been officers in the Dutch army, Crawford, Ramsay and many other Scots in the Swedish. It was not trained officers who were wanting in the two armies, but trained soldiers.

At first each party tried to make use of the existing military organization of the country. The King by his Commissions of Array, the Parliament by its Militia Ordinance, summoned the trained bands to fight. All over England the struggle began with an attempt to obtain possession of the county magazine in which the powder and the arms of the local trained bands were stored. Clarendon's account of the attempt of Colonel Hastings to seize the magazine at Leicester, and Mrs Hutchinson's account of her husband's defence of that at Nottingham, are typical instances.[1] It was with the Yorkshire trained bands that King Charles laid siege to Hull in July 1642, and with the Cornish trained bands

[1] Clarendon, *Rebellion*, v, 417; *Old Parliamentary History*, xi, 276; *Life of Col. Hutchinson*, i, 142, 347–52.

that Hopton drove the Parliamentary militia commissioners out
of Cornwall in the following October. But the trained bands held
it their chief privilege not to be compelled to march out of their
country. Those of Cornwall declined to follow Hopton into
Devonshire, and in their place he had to enlist volunteer regiments commanded by gentlemen of the country, such as Slan-
ning and Grenville. Nor would the Yorkshire trained bands join
the King's army in its march to Edgehill, though two regiments
drawn from their ranks fought in that battle under Bellasis and
Pennyman.[1]

Charles therefore was obliged to fall back on another expedient. Wherever he came he disarmed the trained bands and
used their weapons to arm his volunteers. In Nottinghamshire,
for instance, he mustered the trained bands, and told them that
'because of the harvest and of their wives and children it should
suffice to lend him their arms, and that on the word of a king
he would return them when he had settled the kingdom in
peace'. In the same way he borrowed, as his phrase ran, the arms
of Leicestershire and Derbyshire.[2] Parliament made the same

---

[1] Clarendon, *Rebellion*, v, 436; vi, 62, note (ed. Macray); vi, 241–4.

[2] 'The greatest difficulty was to provide arms; of which indeed there was
a wonderful scarcity, the King being exceedingly disappointed in his
expectation of arms from Holland, a vessel or two having been taken by his
own ships under the command of the earl of Warwick; so that, except 800
muskets, 500 pair of pistols, and 200 swords, which came with the powder
which was landed in Yorkshire, as is before mentioned, the King had none
in his magazine; so that he was compelled to begin at Nottingham, and so
in all places as he passed, to borrow the arms from the train-bands; which
was done with so much wariness and caution, (albeit it was known that
those arms would, being left in those hands, be employed against him,
or at least be of no use to him,) that it was done rather with their consent
than by any constraint, and always with the full approbation of their commanders. And therefore in Yorkshire and Shropshire, where the gentlemen
very unskilfully, though with good meaning, desired that the arms might
still be left in the countrymen's hands, there was none of that kind of
borrowing. But in all places the noblemen and gentlemen of quality sent the
King such supplies of arms out of their own armories, (which were very
mean); so that, by all these means together, the foot, (all but three or four
hundred who marched without any weapon but a cudgel,) were armed with
muskets, and bags for their powder, and pikes; but in the whole body there
was not one pikeman had a corslet, and very few musketeers who had
swords. Amongst the horse, the officers had their full desire if they were able
to procure old backs and breasts and pots, with pistols or carbines for their
two or three first ranks, and swords for the rest; themselves (and some
soldiers by their examples) having gotten, besides their pistols and swords,
a short pole-axe' (Clarendon, *Rebellion*, vi, 73; cf. *Life of Col. Hutchinson*, i,
351, ed. 1885).

attempt to use the trained bands and it ended in a like failure.
It was easy to muster them, too impossible to make them serviceable. 'The trained bands,' says the contemporary historian
of the war in Gloucestershire, 'accounted the main support of
the realm and its bulwark against unexpected invasion, were
effeminate in courage and incapable of discipline, because their
whole course of life was alienated from warlike employment,
insomuch that young and active spirits were more perfect by the
experience of two days. Wherefore these men might easily repine
at oppression, and have a will to preserve themselves, yet a
small body of desperate Cavaliers might overrun and ruin them
at pleasure.'[1]

Sometimes, though they might be persuaded to march out of
the county, the trained bands would refuse to fight. Essex and
Hertfordshire were counties well affected to the Parliament, and
in the summer of 1644 the trained bands of those two counties
under the command of Major-General Browne joined Sir William
Waller after his defeat at Cropredy. 'They are so mutinous and
uncommandable,' reported Waller, 'that there is no hope of
their stay.' Indeed it was hardly desirable. 'Yesterday,' said he,
'they were like to have killed the Major General, and they hurt
him in the face. Such men are only fit for a gallows here and a
hell hereafter.'[2]

The one exception to the rule that the trained bands were
worthless was furnished by those of London. Counting in the
three regiments of the suburbs, the six regiments of the city,
and the six regiments of auxiliaries, they amounted in 1643 to
18,000 men.[3] They were the reserve on which the Parliament
relied in every emergency. Without their aid, Essex could not
have relieved Gloucester, nor could Waller have repulsed Hopton's invasion of Sussex. They were not very well disciplined,
and were too much accustomed to good food and good beds to
support with patience the hardships of a campaign, but they
were well drilled. Men who had laughed at the citizen-soldier
for 'the easy practice of their postures in the artillery garden',
admired the skill and the steadiness with which they beat back

[1] *Bibliotheca Gloucestrensis*, p. 10.
[2] *Cal. State Papers, Dom.*, 1644, pp. 324, 326.
[3] Masson, *Life of Milton*, ii, 447.

B

the furious charges of Rupert's horse at Newbury. 'Of so
sovereign benefit,' says Clarendon,[1] 'is that readiness, order,
and dexterity in the use of arms which hath been so much
neglected. . . .'

As the trained bands in general were unserviceable, each party
raised the army with which it began the war by voluntary enlistment. Both began by appealing for subscriptions of men and
horses. The Lords and gentlemen of the Privy Council engaged
to maintain 1,695 horse for three months, in proportions ranging
from the 100 promised by the Duke of Richmond to a score promised by Secretary Nicholas.[2] Members of Parliament who
remained at Westminster made similar promises. Hampden engaged to furnish three horsemen and £200; Marten, six horsemen; Cromwell, £500, and so on. Anyone providing a horse and
arms for the Parliament's service was promised interest on their
value at the rate of 8 per cent.[3]

This was but a temporary expedient. The next step was to
issue commissions to officers authorizing them to raise regiments.
In the King's commissions the usual number of men specified
for a foot regiment was 1,200, for a cavalry regiment 500. In the
army under Essex the regiment of foot was also fixed at 1,200,
but the horse was raised at first in single troops consisting of
about sixty rank and file apiece. As the Parliament had plenty
of money, each captain who undertook to raise a troop received
£1,100, under the name of 'mounting-money', to enable him to
provide arms and horses. It was divided in this way: the captain
got £140, the lieutenant £60, the cornet £50, the quartermaster
£30, while about £15 apiece sufficed to equip the private troopers
and non-commissioned officers.[4] In the same way the colonels
of foot regiments were paid a certain sum as 'levy money' as
soon as they had enlisted a certain number of men. The King
on the other hand was hardly in a position to advance money
in this way. As a rule the regiments raised for his service seem
to have been equipped at the expense of their officers, and they
were generally raised in the district where the colonel's estates

[1] Clarendon, *Rebellion*, vii, 211.
[2] Ibid., vi, 375; Peacock, *Army Lists*, p. 7.
[3] *Tanner MSS.*, lxiii, 57; Husbands, i, 339, 825.
[4] *Cal. State Papers, Dom.*, 1641–3, p. 362.

lay.[1] Lord Paget's regiment, for instance, was raised in Staffordshire, the Earl of Northampton's in north Oxfordshire.[2]

At the beginning of the war there was no lack of volunteers on
either side. Young courtiers like Sir Philip Warwick enlisted
in the King's troop of guards, 'so gallant a body', asserts Clarendon, 'that upon a very modest computation, the estate and
revenue of that single troop might justly be valued as at least
equal to all theirs who then voted in both Houses under the
name of Lords and Commons'.[3] The young gentlemen of the
Inns of Court, such as Ludlow, Fleetwood and Rich, entered the

[1] Many commissions are given out, but no money, to raise regiments of
horse. Sir Arthur Aston, the governor of Reading, has one; Sir W. Pye has a
commission to be his lieutenant-colonel for raising a troop upon his own
charge. Sir Thomas Ashton raiseth a regiment, and some others also to ten
or twelve new regiments; my Lord Capel raiseth a regiment, and Sir B.
Throgmorton to be his lieutenant-colonel upon the like terms. My Lord
Chandos also raiseth a regiment' (Warburton, *Prince Rupert*, ii, p. 69).

[2] Clarendon, *Rebellion*, vi, 62. The process is further illustrated by the
following passage from Sir Richard Bulstrode's memoirs:—
'When the King had settled his Court at Oxford, recruited his Army, and
fortified his Garrisons in all Parts, he gave Banbury, and that Part of the
Country, to the Earl of Northampton, who was commanded to raise a
Regiment of Horse, which was given to the Lord Compton, his eldest Son,
and Sir Charles, his second Son, was made Lieutenant Colonel of it: To Sir
William Compton, his third Son, was given the Castle of Banbury: one
troop in his Regiment of Horse was given to Captain James Chamberlain,
Brother to Sir Thomas, who was then High Sheriff of Oxfordshire: to
Captain James Chamberlain were given the two Villages of Upper and Lower
Heyford, opposite to North and Steeple Aston, in Oxfordshire, for his
Quarters, while he raised the said Company. Mr Herbert Jeffries, of Here-
fordshire, was his Lieutenant, and I was his Cornet. This Company was
soon raised, and the first Time the Captain went out with it, he was killed
near Northampton, by one Captain Lawson' (Bulstrode, p. 192).
The King had also a certain number of foreign troops in his service. A
French regiment was serving in 1644 in the west of England (*Trevelyan
Papers*, iii, 248). A French brigade, consisting of three regiments, surrendered to Fairfax in March 1646 (Sprigge, *Anglia Rediviva*, pp. 226, 227).
On 18th November 1643 Rupert contracted with one John Van Haesdonck to bring over 200 foreign soldiers of experience in the wars in the
Netherlands to form the nucleus of a regiment of foot. According to the
very curious contract half the plunder they might get was to go to the
soldiers, a fourth to the Prince, and one-eighth to Van Haesdonck (*Cal.
State Papers, Dom.*, 1641-3, p. 500).

[3] Clarendon, *Rebellion*, vi, 74, 82. Sir Philip Warwick and Clarendon both
mention their service at Edgehill:
'It was the more strange, that the reserves would thus precipitately
engage themselves, when they saw the King had given leave unto his own
Volunteer-Guard of Noblemen and Gentlemen, who with their attendance
made two such Troops, as that they consisted of about three hundred
Horse: for a vanity had possest that Troop, (upon a little provocation, or
for a word of distaste the day before, or being called, The Troop of Shew)

bodyguard of the Earl of Essex, while the young tradesmen and apprentices of London filled the regiments of Lord Brooke and Denzil Holles.[1]

The apprentices were encouraged to enlist by a Parliamentary order which secured them against forfeiting their indentures thereby. Their zeal is illustrated by the letters of one of them, Sergeant Nehemiah Wharton, which are preserved amongst the State Papers. His master had already provided a man and horse for the Parliament, but he encouraged his apprentice to engage himself. His master's wife gave him a scarf, which he promised never to stain save in the blood of Cavaliers; and the ancient maid-servant of the household wept for joy when she saw him in his sergeant's uniform.[2]

In Oxford there was equal zeal for the King's cause. 'Many days together,' says a complaining letter from the two Puritan members for the city, written in September 1642, 'the scholars and privileged persons, with such weapons as they had, trained up and down the streets in Christ Church College quadrangle and other College quadrangles and kept no good rule either by night or day.'[3]

An undergraduate of the period who wrote a history of the Civil Wars in verse tells us the result:

> When first to Oxford, fully there intent
> To study learned science I went,
> Instead of Logicke, Physicke, school-converse
> I did attend the armed troops of Mars,
> Instead of books I sword, horse, pistols bought,
> And on the field I for degrees then fought.

to desire this honour of being engaged in the first charge; and I had the honour to be of the number, and to be one of the most inconsiderable Persons of it; and when wee valued the estates of the whole troop, wee reckoned there was 100000£. per ann. in that Body, stak'd that day in that engagement against men of very disproportionable quality' (Warwick, *Memoirs*, p. 230).

[1] Ludlow, *Memoirs*, i, 39, ed. 1894; Vicars, *Jehovah Jireh*, pp. 195, 200, 215; *Old Parliamentary History*, xi, 475, 480.

[2] Wharton's letters are printed in full in *Archæologia*, vol. xxxv, and at almost full length in *Cal. State Papers, Dom.*, 1641–3.

[3] *Duke of Portland's Papers*, i, 57. See *Life and Times of Anthony Wood*, ed. by A. Clark, vol. i, pp. 52–68.

My years had not amounted full eighteen,
Till I on field wounded three times had been,
Three times in sieges close had been immured,
Three times imprisonment's restraint endured.
In those sad times these verses rude were writ.[1]

By the time the war had lasted a year, each party found the
zeal of its supporters insufficient to fill the ranks of its army.
Both resorted to impressment. On 10th August 1643 Parliament
passed an ordinance authorizing the county committees to impress whatever soldiers, gunners and surgeons should be needed,
and a few days later it appointed 2,000 men to be impressed in
London, and 20,000 in the eastern counties.[2] The King adopted
the same plan, and during 1643 and 1644 he issued commissions
for impressing men in twenty-nine different counties.[3]

In these Parliamentary ordinances for impressment there were
as usual a number of exceptions. Clergymen, scholars, students
in the Inns of Court and the Universities, the sons of esquires
and persons rated at five pounds goods or three pounds lands in
the subsidy books were exempt, as were sailors, certain government officials, and the servants of Members of Parliament. All
other persons between the ages of eighteen and fifty were liable
to impressment. In the King's instructions for pressing there are
some additional rules laid down—probably traditional ones.
Mechanics were to be selected rather than husbandmen, those
who were not householders rather than those who were, single
men in preference to the married.[4] One is reminded of the old

[1] Anthony Cooper's *Stratologia, or the History of the English Civil Warres
in English Verse*, 1662, 12mo. Cooper served in the regiment of Lord Darcy
and fought mainly in the north of England.

[2] Husbands, *Ordinances*, ii, 282, 288; cf. Clarendon, *Rebellion*, i, 87; ii, 88.

[3] See Black's *Oxford Docquets*, pp. 110, 293; Walker, *Historical Discourses*, p. 43; *Diary of Richard Symonds*, p. 36.

[4] The following proclamation shows the method in which men were levied
and the rules laid down:
'Wilts – Whereas, by virtue of his Majesty's commission under the great
seal of England to us and others directed, for the impressing of six hundred
and sixty-seven able men within the said county of Wilts; and whereas also
it is conceived that twenty-one is a proportionable number for the Hundred
of Potterne and Cannings: These are therefore to will and require you, and
in his Majesty's name straightly to charge and command you that presently
upon sight hereof, you impress within your said Hundred the said one and
twenty able men, and bring them to us his Majesty's commissioners at the
Devizes, on Friday next, by one of the clock in the afternoon, there to be

ballad on Agincourt, in which King Henry the Fifth says, summoning his archers:

> Recruit me Lancashire and Cheshire both,
> And Derbyshire hills that are so free,
> But no married man, nor no widow's son,
> For no woman's curse shall go with me.[1]

In spite of the large numbers of men whom each party raised
and armed—amounting it is probable to 60,000 or 70,000 on each
side – the numbers engaged in the chief battles were comparatively small. At Marston Moor in the summer of 1644, Rupert
had about 18,000 men under his command, and King Charles
had about the same number with him in Cornwall when Essex
was forced to capitulate. But in both cases these numbers were
got together by the junction of two or three independent armies.
The field army under the King's immediate command tended to
diminish as the war continued. At Edgehill the King had about
14,000 men, at the first battle of Newbury about 12,000, at the
second between 9,000 and 12,000, at Naseby not much over
8,500 or 9,000. The same thing occurred on the other side. About
26,000 Parliamentarians fought at Marston Moor, where the
three armies of Leslie, Fairfax, and Manchester were united, and
at the second battle of Newbury the combined forces of Manchester, Waller, and Essex amounted to 19,000. The army raised
for Essex in the summer of 1642 amounted on paper to some
24,000 foot and 5,000 horse, but it never came to much over
20,000 in reality, and at Edgehill he had at the outside only

received. Hereof fail not at your uttermost peril. Given under our hands
and seals this four and twentieth day of April, Anno Domini, 1644.
  'First. The persons you are to impress for this service, you shall make
choice of such as are of able bodies.
  'Secondly. Such as are for their quality fit to be common soldiers.
  'Thirdly. Such as are fit for their age.
  'Fourthly. Such as are single men rather than married men.
  'Fifthly. Such as being single men, are not housekeepers.
  'Sixthly. Such as not being housekeepers, are out of service rather than
such as are in service.
  'Seventhly. Such as are mechanics, tradesmen, or others, rather than
husbandmen; but no mariners.
  'Eighthly. Next you shall take care that they be conveniently apparelled
either of their own or by the assistance of the parish where they are impressed' (Waylen, History of Marlborough, p. 205).
  [1] Child's English and Scottish Popular Ballads, iii, 322-3.

13,000 or 14,000 under his command. In April 1643 he began the campaign with about 16,000 foot and 3,000 horse; by July his army was reduced to 6,000 foot, half of whom were sick, and 2,500 horse.[1] In May 1644 he had 10,000 men, by December less than 5,000.

The reason for this was that on neither side was any systematic provision made for recruiting the losses of the army in the field. In both armies, too, the pay of the soldiers was continually in arrears, and the loss from desertion was excessive. 'My desire is,' wrote Essex in December 1643, 'that if there be no pay like to come to me by the latter end of the week I may know it; I not being able to stay amongst them to hear the crying necessity of the hungry soldiers.'[2] In April 1644 he complained to Parliament that 'now the speech is general of his Majesty's taking the field, and by reason of the condition which the long delay of recruiting my army and ill payment have brought me to, I am

---

[1] The officers of Essex's army made the following representation:
'The number of Foot are 3,000 marching Men, and at least 3,000 sick, occasioned by the Want of Pay, ill Cloathing, and all other Miseries which attend an unpaid sickly Army.
'The Number of the Horse 2,500 (3,000 last Muster) occasioned by the Loss of Horses upon hard Duty and Service, and other Casualties incident to Horse in Service; Recruits of Horse, though often desired, not performed. Besides, by reason of a new Army, the officers find themselves neglected, the present regiments much lessened, listing themselves elsewhere for the new army expecting better Pay and Cloathing; and, upon their going hence, are entertained and protected: and great Discouragements and Scandals put upon his Excellency, the Officers, and Army, either through false Suggestions of some amongst us, or the Misunderstanding of others; poisoning the Affections of the People, which hinders Recruits and Contributions' (Old Parliamentary History, xii, 350).

[2] Every part of his army was unpaid:
'I have likewise another Week's Pay for the Foot, from the Sergeants downwards, for To-morrow, which is all the Money that is left, tho' I have paid nothing else but what bleeding Necessity compelled me to, of which I am ready to give an account; having not been able to relieve divers, whereof some are Captains of my own Regiment, that, thro' Sickness and Hurts, are ready to perish; and how the other Officers will do for Want of Pay, I know not.
'The Train of Artillery, who have done real and faithful Services to the State, are grown to that Necessity, as you may perceive by the Petition inclosed, that if there be not Pay provided for them by the latter End of this Week, both for those here and those that come from Newport, I shall never be able to keep them together without plundering the Country.
'Col. Behre is gone with the Horse, though they have been long without Pay; and if the Horse in Sir William Waller's Brigade be paid, and they unpaid, I fear the Issue; though, otherwise, I never saw Men better contented with so little Pay as the Horse have generally been' (Old Parliamentary History, xii, 470).

grown the pity of my friends and contempt of my enemies, having as yet no forces to take the field with. . . .' '. . . It grieves me exceedingly to see so fair an opportunity lost of prosecuting the advantage which, by God's goodness, we have gotten upon the enemy at this time,[1] because the army is not recruited; so as I am altogether disenabled to move, but must sit still and see this opportunity pass from me, I verily believe, of ending the bleeding miseries of this destructive war; whereas now the enemy will have time to recover and repair themselves before I can get into a condition to advance towards them.'[2]

The chief reason for this neglect to supply and recruit the main army under Essex was the multiplication of separate local forces. Each county had its garrisons raised by the county committee, and each group of associated counties had each their major-general and their field army. During 1643 and 1644 there were four such armies of considerable size, besides smaller bodies; namely, those of the Earl of Manchester, Lord Fairfax, Sir William Waller, and the Earl of Denbigh. Moreover, the army under Manchester was larger than that of the commander-in-chief, for while Parliament, in April 1644, fixed Essex's army at 10,000 men, Manchester had been authorized to raise at first 14,000 and afterwards 21,000.[3] Add to this that the raising of each new army, as Essex and his officers complained, depleted the ranks of the existing armies, not only by depriving them of possible recruits, but by encouraging desertion. Massey, the governor of Gloucester, put the case plainly. 'All my best men,' he declared, 'run away for lack of clothing, and other requisites, and take service in other parts and associations where they may have a better and surer entertainment. For it seems there is such a liberty given that all comers are entertained by every association without enquiry so that they be well mounted or appointed. The consequence is that in some armies it is personally more advantageous to be traitors, cowards, and runagates, than to be faithful, resolute, and constant soldiers to any one place or service, which state of things tends to the great detriment of the service and discouragement of all gallant and faithful soldiers.

[1] Waller's victory over Hopton at Cheriton, 29th March 1644.
[2] *Old Parliamentary History*, xiii, 152–3.
[3] Husbands, *Ordinances*, 1646, folio, pp. 286, 413, 442.

Notice is taken thereof by most of our private soldiers, and when one has been punished for example to others, and cashiered from us for cowardice or other crime, it is customary for him to find a better entertainment elsewhere, and some obtain offices and advancement. . . . The desertion of our soldiers to seek new entertainment upon any new levies being heard of, is the true reason. I conceive, why our armies moulder away from great strengths to nothing.'[1]

The King's army suffered from the same cause, but not to the same extent. It had special defects of its own which were equally fatal in their consequences. One serious evil was the reckless issue of commissions. Instead of adopting some systematic method of filling up the ranks of existing regiments as they were thinned by the war, the losses of the King's army were supplied by raising new regiments. During 1643 and 1644 the King issued to various colonels forty-nine commissions for regiments of foot, and forty for regiments of horse, making up a total of about 68,000 men.[2] And besides this, the chief local commanders, such as Newcastle, had also power to grant commissions, of which they too liberally availed themselves.

Take for instance Sir Philip Warwick's account of Newcastle's proceedings in the northern counties:

'His army, tho' considerable, was soon weakned by a false policy; for he endeavoured to raise the reputation of it by multiplying his commissions for new regiments, troops, and companies, for which they received some advance-money, and quarters assign'd to them for their men; which they scarse ever raised in such a number, as to embody; and yet in such a number, as did harrass and impoverish the country, and lying with their few men scattered and thin, they were often surprised, and then the enemy had the reputation to have defeated a regiment, where there was perchance but halfe a company or troop. And this, I believe, was a very great wound to him from the first; for had he recruited his first or old troops and companies, and not thus loosly aimed at new, his army would have bin more powerfull tho'

[1] *Cal. State Papers, Dom.*, 1644–5, p. 131.
[2] See the list of the commissions issued by the King whilst he was at Oxford (Black's *Oxford Docquets*, pp. 295, 296). This list does not include those issued when the King's army was originally raised, nor those issued during the last year of the war.

nominally less numerous, and could have lain closer together; and so consequently have bin stronger in itself, and more active upon the enemy.'[1]

After a few months' fighting the Royalist army was full of colonels whose regiments were no stronger than a troop or a company. In September 1644 the Earl of Cleveland's brigade of foot in the King's army in Cornwall consisted of six regiments, but numbered only 800 men. At Naseby in 1645 Thomas Howard's brigade of horse amounted only to 880 men, though it contained seven regiments. Howard's own regiment was but eighty strong.[2] In the Parliamentary army, on the other hand, when a regiment fell below a certain minimum strength it was usually incorporated into another, or, as the phrase was, reduced into it, and the superfluous officers became what were called 'reformados'.[3]

Another cause which led to the diminution of the King's field army was the multitude of Royalist garrisons. This was partly due to financial causes. As the King was unable to pay his forces he was obliged to subsist them on the country.[4] Sometimes an agreement was made with the county in which they were quartered to pay a fixed sum every month for their maintenance.

[1] Warwick, *Memoirs*, p. 236; see also *Life of the Duke of Newcastle*, ed. 1886, pp. 23, 160–6.

[2] *Diary of Richard Symonds*, pp. 102, 166, 181.

[3] Husbands, *Ordinances*, 1646, folio, pp. 446, 457.

[4] Order from the King to Prince Rupert, 27th Nov. 1642:
'CHARLES R.,
    'Right dear and entirely beloved nephew, we greet you well, and do hereby will and authorize you to give order to all the colonels of the horse and dragoons of our army, to quarter and billet their respective regiments in such places as we have assigned, and there to take up such necessary provision of diet, lodging, hay, oats, and straw, as shall be necessary for them. And if there shall not be sufficient for such their supply in their quarters, then they are to send forth their warrants to the several hundreds and parishes adjacent, requiring the inhabitants to bring in all fitting provisions for their daily supply. For all which, as for that taken up in their quarters, they to give their respective tickets, and not to presume, upon pain of our high displeasure, to send for greater quantities than will suffice for their numbers of men and horses, and such as may be proportionable to half of each officer's pay by day for diet only, their horse-meat being to be daily supplied by the counties adjacent to each quarter. In this manner we will that you proceed and continue until such time as the counties wherein they are quartered shall agree of and settle some other course for their constant and daily supply . . .' (Warburton, *Prince Rupert*, ii, 70–71; cf. Clarendon, *Rebellion*, vi, 166, 272).

Berkshire, for instance, in October 1643, agreed to pay £500 a week in money and £500 a week in provisions for that purpose.[1] More often a particular district was assigned to a particular regiment or garrison for its support. This led to all sorts of abuses. One Royalist commander was always seeking to extend the area from which he drew his supplies at the expense of another, and there were frequent quarrels.[2] The amount levied varied a good deal according to the discretion of the commander,

[1] Money, *The Battles of Newbury*, 2nd ed., p. 125; cf. Warburton, *Prince Rupert*, i, 334.

[2] Col. John Cochrane to Prince Rupert, from Towcester, 16th December 1643:

'I have encountered many difficulties in the establishing of this garrison, but now I am reduced to greater perplexities than before; since those hundreds which were by your Highness allotted for the maintenance of this garrison, are by his Majesty's express order withdrawn, and assigned to my Lord of Northampton for the entertainment of the garrison of Banbury, and nothing left to me but the Hundreds of Clely, Towcester and Norton, the two last whereof are so ruined by the long abode of the horse amongst them, that they can contribute little or nothing. Clely is possessed by Sir John Digby, and nothing can be exacted from thence till he be removed; and when he is removed, the contributions that can be levied here will not pay the half of that which is requisite, so that unless there be means found to supply this garrison with a weekly supply of three hundred pounds, it will be altogether impossible to preserve it.'

Col. Robert Howard writes in a similar strain from Camden, on 30th Jan. 1645:

'This last night came to me of the Queen's regiment, to share with me in Rifsgate hundred: they shewed me your Highness's order, and, indeed, I received another to the same effect, which I have sent back again to your Highness; resolving to keep nothing by me that shall hang me. Indeed the commander of the party, so soon as he saw my strength in horse and foot, and how environed with enemies, blushed to see the unreasonableness, and asked me how many hundreds I had besides; which, when I truly informed him, out of mere pity he left the hundred. I am sorry, sir, to see myself pitied of a stranger I never saw before, and your Highness so little value me. I'm sure 'twas otherwise when you first sent me hither, then you were pleased to give me all Rifsgate hundred, and so soon as I sent you a list of the state of the garrison, I should be allotted more. God have mercy. upon me, for I see your Highness will leave me; yet I shall once more look up to heaven and send in my list. What horrid crime have I committed, or what brand of cowardice lies upon me and my men, that we are not thought worthy of a subsistence? Shall all the Queen's seventy horse have Westminster hundred, Tewkesbury hundred, and God knows what other hundreds, and yet share half with me in Rifsgate, who has at this very present a hundred horse and five hundred foot, besides a multiplicity of officers? Sir, at my first coming hither, the gentry of these parts looked upon me as a man considerable, and had already raised me sixty horse towards a hundred, and a hundred foot, and were continuing to raise me a greater number. But at the sight of this order of your Highness, I resolved to disband them, and come up to Oxford, where I'll starve in more security' (Warburton, *Prince Rupert*, ii, 335; iii, 56).

and it was exacted with an unsparing hand. 'Know,' says a
letter from the Royalist governor of Worcester to some default-
ing parishes, 'that unless you bring to me (at a day and a house
in Worcester named) the monthly contribution for six months,
you are to expect an unsanctified troop of horse among you,
from whom if you hide yourselves, they shall fire your houses
without mercy, hang up your bodies wherever they find them,
and scare your ghosts.'[1]

This system of maintenance ruined the discipline of the King's
army as well as ruining the country. In every county there were
a number of superfluous garrisons established for financial rather
than military reasons. Oxfordshire, for instance, in 1645 paid
contributions to eighteen garrisons, many of them very small
ones it is true, but these little garrisons were often the most oppressive.[2] There is a picture of the state of the country in a play
called *The Old Troop*, written by Lacy, an actor who fought in
the King's army. He describes a troop of Royalist horse living
at free quarters on the county: their captain stays at Oxford
in comfort, while his officers Flay-Flint and Ferret-Farm plunder
the countrymen at their pleasure for the benefit of the troop.
Hard by their quarters is Thievesden House with a Parliamentary garrison under Captains Holdforth and Tubtext. The Roundhead captains live by enforced contributions also, but they have
a more original device for raising money. Rumours are spread
of the approach of the enemy, and the people are persuaded to
bring their valuables into Thievesden House for the sake of
security. Thereupon the captains designed to surrender the garrison, on condition that their private property should be respected, and to march off with the valuables of the countrymen
under cover of that phrase. Such things were possible, and there
is no doubt that they sometimes took place.[3]

These petty garrisons in country houses and country towns
were of no military value. They tended, as a Parliamentary
general, Sir John Meldrum, said, to foment rather than finish
the war, as the example of Germany during the Thirty Years'

---

[1] Whitelocke, *Memorials*, i, 540, ed. 1853.   [2] Ibid., i, 511.

[3] *The Old Troop, or Monsieur Raggou,* by John Lacy, 1672. Lacy's *Works*
reprinted by Patterson in *Dramatists of the Restoration*, 1875, pp. 132, 140,
152, 168, 181.

War had shown.[1] Soldiers who might have reinforced the King's marching army were wasted in maintaining unnecessary posts. Experienced Royalist leaders knew this, and in the later years of the war castles were dismantled and houses destroyed to save the cost of men and money required to keep them. Rupert gave Sir Thomas Hanmer the choice between garrisoning his residence (Appley Castle in Shropshire) at his own cost, or blowing it up.[2] He burnt Camden House in Gloucestershire in order to draw off the 300 men who held it. Another old soldier, Sir Richard Willis, the Royalist governor of Newark, proposed in September 1645 that the King should dismantle and evacuate all the inland fortresses, and limit himself to holding the sea-ports. Thus he would be able to meet Fairfax and Cromwell in the field with equal numbers, and to retrieve the disaster of Naseby.[3]

[1] Sir John Meldrum to the Committee of Both Kingdoms, 2nd November 1644: 'I cannot forbear that accustomed freedom I have taken to acquaint your Lordships with what, in my apprehension, I conceive may be both dangerous and unprofitable to this State, which is to keep up forts and garrisons, which may rather foment than finish a war. France, Italy, and the Low Countries have found by experience during these three hundred years what losses are entailed by places being fortified, while the subjects of the isle of Britain, through absence thereof, have lived in more tranquillity. If Gainsborough had not been razed by my order, the enemy might have found a nest to have hatched much mischief at this time. Reading might have produced the same effects if the fortifications had not been demolished. If there be a garrison kept at Liverpool, there must be at least 300 men, which will make the jealousies and emulations amongst those gentlemen endless and chargeable. The place itself is one of the strongest that I have seen in England, which makes me to be the more apprehensive of danger, as well in regard of the partialities and factions amongst the gentlemen of the country as of the Papists in that county, who would find it an easier task to maintain a strong fortification made to their hand, if they could make themselves masters of it, than to raise a new fortification, upon any new commotion that may arise. I desire your resolution herein' (*Cal. State Papers, Dom.*, 1644–5, p. 91; see also Sprigge, *Anglia Rediviva*, p. 16).

[2] Webb, *Civil War in Herefordshire*, ii, 50; 'Mr. Hanmer is to consider whether he will man and mainteyne Appley Castle himselfe at his own charge, or leave it to another or have it blowne up. And if he shall choose to keepe it himselfe and hereafter lose it to the Rebel Enemy that then the damage that shall accrewe to the King in the recovery thereof shalbe refunded out of his estate.' On Camden House, see Clarendon, ix, 32; *Diary of Richard Symonds*, p. 166; Walker, *Historical Discourses*, p. 126.

[3] 'The King coming to Newarke, as afore said, and at a councel of warr proposing what was to be done, Sir Richard propounded that his Majestie would putt all his garrison soldjers in a body and march after Fairfax, then about Taunton. Newarke river was fordable, and in it 4,000 good foot.

Willis gave this advice in September 1645, but it was too late then. The issue of the war depended on the question whether King or Parliament could soonest organize an effective army. When the war began each side had to improvise an army somehow, and thanks to its greater resources the Parliament created a much larger and better equipped force than Charles could put in the field. But partly through the fault of the general who commanded it, and partly through the inferior quality of its troops, Parliament lost the advantage which it at first possessed, and the defects of its military organization and administration prevented it from regaining this superiority during the campaigns of 1643 and 1644. Fortune gave the King an opportunity, but he could not utilize it, for his own army was even worse organized than that of the Parliament. So there were two years of indecisive fighting, and when they ended the conclusion of the war seemed no nearer. True, each side by collecting its local forces and joining them to its main army could get together a body of troops strong enough to defeat its opponents in a battle, but these temporary successes produced no permanent results; for neither side could keep together an army strong enough to carry a campaign to a triumphant and decisive conclusion. To organize an effective army, to feed it, to clothe it, to pay it, and to recruit it, so as to maintain its fighting power and its numbers for any length of time, seemed beyond the skill of either.

'Our victories,' said a Parliamentary orator, in December 1644, 'the price of blood invaluable, so gallantly gotten and, which is more pity, so graciously bestowed, seem to have been put in a bag with holes; what we won one time, we lost another. The treasure is exhausted; the country is wasted. A summer's victory has proved but a winter's story. The game, however, shut up in autumn has to be new played again the next spring; as if the blood that has been shed were only to manure the

'There was then Newarke, Ashby, Tutbury, Lichfield, Belvoir, Werton, Bridgnorth, Denbigh, and other garrisons. Slight them all and all inland garrisons, keep your ports, as Exeter and Bristoll, &c., and you will have canon and a very considerable army to fight Fairfax. Besides, Goring's army in the West was then good too.
'The King likt it well; Ashburnham embraced Sir Richard for the proposition, and so did Lord Digby like it' (*Diary of Richard Symonds*, p. 270).

ground for a new crop of contention. Men's hearts have failed them with the observation of these things.'[1]

It was at this crisis of the war that Cromwell carried through the scheme for the reorganization of the Parliamentary forces which led to the formation of the New Model, and gave the Parliament that efficient army which secured the triumph of its cause. Yet though the realization of the scheme was mainly due to Cromwell's energy, and Cromwell's singleness of purpose, the idea of such a reorganization was not exclusively his. Sir William Waller in June 1644 had plainly told Parliament that an army compounded out of local levies would never do their business. 'Till you have an army merely your own,' said he, 'that you may command, it is impossible to do anything of importance.'[2] Massey also said much the same thing.[3]

Parliament perceived the necessity for such an army. It had hoped to secure it by remodelling Essex's army three months before Waller wrote. The ordinance passed on 26th March 1644, fixing Essex's army at 10,500 men and promising them constant pay, was a sort of anticipation of the New Model.[4] But the army was too small for its work, and the promise of constant pay was not kept. By the end of 1644, not only was the army of Essex reduced to half its numbers, but the armies under Waller and Manchester, which were co-operating with it, were in no better condition. 'The army,' wrote its three commanders about three weeks after the second battle of Newbury (15th November 1644), 'is much weakened both in horse and foot. The horse are very unable for marching or watching, having now for so long time been tired out with hard duty in such extremity of weather as hath been seldome seen; so that if much more be required at

---

[1] Rushworth, vi, 4.   [2] Gardiner, *Great Civil War*, ii, 5.

[3] 'I must be bold to present to your Lordships my opinion concerning the prosecution of this war, that I conceive the course now taken not to be the way to bring the same to so speedy an end or issue as is to be desired. For by this way of raising citizens (as soldiers) or taking in auxillary forces, the war must of necessity either lie near them, or the despatch of the present designs must answer their expectations, else away they are gone, being impatient of delay and absence from their families. It follows that the longer they march and the remoter (they are) from London, the slenderer still will their army grow; and the more his Majesty's armies show themselves abroad and the further they march the stronger they grow' (*Cal. State Papers, Dom.* 1644–5).

[4] Husbands, *Acts and Ordinances of Parliament*, folio, 1646, p. 442.

their hands you will quickly see your cavalry ruined without
fighting. The foot are not in better case. Besides the lessening of
their numbers through cold and so hard duty, we find sickness
to increase so much upon them, that we cannot in duty conceal
it from you, nor indeed with that Christian consideration which
we owe to them whose extreme sufferings we daily look upon
with not a little sorrow, the places we are in not affording firing,
food, or covering for them; nor is the condition of the people
less to be pitied, who both in our horse and foot quarters are so
exhausted, that they have so little left for themselves that we
may justly fear a famine will fall upon them.'[1]

It was obvious that no time was to be lost, and Parliament
promptly ordered the Committee of Both Kingdoms to 'consider the state and condition of all the armies and forces under
the Parliament'. Four days later it repeated this order, bidding
the committee also to consider 'of a frame or model of the whole
militia and present it to the House' (23rd November 1644). The
committee made no haste to obey; its time was taken up with
the daily details of administration, and Cromwell's quarrel with
Manchester filled the minds both of committee and Parliament.
It seemed as if the need for army reform would be forgotten
and thrust out of sight amid the sterile recriminations of the
Parliamentary leaders. Cromwell felt this.[2] On 9th December he
suddenly suspended his attack upon Manchester, declaring emphatically that it was more needful to 'put the army into a new
method' than to examine the faults of any of its generals. Then
followed the Self-Denying Ordinance, proposed by Cromwell on
9th December 1644, introduced into the House on 11th December, and read a third time by the Commons on 19th December.
The Lords delayed to consider it, and protested against passing
it. One reason they gave was that its passage would produce
such an alteration in the armies as would be of dangerous consequence to the cause. 'Till a new model be propounded to
succeed, they cannot but think the present frame better than
such a confusion which is like to follow' (7th January 1645).

[1] Gardiner, *Great Civil War*, ii, 61; *Cal. State Papers, Dom.*, 1644–45,
p. 125.

[2] Gardiner, *Great Civil War*, ii, 79, 82; see also Bruce, *Manchester's
Quarrel with Cromwell*, lxvii.

When the Commons persisted in pressing them to pass the ordinance they finally threw it out (13th January 1645).[1] Meanwhile the scheme for the reorganization of the army was nearing completion. The Committee of Both Kingdoms was slow to take the matter in hand, and did not seriously set to work till 31st December. But it was able to report to the House on 9th January 1645, and two days later the outline of the scheme was voted. There were to be ten regiments of horse of 600 men each, twelve regiments of foot of 1,200 apiece, and 1,000 dragoons. An eleventh regiment of horse was added in 18th January, making the total of the army up to 22,000 men. On the same day the ordinance establishing the army and imposing an assessment of about £56,000 per month on certain specified districts for its maintenance was read a first and second time. On the 21st January Sir Thomas Fairfax was appointed general by 101 votes to 69, Cromwell and the younger Vane being the two tellers for the yeas. The ordinance passed its third reading on the 27th January, and was sent up to the Lords on the following day. The Lords passed it on 15th February, but a new struggle between the two Houses took place over the names of the officers nominated to command under Fairfax, and though the Lords finally gave way, it was not till April that the organization of the new army was completed, and not till May that the New Model could set forth on its career of conquest.[2] After much hesitation, many delays, and many mistakes, the Long Parliament had at last solved the problem which the times imposed upon it.

[1] Gardiner, *Great Civil War*, ii, 89, 92, 117, 118.

[2] Ibid., ii, 117, 119, 128-9, 186-90. For the ordinances, see Husbands, *Acts and Ordinances*, 1646, folio, pp. 599, 623, 627, 629. For the scheme of the Committee of Both Kingdoms for remodelling the army, see *Cal. State Papers, Dom.*, 1644-5, p. 232.

CHAPTER III

The New Model

AT FIRST THE New Model was only one of several armies in the service of the Parliament. In 1645 there were also the Scots under Leslie numbering not less than 21,000 men. Nottingham-shire and the six northern counties had a separate army of 10,000 men under Major-General Poyntz, while Major-General Massey, who commanded the forces of Wiltshire and the four western counties, had probably as many more. Besides these there were smaller bodies of troops in North and South Wales, about 5,000 horse and foot in the eastern counties, and the local levies of the Midlands under Major-General Browne. There must have been, at least, 60,000 or 70,000 men in the pay of the Parliament in 1645, without counting the Scots.

By a gradual process these separate armies either disappeared altogether or were absorbed in the New Model. The local levies were dismissed to their homes at the conclusion of the first Civil War. Massey's force was disbanded in the autumn of 1646, and the northern army was placed under the command of Fair-fax in the summer of 1647. On 19th July 1647 Fairfax was made commander-in-chief of all the forces in England and Wales, and he continued to hold that post till his resignation on 26th June 1650.[1] By the incorporation of certain regiments from these other armies into the New Model, and by the addition of some new regiments raised during the second Civil War, the army under Fairfax's command rose to double its original size. In March 1649 the Commonwealth had in England 44,373 soldiers, besides 2,500 more who were to be disbanded.[2] The reconquest of Ireland and the war with Scotland necessitated a further increase. In July 1652 there were over 34,000 men in Ireland, and about the

[1] *Lords' Journals*, ix, 339; *Commons' Journals*, vi, 430–32.
[2] *Cal. State Papers, Dom.*, 1649–50, p. 28; *Commons' Journals*, vi, 157.

same number in England and Scotland, so that the Common-wealth had then nearly 70,000 soldiers in arms.[1] From 1652, however, the number steadily decreased. Two years later the forces on foot in the three kingdoms were rather less than 53,000 men.[2] Further reductions took place in 1655 and in 1657, and by the end of the Protectorate the army, including the forces in Flanders and Jamaica, was not much more than 42,000 men.[3] Finally, in February 1660, on the eve of the Restoration, its numbers were fixed at 28,342.[4]

Having traced the growth of the army and shown what its numbers were at different times, the next thing to consider is, how it was raised, and of what sort of men it was composed.

The New Model was originally formed by incorporating what-ever remained of the armies of Essex, Manchester, and Waller at the time of its formation. But these armies were so reduced by the campaign of 1644 that they could not supply half of the 14,400 infantry required for Fairfax. A calculation of the men available from these sources in March 1645 showed that Waller's army could supply about 600 foot, that of Essex about 3,000, and that of Manchester about 3,500.[5] To fill the gap it was re-solved to raise about 8,500 men (in London, in the Eastern

[1] *Commons' Journals*, vii, 224; Ludlow, *Memoirs*, i, 295, 360, 497, ed. 1894.

[2] *Antiquarian Repertory*, ii, 12, 2nd edition.

[3] The establishments for the forces in England and Ireland are missing, so that it is impossible to give the exact figures. The establishment for Scotland exists, and there is a paper presented to Parliament in the spring of 1659 showing the pay due to the army, and approximately the strength of the forces in the three nations (*Commons' Journals*, vii, 628; *Scotland and the Protectorate*, p. 373). Taking these as a basis, I calculate that there were in September, 1658:

In England (officers and men, excluding garrisons) about 10,000
In Scotland 10,400
In Ireland . . . . 14,000 or 15,000
In Flanders 6,600
In Jamaica 1,500

Total, 42,500 or 43,500

The strength of the companies and troops in Ireland is not exactly stated in the estimate for pay, but it was considerably higher than in England or Scotland. Moreover, by the spring of 1659 the number of troops in Flanders was about 3,000 less than in 1658, so that under Richard Cromwell the army was probably about 40,000 without counting the garrisons in England.

[4] *Harleian MS.*, 6,844, f. 182; Establishment of 27th February 1659-60.

[5] *Report on the MSS. of the Duke of Portland*, i, 215.

Association, and in the south-eastern counties) by the familiar
process of impressment. The *quota* of each county was fixed, and
its authorities were ordered to send their men to headquarters
by a certain date.[1] As it happened, however, not much more
than half the men required were actually sent, and at the end of
June it became necessary to impress a further 4,000. More than
half the infantry of the New Model were therefore pressed men,
and yet, when the army took the field in May 1645, it was still
3,000 or 4,000 below its proper numbers.[2]

There was no zeal amongst the men thus forced into the ranks,
and at first they deserted and ran home again in great numbers,
and, as Fairfax complained, with perfect impunity.[3] But physically they were good material for soldiers, and after the first few

---

[1] *Cal. State Papers, Dom.*, 1644–45, pp. 381, 625; Husbands, *Acts and
Ordinances*, ii, 623.

[2] A circular letter sent by the Committee of Both Kingdoms to various
counties proves this: 'It is now three months and more since that we
did by our letters, according to an Ordinance of Parliament, appoint you
to cause 1,000 able and serviceable men for the wars, to be levied and
impressed within your county for recruiting the Parliament's army under
the command of Sir Thos. Fairfax; and though we have since constantly
urged that the numbers behind might be supplied, and have cleared up all
doubts retarding that service, yet we find that you, as also the Committees
of other counties, come far short in the delivery of your proportion of
recruits. The army, relying on the recruits assigned, very early in the spring
took the field, and has since been engaged in several actions; and lately in a
battle (Naseby) with the enemy. Though it pleased God to give them a happy
victory, yet wanting their full strength . . . the army hath not been of such
force as to improve that success to the most advantage, and hath been
forced to desert the design against Oxford to our great sorrow. And by this
late encounter the strength of our army cannot be but much weakened, so
as we conceive to carry on the war this summer, the army requires not only
the first intended levy, but an increase of recruits to complete the army
according to the establishment. We therefore appoint you to cause 500 able
men to be levied by press within your county, and sent to Reading by the
16th July, to be clothed as formerly directed, the charge of all which you are
to pay yourself out of the assessments' (*Cal. State Papers, Dom.*, 1644–45,
p. 625). In another letter the committee say 'there have been so many miscarriages by retardings, defective numbers, and running away, that the
army has never yet had the numbers assigned by the establishment' (ibid.,
1645–7, p. 99).

[3] In a letter dated 26th June 1645, Fairfax says that he believes he has
not half the number of foot he should have according to the establishment:
'The difficulty of raising recruits in the Associated Counties, which are so
populous, and their suffering men that run from the army to return and
continue unquestioned among them, and unsent up to the army, as this
seems strange, so the latter, if no course be taken to redress it, will certainly
be such an encouragement to those in the army to quit it, that it will be
impossible for me to keep it up, though I should be recruited every day'
(*Old Parliamentary History*, xiii, 518).

months little is heard of their desertion. The last great press for the army took place in 1651, when Parliament ordered 10,000 men to be raised to reinforce its troops in Ireland. It was then remarked that the men raised by impressment for that service were better than those who had voluntarily enlisted. They were, said a newspaper, 'choicer men for bodies' than the volunteer regiments, which were 'so full of children, that the officers have abused their trust, in bringing such who are fitter for school than manlike exercises'.[1]

Impressment for the army of the Commonwealth stopped in 1651, and it was not resumed under the Protectorate. From that date to 1660 the ranks of the army were filled by voluntary enlistment. Between 1645 and 1647 the army also derived many recruits from an unexpected source. A considerable number of the King's soldiers, after the surrender of the garrisons or detachments to which they belonged, enlisted in the New Model.[2] The fact is attested by Fairfax himself. After the surrender of Oxford, Fairfax told Sir Philip Warwick that the best common soldiers he had came out of the Royalist army. 'I found you had made them good soldiers,' said Fairfax, 'and I have made them good men.'[3] Nevertheless, in July 1647 Fairfax found it necessary to order that all Cavaliers who had enlisted in the army during the last two months should be struck out of the muster-rolls.[4]

From the time of the battle of Worcester to the close of the Protectorate it was easy to obtain all the volunteers who were

[1] See Ludlow, *Memoirs*, ed. 1894, i, 278; cf. *Mercurius Politicus*, pp. 890, 891.

[2] In 1647 Lord Pembroke asserted that there were 4,000 ex-Royalists in the army. The soldiers answered thus:
'It is trouble unto them, that it should be said, that the Army is no more a new Model, that 4,000 Cavaliers are in it; when as all the World cannot tax the Army (consisting of 21,000 Men) for having one commissionate Officer, that ever was on the King's side against the Parliament, but one, and he was by one or both Houses intrusted in business of Concernment after his coming in, and made a Colonel by them, and afterwards recommended by Authority derived from them to the Army; as for the common Foot Soldiers that are in the Army, who being taken Prisoners listed themselves in the Army, they have been engaged in several desperate Services, as in storming of Towns, and proved valiant and faithful to their Trust' (Rushworth, vi, p. 480; cf. Sprigge, *Anglia Rediviva*, pp. 135, 205).

[3] Warwick, *Memoirs*, p. 253.

[4] Rushworth, vi, 639. Order dated 21st July 1647.

needed. There were numbers of old soldiers scattered through the country who were willing to return to the colours.[1] Officers who wanted recruits employed an agent in the district in which the regiment was originally raised, and found no difficulty in getting them.[2] For though there was no real territorial system in existence, certain regiments had an original connexion with certain counties, which, in some cases, continued to exist. Lambert's regiment of horse, for instance, was a distinctively Yorkshire regiment; Montague's foot was a Cambridgeshire regiment; Ingoldsby's was connected with Buckinghamshire and Oxfordshire; and the Protector's own regiment of foot was a Lancashire regiment.[3] Recruits for the infantry were habitually raised

---

[1] In 1655 the threat of a Royalist rising led to a sudden increase of the army. Major William Boteler (of Berry's horse) wrote to Thurloe on 24th February 1655, asking to know the Protector's pleasure concerning the recruiting of his two troops to 100. 'I confess I have done nothing yet, for that I was a stranger in theise parts, and could not get such men as I might elsewhere; and yet I would be loath to call any poore men from their callings and familyes, unless there were most absolute necessity, and I might assure them pay. And rather then not fill up our troopes with such as we know to be honest confiding men, some of us had rather adventure our lives with those we have already.' Captain Hope of the regiment of Colonel Saunders, wrote on 24th March: 'It hath been my endeavour, according to your highnes orders, to complayte my troope to a hundred; for that purpos I sent into Darbyshire to ingage what soldyers I could that had heretofore bin in servis, and others that weare well affected; yett there are manye that are acted from a good principall that have listed themselves, and beyond there abilletyes have layd out what they could procure from frendes to furnish themselves with horses and arms' (Thurloe Papers, iii, 172, 297).

[2] Colonel Robert Lilburne writes in April 1651, to Captain Adam Baynes: 'I conceive if we had money for recruits, they might with more conveniency be raised in Yorkshire, and put the state to no charges for an officer to conduct them; but if you will please to do me the favour to receive the money, and confer with Capt. Peaverell and Cornt Sanderson about the raising 40 or 50 honest and stout men, they might be sent with some other recruits that come from London; and for the rest I think we shall get them in the north parts of England very well, and for paying them that advance which is allowed, I shall disburse it here and charge it upon you by bill.' In a second letter he adds: 'I have agents at work in our northern counties, and many come to us very well appointed, and I think if I rest here about ten days longer my regiment will be reasonable complete' (Letters from Roundhead Officers in Scotland, pp. 19, 23).

[3] Lambert's regiment of horse had been part of the army of the Northern Association, as had Robert Lilburne's horse referred to in the last note. Montague's commission from Manchester in 1643 authorized him to raise men in Cambridgeshire and the Isle of Ely (Collins, Peerage, iii, 449), and on the incorporation of the regiment into the New Model the pressed men of that particular district were assigned to it (Cal. State Papers, Dom., 1644–5, p. 467). Ingoldsby's foot represented the regiment raised by Hampden in 1642 to serve under Essex, and as it had been raised in Oxford,

during the Protectorate by the employment of sergeants selected
for that purpose.[1]

It was always much easier to raise men for the cavalry than
the infantry. The disinclination for mounted service which Cecil
had complained of in 1630 had vanished entirely. When a regiment of horse was wanted to serve in Flanders in 1658 it was
enough for the captain to advertise the fact in the newspapers.
'The captain,' says one of these advertisements, 'being an old
soldier, chooseth rather to accept of such in the service; therefore any that are old soldiers, or gentlemen, if they repair to
the Bell Inn in King Street, Westminster, or to the sign of the
Pelican in Speenhamland at Newbury, may be entertained into
the said troop, and each man shall receive back, breast, headpiece, pistol, holsters, and a considerable advance. And in case
any horse miscarry in the said service, it shall be made good to
him that sustains the loss, who shall be furnished with another.[2]

As a rule a recruit for the cavalry brought his own horse with
him, and often his own arms too. Monck, in ordering his major

---

Berks and Bucks, so it was generally quartered in those counties during the
Commonwealth and Protectorate. The particular foot regiment of Cromwell's referred to was one raised for him in 1650 and specially ordered to be
raised in Lancashire (*Commons' Journals*, vi, 428).

[1] Monck's *Order-Book* contains the following entry:
'Sept. 2, 1659, Instructions of Sergt. Henry Owram of Col. Fairfax's
regiment who is employed into England for getting of recruits. He is to be
careful as near as he can to entertain such soldiers as have served the
Parliament, or at least such as are well affected to the Parliament, and if he
entertain them in a town is he to get a certificate under the hand of the
magistrates what day they were entertained, and if in the country under
the hand of one or two of the Justices of the peace, which certificates he is
to bring along with him and deliver them to the Commissary of Musters,
and he is to take care that the soldiers carry themselves civilly in their
march, and in case he be not careful of this he must expect to be questioned
for it. And the officers of the Army, Justices of the Peace, and Constables
are hereby desired to be assisting to him in raising and conducting the said
men.
'The like to seven other sergeants.'

[2] *Mercurius Politicus*, 15th to 22nd July 1658. Here is another from the
same paper, 3rd to 10th March 1659:
'Whereas divers persons have expressed a willingness (if they might have
an opportunity) to serve his Highness and the Commonwealth in this
campagne in Flanders.
'These are to give notice, that there is a troop of horse in the regiment
under the command of his Excellency the Lord General Lockhart, the
number whereof is not compleat; and if the persons which are inclined to
this service, shall repair to Capt. Richard Mill in Gardiner's lane, Westminster, within six days, they will by him be satisfied, upon what terms
they may be employed.'

to recruit each troop in his regiment up to eighty men, tells him
to take care 'that such as he entertains be well affected persons,
well mounted and armed, and (as near as he can) old soldiers'.[1]
Another of Monck's orders runs thus: 'The captain or chief
officer of any troop of horse in the service here, wherein there is
a vacancy, is desired to admit of Mr. Robert Rasell thereinto, he
bringing with him a horse and arms fit for service.'[2] A trooper in
a cavalry regiment was therefore a capitalist in a small way, and
as also his pay was three times that of a foot soldier, and since
he was for these reasons a volunteer and not a pressed man, he
generally came from a higher social class. 'The old decayed
serving-men, tapsters, and such kind of fellows,' of whose presence in the ranks of Essex's cavalry Cromwell had complained
to Hampden, had now disappeared. According to an army chaplain, many of the troopers in the army with which Cromwell
invaded Scotland were men 'of good parts and learning'; for
'it was there a good employment for a gentleman, and as competent provision, to have near twenty shillings by the week,
and live well and gentlemanlike, keeping themselves and their
horse for some six shillings a week; and there were known many
young physicians and students in other liberal arts that thought
it a preferment'.[3]

The chaplain exaggerates a little, but it is clear that the
cavalry were the aristocrats of the army. There were many men
of some education amongst them, and in the political movements of 1647 and subsequent years it was always the troopers
of the cavalry who took the lead.[4] In the infantry, on the other
hand, the majority of the men could not even write their names.
When petitioning or attesting the evidence given before courts-
martial, most of them make their mark instead of signing.

Both in the infantry and cavalry men of education could rise
from the ranks to a commission. Of the 'Agitators' elected by
the private soldiers in 1647 to represent their grievances, five,
if not more, subsequently became officers. One, William Allen,
of Cromwell's regiment, became adjutant-general of the horse
in the Irish army. Another, Edward Sexby, rose to the command

---

[1] *Order-Book*, 9th August, 1659.   [2] Ibid., 21st September 1654.
[3] Gumble, *Life of Monck*, p. 34.
[4] *Clarke Papers*, i. xv, 33, 430; Rushworth, vi, 474.

of a regiment of foot, and died in the Tower for plotting Cromwell's assassination.[1] It was naturally easiest to get a commission in a regiment intended for foreign service in an unhealthy climate. In 1655 Monck sent four companies of foot from Scotland to serve in Jamaica, out of whose twelve officers six were promoted privates.[2] But a good non-commissioned officer could obtain a commission in the ordinary course of promotion. There is a curious letter written by a Captain Baynes, who was serving under Monck in Scotland. Baynes was anxious to give his brother Richard a commission, and there was a lieutenant's place vacant in the company. 'But,' said he, 'my brother Richard being young and raw, I cannot without too much appearance of partiality bring him over the head of my ensign.' Nor could he promote the ensign and give Richard the ensign's place – 'For my eldest sergeant is so deserving that I cannot well be his hindrance, especially now when experienced soldiers is to be made use of.' And so Sergeant William Robson obtained the commission.[3]

There is another letter from General Monck himself to Cromwell, recommending the senior corporal of a certain troop in his regiment. 'He is a godly man, a stout soldier, and faithful to your Highness and the government; I humbly desire your Highness that a commission may be sent for him to be quartermaster.'[4]

More instances might be added, but these are sufficient to prove that a private soldier in the Cromwellian army might rise from the ranks, and that he not infrequently did so. After the restoration it became impossible. Colonel Clifford Walton in his most admirable history of the British army from 1660 to 1700 says emphatically, 'Among the many recommendations to commissions that I have perused, I have not met with a single instance of the actual or contemplated promotion of a soldier from the ordinary ranks.'[5]

---

[1] For a list see *Clarke Papers*, i, 436. On Allen, see ibid., p. 432. On Sexby, see the *Dictionary of National Biography*. Another, John Bremen or Braman, became a major (*Clarke Papers*, i, 79).

[2] See *Rawlinson MSS.*, A, xxvi, 206, Bodleian Library.

[3] *Letters from Roundhead Officers*, p. 66.

[4] *Clarke MSS.*, l. 105, 14th April 1655.

[5] Clifford Walton, *History of the British Standing Army*, p. 587.

Having described the composition of the rank and file of the army, the next thing to consider is the organization of the regiment, and the character and position of the regimental officers.

The eleven regiments of horse in the New Model consisted of 600 men each, exclusive of officers, and were divided into six troops of 100 men each.[1] The field-officers were a colonel and a major; and the commissioned officers of each troop were four: a captain, a lieutenant, a cornet, and a quartermaster. The non-commissioned officers of the troop were three corporals, for there were no sergeants in a regiment of horse. In this it resembled the Household Cavalry of to-day. 'Sergeant Obadiah Bind-their-kings-in-chains' of Ireton's regiment, into whose mouth Macaulay puts his poem on Naseby, ought to have been styled corporal.

Though there were six troops in the regiment of horse, the names of only four captains appear in the lists of officers.[2] The colonel and major had each the command of a troop, and drew pay in the double capacity of captains and field-officers. A colonel's pay, for instance, in 1647 was twelve shillings a day as colonel, and ten shillings as captain, and the major's was calculated in the same way.[3] The command of the colonel's troop was practically in the hands of his lieutenant, who was called a captain-lieutenant, ranked as junior captain, and had a prescriptive claim to the first vacancy in the command of a troop in

[1] The cavalry under Essex had been raised in single troops which were afterwards formed into regiments. This was the old practice. Sir James Turner says: 'Seventy or eighty years ago there were no Regiments of Horse (properly so called), only Troops or Companies, and these sometimes were two hundred strong, sometimes one hundred, and sometimes not so many, and upon occasion of service, Troops were join'd together, and the command of some of them given for a time by the Prince or State to some person of great quality, whom they thought fit for that employment. Sometimes three troops were join'd together, sometimes five or six, yet they had not the name of a Regiment, nor had he who commanded that Body so composed, the title of Colonel. The Estates of the United Provinces used this much, but now they levy Regiments. The furious wars which began in Christendom in the year of our Lord 1618 (whereof in process of time we had a deep share at home), reversed many good old customs and constitutions, and with other changes introduced Regiments of Horse' (*Pallas Armata*, p. 232). The horse of the New Model were from the first raised in regiments.

[2] See the list at the end of Sprigge's *Anglia Rediviva*, reprinted in Peacock's *Army Lists of Roundheads and Cavaliers*.

[3] *Lords' Journals*, x, 66. See the chapter on the 'Pay and Maintenance of the Army,' p. 183, *post*.

the regiment.[1] The strength of each of the twelve regiments of foot in the New Model was 1,200 men. The regiment consisted of ten companies, but the companies were not of equal size. The colonel's company numbered 200 men; the lieutenant-colonel's 160; the major's 140. The remaining seven companies were each 100 strong.[2]

As in the cavalry, the field-officers were also captains of companies, and received pay in both capacities. A colonel of foot drew twelve shillings a day as colonel and eight shillings as captain, and the lieutenant-colonel and major in proportion. The commissioned officers of the foot company were three: a captain, a lieutenant, and an ensign, and the lieutenant of the colonel's company was styled a captain-lieutenant.

The non-commissioned officers of a foot company of 100 men consisted of two sergeants, three corporals, and a gentleman-at-arms. In the larger companies of the three field-officers the number of sergeants and corporals was increased.[3]

Attached to the New Model was one regiment of dragoons

[1] 'The Colonell in times past hath had the power to elect or at least to nominate all his own captaines, but since it hath been assumed and taken from him by the power of the Generall; so that now though he command all in his regiment, yet he electeth none but his own lieutenant, who in curtesie hath the title of a captaine, and in all meetings may take his place as the punie captaine of that regiment' (Markham, *Decades of War*, 1622, p. 163). The lists of officers present at courts–martial and similar documents show that the captain–lieutenants of the New Model held the position Markham describes. The grade still existed in the army of Charles the Second (see Clifford Walton, p. 409).

[2] *Lords' Journals*, x, 69. The original establishment of the New Model is missing, but that of 3rd November 1647, which is printed in the *Lords' Journals*, reproduces the details of its predecessor with very little alteration. Some changes were made, but excepting in the number of regiments, and amongst the miscellaneous officials of the staff, there was no important alteration. For the New Model, instead of a detailed establishment, we have only some general votes passed by Parliament or the Committee of Both Kingdoms (see *Commons' Journals*, iv, 27; *Cal. State Papers, Dom.*, 1644–45, p. 232).

[3] The 'gentleman-at-arms' must be distinguished from the 'gentleman of a company'. The latter was something between a lance-corporal and a private, being a soldier on probation for promotion, acting generally as a file leader or 'sentinel-perdue' (see Colonel Clifford Walton's quotation from Elton's *Complete Body of the Art Military*, in his *History of the British Standing Army*, p. 416; cf. Markham, *Decades of War*, 1622, pp. 49, 65). The gentleman-at-arms was 'simply a sort of storekeeper for the regimental arms and ammunition; he was responsible for the preservation, repair, and marking of all arms' (Clifford Walton, p. 415). In the establishment of 1647 there is one 'gentleman-at-arms' in every company of foot. After 1655 he seems to have disappeared.

consisting of 1,000 men divided into ten companies. It was considered as mounted infantry rather than cavalry, but its regimental organization was a mixture of the two. It had the commissioned officers of a horse regiment and the non-commissioned officers of a regiment of infantry.

In addition to these company officers there were attached to each regiment certain others, described sometimes as 'general officers of the regiment' and at other times as 'staff'. Cavalry and infantry regiments alike had a provost-marshal, a surgeon, a clerk,[1] and a chaplain. The infantry had in addition a regimental quartermaster, and a drum-major.[2]

Each troop or company had its musicians. In the cavalry there were originally three trumpeters to each troop; in the infantry two drummers in a company; the dragoons like the infantry had two drummers to each company. The musicians were habitually employed as messengers as well as for their proper function. 'Trumpeters,' says Sir James Turner, 'because they are frequently sent to an enemy, ought to be witty and discreet, and must drink but little, that so they may be rather apt to circumvent others, than be circumvented; they should be cunning, and wherever they are sent, they should be careful to observe warily the works, guards and sentinels of an enemy, and give an account of them at their return.'[3] In 1643 when Rupert was threatening Bristol he sent in a trumpeter, ostensibly to demand the dead bodies of two Royalists, in reality, thought the Parliamentarians, as a spy. The trumpeter also inquired for a particular officer of the garrison, and said that the Earl of Cleveland, who had a command under Rupert, would be obliged if he would send him a pound of tobacco. 'I being out of the way,' says the narrator, 'Col. Fiennes sent him one pound, and Col. Popham another.'[4]

Drummers were employed in the same way. 'If they can carry a message wittily to the enemy,' says Sir James Turner, 'they

---

[1] The duties of a clerk are set forth in the *Life of Adam Martindale*, p. 37 (Chatham Society, 1845).

[2] The drum-major, appears in the establishment of November, 1647, at 1 s. 6d. per diem. He disappears from the Scotch and probably from the English establishment in 1657 (*Lords' Journals*, x, 68; *Scotland and the Protectorate*, pp. 306, 376). He was reintroduced after the Restoration (Clifford Walton, p. 465). On military music in general, see Grose, ii, 41.

[3] Turner, *Pallas Armata*, p. 235.   [4] *Bibliotheca Gloucestrensis*, p. cli.

may be permitted to be drolls.'[1] Yet it was dangerous to be too witty. When Fairfax, after making a breach in Sherborne Castle, summoned the governor to surrender, the drummer delivered his message very stoutly, and being, as the governor thought, saucy, was threatened with hanging.[2]

The number of flags was much greater than it is in modern armies. Each company of foot or troup of horse had its distinguishing standard.[3] At the beginning of the war the standard of a troop of horse was generally an emblematical device of some kind with an appropriate motto. That of the Earl of Essex's bodyguard bore the motto 'Cave, Adsum,' which the Royalists interpreted to refer to their ignominious flight in their first battle,[4] or to their supposed propensity for plundering. Some captains had elaborate designs almost like political cartoons. One, for instance, painted on his banner a picture of an armed soldier with his sword drawn threatening a kneeling bishop. Out of the soldier's mouth came a label with the words 'Visne episcopari,' out of the bishop's the words 'Nolo, nolo'.[5] A Royalist flag taken at Marston Moor had represented upon it a lion lying down while a small beagle was biting its tail. Out of the lion's mouth issue the words 'Pym, Pym, Pym, Quousque tandem abutere patientia nostra'. Later in the war armorial bearings and less fanciful devices seem to have been preferred. The standards of the infantry were throughout much simpler. The different companies in a regiment of London trained bands all had flags of the same general type, distinguished by some slight additions or variations in the case of each company.[6] A similar system was fol-

[1] Turner, *Pallas Armata*, p. 219; cf. Markham, *Decades of War*, pp. 57–60; Ward, *Animadversions of War*, p. 194.

[2] Sprigge, *Anglia Rediviva*, p. 93.

[3] On standards in general see Grose, ii, 51, 137; Clifford Walton, pp. 457–62; Markham, *Decades of War*, pp. 73, 83.

[4] *Mercurius Aulicus*, 18th June 1643; *A Full Relation of the Late Victory at Marston Moor, together with a list of the cornets and ensigns, etc., sent by Captain Stewart*, 1644, 4to.

[5] See 'Cornets, Flags or Pennons of Sundry Commanders . . . in the Armies of the Commonwealth' (Prestwich, *Respublica Anglicana*, 1787, p. 24). This list is apparently derived from the broadside published by J. Cole, a copy of which is in the Sutherland Clarendon in the Bodleian.

[6] See Lord Dillon's *MS. List of Officers of the London Trained Bands in 1643*, which contains illustrations of the flags in use (*Archæologia*, vol. lii).

lowed in the regular army. In 1650 when Colonel Charles Fairfax was given the command of an infantry regiment intended to serve against the Scots, he wrote to a friend in London to order flags for it. He adopted as his own colours those of his nephew, Lord Fairfax, which were blue and white. All the ten flags were to be made 'of the best taffaty of the deepest blue that can be gotten'. His own was to be 'at least two yards square', and to bear upon it 'within a well-wrought round, these two words one under the other, "Fideliter, Faeliciter"'.[1] The lieutenant-colonel's flag was likewise to be blue, but with the red cross of England in one corner, and the major's 'blue with the red cross and white streaks'. Finally, the eldest captain and the rest of the captains according to seniority were to be distinguished by one or more white mullets (or stars) in a blue field.

Moreover, as neither the regiments of horse nor foot were distinguished by numbers, each was officially designated by the name of its colonel, and was called Colonel So-and-so's regiment. As the command of a regiment often changed hands, and some had four or five different commanders between 1645 and 1660, it is difficult to trace the history of a regiment. Cromwell's regiment of horse in the New Model passed from Cromwell to John Desborough, then to Valentine Walton, and finally to Charles Howard.

The officers of the New Model in general were described by their opponents as factious and low-born sectaries. 'All of them,' wrote Denzil Holles, 'from the general (except what he may have in expectation after his father's death) to the meanest sentinel, are not able to make a thousand a year lands; most of the colonels are tradesmen, brewers, tailors, goldsmiths, shoemakers and the like.'[2] The statement is untrue. It has been calculated that out of thirty-seven colonels and general officers twenty-one were commoners of good family, nine were members of noble families, and only seven were not gentlemen by birth.[3] A large number of the inferior officers belonged to the minor landed gentry, and came from families whose pedigrees and arms were registered in the visitations of the heralds. A good many were

[1] *Proceedings of the Society of Antiquaries*, 1853, ii, 250.
[2] Holles, *Memoirs*, ed. Maseres, p. 149.
[3] Markham, *Life of the Great Lord Fairfax*, p. 199.

drawn from the trading classes in London and elsewhere, but did not generally rise to command regiments till much later in the war.[1] And throughout the whole period the cavalry officers, like the troopers they commanded, were drawn from a higher social class than the infantry officers. It is also a safe generalization to say that the social status of the officers of the army was higher during the first few years of its existence than it became during the Protectorate. For with the conclusion of the wars the country gentleman who took up arms for political or religious motives tended to be replaced by the soldier who made arms his profession.

Another charge which hostile critics brought against the officers of the New Model was their lack of military experience. Robert Baillie, writing at the time of its formation, speaks of it as 'ill commanded' and 'without officers of experience'. 'Few of the officers are thought capable of their places; if they do great service many will be deceived.' The complaint was raised that 'a multitude of good officers,' most of them Scots, had either been left out or put out.[2]

The charge was admitted by the friends of the army. The officers of the New Model, says Sprigge, 'were better Christians than soldiers, and wiser in faith than fighting'. At Naseby, according to him, the King had on his side 'not so few as fifteen hundred officers, that were old soldiers of great experience through long experience in foreign parts'; whereas on the Parliamentary side there were not ten officers who had any military experience 'save what this war had given them'.[3] It did not matter if it was so, replied another army chaplain. 'Some men gain more experience in two years than others in ten, because they are more advertent, and have better parts. And for our English wars our English experience is as good as any, and we have had more experimental service in these three or four years

[1] In a vindication of the army from the charge of intending to sack London, published in the summer of 1647, it is asserted: 'There are verie few of us, but have most of this world's interest in the Citie of London, being chiefly and principally raised thence, and verie many, especially of our officers, being citizens themselves having their wives and children therein' (*Vox Militaris*, p. 13).

[2] Robert Baillie, *Letters*, ed. Laing, ii, 265, 276, 286.

[3] Sprigge, pp. 46, 325.

war in England, than falls out in other parts in a far longer
time.'[1]

Such as they were, the officers were very carefully chosen.
Fairfax was authorized to take into the New Model 'all such
under officers and soldiers' as he thought fit, from the three
armies of Essex, Manchester, and Waller (11th March 1645). The
higher officers were drawn from the same source. Eight of the
twenty-four colonels had served in Essex's army and eleven
under Manchester. Aided by Skippon, his major-general, the
new commander-in-chief went carefully through the lists, and
picked the best men he could find without regard to social
position or political influence. And his freedom of choice was the
wider because in those days an officer could live on his pay.

By the terms of his appointment Fairfax had power to nominate all colonels and other regimental officers, subject to the
approval of the two Houses of Parliament. When the Lords objected to this provision, the Commons answered, that 'by giving
this power to the commander-in-chief to nominate his officers,
he will more oblige his officers, and better enable them to carry
on the work'. Essex had possessed the same right, and the Commons pointed out that this power was 'granted constantly and
usually to every commander-in-chief'. The Lower House carried
its principle, and more than that, when the Upper House sought
to strike out from the list presented by Fairfax the names of two
colonels and more than forty captains to whose opinions it objected, the persistence of the Commons obliged the peers again
to give way.[2]

All commissions in the army, therefore, ran in the name of the
commander-in-chief and bore his signature. Up to 26th June
1650, they were signed by Fairfax; from that date to the end
of 1653 by Cromwell as captain-general and commander-in-chief;
and from December 1653, when the functions of commander-
in-chief and civil head of the State were united, by Cromwell as
Protector.[3] After the fall of Richard Cromwell Parliament took

[1] Edward Bowles, *Manifest Truths*, p. 53.

[2] Husbands, *Ordinances*, 1646, p. 606; *Old Parliamentary History*, xiii
404, 422; Gardiner, *Great Civil War*, ii, 187. For Essex's commission, see
Old Parliamentary History, xi, 297.

[3] A number of specimens of these commissions are in print. Fairfax's
commission to Algernon Sidney as colonel of horse, *Fairfax Papers*, iii,

the appointment of officers into its own hands, entrusting commissioners with the duty of revising the list of officers, and presenting the names of those they thought fit to reappoint to the approval of the House. Commissions were to run in the name of the Parliament of the Commonwealth of England, and to be signed by the Speaker (6th June 1659).[1] But on 25th February 1660 Monck was made commander-in-chief, and the old method of appointment was revived. Thus throughout the period, excepting for about nine months, the commander-in-chief of the army appointed and promoted officers as he pleased.

Promotion by merit, tempered to some extent by seniority, was the rule adopted. In the troop or the company seniority appears to have constituted the chief claim, but in choosing field-officers merit had more weight than length of service. Supposing, for instance, that there was a vacant majority in a regiment of horse, the senior captain was recognized as having a claim to it, but very frequently some more promising senior captain from another regiment was put in over his head. The Protector kept the selection of the higher officers in his own hands, and the generals who commanded local armies in Scotland or Flanders could do no more than recommend their candidates to him, or make temporary appointments. Monck, for instance, writes to Cromwell in 1655, saying that majors are wanted for two regiments of horse, and will his Highness appoint at once. There are also two troops wanting captains, and for one of them he recommends Jeremiah Smith, 'an honest stout man and well affected to your Highness'. Finally, on the recommendation of the colonel of another regiment, he asks that a cornet in it shall be made a lieutenant and a quartermaster a cornet, but does not give any opinion of his own on their merits.[2] Similarly, Lockhart, commander-in-chief in Flanders, writes to

213; commissions from Cromwell to Captain Goldsmith and Lieutenant Wells in 1651, *Cromwelliana*, p. 116; Mackinnon's *Coldstream Guards*, ii, 235; to Fleetwood as commander-in-chief in Ireland (1652), to Monck as commander-in-chief in Scotland (1654), to Venables to command the army sent to the West Indies (1654), *Thurloe Papers*, i, 212; ii, 222; iii, 16.

[1] *Commons' Journals*, vii, 649, 673, 677. The form of the new commission is given on p. 674, and Fleetwood's own commission is printed in the *Thurloe Papers*, vii, 679. He is styled in it 'commander-in-chief under the Parliament'.

[2] *Scotland and the Protectorate*, p. 268.

C

Cromwell in 1658 saying: 'There being several vacancies of field
officers in the regiments here, I esteem it my duty to give your
Highness an account of them, and have taken the boldness to
offer a list of such persons, as I can judge fittest for the vacant
employments.' If the Protector does not approve of the persons
suggested, let him send persons he thinks more fit as soon as
possible, or the service will suffer. In another letter he says that
he has disposed of the vacant companies because the interest
of the service would not admit of any delays, but keeps the
higher posts vacant till he learns the Protector's pleasure.[1]

On the whole this system worked tolerably well. In the first
place, the Protector was admittedly an excellent judge of men,
and knew the personnel of the army extremely well. In the
second place, he generally took the advice of the local commanders about officers serving under them. Monck did not hesitate to remonstrate as well as to recommend. In one letter he
complains to Cromwell that an ensign has just been commissioned to his regiment who is very unsuited for campaigning in
Scotland, he being 'a High Dutchman, who is a sickly man, and
hardly able to endure the hills'.[2] In another letter Lilburne,
Monck's predecessor in the Scottish command, represents to the
Protector that his Highness has appointed a regimental provost-
marshal who had been dismissed for plundering, drinking, and
gaming, and suggests that 'his viciousness is very unlikely to
correct sin in others'.[3]

---

[1] *Thurloe Papers*, vii, 190, 277.   [2] *Scotland and the Protectorate*, p. 224.

[3] 'One Porter, formerly Marshall to Colonel Twistleton's regiment,
bringing an order from your Highnesse for his restoracion to his place,
having for great misdemeanours bin casheered the regiment, and Major
Cambridge and severall other honest officers of the said regiment being
with mee uppon the said Marshall's producing the said order, I finde a great
unwillingnesse in them to receive him uppon those grounds, which I am pers-
waded if they bee reall and throughly knowne to your Highnesse, your
Highnesse would nott thinke him a fitt member to bee continued; and
though hee was casheered cheiflie for oppressing and wronging the Country
then under proteccion, yett they informe [me] that they have charges
of severall natures against him, as for drunkennesse and gaming &c. which
they conceive themselves bound in conscience to prosecute though hee
should bee restored by virtue of this order, and thinke that his viciousnesse
is very unlikely to correct sin in others; and both they and I knowing how
much itt is against your Highnesse' principles and practice (and sometimes
private instruccions to many of your officers) to countenance such a man or
such thinges, the said Major Cambridge, and I thinke all the officers heere
of that regiment, having shewed mee their peticion to your Highnesse that
they may bee heard by your Highnesse or Court Martiall against the said

There was no doubt a certain amount of favouritism from
political or personal motives. Mrs Hutchinson asserts that Cromwell to consolidate his own power weeded out 'godly and
upright-hearted men', and filled up their places with 'pitiful
sottish beasts of his own alliance'.[1] But the charge is unfounded.
A number of good officers, it is true, were turned out of the
army because their stalwart republicanism made them refuse to
accept the Protectorate. But their successors were usually men
of capacity and experience. Some nepotism undoubtedly there
was, and then as now it was an advantage to be the nephew,
or cousin, or son-in-law of somebody in place. In one of Lockhart's letters he recommends a certain William Fleetwood to be
lieutenant of his regiment 'both upon the account of his family,
and his own merit', but there is sufficient evidence from other
sources that his family was his merit.[2]

There was also a certain amount of intrigue and wire-pulling
to obtain promotion, of which instances are supplied by the
Letters from Roundhead Officers in Scotland extracted from the
Baynes correspondence. There is a curious letter from John
Baynes to his cousin Adam Baynes, who was a sort of army
agent and an influential man at Whitehall. John urged Adam
to speak a word in season on behalf of a certain major, who
wished to become a lieutenant-colonel.

'Now that Colo. Alured is off from his regiment, and supposing
Lt. Colo. Talbott will gain it, I earnestly entreat your word in
season in behalf of Maj. Pownal, that he may be Lieut. Colo. A
word to my Lord Lambert in his favour will perhaps be of good
use. It's known sufficiently how well he hath discharged his place
as major, and what care hath been upon him ever since the
regiment was raised. He hath been a constant drudge to it, and
for 15 months bye past had the whole charge of it. His honesty
and faithfulness is undoubted. I shall say no more: you know

Porter before the said order bee putt in execution, and there being a godly
honest man in the place by virtue of a Commission from your Highnesse
of almost one yeares standing, I presume upon your Highnesse' favourable
construccion of my slownesse in restoring the said Porter untill uppon due
information, and consideracion your Highnesse please to signifie your
further pleasure' (*Clarke MSS.*, l, 13).

[1] *Life of Colonel Hutchinson*, ed. 1885, ii, 163, 202.
[2] *Thurloe Papers*, vii, 190.

the man; do as you have opportunity. I speak for him, unknown and unbiassed as to him. Let me know if you need 100^{li} or 200^{li}. I think the Major will have some to spare, if you have occasion.'[1]

It does not appear whether any money passed, but the upshot was that the major got his place, and John Baynes married the major's daughter, writing frankly to his cousin, 'I do wish she had a little more breeding, and had either no mother or one as good as her father.'

A few years later John Baynes was again engaged in pulling the wires, this time for his cousin, Captain Robert Baynes, who wanted the vacant majority in Monck's regiment of foot. 'There is a great contest in General Monck's regiment about the majors place,' wrote Robert Baynes to his brother Adam. 'The General is very much a friend to Captain Morgan, the eldest captain. Major Holmes is for one of his own judgment,[2] a junior captain, and the regiment for the most part closes with the major; but if they must have a stranger, would rather have me than another, or than Morgan, but the General sticks close by Morgan.' Captain Robert sent pressing recommendations of himself from his old commander, Major-General Lilburne, to Fleetwood and to Lambert, and urged his brother to solicit Lambert personally on his behalf for his influence in the matter. Finally he sent his cousin, Captain John Baynes, to see Monck about it.

John Baynes gave the following account of his mission to Robert's brother, Adam: 'This day I was at Dalkeith, and to try the General's mind touching the major's place of his regiment. After some preparatory discourse, I asked him, if he had not heard the report of Capt. Robert Baynes being propounded to be his major; to which he replied, that he had heard of one or more that were in nomination, but did not know that your brother was one. I told him, I had it only by report and common talk; and he said he did know your brother, and spake very civilly and kindly of him, and that he was sorry that your brother happened to be in nomination, for that he had much

---

[1] *Letters from Roundhead Officers*, pp. 109, 119, 122, 128.

[2] Abraham Holmes was the major who was to be promoted to the rank of lieutenant-colonel in the regiment, thereby creating the vacancy Robert Baynes wished to fill. He was an Anabaptist, and was executed in 1685 for his share in Monmouth's rising. Ethelbert Morgan, the senior captain, was a moderate man.

appeared for Capt. Morgan, and had written to several of the
Parliament and committee of nominations, and did hope to
have the privilege of choosing his own officers and that he did
believe to have his desires granted; and further, that if any
stranger did come, he could not well resent it. This is the end. I
find him very strongly bent for Capt. Morgan, and that none
else will be so acceptable to him, although to the regiment I
have reason to believe your brother will be as much or more
welcome then another.'[1]

Though, as we perceive, there are some traces of favouritism
and intrigue, the system of appointment which prevailed during
the Protectorate was on the whole better then than the rule of
the commissioners appointed by Parliament in 1659. They began
by purging the army of all officers they thought unfit, receiving
any kind of evidence against them, and giving the accused in
most cases no opportunity of being heard in their defence. Even
anonymous informations were received: there are many such in
the Bodleian. In most cases moral delinquencies were alleged:
this cornet was 'old and scandalous'; another was 'given to
drinking and horse-racing'; a third was turned out for 'playing
at tables on the Lord's day'.[2] Many were cashiered for political
reasons, and others put in their places who were better republicans or sounder Anabaptists. Monck complained bitterly of the
changes made in the regiments in Scotland, alleging that some
of his best officers had been removed to make room for men of
less military capacity. This was one of the causes of his quarrel
with Fleetwood and Lambert, who were the chief men amongst
these commissioners.[3]

As for the officers of the army, their great grievance, whether
they were under the rule of a captain-general, a Protector, or
commissioners, was always the same. They complained not so

[1] *Letters from Roundhead Officers*, pp. 134, 151.
[2] *Cal. State Papers, Dom.*, 1658–9, pp. 376, 384.
[3] Baker, *Chronicle*, ed. Phillips, p. 670; Gumble, *Life of Monck*, p. 101.
Advancement was very rapid during the revolutions of 1659–60. In the
winter of 1659 Monck lost 140 officers by desertion to Lambert and Fleetwood, and filled up their places very largely with promoted corporals and
sergeants (Gumble, *Life of Monck*, pp. 136, 140; Maseres, *Select Tracts*,
p. 741). When the Long Parliament was restored, Haslerig and its commissioners are said to have displaced 1,500 officers (Ludlow, *Memoirs*, ii,
204, 207, ed. 1894). By the time Charles the Second landed the army had
been almost entirely reofficered.

much of the arbitrary advancement of some as of the precarious tenure by which all held their commissions, and protested against arbitrary dismissal from the service. In their petitions they repeatedly demanded both from Protector and Parliament that no officer should be cashiered except by judgement of a court-martial, but the demand was always made in vain.[1]

After describing the composition of the rank and file of the army, the regimental organization, and the character and position of the regimental officers, it remains to describe the position and functions of the general, the general officers, and the staff.

First, with regard to the authority of the commander-in-chief. Fairfax, like Essex, was appointed by an ordinance of Parliament, but in one respect his authority was less extensive. Essex was commander-in-chief not only of 'the army appointed to be raised' to march under his command, but also 'of all other forces in the kingdom'.[2] Fairfax was at first simply general of the 22,000 men forming the New Model. He did not become commander-in-chief of all the forces in England and Wales until 19th July 1647. Even then, however, the sphere of his authority was narrower than that of his successor. By an Act of Parliament dated 23rd June 1649, Cromwell was appointed commander-in-chief of all the forces in Ireland for the next three years.[3] Then on 26th June 1650 he succeeded Fairfax and was made 'Captain, General and Commander-in-chief of the armies and forces raised and to be raised by authority of Parliament within the Commonwealth of England, until the Parliament shall otherwise order'. Next, in April 1652, when Cromwell's period of command in Ireland should have expired, Parliament voted that his commission as captain-general was to be construed to extend to the forces in Ireland, 'as if Ireland had been therein particularly named'.[4] And as Scotland had been added to the dominions of the Commonwealth by his victories, he was now general of all the forces in the three nations of England, Scotland, and Ireland. Then came in April 1653 the expulsion of the Long Parliament,

[1] Baker, *Chronicle*, ed. Phillips, p. 680; *Old Parliamentary History*, xxi, 464; *English Historical Review*, 1892, p. 107.

[2] *Old Parliamentary History*, xi, 297.

[3] *Commons' Journals*, vi, 176, 238–9.

[4] *Commons' Journals*, vi, 432; vii, 142.

and the dissolution of all civil government. Cromwell being captain-general by virtue of an unrepealed Act of Parliament, regarded himself as the only constituted authority left in being. In his own words, he was 'a person having power over the three nations, without bound or limit set'.[1] Finally, the evolution of the commander-in-chief concludes with the union of the supreme civil and military authority in the hands of the Protector, limited only by a constitution drawn up by the officers of the army.

Even before this exaggerated development of the authority of the commander-in-chief, and before he himself was commander-in-chief of all the forces in England, Fairfax exercised a power to which it is difficult to find a parallel in later English history. From the beginning of his first campaign he had more authority over the New Model than Wellington ever possessed over the army in Spain and Portugal. Fairfax could promote any man he thought fit. 'I,' complained Wellington in 1810, 'who command the largest British army that has been employed against the enemy for many years, and who have upon my hands certainly the most extensive and difficult concern that was ever imposed on any British officer, have not the power of making even a corporal.'[2]

Fairfax could choose his tools, and did not have incompetent officers thrust upon him by the government he served. Wellington did. 'Really,' said Wellington, 'when I reflect upon the character and attainments of some of the general officers of this army, and consider that these are the persons on whom I am to rely to lead columns against the French generals, and who are to carry my instructions into execution, I tremble.'[3]

In another way, too, Fairfax and Cromwell had an advantage which many generals have not possessed. Their military movements were not hampered by the orders of the government they served. They were not obliged to fight battles for political reasons or to maintain untenable positions against their better judgement. It was not so with Fairfax during the first three months of his generalship. At first the Committee of Both Kingdoms claimed authority to direct the movements of his army, as it

[1] Carlyle, *Cromwell*, Speech iii.
[2] Wellington, *Despatches*, vi, 305.   [3] Ibid., vi, 582.

had claimed to do in the case of Essex.[1] It ordered his army
to relieve Taunton, and when he was nearly there it sent him
counter orders, bidding him detach part of the army to the relief
of Taunton and return with the rest to besiege Oxford. He
thought that both the division of his forces and the siege of
Oxford were blunders, but he had to obey, and to leave the
King's army to do what it would.[2] When Charles stormed
Leicester there was a panic in London, and the City petitioned
that the general might be left free to act as he thought best,
'without attending commands and directions from remote
councils'.[3] The amateur strategists of the Committee of Both
Kingdoms had to yield to public opinion, and to abdicate
functions which they ought never to have assumed. 'We have
thought fit,' they informed Fairfax on 9th June 1645, 'to take
off all limitations or restrictions under which you may be placed
by former letters, leaving it wholly to you who are upon the
spot to do what by the advice of your council of war you shall
judge most conducive to the public interest.'[4]

The freedom of action which Fairfax thus obtained Cromwell
possessed in a still larger measure. For the government which
he served was to a certain extent his own creation; at all events
it knew that its continued existence depended on his success.
Therefore all the resources of the nation were at his disposal.
His position, in fact, was more like that of Marlborough than
that of Wellington. One might almost say of Cromwell in Ireland

[1] For instance, in June 1644, when the King and his army escaped from
Oxford, which Essex and Waller's armies were endeavouring to blockade,
the committee ordered Essex to pursue the King, and Waller to undertake
the relief of Lyme and the Parliamentarians of the West. For military
reasons which seemed to him sufficient Essex had marched into the West
himself, leaving Waller's army to pursue the King. He disregarded the
reiterated orders of the committee and of Parliament to return, or to send
only a portion of his forces, answering that 'by the discipline of war and the
rules of reason' it would be a mistake to divide his army as they wished.
'If,' he added in another letter, 'you shall call me back, as one that is not
fit to be trusted any longer in a business of such high concernment, I will
come and sit in Parliament, as not knowing any military employment
which is worthy of my presence' (Devereux, *Lives of the Earls of Essex*, ii,
400, 403, 406, 410; Rushworth, v, 683; Gardiner, *Great Civil War*, i,
354–8).

[2] *Fairfax Correspondence*, iii, 228.

[3] *Old Parliamentary History*, xiii, 491.

[4] *Cal. State Papers, Dom*, 1644–5, p. 580.

and Scotland, as Wellington said of Marlborough in Flanders, 'he was the government.'[1]

On the other hand, while Fairfax was freed from the control which the Committee of Both Kingdoms had exercised over his movements, it is important to notice the clause in Fairfax's instructions which directed him to take the advice of his council of war.

Nothing is more remarkable in reading the contemporary account of the Campaigns of 1645 and 1646 than the conspicuous part played by councils of war. Without consulting a council Fairfax undertook no important operations. Before the battles of Naseby, Langport, and Torrington, before the assaults on Bridgwater and Bristol, and during the sieges of Oxford, there were in each case one or more councils held to consider what course to take to engage the enemy, or how best to reduce the besieged place. These councils were large bodies. That held at Marston on 9th June 1646 was attended by over thirty persons, and it included all the general staff of the army and all commanders of regiments. Their resolutions were not simply dictated by the general, but the result of full and free discussion. They were arrived at, we are told, 'after much dispute', 'after long consultation and debate', after 'a long and serious debate'. To take an instance, on Tuesday, 2nd September 1645, before Bristol 'a council of war being called and all the colonels present, after a long debate whether to storm Bristol or no, it was put to the question and resolved in the affirmative; and for the manner of the storm it was referred to a committee of the colonels of the army, to present in writing to the general the next morning, to be debated at a general council of war'. Accordingly the report was presented, agreed to, and acted upon.[2]

When Cromwell succeeded Fairfax as commander-in-chief the same system continued. Councils of war were held just before the battle of Preston and the battle of Dunbar; and there must have been many others of which no record remains.[3] So accustomed were the officers of the army to be consulted in this way

---

[1] Stanhope, *Miscellanies*, 1863, p. 102.

[2] Sprigge, *Anglia Rediviva*, ed. 1854, pp. 32, 35, 69, 76, 97, 102, 104, 157, 160, 174, 176, 191, 195, 206, 283.

[3] Carlyle, *Cromwell*, Letters lxiv, cxl.

that the neglect of General Venables to do so during the West Indian expedition was denounced as unconstitutional. 'Much discontent,' we are told, was 'occasioned by his irregular acting.' The colonels who served under him 'have not so much power here as his Highness allowed the captains under his conduct both in England, Scotland and Ireland'. Not twice in the two months since their landing in Jamaica had he summoned them to consult together. 'Nay, that which is worst of all, he acteth as his will leadeth him, notwithstanding the vote of the council.'[1]

Yet the significance of these councils must not be over-estimated. The army was not a republic of which the general was merely the president. Fairfax might ask the advice of his officers but if he chose to take the responsibility of disregarding it they could only grumble. Sometimes he did so. 'I have observed him at councils of war,' writes Whitelocke, 'that he hath said little, but hath ordered things expressly contrary to the judgment of all his council.'[2]

When Cromwell was general we may be sure that his will made itself felt still more effectively, and that the council was completely under his influence. At Dunbar, for instance, we see Cromwell first deciding his plan of battle with Lambert and Monck, and then calling a council and explaining to the officers, by the mouth of Lambert, why they must give battle, and how the battle is to be fought. It is he who determines what is to be done, and if he submits his plan to discussion, it is in order to convince their judgements, and to secure not mere obedience to his orders but intelligent co-operation.[3]

Historically, the council of war is more important from a political than a military point of view. Its military importance tended to diminish; its political importance to increase. As soon as the army began to intervene in State affairs it became the organ through which the general opinion of the army found expression. Out of it sprang two institutions which from 1647 to 1660 exerted an immense influence on the course of English

---

[1] *Narrative of General Venables*, ed. Firth, p. xxix.

[2] Whitelocke, *Memorials*, ii, 20, ed. 1853.

[3] Carlyle, *Cromwell*, Letter cxl; *Autobiography of Capt. John Hodgson*, ed. 1806, p. 144; cf. *Transactions of the Royal Historical Society*, 1900, pp. 34–37.

politics. One was the representative General Council of the Army which existed in 1647 and 1648. The other was the General Council of Officers which existed from 1648 to 1660. But the political history of the army is a subject too large to be treated here, and demands separate treatment.

Closely connected both with the council of war and the commander of the army, as being secretary to both, was the office of secretary to the general. In the New Model these two posts were held by John Rushworth.[1] The general's secretary was always a civilian, and as he conducted the general's correspondence, much of the administrative work of the army was transacted through him. Fairfax habitually appointed committees of officers, either to consider some special subject, such as the garrisons necessary to be maintained, or to consider and advise upon the business which in the ordinary routine would come before the commander-in-chief.[2] But much remained for the general himself to do, and so, though the secretary had no authority of his own, his influence continually increased. Rushworth in his capacity as secretary to the council of war, became in 1647 a personage of political importance. William Clarke, one of Rushworth's assistants, who was Monck's secretary when he commanded in Scotland, occupies a still more important place in the history of English military organization. By his industry, trustworthiness, and knowledge of army administration and finance he made himself so indispensable to Monck that after the Restoration, when Monck became commander-in-chief of the army of Charles the Second, he had Clarke appointed Secretary at War.[3] His successors in the office augmented its authority, and by degrees the Secretary at War, from being a private secretary with no active control over military affairs and no independent power, became a Secretary of State responsible for the administration of the army, to whom many of the ordinary powers of the commander-in-chief were transferred.[4]

---

[1] Peacock, *Army Lists*, p. 101.   [2] *Clarke Papers*, i, 217, 223.

[3] See the life of William Clarke in the *Dictionary of National Biography*, the *Clarke Papers* published by the Camden Society, and the two volumes entitled *Scotland and the Commonwealth* and *Scotland and the Protectorate*, published by the Scottish History Society.

[4] See Clifford Walton, *History of the British Standing Army*, p. 767; Clode, *Military Forces of the Crown*, i, 71–73, 472.

From the commander-in-chief I pass to the other general
officers of the army and to the staff. Next in rank to the commander-in-chief came the lieutenant-general. 'A general's lieutenant standeth as his second in all powers and authorities whatsoever,' says a military writer of the time, adding that 'to all
great officers of the army' he is 'the interpreter of what the
general intendeth.'[1] In the New Model, which in this respect
followed the practice of the Dutch, the post of lieutenant-general
carried with it the command of all the cavalry of the army.[2]
Cromwell, for instance, was appointed lieutenant-general to Sir
Thomas Fairfax on the ground that the horse of the New Model,
'being as great a body as ever the Parliament had together in
one army', had no general officer to command it.[3]

Under the lieutenant-general as commander of the cavalry
were the commissary-general of the horse, two adjutant-gen-
erals of the horse, a quartermaster-general of the horse, a
markmaster-general, a muster-master-general, and the commissary-general of horse provisions. The most important of these
was the 'commissary-general of horse', who was second in
command of the cavalry.[4]

[1] Markham, *Decades of War*, 1622, pp. 193, 194. Markham distinguishes
between the lieutenant-general of the horse and the lieutenant-general of
the army (p. 177).

[2] Turner, *Pallas Armata*, p. 248.

[3] *Old Parliamentary History*, xiii, 497.

[4] The title came originally from the Spanish service: 'And now because
wee have chanced upon these two names, of Commissary-Generall of the
Cavallery; and General-Adjutant: it shall not be amisse (I hope) for the
understanding of our storie the better, to digresse a little, for the expound-
ing of these two offices. I take it, that this Commissary-General of the
Cavallerie is not altogether unlike a Sergeant Major of the horse, in the
Swedish discipline; beyond whom, he hath the power of a Commissarie,
for the provision of the troopes, over which he is Major. Hee is called
Commissary-Generall because his command is not in a single Regiment
alone, but either over all the horse of the Armie, or some Brigade at least in
it. Which Brigade in the Spanish discipline is not so small a Bodie of men,
as the Swedish Brigades be: but it is a full Tercio (so the Spanish call a
Brigade) that is, a whole third part of the Armie, how many soever the
Armie be. The General-Adjutant, that was Leiftenant to this Commissary,
was the Leiftenant Colonel to his Regiment. The General-Adjutants office,
is to bee assistant to the Generall: That is to be sent abroad for the giving
or speeding of the Generalls commands, to the rest of the armie. He is
commonly some able man, or some favourite at least unto the Generall.
His place in the Armie, is that of a Leiftenant-Colonel; of whom hee hath
precedence, but is behinde all Colonels. A General-Adjutant is the same
officer, which in our English discipline, wee call a Corporall of the field.

Just before the battle of Naseby, Cromwell obtained from Fairfax, 'that seeing the horse were near six thousand, and were to be fought in two wings, his excellency would be pleased to make Colonel Ireton commissary-general of horse, and appoint him to command the left wing that day; the command of the right wing being as much as the lieutenant-general could apply himself unto'.[1]

The third officer in rank was the major-general, or sergeant-major-general. In the New Model this post was held by Skippon, who had served in the same capacity under Essex. The sergeant-major-general was the commander of all the infantry of the army, and was sometimes styled the major-general of the foot. One of the functions of the major-general was the drawing up of the army on the field of battle. To draw up an army in the elaborately formal battle array recommended by military writers of the time required great technical skill, and the major-general was usually a veteran of long experience. 'In his memory,' says Markham, 'he must ever carry ready framed the forms and proportions of sundry battailes, any of which he is to sort or fashion to the ground, according as the necessity of the place requireth.'[2] Six days before the Battle of Naseby took place Skippon was desired by Fairfax and the council of war 'to draw the form of a battle', i.e. to make out a plan for the coming engagement.[3]

The French call him Un aide de Camp: an Aide or Assistant of the Field' (*Swedish Intelligencer*, iv, 6–7).

Colonel Clifford Walton mistakes the meaning of the title of commissary-general, and treats of the office in connection with the commissariat. The commissary-general of the horse must not be confused with the commissary-general of victuals or the commissary-general of horse provisions (*History of the British Standing Army*, p. 633). It should also be noted that in the New Model the adjutants-general of the horse were always regimental captains. According to Sir James Turner the adjutant-general of horse was simply an assistant to the commander of the cavalry, a superior aide-de-camp (*Pallas Armata*, p. 249). I cannot find evidence that he had any administrative duties in the New Model.

[1] Sprigge, *Anglia Rediviva*, p. 39. The choice was the more remarkable as Ireton was the junior colonel of horse. When Cromwell invaded Scotland, Whalley was appointed commissary-general by him (*Portland MSS.*, i, 608).

[2] Markham, *Decades of War*, p. 170; Grose, *Military Antiquities*, i, 210; Turner, *Pallas Armata*, p. 249.

[3] Sprigge, *Anglia Rediviva*, p. 39. It should be noted that the rank and title of sergeant-major-general were usually given to officers commanding the forces of particular districts, as, for instance, to Manchester, Waller,

The two most important subordinates of the major-general were the quartermaster-general of the foot and the adjutant-general of the foot. He had also attached to his person certain officers called corporals of the field, charged to carry his orders to different parts of the army during the battle.[1]

The fourth in rank of the general officers was the lieutenant-general of the ordnance, under whom were the comptroller of the ordnance and the engineer-general.[2]

There were also other officers attached to the staff of the army, and charged with particular departments of its administration. A judge-advocate with two 'marshall generals', or rather provost-marshal-generals, of horse and foot superintended the administration of military justice: a commissary-

---

and Massey. An officer whose position is rather difficult to determine is the field-marshal. He appears but for a moment and then vanishes from the military history of the period. In March 1644, Parliament ordered Essex to find some post for Lord Robartes in his army, and Essex appointed him field-marshal. Abroad the title signified general-in-chief. 'For the present,' writes Sir James Turner in 1673, 'in Germany, Sweden and Denmark, those who command armies royal consisting of cavalry, infantry, and artillery are qualified by the title of Felt Marshals, and have an equivalent authority to the ancient Marshals of France.' The word had come to be used in this sense during the later part of the Thirty Years' War. In England and in the case of Lord Robartes it had no such significance. He held rather the position of the Lord Marshal of the sixteenth century, who is described as third in rank amongst general officers. At least he seems to have been considered as superior in rank to Skippon, though the point is not very clear. After 1644 the title disappears from the lists of the army (Rushworth, v, 690, 704; *Commons' Journals*, iii, 433; Turner, *Pallas Armata*, p. 247; Markham, *Decades of War*, p. 189).

[1] The corporals of the field do not appear in Sprigge's list of the New Model army nor in the later establishments of 1647 to 1660, but when Cromwell set out for Scotland in 1650 he obtained permission to add to the establishment 'for the better carrying on of the service', twenty men 'to be corporals of the field' (*Commons' Journals*, vi, 433). They were to be paid 'according to the accustomed allowance'. An account of these officers and their duties in the armies of the sixteenth and early seventeenth centuries is given by Markham, *Decades of War*, p. 153, and by Grose, i, 233. The latter quotes an Elizabethan treatise called *The Military Art of Trayning*. Turner also mentions them as something equivalent to adjutants in the French service. In England they were evidently becoming obsolete. The above is the only mention I have met with of their employment in the English army of this period, and their precise position is uncertain.

[2] In the New Model, Thomas Hammond (uncle of Robert Hammond, governor of Carisbrooke Castle in 1648) was lieutenant-general of the ordnance, and Captain Richard Deane was comptroller. Markham's master of the ordnance appears to correspond to the lieutenant-general, and his lieutenant of the ordnance to the comptroller (*Decades of War*, pp. 117 185; see also Ward, *Animadversions of War*, p. 107; Turner, *Pallas Armata*, pp. 194–5).

general of victuals was the head of the commissariat: a waggon-master-general took charge of the train and the baggage: two treasurers at war, assisted in the case of the New Model by special commissioners appointed by Parliament for the purpose, managed the finances of the army:[1] and besides these there were medical officers to the army and chaplains to the army, who had a general superintendence of the regimental surgeons and chaplains.

There were two general officers in the New Model whom we do not find in modern armies. One was the commissary-general of the musters, or as he was often called, muster-master-general. William Stane held this post in the New Model, assisted by two deputies, James Standish and Richard Gerard. The duty of the muster-master and his assistants was to keep the rolls of the army, to call over the lists of the different regiments every month, and to see that no more men received pay than were actually present with the colours, and that those present were properly armed and equipped.[2] He was, in short, to act as a check upon the regimental officers on behalf of the treasurer of the army. An officer of much greater importance was the scout-master-general, to whom the intelligence department of the army was entrusted. This officer was peculiar to the English army. 'I have known none of them abroad,' says Sir James

[1] 'This army went on better by two more wheels of treasurers and a committee; the treasurers were men of public spirits to the state and army, and were usually ready to present some pay upon every success, which was like wine after work, and cheered up the common spirits to more activity.
'The committee which the House of Commons formed were men wise, provident, active, and faithful in providing ammunition, arms, recruits of men, clothes; and that family must needs thrive that hath good stewards' (Sprigge, *Anglia Rediviva*, p. 327). The two treasurers at war were Sir John Wollaston and Captain John Blackwell. The four commissioners of Parliament were Colonel Martin Pinder, Harcourt Leighton, Thomas Herbert, and Captain John Potter. Their instructions are printed in *Lords' Journals*, vii, 377, and many letters from the commissioners are in the *Hist. MSS. Comm. Report on the MSS. of the Duke of Portland*.

[2] For the 'Rules and Instructions to the Muster-Masters of the Army', see the *Journals of the House of Lords*, 14th May 1645, vii, 374. There are many specimens of muster-rolls, duly attested and signed, in the Record Office. In the establishment of 3rd Nov. 1647 the muster-master-general **to** the army is entered as receiving fifteen shillings a day, his two deputies three and fourpence apiece, and his two clerks two and sixpence each. The same list adds a 'Mark-master and joint commissary of the musters of horse', who was paid 5s. a day, with three servants paid 2s. each (*Lords' Journals*, ix, 66, 67).

Turner.[1] English military books of the sixteenth and early seventeenth centuries give a detailed account of his functions. His
original business was to send out scouts, and to reconnoitre the
ground round the place where the army was encamped and the
country through which it was to march.[2] In the King's army he
appears to have made this his chief duty. In the campaign of
1639 it was the scout-master who was blamed when the unexpected advance of the Scottish army to within sight of the
royal camp threw the whole of the King's forces into disorder.
'Have not I,' said the King, 'good intelligence that the rebels
can march with their army and encamp within sight of mine,
and I not have a word of it till the body of their army give the
alarm?'[3] The disaster of Naseby was also in part attributed to

[1] 'The English have a General Officer whom they qualifie with the Title of
Scoutmaster-General. I have known none of them abroad, but I hear in
some places of Italy they have something very like him, and that is, Il
Capitano di Spioni, the Captain of the Spies. I cannot believe that this
Scoutmaster, or this Captain, hath any thing to do with that Intelligence
which I called publick, and is got by parties whether of Horse or Foot; for
the commanding these out, and the keeping of the Lists of their Turns or
Toures belongs properly to the Major Generals and the several Majors of
Regiments both of the Cavalry and Infantry, none whereof I conceive will
suffer the Scoutmaster to usurp their Office. They must then only have the
regulation of the private Intelligence, wherein no doubt they may ease the
General of the Army very much' (Turner, Pallas Armata, p. 265).

[2] 'The Scoute maister every evening upon the sounding of the Marshalles
trumpet to the watche, must receive by assignment from the General or
Liefetenant of the Horsemen a sufficient number to scoute, the which by
himselfe must be directed into crosse wayes and other places of perrill in
everie quarter of the campe, he must exhorte them still to silence, and to
have regard to looke about them, and not to forsake theyr places appointed,
till discoverers be put foorth in the morninge to the fielde: Hee is in the
morninge (by lyke assignment) at the discharginge of the watche, to receive
a competent number of men to discover the which he must likewise appoynt
to places of most convenience for the purpose: in like manner when the
campe dooth march he must be styll scouring afore to see the coast be
cleere' (B. Rich, A Pathway, 1587).

[3] 'Presently hereupon, the Lord General the Earl of Arundel, was sent
for to the King; The Scout-Master was much exclaimed against, and he
complained as much of the Souldiers who were sent out as Scouts, and gave
him no timely intelligence. But in the Opinion of the Court and Commanders, the Scout-Master General bore the blame; and his Crime was
aggravated, because he was a Papist.
'The Lord General made this Reply to those Nobles that accused the
Scout-Master, That he made choice of him (by Name Roger Widdrington
Esq.); as the fittest Man in England for the Office of Scout-Master, being
born in that County of Northumberland, and one best acquainted with all
the Highlandmen upon the Borders of Scotland, and who was best able, of
any man he knew in England, to gain Intelligence from thence; and that it
was notoriously known, he was a Gentleman who ever bore a perfect hatred

the negligence of the King's scout-master. Rupert wished to know whether it was true that Fairfax was advancing to fight: whereupon one Ruce the scout-master was sent to discover, 'who in a short time returned with a lie in his mouth, that he had been two or three miles forward, and could neither discover nor hear of the rebels'.[1]

In the New Model and in the armies of the Commonwealth the scout-master-general added to his original function the duty of collecting intelligence of every kind about the movements and intentions of the enemy. He was not only master of the scouts, but generally kept spies in his employment. He was not necessarily a soldier. Though Leonard Watson, the scout-master of the New Model, had the rank of major, his successors were generally civilians.[2] Downing, the scout-master of Cromwell's army in Scotland, had been an Independent minister, and was afterwards an ambassador. Henry Jones, who held the same post under Cromwell in Ireland, was a bishop of the Irish Church.[3]

The scout-master's pay was high – about four pounds a day – but out of it he had to maintain a couple of agents and about twenty men. The business of these was naturally a dangerous one, to their souls as well as their bodies according to one scout-master-general. 'I have not a few times sighed,' wrote William Rowe to Cromwell, 'that men set to work by me have necessarily sinned, and one or two complained thereof to me, and desired

---

to the Scots, and was a stout active man upon Border-Service in the time of Queen Elizabeth; that he was a person of quality, and he doubted not of his Integrity, and that he would justify himself.

'In conclusion this business was hushed up, but great was the murmuring of the Private Souldiers in the Camp' (Rushworth, ii, pt. ii, p. 938).

[1] Walker, *Historical Discourses*, p. 114 (or p. 130).

[2] Watson had been scout-master to Manchester's army, and wrote a valuable narrative of Marston Moor. A letter from him to Manchester announcing Rupert's approach and the numbers of his army is printed in *Fairfax Correspondence*, iii, 111. Just before Naseby, Watson did very valuable service by intercepting Royalist despatches (Sprigge, p. 52; *Portland MSS.*, i, 224).

[3] November 1650. 'Warrant to pay George Downing £84 for three weeks pay as scoutmaster-general, to begin Nov. 1–21 1649.' Signed by O. Cromwell.

November 1650. 'Warrant to pay Dr. Henry Jones, late Bishop of Clogher, as scoutmaster-general, £454 8s. for self, 2 agents and 20 men for 142 days, 24 June to 12 Nov.' The receipt is signed 'Hen. Clogher' (*Exchequer Papers*). In the establishment of 1647, £4 per diem is allowed for the scout-master and his assistants (*Lords' Journals*, ix, 66).

therefore the greater wages, which last never troubled me; and of late the sufferings, maims and injuries of some I have employed, have had their impression more than perhaps needed, but I have in both these respects a melancholy soul.'[1]

In 1657 the Protector's government, in a fit of unwise economy, proposed to abolish the deputy to the scout-master-general who was on the establishment of the army of occupation in Scotland. Against this General Monck protested. No man was better served than he was by his intelligence department, and no one attached more importance to that branch of the service. 'I must confess,' said he, 'that there has been as much good service done for the public by the intelligence I have gotten by the help of a Deputy-Scoutmaster-General, than hath been done by the forces in preventing of rising of parties; so that I think his Highness's affairs in these parts cannot well be carried on without such a man.'[2] Monck gained his point, and this useful official was continued, at a reduced salary.

In conclusion, it remains to sum up the chief points in the history of the New Model.

The New Model, which was in 1645 one of several armies, had by 1649 absorbed and incorporated into itself all the other armies of the Parliament. It was no longer the 'New Model', but the Army.

It was originally composed of the remnant of the armies of Essex, Manchester, and Waller, supplemented by pressed men. At first it was recruited both by volunteering and impressment, but after 1651 by volunteering only.

The rank and file of the infantry had very little education, but the cavalry were drawn from a higher social rank and were often men of some education, and even of some little property. In both cavalry and infantry promotion from the ranks was possible, and by no means uncommon.

As to the officers, a large proportion of them, especially amongst the horse, were gentlemen by birth, but few had any

[1] Nickolls, *Letters and Papers of State Addressed to Cromwell* (generally known as the *Milton State Papers*), p. 16. Many specimens of the intelligence sent to Rowe by his agents in Scotland are printed in the early part of this collection.

[2] *Clarke MSS.*, li, f. 21. For the history of the office after the Restoration, see Clifford Walton, *History of the British Standing Army*, pp. 621, 622.

military training save what they had acquired during the Civil War. All were originally appointed by the commander-in-chief, and looked to him for promotion. Promotion went by merit tempered by respect for the claims of seniority.

The power of the commander-in-chief was very great. All military power was concentrated in his hands: he had absolute freedom as to his movements, and absolute freedom in his choice of officers. Fairfax had a larger authority than Essex had enjoyed, and Cromwell a larger authority than Fairfax. Both during their campaigns had more power in their hands than Wellington had during his. Their authority was to some extent limited by the necessity of consulting their officers in a council of war, but the limitation was more apparent than real.

Next in rank to the general were the lieutenant-general and the major-general, one charged with the command of the horse, the other with the command of the foot. There was also a lieutenant-general of artillery, who commanded the artillery and engineers, and there were on the general staff of the army other officers charged with particular departments. One of the most important of these was the scoutmaster-general, and one of the causes of the success of Fairfax and Cromwell was the efficiency of their intelligence department. Indeed, in its entirety, the army was a compact, well-organized body, working like a machine, and directed by a single will.

CHAPTER IV

The Infantry

THE INCREASING IMPORTANCE of infantry is one of the characteristics of the sixteenth and the seventeenth centuries. No doubt the greater importance of the foot soldier was partly due to the introduction of firearms, but for some time after their introduction infantry were not able to contend against cavalry on anything like equal terms. The reason was, partly that the earliest firearms were not very efficient weapons, partly that it was a long time before a system of drill and tactics was evolved which enabled the infantry to make the best use of their new weapons. 'As our footmen of the new discipline are armed and ordered,' said an Elizabethan writer, 'a thousand horse is able to defeat five times as many such footmen.'[1] All depended on the issue of the fight between the cavalry of opposing armies. It became a maxim, that when the cavalry of an army was defeated, the destruction of the infantry followed as a matter of course.

Sir Francis Vere in his account of the battle of Newport in 1600 notes as a 'strange and unusual' thing, that 'whereas most commonly in battles the success of the foot dependeth upon that of the horse, here it was clean contrary; for so long as the foot held good, the horse could not be beaten out of the field; though, as it fell out, they might be chased to them'.[2]

Before the middle of the seventeenth century infantry had so much increased in efficiency, that soldiers ceased to hold the traditional view that it was more honourable to serve in the horse than the foot. 'My choice,' wrote Robert Monro in 1637, 'shall be ever to command on foot.' If kings took his advice, he added, they would esteem their infantry officers more than their cavalry officers. Then fewer would serve on horseback, more on

[1] Thomas Digges, *Four Paradoxes*, 1604, p. 53.
[2] *Commentaries*, p. 100, ed. 1657.

foot. A king's charges would be less and his profit more; his army
stronger, his victories more frequent, his conquests better maintained.[1]

In England, at the time when the Civil War began, it cannot
be said that infantry was yet as highly esteemed as cavalry, but
as in the rest of Europe it had greatly increased in efficiency, and
therefore in honour.

Since the days of Elizabeth, the armament of English foot
had been simplified and made more uniform. By 1640 an English
foot regiment consisted solely of musketeers and pikemen. A
change had also taken place during the same period in the relative number of musketeers and pikemen which a regiment contained. At first musketeers were in a decided minority, and there
were generally at least two pikemen to one musketeer; then for a
time the number of musketeers and pikemen were equal; and
finally there were two musketeers to one pikeman.[2] This was the
process which went on in continental armies, and England followed their example, but more slowly. Two military writers at

[1] 'Likewise I cannot say, but Horse-men are usefull many times, as they
were here; yet in my opinion, in their service, they are not to be paralleld
to foot: For at the in-taking of Townes, and in hilly and mountainous
Countries, that are straight by nature, they are not usefull, neither can they
doe but little service, yet for their great charges they are much harder to be
entertained: Therefore my choice shall be ever, as most credible to command on foote, and if I were worthy to advise a King, or a Generall following warres, I would wish him to esteeme more of his foot Officers, than of his
horse: then fewer should serve on horsebacke, and more on foote; and as his
Charges should be lesse, his profit should be the more, his Armie the stronger
his Countrey lesse spoyl'd, his contribution to maintaine his Armie the
better payd, his treasure richer, his Victories more frequent, and more
durable, his Conquests the better maintained' (Monro His Expedition,
etc., pt. i, 24; cf. Turner, Pallas Armata, p. 243).

[2] 'Formerly scarce the fourth part of a Company was arm'd with fire-
guns, whether Harquebusses or Musquets. In every one of the seven Legions
which were ordained by Francis the First, to be a constant infantry in
France, there were at most (in the latter end of his Reign) but eighteen
hundred Harquebussers, all the rest of the six thousand were heavily
armed, their offensive weapons being long Poles or Perches, most whereof
were Pikes, to which were added Pistols and Swords. The Forces of the
Emperor Charles the Fifth, and his brother Ferdinand, King of the Romans
at Vienna, when they expected Soliman, were reckon'd to be at least one
hundred and ten thousand Horse and Foot, whereof eighty thousand
belong'd to the Infantry, and of these only twenty thousand were Harquebusiers, the other sixty thousand were heavy armed; and for the offensive
they had such weapons as I have described in another place. Maximilian the
Second order'd (as I told you before) his Companies to be four hundred
strong, whereof one hundred and forty were appointed to be Harquebussiers
(the Musquet not being then in request) with Headpieces and Rapiers,
among whom ten of the lustiest and strongest were to carry each of them

the beginning of Charles the First's reign, Gervase Markham and Sir Thomas Kellie, describe a regiment as consisting half of musketeers and half of pikemen.[1] By 1642 England had reached the third stage. It is probable that in the army under the Earl of Essex two-thirds of every regiment were musketeers, for it is certain that it was so in the case of the regiment which Colonel Harley raised for his army in 1643.[2] This was also the proportion which obtained in the Scottish army which Leslie brought to the aid of the Parliamentary cause in 1644.[3] In the New Model from the very beginning there were always two musketeers to one pikeman. Lieutenant-Colonel Elton, who served in it, definitely says so in his *Complete Body of the Art Military*, which appeared in 1650.[4] Of these two arms the pike was still regarded as more honourable than the musket. Roger Williams in his *Discourse of War*, published in 1590, devotes a chapter to proving this proposition, and Elton writing sixty years later makes the same statement.[5] The pike was held more honourable because it was the more ancient weapon. It was also held more honourable because all adventurous gentlemen who enlisted to see the wars preferred, as the phrase was, 'to trail a pike'. There-

a Harquebuss a Croc, the Calibre whereof was made to receive six Balls cast of one pound of Lead; all the rest of the Company were to carry Pikes, Halberts, and Partizans, and all of them were to be in full defensive arms, with Swords, and each of them a Pistol at his Girdle, or as it is called in the establishment, a short fire-gun. In process of time when Soldiers became expert at the Musquet, Companies how strong or weak soever were divided into three parts, two thirds whereof were Pikemen, and one third Musqueteers; thereafter the Musquet crav'd the half of the Game, and got it, so that each Company was equally divided into Pikemen and Musqueteers. But equality for most part is short liv'd, and so far'd it in this, for very soon the Musqueteers challeng'd the two thirds, and obtain'd them, leaving but one third for the Pikemen, which for most part yet they keep, though in several places (as I have said before) Pikes are sent to look for their fortunes elsewhere' (Sir James Turner, *Pallas Armata*, p. 215).

[1] Sir Thomas Kellie, *Pallas Armata*, 1627, p. 14; Gervase Markham, *The Souldiers Grammar*, 1626, p. 15. 'According to our present discipline,' says the latter, 'a company of 200 men would contain 100 pikemen and 100 musketeers.'

[2] *Report on the Duke of Portland's MSS.*, iii, p. 119.

[3] *Memorie of the Somervilles*, ii, 307; cf. *Generall Lessley's Direction and Order for the Exercising of Horrse and Foot*, 1642, p. 1.

[4] 'Our Companies consisting of one hundred men, two parts being musketeers, and a third pikes' (Elton, ed. 1659, see Appendix A).

[5] 'To prove the pike the most honourable weapon carried by Footmen' is the title of Williams's chapter. Elton's second chapter, headed 'Severall reasons why the Pike is the more honourable arme is reprinted in Appendix B'. See also Turner, *Pallas Armata*, p. 220.

fore the pikeman was regarded as a gentleman compared with the musketeer. There is a curious illustration of this view in Shakespeare's *Henry V*, when the King, on the night before Agincourt, wanders disguised through his camp, and meets Ancient Pistol. 'Art thou officer?' asks Pistol, 'or art thou base, common, and popular?' 'I am a gentleman of a company,' replies the King. 'Trailst thou the puissant pike?' demands Pistol. 'Even so,' is the answer.

A third reason was that pikemen were usually finer men physically than the musketeers. Physical strength was not so necessary for shooting as for managing the pike. Therefore, remarks Falstaff to Bardolph, when he is choosing his men, 'Put me a caliver into Wart's hand . . . O give me always a little, lean, old, chapt, bald shot'.[2] It was a standing instruction to officers to make the biggest recruits pikemen, just as in the next century they were made grenadiers. But the instruction was not always observed, and in 1671 Sir James Turner bitterly complained of the supine carelessness of modern officers 'who take no notice to make a difference of those who are to carry muskets and pikes, distributing them promiscuously to the stronger and the weaker, whereas without all question, the tallest, biggest, and strongest should be ordered to carry pikes, that they may the better endure the weight of their defensive arms'.[3] A pikeman's armour was heavy: compared to the rest of the foot he was as a cuirassier to a light horseman. On his head he wore a combe-cap, as it was termed, that is an iron helmet with a ridge like a cock's comb on the top; a corslet, or 'back and breast'; a gorget to protect his throat; and tassets to cover his thighs.[4] But gorget and

---

[1] Act iv, sc. i.   [2] *King Henry IV*, p. II, act iii, sc. ii.
[3] *Pallas Armata*, p. 169.
[4] See Gervase Markham, *Soldiers Accidence*, p. 162. The passage is quoted by Sir S. Scott, *The British Army*, ii, 58. The schedule of the prices of arms established by Charles the First in 1632 thus fixes the 'Prices of the Parts of a whole corslet or Footman's Armour russetted, *viz.*:

	£	s.	d.
'The breast .		5	6
The backe .		4	6
The tassets .		5	0
The comb'd headpecce lyned		4	6
The gorget lyned		2	6

'The totall of the footman's armour 1 2 0'
—(Grose, ii, 335).

tassets were generally abandoned even in Queen Elizabeth's days, and it is probable that the pikemen who fought under Essex and Fairfax had no armour save the corslet and headpiece. Even so reduced the pikeman's armour was a great burden to him in long marches, and especially in the summer. He was, said a soldier, as it were 'imprisoned in his armour' whereas the musketeer marched 'free and open to the air, which is no small benefit and happiness to him upon such occasions'.[1] Before the Civil War ended, even the corslet was generally abandoned in the English army, and the troops whom Cromwell sent to serve in Flanders in 1657 had none. Lockhart, who commanded the contingent in 1658, was eager to reintroduce them. 'If his Highness,' he wrote to Thurloe, 'could spare twelve or fifteen hundred corslets for our pikemen, I would accustom them to wear them when they mount their guards, and at all other reviews; a stand of five hundred pikes well armed with headpiece and corslet will be a very terrible thing to be seen in these countries.'[2] For by this time the rest of the armies of Europe had generally abandoned the use of defensive armour for infantry in order to secure greater mobility. 'When we see batallions of pikes,' wrote Sir James Turner in 1671, 'we see them everywhere naked, unless it be in the Netherlands.'[3]

Charles the Second's Militia Act specifies only 'back, breast, and headpiece' (Ibid., ii, 339). Monck recommends 'a girdle of buff to be worn under the skirts of his doublet' as safer and more serviceable for the pikeman than taces (*Observations*, p. 27).

[1] 'Adde to these inconveniences, That to be put upon long and quick Marches in hot Summer weather, with Armes compleat as well for Pike as for Corslet (and Soldiers are subject, and liable to such duties), cannot but be wonderfully burthensome, and the more by reason of the excessive heat which he is forc'd to suffer, being (as I may so say) imprison'd in his Armes: whereas the Musquetier marches with a great deale of liberty, and is free and open to the aire, which is no small benefit and happinesse to him upon such occasions' (Lupton, *A Warlike Treatise of the Pike*, p. 106).

[2] *Thurloe Papers*, vii, 215.

[3] 'Our Modern Armies, as the ancient ones, consist of heavy and light armed, as well Horse as Foot. In the Cavalry, the Cuirassier is the heavy armed, and the Pikeman in the infantry. The strength of all Armies ever was and is the Infantry, and the strength of it is the heavy armed. He who is in good Armour fights with courage, as fearing no wounds, and frightens him with whom he fights that is not so well armed. Pikemen then composing the Body of the Infantry, and the men of Arms the Body of the Cavalry, should be armed that they may appear to an enemy (when they come to the shock) as a Brazen or Iron Wall. It is true, a Batallion of Pikes, without Defensive Arms, may, being serr'd together, hinder a Troop of Horse from

The offensive weapons of the pikeman consisted of a pike and a sword. According to Monck and Turner the proper length of the pike should have been eighteen feet, but in practice it was a good deal shorter. A contract for supplying pikes to the Protector's army in 1657 specified sixteen feet as the length required, and the Militia Act of Charles the Second laid down the same rule.[1] On active service soldiers had a habit of cutting their pike-staves shorter to make them more manageable and lighter, which the officers were warned to prevent. English soldiers in Ireland did so, according to an officer who served through the rebellion. 'Some that were not strong enough in the British Army for his pike in a windy day would cut off a foot, and some two of their pikes, which is a damned thing to be suffered.'[2] What the consequences of suffering it were was shown at the battle of Benburb in 1646. The crushing defeat which Owen Roe there inflicted upon the Scottish army was partly due to the inferiority of the Scottish pikes. In the first place, the pikes of the Irish were longer 'by a foot or two' than those of the Scots.

---

getting in among them; but their Heads and Bodies being naked, and having nothing on either of them to resist the force of a Carabine or Pistol-ball (except it be a Buff coat, and for most part, not that), it is not to be fancied, but a Volley of shot from a Body of Horse standing without the danger of the points of Pikes, will make many of the Pikemen fall, which will so disorder their Body, that a sudden Charge of Horse will easily break it. This is a great defect of our Modern Militia, of which most Nations are now guilty; for though in all their Constitutions of War there is an appointment for heavy Armed Horse and Foot, yet when we see Batallions of Pikes, we see them every where naked, unless it be in the Netherlands, where some, and but some Companies, represent the ancient Militia; and we find an Universal defect in the Cavalry, as to the heavy armed, there being but few Cuirassiers in many Armies, and in very many none of them at all to be seen' (Turner, *Pallas Armata*, p. 168).

[1] Sir S. Scott quotes the following from the Ordnance Accounts: '20 Oct, 1657, 3,500 pikes to be furnished at 3s. 4d. apiece; to be made of good ash, 16 feet long, bars to be strong and serviceable, in length to be 2 ft. or 22 inches. The staves to be coloured with aquafortis' (*British Army*, ii, 64). The schedule of the prices of arms issued by Charles the First in 1632 fixes the price of the pike at 4s. 6d., *viz.*:

	s.	d.
'The Staffe	2	6
The Head	1	8
Socket and Colouring		4
'Summe	4	6'

(Turner, *Pallas Armata*, p. 176; Monck, *Observations*, p. 26; Grose, *Military Antiquities*, ii, 335, 339).

[2] *The History of the Warr of Ireland, from 1641 to 1653, by a British officer of the regiment of Sir John Clotworthy*, 1873, p. 49.

In the second place, their pikeheads were of a better shape. 'They were far better to pierce,' says the English officer just quoted, 'being four square and small,' while the pikes of the Scots were 'broadheaded, which are the worst in the world.[1]' Lord Orrery, who served in these Irish wars too, thought lozenge-shaped heads the best, 'because they are sharp to enter, and when entered broad to wound with'. He also insisted that the pikehead should be fastened to the staff by thin iron plates about four feet long; for otherwise it was liable to be accidentally broken off, or to be cut off by the enemy's horsemen with their swords.[2]

The other offensive weapon with which the pikeman was equipped was a sword, but it was not of much use to him. Monck recommended that he should be armed with 'a good stiff tuck', that is, a rapier instead of a cutting sword. 'If you arm your men with swords,' said he, 'half the swords you have in your army amongst your common men will upon the first march you make be broken with cutting of boughs.'[3] The foot soldier's sword was generally of poor quality, 'being for the most part,' said Sir James Turner, 'extreamly base,' and therefore it would be better to provide them with hatchets, so that they might cut wood for making their huts or their fires.[4] Orrery, writing a few years

[1] Ibid., p. 49.

[2] 'I must before I proceed further mind the great carelessness of those who furnish pikes to the companies out of the stores, and those officers who receive them. For 'tis but too common amongst us to have in one regiment pikes of several lengths, and only armed at the point with lozange heads, whereas 16 foot and a half ought to be the general length and standard of all pikes, as 'tis amongst the Switzers; which, if the staff be made of seasoned ash, is not heavy for any ordinary man, and less heavy to pikemen, who are usually the properest and strongest men in our companies. . . . The pikes armed at the points with lozange heads, if the cheeks, or sides of the pikes, are not armed with thin plates of iron four foot deep, are very apt to be broken off near the heads, if the push be vigorous and the resistance considerable. Nor is this all; for unless the pikes be armed with those thin iron plates, they are easily cut off with sharp swords, for the pike, especially toward the end, is carried tapering, to poise it the better, and thereby renders it the more flippent for those who use it; so that the slenderer part of the pike, if unarmed, is the more liable to be cut off, it being there nearest to the enemy; whereas if the pikes were armed with those thin plates, and four foot deep, no cutting swords (which are alwayes of the shortest) could destroy the pikes, since that part of the staff of the pike which is unarmed, would be out of the reach of the horseman's sharp cutting sword: I remember we once carried a fort by storm, because the enemies pikes had not those plates, whereby the heads of them were cut off' (Orrery, *Art of War*, pp. 26–8).

[3] Monck, *Observations*, p. 26.   [4] Turner, *Pallas Armata*, p. 275.

later than Turner, complained that nowadays few pikemen and still fewer musketeers had any swords, declaring that without a sword a man did not look like a soldier.[1] But whatever the case may have been in the army of Charles the Second, the infantry of the New Model, both pikemen and musketeers, were supplied with swords. The accounts for arms supplied in 1645 show that a sword with a Dutch blade, and with a belt added, cost four shillings and sixpence.[2]

Pikemen thus armed and equipped did good service during the Civil Wars. More than once their steadiness turned the fortune of a fight. At the battle of Atherton Moor in July 1643 the day would have been lost for the Royalists had not 'a body of pikes' beaten back Fairfax's cavalry and given the rest of their army time to rally.[3] At Newbury it was the pikemen who beat back Prince Rupert's horse. The muskets of the trained bands would not have stopped his charge: his horsemen, says Clarendon, 'endured their storm of small shot', but 'could make no impression on their stand of pikes', and were 'forced to wheel about'.[4]

At Marston Moor the two regiments of the Earl of Lindsay and Lord Maitland won well-deserved fame by the steadiness with which they beat off the Royalist horse, 'having interlined their musketeers with pikemen, they made the enemies horse, notwithstanding for all the assistance they had of their foot, at two several assaults to give ground'.[5] It was with their pikes that at the close of the same battle Newcastle's Whitecoats made such a desperate stand against the cavalry of Cromwell and Leslie, and Lord Orrery tells us that in the last battle fought in Ireland a body of Irish pikemen, abandoned by their musketeers

---

[1] Orrery, p. 28.   [2] *Exchequer MSS.*, 31.

[3] 'This is memorable, that when the day seemed lost on his side, and many of his horse and foot standing doubtfull and wavering; a stand or body of pikes, which being not usefull, where the two armies were strongliest engaged, came up to the defence of their foot, and charged by Fairfax's horse, repelling them, gave leisure to rally horse and foot, and by the credit thereof entirely defeated Fairfax's army' (Sir Philip Warwick, *Memoirs*, p. 257; cf. *Life of the Duke of Newcastle*, p. 48, ed. 1886).

[4] Clarendon, *Rebellion*, vii, 211.

[5] *A Full Relation of the late Victory, etc.*, sent by Captain Stewart, 1644, p. 8.

and their cavalry, charged the English horse and almost reversed the fate of the day.[1]

Often, too, in the battles of the Civil War we hear of the pikemen of the two armies charging each other. It was so at Edgehill.
At Preston Cromwell's despatch describes his foot as 'often
coming to push of pike and close firing'. At Dunbar it was 'at
the push of pike' that Cromwell's own regiment beat back 'the
stoutest regiment the enemy had there'. At Worcester, too, 'the
dispute was long, and very near at hand, and often at push of
pike'.[2]

Nevertheless, in spite of the services which pikemen performed during the Civil War, it is possible to perceive more
than one sign that the contest between the pike and the musket
would end in the victory of the musket. It was so abroad. Before
the close of the sixteenth century English military writers had
pointed out that the pike was generally abandoned by the
French, and that the English must increase their number of
musketeers if they were to fight them on equal terms.[3] In the
course of the Thirty Years' War the pike fell more and more into
disuse, and in 1642, Lupton, a soldier who had served in Germany, dedicated to the Earl of Essex his *Warlike Treatise of the
Pike*, in which he proposed its complete abandonment in war,
and based his arguments on the experiences of his campaign

---

[1] 'I had also an experiment of the goodness of pikes in the year 1651
when in the last battel we had in Ireland, I had the honour to command
the English forces against the Irish, and though we fought in an open
countrey, and though we had routed (after a smart resistance) all the horse
of their left wing, and above a thousand of their musketeers, which composed the left battalion of their foot, yet about 1,200 pikes of the enemy,
without any shot with them, advanced boldly, and charged our squadrons
of horse so home, after their horse and shot of that wing were routed, that
we had more wounded and killed in that charge than in the whole fight
besides: so that had they guarded their angles when they charged them
round, they had done us much more mischief, if not recovered the day; but
by the angles we broke in, and afterwards the resistance was but small, nor
indeed could it be otherwise' (Orrery, p. 25).

[2] Carlyle, *Cromwell*, Letters lxiv, cxl, clxxxiii.

[3] Sutcliffe, *Practice, Proceedings and Laws of Arms*, 1593, pp. 185–7.
According to Sir William Waad, Lieutenant of the Tower under Queen
Elizabeth, it was the weight of the pike which caused the French to prefer
the musket. He asked a French officer the reason that moved them to give
up the pike, and the officer replied that it was due 'not to any disliking or
other cause, but for that we have not such personable bodies as you
Englishmen have to bear them' (Scott, *The British Army*, ii, 60).

under Sir Charles Morgan in 1627 and 1628.[1] Sir James Turner,
thirty years later, devoted a whole chapter of his *Pallas Armata*
to answering Lupton's arguments, but even he had to admit
that he had seen the pike successively abandoned by Germans,
Swedes, and Danes, and that there had arisen 'an universal
contempt of the pike'.[2] The reason for this was that the rapid
marches of Gustavus and of other contemporary leaders required a mobility in their infantry which could only be obtained
by discarding first the pikemen's armour and then the pike

[1] Knowing by experience that in forraign services, our nation hath been
disabled to performe such execution as they might, in regard of the great
multitude and extraordinary number of pikes which are put in our regiments, whereas the enemy consists most of musquets, and usually outstrips
us in numbers, and so hath performed more against us, then we could
against them' (p. 120; for some of the instance given by Lupton, see
Appendix D).

[2] 'I shall not here speak of the number of Pikemen allow'd to each Company, I shall do that in its due place, but it seems strange to me there should
be so little esteem made of the Pike in most places, it being so useful
and so necessary a weapon. Thirty years ago when the War was very hot in
the German Empire, between the Emperor Ferdinand and the Catholick
League (as it was called) on the one part, and the Swede and the Evangelick
Union (as they call'd it) on the other, I saw such an universal contempt of
the Pike that I could not admire it enough; for though after Gustavus
Adolphus King of Sweden entred Germany, squadrons and Batallions of
Pikes were to be seen in all Regiments and Brigades of both places, and that
Pikemen were still accounted the Body of the Infantry, yet after his
Victory at Leipsick over the Imperial forces under Tilly, the Kings Marches
were so quick in pursuance of his successes, which followed one on the
heels of another, and the retreats also of other Armies from him were so
speedy, that first the Pikemans defensive Arms were cast away, and after
them the Pike itself, insomuch that all who hereafter were levied and
enrolled, called for Muskets. But notwithstanding this, when new Regiments were levied after that great Kings death, Colonels and Captains were
ever order'd to levy and arm Pikemen proportionably to the Musquetiers;
yet after they had endur'd some fatigue, the Pike was again cast away,
and no Soldiers but Musquetiers were to be seen. Whether this was done by
the supine negligence of the Officers, especially the Colonels, or for the
contempt they had of the Pike, I know not. But I am sure that for some
years together I have seen many weak Regiments composed meerly of
Musquetiers, without one Pikeman in any of them, and surely they were so
much the weaker for that. Nor did I find long after that, that the Pike got
better entertainment in other places than in Germany; for in the year 1657,
after the late King of Denmark had lost his best Army, he gave as I said in
this same Chapter, Commissions to five of us to raise each of us a Regiment
of men of one thousand apiece, all strangers. We were bound by the
Capitulation to arm our Regiments ourselves out of the moneys we had
agreed for, and expresly with Musquets, neither would those of the Privy
Council, who were order'd to treat with us, suffer one word to be mention'd
of a Pike in our Commission, though the conveniency, and sometime the
necessity of that weapon was sufficiently remonstrated by us' (Turner,
Pallas Armata, p. 177).

itself. The same cause tended to produce a similar effect in the English Civil Wars. In June 1644, when King Charles made his famous night march from Oxford, escaping by the rapidity of his movements between the two armies of Essex and Waller, he took with him only his cavalry and '2,500 choice musketeers drawn out of the whole foot'. He left all the pikemen of his army behind in Oxford.[1]

To take a second instance. By the conclusion of the Irish rebellion in 1652 the pike appears to have fallen into general disuse amongst the English army in Ireland, simply because the work of the army consisted mainly in sieges and in hunting the rebels out of their fastnesses in the bogs and mountains, for which mobility was the chief requisite. In anything like a battle this placed the English foot at a disadvantage. At a fight near Wexford in 1652 they are described as 'hard put to it'. 'The Irish infantry coming to push of pike with your foot,' says a letter to the Parliament, 'who had no pikes, but were fain to club with their muskets.'[2] In the English army, however, the abandonment of the pike was but temporary, and when the emergency passed it was again adopted. As late as 1692 the proportion of pikes per company was still one-third, and not till 1705[3] was the pike altogether abandoned.

The history of the musketeer and his armament is less simple, and requires more technical details. The musket was the later development of the harquebuse and hackbut, which were the earliest firearms. An intermediate stage was represented by the caliver, which had gone out of use by the time the Civil Wars began. First used in the Italian wars about the third decade of the sixteenth century, the musket was chiefly employed in the defence and attack of fortified places. Its weight long prevented its use by armies in the field, but when the Duke of Alva became governor of the Low Countries he equipped with it a large portion of the Spanish infantry. Its value lay in the fact that it carried a heavier bullet than the harquebuse, and was therefore more effective against the armour of Dutch and German horsemen. 'To frustrate the resistance of their armours,' says Sir

[1] Sir Edward Walker, *Historical Discourses*, p. 19; *Diary of Richard Symonds*, p. 15.
[2] Ludlow, *Memoirs*, ed. 1894, i, pp. 515, 517–18.
[3] Fortescue, *History of the British Army*, i, 584.

John Smyth, 'the Duke did increase his numbers of mosquet-
teers, the blowes of the bullets of which no armour wearable
can resist.'[1] On the other hand, many soldiers of experience still
preferred harquebusiers and caliver men to musketeers for skirmishing purposes. The heaviness of the musket made the use
of a rest necessary. This rest, made of ash wood or some other
tough wood, had at the top a sort of fork to support the barrel
of the musket, and at the other end an iron point, so that it
might be stuck in the ground.[2] In marching the soldier carried it
in his right hand, or hung it on his arm by a loop.[3] At the beginning of Charles the First's reign the rest was in general use.
Markham writing in 1625 and Kelly in 1627 assume its employment, and Ward writing in 1639 does the same.[4] The trained
bands whom Charles the First gathered against the Scots in 1639
were ordered to provide themselves with rests from the King's
magazine at Hull, at a cost of tenpence apiece. Abroad however
it was being discarded.[5] The Swedes abandoned it in the Thirty
Years' War, though the Imperialists retained it for some time
after their opponents had given it up. 'In the late expeditions
in most places of Christendom,' writes Turner in 1671, 'they
have been found more troublesome than helpful.'[6] In England,
if they were used when the Civil War began, they were certainly
no longer employed when the New Model army was formed.
Lieutenant-Colonel Elton, writing in 1649, represents the English
soldiers as saying, 'our rests are of little or no use to us
in time of skirmishing; fit they are we confess in the Military
Gardens, but in time of battle both troublesome and cumbersome'.[7] I have found no mention of rests amongst the payments
made for arms supplied to the New Model.

Coincident with the disuse of the rest there was a reduction

[1] Sir John Smyth, *Certain Discourses*, 1590, pp. 13, 143, 149.

[2] A picture of the rest is given in Sir S. Scott's *History of the British Army*, ii, 274, and in Grose's *Military Antiquities*, i, 160, 360.

[3] See the plates representing the exercise of musketeers in Grose's *Military Antiquities*, i, 358, and the quotation from Davies's *England's Trainings*, ii, 126.

[4] Ward, *Animadversions of War*, p. 215; cf. Monck, *Observations*, p. 25.

[5] Rushworth, ii, 723; cf. Grose, ii, 337.

[6] *Pallas Armata*, p. 175.

[7] 'Thirdly, that the Souldiers present and give fire upon their Rests, not using that slovenly posture of popping their Matches into the Pan, their

in the length of the musket. Sir Thomas Kellie describing the weapons of a musketeer in 1627, says that the barrel of his musket should be four feet long, and Charles the First in the seventh year of his reign ordered all the muskets of the trained bands to be of that length. At the Restoration, however, Charles the Second fixed three feet as the length. It is therefore obvious that the diminution took place during the Civil Wars, though I have found no direct evidence of the fact.[1]

The bullet which the musket fired was, as has been already hinted, exceptionally heavy. It weighed about an ounce and a quarter. Twelve to the pound is laid down by military writers as the correct weight for a musket bullet, and the same figure is fixed in the regulations of Charles the First and Charles the Second for the militia. It is evident, however, that bullets of fourteen to the pound, that is one ounce and one-eighth, were frequently used and tolerated if not approved.[2]

Muskets being on their left sides, which is not only hurtfull unto themselves but much endangers their fellow-Souldiers, and by so doing, they scarce or ever do any execution against an Enemy. But here I meet with an objection framed by the Souldiers after this manner; our Rests are of little or no use unto us in time of skirmishing, fit they are, we confesse, in the Military Gardens, but in time of battail both troublesome and cumbersome unto us, to whom I reply, what if they be a little cumbersome at the first, must they therefore be rejected, and carelessly thrown away, nay, rather they ought frequently to practise themselves in the use thereof, which if they did, they would finde the same very serviceable unto them in time of skirmishing, wherewith they fire better, and in a more comely and gracefull way, far more securing both themselves and fellow-souldiers from danger, and likewise upon their March, it is both a help and support unto them' (Elton, *Complete Body of the Art Military*, 1650, p. 54. The Imprimatur is dated 13th April, 1649).

[1] Kellie, *Pallas Armata*, p. 3; see also Grose, *Military Antiquities*, ii, 337, 339.

[2] Ibid. From the remarks of Lord Orrery it seems that the English army in Ireland used muskets of several sizes. He recommends 'That all our muskets be of one bore, or at most of two sorts of certain bores; the bigger for the stronger, the lesser for the weaker bodies: for want of this, I have seen much hazard undergone; for generally our musket shot is of one certain size, and the bores of muskets are of various sizes, whereby having been once engaged in a fight, which by reason of the many inclosures in which we fought, the musketeers were to be supplied with more shot than they carried in their pouches, and barrels of musket bullets being opened, few of the shot in them would fit the muskets, but were a size too large, whereby we had like to have been worsted; for the soldiers were forced to gnaw off much of the lead, others to cut their bullets; in which much time was lost, the bullets flew a less way and more uncertainly; and which was worse so many pauses animated the enemy by making him think our courages cooled' (Orrery, p. 29).

The musketeer carried his bullets in a little pouch, but in battle generally kept one or two in his mouth for convenience in loading. Orrery describes soldiers on service as taking 'their bullets out of their mouths, which is the nimblest way, or out of their pouches, which is slow'.[1] Ward, in his instructions for drilling, bids the musketeer, after charging with powder, 'having your bullet ready in your mouth, and taking it in your right hand, between your forefinger and thumb, let the bullet drop in with a jog to sink it to the powder, or by ramming it down with the gunstick'.[2] This explains a clause which is frequently found in capitulations. When a garrison surrendered with the honours of war it marched out as if prepared for battle. The garrison of Oxford, for instance, by the fifth article of the capitulation, marched out on 24th June 1646, with 'flying colours, trumpets sounding, drums beating, matches lighted at both ends, and bullets in their mouths, and every soldier to have twelve charges of powder, match, and bullet proportionable'.[3]

The charge which so heavy a ball required was considerable. 'A musket,' says Sir James Turner, 'requires the half weight of her ball in fine powder and two thirds of common powder, that is one pound of fine powder to two pounds of lead, and two pounds of ordinary powder for three pounds of lead.'[4] The musketeer carried two kinds of powder, a fine powder for priming his piece, in what was termed a touch-box or primer, and a coarser powder for loading his piece in his flask. He usually had twelve charges of powder ready made up, contained in little cases like tubes, made of tin, leather or wood, and invented in the Low Countries. These cases were hung from a leather belt worn over the shoulder. The belt was called a bandolier, but the term was often applied to the cases as well as to the belt.[5]

The bandoliers were inconvenient and even dangerous. They rattled so loudly that in windy weather their noise prevented the soldiers from hearing the word of command. Moreover, in surprises, when silence was necessary, their rattling often dis-

[1] See p. 82, note 3.   [2] *Animadversions of War*, p. 317.

[3] Sprigge, *Anglia Rediviva*, ed. 1854, p. 269; see also Clarendon, *Rebellion*, vii, 36.

[4] *Pallas Armata*, p. 175.

[5] For pictures of bandoliers and flask, see Grose, ii, plate 40; Scott, ii, 276. For descriptions, see also Grose, ii, 122–7, 293.

D

covered the intended attack to the enemy. In 1655, for example, after General Venables had landed in Hispaniola his camp was frequently disturbed by night-alarms. The sentinels who gave the alarm declared that the Spaniards were advancing to attack them, and that they heard a sound like the rattling of bandoliers. But on examination the sound turned out to be caused by the land-crabs looking for their food and knocking their horny legs together.[1] Moreover, besides their noisiness, the bandoliers were apt to take fire accidentally; 'and when they take fire,' says Orrery, 'they commonly wound and often kill him who wears them, for likely if one bandolier takes fire all the rest do in that collar'.[2]

The danger of explosion was largely due to the fact that the musket in use was a matchlock. The match used was a small cord made of twisted strands of tow, prepared by boiling in vinegar or the lees of wine.[3] Almost any kind of cord could be

---

[1] *The Narrative of General Venables,* Camden Society, 1900, p. 160.

[2] 'Besides, I have often seen much prejudice in the use of bandeleers, which being worn in the belts for them, above the soldiers' coats, are often apt to take fire, especially if the matchlock musket be used; and when they take fire, they commonly wound and often kill him that wears them, and those near him: for likely if one bandeleer take fire, all the rest do in that collar: they often tangle those which use them on service, when they have fired, and are falling off by the flanks of the files of the intervals, to get into the rear to charge again. To which I shall add, that in secret attempts in the night, their rattling often discovers the design, and enables the enemy to prevent it; and in the day time on service, especially if the weather be windy, their rattling also too frequently hinders the soldiers from hearing, and consequently obeying, the officer's word of command, which must be fatal when it happens: whereas the cartridge boxes exempt those who use them from all these dangers and prejudices: they enable the soldiers on service to fire more expeditiously; they are also usually worn about the waste of the soldier, the skirts of whose doublet and his coate, doubly defend them from all rain that doth not pierce both; and being worn close to his body, the heat thereof keeps the powder dryer, and therefore more fit to be fired in service.
'Besides all this, whoever loads his musket with cartridges, is sure the bullet will not drop out, though he takes his aim under breast high, for the paper of the cartridge keeps it in; whereas those soldiers which on service take their bullets out of their mouths (which is the nimblest way) or out of their pouches, which is slow, seldom put any paper, tow, or grass, to ram the bullet in; whereby if they fire above breast high, the bullet passes over the head of the enemy, and if they aim low, the bullet drops out ere the musket is fired; and 'tis to this that I attribute the little execution I have seen musketeers do in time of fight, though they fired at great battalions and those also reasonable near' (Orrery, quoted by Grose, *Military Antiquities,* i, 160).

[3] Grose, ii, 125; Scott, ii, 291.

made into match if it were properly prepared. When Hopton
and the Cornish forces were besieged in Devizes by Waller in
June 1643, it was suddenly discovered that the match in store
was insufficient to repulse an attack. Accordingly Hopton directed diligent officers 'to search every house in the town and
to take all the bedcords they could find, and to cause them to
be speedily beaten and boiled'.[1] Thanks to this expedient, his
musketeers were provided with sufficient match to fight the
next day.

On service the soldier carried a 'link' of match, that is a coil
of two or three yards of it, hung on his belt, and in his left hand
he had a shorter piece about a couple of feet long, as may be
seen in the pictures given in the old drill books.[2] The piece of
match he carried in his left hand was lit at both ends, and he held
it between his fingers, one end between the middle finger and the
third finger, the other end between the third and the little finger.
When he wished to fire he took one end of the match with the
thumb and second finger of his right hand and fitted it into the
cock of his musket, which was termed cocking the match. He
then opened the pan of the musket, and pulling the 'tricker',
brought the match down into the pan and fired the priming.
Having fired he 'uncocked his match', that is, took it out of the
cock, returned it to its place between the fingers of the left hand,
and proceeded to load again.[3]

It required so many motions to load and fire that the matchlock could only be discharged very slowly. But it had many
worse defects. An immense amount of match was required for
an army, because it was very rapidly consumed. The garrison
of Lyme, for instance, which numbered 1,500 men only, often
used five hundredweight of match in twenty-four hours.[4] Yet it
was impossible to avoid this large consumption of match, for
whenever they were anywhere near an enemy the musketeers had
to keep their matches lighted. Marching in an enemy's country

[1] Clarendon, *Rebellion*, vii, 114.

[2] See the plates in Grose's *Military Antiquities*, i, 156, 358.

[3] The motions are well explained by Ward, *Animadversions of War*
pp. 215–21, and illustrated by the plates in Grose, i, 358, or Hexham's
Principles of the Art Military, pt. i, pp. 10–14, ed. 1642.

[4] *Cal. State Papers, Dom.*, 1644, p. 205.

without matches lighted often proved fatal to a regiment.[1] One
of the charges against the commander of the Covenanters at the
battle of Kilsyth (Major-General Baillie) was that his musketeers
had not got their matches lit when Montrose and his Highlanders
attacked them.[2] The same mistake was one of the causes alleged
for the defeat of the Scots by Cromwell at Dunbar. About mid-
night on 2nd September, the Scottish general, believing that
Cromwell would make no attack that night, ordered all his musketeers to put out their matches with the exception of one man
in every six.[3] At dawn, therefore, when Cromwell suddenly fell
upon the Scots, their musketeers could not at first answer his
fire.

Besides this, the light of the burning match, like the rattling
of the bandoliers, often gave untimely warning of an attack. In
the West Indian expedition the soldiers of General Venables
often mistook the fireflies for the matches of a surprise party of
Spaniards.[4] The matches gave a good deal of light. At the storming of Bristol in September 1645 the Royalist garrison was
warned by a deserter of the intended attack. Consequently, says
one of the Roundheads, 'the enemy stood ready cocked, and the
gunners by their guns, the sight whereof at the first going on
made it so light a man might perfectly see all the men about him
and horses'.[5] To remedy this drawback the Prince of Orange
invented a tin pipe about a foot long to contain the match and
to hide its light: it had holes in the side like a flute to let in the
air and prevent the match from being extinguished.[6] On the

---

[1] See the *Swedish Intelligencer*, iv, 119.

[2] 'It is objected against me only, as if no other officer were to give an
accompt, neither for regiment company nor corporallship, that on this our
unhappie day there were no lighted lunts among the musquetrie. The fire
given by the first five regiments will sufficiently answer what concerns
them; and for the other three, I humbly intreat your honours, to inform
yourself of Generall-Major Leslie, the Adjutant, and the chief officers of
these several regiments: if they doe not satisfie yow therein I shall answer
for myselfe' (Baillie, *Letters*, ii, 422).

[3] Walker, *Historical Discourses*, p. 180; cf. *Transactions of the Royal
Historical Society*, xiv, 41. Walker says only two per company were ordered
to keep their matches lit, another account says only the file-leaders. The
latter is more probable.

[4] *Narrative of General Venables*, p. 160.

[5] *Military Memoir of Colonel Birch*, Camden Society, 1873, p. 22.

[6] A picture of one of these pipes is given in Ward's *Animadversions*
p. 394; see also Turner, *Pallas Armata*, p. 176, and Grose, ii, 294.

other hand, if the matches sometimes betrayed an advance, they
were at other times exceedingly useful in concealing a retreat.
For instance, in Scott's *Legend of Montrose* Captain Dalgetty is
pursued, and almost captured, in his escape from Inverary.
Forgetting that the Highlanders with him are bowmen and not
musketeers, he tells them to 'leave some lighted matches burning on the branches of the trees; it shows as if they were lined
with shot'.[1] If a general wished to march off by night in the
face of an enemy he left some rows of lighted matches to per-
sonate lines of musketeers. It was in this way that Charles the
First in 1644 escaped unperceived from Oxford when he was
hemmed in by the armies of Essex and Waller. 'Our soldiers,'
says a Royalist, 'hung lighted matches at the mill and bridge
near Islip to cheat Essex, and so fairly left that place, the enemy
shooting many times that night at the matches in vain.'[2]

In sieges matches were often employed in sham attacks or
fictitious sallies. At the siege of Lathom House the Royalist
garrison sometimes stuck lighted matches in balls of clay, and
threw them near the trenches of the besiegers in order to draw
their fire. At other times, in spite of the sentinels of the Roundheads, 'they would steal a cord about some tree near the enemy,
and would make it terrible with many ranks and files of lighted
matches'. Once they out-turned an old horse 'handsomely
starred with matches, which appeared in the dark night like
young constellations'.[3]

But the occasional advantages to be derived from matches
were far outweighed by their drawbacks. The matchlock was a
very uncertain weapon, and often missed fire. Sir Thomas Kellie
says that he had often seen the muskets of four men out of ten
fail to go off.[4] In rainy or windy weather this happened still more
frequently, either the match was damped and would not burn,

---

[1] Chapter xiv.   [2] *Diary of Richard Symonds*, p. 8.
[3] *Lancashire Civil War Tracts*, Chetham Society, 1844, pp. 176, 180; cf.
Memoirs of Sir James Turner, p. 32.
[4] 'A musqueteer may fail of his shot by sundry accidents, as by rolling
out of the bullet, an badde matche, an matche not right cocked, by evill
powder, or wet powder in his pan: and I have often times seen an ranke of
musquetiers having presented and given fire that three or four of ten have
failed of their shot, and ye must know that in service there is no time to
prime againe or to right their match, for they must fall away with the
rest of their ranke, and make place to the next ranke to give fire' (Kellie,
Pallas Armata, 1627, p. 110).

or the priming was blown out of the pan. Fairfax, in a letter written to the Speaker in February 1646, says that he was hindered from advancing into Cornwall by the 'extreme foulness' of the weather, and that if such wet weather had continued it 'would have made our firearms little useful either for assault or defence'.[1] Sir James Turner attributes the disaster of the Scots in the Preston campaign partly to the unseasonable weather. 'That summer was so excessively rainy and wet that it was not possible for us to keep one musket of ten fixed all the time we were in a body in England.'[2]

Added to this, either in fine weather or wet weather, the match was very dangerous. Sometimes a spark from the match of a rear-rank man would fire his musket before the time and wound a comrade in the front rank. Sometimes a spark would set fire to one of the charges in a man's bandolier, explode them all, and kill the wearer. Occasionally 'the budge barrel', as the regimental powder-barrel was called, would be blown up by an accidental spark.[3] 'To add to our misfortunes,' says Sir Richard Bulstrode in his account of Edgehill, 'a careless soldier in fetching powder where a magazine was, clapped his hand carelessly into a barrel of powder with his match between his fingers, whereby much powder was blown up and many killed.'[4]

[1] Sprigge, *Anglia Rediviva*, p. 199.
[2] *Memoirs of Sir James Turner*, p. 59.
[3] 'Budge-Barrels are small barrels well hooped, with only one head; on the opposite end is nailed a piece of leather to draw together with strings like a purse. Their use is for carrying powder along with a gun or mortar, as they are less dangerous and more portable than whole barrels; they are also used on a battery of mortars to contain meal-powder.' An illustration of a budge-barrel is appended (*Memoirs of the Marquis de Feuquieres*, 1735, 2 vols., with a military dictionary at the end of vol. ii). The term which had in the eighteenth century become restricted to barrels used for the artillery, was originally applied also to those of the infantry, as the following passage from Lord Orrery's *Art of War* shows:
'Once marching in battalia in a plain countrey to fight the enemy's army and as they marched in like order to meet us, some musketeers of ours running hastily to a budge-barrel to fill their bandeleers, and being careless of their matches, the budge barrel took fire, and blew them up; at which the enemies army shouted; and finding our men did not answer them I rid hastily to the next squadrons and battalions, and commanded them also to shout; which the rest of our forces taking from them, repeatedly did so: soon after the like accident happened to the enemies army, and then our men shouted, but were not answered; which I bid the next troops to take notice of as a sign they were disanimated, and a proof that their loss was considerable by that blowing up' (Orrery, p. 186).
[4] *Memoirs of Sir Richard Bulstrode*, p. 84.

On account of all these defects the matchlock musket was finally superseded by the firelock musket, and though this process of supersession was not complete till the next century, it was already beginning. The generic term 'firelock' covered two distinct varieties of weapons, the wheellock and the snaphanse or flintlock. The earliest of these in date was the wheellock, so called because the spark which fired the charge was produced by the friction of a small steel wheel against a piece of iron pyrites. The wheel was set in motion by a strong spring, which was wound up by a key, or, as it was more often called, a 'spanner'.[1]

Wheellocks, however, were expensive, and very liable to get out of order; for these reasons they were little used in the Civil Wars except for the carbines or pistols of cavalry.

The kind of firelock usually employed during the Civil Wars was the snaphanse or flintlock. In this weapon the spark which fired the priming of the gun was produced by the contact of a piece of flint with a steel plate.[2] This lock was invented in Germany, and the word snaphanse means snapcock, not poultry stealer as some early military writers supposed.[3] Originally it was a fowling-piece, not a military weapon; it carried a smaller ball than the musket proper, and was much lighter. It was much used by the German peasantry during the Thirty Years' War when they had to defend themselves against plundering parties. In 1626 two regiments of Imperialist horse were defeated by the Duke of Brunswick; the remnant took refuge in a wood where they were surrounded and hunted down by the country people. 'What for the hand guns and the firelocks which the Boores carried a soldier could not peep out of the wood, but he was taken off presently. . . . As hunger and courage drives them out they are snapped up by these Boores, who being used to kill crowes and vermin on their own land, are very good marksmen (especially, the aim being better, when the mark is alive) with their firelocks, which are a great deal surer shooters and fitter for their handling than the warlike musket.'[4]

[1] Scott, *History of the British Army,* ii, 280; Grose, *Military Antiquities,* ii, Appendix, plate 40.

[2] Scott, ii, 284, plates 32–5.

[3] See Clifford Walton, *History of the British Standing Army,* p. 331.

[4] *More News from the Duke of Brunswick,* 1626, 4to.

Being cheap and serviceable, the snaphanse or firelock, as it is indifferently termed, was speedily adopted for military purposes. Lord Orrery, who compares it at length with the matchlock, praises its safeness and handiness. It was safer because the dangers caused by the match and its sparks did not exist with the firelock. It was handier because it was simpler. 'It is exceedingly more ready,' says Orrery, 'for with the firelock you have only to cock, and you are prepared to shoot, but with your matchlock you have endless motions, the least of which is as long a performing as but that one of the other.'[1]

During the Civil Wars the firelock was therefore used for two purposes in the armies of the Parliament. In the first place, the carbines and pistols of the cavalry were as a rule fitted with snaphanse locks, as being the cheapest and most serviceable form of firelock. In the second place, each army contained certain unregimented companies of firelocks specially appointed to guard the artillery and ammunition. Essex had 400 firelocks under Lieutenant-General Philibert Emmanuel de Boyes, the general of his ordnance.[2] In the New Model there were two companies of firelocks (if not more) who were distinguished from the rest of the infantry by wearing 'tawny coats' instead of red ones.[3] Fairfax found them so useful that in 1647 he proposed to Parliament to disband his lifeguards and to raise a complete regiment of firelocks in its place. Monck went still further. In his *Observations*, written about 1646, he recommended that the regular cavalry should all have snaphanse carbines, or rather 'a musket barrel of the length of a carbine barrel, well stocked, with a snaphanse, which I hold to be much better than a carbine for service'.[4] As soon as he became commander-in-chief he began to rearm his own regiment with firelocks, and on 14th April 1660 he ordered the four companies of it then in the Tower to exchange their matchlocks for snaphanse muskets.[5]

The snaphanse, in its later form the fusil, became more and more used in the English army during the reign of Charles the

---

[1] See Appendix E.   [2] Peacock, *Army Lists*, pp. 25, 26.

[3] Ibid., p. 106; see also p. 151, *post*.

[4] Monck's *Observations*, pp. 24, 26, 34.

[5] Mackinnon, *Coldstream Guards*, ii, 238; Clifford Walton, *History of the British Standing Army*, pp. 331, 785. Colonel Clifford Walton goes too far in saying that 'the real snaphans musket was never used in our army'.

Second. Special regiments of fusiliers took the place of the old companies of firelocks; the marines were armed with them when they were raised in 1664; the guards were equipped with them in 1683, and a certain proportion of every regiment was given the new weapon. The matchlock was still used in the army during William the Third's wars in Ireland, but by 1700 it was entirely superseded by the firelock, or rather the fusil.[1]

Having described the firearms with which the soldiers of the New Model were armed, it remains to discuss the question of their range and their accuracy. On both points exact data are difficult to obtain. In the controversy of Queen Elizabeth's time between the supporters of the bow and the champions of the musket, the comparative range of the two is often discussed. 'The musket,' says Sir Roger Williams, 'spoyles horse and man thirty score off, if the powder be anything good and the bearer of any judgment.'[2] Apparently he meant 600 paces not 600 yards, but in either case the musket was effective at a longer distance than is generally supposed. Again, just at the outbreak of the Civil War, Lupton, comparing the value of pikes and muskets, speaks of the musket as effective at a range of 400 yards, nor does Sir James Turner in his answer to Lupton deny this estimate.[3] In battle, however, musketeers usually delivered their fire a much shorted distance, though the precise distance is not specifically stated in the military books.[4]

What sort of practice the musketeer made with his weapon it is equally difficult to determine with exactness. Probably the abandonment of the rest did not improve his shooting. An eyewitness of the siege of Bergen-op-Zoom in 1622, thus describes the shooting of the English musketeers who fought under the

[1] 'The difference between the snaphans and the fusil as later adopted was that the former had the pan separate from the rest of the lock, as in the earlier matchlocks, whereas in the fusil the hammer and pan-cover were united to the lock' (Clifford Walton, p. 331; see also pp. 431–4; Fortescue, *History of the British Army*, i, 325, 326; Grose, i, 159; Scott, ii, 250).

[2] *A Brief Discourse of War*, 1590. His opponent, Sir John Smyth, admits that the musket would carry a bullet point blank twenty-four or thirty score yards (or perhaps paces). See also Scott, ii, 271, 279.

[3] Lupton, *Warlike Treatise of the Pike*, p. 48; Turner, *Pallas Armata*, p. 178.

[4] 'When the enemies battalias be approacht within 6 or 8 score, or lesse, then the musqueteers are to give fire' (Ward, *Animadversions of War* p. 261).

Dutch flag. 'I saw them run on and give fire in their enemies faces, and they would levy in leaning on their rests, and look after their shot, as though they had been so many fowlers, which watch to see the fowl fall that they may be sure of the body.'[1] Often, however, the shooting was bad, as Orrery points out, referring to his experience with English soldiers in Ireland. The musketeer used no wads. 'Soldiers,' he says, 'seldom put in any paper, tow, or grass to ram the bullet in, whereby if they fire above breast high, the bullet passes over the heads of the enemy, and if they fire low the bullet drops out ere the musket is fired: and 'tis to this that I attribute the little execution I have seen musketeers do in time of fight, though they fired at great battalions, and those also reasonable near.'[2] Occasionally during the course of the war we hear of very accurate individual shooting, but in such cases it was not generally the ordinary matchlock musket which was employed. At the siege of Sherborne Castle, for instance, in 1645, a marksman in a high tower inflicted great damage on the besiegers and picked off many of Fairfax's officers, but we are expressly told that he used 'a birding-piece'.[3] But both this marksman and another of equal skill were not professional soldiers but 'keepers of parks'.[4] Realizing the fact that the ordinary musket was deficient in accuracy, Monck proposed that six men in every company should be armed with fowling-pieces, suggesting that they might be employed in battle to pick off the officers of the enemy.[5]

The musketeer was obliged to depend on his skill in using his

---

[1] Dalton, *Life of Sir Edward Cecil*, ii, 20.

[2] Quoted by Grose, *Military Antiquities*, p. 160, from Orrery's *Art of War*. Compare Sir James Turner's remarks on the subject. 'The mentioning this victory (Wittstock) puts me in mind to advertise all officers of foot not to teach their musketeers to neglect their rammers, a lesson too often taught and practised: for at this battle I speak of the Imperial foot were upon a hill, up which Leslie advanced with his infantry, but neither his nor the Imperial musketeers made use of rammers, only (as the common custom is) when they charged with ball they knocked the butts of their muskets at their right foot, by which means most of the bullets of the Imperial and Saxish fire-men fell out at the mouths of their musket when they presented them down the hill upon the Swedes whose bullets could not run that fortune being presented upward. And for this reason it was observed that few of the Swedish foot fell' (*Pallas Armata*, p. 306.).

[3] Sprigge, *Anglia Rediviva*, pp. 91, 94, 95; *Report on the Duke of Portland's MSS.*, i, 242.

[4] Ibid., i, 242.　　　　　　　[5] Monck, *Observations*, p. 103.

musket, for unlike the pikeman he had no defensive armour. 'The defensive arms of a musketeer is a good courage,' writes General Monck.[1] Twenty years before the Civil Wars musketeers usually wore combe-caps like the pikemen, that is iron helmets with a ridge like a cock's comb, but during the Civil Wars, or at all events long before the wars ended, they abandoned the helmet. In its place they wore a broad-brimmed hat of felt, perhaps with a plume in it.[2] We hear of Monmouth caps being supplied to the army in Ireland, and doubtless the troops in England adopted them too. A curious proof of the abandonment of the helmet by the British infantry is supplied by General Morgan's account of the battle of the Dunes. As the English soldiers advanced to attack the Spaniards, they gave a great shout and 'cast up their caps into the air, saying they would have better hats before night'.[3]

As musketeers had no defensive arms, and as the bayonet had not yet been invented, they could not resist a serious cavalry charge. Many devices were tried in order to give them some protection against horsemen. The chief of them was what was termed a Swede's feather or swine feather. This was a stake about five feet long with a pike head at each end; one end was stuck in the ground, the other served to keep off the horses of the enemy.[4] It must have been something like the stakes which the English archers used at Agincourt.[5] The Swedish feather was employed by Gustavus Adolphus in the Thirty Years' War, and the Scottish armies who fought in England imitated his example,[6] but it does not seem to have been made use of in the English armies of the time. An attempt was often made to combine the Swede's feather with the musket-rest, by affixing a stout prong to one side of the rest. Monck recommended Swede's feathers with heads of rest fastened to them.[7] But a more practicable device,

[1] *Observations*, p. 26.

[2] Scott, *British Army*, ii, 276; cf. Grose, i, 156, 358–60; Cockle, *Bibliography of English Military Books*, p. 65. See also p. 237, *post*.

[3] *Harleian Miscellany*, iii, 345.

[4] A picture of the Swede's feather is given in Ward's *Animadversions of War*, p. 393; cf. Turner, *Pallas Armata*, pp. 169, 175; Grose, i, 157.

[5] Ramsay, *Lancaster and York*, i, 215, 220.

[6] Terry, *Life of Alexander Leslie*, pp. 65, 110.

[7] *Observations*, p. 26.

which gained the approval of Sir Thomas Glemham and Lord
Wimbledon, was the combination of the musket and the half
pike, so as to make its bearer pikeman and musketeer in one.
This was introduced by William Bariffe about 1637 in the exercises of the Artillery Garden, but though it was highly praised
by many military writers it never got beyond the experimental
stage.[1] Later still Sir James Turner, writing in 1671, recommended the use of 'knives one foot long made both for cutting
and thrusting, the haft being made to fill the bore of the musket'.
Thus at last, but not till the Civil Wars were over, the plug
bayonet appears.[2]

None of these devices obtaining general adoption, the safety
of infantry attacked by cavalry depended on the combined
action of musketeers and pikemen. 'Neither musketeers nor
pikemen alone,' says Bariffe, 'can be singly sufficient of them-

---

[1] 'Having often considered the danger of the Muskettier, and how unable
hee is to resist the Horse, after hee hath poured forth his shot, without hee
bee sheltered, either by some naturall or artificiall defence; And withall
having knowledge, that in severall parts of Christendome divers Captaines
and Souldiers, have oft beene trying conclusions, to make the Muskettiers
as well defensive as offensive. Some by unscrewing the heads of their
Rests, and then screwing the staffe of their Rests into the muzzle of the
Musket, with the arming of a Pike at the lower end, by which meanes they
would use the Musket and Rest together, in the nature of a whole Pike.
But this proved so tedious and troublesome, that it fell without profit.
Another sort had been made Rests with the one end of the forke (or head)
being like a spike, about 18 inches in length: this also proved extreame
troublesome to themselves, dangerous to their fellowes, and of no validity
against the enemy. A third sort had a Halfe-pike of about 7 or 8 foot in
length, using it after the manner of a rest: but all the while the Muskettier
was charging his Musket one of them was enough to trouble a whole file, besides the danger in the recovery. A fourth sort there was (yet better than the
former) that with a hooke was fastned to the girdle, the while the Muskettier
was making ready; but this had his defects also as being both tedious and
troublesome. Many other wayes and conclusions have also been tried; with
successe like the former: which I forbeare to demonstrate, for as their con-
ceits proved uselesse, so the discourse would prove as fruitlesse. Lastly, my
selfe, with another Gentleman of our ground (both well affecting the use of
the Musket) found out a way, to use the halfe-pike and Musket, with so
much facility and ease, that it is farre lesse troublesome than the rest: and
yet of a greater length, than any of the former rests, or halfe-pikes, as being
compleat 10 foot in length, with the arming' (Bariffe, *Young Artilleryman*,
p. 349; for the exercise, see p. 368). Lupton devotes the eleventh chapter of
his *Treatise of the Pike* to this invention. He says: 'There can scarce be a
fairer conjunction of offensive and defensive weapons to be practised by one
soldier with such ease and pleasure.'

[2] *Pallas Armata*, p. 375. On the history of the development of the
bayonet, see Grose, ii, 340; Scott, ii, 315–26: Fortescue, i, 327; Clifford
Walton, pp. 340–9.

selves to withstand the able and resolute horseman (without
great advantage of ground). On the contrary musketeers and
pikes being conjoined in one body and being well ordered they
are not only able to defend themselves against their fury, but
also to put them to the worst.'[1]

All depended therefore on the 'well ordering' of the regiment,
on the skill with which the captains combined the movements
of the two arms, and the promptness with which the musketeers
and pikemen obeyed their orders. Only a well-drilled and disciplined regiment could therefore hope to resist a charge of
horse. Such a regiment, according to Robert Monro, was the
Scottish regiment in which he served at Leipsic and Lützen.
'You would think,' says he, 'a whole regiment disciplined as this
was, were all but one body, and of one motion, their ears obeying the command all as one, their eyes turning all alike at the
first stroke given, their hands going to execution as one hand.'[2]
Such, doubtless, were the two splendid regiments of Maitland
and Lindsay which at Marston Moor, when more than half the
Scottish infantry broke and ran, beat back three successive
charges of the King's horse.[3]

At the beginning of the war, as we should expect, the soldiers
of the Parliament were very badly drilled. Essex, for want of
time to get his men thoroughly drilled, ordered his officers not
to attempt too much with them, but 'to bring them to use their
arms readily and expertly, and not to busy them in practising
the ceremonious forms of military discipline'. It would be
enough if they were 'well instructed in the necessary rudiments
of war', and knew how 'to fall on with discretion', to retreat
with care, and to make good their ground.[4]

Nor does the drill of the New Model itself seem to have been
very elaborate. Military books, such as Bariffe's *Young Artilleryman* and many others, are full of complicated and fantastic
marches and counter-marches, and of curious formations which

[1] Bariffe, *Young Artilleryman*, ed. 1643, p. 294.

[2] *Monro His Expedition of the Worthy Scots' Regiment Called Mackay's*,
i, 37.

[3] *A Full Relation of the Late Victory*, etc., sent by Captain Stewart, 1644;
cf. 'Marston Moor,' *Proceedings of the Royal Historical Society*, 1898, p. 51.

[4] *A worthy speech spoken by his Excellence the Earl of Essex at the head of
his army*, 24th September, 1642, 4to; cf. Webb, *Civil War in Herefordshire*,
i,141.

were never practised in war, which expert soldiers banished even from the parade-ground. The best account of the drill of the Cromwellian infantry is contained in Lieutenant-Colonel Elton's *Complete Body of the Art Military*, published in 1650, where he sets down 'the plain way of exercising a company as it is usually practised in the army'.[1]

From Elton we also learn that the ordinary formation of the infantry of the New Model was six deep. It is important to remember this because it is a point on which even the most recent and the most careful historians of the army have fallen into error. The military writers of the period just preceding the war, Markham in 1626, Kellie in 1627, Ward in 1639, all give ten deep as the usual formation both for drill and battle.[2] For the depth of the file was determined by the time which a musketeer needed to charge and discharge his piece. The old plan was for the first rank to give fire, and then to fall back to the rear of the other nine to reload, and for the other nine ranks to repeat this manœuvre in succession. It was calculated by men of experience that the average musketeer could not reload within a less time than ten men required thus to fire and to retreat.[3] Gustavus Adolphus however taught his soldiers to load more quickly, and so found it possible to fight the Imperialists with files six deep as against their files of ten deep. Before the Thirty Years' War ended all other armies except the Dutch followed his example.[4]

[1] See Appendix A.

[2] Markham, *The Souldiers Grammar*, p. 9; Kellie, *Pallas Armata*, p. 7; Ward, *Animadversions*, p. 215; see also Thomas Fisher's *Warlike Directions*, pp. 9, 10.

[3] Markham writes as follows: 'Now it is to bee considered in what space of time a man may Charge and Discharge his Peece, moving from the Front to the Reare, and so Ascending up to the Front againe; and it is found by the experience of all well Judging Souldiers, that the depth of Tenn men is the absolute best number. For the first man Discharging in the Front, in the space that nine more shall come and doe the like, the first shall make his place good againe, and so continue the Volley *ad infinitum*. Now there are some which strongly hold opinion, that Eight in depth of File shall doe as much as ten, and with as litle Difficultie make readie and Present; which no question, may be possible, in expert, old, and readie Soldiers, and so a competent and sufficient File; But in raw, Ignorant, and half exercised men it cannot be so, Neither can it be hoped that dutie shall so sudainly be performed' (*Souldiers Grammar*, p. 10).

[4] 'Before the reign of the Great Gustavus Adolphus, for any thing I could ever learn, Foot Companies were Marshal'd ten deep almost universally, but he marshal'd all his Infantry in six ranks. And after he had invaded

Officers who had served in Holland (as Markham and Ward had done) recommended the Dutch formation, but from the moment the Civil Wars began both parties seem to have adopted the Swedish. At Edgehill we are expressly told that Rupert drew up the King's infantry six deep.[1] There are no similar details as to the formation of the Parliamentarians in that battle, but we know that a year later they were usually drawn up six deep. A sergeant of the London trained bands describes the army of Essex on its march to Gloucester as 'advancing to engage in a body about 800 or 1,000 abreast, six deep'.[2] Added to this, a Royalist captain, who fought at Newbury, says that he saw lying on the field amongst the Parliamentary dead 'a whole file of men, six deep, with their heads all struck off by one cannon shot of ours'.[3] Finally, as to the custom in the New Model itself, Lieutenant-Colonel Elton writing in 1647 expressly describes the files as 'being always six deep in the armies of England, Scotland and Ireland'.[4]

There were occasional exceptions to this rule in actual fighting. Lord Orrery, who served for many years in the Irish wars, says that he frequently formed his infantry four deep, and that with good results. He recommended the introduction of that practice into the army of Charles the Second.[5]

For defensive purposes, when a small body of infantry was attacked by a larger number, it was not unusual to reduce the

---

Germany, the Emperor with most of the European Kings and Princes kept their Foot still at ten deep; but before the end of that War which he began, all of them follow'd his way, and made the file of their Foot to consist of six men, except the Prince of Orange, who still kept ten in file: I should except likewise the Earl of Strafford, who in his Instructions for the better Discipline of his Army, order'd every Captain of Foot to draw up his Company eight deep' (Turner, *Pallas Armata*, p. 216).

[1] Bulstrode, *Memoirs*, p. 80.   [2] *Bibliotheca Gloucestrensis*, p. 258.

[3] *Military Memoirs of John Gwynne*, p. 47.   [4] See Appendix A.

[5] Orrery criticizes 'the drawing up our shot and pikes six deep; and our horse, three deep. And this I should not presume to do, had I not been emboldened to it by some experiments of my own, which God did bless with success: for when I found myself over winged by the enemy they drawing up their foot 6 deep and their horse 3 deep: I judged it best for me to fight my foot 4 deep and my horse 2 deep; whereby I added one-third of more hands to the front and breadth of my battalions and squadrons. . . . I should therefore humbly desire that fighting no deeper than 4 for the foot and 2 for the horse, where the ground is fit, might well be considered' (*Art of War*, p. 36).

files of six deep to files of three deep, in order to prevent being outwinged by the enemy. This was called 'doubling' the files. General William Baillie adopted this plan at the battle of Alford against Montrose, but with disastrous results.[1]

For offensive purposes, the files were also reduced from six to three in order to secure a broader front, and so to deliver a heavier fire. Gustavus Adolphus habitually adopted this formation for this reason, and he was imitated by Montrose. In battle the method in which the musketeers delivered their fire was usually one of the following ways.

The old way was to give fire in successive ranks. The first rank fired and then fell off to the right or left, and marching down on the outside of the other five ranks placed themselves behind them, and so became the rear rank. Then one after another the other five ranks followed their example until all had discharged their muskets. This was the most primitive and simplest method; a variation of it was to give fire advancing instead of retiring. The first rank discharged their muskets but kept their station after they had fired, then the second rank advanced in front of the first, and discharged and kept their ground, and the remaining ranks in succession imitated them.[2]

In both these cases only one rank gave fire at a time. It was soon found more effective to make two ranks fire at once.[3] Monro describes how this was done in the Swedish service. 'Two ranks having made ready alike, they advance ten paces before the body, being led up by an officer that stands in even front with them, the cannon or mouth of their muskets of both ranks being past his body. The second rank being close to the back of the foremost both gives fire alike; priming and casting about their muskets they charge again where they stand, till the other

---

[1] Baillie in his account of the battle says that the Royalists were a little above his strength in horsemen and twice as strong in foot. His horse were routed at the beginning of the action. 'Our foot stood with myselfe and behaved themselves as became them, untill the enemies horse charged in our reare, and in front we were overcharged with their foot; for they having six in fyle, did overwing us, who, to equall their front, had made the half ranks advance, and so receaved the charge at three deep' (Robert Baillie, *Letters*, ii, 419, ed. Laing).

[2] See the quotation for Makham on p. 93, note 4.

[3] See Elton, p. 260; *Monro His Expedition*, pt. ii, p. 190. In the passage quoted the first words are in the original erroneously printed 'to ranks' instead of 'two'.

two ranks advance before them and give fire after the same manner till the whole troop (company) hath discharged, and so to begin again as before after the order of the through countermarch; ever advancing to an enemy, never turning back without death or victory. And this is the form that I esteem to be the best.'

Gustavus Adolphus went a step farther and taught three ranks to give fire at a time; the first rank kneeling upon their knees, the second stooping forward, the third rank standing upright and firing over the shoulders of the second.[1]

Last of all, instead of making his six ranks fire at two several times, three ranks at each time, he taught all six ranks to fire at once. It was done in this way. The six ranks were first of all reduced to three by the process of doubling, and then the three kneeling, stooping, and standing delivered their fire in the manner just described. A volley of this kind, or a 'salvee' as it was often called, was far more effective than making the six ranks fire in two divisions. 'For thereby,' writes Sir James Turner, 'you pour as much lead in your enemies bosom at one time as you do the other way at two several times, and thereby you do them more mischief, you quail, daunt, and astonish them three times more, for one long and continuated crack of thunder is more terrible and dreadful to mortals than ten interrupted and several ones.'[2]

This method of firing was practised by Gustavus in 1631 at the battle of Leipsic with the most complete, and to the Imperialists most startling, success.[3] It was adopted by Montrose

[1] 'On Wednesday, May 9th, the King held a generall Muster before the City; himselfe (to show some content to the Bavarians) drilling and exercising his souldiers: teaching them especially how to give a Charge or Salvee; some upon their knees, others behind them stooping forward; and the hindmost ranke standing upright, and all to give fire at once, the hinder man over his foremans shoulder' (*The Swedish Intelligencer*, ii, 169).

[2] Turner, *Pallas Armata*, p. 237. He declares that the manner of 'six ranks to fire at two several times is not at all to be used'.

[3] 'The Scots ordering themselves in severall small battagliaes, about 6 or 700 in a body, presently now double their rankes, making their files then but 3 deepe, the discipline of the King of Sweden beeng neuer to march aboue 6 deepe. This done, the formost ranke falling on their knees; the second stooping forward; and the third ranke standing right up, and all giuing fire together; they powred so much lead at one instant in amongst the enemies horse that their ranckes were much broken with it' (*The Swedish Intelligencer*, i, 124).

in some of his victories in Scotland.[1] And it formed part of the
ordinary drill of a company of infantry in the New Model when
Lieutenant-Colonel Elton wrote.[2] The English musketeer of the
New Model was in general very expert in the use of his weapons,
thanks no doubt to steady drilling. According to the testimony
of contemporaries, both friends and opponents, he was what was
called 'a good fireman' and a good skirmisher.

In 1648 when Hamilton and the Scots invaded England, and
were deliberating whether to march south by way of Lancashire
or Yorkshire, Sir James Turner advocated Yorkshire, giving
the following reason. 'I was for Yorkshire,' he says, 'and for this
reason only, that I understood Lancashire was a close country,
full of ditches and hedges, which was a great advantage the
English would have over our raw and undisciplined musketeers,
the Parliament's army consisting of experienced and well trained
sojors and *excellent firemen*; on the other hand Yorkshire being
a more open countrey and full of heaths, where we both might
make use of our horse, and come sooner to push of pike.'[3] So it
turned out. In the Preston campaign the good shooting and skill
in hedge-fighting of Cromwell's men gave them a great advantage. Take for instance this little picture from Captain Hodgson's
account of the skirmishing between Stoneyhurst and Preston:
'We drew over a little common, and came to a ditch, and the
enemy let fly at us (a company of Langdale's men that was newly
raised). They shot at the skies, which did so encourage our men
that they were willing to adventure upon any attempt; and the
major orders me to march to the next hedge, and I bid him order
the men to follow me, and then drew out a small party, and we
came to the hedge end, and the enemy, many of them, threw
down their arms, and run to their party where was their stand
of pikes.' This is a good instance of the usual method of handling

[1] At Tippermuir, for instance, in 1644, 'Montrose perceiving the great
strength of the enemy . . . he caused his army to be drawne out to as open an
order as could be possible, and makes his files onely three deep. He commands the ranks all to discharge at once, those in the first ranke kneeling,
in the second stooping, and in the hindmost where he placed the tallest men
upright' (*History of the King's Affairs in Scotland under the Conduct of the
Marquis of Montrose*, 4to, 1648, p. 24).

[2] See chapter lix of Elton's book, headed 'Severall Firings to be performed with any number of Men'.

[3] *Memoirs of Sir James Turner*, p. 62.

a regiment; the musketeers advanced in front of the pikes to skirmish, and took shelter behind the pikemen when beaten back.[1]

The skill of the English infantry in hedge-fighting appeared again at Worcester. 'We beat the enemy from hedge to hedge till at last we beat into Worcester,' says Cromwell's narrative of the battle.[2] Practice in this kind of fighting gave English soldiers a great confidence in themselves when they came to be matched against continental troops not accustomed to fight in the enclosures with which Englishmen were familiar. In 1657, at the opening of the campaign in Flanders, Reynolds, who commanded the English auxiliaries, offered Turenne to attack the whole Spanish army with his 6,000 foot, if they were supported by but 2,000 French cavalry. 'Thinking that number of horse sufficient in that enclosed country, and relying on the bravery of his English foot, who had been accustomed to hedge-fighting, to supply their want of numbers. But Mons. de Turenne refused to give him his consent.'[3]

At times this skirmishing developed into an unintended battle. At Torrington, for instance, Fairfax's skirmishers were 'engaged so far as they could not well draw back'. He was obliged 'to send up stronger parties, to make them good where they were or draw them off'. And so accidentally and by degrees the army in general was committed to an attack upon the Royalist position which ended in a complete victory.[4]

A deliberate engagement between two armies was a formal and elaborate business, in which there were various preliminary stages to be gone through before the actual collision of the main bodies took place. First of all, after the army as a whole had been drawn up in order, or as the phrase was, 'embattelled' by the major-general and his assistants, it was customary to give out the word and the sign for the day.[5] The 'field word' and

---

[1] *Autobiography of Capt. John Hodgson*, ed. 1882, p. 32.

[2] Carlyle, *Cromwell*, Letter clxxxii.

[3] *Life of James II*, i, 309.

[4] Sprigge, *Anglia Rediviva*, p. 200.

[5] In his vindication concerning the battle of Kilsyth, Lieutenant-General Baillie says: 'It is said, I did give neither word nor syne. Whereunto I answer, at our first imbatteling it wes not yet tyme; then we saw no enemy but the outerguard, neither wes it resolved to fight, bot most men thought the rebells were marching west. After we left our ground we had not tyme to imbattell compleatlie; which Souldattis thinks necessarie to be done

'field sign' were employed to distinguish the men of the two armies in the fighting, and were specially indispensable when the combatants were of the same nation.[1] They were habitually used during the Thirty Years' War. At Leipsic, for instance, the watchword for Tilly's army was 'Sancta Maria', the token to know each other by was white strings or ribbands about their arms and in their helmets, while the word in the Swedish army was 'Gott mit uns', and their token green branches in their head-pieces.[2]

The English armies during the Civil War copied this foreign custom. At Edgehill, Essex's forces wore orange scarfs, at Newbury they had green boughs in their hats. At Marston Moor the Parliamentarians wore a white handkerchief or a piece of white paper in their hats, and their word like that of the Swedes at Leipsic was 'God with us', but the sign of the Royalists was to

before the giving of word or syne, neither had it been possible to have given them unto all the regiments in ane poynt of tyme. Farder, it cannot be alleadged, that the want of them made us lose the day, or that by the enemies signe we could not be knowne one from another' (Baillie, *Letters*, ii, 423).

[1] 'And because such Field Marks, wherever you place them, are not still visible on all sides of the Head or Body of every one who wears them, the Field Word is also given: For it often happens that in a Battel, the Field Mark is by accident lost by many out of their Helmets, or Hats, and then if they had not the Field Word, they might be kill'd by those of their own Party who knew them not personally.

'Besides, the Field Mark of each Army is seen by All of both Armies before they engage, and the matter of it, being to be had in all places by private Soldiers, (as a green Branch, a piece of Fern, or a handful of Grass, or a piece of white Paper, &c.). If you Rout your Enemy, he may, while he is pursued, take off his own Field Mark, put up yours in the stead of it, and so scape, if not do you hurt. But the Field Word he cannot know, unless it be told him by some of your own men; and therefore the giving of both before the Battel, must never be omitted. I remember once when some Forces I had the Honor to Command, obtain'd, by the blessing of God, the Victory against the Enemy; an Officer of mine, having killed an officer of the Enemies, and finding he had a good Beaver, he tyed his own helmet to his Saddle Bow, and put on so hastily the dead Mans Beaver, as he forgot to take out of it the green Branch which was their Field Mark, and to put on a white Paper which was our Field Mark; and following the Execution with his Sword all bloody, a Captain of Horse of my own Regiment, taking him by his Field Mark for one of the Enemy, and judging he had done no little slaughter by his Sword being all gored to the Hilt, overtook him in the pursuit, and turning short on him, before he could see his face, ran him through and through with his Tuck, whereof he dyed in a few minutes. But finding the Enemies Field Mark had caused his death, he own'd his fault, and so acquitted my Captain from any Guilt' (Orrery, *Art of War*, p. 186; see also Turner, *Pallas Armata*, p. 304).

[2] *Swedish Intelligencer*, i, 121.

wear no bands or scarfs, and their word was 'God and the King'.[1]
Even when the Parliamentary armies had adopted a distinctive
uniform, which might have seemed to render other distinctions
unnecessary, these customary usages were still observed. At
Naseby the field-word of Fairfax's army was 'God our strength',
and that of the King's 'Queen Mary'. At Dunbar the word of
the Scots was 'The Covenant', that of Cromwell's army 'The
Lord of Hosts', and the sign of the English in the same battle
was 'to have no white about them'.[2]

When the two armies drew near, English soldiers invariably
cheered or shouted. 'The English,' writes Lord Orrery, 'are so
much inclined to it, as I have but once in all the actions I have
been in seen them omit the doing it as soon as they came within
cannon shot of the enemy they were to fight with.'[3] Apparently
the practice of foreign armies varied. The Imperialists were wont
to attack with a shout of 'Sa, Sa, Sa', and Monro speaks with
contempt of their custom of 'entering on service shouting like
Turks, as if crying would terrify resolute soldiers.'[4] The Danes
and the Swedes and the Scots advanced in silence. The French,
according to Morgan's narrative of the Battle of Dunkirk, were
surprised to hear the English shout when they caught sight of
the Spanish army.

'Major-General Morgan, seeing the enemy plain in battalia,
said, before the head of the army, "See! yonder are the gentlemen you have to trade withal." Upon which the whole brigade
of English gave a shout of rejoicing, that made a roaring echo
betwixt the sea and the canal. Thereupon the Marshal Turenne
came up, with above an hundred noblemen, to know what was
the matter and reason of that great shout. Major-General Morgan told him, "It was an usual custom of the red-coats, when
they saw the enemy, to rejoice."

'Marshal Turenne answered, "They were men of brave resolution and courage."'[5]

A battle was also usually preceded by a movement termed

---

[1] Clarendon, *Rebellion*, vi, 86; *Bibliotheca Gloucestrensis*, p. 266; Ashe's
Relation of Marston Moor.

[2] Sprigge, *Anglia Rediviva*, p. 40; Carlyle, *Cromwell*, Letter cxl.

[3] Orrery, *Art of War*, p. 186.   [4] *Monro His Expedition, etc.*, i, 68, 70.

[5] *Harleian Miscellany*, iii, 344.

getting the wind of the enemy.[1] Before Naseby, for instance,
the Parliamentarians saw plainly the Royalists advancing to
attack them, 'and the wind blowing somewhat westwardly, by
the enemy's advance so much on their right hand it was evident
he designed to get the wind of us', which was accordingly met
by a counter movement.[2] The object of this movement was to
get such a position that the wind should blow the smoke of the
enemy's guns and muskets back upon his own troops, under
cover of which he could be attacked with less loss. At Benburb,
in 1646, one of the minor causes of the defeat of the Scots was
that 'the sun and wind was against them, and blew the smoke
in their faces, so that for a little moment the musketeers could
not see'. This moment the Irish pikemen utilized to make the
charge which decided the fate of the battle.[3]

As a rule the struggle between the main body of the infantry
of two armies was begun by what was called a 'forlorn hope',
that is a strong body of musketeers stationed about a hundred
yards in advance of the first line. At Naseby, for instance, we are
told that:

'Upon the enemy's approach, the parliament army marched
up to the brow of the hill, having placed a forlorn of foot, consisting of about 300 musketeers, down the steep of the hill towards the enemy somewhat more than a carbine shot from the
main battle, who were ordered to retreat to the battle whensoever they should be hard pressed upon by the enemy.'[4] In this
case the Parliamentary army was receiving an attack, and the
duty of the forlorn was to break the first force of the attack, and
to throw the advancing enemy into confusion by a volley. The
employment of 'forlorns' in this way seems to have been a peculiarity of English tactics, and had been abandoned abroad.
When the English contingent attacked the Spanish army at the
battle of the Dunes, the Duke of York noticed the employment of

---

[1] You must strive to seize upon the most advantageous ground to range
the army into battalia, having regard to the wind, to avoid the dust and
smoke and to drive it into their eyes, and to the sun, that you be not
dazled' (Du Praissac, *Art of War*, translated by Cruso, p. 27, 1639).

[2] Sprigge, *Anglia Rediviva*, p. 38.

[3] *The History of the War of Ireland*, 1641–53, by a British officer of Sir
John Clotworthy's regiment, p. 48.

[4] Sprigge, *Anglia Rediviva*, p. 39.

this device by Cromwell's soldiers. 'Before each battallion of this first line they had commanded musketeers, which was the only time that I ever knew forlorn hopes used beyond the seas in any battle.' In this way they advanced towards the sand-hill where the Spaniards were posted, these 'commanded musketeers' going before them firing. When they reached the foot of the sand-hill the regiments halted to take breath and prepare to climb it, and 'while they were thus preparing themselves, their commanded men, opening to the right and left, were continually firing'.[1]

After the forlorn on each side had given fire and fallen back, the infantry regiments of the first line came to close quarters. Usually the musketeers gave a couple of volleys, and then the pikemen levelled their pikes and charged home. At the battle of the Dunes, for instance, the English foot, after the momentary halt at the foot of the sand-hill, 'on hands and knees crept up the hill, and gave the enemies foot two good vollies, and with our pikes forced them to retreat'.[2] They 'stopped not', says the Duke of York, 'till they came to push of pike; where, notwithstanding the great resistance which was made by the Spaniards, and the advantage they had of the higher ground as well as that of being well in breath when their enemies were almost spent with climbing, the English gained the hill and drove them from it'.[3]

It might perhaps happen that neither party could drive the other back, and that both would recoil a few paces and carry on the fight with the muskets. This is what the Duke of York describes as happening at Edgehill:

'When the royall army was advanced within musket shot of the enemy, the foot on both sides began to fire, the king's still coming on and the rebell's continuing only to keep their ground, so that they came so near to one another that some of the batalions were at push of pike, particularly the regiment of Guards commanded by the Lord Willoughby and the general's regiment, with some others; insomuch that the Lord Willoughby with his pike killed an officer of the Earl of Essex his regiment, and hurt another. The foot being thus engaged in such warm and

[1] *Life of James II*, i, 346, 348.
[2] *Clarke Papers*, iii, 157.   [3] *Life of James II*, i, 348.

close service, it were reasonable to imagine that one side should
run and be disordered; but it happened otherwise, for each as if
by mutuall consent retired some few paces, and then stuck down
their coulours, continuing to fire at each other even till night, a
thing so very extraordinary as nothing less than so many wit-
nesses as were there present could make it credible.'[1]

As a rule when the pikemen charged, the musketeers, instead
of halting to reload, fell upon the enemy side by side with them,
using their muskets as clubs. 'The foot on either side,' says a
Royalist account of Naseby, 'hardly saw each other till they
were within carabine shot, and so only made one volley; ours
falling in with sword and butt end of the musket did notable
execution, insomuch as I saw their colours fall, and their foot
in great disorder.'[2] Generally the swords of the musketeers seem
to have been little used; the butt end of the musket was more
effective, and the English soldier knew how to handle it. When
he was at close quarters with the enemy he preferred what
Major-General Morgan calls 'clubbing them down'.[3] Hence the
phrase used in describing a hand-to-hand fight between two
bodies of infantry – a phrase which appears in the narratives of
Torrington, Dunbar and other battles – that they were 'at push
of pike and butt end of musket'.[4]

A most vivid and detailed account of close fighting between
two bodies of infantry is given by an English officer who took
part in the battle of Leipsic, as second in command of Lumsden's
regiment of Scots. What he describes is exactly what must have
happened in any English battle during the Civil Wars.

'The first [battalion] of Lumsdell's muskettiers was led on by
his Leiutenant Colonell Muschamp, our daring and valiant countryman: who with much courtesie related this whole pasage
thus unto me.

'First (sayth he) giving fire unto three little feild pieces that
I had before me, I suffered not my muskettiers to give their
volleyes till I came within pistoll shot of the enemy; at which
time I gave order to the three first rancks to discharge at once;

[1] *Life of James II*, i, 12.
[2] Sir Edward Walker, *Historical Discourses*, p. 130; cf. Sprigge, *Anglia
Rediviva*, p. 43.
[3] *Harleian Miscallany*, iii, 346.
[4] *Autobiography of Capt. John Hodgson*, p. 44.

and after them the other three; which done we fell pell mell into
their rancks, knocking them down with the stock of the musket
and our swords.

'The enemy notwithstanding wee were alreadie within their
ranckes, gave us two or three salvees with their musketts: and
at our first falling on, foure gallant troupes of cuirassiers advancing themselves before their owne foote and comming close
up to the head of our pikes, at one volley or two of their pistolls,
shot all the Scottish ancients dead upon the place; so that
strange it was to see how so many colours fell at one instant into
the field. And our men, I thinke payd theirs as well home againe.
A brave commander of theirs all in scarlet and gold lace there
was right before us; whom we might discerne to lay on upon his
own mens pates and shoulders; to cut and slash divers of them,
with his sword, because they would not come on upon us. This
gentleman maintained the fight a full houre, and more against
us; but he being slaine, wee might perceive their pikes and
colours to topple downe, to tumble and fall crosse one over
another; whereupon all his men beginning to flee, wee had the
pursuit of them even until the night parted us.'[1]

In this narrative we see how horsemen attacked infantry in
a battle, but the method in which infantry repulsed a cavalry
charge is not so clearly explained. The pikemen did not, as it is
sometimes supposed, form a hollow square with the musketeers
in the centre. For in that case the horsemen would have ridden
up, halted just outside the reach of the pikes, and fired their
pistols into the pikemen till they made an entrance for themselves, while the musketeers would have been unable to answer
their fire on account of the intervening ranks of pikemen. The
best method for receiving cavalry was that which is set forth by
Monck in his *Observations*.[2] The pikemen, drawn up in close
order, were in the centre, and outside the pikemen, drawn up
two deep, were the musketeers. The first rank of the musketeers
knelt, and the second presented their muskets over the heads
of the first rank, and they gave fire, either both ranks together
or in succession according to command. They were instructed to

[1] Third part of *The Swedish Discipline*, p. 24 (account of the battle of
Leipsic).

[2] Pp. 55–8.

reserve their fire till the cavalry came within twenty yards or so, and to aim low. 'The musketeers when they are to give fire,' says Monck, 'should always take aim at the horses' legs.'[1] If the cavalry were not stopped by the volley but still charged on the pikemen protected the musketeers from their charge. The sixteen-foot long pikes projecting beyond the two ranks of musketeers in front of them served as bayonets to keep off the horsemen. And like the musketeers the pikemen were instructed to direct their weapons against the horses rather than the riders.[2]

If the square was broken the last resource of the musketeers was the butt end of their muskets, and sometimes with this weapon alone, though the odds were terribly against them, they succeeded in beating off cavalry.

'"Tis very observable,' says the Duke of York, describing a charge made by his troop of horse on an English regiment at the battle of the Dunes, 'that when we had broken into this battalion, and were gott amongst them, not so much as one single man of them asked quarter, or threw down his arms, but every one defended himself to the last; so that we ran as great a danger by the butt end of their musketts as by the volley which they had given us.' 'And one of them had infallibly knocked mee off my horse, if I had not prevented him when he was just ready to have discharged his blow by a stroke I gave with my sword over the face, which laid him along upon the ground.'[3]

One more point remains to be considered, and that is the marching power of the infantry. In comparing the marches made by the soldier of that day and the soldier of our own day, it is necessary to take into account the weight which the soldier carried then compared with the weight which he carries now. At

[1] P. 58.

[2] Elton describes the manner in which pikemen alone should meet cavalry: 'In my opinion the best way of opposing the Horse charge is that which we learned of our ever honoured Captain, Major Henry Tillier, in the Military Garden; which was, Files closing to the midst to their closest Order, insomuch that there was not above half a foot intervall of ground between File and File, the Pikes Porting, and after closing their Ranks forwards so close, that they locked themselves one within another, and then charged on. Which in my judgement is so secure a way from routing, that it is impossible for any Body of Horse to enter therein' (Elton, *Complete Body of the Art Military*, ii, 3).

[3] *Life of James II*, i, 351.

present the soldier carries about forty pounds. During the Peninsular War, according to Wellington, he carried a weight of about
sixty pounds.[1] The foot soldier of the seventeenth century probably carried a heavier weight than either. For both the pike
and the matchlock were cumbrous and weighty weapons. The
ammunition of the musketeer, taking into account flask, match,
bandoliers, and the pouch with its heavy bullets, must also have
been proportionately heavy. The helmet and the corslet of the
pikeman must have been an intolerable burden on a long march,
and the abandonment of the pikeman's defensive armour was
due to this fact. Finally, both pikemen and musketeers had their
knapsacks in which they frequently carried as much as seven
days' provisions, and during their campaigns in Ireland and
Scotland they sometimes carried in addition a portion of a tent.[2]
    The table of the marches of the New Model printed at the
end of Sprigge's *Anglia Rediviva* shows the distance the army
covered in the campaigns of 1645 and 1646. On 30th April the
army started from Windsor to relieve Taunton, and by 8th May
it had reached Wichampton in Dorsetshire, marching according
to Sprigge's computation seventy-eight miles in nine days with
one day's halt. From Reading to Blandford they marched 'the
whole seven days and some of them very long marches without
intermission, so willing were the soldiers to come timely to the
relief of distressed Taunton'. They were then recalled and returned to Newbury, where they rested a day or two 'sore galled
with a hard and tedious march to and fro, having had but one
day's rest in 14 days march'. In their second march to Taunton
they covered sixty-two miles in five days, and at the end of the
last day the foot, hearing that Goring was again assaulting the
town, 'were eager to march all night, so far did their compassion
to Taunton and our party then carry them beyond consideration of themselves'. Still readier were they when there was any
prospect of fighting. 'They marched that day but to Crewkerne,
some 6 miles' (it was a very hot season, being the middle of
July), 'the foot weary with their long and tedious march, the
carriage horses tired out, the way ill and narrow, being all enclosures.' When they reached Crewkerne 'intelligence came that

[1] Stanhope, *Conversations with the Duke of Wellington*, p. 24.
[2] See pp. 224, 249, *post.*

made them pull up their stumps as weary as they were[1]. The cavalry of the army was engaged with the enemy, so five regiments of foot were ordered to advance to support the horse, whereupon the foot 'notwithstanding their weary march, leaped for joy that they were like to be engaged.[1]

It is evident from the table given by Sprigge that the army could move at the rate of ten miles a day for a week together, that it very frequently marched twelve miles in the day, and that the longest march was about thirteen miles.

In the later campaigns of the army in Scotland and Ireland, when it is probable that the corslet had been definitely abandoned, the mobility of the infantry was probably much greater. Colonel George Cooke, writing in 1652, and describing a raid made by his troops into the quarters of the Irish rebels, gives the following account of the marching power of his men:

'For my foot, I think they are as good as ever marched, either for fighting, searching woods and bogs, or for long and speedy marching. I dare say they marched, last Wednesday and Thursday, before they rested, at least thirty miles, and much of it through woods and bogs, almost never in a road, continuing marching night and day. All this march, I never heard any of them complain he was weary or lame; it was hard to keep them from straggling before, but very easy to keep them up in the rear. Our horsemen did all confess, their horses were not able to continue a march with them; almost one half of our horse being lame and tired, though they had every night good lodging, and as good provision of oats and hay as they could desire. My foot were many times beating the woods and bogs, when the horse stood still and looked on.'[2]

I have dwelt at length on the characteristics of the infantry because the development of the efficiency of the foot soldier was the most important and permanent result of the war for English military history. Each of the changes which took place during the period testifies to his increased efficiency. The diminution of the number of pikemen and the increase of the number of musketeers meant an increase in the offensive power of the regiment. The reduction in the depth of the file meant a broader

---

[1] Sprigge, *Anglia Rediviva*, pp. 16, 22, 63, 68, 332.

[2] Carey, *Memorials of the Civil War*, ii, 421.

front, a heavier fire, and increased rapidity in loading and firing. The abandonment of defensive armour meant increased mobility. All proved one thing, that the tactics of infantry were becoming more and more aggressive, and that the days of purely defensive tactics for infantry had disappeared.

Only two things were needed to convert the infantry of the Commonwealth into the infantry of Marlborough and Wellington. One was the substitution of the flintlock for the matchlock, a process which was already beginning. The other was the replacement of the pike by the bayonet, which began about twenty years after the Restoration.

CHAPTER V

The Cavalry

IN THE ARMIES of the seventeenth century the proportion of cavalry to infantry was far larger than it is in modern armies. Tradition and the theory of the art of war, as set forth by military writers of the time, demanded that it should be so, and the practice of English military leaders agreed in the main with the theory. Monck writing about 1645 laid down the principle that an army operating in the field ought to consist of one horseman to every two footmen, and if it was intended to be employed in sieges, of one horseman to every three footmen.[1] During the early part of the Civil War the Royal armies were much stronger than the Parliamentarians' in cavalry,[2] and the number of their

[1] He says: 'Where your Service lieth in Campagnia, the proportion of your Army ought to be two Footmen to one Horseman, besides your Dragooners. But where the Service of your Army shall be most in Sieges, there you ought to have three Footmen unto one Horseman; and sometimes four Footmen to one Horseman, besides your Dragoons; provided your Enemy be not able to overmaster you in Horse. But for your Body of Foot, when your Service shall chiefly consist in the Campagnia, then you ought to have as many Pikemen as Musqueteers amongst your Foot, besides your Dragooners. But where your Service lieth most in Sieges, there you ought to have in your Body of Foot besides your Dragoons two Musqueteers to one Pikeman: and to every eight hundred Horse you ought to have an hundred and fifty Dragooners. And always to an Army of twenty thousand, or thirty thousand men, you ought to have a thousand Pioners; whereof an hundred ought to have horses, as a necessary part of the Army upon a March, a .etreat, drawing off Cannon in a Battel, and at Sieges' (*Observations*, p. 21). The Duke de Rohan in his *Complete Captain* (p. 111 of Cruso's translation), says that in open country the rule should be one-fourth horse and three-fourths foot; in enclosed, one-sixth horse and five-sixths foot. Robert Ward in his *Animadversions of War* (p. 293) says that the rule of the Prince of Orange was three horsemen to ten or twelve foot.

[2] Essex writes on 9th July 1643, apologizing for his inaction as follows: 'The Enemy's chief strength being in Horse, and this Army neither recruited with Horses, nor Arms, nor Saddles, it is impossible to keep the country from being plundered; nor to fight with them, but when and where they list; we being forced, when we move, to march with the whole Army, which can be but by slow Marches; so that the Country suffers much Wrong, and the Cries of the poor People are infinite' (*Old Parliamentary History*, xii, 328).

horse frequently exceeded this proportion. At Marston Moor, for instance, Rupert had about 7,000 horse to 11,000 foot, while at Naseby the King's army consisted of about 4,000 horse to not more than 4,000 or 5,000 foot. In Essex's army, on the other hand, as it was reorganized in 1644, there were only 3,000 horse to 7,500 foot. When the New Model was organized, the number of horse was increased till it reached the proportion which Monck recommended as theoretically desirable. Fairfax's army consisted of 14,400 foot and 7,600 horse, and when Cromwell invaded Scotland in 1650 his army of 16,000 men contained 5,400 horse.[1]

Thus the organization of the New Model in 1645 was marked by an increase in the proportion of horse forming part of the Parliamentary armies. It was also marked by the introduction of greater simplicity and uniformity in the armament of the horse. In the continental wars of the sixteenth century every variety of cavalry was employed. There were heavily armed cuirassiers and lancers, lightly armed horsemen equipped with swords or spears, and several varieties of mounted men equipped with firearms, whom the English termed generically 'shot on horseback'.[2] The German *Reiters*, who had each a pair of long pistols, were for a time the most effective cavalry in Europe, and revolutionized cavalry tactics by the introduction of a new method of fighting. To meet them arquebusiers and dragoons were introduced. In England, which took very little part in these

---

[1] *Transactions of the Royal Historical Society* (New Series), xii, 23; xiv, 24.

[2] 'Cavalary ... hath been devided in foure kindes, the first men at armes, them selves armed complet, and theyr horses likewise barbed, and were to give the first charge to discover the squadrons or batalions of pikes. The second launces, lighter armed with corselets, and to breake in with the men at armes where they hadde made way, or otherwise as they could see advauntange. The thirde light horsemen, commonly armed with a coate of plate, with a light staffe charged on the theigh, serving for many purposes, as to scoute, to discover, to breake foreray, or to followe a chace that is put to a retreat. The fourth and last called shot on horsebacke, but now lately called carbines, commonly light horsed without armour, serving either with pistoll or petronell; and as the shott on foote beeinge charged doo retire for succours to theyr pikes, so these carbines may skyrmidge loosely, and delivering theyr their volleies are not able to stand any charge, but must retire to the launce for his safety" (B. Rich, *A Pathway to Military Practice*, 1587).

'There is another sort of horsemen lately come into use,' writes Sutcliffe in 1593. 'We call them carbines, pedrinals, or argoletiers, which use fire-locke peeces on horsebacke, and are commonly armed to the proofe of their peece' (*Practice, Proceedings and Lawes of Armes*, p. 181).

continental wars, there were fewer varieties of horse, and firearms held a less important place in the equipment of cavalry. In
the forces which Queen Elizabeth raised to resist the Spanish
Armada the horse were divided into three classes.[1] First came
the heavy cuirassiers, indifferently termed lances or demi-lances,
who were the lineal descendants of the men-at-arms of medieval
warfare. The second class consisted of the light horsemen, armed
with a spear and a single pistol, and wearing a light coat of mail.[2]
The third class corresponded to the 'shot on horseback', and consisted of mounted men equipped with some species of carbine,
who were termed in the military musters of the period 'pet-
ronels'. The petronel is defined as 'a sort of harquebus, shorter
than the musket, but of greater calibre'.[3]

By 1645, however, when the New Model was organized, a
great change had taken place. The heavily armed cuirassier had
become obsolete, the light horseman with his spear had vanished from English armies, and the cavalry of the New Model
consisted entirely of the two classes technically described as
harquebusiers and dragoons.[4]

The disappearance of the cuirassier was due to the cumbrous-
ness of his armour. It was difficult to get horses strong enough
to bear its weight. Monck, writing in 1645, does not think it
necessary to describe how a cuirassier should be armed, because,
he says, 'there are not many countries that do afford horses fit
for the service of cuirassiers'.[5] The cuirassiers' armour was too
ponderous for the man as well as for the horse. In 1638 the King
summoned Sir Edmund Verney to attend him against the Scottish rebels, armed 'as a cuirassier in russet arms with gilded

[1] See *Fifteenth Report Historical MSS. Commission*, pt. v, pp. 20, 21, 37;
W. M. Noble, *Huntingdonshire and the Spanish Armada*, p. 55.

[2] 'Upon the borders between us and the Scots,' writes Sutcliffe, 'horsemen have staves . . . and for their armes jackes of male' (p. 81). 'Against the
French who abound with shotte and have fewe pikes, the launce and light
horseman's staffe of the north is singular good, and especially in the plaines'
(Digges, *Stratioticon*, p. 144).

[3] Grose, *Military Antiquities*, i, 108.

[4] Markham, writing in 1626, says that in the cavalry of that time 'the
launce, the light staffe, and the short pistoll are taken away' (*Souldiers
Grammar*, p. 42). So the process had begun twenty years before the formation of the New Model.

[5] *Observations*, p. 25. On the cuirassiers' arms, see Ward, p. 293; Hexham,
pt, ii, p. 4; Grose, ii, 317. 325; Scott, *British Army*, ii, 27.

studs or nails'. Verney obeyed the King's summons, but rebelled at the thought of a campaign in full armour. 'It will kill a man,' he said, 'to serve in a whole cuirass.'[1] Edmund Ludlow, who fought at Edgehill as one of Essex's lifeguard, found his armour a great hindrance to him. 'Being dismounted,' says he, 'I could not without difficulty recover on horseback again, being loaded with cuirassiers' arms, as the rest of the guard also were.'[2] For these reasons the fully armed cuirassiers disappeared from the Parliamentary army, though they were for a moment employed in the early part of the Civil War. Essex, as we have seen, had a lifeguard of cuirassiers, and during 1643 and 1644 a regiment of cuirassiers raised by Sir Arthur Haslerig served under Sir William Waller, and did good service at the battles of Lansdown and Cheriton. They were 'so prodigiously armed', says Clarendon, 'that they were called by the other side the regiment of lobsters, because of their bright iron shells with which they were covered, being perfect cuirassiers; and were the first seen so armed on either side, and the first that made any impression on the king's horse, who being unarm[our]ed were not able to bear a shock with them; besides that they were secure from hurts of the sword, which were almost the only weapons the other were furnished with'.[3] Nevertheless, the arguments against the employment of such heavy cavalry outweighed in the opinion of soldiers the advantages which might occasionally be derived from their use, and ere long the cuirassier vanished not only from the English, but from other European armies too. Sir James Turner, writing in 1670, lamented their disappearance as a defect which had become universal, 'there being but few cuirassiers in many armies, and in very many none of them at all to be seen'.[4]

Just as there were no cuirassiers in the New Model, so there were no lancers. The lance proper, the weapon of the heavy

---

[1] *Verney Papers*, pp. 205, 227. 'I am resolved,' he continues, 'to use nothing but back, breast, and gauntlet. If I had a pott for the head that were pistoll proof, it may be I would use it, if it were light, but my whole helmet will be of no use to me at all.' He preferred, in short, to equip himself 'after the manner of a harquebusier,' as he was ordered to equip his attendants.

[2] Ludlow, *Memoirs*, i, 44.   [3] Clarendon, *Rebellion*, vii, 104; viii, 13.

[4] *Pallas Armata*, p. 169. This book was written in 1670–1, though not published till 1683.

E

man-at-arms, disappeared even before the cuirassiers, who represented the later development of the man-at-arms. The spear, or
light horseman's 'staff', as it was termed in Elizabeth's days,
had vanished too, and neither in the army of Essex nor in that
of Fairfax is it ever heard of. On the other hand, this 'staff' or
light lance was the special weapon of the English borderers, and
it was habitually used by the Scottish cavalry, and especially
by that part of it which was recruited from the border counties.
Its value was often proved in the battles of the Civil War. At
Marston Moor, when the Royalist horse routed the rest of the
cavalry forming the Parliamentary right wing, one squadron of
Lord Balgony's regiment escaped and cut its way through to
Cromwell's victorious cavalry on the left; for 'being lancers they
charged a regiment of the enemies foot, and put them wholly to
the rout'.[1] At Dunbar the front rank of the Scottish cavalry
consisted of lancers, and thanks to them Cromwell's horse was
at first repulsed and disordered.[2]

Against the Irish rebels the lances of the Scottish contingent
employed in Ulster were still more effective. 'What would you
give,' said Lord Castlehaven to his Irish troopers, 'to come to a
day's work with the enemy?' They answered him that 'they
would be glad of it, if their doublets and skins could be made
proof against the launces of the Scots'. Castlehaven took the
hint, and succeeded in providing defensive arms sufficient to
protect the two front ranks of his horsemen.[3] For the same
reason Owen Roe adopted the expedient of equipping his regiments of cavalry with pistols for four troops and lances for one.[4]

Lances proved effective once more in Hispaniola against the
infantry whom Cromwell sent to attack San Domingo. The
lances of the Spaniards were light and were about twelve feet
long, shorter therefore than the sixteen-foot pike used by the
English foot soldiers, which was too long and too top-heavy to
be serviceable in the tropical woods, and longer than the half
pike with which others amongst the infantry were equipped. So
eighty or a hundred Spanish lancers put half the army of General

[1] *A Full Relation of the Late Victory*, *etc.*, *sent by Captain Stewart*, 1644,
p. 7.
[2] Carte, *Original Letters*, i, 383.
[3] Castlehaven, *Memoirs*, p. 60, ed. 1753.
[4] *The History of the Warr of Ireland*, 1641–53, p. 44.

Venables to flight, and killed the fugitives till they were weary of killing. All contemporary accounts of the expedition insist upon the effectiveness of the lance in Spanish hands. It is, says one, 'a most desperate weapon, they are very sharp, and so broad that if they strike in the body it makes such a large hole that it lets the breath out of the body immediately'.[1]

Yet in spite of these practical examples of its value, no attempt was made to reintroduce the lance either in the armies of the Parliament or the Protector. It had fallen into the same disuse all over Europe, and its retention by the Spaniards was regarded by most military writers of the seventeenth century[2] as a piece of foolish conservatism. They adhered to the lance, said one, 'more for gravity than for reason'.[3] But Sir James Turner, who laments over its disuse, wondered in 1670 why it was not revived, justly observing that the general abandonment of defensive armour had rendered it more effective than ever.[4]

Thus all over Europe, and not in England only, the old heavy cavalry composed of lancers and cuirassiers had either become obsolete already or was rapidly becoming so, and the lance or spear was no longer used even by light cavalry. The place of lancers and cuirassiers had been taken everywhere by what the Elizabethan writers termed 'shot on horseback'. The new kind

[1] *Narrative of General Venables*, Camden Society, 1900, xxxvi, 155.

[2] Lord Orrery says: 'The five offensive Arms in use amongst us, are the Sword. the Pike, the Musket, the Pistol, and the Carrabine. For I look on the Lance as now wholly laid by, and I think, with reason; for the Lance does little, unless it be by the force of the Horses Course, or Carreer, and even then, only the Front is useful; so that their best order to Fight in, seems to be to charge a Rank at a time, which yet can hardly resist Squadrons of Horse, especially if Riders be in Armor: But if the Lanceers Fight in Squadrons also 'tis much more likely they should discompose themselves, than hurt those they Fight against; which are such apparent inconveniences, as have made me admire, that King Henry IV of France, most justly Surnam'd the Great, Alexander Ferneze, Prince of Parma, and Charles of Lorrain, Duke of Mayen, three the greatest Captains of the latter Age, nay, it may be of any Age, would often lament, that Lances were then throwing aside, as Davila in his excellent *History of the Civil Wars of France* does observe with this addition, That Henry the Great, and all his chief Commanders, more apprehended those thousand Lanceers, led by Count Egmont, at the Battel of Ivry, than double the number of any of the Leagues Cavalry' (*Art of War*, p. 24).

[3] Rohan's *Complete Captain*, translated by Cruso, p. 110. Rohan adds, 'for the lance hath no effect but by the violence of the careir of the horse, and besides there is but one rank can make use of it'.

[4] *Pallas Armata*, p. 171.

of horsemen of which the bulk of seventeenth-century cavalry
consisted were known in England under the technical name of
harquebusiers.

Originally the harquebusier was a foot soldier armed with a
crossbow. In the next stage, about the end of the fifteenth century, he exchanged the crossbow for a firearm which was still
called by the old name of harquebus. The third step was to
mount the harquebusier on horseback, and this the French did
in their Italian wars and the wars of religion. Finally the harquebusier became the typical light cavalryman of the armies of
Western Europe. In the military books of the early part of the
seventeenth century his equipment is minutely described.[1] His
chief offensiue weapon was a harquebus or a carbine. Its length
according to Gervase Markham, writing in 1625, was three feet
three inches; according to Hexham. who described what he saw
in the Dutch service, and wrote in 1639, three feet long;[2] according to Vernon, writing in 1644, two and a half feet long.[3] It
carried a bullet nearly an ounce in weight, seventeen to the
pound, says Hexham, twenty to the pound says Markham. Carbine and harquebus differed in bore rather than length, the

---

[1] Gervase Markham in *The Souldiers Accidence*, 1625, describes the
narquebusier as follows (p. 42). 'The second sort (of which many Troopes of
Horse are compounded) are called Hargobusseirs, or Carbines, these men
ought to be the best of the first inferior degree, that is to say, of the best
yeomen, or best Serving-men, having actiue and nimble bodies, ioyned
with good spirits and ripe understandings; these men shall haue for
defensiue Armes, Gorgets, Curats, Cutasses, Pouldrons, Vambraces, and a
light headpeece, wide sighted, and the Bever to let downe upon barres of
Iron; for offensiue Armes, he shall haue an Hargobus of three foot, three
inches long, and the bore of twentie Bullets in the pound, with Flaske,
Priming-boxe, and moulds; or in stead of these, Cartalages which will
serue either for this or any other peece on horsebacke; also a good Sword,
and other accouterments according to his place. His horse shall be either a
fayre stoned trotting horse, or a lustie strong Guelding well ridden, he shall
be armed with a Morocco Saddle, Bridle, Bit, Petrell, and Crooper, with the
rest before shewed necessarie to his place.'

[2] Hexham, *Principles of the Art Military*, ed. 1642, pt. ii, pp. 4–8. Hexham's first edition was published in 1639. Hexham speaks of casque, back
and breast, and gorget only, not mentioning the additional defensive equipment described by Markham.

[3] John Vernon, *The Young Horseman, or The Honest Plain Dealing
Cavalier*, 1644, p. 8. Vernon speaks of the harquebusier as armed with a
carbine, a sword, and a pair of firelock pistols, but does not mention a
gorget as part of his armour. There is another description of the harquebusier's arms in the *King's Instructions for Musters* in 1639 (Rushworth,
vol. iii, Appendix, p. 137).

carbine was of larger bore than the harquebus, and for both wheellocks or flintlocks were generally employed. The harque-busier's other offensive arms were a sword and a pair of pistols. The pistols were usually what were termed firelocks. Like the carbine or the harquebus they were loaded either from a flask or with cartridges containing powder only, and were discharged by some form of firelock, either by an ordinary flint and steel-lock, or by the more elaborated wheellock. But the drawback of the wheellock was, that if carelessly handled the machinery was apt to get out of order.[1] Moreover soldiers had to be cau-tioned not to wind np or span their pistols too long beforehand, lest the spring of the wheel should become stiff and decline to work. At the siege of Wardour, for instance, Ludlow found him-self in an awkward position. The explosion of a mine by the Royalists had made a breach in the wall of his room, and for the moment he was cut off from his men and had to face the assault of the besiegers alone. 'I was forced,' he says, 'to trust to the sword for the keeping down of the enemy. . . . My pistols being wheellocks and wound up all night, I could not get to fire.'[2]

Besides his pistols, his carbine, and his sword, the harque-busier sometimes carried a small pole-axe.[3]

[1] 'The principall weapones on horsebacke are pistolls, petronells or dragons, and all these are with firelockes, and those firelockes for the most part snaphances, because the other are too curious and too soon distempered with an ignorant hand' (Markham, *Souldiers Accidence*, 1625, p. 53). Hexham, writing in 1642, says, 'Now concerning the snaphane pistoll or snaphanes carabine (more usual in England than in these countries)' (p. 8). Both Vernon and Hexham give instructions how to make and to load with cartridges, though the former recommends loading with the flask as more certain.

[2] Ludlow, *Memoirs*, i, 72. Vernon cautions the horse soldier thus: 'Never prime before you have spanned, and never span before you have need, because many times the firelock pistols will not go off, if they have stood long spanned' (*Young Horseman*, p. 11). He evidently refers to wheellocks.

[3] Vernon gives his harquebusier 'a good poll axe', saying: 'A poll axe is very necessary for a trooper, for if you should encounter a troop of Curassiers where your sword can do no good but little execution, your poll axe may be an advantage unto you to offend your enemie' (*Young Horseman*, p. 2). The poll axe, however, was a weapon more used by the Royalist than the Parliamentary cavalry (see Clarendon, *Rebellion*, vi, 73, and Bulstrode, *Memoirs*, p. 82). A curious account of it is given by Sir Edward Southcote, derived apparently from his father, who fought in the King's army:
'This was the first occasion he had to make use of his little battleaxe, a weapon all the King's troops made use of, hanging in a ribbon that was tied about their wrists, which did not hinder their arm from making use of their pistol or sword as need required, and was a dead doing thing whenever the

The defensive arms of the harquebusier consisted of a light headpiece, which was open in front ('a casque open before'), but sometimes had plates to cover the cheeks ('an open headpiece with cheeks'). This was known amongst English soldiers as a 'pot'. The rest of his defensive armour was a light cuirass, known as a 'back and breast', to which a gorget to protect the throat was sometimes added. Underneath the cuirass, or even as a substitute for it, he generally wore a buff coat of leather.[1]

Looked at from one point of view, the harquebusier might be regarded as a cuirassier relieved of a part of his armour; from another he might be regarded as a development of the mounted infantryman.

When the Civil War began, the cavalry of the Earl of Essex was, with the exception of his bodyguard and few troops of dragoons, entirely composed of harquebusiers. Cromwell's troop, for instance, is described as harquebusiers in a warrant issued by Essex for its payment, and the same term is employed in commissions and in other formal documents.[2] Nevertheless this term harquebusier speedily became a misnomer. Essex's horse appear, from the accounts of Edgehill and other early battles, to have been provided with carbines. At all events a certain number of them possessed those weapons. But in the army of the Earl of Manchester, and probably in the other local armies of the Parliament, carbines were the exception, not the rule.

The accounts for weapons supplied to equip Manchester's army prove conclusively that his troopers in general had no firearms save pistols. Cromwell's Ironsides, the typical cavalry regiment of the army of the Eastern Association, had no carbines. This fact is illustrated by Cromwell's letter to the young

horse broke in among the foot. It was very like the masons' lathing hammers, had a sharp little axe of one side, and a hammer of the other, but most commonly made use of the hammer which was sure to fell them to the ground with one rap upon their round heads' (Morris, *Troubles of Our Catholic Forefathers*, i, 388).

[1] Pictures of buff coats are given by Grose and by Scott (ii, 446). 'They are exceeding dear,' writes John Turbervill in September 1640, 'not a good one to be gotten under £10, a very poor one for five or six pounds' (*Trevelyan Papers*, iii, 194). Capt. John Hodgson complains that in 1662 his buff coat was taken away from him by a Royalist official, adding, 'I would not have taken ten pounds for it' (*Life of Captain Hodgson*, ed. 1882, p. 57).

[2] See 'The Raising of the Ironsides,' *Transactions of the Royal Historical Society*, 1899, pp. 4, 22.

men and maidens of Norwich as to the disposal of the subscriptions they had raised to equip soldiers. Telling them that if they
would spend the money on arming a troop of horse, it should
form part of his regiment, he added: 'Employ your twelve score
pounds to buy pistols and saddles, and I will provide four score
horses'. There is not a word said about providing the proposed
troopers with carbines.[1]

When the New Model was formed the whole of the cavalry of
Manchester's army was incorporated in it, and Manchester's
regiments seem to have become the type to which the rest of
the regiments of horse in the New Model conformed. Neither
the accounts for the equipment of the New Model nor the narratives of the campaigns of 1645 and 1646 afford any evidence that
the regular cavalry of Fairfax's army had any firearms except
pistols. In the second Civil War their armament was unaltered.
The fate of Thompson, the leader of the mutiny of the Levellers,
in May 1649, supplies an illustration of this. Deserted by his followers, Thompson took refuge in a wood near Wellingborough,
where he was surrounded by a party of horse and summoned to
surrender. Twice he tried to break the cordon and escape,
wounding several of his opponents with his pistols. At the third
attempt a corporal borrowed his colonel's carbine, which was
charged with seven bullets, and gave Thompson his death-
wound.[2]

From this incident it seems clear that the officers were armed
with carbines, and that the men were not, and there is other
evidence tending to confirm this conclusion.[3]

Between 1649 and 1660 a change took place, and the regular
regiments of horse were once more armed with carbines. In
England the fortune of the war had been decided by pitched
battles in which, as at Marston Moor and Naseby, an encounter
between two large bodies of cavalry often determined the fate

[1] Carlyle, *Cromwell*, Letter xiii; 'The Raising of the Ironsides,' p. 21.

[2] 'The third time he came up (for he said he scorned to take quarter)
Major Butler's corporal had Col. Reynolds his carbine, which being charged
with 7 bullets gave Thompson his death's wound' (*The Moderate*, 15th to
22nd May 1649, p. 518).

[3] Richard Symonds, describing a skirmish between the King's troops and
some Eastern Association horse in August 1645, says the rebels had all of
them back and breast, headpiece, brace of pistols, 'officers more', meaning,
I have no doubt, carbines in addition.

of the day. But in Ireland there were few pitched battles, and
still rarer were these deliberate encounters between two bodies
of cavalry. Lord Broghil, describing a fight which took place in
June 1651, near Castle Lions in Ireland, says, 'This is the first
time, as I remember, that ever horse to horse fought in Ireland'.[1]

In consequence of this change in the character of the war a
change took place in the tactics of the cavalry. They were employed rather as mounted infantry than cavalry, and tended to
be assimilated to dragoons. Naturally a corresponding change
took place in their armament, and once more they were given
carbines or firelocks to enable them to fulfil the new duties imposed upon them. In November 1650 the Council of State, at
the request of Lord-Deputy Ireton, ordered 3,000 carbines to be
sent over for the use of the English cavalry in Ireland, 'as without them the forces cannot vigorously prosecute the enemy, who
with flying parties (which our foot cannot reach) infest the quarters and commit frequent murders and depredations, and the
horse for want of carbines cannot at passes or bogs do such
execution as they might'.[2]

In January 1651, when Ludlow went to Ireland as lieutenant-
general of the horse, he took with him a troop of 100 horse raised
to accompany him, and equipped not only with swords, pistols
and defensive arms, but also with 'musquetoons'.[3]

Similarly in Scotland, during the Royalist insurrection headed
by the Earl of Glencairne in 1653 and 1654, the government
found it necessary greatly to increase the number of dragoons
at its disposal by mounting foot soldiers on horseback and arming them with firelocks. At the same time carbines or firelocks
were issued to the regiments of horse then in Scotland.[4] Monck,

---

[1] *Mercurius Politicus*, 26th June to 3rd July 1651, p. 896.

[2] The experiment was also tried in the West of England some months
earlier. The Council of State, on 6th May 1650, resolved 'to issue for Col.
Desborow's regiment of horse, 300 backs, breasts and potts; and as the
number of foot in those parts is small, 300 carbines and belts for the troopers, whereby they may be enabled to keep a pass or any such like service'
(*Cal. State Papers, Dom.*, 1650, pp. 144, 433, 446).

[3] Ludlow, *Memoirs*, i, 258; cf. *Cal. State Papers, Dom.*, 1650, p. 426.

[4] Lilburne, Monck's predecessor, asked him to send down 'some more
firelocks, with a reasonable quantity of carbines, which the troops are
willing to carry and pay for' (21st Jan. 1654). Many entries relating to the
issue of these arms and their return at the end of the campaign are in the
order books of these two officers amongst the *Clarke MSS*. See also *Scotland
and the Commonwealth*, pp. 274, 299; *Scotland and the Protectorate*, p. 21.

who took command there in May 1654, was strongly of opinion
that cavalry should have firearms, and in his *Observations* laid
down the rule that a horseman should have besides his sword
and pistols 'a carbine, or musquet barrel of the length of a
carbine, well stocked with a snaphance; the which I hold to be
much better than a carbine for service' (doubtless because its
range was longer).[1] He carried out this principle in the army
under his command, and in February 1660, when he entered
London a spectator noticed that in the two regiments of horse
who came with him every second man had a carbine by his
side, besides his sword and his pair of pistols.[2] In the army of
Charles the Second Monck's practice was followed, and both the
Lifeguards and the Blues had carbines as well as pistols.[3] There
was, in short, a reversion to the original type of the harquebusier,
at least so far as offensive armament was concerned.

On the other hand, during the same ten years (1649–60) a
change of another kind was also taking place. In the cavalry
just as in the infantry there was a tendency to the disuse of
defensive armour.[4]

[1] *Observations*, p. 24. Carbines and musketoons did not carry far. In
August 1650, near Leith, some parties of Scottish horse threatened Cromwell's outposts. 'His excellency in person drew out a forlorn, and went
before them; when he came neer them one of them fired a carbine; upon
which his Excellency called to him, and said: If he had been one of his
souldiers, he would have cashiered him for firing at such a distance; whereupon he that fired, having formerly served Lieut.-Gen. Lesly, coming up,
told him, he was Cromwell himself, and that he had seen him in Yorkshire
with his master' (Appendix to the *Memoirs of Captain Hodgson*, ed. 1806,
p. 254). On 29th July 1654, I find Monck ordering an officer to exchange
musketoons for large firelocks (*Order-Book*).

[2] *Report of the Hist. MSS. Comm. on the Manuscripts of Mr Leyborne-
Popham*, p. 144.

[3] Clifford Walton, *History of the British Standing Army*, p. 419.

[4] There is a good article on the subject by Mr Julian Corbett, entitled
'Firearms and Armour', in *Longman's Magazine* for 1899, p. 159. During the
Civil Wars there are instances of the tendency to slight the value of armour
both amongst Royalists and Parliamentarians. At the second battle of
Newbury, for instance, Colonel George Lisle according to *Mercurius
Aulicus*, 'had no armour on besides courage and a good cause, and a good
Holland shirt; for as he seldom wears defensive arms, so now he put off his
buff doublet, perhaps to animate his men that the meanest soldier might see
himself better armed than his colonel, or because it was dark they might
better discern him from whom they were to receive both direction and
courage' (Rushworth, v, 729). Colonel Hutchinson, at the assault of Shel-
ford House in 1645, 'put off a very good suit of armour which he had,

The tendency was of old standing, and was not confined to the English army. Monck writing in 1645 lamented and condemned it; Lord Orrery and Sir James Turner writing after the Restoration echo his complaint.[1] When this gradual abandonment of defensive armour first began to show itself in the army of the Commonwealth it is not easy to say. In 1654 when Monck undertook the suppression of the Royalist rising headed by the Earl of Glencairne, he found most of the cavalry regiments in Scotland unprovided with backs and breasts. On 6th May 1654, he wrote to the Protector urging that the reinforcements of horse who were to be sent might be ordered to bring their defensive arms with them.[2] Three days later he issued a general order, reciting that 'whereas several inconveniences may probably happen to the soldiers in the several regiments of horse in Scotland from not wearing defensive arms, therefore the muster masters in future are to pass none but those that have them'.[3] His order-book for that month is full of instructions for the delivery of backs, breasts and pots to various regiments, and when the campaign was ended it is filled with instructions for their redelivery to the storekeepers. The custom during the Protectorate appears to have been, that when a regiment was ordered from England to Scotland its defensive arms were given up and stored in the magazine in the Tower. It set out on its march without them, and was supplied, if needful, with others from the magazines in Scotland. Often, however, when the

which being musket proof was so heavy that it heated him, and so would not be persuaded by his friends to wear anything but his buff coat' (*Life of Colonel Hutchinson*, ii, 86). When Gustavus Adolphus saw some of his officers preparing for an assault in this way, he commanded them to put on their armour, 'For (saies he) he loves not the King that will not do so, for if my officers be killed who shall command my souldiers?' (*Swedish Intelligencer*, i, 89).

[1] Monck, *Observations*, p. 230; Turner, *Pallas Armata*, p. 168; Orrery, *Art of War*, p. 32. 'Whereas,' says Monck, 'the defensive arms of horsemen and pikemen are much slighted by some in these times, I would have such know that souldiers ought to go into the field to conquer, and not to be killed; and I would have our young gallants to take notice that men wear not armour because they are afraid of danger, but because they would not fear it.'

[2] *Scotland and the Protectorate*, p. 101; cf. p. 21.

[3] Monck, *Order-Book*, 9th May 1654; *Clarke MSS*, xlvi.

troopers gave up their cuirasses they were allowed to retain their pots.[1]

So far did this abandonment of defensive arms go that in July 1658 Sir William Lockhart's regiment was sent to serve in Flanders with no weapons but swords. Lockhart wrote to Thurloe before they came, begging that his Highness would allow them all backs, breasts and carbines. But when they came they had none of these things. 'I beseech your lordship,' wrote Lockhart once more, 'to give order that they may forthwith be provided with pistols and carbines; defensive arms may be forborne a little longer, if they be not ready.'[2]

Besides its eleven regiments of regular cavalry the New Model contained one regiment of dragoons, numbering a thousand men. The dragoons were simply mounted infantry. It is said that they were of French origin, and were first introduced into the French service about 1554, during the war in Piedmont. They derived their name from their weapon, the dragon, which Markham, writing in 1625, describes as 'a short piece with a barrel sixteen inches long of full musket bore, fitted with a snaphaunce or firelock'.[3] But this special weapon was not essential to the character

[1] 13th September 1655: 'Order to the storekeeper at Sterling to receive such defensive arms to wit, backes and breasts, as Capt. Hatfield's troop shall give him, they being to keep their potts or headpieces as formerly'. 14th April 1654: 'Order to Commissary of Ammunition to give Capt. Dale 177 backs, 177 breasts, & 119 pots, for so many delivered in the public stores in the Tower February last'. Other orders show that backs and breasts were sometimes issued to half a regiment only, pots to all (30th May 1654. Also that when they were returned to the stores, missing arms were charged to the account of the regiment, unless proved to have been lost in service (29th and 30th September 1656).

[2] *Thurloe Papers*, vii, 215, 274.

[3] On the history of dragoons, see Scott, *British Army*, ii, 29–36. Markham in his *Souldiers Accidence*, 1625, describes them thus: 'The last sort of which our horse-troopes are compounded, are called Dragons, which are a kind of footmen on horsebacke, and doe now indeed succeed the light Horsemen, and are of singular use in all the actions of Warre; their Armes defensiue are an open headpeece with cheeks, and a good Buffe coat with deepe skirts; and for offensiue armes, they haue a fayre Dragon fitted with an Iron worke, to be carried in a Belt of leather, which is buckled over the right shoulder, and under the left arme, hauing a Turnell of Iron with a ring through which the peece runneth up and downe; and these Dragons are short peeces of 16 inches, the Barrell, and full Musquet bore, with firelockes or snaphaunces: also a Belt, with a Flaske, pryming-boxe, Key, and Bullet-bag and a good Sword: the Horse shall be armed with a Saddle, Bridle, Bit, Petrell, Crooper, with Straps for his sacke of necessaries, and the Horse himselfe shall be either a good lustie Guelding, or a nimble stoned Horse. These Dragons in their marches are allowed to be eleauen in a Range or

of a dragoon, and the title was freely given to mounted men armed with any kind of musket or firelock.

Dragoons were a cheap form of cavalry much used during the French Civil Wars of the seventeenth century, and in Germany[1] during the Thirty Years' War. In France, according to the Duke de Rohan, 'they ruined the infantry, every man desiring to have a nag that so he might be the fitter to rob and to pillage'.[2] In England, during the first Civil War, both parties raised large numbers of dragoons. No garrison was complete without a company of them. They cost little to equip, for as they usually fought on foot, any sort of horse that could carry a man was good enough for them. In Lacy's *Old Troop* a Royalist officer rebukes some of his comrades for their plundering habits. 'Rascals,' says he, 'did I not know you at first to be three tattered musketeers, and by plundering a malt-mill of three blind horses, you then turned dragooners.'[3] Even in the New Model, while the horse of the ordinary trooper in a cavalry regiment cost eight or ten pounds, half that sum was enough to provide a horse, or as it was often called 'a nag', for a dragoon.[4]

The dragoon was as cheaply armed as he was mounted. Like the musketeer he wore no defensive armour. It is probable that the dragoons of the New Model had no buffcoats, but simply the

File, because when they serue it is many times on foote, for the maintenance or surprising of strayt wayes, Bridges, or Foords, so that when ten men alighteth to serue, the eleventh man holdeth their Horses : So that to every Troope of an hundred, there is an hundred and ten men allowed (p. 42). See also Ward, *Animadversions of War*, p. 295.

[1] In Wallenstein's marches 'The dragooners with their muskets, shovels, and mattocks (with which they still ride) were ever sent before to make good the passes'. Gustavus also employed 'dragoones or musketeers on horseback' (*Swedish Intelligencer*, i, 103 ; iii, 83).

[2] *Complete Captain*, translated by Cruso, p. 110. For this reason, says Rohan, 'musketeers on horseback or dragoons . . . are in a manner left off'.

[3] Act i, sc. i ; *Works*, p. 132.

[4] The cost of equipping the dragoons of the New Model is shown by the following extract from the accounts for July, 1645 :

'200 dragoone musquetts with snaphaunce locks at 15s. 6d. a piece.
 50 dragoone saddles at 7s. 10d. a piece.
 200 dragoons horse at £4 a piece.'

The accounts also show that two drummers were allowed to each company of dragoons (*Exchequer Papers, Commonwealth*, bundle 31).

red coat of the infantry.[1] It is also probable that they wore hats instead of helmets.

The offensive arms of the dragoon were a sword and a musket or firelock. Unlike the regular cavalry they had no pistols except perhaps in the case of officers.[2] As a rule the dragoon dismounted and fought on foot, one out of every ten men remaining behind the firing-line to hold the horses. When he was armed with the matchlock musket it was absolutely necessary to dismount, because it was difficult, if not impossible, to fire it on horseback. When he had a firelock he could make use of it either on foot or horseback as he chose. It was for this reason that Monck recommended the use of a musket barrel fitted with a snaphance lock.[3] The muskets used by the dragoons of the New Model were commonly fitted with these locks, and are therefore often spoken of as firelocks.

The special services which dragoons were expected to perform are set forth by Sir James Turner with great clearness.[4] In an advance they were sent before the rest of the army to secure passes or bridges until the infantry could come up. In a retreat they were used in the same way to hold defensible positions and cover the retirement of the army. When the fighting was in an enclosed country they were employed to line hedges and ditches and to possess enclosures. If it was in open country they might be called on to dismount and co-operate as musketeers with the regular cavalry. 'They ought to be taught to give fire on horse back,' says Turner, but he emphatically declares, 'their service is on foot, and is no other than that of musketeers'.

The narratives of the Civil War supply many illustrations of these propositions. Lilburne, who commanded Manchester's dragoons, says, speaking of the Marston Moor campaign: 'I and

---

[1] John Lilburne, lieutenant-colonel of the Earl of Manchester's regiment of dragoons, is described as wearing a 'short red coat' (*A Declaration of some Proceedings of Lieut.-Col. John Lilburne*, 1648, p. 17).

[2] Vernon, writing in 1644, says, 'The dragoone's arming is only offensive having a good fire and cock musket, something a wider bore than ordinary, hanging in a belt by a swivel ("sweble") at his side, with a good sword and ordinary horse, it being only to expedite his march, for he must perform his service on foot' (*Young Horseman*, p. 8). Neither he nor Monck mention pistols, and the accounts of the New Model do not show that any were supplied to dragoons.

[3] *Observations*, p. 27.   [4] *Pallas Armata*, p. 236.

my regiment of dragoons were constantly quartered in the van of the whole army; always nigh the enemies' garrisons, where constantly in a manner we fought both for horse meat and man's meat, or else with a great deal of vigilance stood upon our guard'.[1] Okey, colonel of the dragoon regiment of the New Model, speaking of the period just before the battle of Naseby, describes himself as 'watching every night with my regiment upon their quarters, having the forlorn guard every night'.[2] In the following winter, during the blockade of Exeter, it was Okey's dragoons who had to hold all the most exposed posts between the besieging army and the Royalist army of the West. In short, during the campaigns of the New Model the bulk of the outpost work of the army seems to have fallen to the dragoons. One reason for this was that, as I have shown already, the regular cavalry of the army had at this period no firearms save pistols. Afterwards, when the regular cavalry were provided with carbines or firelocks, they could perform these duties just as well as the dragoons, and there was no longer any reason why the latter should do all the work.

Now to take some examples of the method in which the dragoons were usually employed in a battle.

At Edgehill each army stationed its dragoons on its extreme flank. On the Parliamentary right were some briers and hedges held by dragoons and musketeers; on their left smaller detachments were posted in ground of the same nature. In each case the King's dragoons had to clear this ground to enable the horse to charge. On the King's right the task fell to Colonel Washington and his regiment; on the left, where the greater part of the Royalist dragoons were stationed and where the Parliamentary position was stronger, the hedges were cleared by Colonel George Lisle and Sir Arthur Aston.[3]

Marston Moor affords another instance of the same tactics. On the right of Prince Rupert's position there was what the accounts call 'a cross ditch', where he had posted a body of musketeers. Opposite to them on the Parliamentary left there

[1] Lilburne, *Innocency and Truth Justified*, 1645, p. 25.

[2] *A more Particular and Exact Relation of the Victory, etc.*, 1645, British Museum, E. 288, 38; Sprigge, *Anglia Rediviva*, pp. 172–3.

[3] Clarendon, vi, 82, 85; *Memoirs of Sir Richard Bulstrode*, pp. 80–82.

was a regiment of Scottish dragoons under Colonel Frizell or Frazer, said to be one of the best regiments in the Scottish army. When the battle began, the dragoons prepared the way for the advance of Cromwell's horse by driving the musketeers out of this cross-ditch. 'By the good management of Col. Frizell, they acted their part so well that at the first assault they beat the enemy from the ditch, and shortly after killed a great many, and put the rest to rout.' They were again called upon at the end of the battle, when Newcastle's Whitecoats, taking up their position in a piece of enclosed ground, beat off all the attacks of Cromwell's horse. 'At last a Scots regiment of dragoons under Frizell was brought up, and by their shot made a way for the horse to enter and put them to the sword.'[1]

But the best account of the services of dragoons in battle is contained in Colonel Okey's narrative of Naseby. Okey was half a mile behind the Parliamentary army in a meadow distributing ammunition to his men when Cromwell came and ordered him with all speed to remount his men, and take up a position on the left flank of the Parliamentary line. The picture-plan of Naseby battle in Rushworth and Sprigge shows a long hedge running from the Parliamentary to the Royalist position, with the inscription, 'Lantford hedges lined with dragoons'. Behind the dismounted dragoons, who are running up to the hedge, from which some are already firing on Rupert's advancing cavalry, are little groups of horses with a man in the centre of each holding them. 'By that time,' says Okey, 'I could get my men to light and deliver up their horses in a little close, the enemy drew towards us, which my men perceiving, they with shooting and rejoycing received them, although they were encompassed on the one side with the king's horse and on the other side with foot and horse [trying] to get the close; but it pleased God that we beat off both the horse and the foot . . . and kept our ground.' Rupert's charge drove the Parliamentary left back for about a mile and exposed Okey's regiment to the danger of an attack from its rear. 'After this,' he says, 'we gave up ourselves for lost men, but we resolved every man to stand to the last.' But Cromwell's

[1] *A Full Relation*, p. 44; *Memorie of the Somervills*, ii, 347; cf. paper on 'Marston Moor', *Transactions of the Royal Historical Society*, 1898, pp. 42, 55.

success on the right drove the Royalists back and extricated the dragoons. 'Which I perceiving,' continues Okey, 'caused all my men to mount and to charge into their foot, which accordingly they did, and took all their colours and 500 prisoners.' Finally, when the King's horse rallied and made a stand, Okey and his dragoons joined in the attack upon them, and took part in the pursuit towards Leicester. He concludes by saying, 'I lost not one man, and had but three men wounded in all my regiment', which seems to prove that his dragoons never came to close quarters with the Royalists till both foot and horse were completely broken.[1]

The method of fighting in use amongst the regular cavalry is more difficult to describe than that of the dragoons, for the evidence is less clear and less consistent. During the latter part of the sixteenth century and the early part of the seventeenth, a great change had taken place in cavalry tactics, and its effects were not yet exhausted. The general disuse of the lance brought with it an alteration in tactics. Lancers like the old men-at-arms had been accustomed to give the charge at full gallop, 'to the intent to give the greater blow and shock, to the overthrowing and breaking of their enemies'.[2]

Opposed to this was a new system of which the German *Reiters* were the exponents, a system which was the consequence of the introduction of firearms. The *Reiters* made the pistol the chief weapon of the cavalryman. 'We must grant them,' says De la Noue, 'the honour of being the first that brought the pistol into use, which when a man can well handle I take to be very dangerous. The Germans among all sorts of horsemen that use this weapon do carry away the prize.'[3]

It is certain that the method of the *Reiters* met with great success. Against infantry such as the Swiss it was very effective. Rank after rank trotted up in succession and discharged their long pistols into the serried mass of pikemen till an entrance was made. 'I like well the manner of the Germans,' says an Elizabethan writer, 'who keep always their main troop standing, and

---

[1] *A more Particular and Exact Relation, etc.,* 1645.

[2] Sir John Smyth, *Instructions, Observations and Orders Military,* 1595, p. 167.

[3] *Politicke and Military Discourses,* 1587, p. 199

cause only one rank from the front to charge, and the same being
repulsed to retire to the tail of the standing troop, and then
another to charge and retire to the tail of the former, whereby
they maintain the whole troop in full strength till they see the
footmen sway or break, and that the horsemen enter. Then presently they back them with another rank, and those again with
another, till they see cause to follow with the whole troop or to
stay. And this is the surest and most orderly form of charging
of all others.'[1]

The tactics of the *Reiters* were equally successful when they
were matched against cavalry armed only with swords, but
against lancers the result was more doubtful. De la Noue declared that a squadron of *Reiters* properly handled ought to beat
a squadron of lancers every time, but he owned that this was a
paradox, and that military opinion was against him. 'Amongst
those who profess arms,' he admitted, 'it is so assured a principle that a troop of spears should beat and overthrow a troop
of pistols, that whoso seemeth to doubt thereof is taken for a
meanly practised soldier.'[2]

Sir Roger Williams, writing in 1590, undertook in his *Discourse
of War* to refute De la Noue's paradox. In his view it was not a
question of the relative value of the two weapons, but of the
relative merits of two methods of attack. The pistol might be
more destructive than the lance, but the *Reiters* hardly ever
charged home. 'Seldom or never at all shal you find pistolers
charge or enter a squadron either horse or foot on the spur like
unto the lancers, but softly on a trot or soft pace.' On the other
hand: 'the charge of the lancers is terrible and resolute. . . .
Considering the resolute charge done with the might of their
horses the lancers are more terrible.'[3] Consequently the lancers
almost invariably routed the *Reiters*. 'It hath bin seldom or
never heard that lancers gave place unto Rutters, but I was

---

[1] Digges, *Stratioticos*, p. 110, ed. 1579.

[2] De la Noue, *Politicke and Military Discourses*, p. 198.

[3] Roger Williams, *Art of War*, 'The Difference between Launtiers and
Pistolers'. Davila, in his account of the French wars of religion, asserts that
either cuirassiers or light cavalry must 'yield to the violence of lances',
giving many instances (Cotterell's translation of Davila, 1647, pp. 900,
952-3, 968, 1379, 1469).

often in their company, when they ran away, three from one
lancer, both in great troops and small.'

When the lance fell into disuse, the tactics of the *Reiters* influenced the tactics of all other horsemen armed with firearms,
whether cuirassiers, harquebusiers, or any other sort of cavalry.
All learnt to trust to their pistols and carbines rather than their
swords, and to attack at a trot rather than a gallop. English
volunteers serving in Holland saw these tactics practised there,
and taught them to their countrymen at home. In his *Commentaries* Sir Francis Vere relates how he, with 1,000 English and
Dutch horse, routed 4,000 Spanish infantry at the battle of
Turnhout in 1597. 'We charged their pikes, not breaking through
them at the first push (as it was anciently used by the men-at-
arms with their barbed horses), but as the long pistols, delivered
at hand, had made the ranks thin, so thereupon the rest of the
horse got within them.'[1]

This was the system of tactics recommended by English military writers of the period just before the Civil War. Charges were
to be made slowly. 'A cuirassier,' wrote Robert Ward in 1639,
'usually giveth his charge upon the trot, and very seldom upon
the gallop.' Both the cuirassiers with their pistols and the harquebusiers with their carbines were to deliver their fire after the
manner of the *Reiters*. 'We are to give fire upon the enemy by
ranks,' says Ward, 'and so fall off into the rear, so that all the
ranks shall come up and give fire by degrees upon the
enemy.'[2]

The fighting formations which the books recommended for
cavalry were very deep; the file consisted of five or six men or
even of more. Gervase Markham, writing in 1625, says with the
air of a man who is refuting a popular error, that a file ought
never to be above six deep, because 'that number is sufficient
for duty and more are cumbrous'.[3] The Dutch, however, under
Prince Maurice and Prince Frederick Henry arrayed their cavalry five deep. It was argued that as each man had two pistols,

[1] *Commentaries*, ed. 1657, p. 79; Arber, *English Garner*, vii, 116.

[2] Ward, *Animadversions of War*, pp. 301, 315, 317, 319.

[3] *The Souldiers Accidence*, ii, 48.

their firing power would equal that of a body of infantry drawn
up ten deep and having one musket apiece.[1]

Nevertheless by the time the Civil War began the method of
fighting which English military books set forth, and English
officers trained in the Dutch school recommended, was becoming
obsolete. The innovations of Gustavus Adolphus affected cav-
alry-fighting as well as infantry-fighting.[2] He formed his horsemen three deep instead of six deep, taught them to reserve their
fire when they charged, to charge at a more rapid pace, and
always to charge home. During the English Civil War Swedish
teaching influenced the tactics of both armies, of the Royalists
as well as the Parliamentarians.

There was a short struggle between the adherents of the
Swedish system and the adherents of the Dutch system, but it
ended in the complete victory of the former. This is the true
explanation of the quarrel between Prince Rupert and the Earl
of Lindsey at the battle of Edgehill. As commander-in-chief of
the Royalist army Lindsey drew up a plan of battle after the
Dutch manner, 'preferring,' in Clarendon's phrase, 'the order
he had learned under Prince Maurice and Prince Harry'. Rupert
was merely general of the horse, but the King took Rupert's
advice instead of Lindsey's, and adopted his nephew's plan of
battle instead of his general's. At Edgehill, therefore, the King's
army was drawn up after the Swedish system, not after the
Dutch.[3] Like the Swedes at Leipsic and Lützen the Royalists
fought with their foot six deep and their horse three deep.[4] Nor
can it be doubted that under Rupert's leadership the King's

[1] Hexham, *Principles of the Art Militarie*, 1642, p. ii, p. 10; Ward, p. 293.
Ward himself argued in favour of files six deep (p. 315).

[2] By 1670, at the latest, the Swedish order was universal. 'Many would
have the file of horsemen to be 5 deep. . . . Others will have it six. . . . The
late Earl of Strafford as he appointed in his military instructions the foot to
be eight deep, so he ordered his troops of horse to be 4 in the file. But
universally now for anything I know (unless it be in the Low Countries)
the horse are marshalled three deep' (Turner, *Pallas Armata*, p. 234).

[3] Clarendon, *Rebellion*, vi, 78; *Memoirs of Sir Richard Bulstrode*, p. 80.
The latter says: 'Our whole army was drawn up in a body, the horse three
deep in each wing, and the foot in the centre 6 deep'.

[4] Of the battle of Lützen we are told: 'The King was no more but 6
deepe of foote, and of horse but three or four deep, according as the brigades were either stronger or weaker' (*Swedish Intelligencer*, iii, 132).

cavalry adhered throughout the war to this formation. On the
other hand, the accounts of the battle afford no evidence as to
the formation adopted by the Parliamentary cavalry at Edgehill. Some of their commanders were men trained in the Swedish
school, as for instance Sir James Ramsay, commissary-general
of the horse, who commanded the cavalry of the left wing.[1] It is
very possible therefore that the Parliamentary cavalry may have
been drawn up in the Swedish manner as well as the King's
cavalry, but there is no proof. Whatever may have been the case
at Edgehill, there is evidence that in one at least of the earlier
battles of the war the Parliamentary cavalry fought in the older,
deeper formation. This fact perhaps explains some of the early
successes of the Royalist horse. At Roundway Down in July,
1643, says a Royalist, 'we advanced a full trot, three deep, and
kept in order: the enemy kept their station, and their right wing
of horse, being cuirassiers, were I am sure five, if not six deep,
in so close order that Punchinello himself had he been there
could not have got in to them'. The result was that the cuirassiers were outflanked and routed. 'They being six deep in close
order, and we but three deep and open (by reason of our sudden
charge), we were without them at both ends.'[2]

However, though the Parliamentary leaders may have been
slower than the Royalists to adopt the Swedish formation, they
certainly did adopt it, and by 1644 at the latest it was universally practised. In 1644 John Vernon, writing a handbook for
the cavalry officers of the Parliamentary army, laid down the
rule that three deep was the proper battle order. Monck writing
about a year later assumed the same principle. Lord Orrery who
had served in Ireland both under Ormond and under Cromwell,
and was when he wrote his book a major-general in the army
of Charles the Second, describes three deep as the recognized
formation in the English army. Finally, Sir James Turner, writing in 1671, says that cavalry are marshalled three deep in every

[1] This was not the James Ramsay who had been governor of Hanau
from 1634 to 1638. See an article on 'Black Ramsay of Hanau' in *Black-
wood's Magazine* for June 1907.

[2] *The Vindication of Richard Atkyns*, 1669. At Rupert's relief of Newark
in March 1644, a Royalist narrative says: 'The rebels doubling their files
from 3 to 6 deep charged our two outmost troops so hard upon the flanks,
that they were nearly broken' (*Mercurius Aulicus*, 23rd March).

European country except Holland.[1] It is certain therefore that Cromwell's troopers fought in this order from Naseby to Dunbar, and probably at Marston and Gainsborough too.

A second point in which Rupert copied Swedish tactics was in teaching his cavalry to reserve their fire. At Breitenfeld, says Monro, 'the resolution of our horsemen on this service was praiseworthy, seeing they never loosed a pistol at the enemy till first they had discharged theirs'.[2] Rupert's instructions to his troopers at Edgehill are on record. 'Just before we began our march,' says Bulstrode, 'Prince Rupert passed from one wing to the other giving positive orders to the horse, to march as close as possible, keeping their ranks with sword in hand, to receive the enemy's shot without firing either carbine or pistol till we broke in amongst the enemy, and then to make use of our fire-arms as need should require; which order was punctually observed.'[3] Another Royalist, Lord Bernard Stuart, describes what followed. The Parliamentary horse, 'stood still all the while upon the hill, expecting the charge, so that we were fain to charge them up hill, and leap over some 5 or 6 hedges and ditches; upon our approach they gave fire with their cannon lined amongst their horse, [their] dragooners, carbines and pistols, but finding that did nothing dismay the king's horse, and that they came more roundly to them with all their fire reserved, just when our men charged they all began to turn head'.[4]

At Edgehill the Parliamentary cavalry fired too soon. In the fight at Worcester, a month earlier, they stood with more

[1] Vernon, *Young Horseman*, p. 42; Monck, *Observations*, p. 61; Orrery, *Art of War*, p. 36; Turner, *Pallas Armata*, p. 234; see p. 131, *ante*, note 2.

[2] *Monro His Expedition*, pt. ii, p. 69.

[3] Bulstrode, *Memoirs*, p. 81. Montrose did the same at Auldearn. 'My Lord of Gordon by this time charges the left wing, and that with a new form of fight, for he discharges all shooting of pistols and carbines, only with their swords to charge quite through their enemies' (Gardiner, *Great Civil War*, ii, 226, apparently quoting Patrick Gordon). A curious traditional account of Rupert's methods is given by Sir Edward Southcote. He says that the Prince's 'way of fighting was, he had a select body of horse who always attended him, and in every attack they received the enemy's shot without returning it, but one and all bore with all their force upon the adversaries till they broke their ranks, and charged quite through them: then they rallied, and when they were in disorder fell upon their rear, and slaughtered them with scarce any opposition' (Morris, *Troubles of our Catholic Forefathers*, i, 392).

[4] *Harleian MS.*, 3,783, f. 60.

resolution. Captain Nathaniel Fiennes, or someone who fought in his troop, thus describes the reception of the Royalist charge by that troop. 'As soon as Sir Lewis Dive's troop had discharged upon us, we let them come up very near that their horses' noses almost touched those of our first rank before ours gave fire, and then they[1] gave fire, and very well to my thinking, with their carbines, after fell in with their swords pell mell into the midst of their enemies, with good hope to have broken them (being pretty well shattered with the first charge of their carbines). But of a sudden we found all the troops on both sides of us melted away, and our rear being carried away with them.'[2]

Both at Edgehill and Worcester the Parliamentary horse waited to receive the attack instead of attacking, and both times they were routed. It was an axiom with some of the military writers of the period that it was often better to allow the enemy to charge than to charge yourself. 'When the enemy shall charge you with one of his troops,' says Colonel Ward, 'do not you rush forth to meet them, but if your ground be of advantage keep it.'[3] Rupert knew better, and he never waited to be attacked, but always took the initiative himself in spite of apparent disadvantages of position. A good instance of his tactics is supplied by the battle of Chalgrove Field, the official narrative of which is the most detailed account of any cavalry fight during the war.

The position of the two forces was this: Prince Rupert was retiring to Oxford, and preparing to cross Chiselhampton Bridge. He had lined the hedges leading up to it with musketeers to cover the withdrawal of his horse, and hoped to lead the Parliamentarians into the trap. Between the advancing Parliamentarians and the retreating Royalists there was only a hedge, which the Parliamentary dragoons had seized and lined. In the open field behind were eight troops or more of Parliamentary horse, and some way farther back a reserve of three more troops. The Roundheads were pressing too closely on Rupert's rear for it to be safe for him to continue his retirement.

[1] 'They,' i.e., 'our men'.

[2] *A Letter Purporting the True Relation of the Skirmish at Worcester*, 1642.

[3] *Animadversions of War*, p. 281. 'If not,' continues Ward, 'advance softly forwards, untill the enemy be within 100 paces of you, and then fall into your careire; by this meanes your horse will be in breath and good order, whenas the enemie will be to seeke.'

"'Twas divers of the commanders counsells that the Prince should continue on the retreat, and so draw the rebells into the ambush, but his Highnesse judgment overswayed that; for (saith he) the Rebells being so neere us, may bringe our reere into confusion, before we can recover to our ambush. Yea (saith he) their insolency is not to be endured. This said, His Highnesse facing all about, set spurrs to his horse, and first of all (in the very face of the dragooners) leapt the hedge that parted us from the rebells. The Captaine and the rest of his troop of Lifeguards (every man as they could) jumbled over after him: and as about 15 were gotten over, the Prince presently drew them up into a front till the rest could recover after him. At this the rebells dragooners that lyned the hedge, fledd; having hurt and slaine some of ours with their first vollie.

'Meanetime Lieutenant-Colonell O'Neale having passed with the Princes regiment beyond the end of the hedge on the left hand, had begun the encounter with 8 troopes of rebels. These having before seene ours facing about, took themselves off their speed presently, and made a fair stand till ours advanced up to charge them. So that they being first in order gave us their first vollie of carbins and pistolls at a distance, as ours were advancing: yea they had time for their second pistols, ere ours could charge them. . . . To say the truth they stood our first charge of pistols and swords, better than the rebels have ever yet done since their first beating at Worcester; especially those of the right wing: for their left gave it over sooner: for that the Prince with his life guard with sword and pistoll charging them home upon the flank put them in rowte at the first encounter. . . . As on the other wing did Major Daniel with the Prince of Wales his regiment: so that now the rebells were wholly routed. . . .

'The rebells now flying to their reserve of three colours in the close by Wapsgrove House, were pursued by ours in execution all the way thither, who now (as they could) there rallying gave occasion to the defeat of these 3 troopes also, so that all now being in confusion, were pursued by ours a full mile and quarter . . . from the place of the first encounter.'[1]

[1] *His Highnesse Prince Ruperts late beating up the Rebels Quarters at Postcomb and Chinner in Oxfordshire and his victory in Chalgrove Field on Sunday Morning, June 18 1643*, Oxford, 1643, 4to, p. 8.

There is one more point in Rupert's tactics which requires special notice. The Prince frequently placed small detachments of musketeers amongst his cavalry, a proceeding which was termed 'interlining' the horse with musketeers. Both at the battle of Leipsic (or Breitenfeld) and at that of Lützen, Gustavus Adolphus had done the same. According to Monro it was one of the chief causes of his success at Leipsic. 'The fourth help to this victory was the plottons of musketeers his majesty had wisely ordained to attend the horsemen, being a great safety to them and a great prejudice to the enemy, the musket ball carrying and piercing further than the pistolet.' In a second passage he describes the part which these detachments played in the battle: 'By halfe three, our Cannon a little ceasing, the Horsemen on both wings charged furiously one another, our Horsemen with a resolution abiding unloosing a Pistoll till the enemy had discharged first, and then at a neere distance our Musketiers meeting them with a Salve; then our horsemen discharged their Pistolls, and then charged through them with swords; and at their returne the Musketiers were ready againe to give the second Salve of Musket amongst them; the enemy thus valiantly resisted by our Horsemen, and cruelly plagued by our Plottons of Musketiers, you may imagine, how soone he would be discouraged after charging twice in this manner, and repulsed.'[1]

Rupert imitated this device both at Marston Moor and Naseby. In the plan of Marston, drawn up by his quartermaster-general, each squadron of one hundred horse in the front line of the Royalist cavalry is backed by a detachment of about fifty musketeers, and the same officer's plan of Naseby shows a similar arrangement.[2] On the Parliamentary side, however, it was a device which was very rarely practised. Edgehill affords the only recorded example of its adoption. In that battle Sir James Ramsay, who commanded the horse of Essex's left wing, describes himself as 'interlining the squadrons with a convenient

[1] *Monro His Expedition*, p. ii, p. 65; cf. *The Swedish Intelligencer*, iii, 128, 165.

[2] The map is reproduced in the paper on 'Marston Moor' in the *Transactions of the Royal Historical Society* for 1899. The origins of it and of that of Naseby are in a volume of plans by Sir Bernard de Gomme in the British Museum (*Addit. MS.*, 16,370).

number of musqueteers', but the result was not encouraging. 'At the approach of the enemy,' complained his officers, 'our troops did discharge their long pieces afar off and without distance, and immediately thereafter wheeled all about and ran disorderly, leaving the Musqueteers to be cut in pieces by the enemy.' After Edgehill there is no evidence that 'interlining' was practised by Parliamentary commanders, and there is no mention of it in any battle where Cromwell was in command.[1]

A comparison between the tactics of Rupert and Cromwell is not easy to make. There is no such exact record of Cromwell's instructions to his troopers, no such detailed description of the way in which he led them, as we have in the case of Rupert. The prominent position which Rupert held from the very beginning of the war attracted an attention to his methods of fighting which Cromwell's did not obtain. It is mainly from Cromwell's own letters that an account of his tactics has to be drawn, and the actor is often less explicit than the spectator, and takes more for granted. One thing however is clear. Rupert started with a definite system of tactics in his mind, and with a certain amount of military experience and military knowledge. Cromwell had no practical experience and little theoretical knowledge; he learnt how to fight as he went along. Rupert's tactics are the same in 1645 as in 1642; in Cromwell's a certain process of development is visible.

In the fight at Grantham in April 1643, the first engagement in which Cromwell commanded, it is evident that he had hardly yet realized the advantages of taking the initiative, and charging without firing during the advance. The Royalist leader hesitated to attack, and the two bodies of horse faced each other for half an hour whilst the dragoons on both sides exchanged shots. At last Cromwell made up his mind to attack. 'They not advancing towards us we agreed to charge them. And advancing the body after many shots on both sides, we came on with our troops a pretty round trot, they standing firm to receive us; and our men

---

[1] *The Vindication and clearing of Sir James Ramsay*, folio. This contains the decision of a Council of War held at St Albans on 5th November 1642, on Ramsay's conduct at Edgehill. It is odd that no modern writer on the battle has noticed it and that it is not mentioned in Colonel Ross's discussion of the authorities in the *English Historical Review*, 1887, p. 533.

charging fiercely upon them by God's Providence they were immediately routed, and all ran away.'[1]

At Gainsborough, three months later, Cromwell's tactics were much more like those of Rupert at Edeghill. In spite of disadvantages of position he did not hesitate to attack, and his troopers seem to have reserved their fire till they came to close quarters. At least there is no mention of any half-hour's preliminary firing as there was at Grantham. Having climbed the slope which led to the Royalist position, 'we endeavoured', writes Cromwell, 'to put our men into as good order as we could. The enemy in the meantime advanced towards us to take us at disadvantage, but in such order as we were we charged their great body. . . . We came up horse to horse, where we disputed it with our swords and pistols a pretty time; all keeping close order, so that one could not break the other. At last they a little shrinking, our men perceiving it pressed it upon them, and immediately routed this whole body.'[2]

In Cromwell's next battle, at Winceby in October 1643, the dragoons of the two parties began by exchanging shots and then the horse attacked. 'Colonel Cromwell fell with brave resolution upon the enemy, immediately after the dragooners had given him the first volley, yet they were so nimble as that within half pistol shot they gave him another. . . . Truly this first charge was so home given, and performed with so much admirable courage and resolution by our troops, that the enemy stood not another, but were driven back upon their own body which was to have seconded them, and at last put these into a plain disorder; and thus in less than half an hour's fight they were all quite routed.'[3]

[1] Carlyle, *Cromwell*, Letter x; cf. Baldock, *Cromwell as a Soldier*, p. 77; Hoenig, *Oliver Cromwell*, ii, 96.

[2] Carlyle, *Cromwell*, Letter xii. For comments, see Colonel Baldock's *Cromwell as a Soldier*, p. 105; Hoenig's *Oliver Cromwell*, ii, 101. 'Wir entnehmen,' says the latter, quoting Cromwell's despatch, 'das Cromwell die heutigen Treffen gekannt haben muss.'

[3] Vicars, *Parliamentary Chronicle, God's Ark*, p. 46. Another account, written by the Earl of Manchester, says that Cromwell and Manchester's own regiments formed the first, and that Sir T. Fairfax led the second line (*Old Parliamentary History*, xii, 422). A third narrative says that 'Sir Thomas Fairfax, being in the rear of Col. Cromwell's regiment with his first body, fell in towards the flank of the enemy's body; which they perceiving the enemy's body broke, and so Sir Thomas had the chase and execution of them a great way' (*Fairfax Correspondence*, iii, 64). As Manchester also speaks of a second charge, it is clear that the victory was not solely due to the success of the first line under Cromwell.

Some military writers have seen in this description evidence of a
further development in Cromwell's methods of fighting, and an
anticipation of modern shock tactics. 'There is no mention,'
comments Colonel Baldock, 'of a dispute with sword and pistol
before the royalists gave way as at Gainsborough. The well
ordered charge of the heavy Roundhead cavalry broke by sheer
weight of man and horse through the looser ranks of their lighter
armed opponents.'[1] It is not safe, however, to lay too much
stress on the silence of the authorities, or to infer from the imperfect evidence we possess that there was a real difference
between the tactics of Winceby and Gainsborough. In any case,
the 'dispute with sword and pistol' fills a very prominent place
in the accounts of Cromwell's part in the battle of Marston
Moor. After Cromwell charged Prince Rupert's division of horse
'they stood', says Scout-master Watson, 'at sword's point a
pretty while, hacking one another, but at last as it pleased God
he brake through them, scattering them like a little dust'. 'The
enemy,' says another narrative, 'being many of them, if not the
greatest part, gentlemen, stood very firm a long time, coming to
a close fight with the sword, standing like an iron wall so that
they were not easily broken.' 'The horse on both sides,' adds a
third, 'behaved with the greatest bravery, for having discharged
their pistols and flung them at each others heads they fell to it
with the sword.'[2]

The impression which these accounts produce is, that the
success of the charge was due not so much to its momentum as
to the superiority of Cromwell's troopers in the hand-to-hand
fighting which took place when the two bodies came into collision. Cromwell's despatch on the skirmish at Islip in April 1645
seems to confirm this conclusion. 'I drew forth,' he writes to

[1] Baldock, *Cromwell as a Soldier*, p. 120; cf. Hoenig, ii, 123–4. Neither of
these writers does justice to the share of Fairfax and the second line. Mr
Fortescue argues that the speed of Cromwell's charge must be overrated by
modern critics. 'The range of the old musket was short enough, and the
weapon took a long time to reload, so it is plain that Cromwell could not
have advanced to the attack very swiftly' if the Royalist dragoons managed
to fire two volleys during his advance (*Macmillan's Magazine*, July 1894,
p. 199). As to the question whether the Royalists were really 'lighter
armed' than their opponents, see p. 143, *post*.

[2] Leonard Watson's *More Exact Relation of the late Battaile neere York*;
Lord Saye's *Vindiciæ Veritatis, or the Scots' Designe Discovered*; cf. *English
Historical Review*, 1890, p. 352; Ludlow, *Memoirs*, ed. 1894, i, 99.

Fairfax, 'your Honour's own regiment, and commanded your
Honour's own troop therein to charge a squadron of the enemy.
Who performed it so gallantly that after a short firing they
entered the whole squadron, and put them to a confusion. And
the rest of my horse presently entering after them, they made a
total rout of the enemy.'[1]

One of the most remarkable cavalry charges in the war was
that which decided the battle of Langport on 10th July 1645.
An account of it by an eye-witness, Lieutenant-Colonel John
Lilburne, will serve as a companion-picture to the account of
Rupert's charge at Chalgrove. The Royalists and the Parliamentarians occupied opposite ridges, and between them lay a
valley and a stream crossed by a narrow ford and a lane leading
up to the plateau held by General Goring and the King's forces.
The enclosures on each side of the lane were held by Goring's
musketeers. Fairfax with his own musketeers cleared the enclosures of the enemy, and with his guns obliged Goring to draw
his cavalry a little farther back from the edge of the plateau and
the point where the lane debouched upon it. Then he ordered
Major Bethell to charge 'with his forlorn of horse'. It consisted
of six troops, those of Bethell himself, Captain Evanson, and
Captain Grove, all of Colonel Whalley's regiment; and of three
troops of Fairfax's own regiment under Major Desborough. All
six had once formed part of the regiment of Ironsides which
fought under Cromwell at Marston Moor.

'Bethell upon command given, led on his own troop through
the water, which was deep, and dirty, and very narrow, the
enemy having a very large body at the top of the lane many
times over his numbers, charged them with as much gallantry
as ever I saw in my life, forcing them with the sword to give
ground; which made way for Capt Evanson's troop to draw out
of the lane and front with him, driving the enemy's great body
and their reserve up the hill; but a very great fresh body of the
enemy's horse coming upon them forced them to retreat to Capt
Grove who was their reserve, who drawing his men close received
the enemy with much bravery and resolution, and gave liberty
to his friends to rally and front with him, who all three charged
the enemy's numerous bodies very furiously, and routed them

[1] Carlyle, *Cromwell*, Appendix 7.

quite; which made way for our musketeers to run up the hedges and gall the enemy, and for Major Desborough to draw his three troops out of the lane and front with Bethell. Upon which six troops divers mighty bodies of the enemy's came, and having disputed it soundly with their swords, the foot marching up furiously, and the other troops careered, God took away the enemy's courage and away they run. Of which charge of Major Bethell's, I heard the General, Lieutenant-Generall, and all the chief officers that saw it, say, it was one of the bravest that ever their eyes beheld.'[1]

Taking all these instances together, the permanent characteristics of Cromwell's tactics as a cavalry leader appear to have been two. In the first place, he invariably took the initiative, and charged the enemy instead of letting them charge him. In the second place, he taught his troopers to reserve their fire till they came to close quarters. Rupert did both these things, but at Edgehill and Chalgrove Field the cavalry of the Earl of Essex had acted on the opposite principles, and in each case they had been routed, while the cavalry of the Eastern Association had been invariably successful. The fact that Essex's troopers had carbines whilst Cromwell's troopers had not, accounts in part for the difference in their tactics. When the New Model was formed the bulk of its cavalry was drawn from the army of the Eastern Association, and the mode of fighting Cromwell had taught his men to practise was adopted by the cavalry in general. Though the carbine was reintroduced during the wars in Scotland and Ireland there seems to have been no reversion to the old tactics. In 1654 Major-General Morgan's instructions to his troopers in Scotland were, 'that no man should fire till he came within a horse's length of the enemy, and then (after firing) to throw their pistols in their faces, and so fall on with the sword'.[2]

[1] There are several accounts of this charge, viz.: *An exact and Perfect Relation of the Proceedings of the Army under Sir Thomas Fairfax from 6 to 11 July 1645*, British Museum, E, 292, 28; *A true Relation of a victory obtained over the King's forces . . . near Langport*, E, 292, 30; *A more full relation of the great battle fought between Sir T. Fairfax and Goring, made in the House of Commons by Lieut.-Col. Lilburne*, E, 293, 3. See also Sprigge, *Anglia Rediviva*, p. 72; *Reliquiæ Baxterianæ*, p. 54; Carlyle, *Cromwell*, Appendix 9.

[2] Quoted by Mr Fortescue, *Macmillan's Magazine*, 1894, p. 201, from a pamphlet published in 1654 called a *Bloodey Battaile*. 'The men deserve very well,' says a captain serving in Scotland, in 1655, 'who after they were

The practice of reserving fire, instead of firing during the advance, naturally led to an acceleration of the pace at which the charge was made. Not that it became as rapid as a modern cavalry charge. At its fastest the pace seemed to have been a trot rather than a gallop. Repeatedly we hear of charges made at 'a full trot'.[1] In an account of the battle, of the Dunes in 1658 we are told that Major-General Morgan, who was charging side by side with the French horse, led his English troopers 'at a good trot, but it was faster than the Monsieur's gallop'.[2]

The charge was always made in close order. 'Those troops that are to give the first charge,' writes Vernon in 1644, 'are to be at their close order; every left-hand man's right knee must be close locked under his right-hand man's left ham.'[3] The same statement is made by Lord Orrery writing after the Restoration: 'When the squadrons advance to charge the trooper's horses and their own knees are as close as they can well endure.' He

---

commanded to discharge their firelocks at a reasonable distance, did it very well, and afterward discharging their pistols when we were very close threw them at the enemy, and then fell in with the sword, which continued near half an hour after we had broken them' (*Report on the MSS. of Mr Leyborne Popham*, p. 110).

[1] Carlyle, *Cromwell*, Letter x. In Monck's directions for a cavalry charge, he represents three sub-divisions of a troop of horse as charging an enemy; two of them advance at 'an easy trot', the third 'at a walking pace'. When the first two are seen 'to be mingled with the enemy,' the third is to 'advance upon a round trot and charge' (*Observations*, p. 61).

[2] *Thurloe Papers*, vii, 150.

[3] Vernon's directions for 'charging the enemy in the field' are as follows: 'In grosse bodies, if you have field room enough, all the troops are to be drawn up into battalia, each being not above three deepe; likewise each troop must be at least a hundred paces distance behind each other for the better avoiding of disorder; those troops that are to give the first charge being drawn up in battail as before, are to be at their close order, every left hand man's right knee must be close locked under his right hand man's left ham. . . . In this order they are to advance toward the enemy with an easie pace, firing their carbines at a convenient distance, always aiming at their enemies breast or lower, because that powder is of an elevating nature, then drawing neere the enemy they are with their right hands to take forth one of their pistols out of their houlsters, and holding the lock up are most firing as before (always reserving one pistoll ready charged, spann'd, and primed in your houlsters, in case of a retreat), having thus fired, the troops are to charge the enemy in a full career, but in good order with their swords fastned with a riband or the like unto their wrists, for fear of losing out of their hand if they should miss their blow, placing the pomell on their thigh, keeping still in their close order, close locked as before' (*Young Horseman*, p. 43).

speaks also of 'the close uniting of the rank which is so necessary to make the charge effectual'.[1]

A third element in the effectiveness of the charge was the weight of horse and man. In Lord Saye's comments on the battle of Marston Moor, he speaks rather disparagingly of the 'light but weak nags' on which the Scottish cavalry were mounted, contrasting them with the stronger, heavier horses of Cromwell's troopers, and giving this difference as the reason why the cavalry of the Eastern Association bore the brunt of the fighting. Rupert's cavalry, on the other hand, were as well mounted as Cromwell's, 'both horse and men being very good'.[2] In this respect the cavalry of Prince Rupert and the cavalry of Cromwell were on an equality. Both too were on an equality with regard to armament, for each were harquebusiers equipped with back and breast, with sword and pistols. The view that Rupert's horse were light cavalry and Cromwell's heavy cavalry lacks proof.[3] When they met at Marston Moor and at Naseby, the only important difference was in their

[1] Lord Orrery adds some remarks on the proper position of officers during a charge. As the whole passage throws some light on the method of fighting amongst English cavalry during the war, and is too long for a footnote, it is added in Appendix G.

[2] See for the whole passage *English Historical Review*, 1890, p. 352, or Lord Saye's *Scots' Designe Discovered*, 1654, p. 80. Undoubtedly, at the beginning of the war the King had more difficulty than the Parliament in providing his horse with the necessary arms. At Edgehill it is probable that not more than half of the King's horse had 'backs and breasts' (Clarendon, *Rebellion*, vi, 73). The local levies probably continued to be imperfectly equipped with defensive armour (Ibid., vii, 104; cf. Rushworth, v, 281; Symonds, *Diary*, p. 231). But it is probable that the best regiments of the King's marching army, and especially those serving under Prince Rupert, were just as much entitled to be termed cuirassiers (or rather fully armed harquebusiers) as Cromwell's men were. Lord Saye speaks of the Royalist horse at Marston as standing 'like an iron wall', which would scarcely apply to light-armed horse. The truth is both were of the same type, but one army was more completely equipped than the other because it had larger resources. It is possible that this may have led the Royalists to rely more upon speed than solidarity in their charges, as Colonel Baldock holds that they did, and I think correctly.

[3] Colonel Baldock says definitely that the cavalry of Rupert and Cromwell represented two different types. 'The former was a light cavalry man. His troopers discarded all defensive armour on account of its weight. Their charge was prompt and rapid. On the other hand, Cromwell's favourite troops were cuirassiers, big heavily armed men and therefore slower' (*Cromwell as a Soldier*, p. 240). This is overstated. The regular cavalry of the King's army were technically described as harquebusiers just like those of the Parliament (see Colonel Haggerston's Commission, *Tanner MSS.*, lxii, 51).

tactics. 'Both,' sums up Colonel Baldock, 'had discarded the evil practice of halting to fire before charging.' But if the general impression which accounts of the battles produce may be trusted, the rapidity of the charge was greater with Rupert's troops than with Cromwell's. 'While the former relied for momentum and striking power on pace, the latter depended on solidarity and weight.'[1] This fact, added to the superiority of their discipline, helps to explain how it was that Cromwell, after a first charge, could succeed in getting his men together for a second, while Rupert could not. 'Though the King's troops,' says Clarendon, 'prevailed in the charge and routed those they charged, they seldom rallied themselves again in order, nor could be brought to make a second charge the same day . . . whereas the other troops, if they prevailed, or though they were beaten and routed, presently rallied again, and stood in good order till they received new orders.'[2]

[1] Baldock, *Cromwell as a Soldier*, p. 240. [2] *Rebellion*, ix, 41.

CHAPTER VI

Artillery during the Civil War

ENGLISHMEN ARE SLOW to accept new ideas, and foreign soldiers were much quicker to appreciate the importance of artillery in general and the way in which it should be employed. 'We may say of artillery,' wrote the Duke de Rohan in his commentaries on Cæsar, 'that it hath even in a manner altered the manner of making war.'[1] This truth was admitted by English soldiers, but it was long before its full significance was realized. Artillery, it was thought, was of course indispensable in sieges, but of no great value in battles. All experienced soldiers, said one Elizabethan writer, knew that 'great artillery very seldom or never hurt' any foot soldiers 'that upon their giving fire do but abase themselves on their knee till the volew be passed'.[2] A second writer was still more emphatic. 'Let it do the utmost it may, being employed by judicious gunners, yet never was victory obtained by great ordnance in open field, nor the force of the enemy coming resolutely to the charge thereby stopped.'[3]

English soldiers, like the rest of Europe, were taught the value and the right use of guns in battle by Maurice of Nassau and

[1] Rohan, *The Complete Captain*, p. 154, translated by J. Cruso, 1640. The original was published in 1636.

[2] Thomas Digges, *Four Paradoxes, or Politique Discourses concerning military discipline*, 1604, p. 63. Digges died in 1595, and the work was published by his son.

[3] Matthew Sutcliffe, *The Practice, Proceedings and Lawes of Armes*, 1593. 'Great artillery against troupes standing thicke and in even ground worketh great effects. But in other places and against men ranged otherwise, the sound is greater than the hurt. At Moncontour the King's ordonance beating among the horsemen ranged hedge-wise, did not in twentie shot hit once. Neither did it anie hurte to the footemen by reason of the vneuenesse of the ground. For eyther it fell lowe, or high. If the same be placed in the front of our armie, yet can not the same be employed past one or two volies. For at the ioyning of the battell, it ceaseth. And if our men march forward it breaketh their arrayes. If the same be placed upon some hill, yet lying out of leuell and shooting downeward, it doth no great hurt.
'But let it doe the utmost,' etc. (p. 190).

F

Gustavus Adolphus, but it was a lesson which they were somewhat slow to learn. Prince Maurice of Nassau, writes John Ward
in 1639, 'had 50 or 60 small field pieces cast, which he used to
place between his battalions, which were of great service in time
of fight, for two or three men could wield one of them as they
pleased, both in advancing it forwards and drawing it back, as
occasion served.'[1] The army of 24,000 men with which Maurice
marched to relieve Bergen-op-Zoom in 1622, was accompanied
by seventy guns great and small, and to every battalion there
was allotted 'two of his Excellency's new devised pieces called
Drakes'.[2] Ten of these newly invented guns Sir Edward Cecil
bought in 1625, for use in the expedition to Cadiz, and these
seem to have been the first pieces of the kind ever introduced
into England.[3]

The campaigns of Gustavus Adolphus supplied still more
cogent proofs of the power of guns in battle.[4] At Leipsic the
swiftness with which the light field-pieces of the Swedes were
charged and fired threw Tilly's infantry into confusion, and was
the chief cause of their defeat. Tilly, wrote Robert Monro, had
'prided himself all his lifetime on his dexterity of his great
cannon,' but there he was 'cunningly overshot' by Gustavus,
and 'from a master turned into a prentice.' A second example
was the passage of the Lech in face of Tilly's army, which was
attributed entirely to the effect of the seventy-two guns which
Gustavus concentrated upon the entrenchments of the Imperialists. 'Here we see the great force of artillery,' comments Monro,
'for this victory was obtained by the force of our cannon alone.'[5]
At the battle of Lützen, to take a third instance, before each of
the eight brigades of foot forming the main body of the Swedish

[1] Ward, *Animadversions of War*, ii, 26.

[2] Dalton, *Life of Sir E. Cecil*, ii, 28.

[3] Ibid., ii, 100. In sending the drakes Cecil says that they 'shoot 70
musket bullets', and expresses the hope that 'they will prove the profitablest
pieces that were ever used in the quarrel of his Majesties friends'.

[4] 'The Swedish trains of artillery since their first footing in Germany have
had the reputation to be the most exactly composed, and conducted by the
most experimented artists of any in Christendom. And no doubt but their
artillery helped them much to take so deep a footing in Germany, that they
have not been since expelled out of it, though that hath been much endeavoured' (Sir James Turner, *Pallas Armata*, p. 174).

[5] *Monro His Expedition of the worthy Scots regiment called Mackay's*,
1637, pt. ii, pp. 68, 118.

army 'marched six pieces of greater ordnance'. On each wing, posted between the cavalry regiments, were five small bodies of picked musketeers, 'every one of which bodies had two small drakes or fielding pieces, which advanced playing still before them'.[1]

In all Gustavus had sixty-eight guns, but nevertheless in the preliminary cannonade with which the battle opened the artillery of the Imperialists was more effective than that of the Swedes. For Wallenstein's guns, fewer and heavier, were 'planted upon steady and fixed batteries', while the lighter and more mobile guns of the Swedes gave fire 'in motion still and advancing'.[2] Mobility indeed was one of the qualities which Gusatavus valued most highly in artillery and sought most to develop. In addition to the light field-pieces carrying balls of from six to three pounds in weight he introduced a still lighter weapon, the so-called leather gun. These guns consisted of a tube of copper, or rather bronze, strengthened by rings of iron and covered with a leather skin. They were very portable and easy to work, but proved too weak for much service, and he finally substituted for them light iron guns of the same size, invented by Alexander Hamilton, one of the many Scots in the Swedish service.[3]

The Scottish officers who had served in the Thirty Years' War taught Englishmen the lessons they had learnt from Gustavus, and soon convinced them by hard experience of the value of field-guns. When the Covenanters took up arms against Charles

[1] *The Swedish Intelligencer*, p. iii, p. 128.

[2] 'The Armies being comme within Cannon shot, the great Ordnance, began to play one upon another, terribly. The aire roar'd, and the earth trembled: and those manly hearts that feared not dying, were yet very loath to have no more play for their lives, then to be beaten to pieces with the bullet of a Cannon. And here had Wallenstein, surely, a great advantage over the Kings Army: for his Ordnance being all ready planted upon steaddy and fixt Batteries the Canoniers traversed their peeces, and delivered their bullets with more aime, then the Kings men could possibly: who gave fire in motion still, and advancing. His Majesties Cannon, ever as a peece was discharged, was there left to be brought after: the Army still advancing, and marching away from it. Plainely, the King liked not this sport: for that the Imperiall Cannon did his men farre more spoile and execution then he possibly could againe returne them' (*The Swedish Intelligencer*, iii, 133).

[3] On these leather guns, see Turner, *Pallas Armata*, p. 189, and *Précis des Campagnes de Gustave Adolphe*, 1887, pp. 48–51. Hamilton's gun is to have been four feet long and to have weighed not more than 625 pounds. On the artillery of Gustavus, see also *The Swedish Intelligencer*, i, 89; ii, 235; iii, 5.

the First, Alexander Hamilton ('Dear Sandy', as he was styled by his contemporaries) placed his inventive talent at the disposal of his countrymen, and set up the manufacture of guns in Edinburgh.[1] The King soon discovered that the rebel forces were better equipped than his own. The battle of Newburn, and with it the fate of the campaign, was decided by the superiority of the Scots in artillery.[2] Lord Conway, who sought to defend the passage of the Tyne against Leslie, was greatly outmatched in numbers, and had at most only eight guns, of which the heaviest were sakers or six pounders. Leslie, who undertook to force the passage, had ten demiculverins carrying a ball of about nine or ten pounds. And besides these he had a number of lighter pieces, such as drakes or three pounders, and some of Hamilton's famous leather guns. Leslie battered Conway's entrenchments till his raw infantry left their guns and ran, and the Scottish horse and foot crossed the ford with little resistance from the English cavalry.[3]

In August 1641, when the King reviewed Leslie's army at Newcastle prior to its disbandment, he was shown sixty pieces of ordnance, whose gunners as he passed 'gave such true fire as it is believed since the invention of guns never better was seen or heard; they discharged wondrous swift, but with as good order and method as your skilfullest ringers observe with bells, not suffering the noise of one to drown the other'. He saw also distributed amongst the lines of musketeers and pikemen the machine-guns of the period, 'those dangerous short guns invented

---

[1] On Hamilton, see *Monro His Expedition*, ii, 1; Terry, *Life of Alexander Leslie, Earl of Leven*, pp. 45, 74, 121. Burnet speaks of the Scots as having 'guns of white iron tinned and done about with leather, and corded so that they would serve for two or three discharges. These were light, and were carried on horses' (Burnet, *Own Time*, ed. Airy, i, 45).

[2] The battle of Newburn was on 28th August 1640. In September Sir Henry Slingsby, on his journey to Hull, 'found the wayes pestered with carriages of all manner of preparations for warr; 30 peices of ordinance I met coming from Hull and abundance of wagons, with all things belonging to pouder, shot, and match, tents, pikes, spades, and shovels. It was then too late to march with their train of artillery, for before they could get to Newcastle the Scots had possessed themselves of it' (*Sir H. Slingsby's Diary*, p. 59, ed. 1836).

[3] Mr Terry in his account of the battle of Newburn, says Leslie, 'not only brought heavier guns into action, but also out-numbered Conway in ordnance by at least five to one' (*Life of Alexander Leslie*, p. 121).

by that their famous engineer, Sandy Hamilton, for the sudden execution of horse in case they should assail them'.[1]

With such object-lessons as these before their eyes, and with the campaigns of Gustavus fresh in their memories, English soldiers of the Civil War period were not likely to underestimate the importance of artillery as those Elizabethan writers did whom I quoted at the beginning of this chapter. Artillery played a much more important part in the Civil War than is generally supposed, and its skilful handling exercised considerable influence in deciding the fortune of battles and campaigns. An examination of the use made of field-guns in some of these battles and of the use made of battering-guns on some of the sieges of the period will, I think, serve to prove this.

It is not easy to estimate the services of artillery during the war for many reasons. One is that we possess very imperfect accounts of many of the battles. Many of the narratives we have were written by chaplains or casual civilians who happened to be present, neither of whom had much real knowledge of military matters. Many others were written by officers of cavalry or infantry, whose tendency was to exalt the services of their own particular arm or division at the expense of the others. I do not know of one single account of any English battle of the period which was written by an artillery officer.

A second difficulty is that the guns in use are generally described by highly technical names which have no definite meaning to most modern readers, and were often very loosely employed by our contemporary authorities.

A third and still greater difficulty is my own want of technical knowledge. All I can do is to state as clearly as possible the facts I have gathered from a number of contemporary narratives, and the conclusions to which they lead me, and to submit these results to the judgement of those who understand the subject better.

Speaking generally, the field-guns usually employed during the Civil Wars were of four or five kinds. The heaviest piece habitually used in the field was the culverin. The culverin discharged a ball of from sixteen to twenty pounds in weight, carried point blank about 400 paces, and had an extreme range

[1] *Life of Alexander Leslie*, p. 154.

of about 2,100 paces. It required eight horses to draw it, and
could be fired about ten times an hour or perhaps twelve.

The demiculverin, which was much more frequently employed in the field, fired a ball of from nine to twelve pounds
in weight, and had a range of from 320 to 380 paces point blank
and from 1,800 to 2,000 paces 'at utmost random'. Of these
larger pieces but few were as a rule employed. Commonly
the bulk of the guns used in the battles of the Civil War were
the light field-pieces called sakers, minions, and drakes. The
saker fired a ball weighing five or six pounds, the minion one of
three and a half pounds weight, the drake was probably a three-
pounder, but possibly smaller. These field-pieces could be discharged about fifteen times an hour.[1]

The larger guns described required six or eight horses apiece
to draw them, the smaller three, four, or five. Oxen were frequently employed instead of horses, especially for the heavier
guns. They were sometimes used for that purpose in the West
of England, and by the Scottish army in the North in 1645. In
Ireland oxen were habitually substituted for horses. At the
battle of Dungan's Hill in August 1647, Colonel Michael Jones
captured Lord Preston's train of artillery, which included 'four
demiculverins, each carrying a twelve-pound bullet, and 64 fair
oxen attending the train'. Jones at once bought the captured
oxen from the soldiers whose plunder they were, and employed
them to draw the guns of the English army.[2]

Military books give long and detailed instructions how to load,
aim, and discharge the guns. The crew of a gun usually consisted
of three men.[3] There was a special drill for gunners which
contained thirteen distinct words of command.[4] The powder for
the charge was sometimes made up into cartridges, but very

[1] For a more detailed account of the different field-guns and their
weights, see Appendix H.

[2] *An exact Relation of the great Victory obtained over the Rebels at Dungan's
Hill*, 1647. The oxen were valued at £16 the yoke, that is £8 apiece, whereas
the horses bought for the train of the New Model two years earlier cost on an
average about £6 apiece (Husbands, *Acts and Ordinances*, 1646, folio, p. 627).

[3] 'Every peece hath his gunner, with his coadjutor or mate, and a man to
serve them both, and helpe them charge, discharge, mount, wadde, cleanse,
scoure, and cook the peeces' (Ward, *Animadversions of War*, p. 108).
Detailed descriptions of the method of loading are given by Ward (p. 118),
and in Hexam's *Principalls of the Art Militarie*, pt. iii, pp. 13–15, ed. 1643.

[4] Fortescue, *History of the British Army*, i, 217.

often carried simply in a barrel which was placed somewhere behind the gun when it was in action.[1] In the contemporary picture-plan of the battle of Leipsic (or Breitenfeld), for instance, behind each little group of Swedish guns there is a powder-barrel standing on one end. From this barrel by means of a large iron ladle the gun was charged, and between each discharge it was the business of one of the gun's crew to cover the top of the powder-barrel in order to prevent an explosion.[2] Such accidents were not infrequent, and at the siege of Reading in 1643 a gun was disabled, four men killed, and about a dozen others badly hurt by the blowing up of one of these barrels.[3]

The prevalence of this method of loading guns explains the reason why both in the army of the Earl of Essex and in the New Model the train of artillery was invariably provided with a guard of men armed with firelocks.[4] In time of action it would have been too dangerous to have a guard of musketeers standing about amongst these open powder-barrels, with their matches lighted at both ends.

Lastly, it should be noted that the custom of attaching a couple of light field-pieces to every regiment of infantry, which Maurice had originated and Gustavus Adolphus had habitually practised, seems to have been copied by the English armies of this period. It is explicitly stated by one of the military writers of the time that this was the case, and in contemporary accounts of battles there are indications that the practice existed both in the army of the Earl of Essex and in its successors.[5] It was a

[1] This was the 'budge-barrel', or as Hexham terms it 'pouch barrel' (see p. 86, note 3, *ante*).

[2] See the two plans of the battle of Leipsic by Olve Hans, Quartermaster-General to the King of Sweden, appended to *The Swedish Discipline*, 1634, 4to.

[3] 'In the morning, Sir Anthony St. John, oldest captaine of his Excellency's guards, giving fire to a peece, by chance fired the barrells, and blew up the carriage, and killed 3 or 4 men outright, hurt himselfe and a dozin more though not mortally' (*Sir Sam Luke's Diary of the siege of Reading*, 18th April 1643; Coates, *History of Reading*, p. 32).

[4] Speaking of guns, Elton says: 'Those which are ordained for their guard to be firelocks or to have snaphances for the avoiding of the danger that might happen by the coal of the match' (*Complete Body of the Art Military*, p. 145).

[5] 'To most regiments there is allowed two waggons for the baggage and ammunition, and two fieldpieces or great cannon, besides other carriages which more concern the victual for the soldiers' (Elton, *Complete Body of the Art Military*, p. 145; cf. *Bibliotheca Gloucestrensis*, p. 247; *Memoirs of Slingsby and Hodgson*, ed. 1806, pp. 219, 247).

practice which prevailed in the army of Charles the Second after the Restoration, and in most important points that army merely followed the example of the New Model.[1]

Such being the guns and such the method in which they were worked in battle, the next thing is to trace the share they took in the campaigns of the Civil War.

In 1642, when the war began, it is evident that the Earl of Essex's army was liberally equipped with artillery. His army list contains the names of forty-five officers (including eighteen gentlemen of the ordnance) holding various posts in connexion with the train and the ordnance. Six hundred pioneers and 100 firelocks were attached to the train. It was nominally commanded by the Earl of Peterborough, but his second in command, Philibert Emmanuel de Boyes, was the person really responsible for its direction. Unluckily, the authorities do not state either the number or the calibre of the guns composing it.[2]

The King's army, on the other hand, was at that period of the war very deficient in artillery, but this deficiency was speedily supplied by the efforts of the Queen and other Royalist agents in France and Holland. Before many months the two armies were in this respect on tolerably equal terms. But when Charles first took the field against Essex his train of artillery, says Clarendon, 'was but mean', and not only poorly provided with ammunition but 'destitute of all things necessary for motion', so that the King was forced to seize the horses and waggons collected at Chester for the suppression of the rebellion in Ireland.[3]

At the battle of Edgehill, however, this inferiority was neutralized by the fact, that though Essex had a large and well-equipped train of artillery, half of it was a day's march behind his army.[4] In the cannonade which preceded the fight the Par-

[1] Clifford Walton, *History of the British Standing Army*, p. 733.

[2] Peacock, *Army Lists of Roundheads and Cavaliers*, ed. 1874, pp. 23–5.

[3] 'The train of artillery, which is commonly a spunge that can never be filled or satisfied, was destitute of all things which were necessary for motion, nor was there any hope that it could march till a good sum of money were assigned to it. Some carriage-horses and waggons which were prepared for the service of Ireland, and lay ready at Chester to be transported with the earl of Leicester, Lieutenant of that kingdom, were brought to Shrewsbury by his majesty's order for his own train' (Clarendon, *Rebellion*, ed. Macray, vi, 62 note, 64).

[4] May, *History of the Long Parliament*, p. 257.

liamentary guns did more damage than the King's. 'We gave them two shoots for one,' writes one Roundhead, 'and their ordnance, blessed be the God of battles, did us scarcely any harm, whereas we scarcely discharged away a bullet in vain.'[1] 'How admirably,' exults another, 'the hand of providence ordered our artillery and bullets for the destruction of the enemy, but how seldom or never almost we were hurt by theirs!'[2]

The rationalistic explanation of this phenomenon given by a Royalist writer is that the King's army was the more exposed, because it was descending a hillside, while the Parliamentarians were on the level ground at its foot. 'Being so much upon the descent his cannon either shot over, or if short it would not graze, by reason of the ploughed lands; whereas their cannon did some hurt, having a mark it could not miss.'[3]

In the rest of the battle the artillery played a very unimportant part. On both sides guns were captured and recaptured. Sir William Balfour with Essex's own regiment of horse 'got up to the greatest part of the enemy's ordnance and took them, cutting off the gears of the horses that drew them, and killing the gunners under the guns'. According to Ludlow, Balfour 'nailed', or as we should say 'spiked', some of them, but he was obliged to leave them unguarded in order to attack the King's infantry, and they were retaken by the Royalists later in the day. On their part the Parliamentarians lost six guns, of which they succeeded in recapturing five. But the next day the King's cavalry took four guns which the withdrawal of Essex's army had left exposed to capture, so that the only trophies of the day fell to the Royalists.[4]

When the King entered Oxford after Edgehill he brought with him, according to Wood, twenty-six or twenty-seven pieces

---

[1] *A true copy of a Letter sent unto the Lord Mayor of London, from a trusty friend in the Army.*

[2] *Special news from the Army at Warwick since the fight, sent from a minister of good note.*

[3] *Harleian MSS.*, 3,783, f. 61. Other Royalists deny that they suffered much. 'When we came within canon shot of the enemy,' says Sir Richard Bulstrode, 'they discharged at us three pieces of canon from their left wing, which canon (shot) mounted over our troops without doing any harm, except that their second shot killed a quartermaster in the rear of the Duke of York's troop' (*Memoirs*, p. 82).

[4] Ludlow, *Memoirs*, i, 42, ed. 1894.

of artillery, which were lodged in Magdalen Grove.¹ During 1643
his store of ordnance was greatly increased, not only by the
supplies of arms which the Queen procured from abroad, but by
captures made in battle from the Roundheads.² At Atherton
Moor the Royalists took five guns, at Hopton Heath eight, four
of which were drakes, at Roundway Down '8 fair brass pieces',
while eighty guns are said to have fallen into Rupert's hands
when he stormed Bristol. From the summer of 1643, at least, the
two hostile armies were in this respect upon equal terms.³

In August 1643, when Essex set out to relieve Gloucester, he
was urged, for the sake of expedition, to take only light field-
pieces with him and to leave his heavier guns in London. This
he wisely refused to do, for the King's army was so much superior to his own in cavalry that artillery was more needed than
ever. According to one account he took forty guns, great and
small, with him.⁴ They did good service at Stow-on-the-Wold,
where Rupert attempted to hinder his march to Gloucester (4th
September), and still better service at Newbury. The King had
occupied the high ground of Newbury Wash with his guns the
night before the battle, and until their own heavier guns came
up, the Parliamentary infantry were exposed to the fire of the
Royalists with little power to reply. The London trained bands,
inexperienced though they were, bore the ordeal well, and 'stood
like stakes', said an eye-witness, 'against the shot of the cannon'.⁵ The drakes (that is three-pounders) attached to these

¹ *Life of Anthony Wood*, ed. Clark, i, 68.

² *Mercurius Aulicus*, 1643, pp. 83, 109, 127, 217, 249, 256, 419.

³ Ibid., pp. 147, 350, 371, 378, 403.

⁴ 'The two Houses did desire that he should leave his great artillery
behind him (for they intended not to try his patience in the siege of cities),
and be contented with his drakes and some small field pieces; he utterly
denied to hearken to that learned motion' (*Mercurius Aulicus*, 28th August).

⁵ The two regiments of London trained bands on the Parliamentary right
wing suffered much from these guns. 'The enemy,' says Sergeant Foster,
'had there planted 8 pieces of ordnance, and stood in a great body of horse
and foot, we being placed right opposite to them, and far less than twice
musket shot distance from them. They began their battery against us with
their great guns, above half an hour before we could get any of our guns up
to us: our noble Colonell Tucker fired one piece of ordnance against the
enemy, and aiming to give fire the second time, was shot in the head with a
cannon bullett from the enemy.' Meanwhile the blue regiment of the
London trained bands, forming the extreme right of the line, was attacked
by two regiments of the King's horse and twice beat them off. Foster's own
regiment lost most from the artillery. 'The enemy's canon did play most

regiments, which were loaded with case-shot, were very effective in repelling the charges of the King's cavalry. When Essex's heavier guns, which were demiculverins, came up his artillery speedily gained the upper hand. It was 'placed so unhappily', says Clarendon, 'that it did very great execution upon the King's party both horse and foot', while the King's guns were no use at all. The credit of this achievement the Parliamentary account attributed to Sir John Merrick,[1] who was then in command of Essex's artillery.

Essex may not have been a good general, but it is plain that he attached great importance to the possession and use of a good train of guns. At his disaster in Cornwall in September 1644, when his infantry was obliged to capitulate to the King, the Royalists captured between forty and fifty guns, a very large proportion for an army which numbered at its highest strength not much more than 12,000 men. The train of artillery which passed into the hands of the conquerors consisted of '49 pieces of fair brass ordnance', including a piece termed 'the great Basilisco of Dover'.[2] Sir John Merrick escaped by sea with Essex, and deserted his guns, but the common soldiers of the army seem to have been more sensible to the disgrace of their loss. At the second battle of Newbury some of the infantry who had surrendered in Cornwall stormed the entrenchments of the Royalists on Speen Hill, and captured '9 good brass pieces', six of them, says Skippon, 'being sakers we left behind in Cornwall'. Some of the soldiers 'ran up to the cannon and clapped their hats upon the 'touchholes of them' to prevent the gunners from firing;

---

against the red regiment of trained bands: they did some execution amongst us at the first, and were somewhat dreadful when men's bowels and brains flew in our faces. But blessed be God that gave us courage, so that we kept our ground, and after a while feared them not; our ordnance did very good execution upon them: for we stood at so near a distance upon a plain field that we could not miss one another' (*Bibliotheca Gloucestrensis*, pp. 266, 267).

[1] Clarendon, *Rebellion*, vii, 212; May, *History of the Long Parliament* p. 352, ed. 1854; *Bibliotheca Gloucestrensis*, pp. 245–7, 264, 277; Money, *The Battles of Newbury*, pp. 45, 52, ed. 2. On the position occupied by the artillery of the two armies, see also Money, pp. 36, 39, 57, 75, and Gardiner, *Great Civil War*, i, 210.

[2] Rushworth, v, 701; *Diary of Richard Symonds*, pp. 63, 66; Walker, *Historical Discourses*, pp. 67, 79. The 'Basilisco' has been identified with an ancient gun called 'Queen Elizabeth's Pocket-Pistol', on which were inscribed the lines:

others embraced the guns for joy, 'saying they would give them a Cornish hug'.[1]

The minor armies of the Parliament were less liberally equipped with artillery than the main army under Essex. Waller, who owed his successes mainly to the rapidity of his movements, required mobility more than any other quality in his guns. The commander of his artillery, Colonel Wemyss, introduced therefore a variety of the leather gun, drawn by one horse and carrying a ball of a pound and a half in weight. It was said by the newspapers to be 'the particular invention' of Colonel Wemyss, but was no doubt an adaptation of Hamilton's weapon.[2] These guns did very little service, and at Cropredy Bridge in June 1644 the Royalists captured from Waller not only eleven cannon of the ordinary type, but also 'two barricades drawn on wheels, in each 7 small brass and leathern guns charged with case shot.'[3]

> 'Load me well and keep me clean
> I'll carry a ball to Calais Green'
> – (Deane, *Life of Richard Deane*, p. 149).

[1] Rushworth, v, 722, 728; Ludlow, *Memoirs*, i, 103.

[2] *The True Informer* of 9th December 1643 has the following: 'That renowned and unmatcheable engineere, Colonel Wems, Lieutenant-Generall of the Ordinance and Traine unto Sir William Waller, according to the desire and appointment of the House of Commons in Parliament, went down from London on Tuesday night last, December 5th, with waggons laden with leather pieces of ordinance, and much other ammunition, and is by this time at Farnham with Sir William Waller. These leather pieces are of very great use, and very easie and light of carriage. One horse may draw a peece, which will carry a bullet of a pounde and halfe weight, and doe execution very farre. This is the said Colonel's particular invention, and will be of very great service unto Sir William's army, especially for this winter season' (quoted by Godwin, *Civil War in Hampshire*, p. 96). A petition from Wemyss containing an account of his inventions is in *Cal. State Papers, Dom.*, 1658–9, p. 35.

[3] 'He routed all those Horse and Foot, and chased them beyond their Cannon; all which (being eleven Pieces) were then taken, and two Barricades of Wood drawn with Wheels, in each seven small brass and leathern Guns, charged with case shot. Most of the Cannoniers were then slain, and Weymes General of the Ordnance to Sir William Waller taken Prisoner; a Person (according to his Quality) as ingrateful to His Majesty as either Argile, Lowden, or any of the Scottish Nation now in Rebellion (being His Majesty's own Servant, and by His especial Favour made Master Gunner of England with the Pension of £300 per Annum)' (Sir E. Walker, *Discourses*, p. 32). 'Tooke all their 14 peeces of Ordnance, whereof 11 brasse viz., 5 Sakers, 1 twelve pound peece, 1 demiculverin, 2 mynions, 2 three pound peeces, besides two blinders for muskets and leather guns invented by Col. Weems a Scot who lately made them at Lambeth (in the same place where the gunpowder traytors practised) and received £2000 for them, as appears by writings found in his pocket' (*Mercurius Aulicus*, 29th June 1646).

The army of the Eastern Association, which the Earl of Manchester commanded, had a train of artillery, but as to its composition very little can be discovered. On the other hand, the Scottish army under Leslie, which entered England in January 1644 to assist the Parliamentarians, was exceptionally well provided with artillery. Leslie is said to have had 120 guns, ranging from small field-pieces to twenty-four-pounders. These twenty-four-pounders were intended for sieges, and did not march with the army, but were transported by sea to take part in the siege of Newcastle. The whole of the artillery was under the command of Alexander Hamilton.[1]

When the Scottish army joined Fairfax and Manchester to besiege York they must have had between them a very considerable number of guns, and yet there was hardly any battle in the war in which guns played so unimportant a part as Marston Moor. There was the usual cannonade before the battle began. 'Our ordnance,' says a Parliamentary narrative, 'about two o'clock began to play upon the brigade of horse that were nearest, and did some execution upon them, which forced the enemy to leave that ground, and remove to a greater distance.'[2] This no doubt facilitated the attack of Cromwell's cavalry later. When the general advance of the Parliamentarians began, their guns which had been first stationed on the top of the hill were 'drawn forward to our best advantage'.[3] On both sides guns were captured and recaptured. Rupert lost finally all those he had brought into the field, from twenty to twenty-five in number, of which the largest seem to have been demiculverins and the smallest drakes.[4]

When the New Model was organized it was provided with a

[1] See Terry, *Life of Alexander Leslie*, pp. 178, 228, 304. Hamilton had invented a new gun for the campaign. 'Their chief Ingenier hath formed a new kind of great guns, never before discovered, which were made purposely for this designe, above three quarters of a yard long, or some a yard, that will carry a twelve pound bullet, to doe great execution at a distance, and yet so framed that a horse may carry one of them' (*The Scots March fom Barwicke to Newcastle*, 1644).

[2] Stockdale, *Narrative*.

[3] Ashe, *Relation*. On the part played by the guns, see also Terry, *Life of Alexander Leslie*, pp. 268, 281, and a paper on 'Marston Moor' in the *Transactions of the Royal Historical Society*, vol. xii, pp. 74, 75.

[4] Terry, pp. 269, 272, 278, 282; *Transactions of the Royal Historical Society*, xii, pp. 71, 76.

powerful train of artillery, though there is no very exact account
in existence of the number and weight of the guns composing it.
It is evident, however, that the field-guns attached to it were
principally demiculverins and sakers. This is proved by the
contracts made with shot manufacturers for the supply of the
army, and by a vote of the House of Commons assigning to
Fairfax two brass demiculverins and eight brass sakers formerly
belonging to the navy.[1] In 1647 Fairfax's artillery train contained sixteen demiculverins, ten sakers, fifteen drakes, and
fifteen smaller field-pieces, in all fifty-six guns, besides mortars
and battering cannon intended for use in sieges.[2]

The train and the baggage of the army required 1,038 horses
to draw them, and were guarded by two companies of firelocks.[3]

The 'Lieutenant-General of the Ordnance' was Thomas Hammond, uncle of the Robert Hammond who was jailer to Charles
the First at Carisbrook. But most of the management of the
artillery in battle seems to have been in the hands of Captain
Richard Deane, 'comptroller of the ordnance', who became later
one of the admirals of the Republic, and was killed in battle with

[1] A list of the artillery was read in the House of Commons on 19th April
1645, and was transmitted to the Lords, but unluckily it is missing. The
same day Fairfax was ordered the ten guns mentioned above (*Commons'
Journals*, iv, 117; *Lords' Journals*, vii, 330). A newspaper called *The True
Informer* says, under 29th April, 'Tuesday in the evening these carriages
following went out of London towards Sir Thomas Fairfax, viz. 10 brasse
peeces of ordnance, one mortar peece, 12 waggons and carriages, 5 load of
match, 2 load of bullets, 6 carriages for ordnance'. No doubt he also had the
guns previously attached to the army under Essex.

Another newspaper supplies the following account of the manner in which
Fairfax's army marched:

'Between every regiment is drawne foure pieces of ordnances, and 4 the
next, and so all through the army: the horse march some before and some
behind, some on the one hande and some on the other, as there is occasion
or as is most convenient: the carriages and traine is drawn in the middle of
the army between the regiments and the pioneers, who march before the
train, and make way as occasion serves, some of the pioneers also going in
every place with the ordnance' (*Perfect Passages*, 1st May 1645).

[2] 'We hear of the trayne of artillery being drawn out of Oxford to the
General's headquarters at St. Albanes, together with 16 demy-culverins, 10
sakers, 15 drakes, 15 small field pieces with great store of ammunition, all
which (it is said) was conducted to St. Albanes by a party of horse appointed
for that purpose' (*The last Newes from the armie*, 20th June 1647, *Thomason
Tracts*, E, 393, 14).

[3] *Commons' Journals*, iv, 71, 117; Husbands, *Ordinances*, 1646, folio
p. 627. The firelocks wore 'tawny' coats, presumably something of a khaki
colour; the rest of the infantry wore red coats.

the Dutch in June 1653. Hammond had commanded Manchester's artillery; Deane had served under Essex.[1]

Despite its superiority in artillery, the guns of the New Model did little service at Naseby. The preliminary firing before the two armies came to close quarters was of the briefest description. 'Being come within cannon shot,' says one narrative, 'the ordnance began to play, but that being found at Marston Moor and other places but a loss of time, we resolved not to want daylight as usual, but to charge with the first.'[2] At one time, continues the same account, when the left wing of the Parliamentary army was driven back, the Royalists 'were almost masters of our artillery'. In the end, however, all the guns the King brought into the field were taken, being twelve in all, 'whereof two', says Cromwell, 'were demicannons, two demiculverins, and the rest, I think, sakers'.[3]

The next battle in which the New Model was engaged, that of Langport on 10th July 1645, was one in which artillery played a really important part, and all three arms worked together with great effectiveness. Goring, the Royalist leader, was endeavouring to cover the retreat of his baggage and his train to the fortified town of Bridgwater. Goring's army was posted on one ridge, that of Fairfax on another, and between the two armies lay a valley and a stream through which a narrow lane led up to the Royalist position. Goring had filled the enclosures on each side of the lane with his musketeers, and stationed his horse on the brow

[1] Peacock, *Army Lists*, pp. 100, 101, 106; Sprigge, *Anglia Rediviva*, p. 327.

[2] *A True Relation.*

[3] Carlyle, *Cromwell*, Letter xxix. The Commissioners of Parliament with the army, Leighton and Herbert, say that there were captured 'all their field pieces, of which some are cannon, most of their baggage, mortar pieces, boats', etc. (Ellis, *Original Letters*, I, iii, 309). Fairfax speaks of two demicannons, a whole culverin, and a mortar-piece, besides lesser pieces (Ibid., p. 307). The demicannons were siege-guns used by the King at the siege of Leicester, which served Fairfax to recover it (Sprigge, pp. 45, 54; Hollings, *Leicester during the Civil War*, p. 65). The boats are those referred to in the following extract:

'On the backside of Maudlin College, in a close where his artillery stood, he (i.e., the King) makes choice of what guns should march out with him, and out of them chooseth 14 of bigger and less size. He caused 14 boats to be made for transporting his artillery over any river, and one day makes trial upon the river at Oxford how these boats would carry these guns, causing two of the biggest to be drawn over by them' (*Diary of Sir Henry Slingsby*, p. 142).

of the hill where the lane debouched on the plateau. He had only
two guns on the hill; the rest were on the way to Bridgwater.
Fairfax's artillery began the action, silenced the two guns and
forced Goring to draw his main body farther back. 'A good
while before the foot engaged,' says one narrative, 'our ordnance began to play, doing great execution upon the body of the
enemy's army, both horse and foot, who stood in good order on
the hill about musket shot from the pass, forcing them to draw
off their ordnance, and their horse to remove their ground.'[1]
Thus the musketeers Goring had placed in the valley were left
unsupported. 'Our cannon,' says another account, 'did very
good service, and made the other side of the hill so hot that they
could not come down to relieve their men.'[2] Fairfax's infantry
then drove the Royalist musketeers out of the enclosures, and
made it possible for his cavalry to gallop up the lane and fight
the Royalist horse on the high ground beyond it.

From a military point of view the battle of Preston three
years later was as remarkable as the battle of Langport, but for
a different reason. In it and in the two days' fighting which followed neither army had any artillery at all. Cromwell had
marched too rapidly from Wales to Yorkshire to bring his guns
with him. He expected to be supplied with some from Hull, and
halted three days at Doncaster to wait for them. Nevertheless
he decided to cross the hills into Lancashire and to fall upon the
Scots without these guns. In his despatch he describes his army
as 'having cast off our train, and sent it to Knaresborough, because of the difficulty of marching therewith through Craven,
and to the end that we might with more expedition attend the
enemies motion'.[3] Very likely Cromwell knew that Hamilton's
army had brought no artillery with it. 'We had no cannon,' says
Sir James Turner, 'nay, not one field-piece, very little ammunition, and not one officer to direct it. Dear Sandy being grown old
and doated, and given no fitting orders for these things.' The
train of the army was so badly provided that Hamilton had to

[1] Sprigge, *Anglia Rediviva*, p. 72.

[2] *An exact and perfect Relation of the proceedings of the Army under Sir T.
Fairfax*, 6–11 July 1645.

[3] Carlyle, *Cromwell*, Letter lxiv; *Cromwelliana*, p. 42; *Cal. State Papers,
Dom.*, 1648–9, p. 230; Gardiner, *Great Civil War*, iv, 179, 184.

rely on the horses he could collect in the country to carry his
ammunition. This was one of the reasons why there was so much
hand-to-hand fighting, and why the two armies came so often
'to push of pike' during this short campaign.[1]

It would be wrong to infer from the Preston campaign that
Cromwell underestimated the value of field-artillery. He took
care to be well provided with it when he invaded Scotland in
1650, and the report in the Scottish camp was that he called his
guns his 'Twelve Apostles', and put his whole trust in them.[2]
In the fighting around Edinburgh artillery played a considerable
part, the Scots sticking to entrenchments whose approaches
were covered by their guns, Cromwell seeking to scour their
trenches with his guns, or to lure them into the open. At Gogar
on 27th August the two armies, prevented by bogs and other
obstacles from engaging, cannonaded each other all day long,
the Scots, according to Cromwell, losing four times as many men
as the English. 'Betwixt the armies,' says Captain Hodgson,
'were some sheep-folds, made up of sod walls; and the Scots
drew into them a party of foot to hinder our men from viewing
their army, and they began to fire upon some of ours that were
pickeering betwixt the armies; and Oliver calls for a couple of
guns and batters their shelter about their ears, so that much ado
they had to get off their quick and dead: at which our army set
up an English shout, and begun to play with our great guns upon
their army, from the right to the left wing, and did great execution; and they let fly at us, but God covered our heads. There
was but one shot flew amongst our pikes all the day, and killed
two men and struck down three; but all that were aimed at us
flew over or short.'[3]

[1] Sir James Turner, *Memoirs*, p. 59; Burnet, *Lives of the Hamiltons*, pp.
450, 457; Monro and the troops who came from Ireland had four guns, but
they took no part in the battle, being too far in the rear of the main army
under Hamilton (*Cromwelliana*, p. 45).

[2] *Memoirs of Sir H. Slingsby and Capt. John Hodgson*, ed. 1806, Appendix,
p. 220, 'A large Relation of the fight at Leith'.

[3] Here are two other accounts of the incident: 'We stood in battalia that
afternoon and next morning, the cannons playing hotly on both sides; and
though we were much the fairer mark, standing upon the pitch of a rising
ground, yet it pleased God our loss was much the less: we had only about 4
that died on the place, and about 18 or 19 wounded; and of the enemy about
100 wounded and killed'.

'We drew up our cannon, and did that day discharge two or three hundred great shot upon them; a considerable number they likewise returned

In the retreat to Musselburgh which followed, Cromwell used his guns with some skill to keep the pursuing Scots in check. 'They marched very briskly after us; and our general observing their motion, as though they designed to flank us on the right wing (they were to march down by a mountain end in view of us, and in reach of our guns), he caused two to play upon them in their march. Their van being passed, the rest must follow, and indeed they were sore baffled with our shot, we had such fair play at them.' A couple of days later, as the retreating army approached Dunbar, the Scots made an attempt to fall upon its rear. 'Two guns played upon them,' says Hodgson, 'and so they drew off and left us that night.'[1]

In the accounts of the battle of Dunbar little is said of Cromwell's artillery, but that little is very suggestive. One of the reasons urged in Cromwell's council of war for attacking the Scots was that owing to the nature of their position 'our guns might have fair play at their left wing while we were fighting their right'. And it seems evident that this is what actually happened. Cromwell's guns were so carefully placed that their concentrated fire kept part of the Scottish army in check, and enabled him to throw the bulk of his forces on the other part, and thus to rout an army much superior in numbers to his own.[2]

To sum up this cursory examination of the employment of field-artillery in the Civil Wars, I think we are justified in concluding that inferior though the weapons were which the gunners of that time had at their disposal, the result of their action was not so insignificant as it is often said to have been. When these defective weapons were well handled they were capable of covering a retreat, facilitating a successful attack, or compensating for disparity of numbers. And one of the causes of the success of the Parliamentarians in the Civil War was, that their artillery was more powerful than that of the Royalists and generally better handled in battle.

---

to us,' writes Cromwell. He estimates his own loss as 'near 20', and that of the Scots at 'about four score' (pp. 262, 270, Appendix to *Memoirs of Captain John Hodgson*, ed. 1806).

[1] *Memoirs of Captain John Hodgson*, ed. 1806, pp. 142, 144.

[2] *Memoirs of Captain John Hodgson*, ed. 1806, pp. 145–6; see also 'The Battle of Dunbar,' *Transactions of the Royal Historical Society*, vol. xiv, p. 36.

CHAPTER VII

Sieges

As FIELD-ARTILLERY became progressively more powerful and more efficient, so did siege-artillery. In the early part of the war the defence seems to have had the advantage over the attack. Neither the Royalist nor the Parliamentary army seems to have been adequately provided either with heavy guns or with trained engineers and gunners. Of the two armies, perhaps that of Essex was better equipped in this respect, yet it took him about a fortnight to reduce Reading.[1] When a town was so imperfectly fortified that it could be taken by assault, the King's soldiers successfully stormed it, but when a regular siege was necessary they failed ignominiously. Had the Royalists in the year 1643 succeeded in taking Gloucester and Hull, the event of the war might have been different, but in each case the attack was un-skilfully conducted. The King's mistake in besieging Gloucester lay not so much in the conception of the design as in its execu-tion. Gloucester was weakly garrisoned and imperfectly fortified. Charles invested the city for nearly four weeks with an army overwhelming in numbers and armed with a considerable num-ber of heavy guns; but his mining operations were a failure and his artillery never succeeded in making a practicable breach.[2] Hull was from its position a stronger place than Gloucester,[3] and

[1] For accounts of the siege of Reading, see the histories of that town by Man and Coates, and Clarendon, *Rebellion*, vii, 24–45.

[2] Detailed accounts of the siege of Gloucester are contained in the *Bibliotheca Gloucestrensis*, by John Washbourn, 1825. John Corbet's 'Military Government of the City of Gloucester', and John Dorney's 'Brief and Exact Relation of the Siege' reprinted there, give full particulars from the point of view of the besieged. There is no equally detailed narrative on the Royalist side.

[3] A good account of the siege of Hull might be put together from con-temporary sources, but does not at present exist.

the Parliament's command of the sea enabled it to reinforce
the besieged garrison when reinforcements were needed. But the
failure of the siege seems to have been due to the faults of the
besiegers as much as to the natural difficulties with which they
had to contend. When Sir Philip Warwick visited the intrenchments of Newcastle's soldiers, he found them standing ankle-
deep in mud and at a great distance from the town; they were
more likely, thought Warwick, to rot there than to starve out
the besieged. But when he suggested as much to their commander, Newcastle put him off with a jest. 'You often hear us called
the popish army,' said the earl, 'but you see we trust not in our
good works.'[1]

In the early part of the Civil War, more especially in the
minor local struggles between the two parties, the want of
proper siege-guns frequently led the attacking party to resort to
obsolete methods of attack. At the siege of Corfe Castle in 1643.
and at the siege of Canon Frome in 1645, both Royalists and
Parliamentarians made use of the mediæval machine called a
'sow', which was a sort of covered shed on wheels.[2] It was still
more frequently employed by the Irish rebels, but in no case does
it appear to have proved effective.[3] At the siege of Gloucester
Dr Chillingworth constructed 'great store of engines after the
manner of the Roman Testudines', but Essex relieved the city
too soon for their merits to be determined.[4]

[1] *Memoirs of Sir Philip Warwick*, p. 265.

[2] Bankes, *Story of Corfe Castle*, 1853, p. 187; *Mercurius Rusticus*, No. xi;
Webb, *Civil War in Herefordshire*, ii, 240; Grose, i, 384–87.

[3] Bellings, *History of the Irish Confederation and the War in Ireland.
1641-3*, ed. J. T. Gilbert, i, xlv; ii, 71; Gilbert, *Aphorismical Discovery of
Treasonable Faction*, iii, 229; *Lismore Papers*, second series, v, 79.

[4] 'We understood likewise that the enemy had by the direction of that
Jesuitical Doctor Chillingworth provided great store of engines after the
manner of the Romane Testudines cum Pluteis, with which they intended
to have assaulted the parts of the city betweene the south and west gates.
These engines ran upon cart wheels with a blinde and plankes musquet
proofe, and holes for foure musquetiers to play out of, placed upon the
axeltree to defend the musquetiers and those that thrust it forward, and
carrying a bridge before it; the wheeles were to fall into the ditch, and the
end of the bridge to rest upon our breast-workes, so making severall compleate bridges to enter the city. To prevent this we intended to have made
another ditch out of our workes, so that the wheeles falling therein the
bridge would have fallen too short of our brestworkes into our wet moat.
and so frustrated their intentions' (*Bibliotheca Gloucestrensis*, p. 225).

A favourite method of attacking fortified houses or castles unprovided with outworks, was to apply a petard to the gate and to blow it in. This was the way in which Waller captured Arundel Castle and Farnham Castle in 1642, and Massey nearly succeeded in taking Beverston Castle by the same means.[1] It was by the use of a petard that Leslie, in 1639, effected the capture of Edinburgh Castle, impregnable though it was reputed to be.[2] Military writers of the period give elaborate directions how to prepare and to affix petards,[3] but the most lucid explanation of the process is given by Sir Henry Lee, in the thirty-third chapter of *Woodstock*, to his housemaid Phoebe, while Cromwell is attaching one to the front door of the Manor House. '"What can they be doing now, Sir?" said Phoebe, hearing a noise as it were of a carpenter turning screw nails, mixed with a low buzz of men talking. "They are fixing a petard," said the knight with great composure. "I have noted thee for a clever wench, Phoebe, and I will explain it to thee: 'Tis a metal pot, shaped much like one of the roguish knaves own sugar-loaf hats, supposing it had a narrower brim – it is charged with some few pounds of fine gunpowder."'

Sir Anthony Ashley Cooper's account of his capture of Abbotsbury House, in Dorsetshire, exemplifies another method of assaulting the fortified houses which played so large a part in the minor campaigns of the Civil War.

'We came thither just at night, and sent them a summons by a trumpeter, to which they returned a slighting answer and hung out their bloody flag. Immediately we drew out a party of musketeers, with which Major Bainton in person stormed the church, into which they had put thirteen men, because it flanked the house. This after a hot bickering we carried, and took all the men prisoners. After this we sent them a second summons under our hands, that they might have fair quarter if they would accept it, otherwise they must expect none if they forced us to a storm. But they were so gallant that they would admit of no

[1] *Bibliotheca Gloucestrensis*, p. 65; Vicars, *Parliamentary Chronicle, Jehovah Jireh*, pp. 223, 231.

[2] Terry, *Alexander Leslie*, p. 46.

[3] 'A kind of iron mortar of the form of a truncated cone,' says Grose, who adds an illustration (*Military Antiquities*, i, 408; see also Ward, *Animadversions of War*, pp. 113, 362).

treaty, so that we prepared ourselves for to force it, and accordingly fell on. The business was extreme hot for above six hours; we were forced to burn down an outgate to a court before we could get to the house, and then our men rushed in through the fire and got into the hall porch, where with furse fagots they set fire on it, and plied the windows so hard with small shot that the enemy durst not appear in the low rooms: in the meantime one of our guns played on the other side of the house, and the gunners with fire balls and granadoes with scaling ladders endeavoured to fire the second storey, but, that not taking effect, our soldiers were forced to wrench open the windows with iron bars, and, pouring in fagots of furse fired, set the whole house in a flaming fire, so that it was not possible to be quenched, and then they cried for quarter; but we having lost divers men before it, and considering how many garrisons of the same nature we were to deal with, I gave command there should be none given, but they should be kept into the house, that they and their garrison might fall together.'[1]

In this instance the church near the house was fortified as an outwork, a course which was very frequently adopted. As the church tower sometimes commanded the house, the capture of one often involved the fall of the other, and, for that reason, the church was sometimes destroyed or the church tower pulled down to secure the garrison of the house. At Borstall in Buckinghamshire, for instance, this was done by the King's orders, so that it was not only the Parliamentarians who destroyed churches.[2]

Massey's capture of the church and house of Westbury in the Forest of Dean supplies an example of the method in which these little garrisons were taken.

'Here the enemy held the church, and a strong house adjoyning. The governour observing a place not flanked, fell up that way with the forlorne hope, and secured them from the danger of shot. The men got stooles and ladders to the windowes, where they stood safe, cast in granadoes and fired them out of the church. Having gained the church, he quickly beat them out

---

[1] Christie, *Life of Shaftesbury*, vol. i, p. 62.

[2] Lipscombe, *History of Buckinghamshire*, i, 77; cf. *Mercurius Aulicus*, 12th June 1644.

of their workes and possest himselfe of the house, where he tooke
about foure score prisoners, without the losse of a man.'[1]

These simpler methods of attack might be successful in the
siege of hastily fortified country-houses and small castles, but
walled towns and castles, defended by proper outworks and by
adequate garrisons, demanded more scientific methods. The
closing campaigns of the first Civil War, and the subjugation of
Ireland and Scotland, were marked by a series of systematically
conducted sieges which form a striking contrast to the ineffective
operations of the opening years of the war. The New Model army
was equipped with powerful siege-artillery, which was progressively increased in strength during the Commonwealth. The guns
most used in sieges were the whole cannon or cannon proper, the
demicannon, and the culverin. These may be roughly defined,
the cannon as a forty-eight or forty-pounder, the demicannon as
a twenty-four-pounder, and the culverin as a sixteen-pounder.[2]
When Fairfax besieged Sherborne Castle in 1645 he employed
a whole cannon and several demicannons. When Cromwell
attacked Basing House in the same autumn he brought with
him five great guns, one of which was a whole cannon and two
demicannons.[3] When the siege of Oxford by the New Model
was projected, two demicannon, three whole culverins, and a gun
from Cambridge called 'the pocket pistol' were ordered to be
sent to Fairfax.[4] But against the solid masonry of some old
castles the sixteen-pound ball of the culverin was found too light
to be serviceable. When Cromwell besieged Pembroke Castle

[1] *Bibliotheca Gloucestrensis*, p. 93.

[2] See Appendix H.

[3] Sprigge, *Anglia Rediviva*, pp. 91, 92. 'They that write from Basing, say
that Lieut.-Gen. Cromwell makes the number now before it between 6000
and 7000 horse and foot; he brought with him 5 great guns, two of them
demi-cannons, one whole canon' (*The Moderate Intelligencer*, Monday, 13th
October 1645).

[4] 'Provisions for the siege of Oxford: 2 demi-cannon and 3 whole culverins, ready at Windsor and Northampton; for the piece wanting pro-
pound the pocket pistol at Cambridge. 1,200 spades and shovels at 73£.,
300 steel spades at 45£., 500 pickaxes at 70£. 16s. 8d., 200 scaling ladders
at £60., 500 barrels of gunpowder at 2,250£., 40 tuns of match at 1,360£.,
30 tuns of bullet at 510£., 300 granado shells, lesser size, at 186£. 13s. 4d.,
300 do., great, at 560£., 1,000 hand grenades at 125£., 50 tuns of round shot
at 600£. Total, 5,842£. 10s. 20 carriages for provisions at 210£., 200 horse
harness at 120£., making 330£. Grand total, 6,172£. 10s' (*Cal. State Papers,
Dom.*, 1644–5, p. 515).

he used principally demicannons, and for the siege of Pontefract
in 1648 he asked for six good battering-guns, none of which were
to be less than demicannons.[1]

Besides the battering-guns there were usually mortar-pieces.
One brass mortar-piece weighing about ten hundredweight, if not
more than one, formed part of the artillery train of the New
Model, and shells twelve inches in diameter were provided for
it.[2] When Cromwell besieged Pembroke he had shells manu-
factured in Carmarthenshire fourteen and three-quarter inches
in diameter, and for the reduction of Pontefract Castle he demanded two or three of the biggest mortar-pieces.

The powerful siege-guns of the New Model proved very quickly effective against Royalist castles and garrisons. At Sherborne
in two days Fairfax's guns made a breach in the wall wide
enough for ten men to march abreast, and beat down one of the
towers. At Devizes where the works, 'cut out of the main earth'
on which the castle stood, were 'so strong that no cannon could
pierce them', Cromwell's mortar-pieces, bursting their shell 'in
the midst of the castle (being open above)', killed several men,
threatened to explode the magazine, and frightened the governor
into surrender within a week. At Winchester the battering-guns
made in a day a breach wide enough for thirty men abreast to
enter. 'We played there,' says Hugh Peters, 'with our granadoes
from our mortarpieces, with the best effect that I have seen,
which brake down the mansion house in many places, cut off a
commissioner of theirs by the thighs (the most austere and
wretched instrument in that country), and at last blew up their
flag of defiance into the air, and tore the pinnacle in pieces upon
which it stood.' Next day, though it was Sunday, the bombard-
ment continued; 'the Lord's day', says Peters, 'we spent in
preaching and prayer, whilst our gunners were battering', and
that evening Winchester surrendered.[3]

Equally rapid and destructive was the operation of Cromwell's guns in Ireland. He took with him not less than eleven

[1] See Carlyle, *Cromwell*, Letter lxxxi and Appendix xi. In his letter to the
Committee of Carmarthen, 9th June 1648, he asks them to cast for him some
demicannon shot, and culverin shot, besides the large shells mentioned in
the following paragraph.

[2] Army accounts amongst the Exchequer papers.

[3] Sprigge, *Anglia Rediviva*, pp. 93, 134, 141.

battering-pieces of large size, and their efficiency was proved at the siege of Drogheda.[1] The siege began on the 3rd of September, the batteries began to play on the 9th, they made 'two reason-good breaches' on the 10th, and Cromwell stormed the town on that evening. At Wexford and Ross the governors began to treat on the day when the batteries opened.[2] Though Cromwell was repulsed with loss in his attempts to storm Kilkenny and Clonmel, his artillery appear to have done its part with perfect success, and the checks he received were due to new intrenchments which the besieged had constructed behind the breaches his guns had made.[3] Cromwell's successor, Ireton, was provided with equally powerful artillery. One of his batteries at the siege of Limerick consisted of twenty-eight guns, and he had also four mortar-pieces, one of which is said to have carried a shell weighing two hundredweight. But in spite of this the siege lasted nearly six months, and the town might have held out longer but for treachery within the garrison.[4] This siege introduced a new term into the military vocabulary of English soldiers. The shells which the besiegers termed 'granadoes', the besieged called 'bombs', so that this familiar word is a relic of the Cromwellian conquest of Ireland.[5]

When Cromwell invaded Scotland in 1650, though he had a considerable train of artillery, it does not seem to have included

[1] On 17th July 1649 the Council of State issued a warrant to the ordnance officers to provide Captain Edward Tomlins, the comptroller of Cromwell's artillery, with certain necessaries out of the navy stores. From the list given, the train of guns appears to have consisted of two cannon of eight inches, two cannon of seven inches, two demicannon, two twenty-four-pounders, three culverins, two demiculverins and ten sakers – that is to say, eleven siege-guns and twelve field-pieces. The necessaries required were ladles, rammers, sponges, budge-barrels, lanthorns, etc. (see *Cal. State Papers, Dom.*, 1649–50, p. 237).

[2] Carlyle, *Cromwell*, Letters cv, cvii, cviii, cxii.

[3] Ibid., Letter cxxx.; *Cromwelliana*, p. 81. The various accounts of the siege of Clonmel are collected by Mr Gilbert, *Aphorismical Discovery*, ii, 408–17.

[4] Gilbert, *Aphorismical Discovery*, iii, 238, 239, 253.

[5] A diary of the siege represents the Irish as saying that the English 'laboured to beat them out with bombshells (so they called our mortar shot), but they would beat us away with snowballs,' meaning that the winter would oblige the English to raise the siege (Gilbert, *Aphorismical Discovery*, iii, 253). Colonel Venables is described in 1650 as using 'bumboes' against Toom (*History of the Warr of Ireland*, p. 117).

an adequate number of siege-guns.[1] After his victory at Dunbar Cromwell marched to Stirling, intending to take it by storm, but found it too strong. 'I heard some of the wisest and greatest commanders affirm,' says a letter, 'that had they had great guns they might in all probability have mastered the place.' Cromwell at all events thought so, and on the return of the messenger sent to London with the news of Dunbar, 'asked him among other things for great guns, but received no satisfactory answer: he seemed displeased and intimated a great impatience for them.'[2] Accordingly a number of heavy guns and mortars were sent him in the course of the next two months, which he used to besiege Edinburgh Castle and to reduce strongholds such as Dirleton, Borthwick and Tantallon Castles. Some demicannons were borrowed from the fleet, others were sent from Hull and Newcastle, others from the magazine in the Tower.[3] At Edinburgh the mortars appear to have been most effective in producing the surrender, at Tantallon the heavy guns.[4] Monck, who was lieutenant-general of the ordnance in Cromwell's army, conducted the sieges of Tantallon, Blackness and other minor fortresses, and was left to reduce Stirling and Dundee when Cromwell followed Charles the Second into England.[5] The battering train with which Monck captured Stirling consisted of four guns and two mortars, and the shells of the latter were so effective, that after twenty-four of them had been fired into the castle, the Highlanders who formed its garrison mutinied and forced the governor to surrender.[6] At Dundee Monck had besides these guns

[1] Cromwell was voted a train of artillery sufficient for a marching force of 12,000 men, but what proportion was held sufficient the papers do not state. The train consisted of 690 men, including a company of 100 firelocks (*Cal. State Papers, Dom.*, 1650, pp. 46, 111, 141; *Cromwelliana*, p. 85).

[2] *Mercurius Politicus*, 26th September to 3rd October 1650, p. 289. On their march to Stirling, 'by reason of the badness of the way,' says a letter from Cromwell, 'we were forced to send back two pieces of our greatest artillery' (Carlyle, Letter cxlix).

[3] *Cal. State Papers, Dom.*, 1650, pp. 369, 438–9. Many guns were captured when Edinburgh Castle surrendered. 'I believe all Scotland hath not so much brass ordnance in it as this place,' said Cromwell (Carlyle, Letter clxi). For a list see *Cromwelliana*, pp. 98, 99.

[4] W. S. Douglas, *Cromwell's Scotch Campaigns*, pp. 200–2, 230–3.

[5] Gumble, *Life of Monck*, p. 39.

[6] Firth, *Scotland and the Commonwealth*, 1895, p. 3.

and mortars a battery of ten naval-guns, with which he made
two large breaches in a couple of days, and then took the town
by assault.[1]

From all these instances it seems evident that the efficiency
of the artillery had increased as the organization of the army
improved. The siege-guns used were heavier and more numerous: their fire more accurate and more concentrated. After the
guns had made a practicable breach immediate preparations
were made for an assault. Often, indeed, as at Bristol, Bridgwater and Dartmouth, the assault took place before any breach
had been made. It was characteristic of the strategy of the generals of the New Model that they preferred to storm, whenever
there was the least chance of success, rather than to adopt the
slower and surer method of gradual approaches. For they held
that for political reasons it was necessary to bring the war to a
close as rapidly as possible, and that more lives were lost in the
sickness which a long siege produced in a besieging army than
were expended in one brief and bloody struggle. They chose to
imitate, and that consciously, the methods of Gustavus Adolphus, rather than the more cautious and conservative siege
tactics of Spinola and Prince Maurice. 'This was his order,
mostly,' says *The Swedish Intelligencer* of Gustavus, 'in taking of
a town: he would not stand entrenching and building redoubts at
a mile's distance; but clap down with his army presently, about
cannon shot from it. There would he begin his approaches, get
to their walls, batter, and storm presently: and if he saw the
place were not by a running pull to be taken, he would not lose
above five or six days before it, but rise and to another.'[2]

Fairfax faithfully followed the example of Gustavus. 'He was
still for action in field or fortification,' says Sprigge in his history
of the exploits of the New Model, 'esteeming nothing unfeasible
for God, and for man to do in God's strength, if they would be
up and doing; and thus his success hath run through a line cross
to that of old soldiery, of long sieges and slow approaches; and
he hath done all so soon, because he was ever doing.'[3] Cromwell
pursued the same plan in Ireland, never hesitating to risk an

---

[1] Ibid., pp. 2–12.   [2] *The Swedish Intelligencer*, iii, 188.

[3] Sprigge, *Anglia Rediviva*, p. 324; see the reasons for storming Bridgwater and Dartmouth, ibid., pp. 77, 181.

assault rather than to spend time in a scientific siege or methodical blockade. In the long run, he told the Parliament, such a
course was economical. 'Those towns that are to be reduced,' he
wrote in April 1650, 'especially one or two of them, if we should
proceed by the rules of other states, would cost you more money
than this army hath had since we came over. I hope, through the
blessing of God, they will come cheaper to you.'[1] At Drogheda
and Wexford this plan was successful; at Clonmel, which was
more skilfully defended, it resulted in a bloody repulse in which
Cromwell lost about a thousand men and many of his best
officers.

When a storm was resolved upon, which usually took place
after a debate and a vote in the council of war, detailed arrangements were made, and instructions issued to the officers employed. If the besieged place was defended by a ditch the soldiers
were set to work to collect brushwood in order to make fagots.
At Sherborne Castle, Fairfax ordered 'every soldier to cut his
fresh fagot, whereby in two hours' time they had above 6,000
fagots, with which to fill the trenches and throw stones and
rubbish upon them'. Fagots were used for the same purpose at
the storming of Bristol and Bridgwater. In advancing to the
assault the soldiers usually carried these fagots on their backs,
but Ludlow records that when he took a certain castle in Ireland
he ordered every soldier 'to carry a fagot before him, as well to
defend himself as to fill up the enemy's trenches, or fire his gates,
as there might be occasion'.[2]

At Bridgwater the ditch proved too broad or too deep to be
filled up in this way, so a new device had to be employed.
Fairfax applied to Hammond, the commander of his artillery,
and Hammond, 'a gentleman of a most dexterous and ripe invention for all such things,' devised eight wooden bridges, each
thirty or forty feet in length, to be laid across the ditch by the
storming parties, which bridges proved perfectly effective.[3]

Besides these fagots and bridges it was necessary to construct
scaling-ladders. At Bristol twenty ladders were allotted for every

---

[1] Carlyle, *Cromwell*, Letter cxxx.

[2] Sprigge, *Anglia Rediviva*, pp. 75, 94, 95, 104, 111; Ludlow, *Memoirs*, i,
272.

[3] Sprigge, p. 76.

breach, and two men told off to carry each ladder, who were given five shillings each for that service. Minute directions for the organization of the storming parties, and the duties to be performed by each particular detachment, are contained in Sprigge's account of the storming of Bristol,[1] which affords the best example of the manner in which an assault was conducted.

One rule generally, if not universally, observed was, that the regiments appointed to storm were selected by lot. For example, at the siege of Bridgwater 'lots were drawn for every one to take their posts, some to storm, some to be reserves, others to alarm' (i.e., to make a false attack).[2] Often the storming party was headed by dismounted horsemen. At Dundee, for instance, Monck ordered 300 horse and dragoons 'to fall on with the foot with pistol and sword'.[3] At Clonmel also the stormers were headed by dismounted horse, one reason alleged being that 'the foot were not so well satisfied that the horse, especially in storms, did not run equal hazards with them'. A better reason was that the armour of the cavalrymen enabled them to lead the way with less risk than the infantry. When Ireton stormed a fort at Limerick he drew out one trooper from each troop of horse to head the forlorn hope. 'They were armed with back, breast, and head piece, and furnished with hand grenadoes, and led by a gentleman of the general's life guard.'[4]

[1] Colonel Weldon's brigade, consisting of four regiments which were to attack on the Somersetshire side, was ordered 'to storm in three places, viz., 200 men in the middle, 200 on each side as forlorn hopes, to begin the storm; 20 laders to each place, 2 men to carry each ladder and to have 5s. a piece; 2 sergeants that attended the service of the ladders to have 20s. a man: each musketeer that followed the ladder to carry a fagot, a sergeant to command them, and to have the same reward; 12 files of men with firearms and pikes to follow the ladders to each place where the storm was to be; those to be commanded each by a captain and a lieutenant; the lieutenant to go before with 5 files, the captain to second him with the other 7 files; the 200 men that were appointed to second the storm to furnish each party of them 20 pioneers who were to march in their rear; the 200 men each to be commanded by a field officer, and the pioneers each by a sergeant; (those pioneers were to throw down the line and to make way for the horse); the party that was to make good the line, to possess the guns and turn them; a gentleman of the ordnance, gunners, and matrosses, to enter with the parties; the drawbridge to be let down; two regiments & a half to storm it after the foot if way were made' (Sprigge, p. 105). A file signified, at this time, six men.

[2] Sprigge, p. 77.

[3] *Scotland and the Commonwealth*, p. 11; cf. Sprigge, p. 106.

[4] Gilbert, *Aphorismical Discovery*, ii, 411; Ludlow, *Memoirs*, i, 275.

One more point deserves notice. Just as in battles it was customary for each army to use a 'field-word' and a 'field-sign' to distinguish friends from enemies, so it was usual in sieges to distinguish the assaulting party by a common watchword and by some badge, or some peculiarity in their dress. At Dartmouth in 1646 the word given was 'God with us', and 'the signal of the soldiers was their shirts out before and behind'. At Dundee, five years later, Monck gave his soldiers the same watchword, and their sign was 'a white cloth or shirt hanging out behind'. The utility of this particular device was plain. It gave the soldier the strongest motive for keeping his face to the foe, for if he turned tail he was liable to be taken for an enemy.[1]

Yet, as a precaution against cowardice, it was not needed. One of the chief characteristics of the soldiers of the New Model – and of the soldiers of the Republic and the Protectorate too – was the desperate courage they exhibited in the attack of fortified places. The 6,000 men whom Cromwell sent to Flanders to serve under Turenne against the Spaniards were for the most part newly raised troops, but the boldness with which they stormed the outworks of St Venant, Dunkirk and Ypres, gained the respect and the admiration of their allies. More than once they earned the hearty praise of Turenne. Sir Thomas Morgan's account of the exploits of these 6,000 English soldiers in Flanders is highly coloured, but the facts he relates are confirmed by other evidence. One of the most characteristic passages is his description of the attack on Ypres with which their campaign ended. The Anglo-French army had been only four days before Ypres when news came that Condé with 15,000 men was at hand to raise the siege. Turenne proposed to keep his forces under arms every night ready to fight the relieving army. Such a plan, replied Morgan, would destroy the besieging troops without fighting. Fatigue would soon render them only fit to be knocked on the head. Morgan urged Turenne to assault the outworks of the city at once, 'and so put all things out of doubt with expedition'. 'The major-general had no sooner said this, but Marshal Turenne joined his hands, and looked up towards the heavens and said, "Did ever my master, the King of France, or the King of Spain, attempt a counterscarp upon an assault, where there

[1] Sprigge, p. 181; *Scotland and the Commonwealth*, p. 12.

were three half-moons covered with cannon, and the ramparts of
the town playing point blank into the counterscarp?' Further
he said, "What will the King my master think of me, if I expose
his army to these hazards?" And he rose up, and fell into a pas-
sion, stamping with his feet, and shaking his locks and grinning
with his teeth, he said, Major-General Morgan had made him
mad.' Morgan argued with Turenne, and by degrees persuaded
him to sanction the attempt. It was agreed that 650 English
and 1,300 Frenchmen should attack the three half-moons (or
redoubts) at dusk, and endeavour afterwards to effect a lodg-
ment in the counterscarp. When the time came, the English
redcoats fell on two of the half-moons, 'throwing the enemy into
the moat and turning the cannon upon the town'. Meanwhile the
French, moving more slowly from their approaches, attacked
the other half-moon and were beaten off. Seeing this, Morgan
turned to his officers and soldiers, and told them to give the
French a little help. In response the redcoats cried, 'Shall we fall
on in order, or happy-go-lucky?' The major-general said, 'In
the name of God, go at it happy-go-lucky,' and 'immediately
the redcoats fell on and were on the top of it, knocking the enemy
down and casting them into the moat'. Thus the third half-moon
was taken, and then Morgan lodged his Englishmen on the
counterscarp, and next morning, as he had predicted, Ypres
surrendered.[1]

It would not be wise to accept implicitly Morgan's disparage-
ment of the French troops or his encomium on his own soldiers.
And yet the narrative has its value as representing in a concrete
form the military ideal which a general of the period thought
good to set before the English soldiers of the next generation.

Scarcely equal in what may be called siegecraft to the more
scientific generals of the continent, English leaders supplied its
place by the development of other qualities and the adoption of
different methods.

The engineers were a neglected branch of service in the New
Model army and its successors, and that necessarily influenced
the character of siege operations. As a rule the chief-engineers
were foreigners, especially in the earlier years of the war. The
engineer-general of the New Model was a Dutchman or Walloon,

[1] *Harleian Miscellany*, ed. Park, iii, 347–9.

Peter Manteau Van Dalem, and in Scotland Cornelius Van Bemmel seems to have been Cromwell's chief-engineer.[1] On the King's side, Beckman, a Swede, and De Gomme, a Walloon, are most often mentioned.[2] Englishmen gradually came to the front as the wars continued. Captain Hooper appears on the list of the New Model as engineer-extraordinary. He had served in the garrison of Nottingham under Colonel Hutchinson, and was forced to leave his charge because the local clergy prosecuted him as 'a leader of separatists'. At Banbury and Raglan Hooper 'gave good demonstration of his skill'.[3] At Sherborne Castle the siege works seem to have been under the supervision of Captain Richard Deane, the comptroller of the ordnance, and at Oxford 'the management of the works, lines, and approaches' was entrusted to Major-General Skippon, 'who went through the same with much dexterity.'[4]

But whether native or foreign the chief-engineer was always hampered by the difficulty that he had very little skilled labour at his disposal. It is true that there was one company of pioneers attached to the New Model, but they were labourers of the lowest class, not trained sappers or artificers. A foot soldier who committed a crime deserving disgrace rather than death was usually punished by degradation to the position of a pioneer.[5] The pioneers, therefore, were too few numerically and too unskilled individually to be of great service. Consequently, whenever mining operations were contemplated, it was necessary to call in skilled assistance. At the siege of Sherborne Castle in

---

[1] Sprigge, *Anglia Rediviva*, p. 330. Another engineer was the German Joachim Hane. Cromwell also employed to fortify Mardyke one Christian Denokson, 'a very good artist, especially in wooden works' (Letter ccxxiv).

[2] A life of De Gomme is given in the *Dictionary of National Biography*. Beckman is described by Lord Digby as 'our incomparable engineer' (Rushworth, v, 815).

[3] Sprigge, *Anglia Rediviva*, pp. 259, 297, 302; *Life of Col. Hutchinson*, ed. 1885, ii, 32, 77.

[4] Sprigge, pp. 96, 258.

[5] Markham in his *Epistles of War*, 1622, says: 'When any common soldier shall commit a slight offence savouring either of carelessness, slothfulness, or baseness then presently to take away his sword and make him a pioneer: which in times past I have known so hateful and intolerable to every quick and understanding spirit that they would with more alacrity have run to the rack, the bolts, or strappado, nay even to death itself, rather than to the mortal degradation' (Walton, p. 573).

1645 Fairfax sent for a contingent of Mendip miners.[1] At the siege of Edinburgh Castle in 1650 Cromwell summoned English miners from Derbyshire, and impressed all the Scottish colliers near Edinburgh.[2]

In the same way in formally conducted sieges the country was generally called upon to supply labourers to build forts and intrenchments. The English soldier of the period was very reluctant to dig. Gustavus Adolphus, who was 'a great spademan', taught his soldiers to dig, and obliged them, it was said, 'to work more for nothing than the States of Holland could get wrought in three years, though they should bestow a ton of gold every year'.[3] But even he found it difficult to get the Scottish regiments in his service to work at intrenching themselves as he thought necessary. Monck noted the same disinclination amongst the English soldiers in Scotland; they were too lazy to build their own huts.[4]

In sieges therefore it was generally necessary to give extra

[1] Sprigge, *Anglia Rediviva*, pp. 91, 92, 95.

[2] See Douglas, *Cromwell's Scotch Campaigns*, pp. 199, 200.

[3] 'Likewise his Majestie was to be commended for his diligence by night and by day, in setting forwards his workes; for he was ever out of patience till once they were done, that he might see his Souldiers secured and guarded from their enemies; for when he was weakest, he digged most in the ground; for in one yeare what at Swede, Francford, Landsberg, Brandenburg, Verbum, Tannermonde, Wittenberg, and Wirtzburg, he caused his Souldiers to worke more for nothing, than the States of Holland could get wrought in three yeares, though they should bestow every yeare a Tunne of Gold: and this he did, not onely to secure his Souldiers from the enemy, but also to keepe them from idlenesse.

'Here also we found by experience, that the spade and the shovell are ever good companions in danger, without which we had lost the greatest part of our followers. Therefore in all occasions of service, a little advantage of ground is ever profitable against horse, foote, or Cannon. And for this it was that the best Commanders made ever most use of the spade and the shovell, and that in such ground as was found most commodious for their safeties' (Monro, pt. ii, pp. 41, 42).

[4] From Monck's *Order-Book*, 11th July 1655. 'Letter to Col. Brayne that the Generall would have him endeavour to repaire the souldiers hutts and to make them hold out till the next summer, That hee has written to my Lord Protector to know his pleasure concerning the building of a castle there, but has hadd noe answer to it, and monies are so scarce that wee shall hardly thinke of itt this yeare. Concerning the finding of timber to build the souldiers hutts the Generall is willing to doe itt, butt would have him agree with the souldiers as cheape as hee can for doing them, but in most places where the Generall has bin itt was usuall for souldiers to make uppe hutts for themselves without being paid for them.'

G

pay to the soldiers for their labour on the siege work. Before Sherborne Castle, for instance, 'very freely did the soldiers work in the mines and galleries and making of batteries, every man being rewarded twelvepence for the day, and as much for the night, the service being hot and hazardous'.[1]

There was one part of the engineers' business, however, the bridging of rivers, in which the engineer officers on both sides attained considerable skill. Ward in his *Animadversions of War* gives descriptions of several kinds of bridges employed in continental warfare; some were constructed with flat-bottomed boats or leather pontoons, others built on casks, wooden tressels and ropes; and for each of these he adds a diagram explaining its construction.[2] Similar bridges were used by English generals during the Civil War. At the siege of York the Scots made two, if not three, boat bridges over the Ouse above and below the city, and on his way to join the besiegers Manchester made another bridge of the same kind over the Trent at Gainsborough.[3] At Chester the Parliamentarians who besieged the city made a bridge of boats,[4] while Prince Maurice, on the Royalist side, 'invented a new fashioned bridge' of a sort never seen before in England. 'He placed a boat on each side of the river Dee, and fastened cords to them from one side to the other; and upon the cords laid strong canvas drawn out and stretched so stiff and hard, and which was so firm that three men could walk abreast on it.'[5]

During the campaigns in Ireland the number of rivers and the fewness of permanent bridges made these temporary erections still more necessary. Cromwell astonished the Irish by the bridge which he made across the Barrow at Ross. It is described in a contemporary chronicle as 'a wonder to all men and understood by no man'.[6] Ireton, at the siege of Limerick, employed 'float bridges', evidently pontoon bridges. At the siege of

[1] Sprigge, p. 92.   [2] Ward, pp. 374–6.

[3] Terry, *Life of Alexander Leslie*, pp. 219, 230.

[4] *History of the Siege of Chester* (undated), pp. 90, 103.

[5] Quoted from a newspaper of March 1645, by Mr Fortescue in *Macmillan's Magazine* for August 1894, p. 270.

[6] Murphy, *Cromwell in Ireland*, p. 218.

Carlow he made two bridges, one of which was of timber, while the other is said to have been built of bulrushes. But the best example of the skill of the Cromwellian army in bridge-building was afforded at the battle of Worcester.[1] It was necessary to bridge two rivers, the Teame and the Severn. Accordingly, when Fleetwood and Deane advanced from Upton on Severn towards Worcester, they brought up the river with them twenty great boats and planks. 'My Lord General fell roundly to work, and in half an hour a bridge was made over Severn and another over Teame just where both rivers run into one.'[2]

But to return to sieges. One result of the deficiency of engineers in the English armies of the period was, that when it was impossible to make an immediate breach and to assault at once, the besiegers generally resorted to a blockade. This plan was followed by the Scots and the Northern Parliamentarians at the siege of Carlisle. The siege extended from November 1644 to June 1645, and the garrison held out until they had eaten their horses.[3] At Carlisle the besiegers built several isolated forts, whilst at Colchester, in 1648, Fairfax not only built about ten forts, but connected them by regular lines of circumvallation, so that exit was completely impossible. These are shown in the picture-plan reproduced in Mr Gardiner's history.[4] Though the siege lasted little more than ten weeks, the besieged were reduced to far greater straits than the inhabitants of Carlisle. Horse-flesh, says a Royalist, was by the beginning of August 'grown so delicious a food amongst the soldiers that we could scarcely secure our horses in the stables, for every morning one stable or other was robbed, and our horses knocked on the head and sold in the shambles by the pound; nor was there in a short time a dog left, for it was customary for each soldier to reserve half his ammunition loaf, and in a morning walk the streets, and if he discovered a dog to drop a piece of bread, and so decoy him on till within his reach and then with the butt end of his musquet knock his brains out, and march away with him to his quarters.

[1] Gilbert, *Aphorismical Discovery*, iv, 218, 240, 241, 255.

[2] Carey, *Memorials of the Civil War*, ii, 357.

[3] See Isaac Tullie's *Narrative of the Siege of Carlisle*, which gives a detailed account of its incidents from the point of view of the besieged. Carlisle was defended by Sir Thomas Glemham.

[4] Gardiner, *Great Civil War*, iv, 152.

I have known six shillings given for the side of a dog, and yet but a small one neither.'[1]

At the siege of Limerick, which lasted from June to October 1651, Ireton, imitating Fairfax, built a number of detached forts and connected them by a line of intrenchments. Some of these forts seem to have been still in existence when the troops of William the Third besieged the town forty years later.[2] The garrison of Limerick, like that of Colchester, endeavoured to husband its resources by turning useless mouths out of the town, but Ireton inexorably drove them back, as Fairfax had done.

'Yesterday,' says a letter from Colchester dated 18th August 1648, 'there came out a woman and five children, one sucking at her breast; she fell down at our guards, beseeching them to pass beyond the line, the people in the town looking to see if they had admittance, resolving to follow them; but the guards were necessitated to turn them back again, or otherwise hundreds would come out.' Three or four days later a troop of 500 women came out of Colchester, and boldly marched towards Colonel Rainsborough's quarters. He fired upon them with blank cartridge to frighten them back, but they still came on. Rainsborough then sent out a few soldiers, with orders to strip some of them. They stripped four and the rest ran off, but the garrison refused to readmit them, and they remained between the walls of the town and the Parliamentary lines. Fairfax when he heard of it was greatly enraged, and remonstrated with the Royalist commanders for their cruelty, saying they should answer for the blood of these women, but his remonstrance was unheeded. Luckily for these miserable victims of war, Colchester surrendered about a week later.[3]

Something of the same sort occurred at Limerick. The besieged Irish were suffering from plague as well as famine. 'Great numbers of people,' says Ludlow, 'endeavoured to get out of the town, sent out by the garrison either as useless persons or to

[1] Matthew Carter, *A true relation of that honourable though unfortunate expedition of Kent, Essex and Colchester*, p. 180; cf. pp. 158, 170, 196; Rushworth, vii, 1216, 1221.

[2] See Story's *Impartial History of the Wars of Ireland*, 1693, pt. ii, p. 38 and the plan showing 'Ireton's Fort'. Story also mentions 'Cromwell's Fort', p. 189.

[3] Rushworth, vii, 1232, 1236; cf. Carter, p. 191.

spread the contagion amongst us. The Deputy (i.e., Ireton) commanded them to retire, and threatened to shoot any that should come out for the future; but this not being sufficient to make them desist, he caused two or three to be taken out in order to be executed, and the rest to be whipped back into the town. One of those that were to be hanged was the daughter of an old man, who was in that number which was to be sent back; he desired that he might be hanged in the room of his daughter, but that was refused, and he with the rest driven back into the town. After which a gibbet was erected in the sight of the town walls, and one or two persons hanged up who had been condemned for other crimes, and by this means they were so terrified that we were no farther disturbed on that account.'[1]

[1] Ludlow, *Memoirs*, i, 284.

CHAPTER VIII

The Pay of the Army

THE QUESTION OF the maintenance of the army demands somewhat detailed treatment, especially as it is generally passed over in silence by military historians. It is not easy to give a complete account of the method in which the army was paid, fed and clothed, because many of the necessary documents are missing, and because it never occurred to any contemporary writer to draw up a description of the system of military administration which existed. There is a large amount of information about the financial side of the subject, but even that is in many respects defective. We have, for instance, no budgets showing what money was expended annually upon the army, and how it was expended. Yet there are occasional balance-sheets of the national income and a series of establishments of the army from which an approximate idea of the military expenditure of the period may be gathered.

In the first years of the war all was confusion, and it is impossible to compute the cost of the army which fought under Essex. When it was reorganized in March 1644, and reduced to 10,500 men, £30,000 a month was considered sufficient for its maintenance. Essex then complained that £34,000 a month was allowed for the support of Manchester's army.[1] A year later, with the formation of the New Model, fuller information becomes accessible. The Committee of Both Kingdoms originally estimated that the pay of the 21,000 men of the New Model would amount to £44,955 per month, that is to say £585,000 a year, for as the soldiers were paid every twenty-eight days, the monthly pay must be multiplied by thirteen, not by twelve, in calculating the total for the year.[2] But in reality this £585,000

[1] Husbands, *Ordinances*, ii, 442. The exact sum fixed was £30,504. For Essex's remonstrance, see *Old Parliamentary History*, xiii, 152.

[2] *Cal. State Papes, Dom.*, 1644–5, p. 232; Husbands, *Ordinances*, ii, 599.

was not sufficient. The accounts of the Treasurers at War for the army under Fairfax's command show that they received from 28th March 1645 to 1st March 1647 £1,185,551, and the pay of the army was, nevertheless, many weeks in arrear at the latter date.[1] A report presented to Parliament on 27th March 1647 showed that £331,000 was still owing to the New Model.[2] In the following winter the army was increased by adding one more regiment of horse and three of foot, so that by the establishment of 3rd November 1647 its pay came to £54,226 per month, or about £705,000 per annum.[3] In March 1649 there is, for the first time, an estimate for the cost of not only the New Model, but of all the forces in the pay of the nation both in England and Ireland. A hundred and twenty thousand pounds a month, or £1,560,000 a year, was the sum which the Council of State judged needful.[4] An estimate made about two years later, in August 1651, just before the battle of Worcester, shows a further increase resulting from the war with Scotland; for the sum necessary had then risen to £157,000 per month, or about £2,041,000 per annum.[5] Nor did the battle of Worcester and the complete subjugation of Scotland produce so great or so immediate a reduction of the military charges as might have been expected. A report presented to Parliament on 2nd December 1652 showed that in spite of the recent disbandings £1,443,680 would be required for the maintenance of the army in the coming year.[6] In the autumn of 1654 the cost of the land forces had slightly increased; for it was estimated at £116,000 per month, that is £1,508,000 per annum.[7] Under the rule of the Protector, however, there was a considerable reduction, and in April 1657 Cromwell roughly estimated the pay of the army as coming to upwards of £1,100,000 per annum.[8] This was probably an under-estimate; for, in April 1659, under Richard Cromwell, the army

[1] Grey's *Examination of Neal's 'History of the Puritans,'* iii, Appendix iii, iv.

[2] *Commons' Journals*, v, 126.

[3] This establishment is printed at length in the *Journals of the Lords*, x, 66.

[4] *Cal. State Papers, Dom.*, 1649–50, p. 28; *Commons' Journals*, vi, 157

[5] *Commons' Journals*, vi, 617.

[6] 'Report of Col. Downes,' *Commons' Journals*, vii, 224.

[7] *Antiquarian Repertory*, ii, 12.

[8] Speech xiii in Carlyle, 21st April 1657.

cost about £1,244,000 per annum, the increase being partly due to the cost of the troops serving in Flanders.[1] A year later, when the Long Parliament triumphed over the army and Monck became commander-in-chief, a renewed attempt was made to reduce the military expenditure. The establishment for the forces in England and Wales, dated 27th February 1659-60, came to £638,093, including the cost of the garrisons.[2] But as the forces in Scotland and Ireland cannot have cost much less than £500,000 a year, the real reduction was not much over £100,000. Finally, to complete this series of figures, it may be added that in the autumn of 1660, when the final disbanding of the army took place, nearly £700,000 had to be raised in order to pay off the forces in England and Scotland.[3]

Taking the whole period from the King's death to the Restoration, it is clear that the cost of the army ran from £1,200,000 to about £2,000,000 per annum.

The pay of the private soldier varied slightly at different dates between 1645 and 1660. When the New Model was originally organized the foot soldier was paid eightpence a day, the dragoon one and sixpence, and the trooper in a regiment of horse two shillings.[4] In 1649 a change took place. In 1645 the average price of the quarter of wheat had been about thirty-five shillings, in 1647-48 it was over sixty-two shillings, in 1648-49 it was over sixty-seven shillings, in 1649-50 it was sixty-five shillings and sixpence.[5] Everything was therefore dearer, and the pay of the soldiers was insufficient to defray the cost of their food and lodging. Their whole pay in fact hardly sufficed for the purpose. It was said that in many cases people were 'obliged to allow sixteen-pence per diem or more for a foot soldier, and three shillings for a horse and man, to avoid the quartering of them'. Unless their pay was raised, either the soldiers would be half-starved or the people on whom they were billeted would be ruined. Accordingly on 12th May 1649 Parliament passed an Act raising the pay all round. 'In regard of the present dearth,'

---

[1] *Commons' Journals*, vii, 628-30.   [2] *Harleian MSS.*, 6,844, f. 182.

[3] *Old Parliamentary History*, xxiii, 3; *Commons' Journals*, viii, 176.

[4] *Cal. State Papers, Dom.*, 1644-5, p. 232; *Commons' Journals*, iv, 16.

[5] Rogers, *History of Prices*, v, 826.

an additional penny a day was added to the pay of every foot soldier in a garrison, twopence a day to those belonging to foot regiments in the field, and threepence a day to troopers and dragoons.[1]

A similar sum was also added, under the same conditions, as 'billet-money', in order to enable the soldiers to pay the cost of their quarters. This additional pay, or such proportion of it as he thought fit, the Lord-General was empowered to assign to the different regiments of the army under his command.[2] For the next five years, therefore, there was a considerable increase in the pay of the soldiers. Foot soldiers of the army in Scotland in 1651 got tenpence a day, dragoons two shillings, and troopers half a crown.[3] This lasted till 1655, when, by a resolution of the Council of State on 20th July, the pay of each foot soldier in England and Scotland was reduced to ninepence a day for the field forces and eightpence for those in garrison. At the same time troopers were reduced from two and sixpence to two and threepence per diem, and dragoons from two shillings to one and eightpence per diem.[4] The reduction was reasonable, for the cost of living was now much less than in 1649. In 1653–4 the average price of wheat was twenty-five shillings a quarter, in 1654–5 little more than twenty-one shillings a quarter.[5] Moreover, it was for financial reasons absolutely necessary to economize by diminishing the pay of the army and by disbanding superfluous troops. Naturally, however, it excited some discontent amongst the soldiers, which the opponents of the Protector strove to utilize by representing the diminution as really caused by the extravagance of his court and household.

'Truly,' wrote a pamphleteer, 'my bowels yearn for the poor

---

[1] 'An Act for the more certain and constant Supply of the Soldiery with Pay and for the preventing of any further oppression or damage to the people by free quarter or billet,' 12th May 1649; cf. *Commons' Journals*, vi, 208.

[2] See *The Moderate*, 19th to 26th June 1649, for Fairfax's orders as to the assignment of this additional pay.

[3] Establishment for the Army in Scotland, 20th October 1651, *Clarke MSS.*, xliii, 1.

[4] *Cal. State Papers, Dom.*, 1655, p. 252; Establishment for the Army in Scotland, 26th July, 1655, *Clarke MSS.*, xliii, 54.

[5] Rogers, *History of Prices*, v, 826.

soldiers, who have run so many hazards and fought so many
famous battles, stormed so many towns, waded through so many
rivers with the loss of limbs and blood; besides all the hunger
and cold and lodging on the ground, which they have gone
through during summer service in winter season; and after all
this to have the tenth part of their pay taken away and spent in
your new court, that the gentlemen Ushers, the gentlemen
Waiters, the Grooms of the Stole, gentlemen Sewers, besides the
fidlers and others that I could name which shine in their silver
and gold, and that these might be maintained the poor soldier
must pay a penny a day.'[1]

Two and threepence a day for the horse, one and eightpence
for the dragoons, and ninepence for the foot, continued to be
the regular scale of pay until the Restoration.

There was a slight change however in 1659. Corn suddenly
went up again, and in 1658–9 its average price was nearly fifty-
eight shillings a quarter. Moreover, the death of Cromwell and
the accession of the feeble Richard gave an opportunity to the
discontented in the army. In November 1658 a petition was
circulated in Fleetwood's regiment of horse for an increase of
threepence a day in their pay, so as to restore the rate which had
existed before the reduction of 1655. But a court-martial punished the promoter by expulsion from the army, and no more
was heard of the petition.[2] Nevertheless there was a certain
amount of reason in the demand, and on 31st May 1659 the
restored Long Parliament voted that the foot quartered in
London should receive an additional penny per day and the
horse threepence.[3]

During the same period some changes also took place in the
pay of the officers. That of the infantry officers remained unaltered. From 1648 to 1660 a colonel of foot received a pound a
day, a lieutenant-colonel fifteen shillings, a major thirteen, a
captain eight, a lieutenant four, an ensign three. But the pay of

---

[1] *The Picture of a New Courtier*, 1656, p. 10.

[2] *Clarke Papers*, iii, 170. Bordeaux in a letter to Mazarin, dated 29th
Sept. 1658, says that within the last few days the pay of the foot had been
raised by twopence a day, and that of the horse by fourpence (Guizot,
Richard Cromwell, i, 238). This statement, however, appears to be inac-
curate.

[3] *Commons' Journals*, vii, 669.

officers of horse varied slightly at different periods.[1] A colonel received throughout the period from 1647 to the Restoration twenty-two shillings per diem; a major fifteen shillings and eightpence, a captain ten shillings. A lieutenant's pay, which was five shillings and fourpence a day in 1648, rose to seven shillings in 1655, and finally settled in 1660 at six shillings. A cornet's pay rose from four shillings and eightpence in 1645 to five shillings and fourpence in 1655 and five shillings in 1660. A quartermaster's remained throughout fixed at four shillings a day. In the case of all these officers an additional sum was granted for horses, and varied according to their rank. A colonel, for instance, in 1651 drew pay for six horses at two shillings a day for each, so that he had an additional twelve shillings a day from this source. A major or a captain was at that date also allowed six horses at the same rate, and subalterns from two to four according to their rank. But during the later years of the Protectorate, when England was at peace, a colonel was paid for three horses only and subalterns for two.

From these figures it is evident that the officers both of horse and foot were well paid. As to the private soldiers, troopers in a regiment of regular cavalry were very well paid, but the foot soldier was much less handsomely treated. The infantryman of the New Model with his eightpence a day received, in Mr Gardiner's words, 'only a penny more than the daily remuneration of the agricultural labourer', and no more than had been paid by Queen Elizabeth to her soldiers at the end of her reign.[2] If we take the higher estimate given by Thorold Rogers, who calculates that the average remuneration of the labourer between 1640 and 1660 was from tenpence to a shilling a day,[3] it is clear that the foot soldier, whose pay at its highest never rose to more than tenpence, was comparatively in a still worse position

---

[1] The figures which follow are taken from the establishments for the years mentioned. The only one printed in full is that of 3rd November 1647, *Lords' Journals*, x, 66. Extracts from the Scottish establishments from 1655 are printed in Mackinnon's *History of the Coldstream Guards*, ii, 378–81. The Scottish establishment of 21st December 1657 is printed in *Scotland and the Protectorate*, p. 373, and the establishments of 1651 and 1655 for that country are amongst the *Clarke MSS.*, xliii, 1, 54. That for England, passed in February 1660, is *Harleian MS.*, 6,844, f. 182.

[2] *Great Civil War*, ii, 195.

[3] *History of Agriculture and Prices*, v, 666–9.

than Mr Gardiner supposes. In either case it was not the high rate of pay which attracted men to enlist in the infantry, and the necessity of resorting to impressment becomes easy to explain.

It is not easy to compare the rate of payment in the Cromwellian army with that in force in the army of to-day, because it is extremely difficult to determine the relative value of money then and now. So many different elements have to be taken into account that an exact estimate becomes impossible. Speaking roughly, it may be calculated that the value of money was at least three times as much as it is now.[1] Taking this ratio as a basis, the eightpence or tenpence the private of foot received may be held equivalent to two shillings or two and sixpence a day, that is to fourteen shillings or seventeen shillings and sixpence per week. The trooper's two shillings or half-crown would therefore mean six shillings or seven shillings and sixpence a day, that is two guineas or two guineas and a half per week. It must be remembered, however, that the trooper had to provide for the keep of his horse out of this sum, and that deductions were made from the pay of both infantry and cavalry for their food and clothing. Applying the same calculation to the officers, the comparatively high rate at which they were paid becomes obvious. The colonel of foot with his £1 a day received a sum equivalent to about £1,200 a year, the captain the equivalent of £480, the lieutenant £240, the ensign £180. As to the officers of cavalry, the variation in their pay caused by the different number of horses allowed for at different dates makes the comparison more difficult. If the allowance for horses is included, as it should be, the pay of a colonel of cavalry was, roughly speaking, from £1,600 to £2,000 per annum, and that of a captain from £720 to £1,200, during the period from 1647 to the Restoration.

[1] Mr J. Cordy Jeaffreson, in editing the *Middlesex Session Rolls* for the period of Charles the Second, habitually multiplies the fines imposed on delinquents by five in order to compute their amount in modern money (vol. iv, pp. 59, 267). But taking into consideration the cost of a soldier's maintenance, lodging, and equipment, between 1642 and 1660, and the comparative wages paid in different trades, it appears to me that this would be a great overestimate. I calculate that the shilling was worth between three and four times as much as it is now, so far as the soldier was concerned. In the text, to be on the safe side, I take the lower figure. (Written in 1901, before the fall in the value of money resulting from the war.)

Besides their pay there were special rewards for good service for all ranks of the army.

Parliament was very liberal in bestowing pecuniary rewards upon its generals and officers. Essex was voted lands worth £10,000 a year. Fairfax obtained an estate worth £4,000 a year and £10,000 down;[1] on Cromwell there were bestowed in 1646 lands worth £2,500 a year, and in 1651, after Worcester, lands to the value of a further £4,000 a year.[2] Officers of lower rank and less eminent merit received smaller gifts: Lambert £1,000 a year; Whalley and Monck £500 a year; Okey £300; Alured £200.[3] In all these cases the confiscated lands of the Royalists were the fund from which the gift was furnished. There were some Republicans who regarded this lavish liberality as a waste of public money. When Ireton received the news that Parliament had voted him £2,000 a year, he said: 'They had many just debts which he desired they would pay before they made any such presents: that he had no need of their land and therefore would not have it; and that he should be more contented to see them doing the service of the nation, than so liberal in disposing of the public treasure'. 'And truly,' adds Ludlow, who reports this speech, 'I believe he was in earnest.'[4]

At the same time gifts of money were voted to officers who performed some distinguished service. Major Bethell, who led the desperate charge which won the battle of Langport, was voted a sum of £200.[5] Officers whom the generals sent to bear Parliament the news of a victory were invariably rewarded in this way. Major Berry, who brought Cromwell's Preston despatch, was given £200; Major Harrison, sent up by Fairfax to report Goring's defeat at Langport, was voted a couple of horses.[6]

Parliament also bestowed decorations on both generals and officers. After Naseby, Fairfax was given 'a fair jewel set with rich diamonds of very great value', and a deputation of Members of Parliament 'tied it in blue riband and put it about his neck'. After the victory of Dunbar, Parliament ordered that

[1] *Commons' Journals*, iv, 679; v, 493; vi, 225, 228–9.

[2] Ibid., vii, 15; *Lords' Journals*, viii, 144–6; *Thurloe Papers*, i, 75.

[3] *Commons' Journals*, vii, 14.   [4] Ludlow, *Memoirs*, i, 286.

[5] *Commons' Journals*, iv, 208.   [6] Ibid., iv, 208; v, 680.

medals should be prepared for all, both officers and soldiers,
'that were in this service in Scotland' (10th September 1650).[1]
Thomas Simon was sent to Edinburgh to draw the head of the
Lord-General that it might be engraved on the medals. Cromwell himself suggested that a picture of the Parliament should
be set on one side, and on the other side an army 'with this
inscription over the head of it, "The Lord of Hosts," which was
our word that day'; but he remonstrated against the proposed
portrait of himself, saying, 'it will be very thankfully acknow-
ledged by me, if you will spare the having my effigies in it'.
But Parliament insisted, and the Dunbar medals bore the
victor's image in spite of his wishes.[2]

What makes this vote of Parliament more memorable is that
it was the first time a medal was voted to the common soldier.
The small gold medal preserved in the British Museum is probably a specimen of those given to the higher officers, while the
large silver ones, which are more common, represent those received by officers of lower rank. Perhaps the private soldiers
received their promised medal in copper, but there is no evidence
that they ever received one at all, and it is possible that they
obtained a gratuity instead.

Gratuities in money were indeed the usual method of reward-
ing privates who distinguished themselves by some notable
exploit, or risked their lives in some extraordinary piece of
service. The men who captured Royalist flags at Marston Moor
and at Dunbar were given ten shillings apiece.[3] At the assault
on Bristol the bearers of the ladders for the storming party were
promised five shillings each. At the siege of Sherborne Castle
the besiegers fell short of cannon-balls, so the soldiers 'fetched
off the bullets that we had shot from under the enemy's walls,
and had sixpence apiece for every bullet they so brought off,
which were worth as much to the service at that time.'[4]

A much more important addition to the private soldier's pay
was what was termed 'lawful plunder'. The horse, the arms,

[1] Markham, *Life of the Great Lord Fairfax*, p. 435; Ludlow, *Memoirs*, i,
130; Sprigge, *Anglia Rediviva*, p. 164.

[2] Carlyle, *Cromwell*, Letter clxv; Henfrey, *Numismata Cromwelliana*,
pp. 1–9; *Commons' Journals*, vi, 465.

[3] *Exchequer MSS.*; *Report on the Papers of Mr Leyborne Popham*, p. 75.

[4] Sprigge, *Anglia Rediviva*, pp. 92, 93, 105.

and even the contents of a prisoner's pockets, were regarded as
the legitimate prize of his captor.[1] A newspaper adds to its
narrative of the victory at Naseby the following intelligence.

'We hear Cromwell's sometime regiment are grown wiser, if
it may be so called: for having helped to beat the enemy out of
the field, they did not as at Marston Moor, leave them that
fought least to get most, but fell upon the good booty as well
as others: some had jewels, others diamond rings, others gold,
some were content with silver, good apparel, horses, and what
else they could get.'[2]

A soldier's best chance for lawful plunder was the capture of
a town or fortress by assault. In such cases it was usually given
up to pillage for a definite length of time. When Monck stormed
Dundee in 1651 he allowed his men to plunder the town for
twenty-four hours. 'The soldiers,' says a contemporary narrative, 'had the plunder of the town for all that day and night,
and had very large prize, many inhabitants of Edinburgh and
other places having sent their ware and geer thither.'[3] The ships
taken in the harbour seem to have been originally reserved for
the reward of the officers, and when the commissioners with the
army proposed to sell them for the State's benefit, Monck remonstrated, saying that the officers had no other prize, and that
the soldiers who had the booty of the town would be in a better
condition than the officers, who had had but a fortnight's pay
for a long time, and had no money to buy themselves clothes.[4]

[1] *The Swedish Intelligencer*, describing the capture of a party of Imperialist horse by the Swedes, says, 'Their horses and arms and buff coats were
good spoil to those that took them, and so was their month's means too
(i.e., a month's pay), which by the law of arms they were to pay for ransom'
(iv., 45). In England, Sprigge, narrating the storming of Sherborne, says
the Royalist soldiers threw down their arms and cried for quarter, 'which
our soldiers (inclining rather to booty than revenge) gave them, but stripped
they were to the purpose'. Again, at the capture of a church, which was used
as an outwork to Tiverton Castle, 'our soldiers . . . made all within prisoners,
plundered them, and stripped most of them to their shirts, yet gave them
their lives' (*Anglia Rediviva*, pp. 95, 155).

[2] *Cromwelliana*, p. 19, quoting the *Moderate Intelligencer* for 19th to 26th
June 1645.

[3] *Scotland and the Commonwealth*, p. 12.

[4] *Scotland and the Commonwealth*, p. 18. When the Scottish army under
Leslie stormed Newcastle (October 1645), a method of plundering more
profitable to the officers was adopted. 'After the entrance there was little
bloudshed, but the common Souldier betooke himselfe to what he could,
the Officer almost to what he would. For herein the Scots are more orderly

At the capture of Sherborne Castle in 1645 we are specially told that Fairfax's soldiers got plunder of great value, and that the next day they held a public market and sold what they could not carry away to the country people.[1] Still more vivid is Sprigge's description of the sack of Basing House a few months later.

'The plunder of the soldier continued till Tuesday night. One soldier had 120 pieces in gold for his share, others plate, others jewels: amongst the rest, one got three bags of silver, which (he being not able to keep his own counsel) grew to be common pillage amongst the rest, and the fellow had but one half-crown left for himself at last.

'Also the soldiers sold the wheat to country people, which they held up at good rates a while, but afterwards the market fell, and there was some abatements for haste. After that they sold the household-stuff, whereof there was good store; and the country loaded away many carts, and continued a great while fetching out all manner of household-stuff, till they had fetched out all the stools, chairs, and other lumber, all which they sold to the country people by piecemeal. In these great houses there was not one iron bar left in all the windows (save only what was in the fire) before night. And the last work of all was the lead, and by Thursday morning they had hardly left one gutter about the house. And what the soldiers left, the fire took hold on.'[2]

Incidents of this nature were not frequent, for by no means all the towns and fortresses taken by assault were given up to plunder. The practice had many evil results, though long usage had made it regarded as a sort of right of which the soldiers could hardly be deprived. It was deleterious to discipline, and gave the soldiers a taste for plundering which it subsequently required severe measures to check. It was more destructive to

---

then the English. Among our Armies commonly the Souldier gets the greatest share of the spoile, the Officers generally being not so earnest at the prey; and the English Souldiers are not so easily commanded as the Scots in such a case. For the Scots Souldiers will very orderly stand Sentinell at the dore they are appointed to, and for some small matter preserve a house with its appurtenances for their Commanders, so that the Towne was not (especially the best houses) spoiled in specie, but onely purged by a composition, which was fortuitous, according as the nature of the Chapmen was, some good bargaines, some ill' (Bowles, *Manifest Truths*, 1646, p. 10).

[1] Sprigge, *Anglia Rediviva*, p. 96.   [2] Ibid., p. 151.

property than profitable to the soldiers themselves, for they got little for their spoils when they sold them, and did a great deal of damage to obtain them. Hence in England the expedient of giving the soldiers a gratuity in lieu of the right to plunder was usually adopted, especially when populous towns were to be captured by assault. This composition was known as 'storm-money'. At Bridgwater, for instance, in July 1645, the soldiers of the New Model were promised five shillings a man, and as payment was delayed they finally received six shillings each.[1] At the assault on Bristol in the following September, Fairfax engaged that they should have a fortnight's extra pay in lieu of plunder. 'To prevent,' wrote the commissioners with the army to the Speaker, 'that ruin which must have fallen upon the city by their storming it, had not their appetite been cloyed by the expectation of this promise, than which a more noble act was not to be expected, nor more nobly entertained both by officer and soldier, who obeyed the general's commands therein to the full satisfaction of the city. And the purchase of so great a benefit to a city of such concernment we presume to say was not dear at fourteen days' pay to the soldier.' It would have cost the city, they continued, ten times as much had the soldiers 'been their own carvers'. So clear was this that the citizens willingly advanced £5,000 towards the £12,000 required to fulfil the general's promise.[2]

Even when towns capitulated, a ransom of this kind was often exacted. At the surrender of Reading in April 1643 the soldiers of the Earl of Essex 'to forbear plundering' were promised twelve shillings a man over and above their pay. But the treasury of the Parliament was empty, and as neither pay nor gratuity was forthcoming, a general mutiny was the result.[3] Seven years later, when Cromwell besieged Kilkenny, he informed the mayor in the course of the negotiations which preceded its surrender, that to save the city from pillage 'I promised the soldiery, that if we should take it by storm, the

---

[1] Sprigge, *Anglia Rediviva*, pp. 81, 106. See also *Cal. State Papers, Dom.*, 1645–47, p. 198, Cromwell's warrant to pay five shillings apiece to the foot soldiers present at the capture of Winchester.

[2] *Report on the MSS. of the Duke of Portland*, i, 284.

[3] May, *History of the Long Parliament*, ed. 1854, p. 279.

inhabitants shall give them a reasonable gratuity in money in lieu of pillages; and so made it death for any man to plunder'. Accordingly, when the city surrendered in order to avoid the threatened assault, its inhabitants were obliged to pay a ransom of £2,000 as a recompense for the forbearance of the soldiery.[1]

One more illustration of the importance attached by the soldier to this question of lawful plunder is supplied by the history of the expedition sent by Cromwell to the West Indies. When the army under Venables was preparing to attack San Domingo, a dispute arose about the disposal of the plunder which it was expected to find in the city. The civil commissioners entrusted by Cromwell with a share in the management of the expedition insisted that 'all preys and booties got by sea or land' should be employed for the public service. Venables remonstrated. Ships and large quantities of treasure captured in towns or forts might be so disposed of, but to attempt to reserve captured property of every kind or 'all sorts of pillage' for that purpose would disgust both soldiers and officers, and cause a mutiny. 'For this was so contrary,' says Venables, 'to what had been practised in England as I doubted it would be impossible to satisfy them; and how to bring them from pay and plunder both (which they had in England) to have neither pay nor plunder, without the providing of some fit medium, I thought was impossible. The thing was imparted to the officers, and a fortnight's pay propounded to them in lieu of the pillage of Santo Domingo. The officers being in arrears, and many of them coming in hopes of pillage into a country where they conceived gold as plentiful as stones, demanded three months. I with entreaty drew them to accept of six weeks' pay.' At first, however, the commissioners declined to guarantee the performance of any such engagement of the general's, and when they did agree to a compromise they clogged their promise with many conditions. The result was that a mutinous spirit spread through the whole army, and helped to produce the failure which followed.[2]

In this last case plunder was suggested as a substitute for pay, but generally it was a mere supplement to it, the more important because the soldier's pay was generally in arrears.

[1] Carlyle, *Cromwell*, Letter cxxvi.

[2] *Narrative of General Venables*, pp. xiii, 14, 24.

Throughout the whole period the grievance of the soldier was not that his pay was insufficient, but that it was always over-due. From the beginning of the war the army under the Earl of Essex suffered continually from the want of its pay, and was at times, as we have seen, reduced to great extremities. That of Manchester, which was more regularly paid, suffered also, though in a much less degree. When the New Model army was organized, 'constant pay' was the inducement held out by Parliament to the soldiers and officers who served in its ranks. The pay of the soldier 'was no longer to be at the mercy of the spasmodic efforts of reluctant committee men, or of the scarcely less spasmodic efforts of a popular assembly. It was to be secured on a fixed taxation, for the full amount of which the counties were to be responsible, and lest there should be any difficulty in the first starting of the new financial machinery, the City had agreed to advance no less a sum than £80,000.'[1] The method of taxation adopted was a monthly assessment on real and personal property, levied on seventeen counties, at a rate ranging from £7,000 a month for Norfolk and Suffolk, and £8,000 in the case of Middlesex, to £184 a month for Rutland. This system of monthly assessments, subsequently generalized and extended to the whole country, was the main source from which the pay of the army was derived between 1645 and 1660.[2] The amount levied rose to £120,000 a month, but was finally reduced by the Protector to half that amount. At first the counties were generally behind-hand in the payment of their quotas, and consequently it was impossible to keep the army paid up to date. In March 1647, when the attempted disbandment of the army by Parliament took place, the pay of the foot was eighteen weeks in arrears, that of the horse and dragoons forty-three weeks.[3] Throughout 1647 and the following year the remonstrances of the army and the letters of Sir Thomas Fairfax to Parliament and other public bodies continually complained of the slackness of the local authorities to pay what was due from their counties. Hence the necessity of taking free quarters,

---

[1] Gardiner, *Great Civil War*, ii, 195.

[2] Cf. Dowell, *History of Taxation*, ii, 4. The ordinance for the assessment to maintain the New Model (15th Feb. 1645) is printed by Husbands, ii, 599.

[3] Gardiner, *Great Civil War*, iii, 225; *Commons' Journals*, v, 126.

which was impossible to avoid unless the army was regularly supplied with money. When possible the attempt was made to quarter the troops on the districts which were in default. Fairfax's letter to the Lord Mayor of London in December 1648 supplies an instance. London, as he pointed out, was one of the worst defaulters. 'I am unwilling to take these strict courses, yet having sent so often to you for the said arrears, and desired sums of money to be advanced by you (far short of the sums due from you), yet I have been delayed and denied, to the hazard of the army, and the prejudice of others in the suburbs upon whom they are quartered; wherefore I thought fit to send to seize the said treasuries, and to send some forces to quarter in the City until I may be satisfied for the arrears due unto the Army; and if this seems strange unto you, it is no less than that our forces have been ordered to do by the Parliament in the several counties of the kingdom, where assessments have not been paid, and there to continue until they have been paid.'[1] A few days later Fairfax sent a circular letter to eighteen counties, promising the removal of free quarter as soon as they paid what was due from them. In it he mentioned the introduction of a new system, by which the assessment of a particular county was to be henceforth assigned for the payment of a particular regiment.[2] This method of allocating the contributions of the counties to the support of a definite regiment or regiments instead of to the army in general, appears to have facilitated the levy of the assessments. For when it was possible, the regiment selected was usually one connected in some way with the district paying the tax, either because it had been originally raised there, or was principally recruited there. The tax, therefore, seems to have been more willingly and more regularly paid thenceforward. Nevertheless the needs of the

[1] 8th December 1648; Rushworth, vii, 1356.

[2] Rushworth, vii, 1382. Fairfax says: 'I desire you would cause the Arrears of the Assessments for the Army that is in your Counties to be forthwith brought unto your Treasurers, and the last six Months sessed, levyed, collected, and brought in as aforesaid, to the end it may be ready to supply that Regiment who shall have your County for its Assignations of Pay, by Order and Warrant from the Committee of Lords and Commons for the Army, which you shall have very suddenly. This being performed, I shall take care that the heavy Burden of free Quarter shall be removed from all those who shall duly pay in their Assessments' (Jan. 2, 1649).

State were far in excess of the revenue, and throughout both Commonwealth and Protectorate the pay of the army was again and again in arrears. At the close of the Protectorate, that is, in March 1659, just before the fall of Richard Cromwell, arrears to the amount of about £800,000 were owing to the forces in the three nations. Nearly £224,000 of this sum was due to the forces in England, nearly £94,000 to those in Scotland, over £371,000 to the Irish army, and over £110,000 to the soldiers serving in Jamaica.[1] The forces in England were throughout the Protectorate better paid than those more remote from the seat of government, yet even they were at times reduced to some distress. 'What is the case of your army?' said Cromwell to his Parliament on 25th January 1658. 'A poor unpaid army; the soldiers going barefoot at this time, in this city, in this weather. And yet a peaceable people, seeking to serve you with their lives; judging their pains and hazards and all well bestowed in obeying their officers and serving you to keep the peace of these nations. Yea, he must be a man with a heart as hard as the weather who hath not a due sense of this.'[2]

The position of the troops in Scotland was generally (if not at this particular time) worse than that of those stationed in England, though their hardships were far greater. The contrast heightened the grievance. 'Our wants of money are very great at this time, being now about three months in arrear,' wrote Colonel Lilburne in October 1653, adding significantly, 'I perceive the forces in England are paid up almost to a day.'[3] Monck was more outspoken. 'I desire,' he wrote in June 1655. 'we may be paid and kept on upon an even foot with those in England; for truly I think the forces here have a great deal of reason to expect equal measure (seeing the greatest part of the officers have their wives in England, by which means they are forced to keep two houses, and have a long journey to visit their relations when the service will give them leave); so I must

---

[1] *Commons' Journals*, vii, 630, under 7th April 1659; *Old Parliamentary History*, xxi, 336. This was the sum required to pay the forces in question up to the end of March 1659.

[2] Carlyle, *Cromwell*, Speech xvii.

[3] *Scotland and the Commonwealth*, p. 258; Cromwell in his speech of 22nd January 1655 describes the troops in Scotland as 'near thirty weeks behind in pay'.

intreat your lordship, that if we must suffer for want of moneys it may be upon equal conditions with those in England, which will be a means to cause us to bear it with the more cheerfulness and patience.' In December 1657 Monck complained to the Protector's council that the army under his command was seven months in arrears, and threatened to resign. 'For truly, if your lordship be not pleased to take it into consideration to bring us into some equal foot with the forces in England, I cannot be able to undertake the command of his Highness's forces in these parts, and the officers think themselves very hardly dealt with- all (being they are so much in arrear, so very far distant from their relations and small fortunes, and lie many of them in very remote garrisons where they suffer much hardship), that they are not paid equal with those forces in England.'[1]

Still worse fared the unfortunate regiments who conquered and held Jamaica. In July 1655 they had only received twelve days' pay during the last six months. 'I wish your army were as honest as poor,' wrote its commander to Cromwell. 'I am con- fident there is not an officer in the army hath above forty shillings, hundreds not above five shillings in their purse.'[2] Things grew worse afterwards; some money was sent in little driblets, but the forces in Jamaica were throughout not merely in arrears but practically unpaid. Nor were the provisions and clothing which should have been provided by the government out of the pay of the soldiers supplied with any regularity or in sufficient quantities. 'We are in want of clothes and shoes, so that we appear more like savages than Englishmen,' was Colonel Doyley's report in November 1658.[3] 'How can it be thought,' he asked in another letter, 'a private soldier can give four shil- lings for a pair of ammunition shoes that never received so much these three years?'[4]

Another complaint of officers and soldiers was that the government did not pay their wives and families what it had promised. In November 1654, before the West Indian expedi- tion sailed, the Council of State ordered that a fourth part of the pay due to the officers and soldiers engaged in it should be paid

---

[1] *Scotland and the Protectorate,*, pp. 289, 373.

[2] *Thurloe Papers*, iii, 676.

[3] *Thurloe Papers*, vii, 499.   [4] Ibid., vi, 833.

every four months to the persons named in assignations, signed
by themselves and countersigned by their general.[1] But these
stipulated payments were very irregularly made, as a petition
from some soldiers' wives and other evidence show.[2] Colonel
Doyley, writing in November 1656, says: 'Our officers are much
discouraged to hear from their relations that the fourth part is
not paid, which makes many lay their wives and families at my
door and say that I detain them as prisoners and slaves, and
will not suffer them to return and provide for their families.'[3]
Later still, when these payments had been resumed, there were
complaints amongst the soldiers that some received a fourth of
their pay through their relatives while others got nothing. 'The
bachelors here,' wrote Doyley in July 1657, 'complain much,
that the married men are paid their fourth part, but not they
. . . and in truth my judgment is that it would redound more
to the benefit of the state, if the bachelors were paid; for then
it would be returned hither either in money, goods, or servants;
whereas that given to wives is spent in victuals and clothes.'[4]
But this cynical counsel does not appear to have been followed.

To sum up, neither during the reign of the Long Parliament
nor under the government of the Protector were the soldiers
punctually paid, though they were more punctually paid between 1649 and 1660 than they had been during the preceding
seven years. The reason was simply that the income of the
country was insufficient to defray its expenditure, and more
especially its military expenditure. Though the financial

[1] *Cal. State Papers, Dom.*, 1654, p. 404. The wives of some soldiers serving
in Ireland had been granted a similar allowance as early as 1643 (*Lords'
Journals*, v, 690).

[2] *Carte MSS.*, lxxiv, 484. 'The humble Petition of the wives and freinds
of all those officers who are gone in the fleete of this Commonwealth towards
the West Indies under the command of Generall Venables.

'. . . That according to the promise made unto your petitioners' husbands
and freindes, that during their absence part of their pay should bee delivered unto such persons as they should appoint, they did borrow and lay out
all that they could to fitt themselves for the said voyage upon hopes of
performance of the said promise, whereby all the meanes they had to
help their families and pay their debts have bin utterly spent, and most of
them left miserably poore and indebted, with many children, without either
clothes, food, or hope to continue in any habitation. And although your
petitioners have endeavoured to receave the said moneys they cannot
hitherto find where to make their addresses to obtaine the same, insomuch
as they remayne in a most desolate and inevitably perishing condition.'

[3] *Thurloe Papers*, iv, 603.

[4] *Thurloe Papers*, vi, 391.

administration of the Protectorate was far superior to that of the governments it succeeded, Cromwell could never make both ends meet. He reduced the cost of the army considerably, but then he reduced the taxes too, so there was still a deficit, and the pay of the army fell into arrears in consequence. The Long Parliament had met the difference between its income and expenditure, and paid off a large part of the debts it accumulated, by selling the lands it had confiscated. But when Cromwell became Protector this resource was almost exhausted. 'All your treasure was exhausted and spent when this government was undertaken,' said Cromwell to his first Parliament in September 1654.'[1] 'All accidental ways of bringing in treasure [were] to a very inconsiderable sum consumed; the lands sold, the sums on hand spent; rents, fee-farms, delinquents' lands, Kings, Queens, bishops, dean and chapters' lands sold. These were *spent* when this government was undertaken.' Not only was the capital out of which debts had hitherto been defrayed practically exhausted but there was a debt of £700,000 owing when the Long Parliament was expelled. In view of these facts, and in view of the expensiveness of the Protector's foreign policy, it is not surprising that the pay of the army was always in arrears.

The method in which the Long Parliament had employed these confiscated lands for the purpose of paying its soldiers deserves attention, for it led to important political results both in England and in Ireland, and it also exerted considerable influence in determining the part taken by the army in public events.

From the very beginning of the war Parliament had found itself unable to discharge the whole of the pay due to its soldiers, and had substituted promises to pay of different kinds for payment in cash. In 1644 it adopted the plan of putting all officers above the rank of captain on half-pay during the war, and promising to pay them the other half when the war ended. This system of deferred payment, or 'respiting' the pay of the officers, as it was termed, was applied to Manchester's army by an ordinance passed on 20th January 1644, to that of Essex on

[1] Carlyle, *Cromwell*, Speech ii; see also Speeches v and xiii for Cromwell's finance. The subject is treated at length in my *Last Years of the Protectorate*, ii, 257–69.

26th March 1644, and to the New Model from the moment of its formation (15th February).[1] For the sum thus respited the officer was to receive a certificate, which was termed a 'debenture', secured 'upon the public faith'. At first the system was applied to the officers only, but in 1647 when Parliament undertook to disband the army, it became necessary to extend it to non-commissioned officers and soldiers also. The soldiers demanded payment of their arrears before they were disbanded – a very reasonable demand, seeing that the pay of the infantry was eighteen weeks in arrears, and that of the horse and dragoons forty-three weeks.[2] Parliament offered at first to pay them six weeks', and when pressed for a larger sum eight weeks', pay in cash. Soldiers and officers both were to have debentures given them for the remainder.

The soldiers naturally thought eight weeks' pay a very inconsiderable proportion of what was owing, and they also held that the security offered for the remaining part was very insufficient.[3] 'No visible security was given,' said they, 'for what should not now be paid.' Parliament had voted that the excise should be the security by which the arrears of inferior officers and soldiers should be guaranteed, and that the superior officers should be paid out of the estates of delinquents. To this the soldiers answered, that the security offered was neither visible nor sufficient. The excise was already pledged for £1,000,000, and the estates in question were mostly disposed of already. They

[1] Husbands, *Ordinances*, ii, 414, 446, 602. The ordinance for the New Model declares 'Every Captain both of Horse and Foot, and every other Inferior and Superior Officer, or other, in the said Army, whose Pay comes to Ten Shillings a day, or above, shall take but half the pay due to him, and shall respite the other half upon the Publick Faith, until these unnatural Wars be ended. And every Officer or other that is to have Five Shillings a day, or above, and under Ten Shillings, shall accept of the two thirds of the Pay due to him, and shall respite one third part upon the Publick Faith, until these Unnatural Wars shall be ended. And when there is three Months Pay due to any of them, or more, a Certificate thereof from such Person or Persons as the Houses of Parliament shall afterwards appoint for the receiving of the Moneys to be Levied by virtue of this Ordinance, shall be sufficient to demand the said Moneys owing upon the Publick Faith as aforesaid' (Rushworth, iv, i, p. 12).

[2] Parliament owed the New Model £331,000. *Commons' Journals*, v, 126; Gardiner, *Great Civil War*, iii, 225, 227.

[3] 'We cannot but consider,' said they, 'that whatever the officers expectances upon debentures may prove, the private soldier may well make little account of whatever part of his arrears he receives not before disbanding, (Rushworth, vi, 505).

demanded that the lands and revenues of the cathedrals and the forest lands should be pledged for the purpose. At the close of 1647, after the struggle between army and Parliament had ended in the victory of the army, the soldiers obtained their desire. By the ordinance of 24th December 1647, the bishops' lands and a large part of the estates of delinquents were set aside to pay the soldiers. Eighteen months later, after the King's execution and the abolition of the monarchy, the lands of the Crown, including the forests, were made available for the same purpose.[1]

Sometimes the sum due to the soldier was charged on the general fund derived from the sale of these lands. At other times particular estates were set aside for the payment of particular regiments or brigades. For instance, the brigade which served in Wales in 1648 under Colonel Horton had settled upon it the lands of Mr Barlow and other Pembrokeshire Royalists.[2] In the same way the manor of Hemel Hemstead and other manors belonging to the King were set apart for Colonel Whalley's regiment.[3] The process was applied upon a still larger scale in Ireland, where the forfeited lands of the rebels were used to pay the soldiers for their services and to repay the capitalists who had found the money for the reconquest of Ireland. But there was this difference between the position of the army in England and Ireland. In England the soldier's debenture was a promise to pay a certain sum of money for which the land was merely security. In Ireland the soldier's debenture expressly stated that the sum due was to be paid in land.[4]

In Ireland the process was this: the soldier's accounts were made up and the sum due to him certified. This was called stating his accounts. The confiscated lands were surveyed and divided out. They were valued at a fixed rate, varying according to the province; an acre in Leinster being worth twelve shillings, one in Munster eight shillings, one in Ulster four shillings. Thus a soldier whose arrears came to twelve pounds was entitled to twenty acres in Leinster, or thirty acres in Munster, or sixty

[1] 16th July 1649.   [2] *Commons' Journals*, vi, 308–9.

[3] *Harleian MSS.*, 427.

[4] 'To be satisfied out of the Rebel's lands, houses, tenements, and hereditaments in Ireland, or other lands, houses, tenements, and hereditaments then at the dispose of the Commonwealth of England.' A facsimile of an Irish debenture is given by Prendergast, p. 196.

acres in Ulster. The question in which province a regiment was
to have its share of land assigned to it was determined by lot,
and the exact county or district in the province was determined
in the same way. Each regiment was established upon the land
as a whole, troop by troop and company by company, so that
the colonist would have his old comrades in arms as his neighbours.[1]

This process of liquidation and settlement in Ireland was
naturally very complicated and very lengthy. In England also
the process of selling the Crown and Church lands and providing
money for the payment of arrears was very tedious and very
slow. In the interval which elapsed between the receipt of the
promise to pay and its fulfilment the soldier, and even the
officer, was frequently reduced to great distress. Hence they
were very often driven to sell their debentures to provide for
their present subsistence. Both in England and Ireland a great
trade in debentures sprang up.

In Ireland soldiers sold their debentures for one-fifth or two-
fifths of their value to speculators or to their officers, and this
produced important political results.[2] A number of these officers
obtained great estates and founded families which still exist in
Ireland. On the other hand, these sales frustrated the scheme of
the English government for establishing a Protestant yeomanry
in Ireland – frustrated it not altogether, for many did not sell,
but to a large extent.

Some soldiers, it was complained, were cheated of their allot-
ments by their officers and so left Ireland altogether. Says a
poet:

> *Some private soldiers were by their commanders*
> *Choused of their land and packed away to Flanders.*[3]

Others sank to the position of tenants at will, and more were
replaced by Irish Catholics as tenants of some great proprietor
who had either bought up the debentures or had gradually
ousted the old soldier from his land.

[1] A detailed explanation of the process is given in Prendergast's *Cromwellian Settlement of Ireland*, pp. 187–234.

[2] Prendergast, p. 221.

[3] Ibid., p. 262; quoting a poem called 'The Moderate Cavalier, or the
Soldiers Description of Ireland', 1675. See also pp. 234, 264–8.

In England the history of the debenture-holders was some-what similar, but the result was different. The sale of debentures was in full swing as early as 1649. In October 1649 the Council of Officers addressed a letter to the commander-in-chief, stating that some persons had so far prevailed upon the present neces-sity and ignorance of the soldiers, that they had purchased their debentures at inconsiderable rates, such as three shillings and sixpence and four shillings in the pound. The petition prayed that such proceedings might be put a stop to in the future, and accordingly an order prohibiting the sale or purchase of deben-tures was issued.[1]

However, the prohibition proved a dead letter, and the cor-respondence of the period proves that the officers themselves were most forward in contravening it. An officer usually began by buying up the arrears of his own troop or company. He bought at a low price because he would have a long time to wait before he could realize them, and because the prohibition of the practice made the speculation rather risky. Captain Chillenden, for instance, writes to William Clarke, saying that he has bought up the arrears of his own troop and of part of his colonel's troop, which will come to at least £3,500.[2] Cornet Baynes writes to his cousin Captain Adam Baynes in 1651 on behalf of a brother officer:

'Captain Wisdom tenders his services to you, and intreats you to add some debentures which he bought of his soldiers to the rest of his company in the purchase of Crown lands. The soldiers were, and are still, of his company, and methinks his request is very reasonable. It need not be discovered that they are bought and sold, and if it should hereafter appear to be so, the hazard he is very willing to run and stand to. I pray you therefore deny it not.'[3]

Even the highest officers took part in the traffic. We find Major-General Lambert, who was practically the second man in the army during the early part of the Protectorate, actively buying up debentures in order to invest them in the purchase

[1] Fairfax's letter recommending this petition to Parliament was dated 3rd October; see the *Perfect Weekly Account*, 3rd to 10th October 1649.

[2] *Report on the Papers of Mr Leyborne Popham*, p. 102.

[3] *Letters from Roundhead Officers in Scotland*, pp. 13, 18, 26, 30 (Ban-natyne Club).

of an estate. There is also a letter from Colonel Lilburne offering Lambert, on behalf of his regiment, Nonsuch Park, which had been assigned to it as security for its arrears, and saying that the men would take about twelve shillings in the pound for their debentures.[1] Some perhaps had scruples, but an officer with a scrupulous conscience thought he had done all that decency demanded when he paid something higher than the market rate for debentures.[2] Lieutenant-Colonel Joyce, for instance, plumed himself on the fact that when he wished to buy a certain park in Hampshire, he bought up the arrears of the garrison of Portsmouth, Southampton, and the greater part of the Isle of Wight at seven shillings and sixpence in the pound; 'deeming himself obliged in conscience to allow the soldiers, who had equally ventured their lives with himself, a more proportionable rate than the common prices of one shilling or one shilling and sixpence per pound.'

Naturally these proceedings caused deep dissatisfaction amongst the soldiers. They had suffered great hardships and privations for the want of their pay, and now they saw themselves practically defrauded of the greater part of their arrears. At the same time they saw their officers growing rich by taking advantage of their necessities. Hence the officers lost their influence over their men. In 1647 the army had been united against the Parliament, because officers and men were united by a common pecuniary grievance. In 1659 and 1660 there was no such common bond of self-interest to hold them together. Lambert and Fleetwood's soldiers were not disposed to fight the soldiers of Monck and those who supported the Parliament. They had come to the conclusion that the result of their previous fighting was that the officers always got the oyster and the soldiers the shells, A pamphlet addressed by a soldier to 'his loving fellow soldiers' about January 1660 put the case strongly.[3] He urged his comrades not to be deceived by officers who wished to continue the war for selfish ends. 'Did not most of those officers (by God's mercy now cashiered the army) purchase your debentures (the price of blood) from two shillings to a noble in

[1] Ibid., p. 59.   [2] *Harleian Miscellany*, ed. Park, viii, 305.

[3] *Truth seeks no Corners; or advice from a non-interested soldier to his loving fellow-soldiers that were under Fleetwood and Lambert*, 1660, 4to, p. 2.

the pound to enrich themselves and perpetuate your slavery?
And through their cruelty many of our fellow soldiers, who were
wounded in battle and made unserviceable, with wives and
children starved in the streets for want of bread, while they
lorded over you tyrant like. Now examine yourselves whether
when you have demanded your pay, you were not had before
Court martials and hanged to all your shames, while they
robbed you and the Commonwealth of your dues.'

It was the existence of this feeling which enabled Monck
when he became commander-in-chief to remove the officers
from their commands as he thought fit, and so to prepare the
way for the Restoration of Charles the Second.

On the other hand, nothing did more to facilitate the return
of Charles the Second than the promise made in his Declaration
at Breda to agree to any Acts of Parliament ' for the full satisfaction of all arrears due to the officers and soldiers of the army
under the command of General Monck.' The King's promise was
faithfully kept. In the autumn of 1660 the army was paid off,
and the soldiers and officers then serving received their arrears
of pay in full. By this time, however, the officers of the old army
– the army of the Commonwealth and Protectorate – had mostly
lost their commissions, so that they did not benefit by the fulfilment of the King's promise. Consequently the officers in England lost greatly by the Restoration. The Crown lands and
Church lands in which they had invested the debentures they
purchased from their men returned again to the King and the
bishops, and they lost the money they had sunk in the speculation. In some cases perhaps an officer obtained a favourable
lease of the Church lands of which he had imagined himself the
proprietor; in most he obtained nothing.[1] The same fate befell
those who had purchased the lands of Royalists which had been
confiscated and sold by the State. Only those sales held good
which Royalists themselves had made in order to raise money
to pay their fines to the government.

In England, therefore, the new landed aristocracy created by
the changes of the Civil War – that is, the class of officers who
had purchased confiscated estates – disappeared entirely at the

[1] For an instance, see *Military Memoir of Col. Birch*, pp. 154, 197
(Camden Society, 1875).

Restoration. In Ireland, on the other hand, it continued to exist, for there the confiscations made by the State were maintained with but little alteration. In one country, therefore, the Cromwellian officers maintained their possessions and exerted a permanent influence on its later development; in the other, they returned to their original position.

CHAPTER IX

The Commissariat

IN THE SEVENTEENTH century the art of feeding an army was
not very highly developed. Comparatively little is said of the
subject in the military books of the time, and it is evident that
the organization of the commissariat was somewhat rudimen-
tary. Yet some of the great generals of the time gave special
attention to the subject, notably Wallenstein. Wallenstein was
held to be inferior to Gustavus in the art of making and utilizing
intrenchments. It was said that he was 'none of the best spade-
men'. On the other hand he was considered more skilful than
his rival in providing for the maintenance of his troops. 'The
Duke of Friedland's masterpiece,' says *The Swedish Intelligencer*,[1] 'is to be a good provisioner, and he hath a singular
good catering wit of his own.' In general, armies lived almost
entirely upon the country in which they were operating, and
the problem which a commander set himself to solve was how
to make the resources of the country last as long as possible by
the systematic collection and distribution of the supplies it
afforded.

Sir James Turner's account of the method of maintaining
troops in vogue upon the continent refers specially to the
German, Swedish, and Danish armies with which he had served,
but it is worth quoting at length:

'Since money is generally scarce in the wars, in so much that
soldiers cannot receive their wages duly, let us see what allowance
of meat and drink (ordinarily called proviant) princes allow their
soldiery; to furnish which every army should have a general
proviant-master; and truly I conceive him to be an officer as
necessary and useful, if not more, in the fields, where mostly our
modern armies are entertained with proviant, as either a general

[1] *The Swedish Intelligencer*, pt. iii, p. 11.

commissary, or a treasurer: his charge is to provide victuals, corn, flesh, wine, bread, and beer; he hath the inspection of them, and should see them equally and proportionably divided to the regiments, according to their several strengths; for which purpose he should have all the rolls and lists by him, which his secretaries should carefully keep. He hath no power to sell any proviant under what pretence soever, without the general's express warrant. All mills where the army comes are under his protection, and he is obliged to protect them. He hath the ordering of all the magazines for victuals, and to him belongs the care of seeing the garrisons and fortified places sufficiently provided with such meats and drinks as are most fit to preserve; these are, corn, grain and meal of several kinds, stock-fish, herrings, and all other salted fishes; salted and hung fleshes, especially beef and bacon, cheese, butter, almonds, chesnuts and hazel nuts, wine, beer, malt, honey, vinegar, oil, tobacco, wood and coal for firing, and as many living oxen, cows, sheep and swine, hens and turkeys, as can be conveniently fed; for which purpose, as also for horses, he is to provide straw, hay, and oats. This general proviant-master hath under him a lieutenant, a secretary, a clerk, a smith, a waggon-master, and a waggon-maker, a quarter-master, and some officers who are called directors.

'There are few princes who have not their particular establishment for their proviant, both in field and garrison, as well as for money; the order whereof commonly is this: they allow so much bread, flesh, wine or beer to every trooper and foot soldier, which ordinarily is alike to both, then they allow to the officers, according to their dignities and charges, double, triple, and quadruple portions; as to an ensign four times more than to a common soldier, a colonel commonly having twelve portions allowed him. The ordinary allowance for a soldier in the field is daily, two pound of bread, one pound of flesh, or in lieu of it, one pound of cheese, one pottle of wine, or in lieu of it, two pottles of beer. It is enough, cry the soldiers, we desire no more, it is enough in conscience. But this allowance will not last very long, they must be contented to march sometimes one whole week, and scarce get two pounds of bread all the while, and their officers as well as they; who, if they have no provisions

H

of their own carried about with them, must be satisfied with
commis-bread and cold water, as well as the common soldier,
unless they have money to buy better entertainment from
sutlers.'

Want of money, continues Turner, frequently obliged princes
and their generals to fall back on the plan of quartering their
troops on the country. 'This proves oft the destruction of a
country: for though no exorbitancy be committed, and that
every man both officer and soldier demand no other entertainment than what is allowed by the Prince or State where they
serve; yet when an army cannot be quartered but close and near
together, to prevent infalls, onslaughts, and surprisal of an
enemy, it is an easy matter to imagine what a heavy burthen
these places bear. . . . And withal it is very hard to get soldiers
and horsemen kept within the limits of their duty in these
quarters after they have endured hunger, thirst, and other hardships in the field. It is true, all Princes who for preservation of
their armies from extream ruin, and for want of treasure, are
necessitated too often to make use of this free quarter, do not
only make strict laws and ordinances, how many times a day
officers and soldiers are to eat, and how many dishes every one
according to his quality is to call for, but likewise set down the
precise rates, and values of the dishes, that the host be not
obliged to do beyond those limitations, yet the grievance continues heavy and great.

'The ordinances concerning free quarter of the Emperor, the
Kings of Denmark and Sweden, and German Princes, are upon
the matter with little difference all one, as thus: A colonel is to
have twelve dishes of meat, each at the rate of the eighth part
of a dollar, ten pound of bread, and ten measures of wine. A
lieutenant-colonel, eight dishes, eight pound of bread, and six
measures of wine. A major or captain six dishes of meat, six
pound of bread, and six measures of wine. A lieutenant and ensign, each of them four dishes, four pound of bread, and three
measures of wine. Every sergeant three dishes of meat, two
pound of bread, and one measure and a half of wine. Every corporal and every drummer two dishes of meat, two pound of
bread, and one measure and a half of wine. A common soldier or
trooper so much flesh, bread and wine as I spoke of before, when

I told you what proviant was allowed him. If the Army be not in a wine country, then all those I have spoke of, have a double allowance of beer. This is besides the hay, straw and oats the country is bound to furnish to the horses, not only of the cavalry, artillery, and general officers, but to those horses likewise that belong to the infantry. And this grievance of fodderage proves many times heavier than the free quarter, all being often eaten up in a short time wherewith the inhabitants should maintain their horses and beasts.'[1]

Francis Markham writing about fifty years earlier than Turner, and describing apparently the system existing in the Dutch army when he served there, gives a similar account of the duties of the victual-master, proviant-master, or purveyor of victuals, and adds some details as to the amount and nature of the soldiers' rations. 'For example's sake,' says he, 'and according to the experience of those wars which I have seen, half a pound of biscuit and half a pound of butter hath been a fit day's proportion for one man, or a pound of bread and half a pound of beef or else bacon a full day's proportion; or otherwise half a pound of biscuit and a pound of cheese; likewise a pound of biscuit and a poor John between two men for one day, or two pounds of biscuit and a haberdine between four men for one day is a great proportion; half a pound of biscuit and four herrings is one man's allowance for one day, and so is a quart of peas boiled, or a pint of rice with the ordinary allowance of biscuit.'[2]

In the French army, according to Du Praissac's *Art of War*, published in 1625, 'to every soldier is given usually two loaves of bread a day, of ten ounce weight apiece, and one pint of wine Paris measure'. This bread, known as munition or ammunition bread, was composed two parts of wheat and a third part of rye, and the bran and meal were mixed together in making it.[3] But the French were far behind the Dutch in the art of supplying an

---

[1] *Pallas Aramata*, p. 201.

[2] Markham, *Decades of War*, 1622, p. 103.

[3] *The Art of War, or Military Discourses*, translated by J. Cruso, 1639, p. 143. Captain Cockle describes the French edition of 1625 as being the fifth, so the original must have been published much earlier (*Bibliography of Military Books*, pp. 116, 164). See Avenel's *Richelieu et la Monarchie Absolue*, iii, 131, for the food of the French soldier between 1620 and 1660. He gives the nominal ration as a pound and a half of bread, a pound of meat, and an allowance of wine, cider or beer.

army, and during the wars of Louis the Thirteenth the commissariat of his armies was invariably defective, nor did it
become efficient until Louvois reformed the military administration of France.[1]

In England the development of all branches of military organization was slow, much slower than on the continent, and as
the government had no experience of great wars the commissariat was much neglected. The history of the naval and military
expeditions of Queen Elizabeth's reign and that of the expedition
to Cadiz in 1625 suffice to prove this. Bad food and very little of
that was the one invariable complaint. When the Civil War
began, the methods in which the army was provisioned were
those which had prevailed in the days of Elizabeth. As there
were no government manufacturing establishments, any provisions needed were either bought by officials in the open market
or supplied by contract. The army employed to suppress the
rebellion in Ireland, like that which Elizabeth had sent against
Tyrone's rebellion forty years earlier, was mainly supplied by
contract.[2]

According to contemporary pamphlets the contractors in
some cases defrauded both the State and the soldier,[3] but up to
1646, at all events, the real cause of the sufferings of the troops
in Ireland was the insufficiency of the supplies sent over by the
Parliament, rather than any defects in the system by which
they were provided. During 1642 and 1643 the impossibility of
victualling the army for a campaign in the field obliged it to
remain stationary at Dublin or to confine its operations to brief
forays.[4] Thus the rebellion was enabled to spread and to grow
strong when it might have been crushed at the beginning.

The state of affairs was little better in 1647, though the cessation of the war in England had set the hands of the Parliament
free. Sir Charles Coote wrote from Londonderry in June 1647

[1] See Rousset, *Louvois*, i, 248, ed. 1879.

[2] Specimens of these contracts may be found printed in the *Journals of the
House of Lords*, cf. vii, 377.

[3] See *The State of the Irish Affairs, represented from the Committee of
Adventurers in London*, 1645, 4to, p. 25; Lilburne's *Regal Tyranny Discovered*, 1647, pp. 103–8.

[4] Clarendon, *Rebellion*, vii, 357; *Report on the Duke of Portland's MSS.*,
i, 37, 115.

that many of the soldiers under his command in Ulster had died
'for want of bread to sustain nature', he 'having not been
able for many months past to afford them but five or six pounds
of oaten meal a week, and if God had not miraculously blessed
us this winter by getting beef from the rebels with the little salt
we had in store, we had perished'.

Little better was the condition of Lord Inchiquin's army in
Ulster at the same date. 'Bread and pease – other provisions we
have none' – was the food of his soldiers, and very short allowance of both.[1] He might capture cattle from the Irish, but they
were usually 'embezzled' by the soldiers, that is, devoured in a
disorderly manner instead of being handed over to the authorities. He could lay waste the cornfields in the enemy's quarters,
but as in spite of repeated applications his army was not supplied
with handmills, he could make little use of the corn to subsist
his men.[2] Cromwell succeeded where Inchiquin and Coote failed,
not only because his men were better soldiers and better led,
but because they were better fed.

To supply an army operating in England was a comparatively
easy task, and yet the army which fought under the Earl of
Essex was never well supplied. His commissariat was under the
charge of a 'commissary for the provisions', and his train under
a 'carriage-master-general'.[3] The train must have been extremely small. Two waggons per regiment for the sutlers appears
to have been the official allowance, and forty were apparently
held enough for the whole army. Others were hired with their
teams as wanted, or, if necessary, were impressed. Whenever
possible, water-carriage was substituted for land-carriage.[4]
When Essex laid siege to Reading in April 1643, the Militia
Committee of London was ordered to take up boats, barges,
carriages and carts in and round London to convey provisions to
the besieging army. The orders were carried out, and, according
to Clarendon, 'vast quantities of victual ready dressed were

[1] *Portland MSS.*, i, 422, 424.

[2] Carey, *Memorials of the Civil War*, i, 352, 366.

[3] Peacock, *Army Lists of Cavaliers and Roundheads*, pp. 20, 24. The
duties of the waggon-master are explained by Markham, *Decades of War*,
p. 93, and Turner, *Pallas Armata*, p. 276.

[4] *Cal. State Papers, Dom.*, 1641-3, pp. 408, 439, 459.

every day sent in waggons and carts from London', besides forage and other supplies which came by way of the Thames.[1]

In the main, Essex relied upon the goodwill of the country people and upon the resources of the country for provisions, far more than upon any organized system of forwarding supplies. Speaking of the King's motives for fighting at Edgehill, Clarendon observes that all the country was so devoted to the cause of the Parliamentarians, 'that they had all provisions brought to them without the least trouble', whereas the people were so hostile to the Royalists that 'they had carried away or hid all their provisions, insomuch that there was neither meat for man or horse'. Consequently the King's army was reduced to such extremity, that there were very many companies of the private soldiers who had 'scarce eaten bread in forty-eight hours' before the battle.[2] In November of the same year it was the turn of the citizens of London to show their zeal. After the King's forces had surprised Brentford (11th November 1642), Essex mustered his forces on Turnham Green. The Lord Mayor of London 'with some prime well-affected citizens, taking into their serious consideration that the soldiers ... could not but be destitute of victuals to refresh them', appealed to the City to supply their needs. 'The ministers therefore were moved by a motion from the said ever to be honoured, pious, and prudent Lord Mayor, on the said Lord's day in their morning sermon in their pulpits, to encourage and incite the people to spare some part of their diet, ready dressed for that present dinner, and to bestow it upon the soldiers aforesaid. Whereupon after the sermon was done, carts being ordered to stand ready in the streets in every parish throughout the City, to carry presently away what was sent, there were sent at least an hundred loads of all manner of good provision of victuals, bottles of wine, and barrels of beer instantly carried to them, and accompanied by honest and religious gentlemen, who went to see it faithfully distributed to them. And this was done so freely and with such willingness and cheerfulness, that not only the liberal contribution itself, but the forwardness therein, deserves a perpetual memory.'[3]

[1] Clarendon, *Rebellion*, vii, 25, 26; Husbands, *Ordinances*, ii, 40.

[2] Ibid., vi, 83.

[3] Vicars, *Parliamentary Chronicle*, i, 216.

All districts were not equally enthusiastic for the Parliamentary cause, and many parts of the country were not sufficiently populous or fertile to provide food for an army. In such cases the commissariat of the Earl of Essex invariably broke down. During the march of Essex to the relief of Gloucester his troops subsisted in the most haphazard manner, and it is clear that he had no proper provision train. Sergeant Foster in his relation of the march of the London trained bands says:

'At Chesham we were well accomodated for beer, having great plenty; at Aynhoe we were very much scanted of victuals; at Chipping Norton our regiment stood in the open field all night having neither bread nor water to refresh ourselves, having also marched the day before without any sustenance.' When the army reached Cheltenham 'we had by this time marched 6 days with very little provisions; for no place where we came was able to relieve our army, we leaving the road all the way and marching through poor little villages'.

On the return march it was much the same: 'we could get no accomodation either for meat or drink, but what we brought with us in our snapsacks, . . . we had no provision but what little every one had in his snapsack'. Fortunately at Cirencester, at the beginning of the march, two Royalist regiments of horse were surprised, and 'forty loads of victuall' were taken, 'which under God's providence was the preservation of the army till the day we fought the great battaile'. On reaching Swindon 'we drove along with our army', says Foster, 'about 1000 sheep and 60 head of cattell, which were taken from malignants and papists in the country for the maintenance of our army; 87 sheep was allotted for our red regiment, but we afterwards lost them all when we came to fight'.[1]

Things were little better in the other armies of the Parliament. Both before and after the battle of Marston Moor the Parliamentary forces were very short of provisions. After the battle Manchester told his men, 'That although he could not possibly that night make provision for them, according to their deserts and necessities, yet hee would without faile indevour their satisfactions in that kind in the morning.

[1] *Bibliotheca Gloucestrensis*, pp. 241, 261, 263, 265.

'The souldiers unanimously gave God the glory of their great
deliverance and victory, and told his Lordship with much cheer-
fulnesse that though they had long fasted and were faint, yet they
would willingly want three daies longer, rather then give off the
service, or leave his Lordship. And heere,' adds Ashe, 'I would
move your compassions towards poore souldiers, if I should
largely relate the wants, which that night (and some time since)
they were pinched withall. They having drained the wells to the
mud, were necessitated to drinke water out of ditches and out
of places pudled with the horse feet. Yea, through the scarcity
of accomodations, very few of the common souldiers did eate
above the quantity of a penny loafe, from Tuesday till Saturday
morning; and had no beere at all.'[1]

The arrangements of the Earl of Essex were no better in the
campaign of 1644. Just before the second battle of Newbury
the Commissioners of Parliament with the army reported to the
Speaker that for most part of its march from Portsmouth to
Reading it had suffered from want of provisions, 'partly
through the indigency of the country through which we passed,
and partly through want of commissaries, whose continued absence is of extraordinary prejudice, it being an employment both
of care and pains'.[2]

From the want of a proper commissariat arose the practice
of quartering troops on the country adopted in every one of the
Parliament's armies and prevalent from 1643 to 1651. The
householder was obliged to provide food and lodging for a certain number of soldiers at a fixed rate. In return, a ticket was
given him by the commissary, or some other officer, specifying
the number of soldiers quartered on him, the time they were
maintained, and the amount due for their entertainment. This
is what was meant by the phrase 'free quarter' which becomes
so painfully familiar in the complaints of the country. It did not
mean that food and lodging was provided gratis, but that pay-

---

[1] Ashe's relation of the battle of Marston Moor. Bills for the supply of
Manchester's army during the siege of York show that there had been no
lack of provisions in his camp before the battle, so that considering how
near the battlefield was to his late headquarters it is clear the system of
distribution must have been at fault. But probably the provision waggons
had been sent on to Tadcaster in advance of the army.

[2] *Report on the Duke of Portland's MSS.*, i, 189.

ment for them was deferred.[1] In the Record Office there are hundreds of such tickets receipted as paid by the treasurer of the Earl of Manchester's army. A certain sum was deducted from the soldiers' daily pay for this object, usually about half the pay of the private, and one-third of the pay of the officers.[2] In an ordinance for making up the accounts of the soldiers of the New Model, passed in 1647, one shilling a day was the deduction to be made from the pay due to every trooper, ninepence from that of each dragoon and fourpence a day from the foot soldiers.[3]

This method of maintaining the army naturally led to loud complaints from the country. The burden it imposed on the householder in city or country was very heavy; the prospect of repayment was somewhat doubtful and in any case remote. In order to prevent abuses Parliament drew up an elaborate series of rules for the New Model. The quartermaster was to show the householder by what authority he acted, and to produce his commission if required. He was also to give the involuntary host a ticket specifying the number of men quartered and the length of time for which they remained there. Neither quarters nor provisions were to be taken without payment, except in case of necessity, and the commanding officer was to give a certificate showing the amount of provisions taken and the regiment for which they were required. The rates for entertainment of man and beast on the march were fixed. For the horse, threepence a night for grass and fourpence for hay: oats, fourpence a peck, pease and beans, sixpence a peck, barley and malt, sevenpence a peck. For a trooper, eightpence a day was allowed; for a dragoon, sevenpence; for a foot soldier, sixpence. There was a special proviso also that no householder should be required to furnish the soldier 'with any provision but what he hath in his house of his own'; and that the officer, unless he paid for his quarters, 'should content himself with such ordinary diet as the party with whom he quarters is provided of, without putting the said party to the trouble or charge of seeking

[1] See *Cal. State Papers, Dom.*, 1641–3, 487.

[2] Husbands, ii, 414, Ordinance of 20th January 1644, for Manchester's Army.

[3] Ordinance of 24th December 1647.

abroad'. After examining the certificates given in lieu of payment, debentures were to be made out for the money due, which
were to be cashed by the treasurer of the army, or some other
financial authority.[1]

In spite of these regulations there were, as many enactments
and proclamations show, abuses which it was difficult to check.[2]
Free quarter, however regulated, was oppressive, and the only
way to prevent the inevitable evils to which it gave rise was to
put an end to the system by paying the soldier regularly, and
by obliging him to defray the cost of his food and lodging. From
the time when the New Model was organized there was a per-
sistent attempt made to do this, and though money often ran
short, and the army was from time to time quartered on the
country, these relapses were but temporary. After 1649 free
quarter practically disappeared. In that year an addition of a
certain sum was granted to soldiers on active service as billet-
money and additional pay, and an Act was passed 'for the more
certain and constant supply of the soldiers with pay and the

---

[1] Instructions to the Commissioners with the Army, May 1645, *Lords,
Journals*, vii, 373.

[2] See Fairfax's proclamation of 23rd February 1649. Free quarter was
complained of by the soldiers themselves in a letter from the Council of the
Army to the Speaker on 7th October 1647:

'Nothing is so difficult and grievous to us as to consider how the poor
Soldier (for his mere Subsistence) is compelled to grind the Face of the
Poor, to take a livelihood from them who are fitter to receive Alms, to undo
Families, threaten the Ruin of the whole, and all Propriety, and to be an
abhorring to himself (which some ingenuous of them acknowledge), and
this for want of that constant Supply and Pay, whereby they might cheer-
fully, and with Content to the People, discharge their Quarters, and so
ease both the Country and their own Minds of an intolerable Burthen'
(Rushworth, vii, 838).

A year later a letter from the headquarters of the army at St Albans,
dated 29th September 1648, reiterates the same complaint:

'His Excellency takes all the Care he can to satisfie the Country that
undergoes the great Burthen of free Quarter, Complaints coming daily
concerning the same; and that which adds to Affliction is, That the Soldiers
are not paid, whereby to enable them to discharge their Quarters; some
Regiments having not one Penny Pay these eighteen Weeks past, and none
having had above one Months Pay in all that time, except the two Regiments which were in Kent; and the Soldiers begin to be much discontented,
that the Fault should be imputed unto them, for not satisfying for what
they have in Provisions, whenas they have been so ill paid; it is very much
feared, if some speedy Course be not taken herein, neither the Country nor
the Soldier will with Patience long undergo the same' (Rushworth, vii,
1279).

preventing of any further oppression or damage to the people by free quarter or billet' (12th May 1649).[1]

Side by side with the system of quartering the soldiers on the inhabitants of the country, there existed a system of requisitioning supplies from the district in which the army was quartered, under promise of future payment. It was by this method that Fairfax's army was supported during the siege of Bristol in 1645. Its operation is described by the Commissioners of Parliament with the army in a letter to the Speaker. 'The care for the supply of the army was committed to us amongst others . . . to which purpose we issued out warrants to the counties of Gloucester and Somerset to have provisions brought in, engaging ourselves the country should be satisfied for the same out of the pay of the army, and the success was answerable to our desires and necessities: but the irregularity of the soldier hath prevented that just imposition on themselves which by our instructions the honourable Houses of Parliament have ordered, and begot unto us much more trouble than is fit to trouble you withal. Where we can possibly reduce the charge by ticket or oath to any regiment, troop, or company, we have upon moderate rates given debentures to the parishes for the same. Where we cannot come to an exact rule, we have left it to the committees of the counties to allow out of contributions or assessments upon the several hundreds, without which particular persons will be undone, because they cannot say who hurt them.'[2]

This system of requisitioning provisions, intermittently practised in England during the first and second Civil Wars, fell into disuse afterwards. Cromwell's military chest was apparently better filled than that of Fairfax, for on his march from Scotland to Worcester in pursuit of Charles the Second he was able to pay for what food his army needed. On 18th August 1651 he wrote to the mayor and corporation of Doncaster:

'I intend, God willing, to be at Doncaster with the Army on Wednesday night or Thursday morning: and forasmuch as the

[1] As to the additional pay, see p. 186. In future soldiers billeted on householders during a march, which was under certain restrictions still allowable, were to pay, a foot soldier eightpence a night, a dragoon twelvepence, a trooper fifteen-pence. For Fairfax's instructions, see Appendix I.

[2] 8th October 1645; *Report on the Duke of Portland's MSS.*, i, 283; cf. p. 347.

Soldiers will need a supply of victual, I desire you to give notice
to the country, and to use your best endeavours to cause bread,
butter, cheese and flesh to be brought in, and to be in readiness
there against our coming; for which the country shall receive
ready money'.[1]

Under any system of supplying the army something was necessarily left to private enterprise. The Articles of War, both those
for the army under Essex and those for the army under Fairfax,
lay down a number of rules for the regulation of the vintners and
sutlers who accompanied the army. During the campaign of
1645 we hear mention of 'the market, which is appointed to
follow the army with provisions from our rear', and in which
the soldiers could supply themselves with food out of their pay.[2]
The transition from the system of making the country provide
the soldiers with food to the system of making them buy it for
themselves must have been a great spur to private enterprise,
and after 1649 the open market became more and more important to the army. Immediately after his landing at Dublin (24th
August 1649), Cromwell published a proclamation declaring,
'That it shall be free and lawful to and for all manner of persons
dwelling in the country, as well gentlemen and soldiers as
farmers and other people (such as are in arms or office with or
for the enemy only excepted), to make their repair and bring any
provisions to the army, while in march or camp, or unto any
garrison under my command: Hereby assuring all that they
shall not be molested or troubled in their persons or goods, but
shall have the benefit of a free market, and receive ready money
for goods or commodities they shall so bring and sell'.[3]

On 14th September 1650, immediately after his occupation of
Edinburgh, Cromwell published a similar proclamation to the
Scots: 'That all the Inhabitants of the country, not now being
or continuing in arms, shall have free leave and liberty to come
to the Army, and to the City and Town aforesaid, with their
cattle, corn, horse, or other commodities or goods whatsoever;
and shall there have free and open markets for the same; and
shall be protected in their persons and goods, in coming and
returning as aforesaid, from any injury or violence of the Soldiery

---

[1] Carlyle, *Cromwell*, Appendix xxi.

[2] *Duke of Portland's MSS.*, i, 293.   [3] Carlyle, *Cromwell*.

under my command; and shall also be protected in their respective houses. And the Citizens and Inhabitants of the said City and Town shall and hereby likewise have free leave to vend and sell their wares and commodities; and shall be protected from the plunder and violence of the Soldiers.'[1]

Nevertheless, both in Ireland and Scotland, Cromwell could not expect to maintain his army by provisions obtained entirely in those countries themselves, either by payment or otherwise. Ireland was wasted by many years of war, and in Scotland cattle had been driven away and growing crops destroyed. 'The Scots,' says a newspaper, under the date of 15th July 1650, 'have carried away all their corn, and driven the country between here and Edinburgh.' Another observes that 'great stores of all sorts of provisions are preparing to carry along with the army, by reason the Scots have so drained the country, that very little is left in the villages adjacent to Northumberland and Cumberland, which is the chiefest cause our march is retarded at present'. A letter written from Cromwell's camp after the army had entered Scotland, describes the country people as being 'more base in hiding their provisions than the country is barren of producing them'.[2] In Scotland, therefore, as in Ireland, Cromwell's soldiers had to rely almost entirely upon the food which they could carry with them, and the strategy of both campaigns is influenced by the fact that the army relied mainly upon the fleet which accompanied it for supplies. The command of the seas was essential to the success of both campaigns, and at the same time the conditions of the war necessitated a more systematic method of supplying the army than had hitherto existed. Yet, though the commissariat department was better organized than it ever had been before, the army in Scotland was frequently in want of food. Wind and weather often prevented the ships from landing provisions, or accidents delayed their arrival. Captain John Hodgson describes the results: 'About the 6th of August we retreated to Dunbar for want of provisions; the ships not being come up with recruits and provisions that were hourly expected. At this time we were brought under great distress for want of provisions, and had much what

[1] *Cromwelliana*, p. 83.

[2] *Memoirs of Capt. John Hodgson*, ed. 1806, p. 217.

lost the discipline of the army. It was sad to see the devastation that was made: and the great reason was the timorousness of the Scots, who had plundered their own houses, and had hid their stuff in private places; where the Scots informed them, or they by their own covetous appetites, found them out.'[1]

The constant endeavour of the Scots was to interpose between the English army and the coast, and thus cut off its provisions. 'Our victual failing,' writes Cromwell, 'we marched towards our ships to recruit our want. . . . The enemy quarters himself in a posture easy to interpose between us and our victual. But the Lord made him to lose the opportunity. And the morning proving exceeding wet and dark we recovered, by that time it was light, a ground where they could not hinder us from our victual: which was an high act of the Lord's providence to us.'[2] One of the reasons which led Cromwell to resolve to fortify Dunbar was, that it 'would be a good magazine, which we exceedingly wanted, being put to depend upon the uncertainty of the weather for landing provisions, which many times cannot be done though the being of the whole army depended upon it, all the coasts from Berwick to Leith having not one good harbour'.

On the question of the amount of food the Cromwellian soldier carried during these campaigns there is very good evidence. When Cromwell's army marched to Stirling after its victory at Dunbar, 'They took a week's provisions along with them, it being the masterpiece of the Scotish policy to defeat their enemies sooner by famine than by the sword, driving all away still before them, whereby they make the country a verier wilderness, so that the soldier hath little to subsist upon besides his own provender which he carries in his knapsack; and therefore about 7 dayes hence we expect their return back here'.[3] Seven days' provisions was the usual quantity issued during these campaigns in Scotland both by Cromwell in 1650–1 and by Monck in 1654. Once, however, one hears of ten days' provisions being issued. Napier in his *History of the Peninsular War*

[1] *Memoirs of Capt. John Hodgson*, p. 138.

[2] Carlyle, *Cromwell*, Letter cxl.

[3] A letter from Edinburgh, 18th September 1650, printed in *Mercurius Politicus*, No. 17; cf. Hodgson, *Memoirs*, p. 316.

holds up for imitation the example of Napoleon's soldiers, who frequently carried rations for a fortnight. 'French soldiers only,' says he, 'are accustomed to carry so much bread. Other nations, and notably the English, would not husband it.'[1] But Cromwell's men apparently were more thrifty than Wellington's.[2]

As to the nature of the food supplied to Cromwell's soldiers during these campaigns, it is evident that it consisted exclusively of bread (or rather biscuit) and cheese. Bread and cheese in fact is freely used as a synonym for provisions. Where Cromwell describes the Scots as 'seeking to interpose between us and our victual,' an officer says 'the enemy would have interposed between us and our bread and cheese'.[3] In garrison the soldiers could supplement their rations by buying meat in the markets out of their pay, but both there and in the field nothing was issued to them but cheese and biscuit, or bread, though captured sheep or cattle sometimes afforded them a change of diet. 'Nothing is more certain than this,' wrote an officer who remembered Cromwell's campaigns to William the Third in 1691, 'that in the late wars both Scotland and Ireland were conquered by timely provisions of Cheshire cheese and biscuit.'[4]

The Cromwellian soldiers became so used to this diet that those employed in Flanders during 1657 and 1658 grumbled greatly because of the alteration which took place in their food now that they were in the French service. They disliked the 'ammunition-bread' which they got in place of it. 'We find a great want of cheese,' wrote an officer, 'which I hope will be supplied, brown bread and water being strange to our soldiers.'[5] After the capture of Dunkirk, General Lockhart found himself in great need of provisions. 'I have been forced,' said he, 'to make

[1] Napier, *Peninsular War*, ed. 1886, p. 35.

[2] However, in the description of the movements of Cromwell before Edinburgh, we are incidentally told that 'divers of our men cast away their biscuit out of a confidence they should then fight' (Hodgson, p. 266).

[3] Hodgson, *Memoirs*, pp. 132, 271, 292.

[4] *Calendar of Domestic State Papers, William III*, 1691–2, p. 75. The writer was very likely Dr Robert Gorges who had once been secretary to Henry Cromwell (cf. *Cal.*, 1690–1, p. 398). Besides Cheshire cheese Suffolk cheese is occasionally mentioned. The biscuit, or 'biscake' as it is sometimes called, was made anywhere where ovens could be got (see *Letters and Papers of State Addressed to Cromwell*, edited by J. Nickolls, pp. 11, 78; *Mercurius Politicus*, 1650, pp. 186, 207; also Firth, *Scotland and the Commonwealth*, pp. 82, 149, 258).

[5] *Clarke Papers*, vol. iii, 111.

the soldiers bread of some old rye I found here, and to buy as
much wheat to mix with it, the soldiers not being able to eat the
ryebread without a mixture of wheat in it.'[1]

The account of a court-martial which took place at Dundee
in 1651 gives us a glimpse of the way in which provisions were
issued to the men. A couple of officers assisted by a sergeant
were giving out the rations in an upper room, but the room was so
full they could hardly move. Ensign Kent ordered some of them
out. 'Get you out,' said Lieutenant Woodward to a man who
was pressing forward, and as he continued to shove, he gave him
a blow on the neck, and thrust him downstairs. 'What,' shouted
the private, 'shall we not see our biscuit and cheese weighed,
I hope to see such officers as you disbanded before long.'[2]

What quantity of cheese and biscuit formed the soldier's daily
allowance it is not easy to determine. The best evidence on these
points is supplied by Monck's *Order-Book*. During his campaign
in the Highlands in the summer of 1654 the infantry under his
command usually carried seven days' provisions in their knapsacks, at the rate of a pound of biscuit per diem for each man.
How much cheese they received per diem is not specified;
probably half a pound.[3]

The cheese was carried upon pack-horses,[4] who sometimes
carried also an additional supply of biscuit. 'The general,' says

[1] *Thurloe Papers*, vii. A French writer observes that while French soldiers
were content with little, the English auxiliaries demanded a good deal:
'huit sous par jour et le pain ne suffisent pas à cette nation carnassière,
parcequ'elle n'est pas satisfaite du pain de munition, n'y étant pas accoutu-
mée, et en ayant toujours eu d'autre' (Avenel, *Richelieu et la Monarchie
Absolue*, iii, 133).

[2] *Clarke MSS.*

[3] Monck wrote to Colonel Cooper, 22nd May 1654, ordering him 'to
furnish the horse under his command with 14 days provisions, the soldiers
snapsacks with 7 days bread and the cheese to be carried on horseback, and
as much bisquett besides the cheese as the horse can well carry'.

A second order on 7th June directs the issue by the storekeeper of 590
pounds of cheese each company of foot, and 295 to each troop of horse.

'7 days provisions to be in each knapsack and 200 weight of biscuit to be
carried on each baggage horse.'

On 4th July three regiments of foot are ordered ten days' provisions
'at 1 lb. of bisquett for each man per diem' (*Order-Book, Clarke MSS.*). See
also *Cal. State Papers, Dom.*, 1658–9, pp. 20, 75.

[4] Pack-horses had also been used by Fairfax, in 1646, when the New
Model advanced into Cornwall where no roads were to be found (Sprigge,
Anglia Rediviva, p. 175). Major-General Deane on his expedition into the
Highlands in 1652 was accompanied by '400 baggage horse led by the
country people, laden with biscuit and cheese' (*Scotland and the Common-
wealth*, p. 361; see also *Scotland and the Protectorate*, pp. xl, 150).

Gumble in his *Life of Monck*, 'did take great care for provisions for his forces, which were carried upon baggage horses, forty sometimes of them lost in a morning in a bog.'[1] Gumble gives also the following picture of Monck's manner of living during the campaign.

'His custom was after guards were placed to fall upon his cold meat (of which he had store dressed the night before), and [sit] upon the grass in the midst of his officers, and throw them joynts of meat very bountifully; and at nights there were great provisions of all kinds of meat that could be got, and free welcome to all the officers, with better state in his tent, and great preparations made for the next day's dinner.'[2]

When the food carried in the knapsacks and on the pack-saddles was exhausted, they were replenished from the magazines which had been established at various points in the Highlands.[3] Monck, who was undoubtedly the best English military administrator of the period, was always careful to keep his fortresses so well victualled that they could provide not only for their own garrisons, but if need be contribute supplies for a force in the field. Monck's aim was, whilst he commanded in Scotland, to keep his garrisons with stores enough to last them for ten months. Then if a Royalist rising or a foreign landing took place in England, he could draw his marching army out of the country and leave the fortresses to shift for themselves. If, on the other hand, there was another rising in Scotland itself, his flying columns could draw upon the stores in the fortresses to enable them to keep the field.[4]

[1] Gumble, *Life of Monck*, p. 82.   [2] Ibid., p. 85.

[3] Gumble says 'at several stages he had laid up stores of biscuit and cheese' (p. 82; cf. *Scotland and the Protectorate*).

[4] *Scotland and the Protectorate*, pp. 261, 319, 369. Monck's *Order-Book*, under 15th January 1656–7, contains the following entry:

'Letter to Col. Daniell to come and cleare all accounts with the Commissary for provisions of his garrison for that he is forthwith to furnish his garrisons of S. Johnston's (Blaire, Finlarick, and Balloch included) with 10 monthes stores of bread or wheate and cheese for 9 companies, accompting 80 men (officers and soldiers) to each companie, allowing to each man 2 lb. of bread and a quarter of a pound of cheese per diem, or for each 112 lb. of bread one boll of wheate, and to pay into the Treasury soe much of the monies now in his hands uppon the old account as will appeare uppon his account (when stated) to bee the true difference betweene the old and new stores, which said new stores he is betwixt this and the last of May next to get compleate into his garrison, according to the proportion above said'.

Whatever provisions regiments in the field might draw from
the magazines of the garrisons they had to pay for or to replace.
On 31st January 1657 Monck wrote to Colonel William Daniel,
ordering him 'that whereas there may bee occasion for the
Field forces in Scotland for to be supplied with provisions out
of the stores in the garrison of St. Johnston's, that he take care
that such regiments or companies as shall receive provisions out
of his stores doe either lay in the same proportion in kinde, or
else agree with the storekeeper to pay for the same at reasonable
rates'.[1]

In the same way the daily rations issued to the soldiers of any
particular regiment or company were charged to its account,
and deducted from the pay due to it when the regimental
accounts were made up. This rendered the business of making
up the accounts of a regiment very complicated, and was one
of the difficulties which prevented individuals from obtaining
their arrears of pay as quickly as they ought to have done.[2]

The system thus outlined was adopted in all the armies of the
Commonwealth and Protectorate. It is probable, however, that
troops quartered in England were more frequently left to provide their food out of their own pockets instead of being supplied
with rations by the government. The greater simplicity of this
latter plan was a strong recommendation, but it was only pos-

[1] Monck's *Order-Book* also contains the following entry:
18th September 1654. 'Letter to Mr. Bilton, that Lt. Col. Blunt having
acquainted him with a note of severall provisions of biskett and cheese
delivered to the northern regiments out of the stores at Inverness, to
deduct soe much out of the pay of those regiments as they have received,
that it may bee reimbursed to the garrison, and in the mean time to let
Lieut. Col. Blunt have what hee can spare for a stock of provisions. The rate
of provisions, 4d. a lb. of cheese & 15s. each bagge of biskett.'

[2] The commissary of provisions had to come to a settlement with the
various regiments. In 1655, when it was proposed to abolish one of these
officials, Monck urged his continuance, writing as follows:
'What allowance yow will give him your Lordship may consider of, but
being hee has a charge of provisions in his hands, and many accounts to
make upp betweene the regiments and himselfe, which cannot quickly bee
done, I thinke your Lordship may doe well to continue him for a yeare, till
the souldyours have eaten upp their provisions, and that hee has cleared off
the accounts with the regiments, which as yet wee cannot doe because the
souldjers have not soe much monie to spaire to eaven theire accounts'
(*Scotland and the Protectorate*, p. 300). It should be noted that the government seems to have charged the soldiers one-fourth more than the provisions issued actually cost, as an allowance for waste (*Cal. State Papers,
Dom.*, 1658–9, p. 183).

sible when the soldiers were punctually paid, and the troops in England were always paid with greater regularity than those abroad. Lockhart, however, writing from Dunkirk just after its capture, expressed himself anxious to introduce the plan there. 'I shall much desire,' he said, 'that when money comes, the soldiers may be as much taken off provisions as may be, and left to make their own markets; it will keep counts more distinct and clear, and be more satisfaction to the soldiers.' It is not probable that Lockhart could ever make the change he proposed, for the pay of the garrison of Dunkirk was constantly in arrears, and unless the soldier had money in his pocket the experiment could not be tried.[1]

On the whole, after making due allowances for their failures, the administrators of the Commonwealth and Protectorate solved the problem of feeding their forces with a fair amount of success. The army appears to have been better fed than the navy was during the same period.[2] At all events complaints are fewer. The commissariat department, it is evident, was far better organized than it had been in the earlier part of the Civil War, and the system compared favourably with that existing in most foreign armies at the time.[3]

One great exception to this comparative success is afforded by the history of the expedition to the West Indies in 1655. English governments had no experience of distant expeditions in tropical climates, and the little army sent under Venables was

[1] In the same letter (*Thurloe Papers*, vii, 216) Lockhart gives the following account of his measures for victualling Dunkirk. It was cheaper, he thought, to buy provisions in Flanders than to get them sent from England. 'I shall go abowt the buying of wheat and rye, to make bread for the present subsistence of the forces, and shall keep the months provisione of biskitt in store, least at any tyme, either by seege or otherwayes, we should be putt to a pinch; and once in a yeare, the maggazine of bread, I mean the month's biskitt for 4000 men, must be renewed, and the old given owt, and rebaitted of the soldiers pay; but before the old stock of biskitt so laid in be meddled with, the new stock to the same quantity must be first in store; and so this place will never want six weekes provisione of bread, which is the staff of man's life. If I find the butter and cheese may be kept without spoyling, I shall lykewise save it; but I think, for provisions that are not to be made use of save once in a year, all cheese, or at least salt beefe and bacon, or pork in lieu of the butter will be best.'

[2] See Mr Oppenheim's article on 'The Navy of the Commonwealth', *English Historical Review*, 1896, pp. 41–4.

[3] See besides the passages already quoted from Turner's *Pallas Armata*, Avenel's *Richelieu et la Monarchie Absolue*, iii, 127–46, and Rousset's *Louvois*, i, 248, ed. 1879.

badly organized, badly equipped, and still worse provisioned. The provisions supplied originally were bad in quality and insufficient in quantity. They were supplied by the victuallers of the navy, and Venables asserts that when he complained of their unsoundness General Desborough, who had charge of the preparations, refused to hear him. He goes on to say that Desborough was secretly in league with the victuallers, and had a share in their profits. At Barbadoes, where more provisions were bought, all that could be obtained were some which had been refused by the fleet in England, and therefore sent to Barbadoes by the victuallers to be sold. On the voyage from Barbadoes to Hispaniola the soldiers were reduced to half rations, and their bread or biscuit was 'most beastly rotten,' insomuch that they were greatly weakened by the time they landed. When they marched to attack the city of San Domingo, instead of carrying in their knapsacks rations for seven days like Monck's or Cromwell's soldiers, they had only food for three days, and often not that, so that they were starving by the time they reached the city, and had to fall back upon their ships at once for fresh supplies. The food they had was unsuitable in character. 'The worst saltest beef, unwatered,' says a soldier, 'with all the broken, mouldy, dusty sweepings of the ship's biscuit the false steward could give us.' Many died in Hispaniola from eating unsuitable food, more in Jamaica after they landed there. 'For these seventeen days,' wrote an officer on 4th June 1655, 'we have had but three biscuits of bread per man, neither officer nor soldier, and sometimes little or no meat for two or three days together, and when God will send us supplies we know not.' General Venables reported on 13th June that he could only allow the soldiers half a biscuit per diem, and that even that allowance would come to an end in five weeks. When they landed in Jamaica the English army found abundance of cattle, but fresh meat without any other food proved very unwholesome. 'Fresh flesh and roots,' wrote Venables, 'put them into fluxes which sweep them away by ten and twenty per diem frequently.'[1] Later still the cattle being driven into the mountains by the Spaniards, or shy and difficult to catch, even meat

[1] *The Narrative of General Venables, etc.*, edited by C. H. Firth, pp. xxxii, 4, 13, 41, 49, 142; *Seventh Report Hist. MSS. Comm.*, p. 574.

became scarce. The soldiers were driven to eat horses and asses. 'The last flesh,' says an officer, 'I conceived the best, and did eat heartily of it.' The dogs that accompanied the army were eaten too – 'Not one walks the streets that is not shot at, unless well befriended or respected'. Out of about 7,000 men who landed at Jamaica in May 1655, not more than 3,700 were alive in the following November.

Yet the inferior quality of the provisions supplied was only one amongst the many causes of the disasters which overtook the expedition. The deficiency in quantity was in part due to the accident by which the store-ships became separated from the rest of the fleet, and to the mistake committed by General Venables in enlisting more men at Barbadoes and in the islands than he had provisions to feed. The organization of the expedition was defective from the beginning, partly from the negligence of those entrusted with its equipment and preparation, partly from their ignorance of the conditions necessary for the success of oversea campaigns and war in the tropics. Nor was its commander a man of sufficient energy and ability to compensate for these defects and neglects.

CHAPTER X

Clothing, Equipment and Mounting of the Army

THERE ARE MANY popular misconceptions about the Cromwellian army which it is almost impossible to remove. Some which relate to its character and composition have already been touched upon. Others which concern its appearance and externals remain to be dealt with. A modern artist charged to depict a scene from the history of the Civil Wars usually distinguishes the soldiers of the two parties by depicting the one with long hair and the other with short. In reality there was very little difference between Cavaliers and Parliamentarians in this respect. Amongst the numerous portraits of Parliamentary officers which have been handed down to us, there is hardly one in which the subject is not wearing the long locks supposed to distinguish his opponents. Cromwell, Lambert, Harrison, Hutchinson, and many others, all are represented with hair which touches or almost touches their shoulders. It was not so, according to Mrs Hutchinson, when the Civil War began. At first the name of Roundheads seemed apt enough for the Parliamentary army. They 'marched out so', says she, 'as if they had been only sent out till their hair was grown'. But 'two or three years after, any stranger that had seen them, would have inquired the reason of that name'.[1] Not only the officers but the rank and file too had ceased to resemble the typical Roundhead of satires and caricatures.

Another deeply rooted popular error is the belief that the soldiers and officers of the King's army were better dressed than those of the Parliament's. It was current in the next generation, and finds expression in Shadwell's play, *The Volunteers*, which was published in 1693. Shadwell brings upon the stage one

[1] *Life of Col. Hutchinson*, i, 170, ed. 1885.

Major-General Blunt, a soldier who had fought for the King at Edgehill, and is now entertaining at dinner some of his old companions in arms and with them a certain Colonel Hackwell who had served under Cromwell. 'You have not forgotten,' says Blunt to his comrades, introducing Hackwell, 'how this gentleman and his demure psalm-singing fellows used to drub us?'

'No gad,' replies a Cavalier, 'I felt 'em once to purpose.'

'In high-crowned hats,' rejoins Blunt, 'coller'd bands, great loose coats, long tucks under 'em, and calves-leather boots, they used to sing a psalm, fall on, and beat us to the devil.'

'What a filthy slovenly army was this,' says a young beau, 'I warrant you not a well-dressed man among the Roundheads.'

'But these plain fellows,' adds Blunt, 'would so thrash your swearing, drinking fellows in laced coats (just such as you of the drawing-room and Locket's[1] are now), and so strip 'em, by the Lord Harry, that after a battle those saints looked like the Israelites laden with the Egyptian baggage.'[2]

There was some element of truth in this. The King's officers in general probably wore more lace and feathers than their adversaries, and perhaps gayer cloaks, but to a modern judge the simple and serviceable dress of the officers of the New Model would have been more attractive, and the uniform of the rank and file would have been decisive. The familiar red coat is a relic of the New Model, and it was first generally adopted in 1645. At the beginning of the war the soldiers of both armies were dressed in whatever colour their colonels chose to select. At Edgehill every variety of hue was visible on the backs of Essex's army. The regiments of Denzil Holles and Lord Robartes had red coats, Lord Brooke's regiment purple coats, Lord Saye's blue, Colonel Ballard's grey, Colonel Hampden's green.[3] Amongst the ranks of the Royalists there was the same diversity of tint.

---

[1] A fashionable ordinary, which stood on the site of Drummond's Banking House at Charing Cross, and was so called from Adam Locket, the landlord.

> '*At Locket's, Brown's, and at Pontack's enquire*
> *What modish kickshaws the nice beaux desire.*'
> – (Mrs Centlivre).

See Wheatley and Cunningham's *London*, ii, 413.

[2] Act iii, sc. i.

[3] Vicars, *Jehovah Jireh*, p. 200; cf. *Life of Col. Hutchinson*, i, 208; Warburton, *Prince Rupert*, i, 428.

In that battle the two sides were distinguished simply by the
fact that Essex's men wore orange scarfs and those of the King
red. In the absence of these scarfs it was impossible to determine
whether a man belonged to one army or the other. At Marston
Moor when Sir Thomas Fairfax, in consequence of the defeat of
the cavalry he commanded, found himself alone amongst the
enemy, he took the white handkerchief out of his hat (which was
the sign of the Parliamentarians that day) and 'passed through
for one of their own commanders' till he reached Cromwell's victorious troops.[1] At Edgehill, where Sir Faithful Fortescue's
troop deserted in a body to the King's army, seventeen or
eighteen of them were killed by their new allies 'by their negligence of not throwing away their orange tawny scarfs'.[2] In the
same battle the King's standard, which had been taken and delivered to the keeping of Essex's secretary, was recovered by
Captain Smith and two other Royalists, 'who, disguising themselves with orange-coloured scarfs, and pretending it unfit that
a penman should have the honour to carry the standard, took it
from him and rode with it to the King'.[3]

Gradually, however, greater uniformity in the colour of the
soldiers' clothing became the rule amongst the Parliamentarians.
At Marston Moor Rupert's own regiment had blue coats and that
of Colonel Tillier's green coats, while Newcastle's foot wore
white coats.[4] But amongst the infantry of the Eastern Association whom he was fighting red was rapidly becoming the usual
wear. At the relief of Newark in March 1644 we hear of the
'Norfolk Redcoats'.[5] About the same date there is a bill for
supplying Colonel Montagu's regiment, raised in Cambridgeshire
and the Isle of Ely, with red coats faced with white.[6] The regiments raised in Essex were dressed in red coats lined with blue.[7]

---

[1] Fairfax's *Short Memorial*, reprinted in Arber's *English Garner*, viii, 608.

[2] Clarendon, *Rebellion*, vi, 86.   [3] Ludlow, *Memoirs*, i, 43.

[4] Phillips, *Civil War in Wales*, ii, 195; *Transactions of the Royal Historical Society*, xii, p. 55.

[5] *A Brief Relation of the Siege at Newark*, by Lieut-Col. Bury, 1644, p. 7.

[6] Thos. Buckley's account, 27th March 1644, *Exchequer Papers*.

[7] *Seventh Report Hist. MSS. Comm.*, i, 561. In 1645 the Committee of Both Kingdoms ordered the county of Essex to send its quota of recruits for the New Model 'commodiously provided, as hath formerly been practised, with 1000 red coats lined with blue' (*Cal. State Papers, Dom.*, 1644–5, p. 358).

Another regiment, whose colonel's name is not mentioned, had red coats faced with blue.[1] Finally, Manchester's own men had green coats faced with red.[2] It is evident, therefore, that by 1644 red coats must have been the prevailing wear in the army of the Eastern Association, though they were not universal.

On the formation of the New Model in 1645 the final step was taken, and the whole of the army under Sir Thomas Fairfax's command was from the first dressed in red.[3] A newspaper called *Perfect Passages*, published on 7th May 1645, definitely says: 'The men are Redcoats all, the whole army only are distinguished by several facings of their coats'. As Fairfax's own colours were blue, his regiment had blue facings.[4] From the contract made in October 1649 for the clothing of the army in Ireland, we get the further information that the coats were of 'Venice colour red', and the breeches 'of grey or other good colour'.[5]

Throughout the Protectorate the same colour was adhered to. The troops whom Cromwell sent to Flanders in 1657 were equipped with new red coats when they left England,[6] and in November 1658 the Protector Richard gave all the foot soldiers about London 'new red coats trimmed with black' to wear at his father's funeral.[7] In the literature of the Commonwealth and Protectorate 'redcoat' and 'soldier' are used as synonymous terms.[8]

The clothing and equipment of the troops were supplied by the government. Parliament, the Council of State, or the Committee for the Army purchased what was needed, or more frequently contracted for it with the manufacturers, and handed it over to the regiments for which it was required. The cost of

[1] Buckley's account.

[2] On 2nd October 1643 Manchester writes ordering coats for his regiment, 'being 2100 and odd men, and that the coats be of green cloth lined with red' (*Seventh Report Hist. MSS. Comm.*, i, 565).

[3] The credit of being the first to make this clear belongs to Mr Fortescue. See 'A Chapter on Red Coats', *Macmillan's Magazine*, September 1893.

[4] *Perfect Passages*, 7th May 1645, under 1st May.

[5] *Cal. State Papers, Dom.*, 1649–50, p. 343.

[6] 'They had new red coats given them for the terrible name thereof' (Heath, *Chronicle*, ed. 1663, p. 720).

[7] *Clarke Papers*, iii, 168.

[8] See *The Red-Coats Catechism*, 4to, 1659.

the clothing thus supplied was deducted from the pay of the men. On 10th September 1642 Parliament, in a contract for 7,500 suits for the English troops in Ulster, stipulated that the cost of the suits, which came to forty-two shillings and sixpence apiece, should be deducted from the pay of the soldiers at the rate of twopence per diem.[1]

The same system prevailed under the Protectorate, but the clothing was rather cheaper. Ninepence a week was deducted for clothing from the forces in England and Ireland, so that thirty-nine shillings a year sufficed. One suit a year was the rule, and it seems to have been usually issued about October.[2] It was not always punctually supplied, and in the spring of 1655 Monck complained that his soldiers were 'out of shoes, stockings, shirts and clothes'. 'Unless,' he said, 'we can have a fortnight's pay to give together to the soldiers to buy them necessaries, they will be but in an ill condition.' In a second letter he describes divers of the officers as 'enforced to engage their own credit for clothes for their soldiers'.[3]

The nature and quality of the clothes supplied to the army can be gathered from the contracts. The 7,500 suits for the army in Ulster which Parliament contracted for in 1642 included a cap, doublet, cassock, breeches, two pair of stockings, two pair of shoes, and two shirts for each soldier.[4] The contracts made in 1645 for the New Model army and in 1649 for Cromwell's army in Ireland include fewer items, but the quality is more exactly specified. The doublets ordered in 1642 cost six shillings apiece. The shirts which were to be of fine Oxenbrig (i.e., Osnaburgh) linen were two and ninepence each.[5]

The cassock and breeches, or coat and breeches (for the terms coat and cassock seem to be interchangeable), cost, according to the contracts of 1645 and 1649, seventeen shillings together. In the agreement with Richard Downes, the contractor, it is specified that the coats are to be 'of Suffolk, Coventry or Gloucestershire cloth, and to be made three quarters and a nail long [i.e., twenty-nine inches and a quarter], faced with bayes or cotton with tapestrings, according to a pattern delivered to the Com-

[1] Lords' Journals, v, 347.   [2] Thurloe, iii, 536.
[3] Scotland and the Protectorate, pp. 246, 266.
[4] Lords' Journals, v, 347.   [5] Ibid., v, 213, 347, 556, 599.

mittee'. The breeches were to be made of Reading cloth, or other cloth, in length three quarters one-eighth (i.e., thirty-one inches and a half), well lined and trimmed suitably to the pattern presented. Finally, the cloth both of the said coats and of the breeches was to be first shrunk in cold water.[1]

The rest of the clothing bought in 1649 for Cromwell's army in Ireland cost much the same as in 1642. Sixteen thousand shirts were contracted for at £2,400, that is at three shillings apiece.[2] Stockings described as 'of good Welsh cotton' Downes supplied in 1645 at thirteen pence halfpenny a pair, but others, presumably of inferior quality, were obtained at a shilling a pair both in 1645 and in 1649.[3] Shoes for the New Model cost two and threepence per pair, but in 1649 half a crown a pair was the price.[4] These were low shoes, as shown in the wooden figures of musketeers and pikemen of the time at Cromwell House, Highgate.[5] The men paid for their boots as well as for their clothes, and paid a good deal more than the wholesale price. 'How can it be thought,' asks Colonel Doyley, complaining of the unpaid condition of the forces in Jamaica, 'that a private soldier can give four shillings for a pair of ammunition shoes that never received so much these three years?'[6] It was still more unreasonable, as the shoes were probably worth but half a crown.

The headdress of the infantry varied at different times. The helmet was falling into disuse on account of its weight, and had been practically abandoned long before the Restoration.[7] In 1642 the troops serving in Ulster were provided by the Long Parliament with 'Monmouth caps', which were contracted for at the rate of twenty-three shillings a dozen.[8] The best description of them is given by Richard Symonds in 1644. Speaking of

---

[1] Tangye, *Two Protectors*, p. 276; *Cal. State Papers, Dom.*, 1649–50, p. 343. In September 1645 the suits cost sixteen shillings each according to the *Exchequer Papers*, but the contract with Downes in February 1646 fixed the price at seventeen shillings.

[2] *Cal. State Papers, Dom.*, 1649–50, pp. 369, 597.

[3] Ibid., pp. 369, 514, 594, 599. In September 1645 5,000 pairs of stockings were bought for the New Model at a shilling a pair (*Exchequer Papers*; Tangye, p. 277).

[4] *Exchequer Papers*; *Cal. State Papers, Dom.*, 1649–50, pp. 369, 594, 598.

[5] See the engravings of these figures given in the illustrated edition of Green's *Short History of the English People*, iii, 1162–7.

[6] Thurloe, vi, 833.   [7] See p. 91.   [8] *Lords' Journals*, v, 599.

Bewdley, he says: 'The only manufacture of this town is making of caps called Monmouth caps, knitted by poor people for twopence apiece, ordinary ones sold for two shillings, three shillings, and four shillings. First they are knit, then they mill them, then block them, then they work them with tassels, then they sheer them.'[1] Defoe writing in 1724 describes these caps as 'sold chiefly to the Dutch seamen, and made only at Bewdley'.[2]

But the eventual substitute for the helmet was not the Monmouth cap, but a broad-brimmed hat of some kind, such as is shown in the wooden figures of the musketeer and the pikeman at Cromwell House, Highgate. The felt hat was coming into general use before the Restoration took place,[3] and Colonel Walton's description of the soldiers' headgear just after the Restoration probably applies pretty closely to the period just before that event. 'The buff leather hat, which had superseded the old morion or burgonet, very soon disappeared before the beaver or its black felt imitation, and whereas the crown was previously wont to be high, it was now cut down to a very moderate size. In 1661 the beaver hat was a novelty; but two or three years later all the troops wore imitation of felt, and their officers had them of beaver or velvet.'[4]

There are occasional complaints as to the quality of the goods supplied under these contracts. In 1645 the Committee of London Merchants representing the Adventurers (that is the persons who had advanced money for the reduction of Ireland on promise of repayment in Irish lands) complained of the frauds of a contractor named John Davis and his partners. He not only charged too much both for clothes and provisions, but the quality of his goods was inferior. 'The cloth which was sent thither and furnished for the officers of the army at 18s. per yard, was dear at 8s. per yard. The clothes which arrived there were found to be very coarse shrinking cloth, and most of the suits too little

[1] *Diary of Richard Symonds*, p. 14.

[2] Defoe's *Tour in England*, vol. ii, letter iii, p. 70, ed. 1724.

[3] When Tom Verney enlisted as a pikeman in Colonel Ingoldsby's regiment, about 1653, he asked his brother's agent to provide him with an outfit. It included amongst other things 'a grey Dutch felt', a pair of grey worsted stockings, a pair of strong buck's leather gloves, a black leather sword belt. All of these, including the felt hat, were probably part of the ordinary uniform of his regiment (*Memoirs of the Verney Family*, iii, 160).

[4] Clifford Walton, *History of the British Standing Army*, p. 365.

and unserviceable.' Cassocks and breeches as good as those for which he charged seventeen might be had for ten shillings.[1]

To prevent similar frauds there was subsequently a systematic inspection of all goods supplied, to see that they were of the specified quality. The contract for clothing made with Richard Downes in February 1645-6 contains the following clause: 'That although it is impossible for any person to make the said provisions exactly suitable for goodness to any pattern, for that many may be a little better, and some a little worse, yet it is the resolution of the said contractor and he does hereby promise, that as near as he can none of the said provisions of coats, breeches, and stockings shall be worse than the patterns presented to the said honourable committee, and that the said Committee, or such as they shall appoint to view and supervise the said provisions, shall have power to refuse any of them, against which there is exceptions'.[2] The certificates amongst the State Papers show these inspections to have been duly made, and they were conducted not merely by the officials of the government, but by experts selected for the purpose. For instance, the boots supplied for Cromwell's army in Ireland were examined and passed by the Master and Wardens of the Cordwainers' Company.[3] On the whole there is reason to believe that during the Commonwealth and Protectorate the quality of the clothing thus obtained was tolerably good. Yet there are occasional complaints. Colonel Lilburne, complaining in March 1654 that his soldiers have received so little pay that they cannot provide themselves with clothes and shoes, adds that 'as for sending down anything which they call ammunition stores, the soldier hath been so much cheated in it, that I presume it will be altogether unseasonable at this time'.[4] Apparently he meant that the shoes and clothes provided by the government were bad, and that it would be better to pay the soldier and let him provide his own.

Two minor points in the soldier's equipment remain to be

---

[1] *The State of the Irish affairs . . . as they lie represented from the Committee of Adventurers*, 1645, 4to, pp. 25-6.

[2] Tangye, p. 277; *Cal. State Papers, Dom.*, 1649-50, p. 343.

[3] Ibid., 1649-50, pp. 556, 561.

[4] *Scotland and the Protectorate*, p. 59.

mentioned. The first is the 'knapsack', or as it was usually called 'snapsack', in which he carried his food and his spare clothing, if he had any. The knapsacks of the New Model cost the government ninepence apiece,[1] and were probably, like those used in the army of Charles the Second and William the Third, merely canvas or leather bags.[2]

On the other hand, one article with which the army of William the Third was supplied does not appear in the outfit of the Cromwellian army. The soldiers were not provided with water-bottles. This omission was one of the causes of the defeat of the expedition to the West Indies in 1655. During their long march through the woods to attack the city of San Domingo the soldiers were reduced to the utmost extremity by thirst, and when they reached the city they were unfit to fight, and unable to maintain their ground before its walls. 'Whoever comes to these parts,' wrote General Venables in May 1655, 'must bring leather bottles, which are more needful here than knapsacks in Ireland.' In another letter he asks for 'blackjacks', as these bottles were called, without which 'not one man can march in these torrid regions, where water is precious and scant'.[3]

What has been said of the method in which the army was clothed and equipped applies to the cavalry as well as the infantry, but with certain exceptions. There were necessarily certain differences in their equipment and dress. As to uniform, the dragoon, being but a mounted infantryman, probably wore a red coat like a foot soldier. Lilburne, who was a lieutenant-colonel of dragoons, is described as 'drawing a paper book from under his short red coat' at a public meeting in 1648.[4] But it is not easy to determine whether the troopers of the regular cavalry wore the red coat. Probably their ordinary uniform was the leather 'buff coat', with a scarf or possibly a cloak added. It is significant that in the report of the debates which took place in the Council of the Army during October 1647, 'buff coat' is

---

[1] *Exchequer Papers.*

[2] Clifford Walton, *History of the British Standing Army*, p. 377.

[3] *The Narrative of General Venables*, pp. xxxvii, 49, 65.

[4] *A Declaration of some Proceedings of Lieut-Col. John Lilburne and His Associates*, 1648, 4to, p. 17.

the synonym employed to describe a trooper.[1] The officers perhaps wore red coats when they were not on active service.
Edwards writing in 1647 complains of a lieutenant of a troop of
horse quartered at Bristol who was wont to preach publicly 'in
his scarlet coat laced with silver lace'.[2] On active service, however, or on duty the officers pretty certainly wore buff coats as
their men did. Sir Thomas Herbert in describing Colonel Harrison's meeting with the King, as Charles the First was on his
way to London for his trial, says that Harrison, who came to
take command of the escort, had 'a velvet montero on his head,
a new buff coat upon his back, and a crimson silk scarf about his
waist, richly fringed'.[3] Mrs Hutchinson complains that the same
Harrison, at the reception of the Spanish ambassador in December 1650, was far too gorgeously dressed for a godly Puritan. He
came to that ceremony in a 'scarlet coat and cloak both laden
with gold and silver lace, and the coat so covered with clinquant,
that scarcely could one discern the ground'.[4] On the first of
these occasions Harrison, one would be inclined to infer, wore
the dress appropriate to his rank, and on the second something
devised by his personal taste.

When the cavalryman was not wearing his helmet, a broad-
brimmed felt hat of some kind seems to have been his usual
headgear.[5] A portrait of Essex by Hollar represents him with
his plumed helmet at his feet, and on his head, as a substitute
for the helmet, a broad-brimmed hat with a very square and
high crown, having an ostrich feather at one side.[6]

[1] *Clarke Papers*, i, 235, 258; cf. Clifford Walton, *History of the British Standing Army*, p. 370.

[2] Edwards, *Gangræna*, iii, 111.

[3] *Memoirs of Sir Thomas Herbert*, 1701, p. 97.

[4] *Life of Colonel Hutchinson*, ii, 171.

[5] Lambert, for instance, sent for the following articles when he was in Scotland: 'I must entreat you to buy two handsome sword-belts for the Major General, one with black fringe, a shoulder belt, the other of strong buff for the middle, used to hang a charging sword in. I must desire you to buy him a good French hat of the best sort, and one of an ordinary sort with most fashionable black bands, for gold or silver pleaseth him not. Also to get Mr Kendell our shoemaker to make two pair of handsome walking boots and one pair of summer riding boots, with two pair of Spanish leather shoes' (Capt. W. Walker to Capt. Adam Baynes, 7th May 1651, *Letters from Roundhead Officers in Scotland*, p. 21).

[6] The portrait is reproduced in the illustrated edition of Green's *Short History of the English People*, iii, 1155.

The 'montero' mentioned above in the description of Harrison's costume was also frequently worn by cavalry officers. At Naseby both generals wore it. After Rupert had routed the left wing of the Parliamentary army, he led a party of horse to attack the baggage-guard of Fairfax's army. 'The leader of them being a person somewhat in habit like our General, in a red montero as the General had,' was mistaken by the commander of the baggage-guard for Fairfax. So that officer went up to Rupert 'with his hat in hand, and asked him how the day went, thinking it was the general'. 'The cavalier, who we have since heard was Rupert, asked him and the rest if they would have quarter. They cried "No", gave fire, and instantly beat him off.'[1]

The 'montero' appears to have been made of cloth or of velvet, but its shape is not definitely described. Thomas Ellwood, the Quaker, describes himself as wearing on one occasion, 'a large montero cap of black velvet, the skirt of which being turned up in folds, looked, it seems, somewhat above the then common garb of a Quaker', and therefore he escaped ill usage which otherwise would have befallen him.[2] As in the case of the infantry, a broad-brimmed hat of felt, or some similar material, became the general wear by 1660.

A more distinctive part of the equipment of the cavalry was their boots. Two thousand pairs of boots 'of good neats-leather, well tanned and waxed', were purchased for the horsemen sent to serve in Ireland at fourteen shillings and tenpence a pair in 1649.[3] The dragoons, as they were intended to serve on foot,

[1] From a narrative of Naseby in a pamphlet entitled *A Letter from a Gentleman of Public Employment*, quoted in Markham's *Life of Fairfax*, p. 223.

[2] *History of Thomas Ellwood*, ed. 1885, p. 83. It will be remembered that Corporal Trim had a montero cap, given him by poor Tom, his unfortunate brother. 'The montero cap was scarlet, of a superfine Spanish cloth, dyed in grain, and mounted all round with fur, except about four inches in the front, which was faced with a light blue, slightly embroidered; – and seemed to have been the property of a Portuguese quartermaster, not of foot, but of horse, as the word denotes' (*Tristram Shandy*, vi, 24).

[3] *Cal. State Papers, Dom.*, 1649–50, pp. 412, 594. How to wax boots, and why boots should be waxed, is set forth at length in a sham sermon attributed to Colonel Hewson, entitled *Walk, Knaves, Walk*, published in 1659. It is reprinted in Morgan's *Phœnix Britannicus*, p. 261. Hewson had once been a shoemaker. The text on which the discourse is composed is 'Now because the times are bad, and the winter draws near, therefore buy ye waxed boots'. A composition of tallow and beeswax is recommended by the preacher.

must have worn shorter and lighter boots than the regular cavalry.[1]

As to the saddles of the cavalry, 'troop saddles with furniture' were bought for the horsemen of the New Model in July 1645, at sixteen shillings or sixteen shillings and sixpence apiece. 'Dragoon saddles,' lighter and of inferior workmanship, cost at the same date seven shillings and tenpence, while 'cantle pad saddles', i.e. pack-saddles for baggage horses, cost seventeen shillings. Holsters for holding pistols, a necessary adjunct to the saddles, cost half a crown a pair.[2]

From the saddles one passes by a natural transition to the horses. Horses for mounting the cavalry were provided in many different ways.[3] The first method was purchase in the open market. A captain commissioned to raise a troop received an allowance for mounting it from the State, at the rate of ten pounds per horse.[4] When Ludlow became major to Sir Arthur Haselrig he records that Haselrig bought a hundred horses in Smithfield Market to mount his troop.[5] In 1644 forty-nine horses for Cromwell's regiment were bought at Huntingdon Fair for an average of six pounds apiece. When the war began a considerable number of the Parliamentary cavalry were mounted by subscription. Persons well affected to the Parliament undertook to provide a horse and a man to serve in Essex's army. If they provided the horse only they were paid one and fourpence a day; if the rider also, two and sixpence. But often they undertook to defray the cost of maintaining both.[6] The value of the horse was assessed, and it was regarded as a loan, for which repayment was promised, with interest, at the rate of 8 per cent. When this source of supply proved insufficient, committees were appointed to take horses suitable for military service, valuing them and giving their owners certificates promising future repayment.[7]

---

[1] Clifford Walton, *History of the British Standing Army*, pp. 375, 376.

[2] *Exchequer Papers*, bundle 31; cf. 'Raising of the Ironsides,' p. 23.

[3] I have already treated this subject at some length in a paper on 'The Raising of the Ironsides' (p. 24), published in the *Transactions of the Royal Historical Society*, vol. xiii.

[4] 'Raising of the Ironsides,' p. 2.   [5] Ludlow, *Memoirs*, i, 90.

[6] Husbands, *Ordinances*, i, 341; cf. a pamphlet entitled *The Old Proverb*, 1645, 4to, p. 10.

[7] Husbands, *Ordinances*, i, 339, 358, 456, 773.

The subscription, in short, developed into a forced loan.

A third method of procuring horses, which was adopted in 1643, was to assess a district to provide a given number of horses, according to its size, wealth, and population, and to leave the local authorities to collect the horses and forward them to the army or to certain fixed stations. On 25th July 1643, for instance, 6,500 horses were ordered to be raised from fifteen counties named.[1]

A fourth method of procuring horses, which proved very fruitful during the early years of the Civil War, was to confiscate the horses of persons disaffected to the Parliament. This had the double advantage of at once disarming opponents and completing the armament of friends. Legitimate enough in a time of war, it led, however, to a hundred abuses. Horses were seized without inquiry into the political conduct of their owner, or on slight suspicions and insufficient proofs of the owner's disaffection. Officers were charged by the civil magistrates with taking the horses of persons who were not 'malignants' at all, and they in turn accused the magistrates of sparing the horses of proved 'malignants' for purely personal reasons. So came conflicts of authority and disputes between the civil and military power.[2] The complaint which follows is a specimen of the complaints which came from every county in England.

'The friends of the Parliament are much troubled about taking up of horses, it being left to the discretion of a Quartermaster, or his man, to take what horses he please, and if he account a man a malignant, he takes away his horses, and if he be drunk, or have but a cross word, he takes all that a man hath, not leaving him any to inn his harvest; these are sad things, and so much the sadder, when a little care might prevent them. There is another inconvenience that the poor countreys undergo, and that is, they know not a true warrant from a counterfeit, my Lord General's name being easily counterfeited; and you shall have a fellow come with never a cover to his tail, nor boots to his legs, with a pistol hanging in his scarf, his sword by his side, and he shall fright the poor countryman, and take what he please

[1] Husbands, *Ordinances*, ii, 184, 275.

[2] See Carlyle, *Cromwell*, Letters xvi, xviii. Cromwell's letter to the Committee of Suffolk in defence of Captain Margery is an example of the disputes which were happening all over England.

from him: and besides all this they that have warrants take many and make money of them, and besides take bribes instead of horses: this is not the way to have men long able to afford relief to the war.'[1]

In the spring of 1645 when the New Model was organized, all these different sources of supply were exhausted, or almost exhausted, and practically the only method left was the method of purchase. Horses were bought to mount Fairfax's troopers at seven pounds ten shillings each, at four pounds each for his dragoons, and at six pounds each for drawing his baggage and artillery.[2] Prices rose slightly in later years, but only slightly. Fairfax was also empowered to take such horses as he should think fit for the service of the Parliament in the districts occupied by the enemy.[3]

All these horses, whether bought, requisitioned, or confiscated, were known as 'state's horses', and were branded with the State's mark by the markmaster-general or one of his deputies.[4] The captain of a troop of horse was required to keep an exact account of all the horses received by him for his troop from the agents of the government, and of all that might be bought by him for the service of the State. Negligence in this respect was a frequent source of trouble. The case of Captain (or Commissary-General) Copley illustrates this. Copley was accused of embezzlement of several kinds, and in particular for his conduct with regard to the horses of his troop. Husbands, his cornet, deposed that the captain 'offered to sale and gave away some of the state's horses, viz. one fleabitten nag to Mr Loe the chirurgeon, and one bay gelding with a bald face to this deponent'. It was also alleged that he had defrauded the State in his purchases of horses. When he received money to remount his troop he had bought 'many which were poor, lame, and foundered, some not worth six pounds, some not worth five pounds'.[5]

[1] *The Parliament Scout*, 17th to 24th August 1643; quoted in Webb's *Civil War in Herefordshire*, i. 333.

[2] *Exchequer Papers*; Husbands, *Ordinances*, ii, 627.

[3] Husbands, *Ordinances*, ii, 664.

[4] A copy of the mark is given in the *Lords' Journals* for 23rd March 1643, and any person buying horses or arms bearing that mark was liable to punishment (v, 661–2).

[5] 'Deposition of Azanah,' Husbands, *Exchequer Papers*.

The soldier who received a horse from the State was, like his captain, responsible for its custody, and if he sold it both buyer and seller were liable to punishment. He provided for its maintenance out of his pay, and the rates which he paid for forage were fixed by the government. In May 1645, for instance, the rates to be paid while the army was on the march were 'fourpence a night for hay, threepence a night for grass, fourpence a peck for oats, sixpence a peck for pease and beans, and sevenpence a peck for barley and malt'.[1] When the army was stationary, as in the case of Monck's forces in Scotland, during the latter part of the Protectorate, the custom appears to have been to hire grass-land for the purpose of grazing the horses of a particular regiment, and to assess the district in which the regiment was quartered to supply straw at a fixed rate.[2] The total was then charged to the regiment and deducted from its pay.

The soldier had also to defray the expense of shoeing his horse, and generally he procured the shoes from the regimental store, as the government contracted for horseshoes wholesale and supplied them to the regiments.[3]

The general supervision of the mounting of the army was entrusted to the muster-master and his assistants.[4] Originally the musters were ordered to take place once a month, but under the Protectorate once in six weeks was the usual practice. On these occasions the muster-master inspected the horses of the cavalry regiments, saw that the proper number of horses were produced, and ordered defective horses to be disposed of for the benefit of the State, and replaced by others fit for service. A trooper who appeared at a muster without a horse was reduced to one shilling a day until he procured one.[5] A horse killed or ex-

---

[1] *Lords' Journals*, vii, 377; 16th May 1645.

[2] *Scotland and the Protectorate*, p. 364; Thurloe, vi, 400; see also Appendix N, *post*.

[3] *Scotland and the Protectorate*, p. 83; Ludlow, i, 293; *Eighth Report Hist. MSS. Comm.*, ii, 61.

[4] 'Rules and Instructions to the Muster Masters of the Army,' *Lords' Journals*, vii, 374.

[5] Soldiers with unserviceable horses were obliged to provide better. In Monck's *Order-Book* under 10th October 1656 is the following entry: 'Order to Commissary John Clarke to give notice unto such troopers of the respective troops he musters who have small or bad horses, that they provide themselves with better or more sufficient horses against the muster of the 25th of November, or he is not to pass them'.

pended in the course of a campaign was replaced by the State. During his campaign in Scotland in 1654 Monck regularly paid eight pounds each to various troopers 'for one horse lost on actual service', in order to enable them to remount themselves.[1] On the other hand, a horse which died of disease (except presumably when the disease was the direct result of hard service) had to be replaced by the trooper himself. An epidemic consequently spelt bankruptcy for the cavalry. The petition of the army to Richard Cromwell in April 1659 complains greatly of the poverty of the army, not only because its pay was in arrears, but on account of 'the great and unusual mortality among the horses of the army (insomuch that many troopers have been forced to buy twice over), having brought the horse of this army under exceeding great extremities'.[2]

Such a mortality was the more serious for the soldiers because in many cases the horses were their own property, and had not been originally supplied by the State. It has been shown in a previous chapter that not only at the beginning of the war, but even during the Protectorate, recruits frequently brought their own horses with them when they enlisted. In other cases, men who had originally been mounted by the State had remounted themselves at their own cost. A petition against the terms of disbanding, presented by Ireton's regiment in May 1647, says: 'Many of us have furnished ourselves with horses at our own costs and charges, when the state's horses miscarried, such were our affections to the service'.[3] The question of the disposal of horses of the cavalry therefore became of great importance in any general or partial disbandment of the army. The cavalry regiments which the Parliament attempted to disband in 1647 expected to be allowed to keep their horses, as seems to have been usual, and one of their grievances was that they were not to be allowed to do so. 'We find it provided,' they complain, 'that no trooper is capable of allowance or debenture for arrears, unless he deliver in such horse and arms with which he hath served, or a certificate that such horse and arms did not appertain to the

[1] *Order-Book, passim.*

[2] Army Petition of 6th April 1659; reprinted in the *Old Parliamentary History*, xxi, 343.

[3] *Clarke MSS.*

State, or else was lost in actual service; which extends to the
total taking away from them those horse and arms of the state's
which they have used and preserved in the service, contrary
to the favour allowed, and never (that we know of) denied in the
disbanding of any other army. And if that, being but a matter
of favour, the horsemen in this service be thought unworthy of
it, and must for account of their arrears rebate for such horses
and arms as upon disbanding they thought to have been given
them; yet it seems hard, that such as cannot deliver in those
state's horses and arms, which at disbanding they understood
to be their own, and so perhaps have sold or otherwise disposed
of, should for that lose their whole arrears, or be incapable of
account or debenture for any part thereof.'[1]

In later disbandments a compromise appears to have been
adopted. The disbanded soldier who wished to keep the horse
he had received from the State was allowed to do so on paying
for it at a fixed rate of forty or fifty shillings, which sum was to
be deducted from the arrears due to him.[2] Those who had served
with their own horses could, of course, dispose of them as they
pleased. Monck in 1654, in discussing the question of disbanding
superfluous troops, urged the Protector to draw the cavalry to
be disbanded from Scotland into England for the purpose;
otherwise many of the horse would sell their horses in Scotland,
and the Royalists would probably get hold of them, and use
them against the government.[3] In November 1659, when Monck
purged the army under his command of disaffected soldiers,
before he undertook his march into England, a large number
of the passes issued record the fact that the discharged trooper

[1] Rushworth, vi, 506. *A humble Representation of the Dissatisfactions of
the Army, in relation to the late Resolutions for sudden Disbanding: shewing
the particulars of their former grievances, etc.*

[2] For instance, there is the following entry in Monck's *Order-Book* for
6th August 1655 concerning the disbanding of a troop of dragoons. 'Order
to Capt. John Greene, that in the accompting with the dragooners under his
command what is due unto them respectively, he is to take notice that for
such of his troop as received horses from the state, he take a discount of
50 shillings a man from them for their horses; but giving up their arms to
the states use to the governor of Sterling, he is to receive or discount from
them who so deliver up their arms but 40 shillings; and those who had no
horses from the state, those delivering up their arms to Col. Read they shall
receive 6s. 8d. apiece for their arms.'

[3] *Scotland and the Protectorate*, p. 221.

took his horse with him, proving that up to the Restoration many troopers still owned their horses.[1]

In conclusion, there is one important article in the equipment of an army for the field which appears in an intermittent and irregular way in the records of the Civil War. During the earlier part of the period tents were not used either by the Royalists or the Parliamentarians. The soldiers of the New Model during the campaign of 1645 either bivouacked in the open air or were quartered in villages. 'For the most part,' says an account of the march of Fairfax to the relief of Taunton, 'we took barns and hedges for our night's repose, after our hard and hot days' marches.'[2] The innumerable orders relative to the quartering of soldiers in houses when they were on the march from place to place show conclusively what the usual practice was.

The absence of tents is the more surprising because they seem to have been habitually used in the Scottish armies. When Leslie encamped on Duns Law in 1639 Baillie describes the Scottish method of encamping thus: 'The crowners [i.e., colonels] lay in kennous [i.e., canvas] lodges, high and wide, their captains about them in lesser ones; the soldiers about all in huts of timber covered by divot [i.e., turf] or straw'.[3] An English account describes the Scottish soldiers as lodged in 'dry and handsome huts'.[4] In the camp of the King's army, which lay at a place called the Birks about two miles from Berwick, the principal commanders had tents, while under-officers and soldiers were hutted. In 1640, when the second war began, Leslie provided his army with tents for the rank and file as well as for the officers. According to Baillie, this was done chiefly for political reasons, in order that the friends of the Scots in England might have no cause to complain. 'Because it would be troublesome to these of England, who were much delighted with their planting, if our army should cut down timber for bigging [i.e., building] of our huts, they prayed that the honest women [of Edinburgh] might be tried what webs of harding or sheets they might spare, that every four soldiers might be accommodated in a tent of 8 ells.' Thanks to an inspiring sermon from Mr Rollock, the

[1] Monck's *Order-Book*, November 1659; *Clarke MSS*.
[2] *A brief Narration of the Expedition to Taunton*, 1645, 4to.
[3] Baillie, *Letters*, i, 211.   [4] Terry, *Life of Alexander Leslie*, p. 75.

women of Edinburgh 'gave freely great store of that stuff', and so tents of a kind were provided for the whole army.[1] It is not clear, however, whether the Scots used tents in the campaigns of 1644 and 1645.

In the English army of the period tents were first introduced when it served outside England, in less populous countries such as Ireland and Scotland. Their employment appears to have been an innovation introduced by Cromwell, in order to keep his soldiers in health during his Irish campaign. At the close of his letter on the capture of Drogheda he says, 'We keep the field much, our tents sheltering us from the wet and cold; but yet the country sickness overtakes many'. They were an imperfect shelter, however, and a few weeks later, at the siege of Wexford, when its governor asked for a cessation of arms during the negotiations for its surrender, Cromwell refused, giving as one of his reasons, 'because our tents are not so good a covering as your houses'.[2]

But though Cromwell seems to have been convinced of the advantages of tents, the army with which he invaded Scotland in July 1650 was not supplied with them, and in consequence, as the summer was very wet, its losses from sickness were extremely heavy. About a month after the campaign opened the tents came. 'There is,' says a newspaper dated 13th August 1650, 'for every file a tent, for their better quartering in the field, which they have received this morning.' That means one tent for every six men. These tents were naturally small, and seem to have been carried by the men themselves in parts. A few days later, when a battle was expected, we hear that many of the soldiers 'cast away their biscuit with their tents, upon confidence they should then fight'.[3] The English army of occupation in Scotland under Monck was well supplied with tents, and he was careful to keep them in good repair. He used them in his campaign in the Highlands in 1654, or in summer, when distant garrisons had to be relieved, or when his cavalry regiments went into camp and turned their horses out to grass.[4]

[1] Baillie, *Letters*, i, 255. According to English accounts the Scots had 'a canvas tent for every six soldiers', i.e. every file (Terry, p. 106).

[2] Carlyle, *Cromwell*, Letters cv, cvii.

[3] Terry, *Life of Alexander Leslie*, pp. 466, 472.

[4] *Scotland and the Protectorate*, pp. xlii, 150; see also Appendix N, *post*.

Yet in spite of the experience of the value of tents gained by the campaigns in Scotland and Ireland, neither of the two foreign expeditions which were sent from England during the Protectorate were supplied with them. Both in Hispaniola and in Jamaica the army under General Venables suffered greatly for the want of them. In stating his reasons for not attacking Cartagena as he had been instructed to do, Venables lays great stress on this deficiency. 'Our tents not coming, nor our stores, we doubted the rains (which would kill us all) would overtake us before we could gain any place of shelter or make one, they usually on that coast falling in the beginning of April, and destroying the natives, if lying in the open air as we must.'[1]

In the case of the West Indian expedition tents appear to have been originally promised, but if provided they were embarked on those store-ships which parted company from the rest of the fleet, and did not arrive till long after the expedition had left Hispaniola. In the case of the expedition to Flanders they were not provided at all, or not till the second campaign was practically over. The officers had them, thanks to Mazarin, from the beginning.[2] 'The Cardinal,' writes Lockhart on 31st May 1657, 'hath caused to provide some fourscore tents for the officers of our forces, and hath obliged those of this town [i.e., Abbeville] to furnish them at the rate they call the King's, which is not above half or a third part their worth, so that a tent fit for a captain will be had for some twenty shillings.'[3] In the winter of 1657 the rank and file of the English regiments suffered greatly from this cause, and those in the small and dilapidated fort of Mardyke especially. They had neither tents nor timber to make huts. 'I have been here now these seven weeks,' writes an engineer from Mardyke on 30th November 1657, 'waiting for timber and boards wherewith to erect houses and lodging for our soldiers, but besides empty promises we have got but little hitherto; which neglect makes the condition of the soldiers very

[1] *Narrative of General Venables*, pp. 49, 65.

[2] In the Peninsular War the officers of the English army were supplied with tents as early as 1809, but the rank and file were not provided with them till the campaign of 1813. Three tents, to be carried on a mule, were then issued to each company (Wellington, *Despatches*, vi, 506; *Supplementary Despatches*, vi, 268, 285; vii, 563–4; Napier, *Peninsular War*, v, 86, ed. 1886).

[3] Thurloe, vi, 297.

miserable, and so destructive that we send every day no less than 10, 12, or more to the grave, for we have about 2,000 men, and have not accommodation for 600 of them, hence the shifts we make for lodging are very hard and unwholesome, tending to the destruction of many every day.'[1] Seven months later things were little better. 'Our friends in England have been very care-less of us,' wrote Lieutenant-Colonel Hughes from the camp before Dunkirk, just two days before the battle of the Dunes; 'the thousand tents ordered us by the Council five weeks ago are not yet come, which causes a great sickness amongst us, having not one piece of wood within six miles to hut us with.'[2]

It is surprising that such neglect as this should have existed at a time when a great soldier was head of the State. But as Protector, Cromwell was too much occupied with political busi-ness of every kind to pay adequate attention to the details of military administration, and trusted too much to subordinates. Something no doubt was also owing to the fact that the troops in Flanders were for the time being in the French service, and their lodging might be regarded as the business of the French government.[3]

[1] *Clarke Papers*, iii, 128.   [2] Ibid., iii, 152.

[3] In the French and in most foreign armies tents had by this time fallen into disuse. Orrery, in his *Art of War*, 1667, p. 86, writes as follows: 'In ancient times they used tents instead of hutts, for then the way of making war was in the field, and armies were daily in motion; and in such cases, straw, rushes, or flags, to cover, and wood to make stakes and roofs were not alwayes at hand, nor to frame the roofs easie; but now that for the most part war is made in the besieging of strong places or in standing camps, both soldiers and officers use to hutt, which is more warm, and more lasting than tents'.

CHAPTER XI

Provision for the Sick and Wounded
and for Old Soldiers

THE PROVISION MADE for sick and wounded soldiers is a
subject of which the historians of the Civil War supply no adequate account. Grose, in his *Military Antiquities*, brings together
a number of passages showing that in earlier times English
armies had surgeons and physicians attached to them, but says
nothing of the medical administration of the Parliamentary
armies.[1] Colonel Clifford Walton, in his elaborate account of the
military system of the post-Restoration period, is equally silent
on the system which existed in the twenty years before the
Restoration.[2] The documents dealing with this question of the
provision for the sick and wounded are nowhere collected, and to
give a sketch of the subject it is necessary to collect scattered
notices, and to make the most of fragmentary materials.

It is best to begin by describing the position of what is now
called the Army Medical Corps – that is, the army doctors.
During the Civil Wars military surgeons appear to have been
treated by both parties as non-combatants, and to have enjoyed
certain privileges defined by custom rather than by any positive
regulations. When in the field they probably wore a distinguishing badge, according to the practice of earlier times. 'Surgeons,'
says an Elizabethan writer, 'must wear their baldric, whereby
they may be known in time of slaughter; it is their charter in
the field.[3] They were often allowed to enter a hostile camp or

[1] i, 236–42.   [2] *History of the British Standing Army*, p. 752.

[3] *Ralph Smith's MS.*, quoted by Grose, i, 241. Smith follows Styward's
Pathway to Martial Discipline, p. 40, 1581, using many of his phrases.
Another Elizabethan writer, Barnaby Rich, in his *Pathway to Military
Practice*, 1587, says: 'A good and skilful chyrurgeon is a necessary man to
bee had in a companie, such a one as should work according to arte, not
practisinge newe experiments upon a poore souldier, by meanes whereof

fortress in order to treat wounded men of their own party, though the privilege was sometimes abused.[1] When they fell into the hands of the enemy they were not usually retained as prisoners, and in most cases they made no distinction between Roundheads and Cavaliers if suffering was to be relieved. In 1644, for example, Henry Johnson, surgeon of the King's own troop, wrote to the Parliamentary governor of Newport Pagnell asking for the release of his apprentice who had been captured in a skirmish at Kidlington. 'It is very well known,' said he, 'how careful I have ever been in dressing your wounded men, whensoever they have fallen into our hands. Therefore if you will give him a speedy release and safe pass to Oxford, I am very confident the favour shall not pass without an earnest endeavour of recompense, for if at any time any chirurgeon or wounded men of yours shall fall into our hands, my care of getting release-ment, or dressing those that have need thereof, shall manifest how great a favour you have done to your obliged servant.'[2]

The proclamation about the wounded Parliamentarians which Charles the First published after the battle of Newbury is con-ceived in the same spirit. 'Though they be rebels and deserve the punishment of traitors,' said the King, 'yet out of our tender compassion upon them, as being our subjects, our will and pleasure is that you carefully provide for their recovery, as well as for those of our own army.'[3] So, too, on the other side, Mrs

---

many have been utterly maymed by a chyrurgeon's practice that otherwise might have doon very well'. Turner, writing in 1671, speaks with some distrust of the military surgery of his time, demanding that none but 'good and experienced artists' should be employed. He declares that the surgeon, 'besides his monthly pay, should have his Surgeons Chest furnisht with all manner of Necessaries for curing Wounds of all kinds; and this Chest is to be furnisht at the Princes charge, and all Wounds received in the Prince or States service, he is obliged to cure (if he can) without demanding any thing from the Patients, but all others got accidentally, or by quarrell-ing and Duels, he is not obliged to cure but for payment, in which the Officers are bound to assist him' (p. 223).

[1] See the case of Colonel James Hippesley who, disguising himself as a surgeon, treacherously obtained leave to visit an Irish castle, and after spying out its weak points headed the storming party which took it (Carey, *Memorials of the Civil War*, i, 351).

[2] Ellis, *Original Letters* (Third Series), iv, 226; cf. *Military Memoir of Col. Birch*, p. 208.

[3] *Mercurius Aulicus*, 21st Sept. 1643.

Hutchinson, wife of the governor of Nottingham, bound up the wounds of Royalist prisoners as well as Parliamentarians, doing 'what she thought was her duty in humanity to them, as fellow-creatures, not as enemies.'[1]

In the armies raised by Parliament there were usually two or three medical officers attached to the staff of the general, who supervised and controlled the medical administration of the whole army. There were also regimental surgeons and assistants who were attached to each particular regiment,

In the list of Essex's army, for example, there appear a 'physician to the train and person', Dr St John, and a 'surgeon to the train and person, Laurence Lowe'. In the list of the New Model the names of four medical officers appear amongst the staff, two physicians to the army, an apothecary to the army, and a surgeon-general to the army. The armies in Ireland and Scotland had each a physician-general, a surgeon-general, and an apothecary-general, and this arrangement survived in the post-Restoration army.[2]

The chief of these officials was the physician-general, who was usually a man of some standing in his profession, and was paid accordingly. Dr Henry Glisson, physician-general to Manchester's army, Dr John Waterhouse to Cromwell's army in Ireland, and Dr Samuel Barrow to Monck's army in Scotland, received all three of them ten shillings a day. Next in point of emolument came the apothecary-general of the army, whose salary was six and eightpence a day. Last came the surgeons.

---

[1] 'In this encounter, one of the Derby captains was slain, and five of our men hurt, who for want of another surgeon, were brought to the Governor's wife, and she having some excellent balsams and plasters in her closet, with the assistance of a gentleman that had some skill, dressed all their wounds, whereof some were dangerous, being all shots, with such good success that they were all well cured in convenient time. After our wounded men were dressed, as she stood at her chamber-door, seeing three of the prisoners sorely cut, and carried down bleeding into the Lion's Den, she desired the marshal to bring them in to her, and bound up and dressed their wounds also: which while she was doing, Captain Palmer came in and told her his soul abhorred to see this favour to the enemies of God; she replied, she had done nothing but what she thought was her duty, in humanity to them, as fellow-creatures, not as enemies' (*Life of Colonel Hutchinson*, i, 265, ed. 1885). Compare *Autobiography of Lady Anne Halkett*, p. 62.

[2] Peacock, *Army Lists of Cavaliers and Roundheads*, pp. 26, 27, 101; Clifford Walton, p. 754.

In Cromwell's Irish army James Winter, as 'chirurgeon-general to his excellency's person and train', and Thomas Trapham, as 'chirurgeon-general to the officers of horse', received four shillings a day only. Each had a couple of assistants or 'mates', who were paid two and sixpence a day.[1]

The ordinary regimental surgeon got the same pay as the staff surgeon, and had also his two mates. In 1651 the surgeon's pay rose to six shillings a day; in 1655 it was fixed at five shillings, and the economists cut off one of his mates; in 1657 his pay was again reduced to four shillings a day.[2] Monck considered this sum so insufficient that he ordered the surgeons to be entered as privates in the muster-roll of their regiments, in order to give them an additional ninepence a day.[3] Even before this reduction the pay of a regimental surgeon was too small to secure really able men. Very few of the army doctors of the period are to be found in the roll of the Royal College of Physicians. Some of them were notoriously incompetent. In October 1654 Monck remonstrated with Cromwell for appointing a certain Mr Fish to be surgeon to the artillery train. Fish was a former surgeon's mate who had resigned to avoid a court-martial for misconduct. 'He is one,' complains Monck, 'that was never bound prentice to the profession, and the surgeon-general looks upon him as unfit to take such an employ upon him. . . . I earnestly entreat your highness, that if possible I may have an able surgeon to the train, in regard I know not what occasion I may have to make us of him myself, and I conceive this person not fit to undertake it, as well for his want of skill as former miscarriages.'[4]

Amongst Thurloe's papers in the Bodleian Library there is a curious letter from an army doctor who had been accused of incompetence and neglect of his patients. He replied by for-

---

[1] These particulars as to the pay and names of the medical officers mentioned are derived from the *Exchequer MSS.* in the Record Office. Waterhouse was recommended by Cromwell to the University of Oxford for the Degree of M.D., which he obtained on 12th March 1651 (see Carlyle's *Cromwell*, Letter cxlvii). On Barrow, see Masson's *Life of Milton*, v, 476, 528, 534; vi, 714.

[2] Establishments for the army in Scotland of the dates named (*Clarke MSS.*).

[3] *Order-Book*, 22nd Sept. 1658, *Clarke MSS.*

[4] *Scotland and the Protectorate*, p. 158.

warding a statement in his favour signed by some of the sur-
vivors, and by protesting that it was not his fault if the others
had died.

'Alas, my Lord, what is the physician or surgeon but dame
Nature's handmaid to be aiding and assisting to her, but the
great God of heaven has ordained and appointed severall diseaess
which are incident to men, and they have to attend them one
Death, who does and will prevail, notwithstanding the most
excellent means which the gravest or wisest physician or surgeon
can use in the world, and this we may see by daily experience.
My Lord, I humbly pray your honour that you would be pleased
to take these things into your serious consideration, that your
poor servant Edward Cooke, surgeon, may not lose your former
love, for I can appeal to the Almighty, I have done what I can
for the sick and wounded, according to the best judgment I
have in my calling.'[1]

To supplement the army doctors, and possibly because some
of them were not remarkably skilful, it was customary in important cases to call in other aid. When Skippon was dangerously
wounded at the battle of Naseby, Parliament sent a special
physician to Northampton to attend him.[2] When Cromwell fell
ill in Scotland during the Spring of 1651, Dr Wright and Dr Bates,
two of the leaders of the profession, were despatched to Edinburgh by the Council of State.[3] These eminent men were liberally
paid by the Parliament, but ordinary practitioners employed in
the absence of army doctors, or in moments of special pressure,
were paid by the job. There are bills in existence in the Record
Office which show the rate of payment. One George Blagrave
sends in an account for the wounded soldiers cured by him, in
which each injury is charged for according to its gravity. For
curing 'a sore bruised leg' he asked ten shillings; for 'a cut over
the eye and a sore thrust in the arm', a pound. The highest
charge was one pound ten for a certain John Bullock, 'who had
a very sore cut in the fore part of his head, which caused a piece

[1] *Rawlinson MS.*, A, lx, f. 325, Bodleian Library.

[2] Cf. *Commons' Journals*, iv, 180, 190; Vicars, *England's Worthies*, p. 55;
Report on the Duke of Portland's MSS., i, 187.

[3] *Commons' Journals*, vi, 578; Carlyle, *Cromwell*, Letter clxxiv.

of his skull, the breadth of a half-crown piece, to be taken forth'.[1]

There are similar bills from civilian doctors for the cure of sick soldiers. Mr Frisby, for example, sends in an account amounting to fifteen shillings for physic supplied to a trooper; the cost of each item is given – sixpence for a powder, eighteen-pence for a cordial, two shillings for a purge. In another case a long series of 'dormitive bowls' and 'cordial juleps' are enumerated and charged for.[2]

Army doctors and regimental surgeons, however, made no charge for attendance. While a soldier was in hospital a certain proportion of his pay was stopped to defray the cost of drugs and nursing, but there does not appear to have been any per-

---

[1] Blagrave's bill, which was ordered to be paid on 18th September 1645, runs thus:

'A true note of all those wounded souldiers cured by George Blagrave and his sonne since his last bill, for which he demandeth pay as follows.

Imprimis. At the fight neare Ashe one Tewsday the first of July:

John Cox, 1 cut in his hand and a very soare wound in his arme	1	0	0
Hugh Bande, of Capt. Barton's, a thrust in the arme with a tuck, and shott in the backe	0	13	4
John Bullock of Capt. Barton's, a very sore cut in the fore-part of his head, which caused a peece of his scull the breadth of half crowne peece to [be] taken forth, allsoe a very sore cut over his hand	1	10	0
William Higgot of Major Molynes companye, haveinge a a sore brused legge	0	10	0
Richard Hudson, taken prisoner at Ashby, haveing a sore cut in the shoulder, was sent to be dressed by the governour's command	0	6	8
One John Curson, a Scotsman, Quartermaster, a very sore wound in the head	1	0	0
Robert Moris, of Maior Sanders his comp. haveinge a dangerous cut over the eye, hurt at Kegworth, and a sore thrust thorough the arme	1	0	0
Luke Severne, quarter master to Capt. Hope, a thrust and cutt in the arme, a very dangerous wound	1	0	0
Richard Becke of Liefftenent Corsnalls, a very sore scalded foot	0	5	0
For cureing 10 Caveliers taken at the fight at Ashe, where-of one was shot into the arme in the elbowe joynt and the bullet taken forth in the wrist near the hand. The rest were sore cut in their heads & thrust in the back.	5	0	0
2 Caveliers of Newark			
	12	5	0'

[2] Exchequer MSS.

manent stoppage for these objects.[1] At the opening of a campaign the government provided each regimental surgeon with a medical chest. In 1650, for instance, when Cromwell set out for Scotland, each of the surgeons attached to his regiments was ordered fifteen pounds for a chest, and ten pounds for a horse to carry it.[2] Two shillings a day also was allowed for the keep of the horse and the man who attended it. When more medical stores were needed, the practice appears to have been to issue warrants to the apothecary-general for the supply of internal medicaments, and to the surgeon-general for external medicaments. No doubt the cost of these drugs was charged to the regiment for which they were needed, as was done in the time of Charles the Second.[3]

A subject of greater interest than the question of these payments is the organization of the hospitals. As yet there was no systematic arrangement for the collection and transportation of soldiers wounded in battle. An Elizabethan writer sixty years earlier had proposed the institution of a body of men and carriages to remove the wounded from the field, but the suggestion was not adopted.[4] After a battle the victorious general usually ordered or permitted the people of the country round to carry away the wounded men the enemy had left behind. King Charles issued a proclamation to that effect after the battle of Newbury, and Cromwell after that of Dunbar.[5] The wounded of the victorious army were collected by their comrades, and conveyed in any waggons that could be procured to the nearest town.

[1] By order of 16 June 1653 foot soldiers who were patients in Heriot's Hospital were to pay one shilling a week, horse soldiers two shillings.

[2] *Exchequer MSS.*; cf. *Lords' Journals*, v, 105.

[3] Warrant to Mr Pugh to deliver to Mr Thos. Cosens externall medicaments for 130 men for six months in Dunstaffenage and Dunolly. Order to Mr White to deliver to him a proportionable quantity of internal medicaments for the like number' (Monck's *Order-Book*, 13th March 1654).

[4] 'It were convenient to appointe certaine carriages and men, of purpose to give their attendance in every skirmishe and incounter, to carry away the hurt men to such place as surgions may immediately repayre unto them, whiche shall not only greatly incourage the souldior, but also cause the skirmish to be the better mainteined, when the souldiors shal not neede to leave the fielde to carry away their hurte men. These were called among the Romanes 'Despotati'. And this among many other laudable Romane orders have the Spaniards at this day revived and put in practise, whereby also they conceale from the enemie what losses in any skirmishe they have received' (Digges, *Stratioticon*, p. 154).

[5] Carlyle, *Cromwell*, appended to Letter cxxxix.

There were no movable hospitals attending the army during the campaign. In 1643 Essex sent the soldiers wounded at the siege of Reading up to London to be treated there. An order of Parliament in the following June recites 'that the Lord General hath been enforced to send back many sick soldiers to be billeted in some remote houses and towns, some miles distant from London, till it shall please God to restore them health and ability to return again to his army'.[1] Those who were badly wounded were left in villages nearer the field of battle. Something was usually paid for their quarters, or for attendance on them, as accounts prove;[2] but often they were left entirely to their own resources, and to the charitable care of well-wishers to the cause. There is a petition from a woman named Hester Whyte, stating that after Edgehill she took charge of some of the wounded Parliamentarians, 'who continued at her house in great misery by reason of their wounds for three months. She often sat up night and day with them, and, in respect of her tenderness to the Parliament's friends, laid out her own money in supply of their wants.'[3]

In another case a paymaster sends in a charge of £21 for money 'paid to fifty or sixty poor people in whose houses we were constrained to quarter many of the wounded soldiers, until we could provide better for them'.[4] After Naseby the soldiers wounded in the battle were collected at Northampton and in the

---

[1] Clarendon, *Rebellion*, vii, 27; Husbands, *Ordinances*, ii, 210.

[2] 'A bill of the charges that I am out for Richard Barker for the time of his sicknes and for his buriall who was trooper under Capt. Selby, April 16 1644.

'Item: for his diett and firing and candle for three weekes after
15^d pence a day 1 6 3
for three weekes dyett for the woman that was continually to look to him 12 0
for the woman's wagges for watching with him night &
day for three weekes 14 0
for a sheet to burie him in 7 0
for church duties for the buriall of him . . . 3 0
for washing up my linning and all other thinges belonging to the bed 3 0
'Item: for meate for his horse for a peck of oates a day and
hay for one and twenty days 1 1 0
for seven days ninepence a day 4 3
                                                    _____
                                                    4 10 6'
                         – (*Exchequer MSS.*, bundle 223).

[3] *Cal. State Papers, Dom.*, 1625–49, p. 693.   [4] Ibid., Addenda, p. 345.

villages round it. Doctors were sent from London to attend them, and the Commissioners of Parliament with the army made provision for their care and subsistence.

After the capture of Bristol, in September 1645, the same commissioners took a large house in that city, and set up there a hospital of considerable size. The management of it and the whole responsibility of looking after the wounded seem to have been in the hands of the commissioners rather than in those of the physician-general or surgeon-general.

They procured attendants and surgeons, provided subsistence for patients, and found quarters in neighbouring villages for those whom the hospital could not take in. They also saw to the burial of those who died of their wounds, and provided those who recovered with money to take them to their colours. In a report addressed to the Parliament they enlarged on the fortitude of the wounded, 'no less patient in their sufferings than they were courageous in their undertakings', and begged the House to 'reach forth your arm of comfort to those poor men whose pay will be far short to defray their charges and expenses in this their extremity'.[1]

[1] *Report on the Duke of Portland's MSS.*, i, 309. The letter from the commissioners, Pinder and Leighton, to Speaker Lenthall, runs as follows:

'We shall now make bold to present yow with an accompt of the being and welbeing of such wounded men as were left here, after the taking of the citty and Barclay Castle, for whome according to the Generall's order, and our best judgment, we appointed an hospitall, and placed therein soe many as the house could conteine, with nurses and chirurgiens fitting for them, and as our number increased we added house-roome and attendants to them: which though a house of great receipt yet not sufficient to hold all our foote soldyers, we caused the horse to be quartered in the country which hath byn one addition to theyr burthen, though not in giving free-quarter – which we have paied in money for the most part – yet in disquiet of theyr houses, distruction of theyr beddinge, linnen, and consumption of theyr fiering, which hath byn the more enforced, the generallity of theyr wounds being fractures of bones and dismemberinges by plugg-shott from the enemy, expressing height of malice, rather than martiall prowesse. Sir, we bless God the greater number are returned to the army, well recovered. Such as have dyed of theyr woundes, we have seen decently interred, amongst whom were two gentlemen of worth for theyr valour in health, and Christian conversation in sickness, Majour Bethell of horse, Majour Cromwell of foote, both which had such honorable buriall as the place and theyr rank did require; for whose attendance in theyr sickness and buriall, as for all other charges about the care, attendance, and diett, of the rest that were wounded, we have taken speciall care, and all that have gone to the Army wee have supplied with monyes and other accommodations to carry them to theyr coulers. What we now humbly crave of the honorable Howse is, that as your bounty extended itself to those that were wounded at Naseby and left at Northampton; soe you will please to reach forth your

These hospitals at Northampton, Bristol, and other local centres were only temporary establishments. Throughout the first and second Civil Wars the London hospitals supplied the only permanent provision for the cure of the sick and wounded soldiers. The four great hospitals of St Bartholomew, Bridewell, St Thomas, and Bethlehem were freed by Parliamentary ordinance on 16th November 1644 from all taxes and assessments, on the ground that 'great numbers of sick, wounded, and other soldiers have for the time of twenty months past been constantly kept in the said hospitals, at very great and extraordinary charges, especially for their cure and diet'.[1] Every year, from 1642 to about 1653, these hospitals published printed reports showing the number of soldiers relieved.[2] During 1644 St Bartholomew's claimed to have cured 1,122 'maimed soldiers and other diseased persons', 'all of which', adds the report, 'have been relieved with money and other necessaries at their departure'. A hundred and fifty-two had died, and 249 were still in the hospital. St Thomas's during the same period had treated and discharged 1,063 persons, 'whereof a great number have been soldiers'.

These institutions were not sufficient, for much of their revenue was devoted to educating children and to other charitable objects. Special military hospitals also were necessary, and two were accordingly created by the Parliament. The first was that at the Savoy, which was established about November 1644. The second was at Ely House, which, having been used in the earlier part of the war as a prison, was converted into a hospital

arme of comfort to these poore men whose pay will be farr short to defray theyr charge and expenses in this theyr extremitie, whom we affirme – as eye wittnesses – to have been noe lesse patient in theyr sufferings and constant in theyr resolutions, then they were couragious in theyr undertakings. Sir, we have kept constant musters of them, and did constantly visit them. though to the hazard of our lives, in this place and time of visitation, and can thereby the better judg of theyr wants and deserts, for whome we pray there may be some such course taken, as may encourage them and all others that willingly offer us theyr lives in your service, and we shall assure you to see all theyr scores cleared and every of them paied whatever you shall thus order to the uttmost penny.'

[1] Husbands, *Ordinances*, ii, 587.

[2] A specimen of one of these reports is reprinted in Leonard's *History of English Poor Relief*, p. 369. The originals are to be found in the British Museum (*King's Pamphlets*, 669, f. 10, et seqq.).

in 1648. Between them the two accommodated about 350 patients. The management of the military hospitals, and the relief of wounded soldiers in general, were placed in the hands of the commissioners who governed these two.[1]

Other hospitals were subsequently established at the head-quarters of the armies in Ireland, Scotland and Flanders. In Dublin two were set up in 1649, one in the Archbishop of Dublin's house, the other in 'the mass house in Back Lane'. Between them they held only 200 men, so that they must have been far too small for the needs of the army.[2]

In Scotland during the Commonwealth and Protectorate the English generals utilized the building and revenues of Heriot's Hospital at Edinburgh for the sick and wounded. It was not large, for in 1654 it contained only thirty patients, yet it was expected to serve the whole of the army in Scotland, which rarely numbered less than 10,000 men, and sometimes more. Its annual cost, in 1655, was about £1,300 a year; in 1659, about £587.[3]

In the summer of 1658 Sir William Lockhart, who command-ed the English auxiliaries in Flanders, found himself after the capture of Dunkirk with about 700 sick and wounded men on his hands, and established a hospital at Dunkirk. 'I put all the wounded,' he wrote to Thurloe, 'in some houses near a nunnery, and have bargained with the nuns to wait upon them and furnish them. I pay them one styver by the day for each wounded soldier, for which they put a nun to every eight wounded men, and give them warm broth, meat, bread, and beer, and keep them in clean linen. I shall also allow the sick money for their present subsistence.'

The nuns proved unable to carry out their contract, and a few

[1] Husbands, *Ordinances*, ii, 581; *Commons' Journals*, v, 530-6, 548; *Cal. State Papers, Dom.*, Addenda, p. 643.

[2] *Cal. State Papers, Dom.*, 1649-50, p. 281. The sum spent for physicians, surgeons, nurses, and care of sick and wounded soldiers in Ireland from July 1649 to November 1656 amounted to £29,919 2s. 11d. (*English Historical Review*, 1899, p. 107). The Dublin Hospital cost in 1659 £279 4s. per annum, and £3,000 a year was spent at that time in pensions (*Old Parliamentary History*, xxi, 334-5).

[3] Thurloe, v, 529-30; *History of Heriot's Hospital*, by F. W. Bedford, ed. 1872, pp. 67, 71, 72; *Old Parliamentary History*, xxi, 334. Monck's papers amongst the *Clarke MSS.* contain much information about the administration of the hospital.

days later Lockhart had to adopt a different arrangement. Accordingly, he set up eight small hospitals, one for every regiment, and appointed to each a sutler to supply the inmates with food, and 'a convenient number of women to wait upon them'.[1]

On the internal arrangements of these hospitals a certain amount of information is accessible. The diet of the patients seems to have been tolerably liberal. Of Heriot's Hospital in 1655, a report says: 'There are thirty soldiers in the said hospital, whereof twenty-two have four days in the week each man of beer one Scots pint, of butter five ounces, of cheese five ounces, of bread two pounds. The other three days they have each man $1\frac{1}{4}$ lb. of flesh, with bread and beer as aforesaid, and each man an English pint of gruel or milk to breakfast, which will amount to about 4s. per week for each soldier's allowance. The other eight soldiers being weak have 3s 6d. per week allowed each man in money, and no other provisions.'[2] The scale of diet for the Dublin hospitals is not given, but beer was allowed patients there also.

As to attendance on the inmates, there were no hospital orderlies in those days, and the nursing was entirely done by women. It was an accepted principle that women made the best nurses, especially the wives or widows of soldiers. The nurses of the Savoy Hospital were ordered 'to be chosen from the widows of soldiers so far as fit ones can be found'. When General Venables was censured for taking his wife with him on the disastrous expedition to the West Indies, and for allowing some of his soldiers to be accompanied by their wives, he answered that anybody who had served in the Irish wars knew 'the necessity of having that sex with an army to attend upon and help the sick and wounded, which men are unfit for'. 'Had more women gone,' he concluded, 'I suppose that many had not perished as they did for want of care and attendance.'[3] In Ely House and the Savoy there were twenty-nine nurses to an average of 350 patients; in the Dublin Hospital one nurse was allowed for every ten patients; in the Edinburgh Hospital there was one to every five 'weak men', and one per ward 'where the patients are

[1] *Thurloe Papers*, vii, 179, 186.

[2] Ibid., v, 529–30; *Cal. State Papers, Dom.*, 1649–50, p. 281.

[3] *Narrative of General Venables*, pp. 11, 102.

ambulant'. The nurses were paid ten pounds a year each at
Dublin, and four shillings to four shillings and sixpence a week
at Edinburgh. The authorities of the Savoy Hospital drew up a
series of rules for soldiers and nurses. A soldier who got drunk or
used profane language was to be fined, or for the third offence
expelled. A nurse who neglected her duty or 'made any disturbance by scolding, brawling, or chiding' was to be punished
in the same way. If a soldier married a nurse both were at once
to be expelled.[1]

The question of the medical treatment given to the sick and
wounded belongs rather to the history of medicine than to
military history proper. It is at all events too technical for discussion in these pages. The manual of practical surgery published by John Woodall under the title of *The Surgeon's Mate*,
which went through four editions before 1655, gives a good idea
of the ordinary method of treating wounds.[2] More important
scientifically are the writings of Richard Wiseman, who served
as a surgeon in the Royalist army in the west of England during
the campaigns of 1645 and 1646, and under Charles the Second

[1] 15th Nov. 1644. 'Order by the Committee for sick and maimed soldiers,
for regulation of the patients and nurses in the Savoy and other hospitals.
All who are able are to attend the daily reading of God's Word, and to go
diligently every Lord's Day and Fasting Day to the services at the Savoy
Church, on pain of fine.
    'Every soldier drunk is to be set in the stocks for the first offence, forfeit a
week's pay for the second, and be expelled for the third.
    'Every soldier or nurse using profane language is to be fined, and for the
third offence expelled.
    'Soldiers are only to be admitted on certificate that they received their
wounds in the "King's and Parliament's service".
    'If a soldier marry a nurse they are both to be expelled.
    'No nurses are to be put in or out without the consent of two at least of
the treasurers; they are to be chosen from the widows of soldiers so far as fit
ones can be found, and to be paid 5s. a week.
    'The soldiers in Bartholomew's Hospital and St Thomas's Hospital,
Southwark, are to be paid 2s. per week, and none, in hospital or in friends'
houses, are to receive more than 4s.
    'Those who receive relief yet go about as beggars are to be sent to
Bridewell.
    'If nurses are negligent in their duty, or make any disturbance by scold-
ing, brawling or chiding, they are to be fined, and for the third offence
expelled. Signed by Cornelius Holland' (*Cal. State Papers, Dom.*, 1625–49,
pp. 643, 668–9).

[2] See the article on Woodall in the *Dictionary of National Biography*.
Woodall was the chief surgeon of the East India Company, and drew up
regulations for their surgeons. His *Surgeon's Mate* was first published in
1617, and he also wrote *Viaticum, being the Pathway to the Surgeon's Chest*.

in Scotland and at Worcester. His note-books give particulars of various cases treated by him during this period, and of the nature of the treatment he adopted.[1]

One curious fact in regard to the treatment of the convalescents deserves to be recorded. In May 1652 the Council of State selected 220 soldiers from amongst the patients at Ely House, and sent them to Bath, in charge of two officers, 'for the recovery of their limbs and perfecting their cure' by means of the waters.[2]

Besides these arrangements for the cure of wounded soldiers there was an effort made to provide some support outside the hospitals, both for disabled soldiers and for the widows and orphans of the dead. On 25th October 1642, the day after the battle of Edgehill, the two Houses published a declaration promising such a provision. It recited that whereas there were divers persons serving the Parliament in the present war 'who have little or nothing to maintain themselves, their wives and children, but by their own labours', the Lords and Commons would 'provide competent maintenance for such of them as shall be maimed and thereby disabled', and in case such persons should be slain, 'they will make provision for the livelihood of their wives and children'.[3] Though these promises were imperfectly fulfilled, owing to the financial difficulties of successive governments, a serious attempt was made to carry them out. At first it seems to have been thought that voluntary contributions for the purpose would suffice, and collections were frequently ordered in all the London churches on fast days and thanksgiving days during 1643 and 1644. In June 1644 contributions of old clothes, linen, and woollen stuffs were requested for the use of the wounded, and churchwardens were ordered to contribute all the linen surplices belonging to their parishes.[4]

Private charity naturally proved insufficient, and some systematic method of raising money became necessary. An Act passed in the forty-third year of Elizabeth's reign had imposed

[1] See Sir T. Longmore's *Life of Wiseman*, 1891, pp. 45-7, 58-60, 119, 128, 144, and Dr W. B. Richardson's papers in the third volume of the *Asclepiad*, on 'Richard Wiseman and the Surgery of the Commonwealth'.

[2] *Cal. State Papers, Dom.*, 1652-3, pp. 320, 332, 341, 355.

[3] Husbands. *Ordinances*, i, 673.

[4] Ibid., 951; ii, 42, 184, 210, 243, 305, 504, 581, 594.

the duty of maintaining disabled soldiers upon the parishes to which they belonged,[1] so in March 1643 Parliament passed an ordinance ordering the constables and churchwardens of every parish to levy a rate for its disabled soldiers and for the widows and orphans of those who had fallen.[2] As the parishes showed no great alacrity to assess themselves, Parliament went a step farther, and in November following ordered a special tax of about £4,000 a month to be levied on the counties in its power for the next six months. The allowance to the disabled or their families was not to be more than four shillings a week. The funds raised were to be administered by four 'treasurers for maimed soldiers', who had their office at Cordwainers' Hall in London.[3] In August 1644, after the expiration of this ordinance, £200 a week was charged on the excise, and was ordered to be paid to the treasurers. Three years later half the fines for non-payment of the excise duties were assigned to the same purpose, and other sums of money were from time to time voted.[4] Sometimes, too, the House of Commons granted money to some special case. On 10th February 1648 Richard Cave, who had lost both eyes at the battle of Marston Moor, was ordered £100.[5] On 16th December 1651 the widows of some officers and soldiers killed at the battle of Worcester were voted amounts ranging from £200 for a captain's wife to £20 for a private's.[6] Other sufferers obtained admission to almshouses and similar institutions. Sutton's Hospital – that is the Charterhouse – numbered amongst its indoor pensioners in 1652 thirty-one disabled soldiers, including a

---

[1] The last Act (43 Eliz. c. 3) is summarized by Grose, ii, 84. These Acts gave Elizabeth the undeserved reputation she enjoys in the ballad:

> 'To the souldiers that were maimed
> And wounded in the fray,
> The Queen allowed a pension
> Of fifteen pence a day,
> And from all costs and charges
> She quit and set them free,
> And this she did all for the sake
> Of brave Lord Willoughby.'

[2] The ordinance is reprinted by Grose, ii, 86.

[3] Husbands, *Ordinances*, ii, 376.

[4] Ibid., 533; Scobell, *Acts*, i, 123, 129, 131, 137; *Cal. State Papers, Dom.*, 1654, p. 391. Three Acts passed 28th May, 10th August, and 27th December 1647, supplemented the Elizabethan Act. There was another Act passed on 30th September 1651.

[5] Rushworth, vii, 994.   [6] *Common's Journals*, vii.

colonel and nineteen other officers.[1] Nevertheless the sum of distress was only partially met by these different methods of relief. The treasurers for maimed soldiers found themselves besieged by claimants whom they were unable to help. In May 1650 they petitioned Parliament either for more money or for the appointment of new treasurers. 'Some threaten us,' they said, 'that though they be hanged at our doors or shot to death, they will try whether we be pistol proof or no.'[2]

The question of the fulfilment of the promises of Parliament to its soldiers was naturally one which the army had much at heart. After the expulsion of the Long Parliament the Council of State established by the officers at once began an inquiry into the condition of Ely House and the Savoy, and into the administration of the funds for pensioning maimed soldiers and the dependants of dead soldiers. On the report of these committees one managing committee for both hospitals was appointed, and the administration of the pensions was confided to them. The revenue at the disposal of the commissioners was fixed at about £45,000 a year, of which the greater part came from the excise. Out of this they maintained the two hospitals and paid the pensions, supporting about 6,000 persons. The pensions granted were small – few larger than four shillings a week. A colonel complains that he was only granted eight shillings a week. The commissioners reduced the pension list, and made room for fresh sufferers by sending such pensioners as were not wholly disabled to serve in garrisons.[3] Nevertheless, after a few years the hospitals were again in difficulties. Even before the Protector's death the payments due to them fell into arrear, and in the year of confusion which followed it the government for a time suspended payment altogether. On 7th April 1659 Lord Fairfax

[1] 'Reasons humbly offered as inducements to the freeing of Sutton's Hospitall from the payment of taxes.' It is alleged that 'the Hospitalls of Christ Church, Bartholomewes, Bridewell, Thomas Hospital and others are by the Parliament freed from taxes'; moreover, 'many old and maimed soldiers (at present 31, *viz.*, 1 colonel, 1 major, 12 captaines, 6 lieutenants, etc.) are maintained there as pensioners, and the children of some, who have lost their lives in the Parliament's service as scholers' (*Several Proceedings in Parliament*, 20th to 27th May 1652).

[2] *Report on the Duke of Portland's MSS.*, i, 524, 568.

[3] *Mercurius Politicus*, 12th to 19th August 1652, p. 1804; *Cal State Papers, Dom.*, 1652–3, pp. 299, 332, 363; 1654, pp. 53, 67, 275, 391; 1657–8, p. 364.

presented a petition to Parliament from 2,500 maimed soldiers on behalf of themselves, and for 4,000 widows and orphans, praying for the regular payment of their pensions.[1] Parliament made some temporary grants, but they were insufficient to meet the emergency. It ordered the pension list to be further reduced, invalids who were sufficiently recovered to be sent to garrisons, orphans to be bound apprentices to trades, and everything to be done to reduce the charge on the State. A report presented on 1st March 1660 revealed the fact that the revenues assigned to the hospitals were forty-nine weeks in arrear, and that the pensioners and patients were in the greatest distress, 'insomuch that some have been starved; others have attempted to destroy themselves; and many are daily likely to perish, through imprisonment, hunger, cold, and nakedness. And the sick and maimed soldiers now under care in the said hospital are also ready to perish for want, being not able to stir out of their beds, and having had no pay these four weeks.'[2]

At the Restoration hospitals and pensions came to an end altogether. The 140 soldiers still in the hospitals in September 1660 were discharged. Some 1,500 widows and orphans who had been in receipt of pensions, and 1,700 maimed soldiers who were out-pensioners, were given twelve weeks' pay apiece and dismissed with letters of recommendation to the justices of their respective counties.[3] For the future Parliament fell back upon the principle laid down in the Elizabethan statute, and ordered the justices of the peace and the overseers of the poor to make provision for the relief and livelihood of the widows and maimed soldiers of their particular districts.

So closes the history of the Long Parliament's effort to provide for the soldiers who suffered in the Civil War. It had promised more than it could perform, but it had made a serious attempt to carry out the principle it had laid down in 1642. It recognized the moral obligation of the State to those who suffered

[1] *Commons' Journals*, vii, 627, 655, 667, 682, 741, 761, 771, 792; Burton, *Diary*, iv, 361, 415, 421.

[2] *Commons' Journals*, vii, 856.

[3] Ibid., viii, 212. Of the 140 soldiers in hospital on 13th September 1660, all but four, who were bedridden, had been discharged by 17th December; of 1,782 widows and orphans, 1,458 had received their twelve weeks' pay; of 2,249 soldier pensioners, 1,673 had also been paid off.

in its service, and it was the first English government to do so. At first the government of Charles the Second did nothing to recognize its duty in this respect. Sir James Turner and Lord Orrery agree in the complaint that there was no public provision for old soldiers. The latter lamented that 'that great and wise encouragement which the ancients gave their soldiers, of providing for the maimed or superannuated by feeding and maintaining them or by rewards of lands, is not practised amongst us; only we have some faint representation of the former in our hospitals; but, alas! how few of them are for soldiers. Yet were all of them for that use yet the plaster would be much too narrow for the sore; and would be rather a sign of the thing than the thing itself.'[1]

In 1680, three years after Orrery's book was published, the foundation-stone of Kilmainham Hospital for old soldiers, in Dublin, was laid, and in 1681 that of Chelsea Hospital.[2] Thus at last the example of the Long Parliament bore fruit.

It remains now to consider the case of the able-bodied men who left the army to return to civil life, either of their own freewill or because of reductions and disbandments. In the New Model and other English armies of the period the duration of the soldier's service was not fixed by any law. Men enlisted for the duration of the war or for so long as they were required: the term does not appear to have been precisely specified at the time when they enlisted. Consequently, there were always a very

[1] Orrery, *Art of War*, 1677, p. 53. Turner, *Pallas Armata*, p. 352, speaks as follows: 'I have observ'd in another place, how in many parts of Christendom, Officers, above the quality of private Captains, many times are reduced to beggary; to obviate which, since Princes and States cannot forbear War, or will not live in Peace, it would be a great work of Charity in them, and would much redound to their Honour and Fame, to build some Hospitals, and endue them with some small Revenue, in which those Commanders who are lame, old, and poor, might get a morsel of Bread; which would be an exceeding great relief to those distressed Gentlemen, and much encourage younger people to engage in a fresh War; for alass, though written Testimonies, sign'd and seal'd by the Prince or his General, may be of good use to young and lusty Gallants, who have their Health, and some Money in their Purses, to look for new Fortunes; yet Passes (though never so favourable) to poor old men, are, upon the matter, nothing else but fair Commissions to beg' (cf. Orrery, *Art of War*, p. 15).

[2] France was in this respect before England. Thanks to Louvois, the Hôtel des Invalides was founded in 1670 and opened four years later. On the hospital system and the provision made for sick, wounded, and old soldiers in France during the seventeenth century, see Rousset, *Louvois*, i, 250–5, and Avenel, *Richelieu et la Monarchie Absolue*, iii, 147–51.

large number of experienced soldiers in the ranks of Cromwell's regiments. There exists a table showing the arrears of pay claimed by Colonel Whalley's regiment in 1650, which proves that many of his troopers had formed part of the Earl of Manchester's army, and had therefore been six or seven years in the service. In one troop there were fifty such men, in another sixty or seventy, in the colonel's troop eighty-seven.[1] Monck's *Order-Book* during the years from 1654 to 1659 often mentions soldiers as having served ten or twelve years in the army, who either petitioned their general for their discharge, or were discharged by him as unfit for further service.[2]

After the battle of Worcester, in 1651, it can never have been difficult for a soldier to leave the army if he wished to do so. The government from motives of economy disbanded a large number of men, reducing the company of foot by successive steps from one hundred and twenty to seventy men, and the troop of horse from one hundred to forty-eight men. At any one of these reductions a soldier who wished to return to civil life could easily get his name included in the list of those disbanded. If he missed these opportunities he might petition his general for a discharge, which was usually granted if his regimental officers made no objection, and if he provided a substitute to take his place.[3] It was not difficult to find a substitute, for during the Protectorate the supply of recruits was generally in

[1] *Harleian MS.*, 427.

[2] The following extracts from Monck's *Order-Book* supply examples of such discharges:
'1 Sept., 1658. Whereas the Bearer Francis Fletcher hath served as private soldier in Col. Cooper's regiment for the space of 8 years past, and now by reason of lameness contracted in the service is nott fitt for further imployment, to recommend him to the Committee and Treasurers at Ely House or the Savoy.'
'Feb. 24, 1658–9. Upon a certificate from Major Hubblethorne that Francis Wilson hath served the Commonwealth under several commands as a private souldier ever since the year 1642 till the year 1652, and ever since that time to the date in Major Hubblethornes company, and now by reason of age and sickness contracted in the service is unable for further service, Recommendation to the Hospitall.'

[3] '24 Aug., 1654. Letter to Col. Daniell to discharge Hutton a private soldier in his regiment upon his bringing in a fit person in his room.'
'29 July, 1656. Reference to the petition of John Lewis of Capt. Collinson's company in Col. Fenwick's regiment to Lt. Col. Wilkes, to give him a discharge, in case he put another in his room and the officer of the company be willing to it' (Monck's *Order-Book*).

excess of the demand, and there were always plenty of old soldiers willing to return to the colours. The soldier who obtained his discharge usually received a pass to his native county, and if he required it a recommendation to the local authorities for assistance. He frequently procured also a certificate of good conduct from his regimental officers, in which his length of service was stated.[1]

What became of these old soldiers after leaving the army? In some cases they had a few pounds due to them which enabled them to make a start in civil life; but in most cases very little, and in some nothing at all. On disbanding they received either their arrears of pay or a certificate for them, and generally a small gratuity to pay their journey home. Cromwell, in January 1653, ordered that the soldiers then disbanded in Scotland should be given the foot soldiers a fortnight's pay, the horsemen eight or ten days' pay, to defray the charges of their return to England. But before the order came many had been already despatched. 'I am confident,' wrote Colonel Lilburne, the commander-in-chief in Scotland, 'abundance are gone hence that begs their bread in their way homeward, and hath not a groat in their purses to live upon, which me thinks does much reflect upon the honour of the commonwealth, and something, I fear, upon your Excellency and the chief officers of the Army.'[2]

What became of discharged and destitute soldiers? In Elizabethan times, and indeed much later, a disbandment invariably meant an increase in the number of highwaymen, footpads, and thieves in general, and new dangers for all who travelled the King's highway. Something of the same sort happened after the

---

[1] 'Thes are to sertyfey home it may concern that Edmund Peckover, Gentillmane, served as a Solger in the troupe of Will. Collman, major: after him Joseph Blisitt capting had and hath still the Comand of all the same troupe under the Comand of the Right honorabull Leftennante General Charles Fletewood whom is Colonell in the service of the Comonwellth, both in England and Scotland, from the yeare of our Lord on thousand six hundred forty six untill the yeare on thousand six hundred fifty and five: during which time he behaved him selfvef faithfull ley and honestley, as becom a Solger, in witnes whereof we have here unto set our hands and Seels this Sixen of Aguste, 1655.

'Joseph Blissett,
'Hugh Parrye.'
– (Kingston, *Civil War in East Anglia*, p. 355.)

[2] *Scotland and the Commonwealth*, p. 80.

close of the Civil War. Whitelocke notes in his *Memorials*, under 4th May 1647, letters from the sheriff of Oxfordshire certifying 'that many troopers, Irish and others, who had been in arms against the Parliament, robbed all passengers, and that he had raised the *posse comitatus* and apprehended about one hundred of them'.[1] James Hind, the most famous highwayman of the time of the Commonwealth, 'the great robber of England' as his biographer calls him, had fought for Charles the Second at Worcester.[2] In July 1654, two years after Hind's execution, Hussey and Peck, two gentlemen who had once been officers in the King's army, were hanged at Oxford, 'to the great reluctancy of the generous Royalists then living in Oxon.' 'They were out of commission and employ,' apologizes Anthony Wood, 'and had no money to maintain them, which made them rob on the highway.'[3] Probably some of the disbanded soldiers of the Cromwellian army took to similar courses, but they were less conspicuous in the criminal records of the time.

A more common figure still in the literature of the seventeenth century is the soldier turned beggar. Take for instance the ballad called 'The Maunding Soldier, or the Fruit of War is Beggary'.

> *Good your worship, cast your eyes*
> *Upon a souldier's miseries;*
> *Let not my leane cheeks, I pray,*
> *Your bounty from a souldier stay,*
> > *But like a noble friend*
> > *Some silver lend,*
> *And Jove will pay you in the end.*

He then recites his services and perils:—

> *Twice through the bulke have I been shot,*
> *My braynes have boylèd like a pot:*
> *I have at least these dozen times*
> *Been blowne up by those roguish mines.*

[1] Whitelocke, *Memorials*, ii, 138, ed. 1853.

[2] *Life of Captain James Hind.*

[3] *Life of Anthony Wood*, ed. Clark, i, 156, 186. For the results of disbanding some of the troops of Charles the Second, see *Memoirs of the Verney Family*, iv, 239.

And concludes:

> *I pray your worship, think on me,*
> *That am what I do seeme to be,*
> *No rooking rascall, nor no cheat,*
> *But a souldier every way compleat:*
> > *I have wounds to show*
> > *That prove it so,*
> *Then courteous good sir, ease my woe,*
> > *And I for you will pray,*
> > *Both night and day,*
> *That your substance never may decay.*[1]

In another ballad called 'The Cunning Northern Beggar' an impostor describes how he personates an old soldier:

> *Now like a wandring souldier*
> *(That has i'th warres bin maymed*
> > *With the shot of a gunne)*
> > *To gallants I runne*
> *And begg, 'Sir, helpe the lamed!*
> *I am a poore old souldier,*
> *And better times once viewed,*
> > *Though bare now I goe,*
> > *Yet many a foe,*
> *By me hath bin subdued.'*
> *And therefore I cry 'Good your worship, good Sir,*
> *Bestow one poor denier, Sir,'*
> > *Which when I've got,*
> > *At the Pipe and Pot*
> *I soon will it casheere, Sir.*[2]

A third ballad, 'The Lamentation of a Bad Market, or the Disbanded Soldier,' refers directly to the great disbanding of the Cromwellian army in the summer of 1660.

> *In Red-coat rags attired, I wander up and down,*
> *Since Fate and foes conspired, thus to array me,*
> > *Or betray me to the hard censure of the Town.*

[1] *Roxburghe Ballads*, iii, 111.   [2] Ibid., i, 137.

My buffe doth make me boots, my velvet coat and scarlet,
Which us'd to make me credit with many a Sodom harlot,
Have bid me all adieu, most despicable varlet!
'Alas, poor souldier, whither wilt thou march?'

   .   .   .   .

Into the countrey places I resolve to goe,
Amongst those sun-burnt faces, I'le goe to plough,
Or keep a cow; 'tis that my masters now again must do.[1]

On the other hand, a soldier willing and able to work found great difficulty in obtaining it. Hardly any pursuit but agriculture was open to him. Hence in the army petition of 12th August 1652 it was asked by the Council of Officers 'That some effectual provision may be made for liberty for such poor men as have served the Parliament in the late wars, since the 12th of July, 1642. Who desiring to exercise manual occupations and other means to get themselves a livelihood, are denied the same within several corporations.'[2]

The Long Parliament did nothing to meet this demand, reasonable as it was, and it was left for Cromwell to redress the grievance after he became Protector. On the 2nd of September 1654, he issued an ordinance which was of very great value to old soldiers.[3] The preamble explains clearly the exact nature of the legal hindrances which hampered the soldiers in getting employment.

'Whereas there are divers soldiers who have served the Parliament and this Commonwealth in these late wars, some of which were men that used Trades, others that were apprentices to Trades, who had not served out their times, and others who are apt and fit for Trades; many of which, the Wars being now ended, would willingly imploy themselves in those Trades they were formerly accustomed unto, or which they are apt and able to follow and make use of, for the getting of their Living by their labor and industry, but are hindered from exercising those trades in certain Cities, Corporations, and other places within this Commonwealth, because of certain By-laws and Customs of

[1] *Roxburghe Ballads*, vii, 647.
[2] *Mercurius Politicus*, 12th to 19th August 1652, p. 1801.
[3] Scobell, *Collection of Acts and Ordinances*, 1658, ii, 357, 389.

K

those places; and of a statute made in the fifth year of the late
Queen Elizabeth, prohibiting the use of certain Trades by any
person that hath not served as an Apprentice to such Trades
by the space of seven years.' To remove these obstructions
Cromwell ordained that any soldier who had served in the armies
of the Parliament or the Commonwealth between the year 1642
and the 3rd of September 1651, for the period of not less than
four years, should be free to practise his trade or occupation
in any place within the boundaries of the Commonwealth in
spite of the legal restrictions enumerated. A similar freedom
was given to any soldier who, since September 1651, had served
for two years in the forces employed in Ireland and Scotland.
A soldier who wished to take advantage of this ordinance had to
provide himself with a certificate, signed either by a field-officer
and two commissioned officers of his regiment, or by some general officer of the army, testifying that to the knowledge of the
signatories he had fulfilled the requisite period of service. Notes
of the issue of many such certificates are to be found in Monck's
Order-Book, and many others must have been issued by regimental officers to their men.[1]

This ordinance was evidently a great boon to discharged soldiers. It was confirmed in 1656 by Cromwell's second Parliament,
and was even re-enacted in a somewhat different form after the
Restoration. By Charles the Second's Act all soldiers who had
formed part of the army under Monck's command on the 25th
of April 1660 were allowed to practise trades and handicrafts,
provided they were willing to take the oaths of allegiance and
supremacy.[2]

Cromwell therefore deserves the credit of being the first
English ruler who attempted to find employment for old soldiers,
for the adoption of this plan was due to his initiative. Thanks

[1] The following example is from Monck's *Order-Book*, 1st September
1658: 'That whereas Courtney Manton served for several years as Corporal
in Capt. Benson's company in the regiment then Col. Alured's now Col.
Cooper's before the 20th of November, 1652, and afterwards in his Lordship's regiment of foot, and so is capable of having the benefit of the
ordinance of his Highness bearing date 2 Sept., 1654, to permit him to pass
into any part of England, Scotland, or Ireland, and to follow any handi-
craft or other trade exercised about manufactures in any City, or town
Corporate, or other place, without the lett or molestation of any persons
whatsoever'.

[2] Grose, *Military Antiquities*, ii, 88.

largely to it, the successive reductions of the army which took place during the Protectorate caused no disturbances, and it was also one of the reasons which made the peaceful disbandment of Monck's army so easy in 1660. Without overestimating the scope of the Act, it is clear that the prospect of employment made the soldiers willing to return to civil life. Their good conduct was as remarkable after they had ceased to bear arms as it was during their service. Much was due to the orderly habits which the severe discipline of the army had taught them; as much to the fact that no artificial difficulties intervened to prevent them from earning a livelihood. 'Of all the old army,' said a friend to Pepys in 1662, 'you cannot see a man begging about the streets. . . . You shall have this captain turned shoemaker; the lieutenant a baker; this a brewer; that a haberdasher; this common soldier, a porter: and every man in his apron and frock, etc., as if they had never done anything else.'[1]

[1] *Pepys' Diary*, 9th Nov., ed. Wheatley, 1663, iii, 337.

CHAPTER XII

Discipline

BY THE JUDGEMENT both of friends and foes one of the most striking characteristics of the Cromwellian army was the excellence of its discipline. A pamphlet called *The Honour of the English Soldiery*,[1] published in 1651, drew an elaborate comparison between the good behaviour of the soldiers of the New Model and the misconduct and barbarity of the French soldiers during the wars of the Fronde. 'It was said of King Alfred,' added the pamphleteer, 'that by his severity and diligence he so terrified robbers that a traveller might pass safe all over England with his purse in his hand; the like may be said of our noble Cromwell and his incomparable discipline, that a man may pass through the land without the least prejudice from the soldiery.' Foreign observers, such as the Venetian Sagredo in the relation which he drew up for the Senate of Venice after his mission to England, praised the good conduct of the army.[2] Candid Royalists echoed their praise, and Clarendon, when the army was disbanded, commended not only its courage, but its sobriety and manners.[3] They seemed, he declared, '*in bello pacis gerere negotium*', they 'lived like good husbandmen in the country and good citizens in the city'. Other Royalists admitted the fact with a reservation. 'I remember,' says Sir Philip Warwick, 'what a sober friend of mine told me that he replied to an old acquaintance of his engaged with Fairfax vaunting of the sanctity of their army and the negligence of ours. "Faith," says he, "thou sayest true; for in our army we have the sins of men

---

[1] *Thomason Tracts*, E, 638, 639.

[2] Horatio Brown, *Venetian Studies*, p. 387.

[3] See his speech of 13th September 1660; *Old Parliamentary History*, xxii, 487.

(drinking and wenching), but in yours you have those of devils, spiritual pride and rebellion." [1]

This discipline was a plant of slow growth. It did not spring up in a night, like Jonah's gourd, as soon as the New Model was organized, but was the result of unremitting labour and vigilance for many years. At the beginning of the Civil War the soldiers of the Parliament had not been remarkable for discipline and good conduct, but rather for the opposite qualities. The proclamations issued by the Parliament during the first few months of the war continually refer to their lawlessness. On 18th August 1642 the Lords and Commons inform the world that 'there have been divers complaints made unto us of many disorders committed by the soldiers in their marching, and in such places wherever they have been quartered or billeted, which disorders have been partly occasioned by the neglect of their officers to go along with them'. On 27th August another proclamation declares that 'divers soldiers have in a tumultuous and violent manner broken into divers of the King's subject's houses, pillaged and ransacked them, under colour that they are papists' houses or the houses of persons disaffected'. [2] The letters of Nehemiah Wharton, a sergeant in Lord Brooke's regiment in Essex's army, supply some remarkable illustrations of the absence of all discipline amongst the London volunteers during their march to join the army. They started from London on 8th August 1642, and the next day at Acton, says Wharton, 'several of our soldiers sallied out to the house of one Penruddock, a Papist, and being basely affronted by him and his dog, entered his house and pillaged him to the purpose. This day also the soldiers got into the church, defaced the ancient and sacred glazed pictures, and burned the holy rails.' Two days later, when Wharton and his company reached Hillingdon, they visited the church, but found the van of the regiment had already burnt the rails. 'The rails being gone we got the surplice to make us handkerchiefs, and one of our soldiers wore it to Uxbridge.' [3]

Besides this, Wharton's men requisitioned food freely. 'Every day,' says he, 'our soldiers by stealth do visit Papists' houses,

[1] *Memoirs of Sir Philip Warwick*, p. 253.

[2] Husbands, *Ordinances*, i, pp. 565, 590.

[3] *Cal. State Papers, Dom.*, 1641–3, p. 372.

and constrain from them both meat and money. They give them whole great loaves and cheeses, which they triumphantly carry away upon the points of their swords.' The deer of gentlemen suspected to be Papists or malignants were treated as lawful prey. 'Several of our soldiers,' he writes from Coventry, 'both horse and foot, sallied out of the city to Lord Dunsmore's park, and brought from thence great store of venison, which is as good as ever I tasted; and ever since they make it their daily practice, so that venison is almost as common with us as beef is with you.' The officers were powerless to restrain their men, and often shared the plunder. Sergeant Wharton with a file of his men marched to Sir Alexander Denton's park, 'who is a malignant fellow', and killed a fat buck, which he then had conveyed to the headquarters of the brigade at Buckingham. 'With part of it,' says he, 'I feasted my captain, Captain Parker, Captain Beacon and Colonel Hampden's son, and with the rest several lieutenants, ensigns and sergeants, and had much thanks for my pains.'[1] Obedience to their officers was scarcely to be expected. On the third day of the march from London the regiment mutinied against its lieutenant-colonel. 'Our soldiers,' says Wharton, 'generally manifested their dislike to our lieutenant-colonel who is a Goddam blade and doubtless hatched in hell, and we all desire that either the Parliament would depose him, or God convert him, or the devil fetch him away quick.' So they disobeyed the orders of this ungodly lieutenant-colonel, and soon succeeded in getting him removed and replaced by an officer whose piety was above suspicion; but the lieutenant-colonel and a major-general, who were both, according to Wharton, 'profane wretches', by their 'false informations' to the general prejudiced him against the regiment. 'Indeed,' complains Wharton, 'our regiment is more slighted than any other.'[2]

The disorders to which these letters testify were not confined to a single regiment. The whole army was infected. Hampden and five other colonels wrote to Essex in September 1642, complaining that their soldiers plundered everywhere. 'The truth is unless we were able to execute some exemplary punishment upon the principal malefactors, we have no hope to redress this horrid enormity. We beseech your Excellence to take this into

[1] *Cal. State Papers, Dom.*, 1641–3, pp. 373, 379, 382.
[2] Ibid., pp. 372, 379, 392.

your present and serious consideration, for if this go on awhile, the army will grow as odious to the country as the Cavaliers. And although we take not upon us to advise the Parliament, yet we that are eyewitnesses of the state of this army, do verily believe that without martial law (to extend to soldiers only) it may prove a ruin as likely as a remedy to this distracted kingdom.'[1]

A couple of months later Parliament acted as Hampden desired. On 9th November 1642 it issued a declaration stating that 'Whereas it is found, that great inconveniences have ensued for want of a strict and severe discipline to have been observed in the army now raised by authority of Parliament, under the command of Robert Earl of Essex, and for that the laws and ordinances of war by him set forth for the government of the said army, have not been put in execution: it is now ordained and declared by the Lords and Commons in Parliament assembled, that from henceforth the officers and soldiers of the said army may not expect any further forbearance of such punishments to be inflicted on them for any their offences, as shall be due unto them by the said ordinances. But that the Lord General may and ought to punish them by death or otherwise, according to their demerits.'[2]

These 'laws and ordinances' referred to by Parliament are the 'Articles of War' by which the armies of Essex, Fairfax, and Cromwell were successively governed. It was customary for every commander-in-chief to issue a military code of the kind when he took up his command.[3] The Earl of Arundel, commander of the army which Charles the First sent against the Scots, had issued such a code in 1639,[4] and his successor the Earl of Northumberland did so a year later.[5] These and other

[1] Sanford, *Studies and Illustrations of the Great Rebellion*, p. 559. This letter is misdated by Sanford, but internal evidence shows it belongs to September 1642.

[2] Husbands, *Ordinances*, i, 742.

[3] A list of such codes from the time of Richard the First to James the Second is given by Grose in *Military Antiquities*, ii, 63–72. Some he reprints, including that of James the Second, but the list is very imperfect. Others are given in Captain Cockle's *Bibliography of Military Books*.

[4] *Laws and Ordinances of War for the better government of his Majesty's Army under Thomas Earl of Arundel and Surrey*, Newcastle, 1639; reprinted in Clode's *Military Forces of the Crown*, i, 429.

[5] *Laws and Ordinances of War established for the better conduct of the service in the Northern parts by his Excellency the Earl of Northumberland*, London, 1640.

collections of the same kind served Essex as a model. In his commission (July 1642) Parliament had granted Essex power to
issue rules and instructions for the government of his army and
for the punishment of offenders in it, 'according to the course
and customs of the wars and rule of the land'.[1] Further, on 8th
September 1642, Parliament ordered Essex to take special care
for punishing disorders amongst the soldiers according to the
custom of war. Essex accordingly issued on the same day the
*Laws and Ordinances of War established for the better conduct of
the Army*, and during the next few days they were read and
expounded at the head of the various regiments.[2] These 'Laws
and Ordinances' became the laws under which the New Model
and the armies of the Commonwealth and Protectorate were
governed. Essex's name was omitted in the title, and some additions were made in three or four points, but for the rest the
articles of war issued by Fairfax are identical with those issued
by Essex.[3] In each army every colonel or captain was bound to
provide himself with a copy, and to have it read at stated times
at the head of his regiment or company. A certain number of
these articles of war were embodied in the military regulations
of the Restoration army,[4] and so found their way into the
English military code.

There are several other military codes of the same period,
which may profitably be compared with that governing the
armies of the Parliament. A code for the Royalist army was
printed at Oxford in 1643, entitled *Military Orders and Articles
established by his Majesty for the better Ordering and Government
of his Majestie's Army*.[5] It contains 153 articles, and has ap-

[1] The commission is printed in the *Old Parliamentary History*, xi, 299.

[2] *Cal. State Papers, Dom.*, 1641–3, pp. 387, 391. My copy of these laws is
printed for John Partridge and John Rothwell, 13th May 1643. Essex's
order for publication is appended, dated 8th Sept., and also the Parliamentary proclamation of 9th Nov. 1642 quoted above.

[3] Reprinted in Appendix L.

[4] See the *Rules and Articles for the better Government of their Majesties
Land-Forces*, 1692; reprinted with notes in Clifford Walton's *History of the
British Standing Army*, 808–20. The *Laws and Ordinances* issued by Lord
Peterborough for the garrison of Tangiers in 1662, which are reprinted at
length by Colonel Davis, are in many parts an exact copy of those which
governed the New Model (*History of the Second Queen's Regiment*, pp.
283–96).

[5] Printed by Leonard Lichfield. This code resembles that drawn up by
Northumberland.

pended to it a very lengthy military oath which every soldier was required to take, and proclamations against plunder and against the sale of horses and arms. Next to this in point of interest comes Leslie's code published in 1644, *Articles and Ordinances of War for the present Expedition of the Army of the Kingdom of Scotland*. It is much briefer than the Royalist or Parliamentary code, but ends with the following advertisement: 'Matters that are clear by the light and law of nature are presupposed: things unnecessary are passed over in silence: and other things may be judged by the common customs and constitutions of war, or may upon new emergency be expressed afterward'.[1] Finally, there are two Irish codes. *Laws and Orders of War established for the good conduct of the service of Ireland*, issued by Ormond for the English army there in 1641. The second is the *Laws and Orders of War established for the conduct of the Army designed for the expedition of Ulster*, issued by the Earl of Castlehaven in 1643.[2]

All these different codes resemble in many respects the regulations in force in foreign armies, and are to some extent copied from them. Those foreign models which exerted most influence were the Dutch and Swedish codes.[3] Leslie, as was natural in the case of a soldier who had served under Gustavus Adolphus, followed some of the Swedish regulations very closely in the articles which he drew up for the army of the Covenanters. On the other hand, the Irish Catholics took the regulations of the Spanish armies as their model.

In the New Model the machinery for the administration of military justice was the same as that which had existed in the

---

[1] This code is reprinted in the *Harleian Miscellany*, ed. Park, vii, 475.

[2] Originally printed at Waterford; reprinted in C. P. Meehan's *Confederation of Kilkenny*, Dublin, 1882, pp. 298–307.

[3] Henry Hexham in his *Principles of the Art Military*, 1642, gives a translation of the *Laws, Articles and Ordinances, established for Martial Discipline*, by the States-General of the King of Sweden in 1590, adding the articles published by Prince Frederick Henry in 1631 and 1637. Robert Ward in his *Animadversions of War*, 1639, prints a series of 'Articles and Military Laws to be observed in the Wars,' 167 in number, adding in a marginal note 'by these laws the King of Sweden governed his army' (bk. ii, pp. 42–54). *The Swedish Discipline, Religious, Civil, and Military*, a pamphlet published in London in 1632, contains the forms of prayer used in the Swedish army, the 'excellent orders' observed in it, and the King's commission for levying a regiment.

army of the Earl of Essex.[1] There was first of all an 'advocate
of the army', or as he was called in the New Model 'a judge-
advocate'. In Essex's army this post was held by Isaac Dorislaus, a Dutch lawyer, who had served in the same capacity in one
of the armies of Charles the First, who helped subsequently to
prepare the charge against the King, and was assassinated by
some Royalists in May 1649, when he was acting as envoy from
the Commonwealth to the United Provinces. In the New Model,
John Mills, a much less distinguished person, replaced Dorislaus
in 1645. There was also a deputy-advocate attached to each of
the minor armies of the Parliament and Republic.

The business of the judge-advocate was to draw up charges
and to see that legal formalities were properly observed in the
trials of prisoners.[2] The custody of the prisoners and the infliction of the punishments were in the hands of the provost-
marshal-general of the army.[3] In Essex's army this post was
held by John Baldwin. In the New Model there were two
officials, Captain Wykes, marshal-general of foot, and Captain
Richard Lawrence, marshal-general of horse. The provost-marshal-general had about twenty mounted men to attend him,
who formed the police of the army. Not only the soldiers but all
the civilians who followed the army were under his jurisdiction.
To prevent extortion and quarrelling he was authorized to fix
the prices of the food sold by the sutlers, and to see that they

[1] In the establishment of 3rd Nov. 1647, there appear (1) a provost-
marshal-general of foot at four shillings and five pence per diem with
twenty men at two shillings per day each. (2) An advocate of the army at
ten shillings per diem and his clerk at three shillings and fourpence per
diem. (3) A provost-marshal-general of the horse at three shillings and fourpence per diem with eight men at two shillings per diem apiece for themselves and their horses. (4) Each regiment of horse also has its provost-
marshal at three shillings and fourpence per diem with two men at two
shillings apiece. The provost-marshal of a regiment of foot also receives
three shillings and fourpence per diem for himself, but no assistants are
provided for (*Lords' Journals*, x, 66–9).

[2] The duties of the 'praetor or judge-martial', as Francis Markham calls
him, are set forth at length in his *Decades of War*, p. 111. According to
Markham this official was originally a legal assistant to the lord-marshal of
the army.

[3] The provost-marshal was, according to Markham, commonly appointed
in old times by the lord-marshal, whose under-officer he was. Markham
styles him 'the great and principal gaoler of the army', and gives an account
of his functions (*Decades of War*, pp. 105–8). There appears to be no exact
account of his functions in the Cromwellian army extant. They must be
gathered from the Articles of War and other occasional orders.

gave good weight and full measure to their customers. Finally it was his business to look after the sanitary condition of the camp, and to see that it was kept clean.

Under the marshal-general came the provost-marshals of the regiments of horse and foot, who formed part of the ordinary staff of each regiment both in the army of the Earl of Essex and in the New Model.[1]

As the military code in force was practically the same in both armies, and the disciplinary organization was also the same, it is evident that the cause of the difference between the discipline of the two armies was mainly due to greater vigour in the administration of each.[2] Fairfax and Cromwell used their authority with greater decision than Essex, and they were supported by better officers. They had also a great advantage in the fact that their men were much more regularly paid than those of Essex had been, and that discipline was therefore much easier to maintain. Fairfax also made certain changes in the articles of the Military Code relating to the administration of justice, evidently in order to quicken and facilitate the method of proceeding against offenders.[3] Another change he made was the institution of regimental courts to try minor offences, reserving always to the general court sitting at headquarters the more serious cases.

[1] The functions of the regimental provost-marshal are described by Turner: 'The Regiment Provost-Marshal hath power to apprehend any Soldiers whom he sees transgressing the Laws and Articles of War, from doing whereof no Officer may hinder him; but he hath not power to set any Prisoner at liberty, no not those whom himself hath imprison'd. He is Gaoler, and keeps those who are committed to him, either in Irons, or without Irons, for which he hath a Guard allow'd him. He is to present the Prisoners to the Court of War, and to desire that Justice may be done on them for the crimes they have committed, which he is obliged to specifie, and he is to be present at the execution of every sentence; and when a Soldier is to run the Gatloupe, he is to give him the first lash; he is to impose prices on Wine, Ale, Beer, Mead, Tabaco, and all manner of Meats, according as he receives directions from the Provost-Marshal-General. And if the Victuallers, Sutlers and Mark-tenters transgress he is to make price of those Wares, in venting whereof any of them did fail, the half whereof belongs to the Judg-Marshall, and the other moiety to the Princes Procurator Fiscal, and he hath an allowance of every Hoghead of Wine, Ale, Beer, and Brandy' (*Pallas Armata*, p. 223).

[2] The great improvement which took place is pointed out in *The Honour of the English Soldiery* quoted on p. 276, but it was generally noticed as early as 1646 or earlier.

[3] A comparison of the clauses in the articles relating to procedure proves this.

This took place in the autumn of 1647, and is spoken of as if it were a novelty.[1]

There are many accounts of the proceedings of courts-martial printed in contemporary newspapers and pamphlets, and many others still in manuscript. From these it is possible to form a very accurate idea of the actual working of military justice and of the system of punishment. Incidentally these reports throw a great deal of light on the character of the army, the manners and habits of the soldiers, and the relations of officers and men.[2]

The highest military punishments were death by the rope or bullet, of which the most honourable form was shooting. These were the penalties usually inflicted on the leaders of mutinies. In the first march of the New Model to the West, Fairfax, 'to lay an early foundation of good success in the punishment of former disorders and the prevention of future misdemeanours', called a council of war near Andover, and tried various offenders for their lives. Five were condemned, and two were promptly executed, one as a renegade, and another as a mutineer. Both were hung upon a tree by the road on which the army marched, 'in terrorem'.[3]

Mutineers as a rule were shot.[4] There is a detailed account of the execution of Robert Lockyer, a Leveller, who headed a mutiny in Colonel Whalley's regiment, and was shot by a file

[1] Rushworth, vii, 816; about 20th Sept. 1647; see Appendix M.

[2] A small quarto amongst the *Clarke MSS.* in Worcester College Library (No. 21), which contains an account of the trials by court-martial taking place at Dundee from 17th September 1651 to 10th January 1652, is of special interest. A selection from them was printed in the Miscellany of the Scottish Historical Society in 1919. Grose's chapter 'Of Military Punishments' (vol. ii, p. 103), and Colonel Clifford Walton's on 'Martial Law and Punishments During the Period from 1660 to 1700' (p. 529), supply a general view of the whole subject.

[3] Sprigge, *Anglia Rediviva*, p. 17.

[4] Shooting was also sometimes the penalty for murder, as the following instance shows: 'George Preston was this Sunday condemned to be shot to death in the High Street in Edenburgh, at the high Crosse on Wednesday next between the houres of 9 and 11, for killing a Scotch woman at Netherey, the manner in short thus: Hee, with two of his fellow Souldiers, without leave from their Officers, went out into the Countrey to kill Pigeons, they finding none, shot at a Cock, and kild it, the woman that owned the Cock came for it, and told them if they would not return the Cock shee would follow them to their Officers, and have an order for them to make them return the cock, the said Preston told her if shee would not goe back with her company, they would set fire on their tailes, the woman following them for her cock, hee turned about and shot at her, and about five houres after she dyed' (*Several Proceedings in Parliament*, 1st to 8th April 1652).

of musketeers in St Paul's Churchyard on 27th April 1649.[1] On
19th May of the same year, after the suppression of the mutiny
at Burford, three of the prisoners were shot against the wall of
the church, while their fellow-mutineers were stationed on the
leads to see the infliction of the penalty.[2]

Hanging was another punishment for mutiny, or even for
mutinous words. On 29th May 1651, says a newspaper, 'At a
court of war held at Whitehall one Samuel Gardner foot-soldier
in Col. Ingoldsby's regiment was condemned to be hanged in
Paul's Churchyard on Friday after, for speaking words of sedition, uproar and mutiny, contrary to the laws of war, in
promoting Charles Stuart, and advertising the soldiers and
people not to fight for the state, but for King Charles. This he
spake and uttered the same divers times while he was whipping
through the city for a former offence; he is also afterwards to be
hanged in chains on Turnham Green for example to others that
shall offend in the like kind.'[3]

When several persons were sentenced to death by a court-
martial, it was usual to inflict the extreme penalty on one or
two of them, and to allow them to cast lots for their lives. There
is in Monck's *Order-Book* an answer to the petition of three
soldiers condemned to death, 'that they are to cast lots for their
lives, as in like case hath been accustomed, that two receive
mercy as the lot shall fall, and the other suffer death upon

---

[1] *The Army's Martyr*, 1649, 4to. This is the most detailed account of a
military execution during the period which I have met with.

[2] *The Moderate*, 15th to 22nd May 1649. The three men executed were
Cornet Thompson, Corporal Perkins, and Mr John Church (the last being
apparently a private).

[3] *Several Proceedings in Parliament*, 29th May to 5th June 1651, p. 1345.
Some other examples of trials for mutiny in 1648 may be added. 'From the
Head Quarters at Windsor we had further Intelligence to this purpose,
That on Wednesday last, at a Council of War there was one Bartholomew
Symonds, of Col. Lilburn's Regiment condemned to dye; he was one who
was the chief Ringleader of the Mutiny at the Rendezvous near Ware;
where when Major Gregson spake to the Soldiers of Col. Lilburn's Regiment
to submit to the Discipline of the Army, he cryed out, That the Major was
against the King; and thereupon divers Soldiers in the Regiment threw
Stones at the Major, and broke his Head.
'There was also one Bell condemned to run the Gantlet twice, for being
active in that Mutiny.' Two officers, Major Cobbett and Captain Bray,
were also tried for the mutiny at Ware, and sentenced to be cashiered
(Rushworth, vii, 922, 937, 940, 943).

further order'.[1] In 1649 three officers who had formerly served
the Parliament, but had gone over to the Royalists in the
second Civil War, were sentenced to death by court-martial.
Fairfax ordered them to cast lots which should suffer, and 'by
reason the prisoners were unwilling to draw their own destiny,
three lots were given into the hand of a child; in two of them
was written "Life given by God," and the other a blank. The
child gave the first to Colonel Powell, the second to Major
General Laugherne, in both which life was written, and the
third (being a blank) to Colonel Poyer.' Poyer was accordingly
shot.[2]

Whipping was a very frequent punishment for plundering,
violence to country people, fraud, and various military offences.
A soldier of the garrison of Leith, in 1651, was sentenced to
receive thirty-nine stripes on the bare back under the gallows
'for a high misdemeanour in taking a mutton'.[3] On a march
through the Highlands in 1652 five soldiers were punished for
plundering and straggling from their colours. Two were tied to
a tree and received thirty stripes apiece, another was 'to be
hanged up by the arm pits while the regiment passed by', and
a fourth to be 'hanged so that he may stand on tiptoe, and
receive a lash as each subdivision of the regiment passed by'.[4]

[1] On 30th January 1655. The condemned man was pardoned on 16th
February 1655. Compare the following case: 'From Leith Octob. 2. thus,
This week a stirree hapned among the Souldiers here, for abating twelve
pence a week out of pay towards a store; some were sentenced at a Court
Martial, but upon supplication to the Governour they did cast Lots, and it
pleased God (the disposer of life and death) that it fell upon him who was
the most sedicious, which was very remarkable, yet Divine Mercy further
extended it self, for this day the souldiers being drawne forth to the
Gibbets, and that Souldier fitted for his end, all or most of the wives in this
Garison had petitioned and prevailed with the Governour's clemency for his
pardon' (*Several Proceedings in Parliament*, 2nd to 14th October 1652,
p. 2488).

[2] *The Moderate*, 17th to 24th April 1649.

[3] The criminal was then to 'be turned forth of the Towne, and that if he
should be found in any Regiment in Scotland within a month after, then to
be severely punished'.

Before the sentence could be carried out the criminal escaped from the
custody of the provost-marshal. 'Whereupon the Court receiving notice of
it, it was further ordered by the Court, That the two Souldiers who were the
chief in letting this prisoner escape, should be led with ropes about their
necks to the Gallowes, and thereto tyed halfe an hour, with papers on their
breasts signifying their offence' (*Several Proceedings in Parliament*, 8th to
15th January 1652, p. 1858).

[4] *Several Proceedings in Parliament*, 15th to 22nd July 1652, p. 2301.

Other penalties were frequently combined with the whipping. In September 1651 two soldiers of the garrison of Dundee for beating and robbing two countrymen were sentenced 'to be brought from the prison with ropes about their necks, and their faults upon their breasts, to the gallows at the time of parade, and being tied up by the neck to receive thirty stripes apiece upon their bare backs. Afterwards to ask forgiveness upon their knees for the injury done to the poor men and the army. And after that to be kept with bread and water till they have restored fourfold to the countrymen for what they have taken away.'[1]

Sixty lashes is the highest number awarded in any sentence of a court-martial which I have met with.[2] If a severer whipping was held necessary the culprit was sentenced to run the gauntlet. The 'gatloup', 'gantelope', or 'gantlet' was a form of punishment much used in the Swedish and German armies, and copied from them by the English.[3] For instance, in 1649 the following sentence was passed on two soldiers for deer-stealing: 'That

[1] *Clarke MSS.*, xxi, 10, 23rd September 1651.

[2] Ibid., xxi, 32, 10th October 1651. For an attempted rape.

[3] Robert Monro calls this punishment 'the Loupegarthe' (*Monro His Expedition of the Worthy Scots Regiment called Mackay's*, pt. i, p. 4). Turner, in a list of the minor military punishments, explains the derivation of the word. 'Military punishments, which reach not to Death, are the Strappado, hanging up by the Thumbs, so that only the Delinquents Toes can touch the ground; laying Muskets on their Shoulders, more or fewer, for a longer or shorter time, according to the quality of the fault; to be kept in Prison so many days or weeks with irons on them; and sometimes to be fed only with Bread and Water in Prison. Observe here, that without a Sentence of a Court of War, no Superior Commander, be who he will, can keep an Inferior Officer or Common Soldier longer in Prison than the imprisoned party calls for a hearing. There is also riding the Wooden Horse, on which sometimes the Offender hath his hands tyed behind his back, and sometimes Muskets or other weights tyed to his feet: As likewise to be turned out of the Army by the Hang-man, to have their Ears cut off by the Hang-man, to be whipp'd by the Hang-man, to have their Swords broke by the Hang-man. I have known some who thought, that Souldiers who are whipp'd at Gatloupe, should be turned out of the Army; which is a gross mistake, for they are appointed to be whipped by their Comerades, that they may be kept in the Army, for after an Officer or Souldier is put in a Hang-man's hand, he should serve no longer in any Army. Gustavus Adolphus, King of Sweden, first began it, in imitation belike of the custome the Roman Centurions had to whip their Souldiers. It is a German word, Gaslauf, and comes from Gas, or Gat, which signifieth a Street; and Lauffen, or Louppen, which is, to run; because he who is to be whipp'd, is to run through a Street, between two rows of Souldiers. The Provost Marshal is to furnish Rods, and to give the Delinquent the first lash; but if there be neither Provost, nor Lieutenant, nor Servant of his (who is called Stokknecht), then the Drummers give the Rods' (*Pallas Armata*, p. 348).

they be stripped naked from the waist upward and a lane to be
made by half of the Lord General's regiment of foot and half of
Colonel Pride's regiment, with every soldier a cudgel in his
hand, and they to run through them in this posture, every soldier
having a stroke at the naked breasts, arms, or where it shall
light; and after they have run the gantelop in this manner they
are to be cashiered the regiment'.[1]

A similar punishment was inflicted on six soldiers of Colonel
Lilburne's in December 1648 for their part in the mutiny at
Ware, and on two of Colonel Deane's for a fraud.[2]

A much lighter punishment, and one very frequently employed for minor offences, was riding the wooden horse. The
horse was formed of a couple of boards nailed together so as to
make a sharp ridge or angle, which represented the back of the
horse, while four posts formed the legs. Sometimes it was fixed
on a movable stand, and was adorned with a rough representation of a horse's head and tail.[3] On this sharp ridge the culprit
was seated for half an hour or an hour, according to his offence,
with his hands tied, and with one, two, or three muskets fastened
to each leg. At Dundee, on 17th September 1651, two soldiers
for plundering were sentenced 'to ride the horse for an hour with
a musket at each heel, and the fault writ upon their backs'.
Another a few days later for insubordination was condemned
'to ride the horse an hour with one musket cross under the horse
to keep his legs wide). Sometimes there were additional refine-
ments of disgrace added. On 22nd October 1651 a soldier for

[1] Quoted by Colonel Clifford Walton, *History of the British Standing
Army*, p. 561. He does not give the name of the newspaper quoted.

[2] 'Two new listed Souldiers in Col. Deanes Regiment, Henry Matthews,
and Robert Rowe, were this day tryed by a Court Martial, and sentenced to
ride the Wooden-Horse at the Royal Exchange, for an Hour at Exchange-
time; and on Saturday next at the same place to run the Gantelope through
Col. Deanes Regiment: this was a piece of Justice upon these two for the
Example of others, who under the colour of being Souldiers, care not what
knavery they act. Their Crime was this: These with two more who escaped,
took upon them to apprehend a citizen of London, under pretence of a Warrant from the Council of War, and that they had a great charge against
him, when there was no such matter; but they thought by this means to get
Mony of him. The Citizen forthwith makes some Officers at White-Hall
acquainted therewith, and the Council of War disclaiming the Act, send for
the Souldiers, that made this bold attempt' (Rushworth, iv, ii, 1369).

[3] See Grose, *Military Antiquities*, ii, 106. He adds a picture of the wooden
horse (p. 111).

stealing and killing an ox was condemned not only to ride the horse with a couple of muskets at each heel, but also with a rope about his neck, and the hide of the ox on his back.[1]

For some offences mutilation or branding was the penalty. For blasphemy or cursing, soldiers were occasionally bored through the tongue with a red-hot iron.[2] Sometimes the milder punishment of public degradation was deemed sufficient. In May 1655 a soldier of Colonel Axtell's regiment, for drunkenness, swearing and quarrelling, was sentenced to three days' imprisonment on bread and water, 'and then to stand upon a joint stool with a cleft stick upon his tongue for the space of half an hour, near Mr Henry Halfpenny's door, a victualler in Covent Garden, where he committed his misdemeanour, and to have a paper fixed on his breast, written in capital letters, signifying his offences, and after that to be cashiered the army'.[3] Publicity was one of the chief elements in all military punishments. In 1649 Robert Spavin, Cromwell's secretary, convicted of forging his general's hand to passes and protections, was sentenced by a council of war 'to ride on horseback from Whitehall to Westminster and thence through the City, with an inscription on his back and on his breast, written in capital letters, to signify his crime'.[4] An instance of public degradation followed by expulsion from the army is supplied by the case of five troopers who in March 1649 presented a seditious and mutinous letter to Fairfax and the Council of Officers. The sentence of the court-martial

---

[1] *Clarke MSS.*, xxi, 3, 46.

[2] A letter from Wakefield in September 1647 supplies an instance:
'We begin to do Justice a-pace, keep Councils of War often, punish Offenders. At a Council of War yesterday one Mac Ro an Irish Man, a notorious Drunkard, Swearer, and one that slighted the Commander in Chief, was tried. He was clearly convicted; and it was so bad, that all cried out against it. His Sentence was to be bored through the tongue with a red-hot iron, to suffer Fourteen Days Imprisonment with Bread and Water, to be casheered the Army, made incapable of ever serving the Parliament again, to deliver up his Horse and Arms. Another Delinquent was also tried for being disorderly in his Quarters, and other Crimes, and was adjudged to a Weeks Imprisonment, to stand in the Market-place during the time of the Market at the Head-Quarters for the Space of an Hour with his Faults written in Great Letters on his Breast. These are strange things here, and much gazing at it; ingenuous People both Martial and Civil, are much taken with it. It hath wrought much Good amongst the Soldiers already; the Officers do confess it, and the Country are sensible of it: Money and Justice will work great Reformation' (Rushworth, vii, 809).

[3] *Perfect Proceedings of State Affairs*, 24th to 31st May 1655, p. 4694.

[4] *Cromwelliana*, p. 61.

was: 'You shall ride with your faces towards the horse tails before the heads of your several regiments, with your faults written upon your breasts, and your swords broken over your heads, and so be cashiered the army as not worthy to ride therein: and a proclamation to be made that none shall receive you into any troop, company, or garrison'.[1]

There is one more point which requires mention whilst we are dealing with this question of punishments. In the fifth section of the Article of Duties towards superiors and commanders, it is said, 'that no man upon penalty of death is to resist or to offer to use a weapon against any officer correcting him orderly for his offence'. It is clear from this article, and from the records of trials, that both officers and non-commissioned officers were allowed, with certain restrictions, to strike their men, if they thought such correction necessary. Many instances prove this.

In October 1651, some companies of Monck's regiment being drawn up in the church at Dundee, one Abraham Randall, 'being playing and abusing his fellow soldiers', the sergeant told him that if he continued fooling, he would strike him. 'Do if you dare,' answered Randall. 'I will strike again.' Thereupon the sergeant gave him a box on the ear, upon which Randall struck him several times. A corporal parted them, but afterwards whilst the sergeant was lighting a pipe Randall attacked him again. Randall was found guilty of a breach of the fifth article, 'of duties to superiors', and sentenced to be shot.[2] Another soldier, 'giving reproachful words' to his fellow-soldiers on parade, was told by his lieutenant to hold his peace, and as he disobeyed, the officer gave him two or three strokes with his cane. A scuffle took place in which the soldier struck his lieutenant and both fell down.[3] In this case the court, more lenient, treated the offence as a misdemeanour, and sentenced the offender to sixty stripes, and to make a public apology to his officer at the head of the company. In a third case an ensign struck a soldier with his sword in its scabbard, and the soldier 'swore by

[1] See the narrative of the trials of the petitioners appended to *The Hunting of the Foxes from Newmarket and Triploe Heaths to Whitehall, by five small Beagles*, 4to, 1649. The 'Beagles' were the petitioners. This pamphlet is reprinted in vol. vi of the *Somers' Tracts*, ed. Scott. For the sentences, see p. 57.

[2] *Clarke MSS.*, xxi, 37, 31st October 1651.

[3] Ibid., xxi, 40, 3rd November 1651.

his Maker, that if he had the ensign half a mile out of town he would give him as much'. For this the soldier was given thirty stripes, and condemned to stand half an hour under the gallows with a gag in his mouth.[1] On the other hand, a lieutenant, who in one of these scuffles drew his sword and dangerously wounded a soldier, was ordered to be tried by court-martial if the soldier died.[2]

Turning from the subject of the punishments to that of the offences for which they were the penalty, the most frequent crimes amongst the soldiers were apparently swearing, drunkenness, and plundering.[3]

Plundering the country people, against which Essex had issued so many futile proclamations,[4] was naturally much easier to suppress when the soldiers were paid with tolerable regularity. Under Fairfax and Cromwell it was rigidly put down. Cromwell signalized his landing in Ireland by a proclamation against it, which begins with the confession that heretofore 'upon the marching out of armies or of parties from garrisons, a liberty hath been taken by the soldiery to abuse, rob, and pillage, and too often to execute cruelties upon the country people'. For the future, he announced, he was resolved 'diligently and strictly to restrain such wickedness'.[5] A year earlier, when Cromwell entered Scotland, after Hamilton's defeat at Preston, he published a proclamation prohibiting his soldiers from demanding money and taking horses, goods, or victuals from the inhabitants.[6] His own regiments punctually obeyed his orders, but some of the northern horse, who, says he, 'have not been under our discipline and government', were guilty of very disorderly carriage. As a punishment for this a regiment was sent back into England. A newspaper thus relates the incident[7]:

[1] *Clarke MSS.*, xxi, 45, 13th November 1651.

[2] Ibid., xxi, 80, 30th December 1651.

[3] In the records of the trials which took place at Dundee there are also a certain number of cases in which soldiers were punished for illicit amours with the women of the town. Whipping was the usual penalty. Several sentences of the kind are reprinted in Prendergast's *Cromwellian Settlement of Ireland*, pp. 232–3.

[4] Husbands, *Ordinances*, ii, 43, 24th April 1643.

[5] 24th August 1649; reprinted in Carlyle's *Cromwell*.

[6] 20th September 1648; see also Letter lxxiv in Carlyle's *Cromwell*.

[7] *Cromwelliana*, p. 47.

'Upon our entrance into Scotland, a regiment lately raised in the bishoprick of Durham, under Col. Wren, behaved themselves rudely, which as soon as the Lieut-General had notice of, he caused it to rendezvous upon Tweed Banks, and the Scottish people having challenged several horses taken from them by that regiment, which the Lieut-General caused to be restored back, and the plunderers to be cashiered; a lieutenant that countenanced such deeds, was delivered into the Marshal's hands, and the Colonel himself conniving at them, and not doing justice upon the offenders, when complaints were brought into him, was taken from the head of his regiment, and suspended from executing his place, until he had answered at a council of war, for his negligence in the performance of his duty. This notable and impartial piece of justice did very much take with the people, and the regiment is ordered back into Northumberland.'[1]

An offence as great or greater than plundering the country people was plundering, in breach of capitulation, a garrison which had surrendered upon articles. A notorious instance of this occurred in April 1643, at the surrender of Reading, when the Royalists were robbed as they marched out. This took place, according to Clarendon, 'in the presence of the Earl of Essex himself, and the chief officers who seemed to be offended at it, and not to be able to prevent it; the unruliness of their common men being so great'.[2] This outrage had serious consequences. 'As this breach of articles was very notorious and inexcusable, so it was made the rise, foundation, and excuse for barbarous

[1] In this severity towards plunderers Cromwell had before his eyes his usual model, Gustavus Adolphus. Gustavus when he was encamped at Nuremburg made an oration to the officers of his army against plundering. It was not his own Swedish troops, he said, who had been guilty of this offence, but the Germans in his service. 'Had I known that you Germans had been a people of this temper; of a humour that had borne no more natural affection to your own native country, I would never have saddled horse for your sakes; much less have hazarded mine own kingdom, my life, and estate in your behalfs.' Henceforth, he added in a special proclamation, no man of any degree, general, officer or soldier, should be pardoned if found guilty of this offence. To give weight to his words a lieutenant was immediately hanged, and a soldier suffered the same fate. 'When a Boor having complained of a soldier for stealing his cow from him, there was means made to save the delinquent; "My son," says the king to him, "it is better that I should now punish thee, than that the wrath of God for thy misdeeds, and his judgments, should fall down upon me, and thee, and all of us here present"' (*The Swedish Intelligencer*, 1633, pt. iii, pp. 23–27).

[2] Clarendon, *Rebellion*, vii, 37.

injustice of the same kind throughout the greatest part of the war, insomuch as the King's soldiers afterwards, when it was their part to be precise in the observations of agreements, mutinously remembered the violation at Reading, and thereupon exercised the same licence;[1] and from thence, either side having somewhat to object to the other, that requisite honesty and justice of observing conditions was mutually, as it were by agreement, for a long time violated.'

On the other hand, when Fairfax and Cromwell took the command, similar complaints ceased. Terms of surrender were thenceforth rigidly observed. The punishment inflicted by Cromwell on some soldiers who violated the capitulation of Winchester is a case in point. It is thus related by Sprigge.[2]

'I cannot but observe a remarkable piece of justice done in satisfaction to the enemy, for some injury they had sustained at their marching forth of Winchester, by plunder, contrary to the articles, which was done by some troopers; who being apprehended, were afterwards tried by a council of war, and condemned to die; and after lots cast for their lives (being six of them), he whose lot it was to die was brought to the place of execution, where, with a demonstration of great penitence (so far as the beholders did judge), he suffered death for his offence; which exemplary justice made a good impression upon the soldiery. The other five were sent with a convoy to Oxford (together with a full account of this proceeding, to the governor there, sir Thomas Glemham) to be delivered over as prisoners, and to be put to death, or otherwise punished as he should think fit; which was so well received by the enemy (to see so much right was done them), that sir Thomas Glemham returned the prisoners back again, with an acknowledgment of the lieutenant-general's nobleness.'

To prevent open breaches of capitulations and open robbery was not difficult for Cromwell and his officers. It was not so easy, however, to prevent less public breaches of good order, and petty oppression or violence, though that too was attempted.

---

[1] For instance, at the surrender of Bristol to Prince Rupert in July 1643, at the surrender of Sir John Meldrum's forces at Newark in March 1644, and at the surrender of Essex's army in Cornwall in September 1644.

[2] Sprigge, *Anglia Rediviva*, p. 144.

As soldiers were usually quartered in private houses their misbehaviour in their quarters was a continual cause of complaint.
Since no barracks existed[1] offences of this kind were bound to
occur with great frequency, but every effort was made to put a
stop to them. In the reports of the courts held at Dundee there
are many examples of punishments inflicted with this object.
For instance, a Scotchman living near Dundee complained that
there came into his house 'one Richard Walton, a dragoon with
six others to quarter; after they had supped, . . . the said
dragoon, being full of drink, sent the servants out for drink, and
afterwards beat several of the servants, insomuch that they
durst not stay in the house, but were forced to quit it, by which
means wanting fire and other accomodations the said dragoon
caused the locks of the doors and other wood about the house
to be burnt.' Walton was sentenced for this to ride the wooden
horse 'with two muskets at each heel, and two pint stoups about
his neck'.[2] One soldier was complained of for abusing his host's
mother, terming her 'old jade and old witch';[3] another for saying playfully when his landlady's child cried, 'that he would
boil it, and that it would make good broth'.[4] Such occurrences
are but examples of what must have occurred in innumerable
cases of which nothing is recorded. When the soldiers were unpaid and forced to take free quarters, or to pay for their lodgings
in paper tickets instead of in money, the burden on the inhabitants was heavier still, and misconduct was more common. But
even when they paid for their quarters and conducted themselves
tolerably well soldiers were not agreeable guests for a householder. 'My house,' wrote a gentleman in 1647, 'is, and hath
been full of soldiers this fortnight, such uncivil drinkers and
thirsty souls that a barrel of good beer trembles at the sight of
them, and the whole house is nothing but a rendezvous of tobacco and spitting.'[5]

The misbehaviour of regiments on the march from place to

[1] The citadels built at Ayr, Leith, Perth and Inverness after the subjugation of Scotland served to some extent as barracks, and seem to have
been designed for that purpose as well as for defence.

[2] *Clarke MSS.*, xxi, 53, 9th December 1651.

[3] Ibid., xxi, 54, 9th December 1651.

[4] Ibid., xxi, 77, 27th December 1651.

[5] *Trevelyan Papers* (Camden Society), iii, 257.

place is also often mentioned. The conduct of the old regiments
of the regular army was generally good during their marches,
for their officers kept them under proper control. But from 1646
to 1649 there were continual complaints from the West of England of the plunderings and outrages committed by the new
regiments raised for service in Ireland. A letter written from
Cheshire about May 1649 says that the oppression that county
suffered from these new raised forces on their way to Ireland
was intolerable. 'Several regiments having of late marched
through our parts take free quarter, though we are nothing in
arrear in our assessments; ten, fifteen and twenty are quartered
together in a poor man's house; and when we bring them good
beef, bacon, cheese, butter, and other good fare, they tell us
they must have such joints of mutton and veal, with poultry,
tobacco, and strong beer provided for them. Some of the abler
sort give them considerable sums of money to quarter elsewhere,
which no sooner done but they go to the next village, and get
there perchance as much if not more, and so impoverish the
country.'[1] Fairfax issued a severe proclamation against these disorders, confessing that soldiers on their march for Ireland 'have
and still do harass, plunder and act great violences and in-
solences in the country', and ordering all officers and soldiers
that quartered in or near such places to assist the country people
in the forcible repression of such outrages.[2]

By such stringent measures this evil was repressed, but it
recurred in a modified form in 1650 when various companies of
recruits on the march to join Cromwell's army in Scotland signalized their progress thither by beating the country people and
stealing horses on the way.[3] In these cases the fault lay with the
officers. Some were absent from their duties, others were incapable. Often these detachments were under the command of some
temporary conductor whose only interest was to deliver so many
soldiers for Ireland at the port of embarkation or bring so many
recruits to headquarters. In such cases the conductor was content to wink at a good deal of misbehaviour, provided he could

[1] *The Moderate*, 29th May to 5th June 1649.

[2] Ibid., 13th to 20th March 1649. The proclamation is dated 17th March.

[3] *Order of a Court of War held at Whitehall*, 14th November 1650, printed
for John Wright. The original is in Worcester College Library.

get the men along somehow and keep them together till the journey's end. It became customary therefore to put officers conducting such parties under a bond for the good behaviour of their men.[1]

Recruits picked up anyhow and new to the restraints of discipline might be expected to be troublesome, but old soldiers when they did break loose were much worse. In 1656 a regiment of 500 men was raised out of the army in Scotland for service in Jamaica. Forty were drafted from each regiment, and they were commanded by a few officers out of employment, some promoted non-commissioned officers and privates raised from the ranks. While they were waiting for their ships at Ayr a riot broke out. A soldier of the garrison in some pothouse brawl wounded a man of the Jamaica regiment, whose comrades swore to avenge him. Many of them were drunk, and declared that they would beat the garrison, guards and all, out of the town. In the free fight which followed four men were killed and sixty or seventy wounded. 'I never saw nor heard of the like in all the war in the three nations,' said an officer, 'for no man could tell or give any pretence of the ground of the disturbance, yet it was so high that all the force we had was little enough to suppress it.' The bloodshed would have been greater but that the officers of the garrison acted with great discretion, and their soldiers showed more patience than they had ventured to expect. As for the men of the Jamaica regiment, said the report of the governor of Ayr, 'their officers being most of them strangers to them, do not yet so well know how to deal with them, though they omitted not their best diligence'.[2]

There were two minor breaches of discipline very prevalent amongst the soldiers of the period which must be mentioned in any account of life in the army. One was poaching, the other marriage without leave. The propensity of the soldiers for poaching, noticeable in 1647 and 1648, came to its height in 1649. On 5th September, in that year, Fairfax published a proclamation against it. 'Daily complaints are made,' said he, 'that some disorderly soldiers under my command, contrary to the laws

[1] There are many such bonds amongst the *Domestic State Papers* for 1649–51.

[2] See *Scotland and the Protectorate*, pp. 323–8.

of the nation and discipline of the army, have and still do commit very great outrages and riots, with their arms, entering into
parks, chases, and warrens, and thence stealing all sorts of deer
and conies, menacing the death of the keepers, and all such who
any ways oppose them.'[1] In future, therefore, all field-officers
and captains were desired 'that forthwith they cause to be taken
from their soldiers, all such hounds, greyhounds, and other dogs
which may any ways be hurtful to deer or conies'. Soldiers,
moreover, were not to enter any park or warren or to pass
through it without a written permission from their officer, and
any future transgressors were to be punished in an exemplary
manner.

These measures were apparently successful, at least little or
nothing is heard of this particular offence in England after 1649.
But it appears once more amongst the army of the occupation
in Scotland. It is evident that the British privates of the period
had a taste for sport. In 1653 the commander-in-chief in Scotland issued a proclamation which recited that soldiers 'do
straggle at a great distance from their colours with their
muskets, and kill and destroy rabbits belonging to warrens and
house-pigeons', and prohibited the practice as 'contrary to the
laws of Scotland, dishonourable to the discipline of the army,
and the cause of frays with the country people'.[2] Soldiers, however, could obtain leave to go shooting. In Monck's *Order-Book*
there is a pass for a private in his own regiment 'to carry a
fowling-piece for the killing of fowls for his game, provided he
kill no tame pigeons and rabbits'. Such passes are frequent,
and in one order hares and partridges are added to the list of
exceptions. In another order Monck prohibits the regiment in
garrison at Dundee from keeping more than two greyhounds per
company.[3]

As to the other point, the marriage of soldiers, there were
originally no restrictions imposed upon it. A large proportion of

[1] *The Moderate*, 4th to 11th September 1649. This newspaper says that
about eighty deer had been killed in Eltham Park during the last eight days
by soldiers and countrymen.

[2] *Scotland and the Commonwealth*, p. 139. The order is dated 27th May
1653.

[3] See Monck's *Order-Book* under 14th Nov. 1654; 23rd July 1656; 23rd
March 1659 (*Clarke MSS.*).

the rank and file must have been married men, especially so long as the army was recruited by the process of impressment. The wives and the widows of soldiers are frequently mentioned, and soldiers absent on foreign service were sometimes allowed to assign a portion of their pay for the support of their wives and families.[1] In many cases the wives of the soldiers followed their husbands to Ireland, Scotland or Jamaica, and were encouraged to do so, because they were regarded as the best nurses for the sick and wounded.[2] There are even authentic instances of women who enlisted as soldiers to follow their husbands or lovers. In 1657 the colonel commanding the garrison of Ayr reports that a young Lincolnshire woman, named Anne Dymoke, had served for some weeks past in the ranks of his regiment. 'I can perceive,' he adds, 'nothing but modesty in her carriage since she has been with us.'[3] A ballad written in 1655, called 'The Gallant She-Soldier,' celebrates the prowess of a lady who served some years in the same regiment as her husband under the name of Mr Clarke.[4] Incidentally the ballad shows what the usual amusements of the soldiers were.

> *With musket on her shoulder, her part she acted then,*
> *And every one supposed that she had been a man;*
> *Her bandeleers about her neck, and sword hang'd by her side,*
> *In many brave adventures her valour have been tried.*
>
> *For exercising of her armes, good skill indeed had she,*
> *And known to be as active as any one could be,*
> *For firing of a musket, or beating of a drum,*
> *She might compare assuredly with any one that come.*
>
> *For other manly practices she gain'd the love of all,*
> *For leaping and for running or wrestling for a fall,*
> *For cudgels or for cuffing, if that occasion were,*
> *There's hardly one of ten men that might with her compare.*

[1] See p. 198, *ante*.   [2] See p. 262, *ante*.

[3] *Report on the Papers of Mr Leyborne Popham*, p. 112. Colonel Sawrey's letter is dated 6th April 1657.

[4] There are many later ballads of the same kind; as for instance, 'The Famous Woman Drummer'; 'The Soldier's Delight or the She-Volunteer'; 'The Maiden Warrior'; 'Pretty Polly Oliver'.

Yet civill in her carriage and modest still was she,
But with her fellow souldiers she oft would merry be;
She would drink and take tobacco, and spend her money too,
When as occasion served, that she had nothing else to do.

At last the secret is betrayed, and her military career interrupted by the birth of a young soldier (July 1655). The ballad
concludes with the following advertisement:

'All that are desirous to see the young souldier and his mother,
let them repair to the sign of the Blacksmith's Arms in East
Smithfield, neere unto Tower Hill in London, and inquire for
Mr Clarke, for that was the woman's name.'[1]

The causes which led to the restraint of marriage in the army
seem to have been entirely political. As soon as Cromwell's first
campaign in Scotland was over and the army went into winter
quarters, marriage set in. A letter from Edinburgh dated 1st
December 1650 says that 'our English lads and Scotch lasses'
begin to marry with great frequency. 'So that there is scarce a
day but the bagpipes are heard at a marriage; some private
soldiers have married knights and lairds' daughters, and others
of them marry maid servants of the great citizens of Edinburgh
who are absent, so that we are like to stock ourselves of a new
generation.'[2] After the second campaign, when Scotland was
practically subdued, this epidemic commenced again. On 16th
October 1651 the governor of Edinburgh and Leith issued a
stringent order that no soldier in his regiment should 'presume
to be married to any woman in or of Scotland' without the consent of the governor, deputy-governor, or major of the regiment
in writing. If he did he was to be cashiered from the regiment,
and the minister who performed the ceremony was to be brought
before a court-martial.[3]

The reason for this severity was apparently the fear lest these
Scottish wives might make Royalists of their husbands, or give
intelligence of military movements to the Scots still in arms.

[1] The ballad is reprinted in *Roxburghe Ballads*, vii, 728 (Ballad Society).
Its date is fixed by a reference to the event in the *Faithful Scout* for 13th
to 20th July 1655, under 17th July.

[2] *Mercurius Politicus*, 5th to 12th December 1650, p. 441.

[3] *Scotland and the Commonwealth*, pp. xxxiv, 334.

In Ireland the same thing happened. The Cromwellian soldiers long before the war ended began to intermarry with the Irish women. To a Puritan a Papist was little better than a pagan, and, indeed, much more dangerous. Ireton, the commander-in-chief, published on 1st May 1651 a proclamation against all such marriages.[1] 'I judge it to be displeasing to God,' he declared, 'to join in near relations with the people of such abominations, persons whose principles have led them to the shedding of so much innocent blood as they have done.' It was also, he said, 'a great hazard to the cause and work we are engaged in'. Men faithful before their marriages might be 'led aside by such temptations as they have thereby run themselves into, either to the deserting or betraying their trust'. At all events their union with the enemies of the cause justly rendered such men objects of suspicion. These Irish women, it was true, pretended to be converts to Protestantism, but the general feared it was 'only for some corrupt and carnal ends'.

'I therefore thinke fit to let all know, that if any Officer or Souldier of this Army, shall marry with any of the Women of this Nation that are Papists, or have lately been such, and whose change of Religion, is not or cannot be judged (by fit persons such as shall be appointed for that end) to flow from a reall work of God upon their hearts, convincing them of the falshood and evill of their owne wayes, and goodnesse and truth of that way they turn to; I say that any Officer who marries any such, shall thereby be judged, and held uncapable of command, or trust in this Army; and for any Souldier that married any such, if he be a horseman, he shall be dismounted and cashiered from horse service, to serve onely in foot service (if at all), and a footman so married shall be cashiered from his foot service, and to serve onely as a Pionier, and neither of them be held capable of preferment for the future, unlesse God doe (by a change wrought upon them with those whom they have married) take off this reproach, and so give us ground to restore them.

'And I desire all Officers of this Army, and others under my Command, that they doe their utmost (in the use of all lawfull meanes) to prevent any such sinfull contracts, the issue of which

[1] The proclamation is printed at length in *Several Proceedings in Parliament*, 17th to 24th July 1651, p. 1458.

can be no other than to provoke God to depart from us, or
testifie his displeasure against us some way or other: especially
when such things come to passe from our neglects, or our not
doing what concerns us to do, to hinder any thing of this nature,
as much as in us lyes.'

Such injunctions were repeated from time to time, and sometimes enforced by punishment, but they failed to produce the
desired result. Intermarriage with the Irish still continued.
There were few soldiers who, as a military poet observed,

> *rather than turn*
> *From English principles, would sooner burn;*
> *And rather than marry an Irish wife*
> *Would bachelors remain for term of life.*

And the result of these marriages generally was that the children
became Irish in feeling and education and forgot their father's
language. A pamphleteer, writing in 1697, laments over the
number of children of Oliver's soldiers then in Ireland who could
not speak a word of English.[1]

Hitherto we have considered discipline in its application to
the rank and file; it remains to discuss military punishments and
offences in the case of officers. Officers were subjected to as strict
a discipline as their men. Many of the trials reported are for
neglect of military duties or misconduct in the field. Sir James
Ramsay, who commanded the cavalry of Essex's left at Edgehill, was tried by a council of war, but was acquitted on the
ground that he had taken all reasonable precautions and was
not to blame for their cowardice.[2] Colonel Nathaniel Fiennes, for
surrendering Bristol to Prince Rupert when the place was judged
to be still tenable, was tried and sentenced to death. His sentence ran as follows: 'Colonel Nathaniel Fiennes, you have been
arraigned and convicted before this honourable council for surrendering and delivering up the town and castle of Bristol, with
the forts, magazines, arms, ammunition, victuals, and other
things thereunto belonging, and for not having held the same

---

[1] Prendergast, *Cromwellian Settlement of Ireland*, 2nd ed., pp. 261–6.
The verses quoted are from 'The Moderate Cavalier, or the Soldier's
Description of Ireland', 1675.

[2] *The Vindication of Sir James Ramsay.*

to the utmost extremity, according as by your duty you ought
to have done; For which offense this honourable council hath
adjudged you to be executed according to the tenor of the
articles of War, by having your head cut off. God have mercy
on your soul.'

The trial, which is very fully reported,[1] lasted nine days, and
the charge against Fiennes consisted of articles of impeachment
drawn up by two civilians who acted as accusers, William
Prynne and Clement Walker. Fiennes, though condemned, was
not executed, but received a pardon from Essex, and two years
later when Fairfax and the New Model recaptured Bristol, the
colonels of Fairfax's army drew up a statement declaring that
Fiennes had been unjustly condemned, and that in the then
condition of the garrison and its fortifications he could not possibly have held out. This case also led to the alteration of the
Articles of War so as to make the duty and responsibility of the
governor of a besieged fortress clearer than they had been in
the *Laws and Ordinances* of Essex.

Another interesting example of military justice is the case of
Colonel Tothill. About July 1651, when Major-General Ireton
was besieging Limerick, an attack was made on an outlying fort,
in the course of which about a dozen Irish prisoners were put to
the sword after quarter had been promised them by their first
captor. Ireton was excessively angry at this breach of quarter,
and as a partial reparation released a certain number of Irish
prisoners and sent them into the besieged town. 'For justice
amongst ourselves,' he adds, 'I sent Colonel Tothill that commanded, and his ensign that acted the violation, to be presently
tried by a court of War. But he alleging that he did it partly
from an opinion, that no soldiers or inferior officers had power
to give quarter without consent of himself, then being Chief-in-
command on that quarter, and partly from an apprehension,
that I would be "offended with him if he had spared them"; the
Court thought fit to do no more justice but cashier him and his
ensign for it. But I fear it fell short of the justice God required

---

[1] The best account is Prynne's *True and full Relation of the Prosecution,
etc. . . . of Nathaniel Fiennes*, 4to, 1644. It contains the substance of the
different pamphlets published about the question and the text of the
depositions, but is extremely biassed against Fiennes. Prynne and his
co-editor, Clement Walker, were the prosecutors.

therein to the acquitting of the Army from the guilt of so foul
a sin, the excuses whereof were equally abominable for the base
and servile fear pretended in the latter part, as for the spirit of
pride (I doubt) predominate in the former.'[1]

Cashiering, as in this case, was the usual punishment inflicted
upon officers, except in cases of mutiny, when the penalty was
sometimes imprisonment or death. A young officer writing from
Cromwell's army in Scotland describes the summary way in
which unfit officers were got rid of by the general and their own
colleagues. 'Almost every day,' says he, 'some officer or other is
turning out or articled against upon some account or other. . . .
Nothing is more frequent here than our officers exhibiting articles
against one another: a man must have good footing that stands
here.' Often the accused officer resigned to avoid his trial.
'Lieutenant-Colonel Crooke hath laid down his commission, and
is gone home, and will not answer his articles. Lieutenant-
Colonel Carter is gone off too and will not stay till his articles
come forth. Tippling is the main against both.'[2] Drunkenness in
an officer was punishable with the loss of his commission, and it
is a charge which frequently appears in the records of courts-
martial. For instance, Captain Clement Needham, of Colonel
Hacker's regiment of horse, was accused in 1653 'that when he
was in Scotland he drank so much ale and strong waters, till
he was so drunk that he could not find the way into his chamber',
but in this case the court disbelieved the witness who undertook
to prove the fact. Needham was also charged with indecent and
immoral language, but the cornet on whose evidence the charge
depended had too bad a moral character himself, and was
credibly reported to have said that he did not believe he had
any soul. So this charge too was dismissed. Needham's case supplies examples of another class of offences which brought many
officers to grief. He was charged with making false musters, that
is with drawing pay for men who were not really effective soldiers, or who were not with the regiment when the muster took

---

[1] *Several Proceedings in Parliament*, p. 1487, 31st July to 7th August
1651. Tothill was never employed again. Colonel Axtell, however, who was
temporarily suspended from his command for a similar crime, was subsequently reinstated.

[2] *Letters from Roundhead Officers in Scotland*, pp. 26, 28, 30.

place. The rules about musters were strict, but there were so
many relaxations, and orders were so often issued to muster
some clerk, surgeon, or servant in a soldier's place, that there
was continual trouble about the matter. Needham was able to
prove to the satisfaction of the court that he had acted honestly
in all the instances alleged against him with one exception. He
admitted having mustered as a trooper a boy who acted as his
servant, and having drawn pay for the boy, for which offence
he was fined twenty pounds.[1]

An equally frequent cause of stumbling arose from the fact
that the captain was the paymaster of his troop, as the colonel
was of the regiment. He had the clerk of his troop or company
to help him in keeping the accounts, but he was personally responsible for the proper payment of his men, and was liable to
punishment if he failed to do it. In July 1651 Lieutenant-
Colonel Sexby was cashiered for wrongfully detaining the pay
of seven or eight of his soldiers, though it was not proved that
he did so with fraudulent intent.[2] Similar charges formed part of
the case against Captain Needham in 1653. He confessed in answer that 'there were moneys owing to divers of his soldiers,
and the reason why they had not received it was their neglect
in not demanding it: one of the persons claiming moneys confessed the reason why he neglected to demand it was, because
he stood in no need of moneys, and that he knew it safe while in
the captain's hands. Another of the persons claiming moneys,
being asked if he ever demanded it, he said it was contrary to
an article of war for a soldier to ask his pay.' The upshot of the
matter was that Needham was reprimanded by the court for
carelessness in accounts, and was ordered 'to reckon and set
straight with his soldiers'.

Another case which throws a great deal of light on the army
life of the period, and on the relations which existed between
officers and men and between a colonel and his subordinates, is

[1] See *A Brief Narration of the Trial of Captain Clement Needham*, 4to,
1653. This was written by Needham himself. Also *The Deep Sighs and sad
Complaints of some late Soldiers in Captain Needham's Troop*, by Thomas
Fothergill, 4to, 1653. Fothergill seems to have been the instigator of the
charge.

[2] *Clarke MSS.*, xix, 26, Worcester College Library. It is fair to say there
were other charges against Sexby too.

the case of Captain Francis Freeman.[1] Freeman was a captain in
Colonel Okey's regiment of dragoons, a good officer so far as his
military duty was concerned, but a man of advanced theological
views, and one of the sect called Seekers. His colonel, an orthodox Congregationalist, abhorred Freeman's theology, and
wished to drive him out of the regiment. In fact, Okey told
Freeman and another captain plainly that he would 'root them
out of the regiment'. But Freeman was not to be intimidated
into resigning his commission. When an officer whom he met
told him that Okey was preparing articles against him, 'I told
him,' says Freeman, 'that I did not value a chip any charge that
could be brought against me'. His troop was in excellent order.
'We owed nothing in our quarters,' says he, 'when other troops
owed considerable sums; we were best mounted of any troop,
well clad in good apparel and all accoutrements belonging to
soldiers, stout gallant men, and such as I dare say that the
Colonel never had a gallanter troop in his regiment since he was
Colonel.'

Freeman's troopers had no complaint to make against their
captain. Okey, during his absence, told the troop that their
captain was a dangerous fellow and that he would put an honest
man over them in place of him. The troop, however, answered
him plainly, that they desired no other captain, that they had
long time had experience of Freeman, and that he had always
proved an honest man to them. Okey threatened to disband the
troop in order to get rid of its commander, but though Freeman
offered to resign to prevent this, his men refused his offer and
petitioned the general that he might be tried by a court-martial.

Fairfax promised that Freeman should have this trial, but it
was put off. Cromwell succeeded Fairfax as general, and to him,
since the colonel's persecution continued, Freeman repeated his
request for a court-martial just before Cromwell's army entered
Scotland. Cromwell heard in an informal way what both of them
had to say. Freeman gives a vivid description of the scene.
Okey told Cromwell that Freeman was a base, unworthy fellow,
not fit to be in the army, and railed generally against him.

[1] All the facts relating to Freeman's case, and the passages quoted concerning him, are taken from his own tract, *Light Vanquishing Darkness*,
1650, 4to. I know of no other account of the case, and it evidently attracted
very little attention.

L

Freeman demanded to be brought before a court-martial in order that Colonel Okey might be obliged to give some proof of what he said. Then another officer who was present interposed, and rebuked Freeman for hinting a doubt of his superior officer's veracity. 'Oh,' said he, 'was there ever any officer in the army that ever gave such language to his Colonel!' 'As if,' complains Freeman, 'captains were such low prized officers that they must be subject to bear every burden that their colonels shall lay upon them; to be like Issachar's ass; and to bear all scandalous reproaches and to submit to them with silence.' Another time when Freeman protested the truth of one of his statements, he was again called to order by one of the bystanders: '"As I live it is a truth, Sir," said I, but I was presently reproved for it. "Oh what an expression is there," said one of the colonels, as if it had been a very vile expression.'

Now that he was before Cromwell, Okey changed the nature of the charge. Hitherto he had denounced Freeman as a blasphemer, a charge which was unjust, for he was merely a crazy enthusiast whose theology was mainly an extravagant mysticism. Cromwell might not have thought this sufficient ground for the removal of a good officer, so Okey proceeded to accuse Freeman of immorality. It was asserted that the captain, riding at the head of his troop on their journey to Scotland, had been heard to sing songs of a most unsaintly character, songs that were 'a grief to all godly Christians'. Freeman in reply gave the general a detailed account of the occasion when he sang those songs and why he sang those songs. 'I shall give you a true and perfect relation both of the manner, and also of the occasion of my singing, that you may the better see upon what slight occasions he would take advantage against me. I had a souldier in my troop whose name is *Roger Daniel*, who was formerly a Lieutenant in the State's service, a man whom I loved very well, insomuch that I called him my *Buckingham*, my *favourit*, &c. Who came to my quarters one morning (whilst I quartered at *Morley* near *Darby*) and told me that he had excellent musick at his quarters, and invited me to come that night to hear it. I asked him what musick it was? he told me it was gallant musick, but did not tell me what instruments they were, neither did I at present take any more notice of what he had said, nor never thought of his invitation, till after supper; but then (it coming into my mind, I being musical myselfe, and its well known can sing my part) I went up to his quarters, where I found them at supper; the people of the house bid me welcome, and as soon as they had supt *my Buckingham* (as I call'd him) rose from the Table, and went to a presse-cubboard, where he took out a *fife recorder*, and a *citern*, and delivered the recorder to the old man, and the citern to his son, and they played half a douzen lessons, very well in consort, insomuch, that I thought they could sing prick-song, therefore I desired to know of them, whether they could or not? they answered no, but they had some delight to play upon those foolish instruments (as they call'd them) and so played three or four lessons more, and layd them aside. Now it came to passe, as I sate by them in a chair taking a pipe of Tobacco: one *Ralph Dennis* another Souldier of mine that quartered there, having a very good voice, sung a tune as he walked in the room, *Ralph*, said I, thou hast a very good voice, and so hath *Graves*, which is another of my Souldiers, I care not if I have you two to quarter near me, that I may teach you to sing your song. Captain, said my *Buckingham*, will you not teach me? Why, thou hast no good voice, said I. Yea, but I have a good voice, and I do not think, but I shall learn to sing my part as soon as either of them. Dost thou think thou canst? said I, that shall be tryed, and so began to sing this old song, '*New Oysters*' &c. And after I had sung it once or twice over, I set them their parts, and shewed them their time, and shook time for them with my hand, and found them very tractable, for after twice or thrice singing over, they sung their parts and kept their time very well, insomuch as I conceived the two men of the house who played on the musick before, were much taken with it, and liked our musick very well. Then I sung six or seven songs and catches by myself, whereof one of them was this that my Colonel hath laid to my charge; '*I met with Joan of Kent*,' &c. And this was another. 'There dwels a pretty Maid her name is *Sis*,' &c. And these are the two songs, that goe under the notion of bawdy songs; which I shall appeal to all those that know what they are, and what the musick is. And truly for my part, I sung but merely for the musick sake, not thinking any hurt at all.'

Cromwell listened gravely. He pronounced no opinion on the

character of the songs, but he told Captain Freeman that since he and his colonel could not get on together they had better part. Freeman might have the court-martial he wanted later if he liked, but he could not have it now when they were just about to invade Scotland. Therefore he had better resign his commission, and the captain accordingly did so.

In conclusion, one point of importance must be briefly touched. Throughout the period the military authorities maintained with great strictness their exclusive jurisdiction over offences committed both by officers and soldiers. More than once conflicts took place between the civil magistrates and the commanders of the army over this question. The pamphlet just quoted supplies two instances. Captain Freeman was accused of blasphemy in 1647, was arrested on the charge by the mayor of Taunton, and was obliged to give sureties for his appearance at the next assizes to answer the indictment. He appealed to his general, and Fairfax wrote to the mayor saying that Freeman's recognisances must be delivered up and his sureties discharged. The charge against him must be sent up to the judge-advocate of the army, 'that so he, being a member of the army, may be prosecuted and tried for the same at the headquarters'. A few months later a riot took place at Taunton, in which a townsman was mortally wounded by one of Freeman's soldiers. The townsmen appealed to a local magistrate, demanding that the soldier should be committed to prison for his trial at the assizes. 'Then,' Justice Nicolas said, 'Captain Freeman, it concerns you to do them justice, and if you will not, I must.' 'To which I answered,' says Freeman, 'that it did altogether concern me to do justice upon my soldiers, if they did offend, and that it did in no way concern him at all. And if so be that they could show me the man which they accused, then they should see me do them justice.'[1] He went on to promise that the man should be tried by a council of war, but they continued to require his trial at the assizes, and the dispute only ended when the confrontation of the wounded man and the accused proved that it was a case of mistaken identity.

Disputes of this kind recurred more than once during the Commonwealth and Protectorate. One of them, which took

[1] *Light Vanquishing Darkness.*

place in London, is thus related in a news-letter, dated 14th
June 1651.

'We are in a little kind of contest with the Citty as to Jurisdiction, they have gotten 2 souldiers of Lt. Gen. Fleetwood's
regiment in Woodstreet Compter committed by the foot (though
he knew they were souldiers), for some falling out and kinde of
battery at Whitefryers. We have demanded the men, the sheriff,
Col. Titchburne, refuses to deliver them, saying they are to be
tryed by them, because the fact was committed within their
jurisdiction, and commands the Keeper (notwithstanding our
Court of War writt to him) not to deliver them. Wee claim it as
necessary and our undoubted jurisdiction to try every member
of the Army. On Monday morning some officers treat with the
sheriff heerin, and though wee are very tender of offering or
moving anything that might make differences, yet I think wee
shall nott be so poore spirited as to betray the discipline and
necessary jurisdiction of the Army.'[1]

Another took place in March 1656, also in London, and is thus
described: 'Here is lately grown a feud between the magistrates
of the City and the officers of the Army, about the committing
some disorderly soldiers to the Counter; which was highly
resented by the Army-men, who sent presently 2 or 3 files of
musketeers, and took as many sergeants from the Counter-gaol
and committed them to the Marshall; some of the Aldermen
have wrote to the Lieutenant of the Tower about it, but have
no redress; so they intend to make application to Whitehall,
though it will be to small purpose, the soldiers resolving to out-
brave all persons that are not highly interested with them.[2]

In maintaining their jurisdiction over all offences committed
by soldiers the military authorities were acting in accordance
with the Articles of War then in force. 'No Magistrate of town
or country," said the articles, 'shall, without license, imprison
any soldier, unless for capital offences.' The same article, in an
enlarged form, appeared again in the regulations drawn up by
Monck for the army of Charles the Second.[3]

[1] *Clarke MSS.*, xix, 30, Worcester College Library.

[2] Carte, *Original Letters*, ii, 94.

[3] See Clode, *Military Forces of the Crown*, i, 54, 448, and for the general
subject of military discipline during the reign of Charles the Second,
Clifford Walton, p. 529.

On the other hand, the authorities of the City evidently based their claim on the theory that military tribunals and military law were no longer in force when a state of peace was restored.[1] The exercise of martial law in time of peace, and the denial of the right of the civil magistrate to punish offences committed by soldiers, were amongst the grievances most loudly complained of by the opponents of the government. But without this exclusive jurisdiction all officers agreed it would be impossible to maintain the discipline of the army.

[1] See the arguments of the lawyers concerning the illegality of martial law in time of peace, delivered in 1628 (Rushworth, iii, Appendix, pp. 76–81).

CHAPTER XIII

Religion in the Army

THE CIVIL WAR was a war of creeds as well as a war of parties, and religious differences were as important a factor amongst the causes of the war as political differences. Royalists and Parliamentarians, Scots and Irish, all made the defence and the propagation of their faith one of their reasons for fighting. For that reason, if for no other, the ecclesiastical machinery which existed in these various armies requires description, and the religious life of the New Model demands study just as much as its political life.

In the Articles and Ordinances of War published both by the King and the Earl of Essex the duty of the soldier with respect to religion holds the foremost place.[1] Both begin by declaring that no man shall blaspheme the persons of the Trinity or the Articles of the Christian Faith, under penalty of having his tongue bored with a hot iron, and that any man using unlawful oaths and execrations shall be punished by a fine.[2] Each army was equipped with chaplains. The King's Articles order that every regiment shall have a chaplain who shall read prayers daily and preach every Sunday or Holy-day.[3] Many clergymen

---

[1] See *Laws and Ordinances of War, established by his Excellency the Earl of Essex*, 1643, 4to; Fairfax's 'Articles of War', printed in the Appendix, repeat on this question the regulations of Essex. The *Military Orders and Articles established by his Majesty*, Oxford, 1643, 4to, are even more rigid and detailed.

[2] See Appendix L.

[3] 'That the service of Almighty God be not neglected; it is ordained, That there be a Chaplain appointed for every Regiment, who shall read Prayers orderly, and duly once every day whil'st they are in Leaguer, and shall Preach, or expound some place of Scripture, or Catechisme once at least on every Sunday, and Holiday, in some such convenient place as the Colonell of the Regiment shall appoint, and by the sound of a Trumpet or Drumme notice shall be given of the time, in such manner as the whole Regiment may take notice thereof.'

driven from their livings became chaplains to regiments or commanders in the Royalist army. Fuller, for instance, became
chaplain to Sir Ralph Hopton, and Pearson to Lord Goring's
army.[1] At times, if opportunity offered, a battle was preluded
by some form of religious service. Before the battle of Bradock
Down in January 1643, Sir Ralph Hopton, 'having put his men
in order, caused public prayers to be said on the head of every
squadron (which the rebels observing told their fellows they
were at Mass, to stir up their courage in the cause of religion)'.[2]
At Marston Moor, according to a Parliamentary writer, Rupert,
'that bloody plunderer', in order 'to seem religious', had a
sermon preached before him and his army. His chaplain took
his text out of Joshua xxii, 22. The words were these: 'The Lord
God of gods, the Lord God of gods, He knoweth, and Israel shall
know; if it be in rebellion or if in transgression against the
Lord, save us not this day'.[3]

The Parliamentary army had its chaplains also. Essex's
Articles, however, do not mention chaplains or prescribe daily
services, saying simply that 'all commanders are charged to see
Almighty God reverently served, and sermons and prayers duly
frequented', and that 'all those soldiers who often and wilfully
absent themselves from sermons and public prayer shall be
proceeded against at discretion.' When the war began Essex's
army was very liberally supplied with ministers. A number of
them arrived at his headquarters at Northampton on 7th
September 1642, and next day they set to work. 'Friday morning,' writes Sergeant Nehemiah Wharton, 'worthy Obadiah
Sedgwick gave us a worthy sermon (and my company in particular marched to hear him in rank and file). Saturday morning,
John Sedgwick gave us a famous sermon. . . . Sabbath day
morning, Mr Marshall, that worthy champion of Christ, preached
to us; in the afternoon Mr Ash. These with their sermons have
already subdued and satisfied more malignant spirits amongst

---

[1] Bailey, *Life of Thomas Fuller*, pp. 306, 313.

[2] Clarendon, *Rebellion*, vi, 248. Compare the account of the proceedings
of Gustavus Adolphus before the battle of Lützen. 'The drums' having
beaten the first march, he caused prayers to be read to himself by his own
chaplain, Dr Fabricius; and when there were ministers at hand the same
was done through every regiment of the army' (*Swedish Intelligencer*, iii,
126).

[3] Vicars, *Parliamentary Chronicle, God's Ark*, p. 281.

us than a thousand armed men could have done, so that we have great hopes of a blessed union.' Of the following Sunday, Wharton says: 'Sabbath day we peaceably enjoyed with Obadiah Sedgwick, who gave us two heavenly sermons'. It may be surmised that the preachers did not omit to stir up their hearers against the ritual of the Church and the bishops. A week later when Wharton's force reached Hereford, he relates, 'Sabbath day, about the time of morning prayer, we went to the Minster, where the pipes played and the puppets sang so sweetly that some of our soldiers could not forbear dancing in the holy choir, whereat the Baalists were sore displeased. The Anthem ended, they fell to prayer, and prayed devoutly for the King, the Bishops, etc.; and one of our soldiers with a loud voice said, "What! never a bit for the Parliament", which offended them much more. Not satisfied with this human service we went to divine; and passing by found shops open and men at work, to whom we gave some plain dehortations, and went to hear Mr Sedgwick, who gave us two famous sermons which much affected the poor inhabitants, who wondering said they never heard the like before. And I believe them.'[1]

We get another glimpse of the chaplains at Edgehill. John Vicars informs us that during the battle 'the reverend and renowned Master Marshall, Master Ashe, Master Mourton, Masters Obadiah and John Sedgwick, and Master Wilkins, and divers others eminently pious and learned pastors rode up and down the army through the thickest dangers, and in much personal hazard, most faithfully and courageously exhorting, and encouraging the soldiers to fight valiantly and not to fly, but now, if ever, to stand to it and fight for their religion and laws!'[2] In the Scottish army which marched into England in January 1644 under Alexander Leslie, the religious instruction of the soldiers was still more elaborately provided for. Not only were there to be morning and evening prayers, and sermons on Sundays and Fast-days, both in the morning and afternoon, but a complete system of ecclesiastical jurisdiction was to be established in the army. Church discipline and military discipline were to flourish side by side in it.

[1] *Cal. State Papers, Dom.*, 1641–3, pp. 388, 391, 397, 399.

[2] Vicars, *Parliamentary Chronicle, Jehovah Jireh*, p. 200.

'Kirk discipline shall be exercised, and the sick cared for in
every Regiment, by the particular Eldership or Kirk-Session to
be appointed, even as useth to be done in every parish in the
time of Peace: And that there may be an uniformitie thorowout
the whole Army in all matters Ecclesiasticall, there shall be a
generall Eldership or common Ecclesiastick Judicatory, made
up of all the Ministers of the Camp, and of one Elder direct from
every particular Regiment, who shall also judge of Appellations
made unto them from the particular Sessions or Elderships.'[1]

Here, as in many other respects, Leslie followed the example
of his old master, Gustavus Adolphus, and imitated very closely
the rules laid down for the Swedish army.[2] But in this case, as
in many others, theory and practice were worlds apart. In 1639
the camp of the Scottish army at Dunse Law was full of ministers. There were, says Baillie, 'good sermons and prayers morning and even, under the roof of heaven to which the drums did
call for bells. . . . Had ye lent your ear in the morning, or
especially at even, and heard in the tents the sound of some
singing psalms, some praying, and some reading Scripture, ye
would have been refreshed.'[3]

By 1644, however, the zeal of the Scottish clergy had somewhat abated. From the very beginning of Leslie's campaign in
England it was difficult to get chaplains to accompany his army.
In March 1644 Baillie laments 'that so great an inlack was in
the ministers to come out with the regiments'. In April 1645
he says that he is told 'that by no means ministers will come to
the Army'; and that 'in two and twenty regiments there was
not one minister'. 'You cannot be answerable to God,' he wrote
to one of his brethren, 'if you do not your best quickly to send
up an able minister to every regiment, and at least one half
dozen of the most gracious, wise, and courageous ministers of
the Kingdom.' For not only was the want of religious teaching
one of the causes of the disorders which began to spread in the
Scottish army, but it favoured the growth of heresy in the ranks.
Baillie feared that the Independents of Manchester's army

[1] *Articles and Ordinances of War for the present expedition of the Army of
the Kingdom of Scotland*, 4to, 1644, § 1.

[2] See *The Swedish Discipline*, 1632, and also the reprint of the ordinances
of Gustavus in Ward's *Animadversions of War*, 1639, ii, 42–43.

[3] Robert Baillie's *Letters*, ed. Laing, i, 213–4.

might corrupt their Presbyterian comrades in arms. 'We all conceive that our silly simple lads are in great danger of being infected by their company, and if that pest enter in our Army, we fear it may spread.'[1]

The later history of the army under Essex resembled that of the army under Leslie. After Edgehill most of the ministers went home. In 1645, when Baxter began to examine into the causes for the increase of the sectaries in the army, he attributed it mainly to this cause. 'I saw,' said he, 'that it was the Ministers who had lost all, by forsaking the Army and betaking themselves to an easier and quieter way of life.'[2] Something, perhaps a great deal, was due to this cause, but it was not till the formation of the New Model that Independency made much progress in the army. When Manchester's army was united with that of Essex, and with what remained of Waller's infantry, to form the New Model, the spread of Independency became rapid. But it was not till the close of 1647 that the triumph of Independency was complete. Even Manchester's army had been divided, and probably it contained almost as many Presbyterians as Independents. Manchester's own chaplains, Ashe, Goode, and Lee, were strong Presbyterians, whilst other chaplains attached to his army, such as William Sedgwick and William Dell, were Independents of the most extreme type. So too amongst Manchester's officers there were many staunch Presbyterians besides Major-General Crawford, and Crawford's party was strong enough to counteract Cromwell's influence over Manchester and to check his designs. According to Manchester himself, Cromwell boldly declared to him 'that he would not deny but that he desired to have none in my army but such as were of the Independent judgment.'[3] But he was only partially successful in this design. Four of Manchester's regiments of foot were commanded by Independents, but the four others were officered by Presbyterians. On the other hand, the cavalry was almost entirely composed of Independents.[4]

'If you look upon his own regiment of horse,' wrote an

[1] Baillie's *Letters*, ii, 156, 185, 268, 273.

[2] *Reliquiæ Baxterianæ*, p. 51.   [3] *Camden Miscellany*, vol. viii.

[4] The Independent colonels of foot were Pickering, Rainsborough, Montague, and Russell.

opponent of Cromwell about December 1644, 'see what a swarm there is of those that call themselves the godly; some of them profess they have seen visions and had revelations. Look on Colonel Fleetwood's regiment with his Major Harrison, what a cluster of preaching officers and troopers there is. Look what a company of troopers are thrust into other regiments by the head and shoulders, most of them Independents, whom they call godly precious men; nay, indeed, to say the truth, almost all our horse be made of that faction.'[1]

This was the composition of Manchester's army in the spring of 1645, when it was incorporated into the New Model and passed under the command of Fairfax. At the beginning, amongst the infantry of the New Model the Independents must have been in a minority. For of the 7,200 old soldiers whom the foot regiments contained, half were drawn from the armies of Waller and Essex, and a large part of those taken from Manchester's army were not Independents. Moreover, the 7,000 or 8,000 pressed men added to make up the required numbers cannot be credited with definite theological views of any kind. Of the horse, however, quite half were taken from Manchester's army and may safely be described as Independents of the most pronounced type. When Richard Baxter first became acquainted with the army, soon after the battle of Naseby, he found that the Independents were a minority in its ranks, although it was already commonly described as an army of sectaries. 'Abundance of the common troopers and many of the officers,' says he, 'I found to be honest, sober, orthodox men, and others tractable to hear the truth and of upright intentions. But a few proud, self-conceited, hot-headed sectaries had got into the highest places, and were Cromwell's chief favourites, and by their very heat and activity bore down the rest, or carried them along with them; and were the soul of the Army, though much fewer in number than the rest (being indeed not one to twenty throughout the Army; their strength being in the general's and Whalley's and Rich's regiment of horse, and in the new-placed officers in many of the rest).'[2]

During the two years which followed the formation of the

[1] *Manchester's Quarrel with Cromwell* (Camden Society), p. 72.

[2] *Reliquiæ Baxterianæ*, p. 50.

New Model this Independent minority obtained by degrees complete control of the army. Some of the Presbyterian officers left the army and were replaced by Independents;[1] others were converted to Independency. Amongst the rank and file the views o Cromwell's troopers spread and bore an abundant harvest. In June 1647, when the breach between army and Parliament took place, the strength of the two parties in the army was revealed. Three-quarters of the officers, who may be taken as all or nearly all Independents, adhered to Fairfax and Cromwell. One-fourth of the officers – or to be exact, 167 – left the army to give their support to the Parliament and the Presbyterian leaders. Only a few hundred of the soldiers followed them, and with this secession the dominion of Independency in the army was assured. For the 167 seceding officers lost their commissions, and were all replaced by staunch Independents.[2]

A question which naturally arises is, What were the religious agencies which produced this change in the character of the New Model? Much of course must be attributed to political rather than religious causes, to the democratic spirit which the progress of the Civil War and the nature of the contest produced amongst the soldiers, but much was due to the perpetual propagation of definite religious tenets in the army. Baxter attributed the result mainly to the lack of good chaplains, and in part to the influence of bad ones. To set an example to his brethren and to stay the tide of sectarianism he joined the army himself in June 1645, as chaplain to Whalley's regiment of horse. His days were spent not so much in preaching as in controversial

---

[1] Edwards complains that some efficient officers were turned out of the New Model simply because they were Presbyterians. 'Because a man is a Presbyterian, he shall be turned out of his command, and to compasse it, they have sent as far as Pendennis for an Accuser, to London for another, and Bristow for a third, and all they can say against our Adjutant General Gray (who is an honest godly Scotshman), is, that three quarters of a year since he was met (as they think) drunk, because as they remember, he faultred in his speech, and all because he is Major Generals Officer: Mr Peters said, That was not all, he had made a Faction in the Army by seducing many to the Presbyterian party; so it seems its counted a Faction with them to hold what the Parliament allows' (Edwards, *Gangræna*, pt. iii, p. 70).

[2] See *A Vindication of* 167 *Commission Officers of the Army that are come off from the Army in obedience to the Parliament's Orders*, published 1st July 1647. The names of the dissentients may be gathered from Rushworth, vi, 465.

discussions with officers and men. 'I set myself from day to day to find out the corruptions of the sectaries, and to discuss and dispute them out of their errors both religious and political. My life among them was a daily contending with seducers and gently arguing with the more tractable.' Some success he had. 'I found that if the Army had but had Ministers enough that would have done such a little as I did, all their plot might have been broken, and King, Parliament, and Religion might have been preserved.' But he found it impossible to get fellow-labourers in the work. One assistant he obtained for a month or two, but he soon left again. He had no taste for controversy. 'He was a very worthy, humble, laborious man, un-wearied in preaching, but weary when he had not opportunity to preach.'[1]

The official army chaplains had it all their own way, and though they were few in number, made up for the deficiency by their zeal and activity. In the New Model, when it was first organized, there appear to have been no regimental chaplains such as there had been at first in the army under Essex. In place of them there were a certain number of ministers attached to the staff of the army. Edward Bowles, whom Baxter praises as 'honest and judicious', appears in the list of the New Model as 'Chaplain to the Army', but he did not hold the place many months. The colleagues and successors of Bowles were Independents of the most advanced type, Dell, Saltmarsh, William Sedgwick and the famous Hugh Peters. The narratives of Fairfax's campaigns and the newspapers of the period give occasional accounts of their sermons. Before the assault on Bridgwater 'On the Lord's day, July 20, 1645, Mr Peters in the forenoon preached a preparation sermon, to encourage the soldiers to go on; Mr Bowles likewise did his part in the afternoon. After both sermons the drums beat, the army was drawn out into the field: the commanders of the forlorn hope, who were to begin the storm, and the soldiers being drawn together in the field, were there also afresh exhorted to do their duties (with undaunted courage and resolution) by Mr Peters, who did it (as one says of him) *tam Marte quam Mercurio*.'

In the same way Peters and Dell 'exhorted the soldiers to

[1] *Reliquiæ Baxterianæ*, pp. 53, 56.

their duty' before the storming of Dartmouth in January 1646.[1]
No doubt after the capture of these and other garrisons they
also held thanksgiving services as the Scots did after the surrender of York in 1644.[2] It was customary also in the English as
in the Swedish army to return thanks to God after each victory,
either at once on the actual battlefield or in more formal fashion
on the following day.[3] At Marston Moor, for instance, the conquerors sang a psalm of praise after the battle, and fixed the
next Sunday for a solemn celebration of their great success.
There were also at intervals Fast-days or Days of Humiliation.
On Friday, 29th August 1645, 'a fast was kept through the army
to seek God for a blessing upon the design against Bristol. Mr
Dell and Mr Peters kept the day at the headquarters.'[4] As a rule,

[1] Sprigge, *Anglia Rediviva*, pp. 77, 102, 180. Soldiers who did not do their
duty in battle were duly rebuked by their chaplains. 'As for them of each
nation who went away, they have by their ministers and others been so
sharply reproved, and their fault in such sort aggravated, that there is hope
they will regain their credit by good service upon the next occasion'
(Ashe's *Relation of the Battle of Marston Moor*).

[2] 'When the enemies were departed, our three Generalls went together
into the Citie, attended with many of their officers. The first house they
entered was the Minster-Church, where a psalm was sung and thanks given
unto God by Master Robert Douglas, chaplain to the Lord Leven, for the
giving of that citie into our hands upon such easie terms; at which time
notice was given, that Thursday after should be kept by the whole Army,
as a day of thanksgiving for that great mercy' (*Continuation of True Intelligence*, No. 6).

[3] After the battle of Witstock the Swedish general spent three days
'partly in piety, partly in polity, yet piety preceded and polity followed as
the handmaid. First hee assembled his companies to give thankes to him
who had covered their heads in the day of battell, and blessed the enter-
prize with so good and great successe, singing Te Deum after their manner,
and supplying the want of organs and other church musicke with drums,
fifes, trumpets, canonadoes, and musquetadoes intermingled, not to the
disturbing of the souldiers devotion, but the raysing of their spirits, who
rejoyced that they had now opportunity to spend their powder in triumph
not in an uncertaine fight against the enemy' (*The Passages in Germany*,
1636, p. 35).
Lord Orrery speaks of the custom as follows: 'After the chace is finished
. . . I esteem it an indispensable duty in a general, even in the field of battel,
to draw together all his forces that he can, and with them cause to be
returned to Almighty God their most humble and hearty thanks, for his
blessing, in bestowing on them the victory, and his preserving so many of
them from death; for an unfeigned and publick gratitude to God is not
only what piety, but even what the light of nature does teach, and nothing
does more incline God to bestow future blessings, than to have men really
thankful for the present, and to own him to be the only author and finisher
of them' (*Art of War*, p. 205).

[4] Sprigge, *Anglia Rediviva*, p. 102.

however, the chaplains preached not merely to the officers
gathered at headquarters, but to the army, or so much of it as
could be collected for the purpose. At the siege of Oxford, in
1645, we are told that on Monday 25th May, 'Mr Saltmarsh
preached before the General and the army at Heddington',
while on the Sunday previous 'Mr Dell preached in the forenoon
and Mr Sedgwick in the afternoon; many soldiers were at each
sermon, divers of them climbing up the trees to hear, for it was
in the orchard before his Excellency's tent, and it is very observable to consider the love and unity which is amongst the
soldiers, Presbytery and Independency making no breach.'[1]

Of all these five ministers who were with the New Model
during 1645 and 1646 only one, namely Peters, long continued
to act as an army chaplain. Bowles, as we have seen, left the
army before the end of its first campaign. Dell became in May
1649 Master of Caius College, Cambridge, but he had severed
his connexion with the army at least two years earlier. The
famous sermon on 'The Building and Glory of the Truly Christian and Spiritual Church', which he preached before Fairfax at
Marston on 7th June 1646, was perhaps his farewell sermon.[2]
When he published it a year later he prefixed to it 'A faithful
testimony touching that valiant and victorious Army', praising
the unity, the humility, and the faith of its members. One of the
six things most remarkable in the army, said he, was 'the spirit
of prayer: and this the Lord hath poured forth upon many of
them in great measure; not only upon many of the chief commanders, but on very many of the inferior officers and common
troopers; some of whom I have by accident heard praying with
that faith and familiarity with God, that I have stood wondering
at the grace'.[3]

William Sedgwick, 'Doomsday Sedgwick', as he was called on

[1] *Perfect Occurrences*, Monday 25th May 1646.

[2] London, 1647, 4to. See also *A Vindication of certain citizens that went to
the Leaguer then before Oxford, or their answer to certain passages in a pre-
varicating Epistle, lately published by William Dell*, 1646, 4to; see also
Edwards, *Gangræna*, iii, 63.

[3] Cf. Hodgson's account of the preparations for the battle of Dunbar.
'As our regiment was marching in the head of the horse, a cornet was at
prayer in the night, and I appointed one of my officers to take my place.
I rid to hear him, and he was extremely carried on in the duty. I met with
so much of God in it, as I was satisfied deliverance was at hand' (*Memoirs*,
p. 140, ed. 1806).

account of some unlucky predictions made by him, parted from the army in a less admiring temper. He disapproved of their forcible resistance to disbanding in 1647, and still more of their interruption of the treaty with the King in 1648 and their whole attitude towards both King and Parliament after the victories of the second Civil War. 'You have left God,' he said in a pamphlet addressed to the army in December 1648, 'so he now hath left you. . . . Poor wretches, though angry at you, yet my soul pities you, never were men caught in such a snare of the devil as you are.'[1]

John Saltmarsh, whom Fuller styles a man 'of a fine and active fancy, no contemptible poet, and a good preacher', seems to have stayed longer with the army. The negotiations of the army leaders with the King, during the summer of 1647, and the suppression by them of the extreme democrats, filled him with grief and anger. About Christmas 1647 he left his living in Essex and came to the headquarters at Windsor, saying 'that he had something revealed to him from heaven he must presently acquaint the army withal'. Reaching Windsor, he entered the castle where the General Council of the Army was to sit that day, 'and meeting several officers, told them, that he had formerly come to them as a lamb, but now in the spirit of a lion, to tell them what the Lord had revealed to him from Heaven, that though the Lord had done much by them and for them, yet he had now forsaken them, and would not prosper them, because they had forsaken him, their first principle, and imprisoned Saints, &c., with many other such like expressions.

'Afterwards he met with the General, and told him, with his hat on, that he had formerly so much doted on his person, he had offended God for it; but he had now no command from God to honour him at all: and that God had revealed into him, that he was highly displeas'd with him for imprisoning of Saints, and would not prosper him. And spoke of great divisions to arise in the army, to the ruine of them.

'The like expressions he used to another great officer in the army, with his hat on. And spoke also to a minister of the army, and others, to the same purpose.

'On Tuesday Mr Saltmarsh took his leave of the army, and

[1] *Justice upon the Army's Remonstrance.*

told them, "He had now delivered his message and done his work, and must leave them, never to see the army more".[1]

New men were found to fill the vacant places without difficulty, and the system of having regimental chaplains seems to have been re-established. At all events there was, about 1648, a considerable increase in the number of chaplains attached to the army. On 9th January 1648 the Council of the Army being informed 'of the willingness and readiness of divers godly men of the ministry to bestow their pains to preach the Gospel of Christ in the army', voted 'that some of those whose hearts should most incline to that work should be desired to come to the army for that purpose, and be assured from the council of all encouragement thereto'. In consequence of this vote John Canne became chaplain of Colonel Lilburne's regiment, and other divines attached themselves to other regiments.[2]

In the summer of 1649, when Cromwell set out to reconquer Ireland, he took with him as his own chaplain John Owen, and Hugh Peters as one of the chaplains of the army. Owen soon returned to England to become Dean of Christ Church and Vice-Chancellor of Oxford; nor did Peters stay long in Ireland. A third army chaplain, Thomas Patient, founded a small Independent congregation at Waterford. Indeed the army in Ireland was throughout very poorly supplied with chaplains. Next year, when Cromwell invaded Scotland, he was accompanied by Robert Stapylton as his chaplain, and every regiment appears to have been provided with its minister. As it was hoped to argue the Scots out of their hostility to Independency, as well as to convince them 'by apostolic blows and knocks', chaplains were doubly needed, and great hopes were founded on their persuasive powers. When Stapylton preached in the High Church at Edinburgh before Cromwell and his officers we are told that 'many Scots expressed much affection at the doctrine preached by Mr Stapleton, in their usual way of groans, and it is hoped a good work is wrought in some of their hearts'.[3] Another letter,

[1] Rushworth, vii, 944; cf. *England's Friend raised from the Grave, giving seasonable advice to the Lord General, Lieutenant-General, and the Council of War, being copies of three letters written by Mr John Saltmarsh, a little before his death*, 4to, 1649.

[2] *Clarke Papers*, i, lvii.

[3] *Cromwelliana*, p. 92; *Mercurius Politicus*, 3rd to 10th October 1650.

written in 1652, speaks of disputations between the army chaplains and the Scottish ministers. There was one at Cupar, between Browne, the chaplain of Colonel Fairfax's regiment, and one Mr James Wood, on the results of Adam's sin, the validity of infant baptism, and on universal redemption. 'Although the disputers were not convinced,' concludes the account, 'yet it's hoped a good seed is sown which will sprout forth in such of the auditors who are enquirers of the truth.'[1]

Foreign expeditions were less well provided than the troops serving in England or Scotland. In 1654, when General Venables asked for six chaplains to accompany the regiments sent with him to the West Indies, he was jeeringly offered by some person in authority (apparently Major-General Desborough) six black coats in their place.[2] Eventually, however, he obtained his chaplains. In January 1657 one of them, Nathaniel Lane, wrote to the Protector from Jamaica saying, 'I am the meanest of the Lord's and your Highness' servants, the only survivor of seven ministers. . . . Had not my passionate affections to your Highness, my country's, and the Gospel's service, maintained my resolution, I had long since either wholly desponded or deserted my employment. . . .' In conclusion, he urged Cromwell to provide 'a plentiful and certain maintenance' for ministers in Jamaica, and then he would secure 'faithful and able men'. 'Then will you convince the jealous and too censorious world, that the name and the noise of the Gospel's interest is real, not a base pretence: then will you engage God as a party in your concernments, revive the decaying hopes and expectations of your faithful friends, and elude the malice and strongest confidence of enemies.'[3]

The army employed in Flanders in 1657 was still worse cared for from the religious point of view than the expedition to the West Indies. Apparently the troops had no chaplains at all. 'I find not one minister here,' wrote Lockhart from Mardyke on 7th May 1658, 'and out of charity have sent for my chaplain from Calais; the soldiers need much both to be dehorted from evil and exhorted to good. If you will send over three ministers

---

[1] *Scotland and the Commonwealth*, pp. xl, 53.

[2] *Narrative of General Venables*, p. 6.

[3] *Thurloe Papers*, vi, 24.

they may very well serve the six regiments, and I engage myself
to procure them £180 sterling per annum apiece, which I think
is encouragement enough to any honest man, who hath zeal for
his Master's service or the propagation of his Gospel. The Popish
priests, who go a-begging to vent their errors, will rise up in
judgment against our ministers, who cannot be persuaded even
upon reasonable terms to preach the glad tidings of salvation to
their poor countrymen who have some longings after the ordinances of God.' A couple of months later, Fuller, Lockhart's
chaplain, was called to England by his father's death, and a
successor was needed. Lockhart pointed out how necessary it
was 'to have men of more than ordinary talents in this place,
who by their conversation, doctrine, and learning too may be
able to prevail against adversaries'.[1] The want was to some
extent supplied by Hugh Peters, who spent a few weeks at
Dunkirk after its capture. 'He hath laid himself forth in great
charity and goodness,' wrote Lockhart to Thurloe, 'in sermons,
prayers, and exhortations, in visiting and relieving the sick and
wounded; and in all these profitably applying the singular
talent God hath bestowed upon him to the two chief ends proper
to our auditory; for he hath not only shown the soldiers their
duty to God, and pressed it home upon them, I hope to good
advantage, but likewise acquainted them with their obligations
to his Highness' government and affection to his person.'

Peters thought of settling at Dunkirk 'if he had a call', and
some of the officers wished to get him established there, but
Lockhart thought him too much of a busybody. 'I must give
him that testimony,' he added in a postscript, 'that he gave us
three or four very honest sermons; and if it were possible to get
him to mind preaching, and to forbear the troubling of himself
with other things, he would certainly prove a very fit minister
for soldiers.'[2]

From this sketch of the ecclesiastical establishment of the
Puritan armies it appears that the provision made for the religious needs of the soldiers varied considerably at different
dates. At the beginning of the war it was easy to obtain a
number of eminent divines as chaplains, but it was not easy to

[1] *Thurloe Papers*, vii, 125, 205.

[2] Ibid., vii, 249.

retain their services. The hardships of military life repelled them,
and other ecclesiastical functions called them away. Later it was
always possible to obtain an eminent divine for the post of
chaplain to the general or the army, but it was not easy to get
the requisite number of regimental chaplains, nor is it clear that
the government systematically and continuously sought to procure them. From the pecuniary point of view the situation of a
regimental chaplain was extremely good. In the establishment
of 1648 chaplains were paid six shillings and eightpence per
diem, and on 19th May the regimental chaplains of the army in
Scotland were ordered eight shillings per diem.[1] Both regimental
chaplains and chaplains appointed to particular garrisons appear
to have received regular commissions from the commander-in-
chief.[2] Yet in spite of this their position was somewhat precarious. In 1649 Colonel Okey quarrelled with some officers of
his regiment about various theological points, and finding that
they were supported in their views by Mr Close, the chaplain of
the regiment, he discharged him, saying that he held and
preached dangerous tenets. Close remonstrated, and Okey told
him that he might stay in the regiment as a private trooper, if
he liked, but not as chaplain. To this Close replied with spirit,
'that if he were not fit to be chaplain to the regiment, he was
not fit to ride in any troop'.[3] It is pretty clear that the precise
shade of theology preached in any particular regiment depended
upon the taste of its colonel, and in many cases the chaplain was
chosen by common consent of the officers. Thus in 1643 the
officers of Cromwell's regiment invited Richard Baxter to be
their chaplain, and proposed to form the regiment into 'a
gathered church'.[4]

[1] *Lords' Journals*, x, 66; *Cal. State Papers, Dom.*, 1652–3, p. 338.

[2] See *The Gentleman's Magazine*, 1791, p. 919, for a specimen of a commission from Cromwell to a garrison chaplain.

[3] *Light Vanquishing Darkness*, by Capt. Francis Freeman, 1650.

[4] *Reliquiæ Baxterianæ*, p. 51. Sometimes also an Independent congregation would raise a troop under its minister, as an instance recorded in the
newspapers of 1651 shows: 'Yesterday marched thorough this City towards
Scotland, Col. Walter Cradocke, and very lately Mr Vavasor Powel from
other parts of South-Wales (those eminent Pauls of our time), with 2
troopes of Horse attending them, selected out of their gathered Churches,
after their dear Brethren Mr Jenkin Jones and Mr Morgan Floyd, to fight
the Lords Battell, and questionlesse armed with the shield of Faith that
subdueth nations. They having been Instruments for the expelling of Satan
out of many thousand soules in these parts' (*Special Proceedings*, p. 1476).

One duty the chaplains performed during the first Civil War which seems strange to modern ideas: they drew up narratives of the proceedings of the armies to which they were attached for publication in the press, and were in fact the first war correspondents. Two of Essex's chaplains, Thomas Case and Adoniram Byfield, published accounts of Edgehill.[1] Manchester's chaplains, Simeon Ashe and William Goode, published a detailed history of his campaign during the year 1644, in eight or nine parts.[2] Ashe's narratives of Marston Moor and the second batttle of Newbury are specially valuable. 'For the man's known integrity every word is believed,' wrote Robert Baillie, lamenting that Ashe had unfortunately assigned too much credit to Cromwell and the sectaries in his account of Marston Moor.[3] Edward Bowles wrote several pamphlets on the early proceedings of the New Model in the West of England, and others on the services of Lord Fairfax and the army under Leslie in the North.[4] His colleague, Hugh Peters, wrote half a dozen printed narratives of the battles and sieges of 1645 and 1646. Cromwell employed him to give the House of Commons an account of the capture of Basing, and Fairfax sent him to report to it the surrender of Hopton's army and the state of the West.[5]

To assist and supplement the teaching of the chaplains, there

[1] *A more exact and true relation, etc.*, by T. C., *one of the chaplains in the army. A letter from a worthy divine to the right honourable the Lord Mayor,* Oct. 24, 1642.

[2] *A particular Relation of the several Removes, Services, and Successes of the Earl of Manchester's army.* The fifth part of this series of *Relations*, or as some are called *Intelligences*, deals with Marston Moor. That on Newbury is entitled *A true Relation of the late Occurrences at and since the late Battle at Newbury. Published upon necessity both to undeceive the mistaken Multitude and to vindicate the Earl of Manchester. Penned by Simeon Ashe who, as his chaplain, did wait upon his Lordship in the Western expedition,* 1644.

[3] Baillie, *Letters,* ii, 209.

[4] *The Proceedings of the Army under the command of Sir Thomas Fairfax.* No. 6 is said to be written by Mr Bowles to a friend in London. Sprigge made great use of these letters in compiling his *Anglia Rediviva.*

[5] *Mr Peter's Report from the Armies,* 26 July 1645, *with a list of the chiefest officers taken at Bridgewater,* 4to, 1645. *Mr Peter's Report from Bristol,* 4to, 1645. *The Full and Last Relation of all things concerning Basing House with divers other passages represented to Mr Speaker and divers members in the House. By Mr Peters who came from Lieut.-Gen. Cromwell,* 4to, 1645. *Master Peter's Message from Sir Thomas Fairfax, with the narration of the taking of Dartmouth,* 4to, 1646. *Master Peter's Message from Sir Thomas Fairfax with . . . the whole state of the west and all the particulars about the disbanding of the Prince and Sir Ralph Hopton's Army,* 4to, 1646. *Mr Peter's Last Report of the English Wars,* 1646, 4to. See also Sprigge, pp. 141, 150.

was a class of literature specially designed for the instruction of soldiers of which a few specimens have survived. *The Christian Soldier, or a Preparation for Battle,* published in 1642 is an example. Major-General Skippon published between 1643 and 1645 three books of devotion addressed to his fellow-soldiers. *The Christian Centurion's Observations, Advices, and Resolutions* is the title of one. Another is called *A Salve for every sore, or a collection of Promises out of the whole Book of God, and is the Christian Centurion's infallible ground of Confidence.*[1] In 1644 Robert Ram, minister of Spalding, published what he termed *The Soldiers' Catechism, composed for the use of the Parliament's Army, consisting of two parts wherein are chiefly taught* (1) *the justification and* (2) *the qualification of our Soldiers.*[2] After proving the lawfulness of the military profession and the justice of the war, the author draws a picture of what the ideal soldier of the Parliament should be. Incidentally he defends the conduct of the soldiers in breaking down crosses and images, and in tearing or burning the book of Common Prayer.

'Much may be said in their justification who show themselves so zealous against that book.'

(1) 'It hath been the fomenter of a most lazy, lewd and ignorant ministry.'

(2) 'It hath been the nurse of that lamentable blindness and ignorance which hath overspread many parts of this Kingdom.'

(3) 'It is a great cause of our present calamities, for who are they that side with our Popish enemies, but Common-Prayer men?'

(4) 'It is become the most abominable idol in the land, people generally do doat upon it, as much as the Ephesians upon Diana, and prefer it before preaching in many places, being strangely enraged for the want of it.'

(5) 'It is high time therefore to remove this Brazen Serpent and grind it to powder seeing it is the occasion of so much evil.'

---

[1] See the life of Skippon in the *Dictionary of National Biography.* Skippon's oration to the soldiers at Turnham Green in November 1642 is characteristic. It ends, 'Come, my honest brave boys, pray heartily and fight heartily and God will bless us' (Whitelocke, *Memorials,* i, 191).

[2] A facsimile reprint of this under the title of *Cromwell's Soldiers' Catechism,* edited by Rev. Walter Begley, was published in 1900 by Mr Eliot Stock. For evidence that the author of the *Catechism* was Robert Ram, see *English Historical Review,* 1900, p. 585.

(6) 'It is very likely therefore that God hath stirred up the spirits of some honest soldiers to be his instruments for the destruction of that idol.'

As to the propriety of breaking down crosses and images, the *Catechism* answers that 'nothing ought to be done in a tumultuous manner. But seeing God hath put the sword of Reformation into the soldiers' hand, I think it not amiss that they should cancel and demolish those monuments of superstition and idolatry, especially seeing the Magistrate and the Minister that should have done it formerly neglected it.'[1]

Ram's *Catechism* is one of the many proofs that the iconoclasm of the Parliamentary soldiers was approved and encouraged by their ministers, as it was by too many of their officers. The wanton destruction wrought by Waller's soldiers at Chichester and Winchester Cathedrals are two instances amongst many. At Chichester, whilst Waller's soldiers, under their commander's eyes, were breaking painted windows and defacing monuments, one of the troopers boldly told Sir William, that it was contrary to good discipline to allow it, adding, 'That if his old colonel in the Low Countries were there, and commanded in chief, he would hang up half a dozen soldiers, for example's sake.'[2]

A picture of the Puritan soldier which omits to mention his iconoclasm would be incomplete. It is fair, however, to add that the worst instances of this belong to the two first years of the war: in the later years of the war the soldiers were kept in better order. Much too of the destruction popularly attributed to Cromwell's soldiers was really the work of agents of the civil government specially commissioned to remove all relics of superstition from the churches.

More interesting than Ram's *Catechism* is the little pamphlet of sixteen pages entitled the *Soldiers' Pocket Bible*.[3] Both are the private production of some Puritan divine, and neither has any official character. Yet one has been reprinted as *Cromwell's Soldiers' Catechism*, and the other as *Cromwell's Soldiers' Bible*, though there is no evidence that he had anything to do with either of them. The full title of the second work is *The Soldiers'*

---

[1] Pp. 21, 22.

[2] *Mercurius Rusticus* (Second Series), Nos. ii and iii, p. 141, ed. 1685.

[3] Reprinted in facsimile in 1895 under the title of *Cromwell's Soldiers' Bible*, by Mr Eliot Stock.

Pocket Bible, containing the most if not all those places contained in Holy Scripture which do show the qualifications of his inner man, that is a fit soldier to fight the Lord's battles, both before the fight, in the fight, and after the fight: which Scriptures are reduced to several heads, and fitly applied to the soldiers on several occasions, and so may supply the want of the whole Bible which a soldier cannot conveniently carry about him. This tract, published in August 1643, consists of a selection of texts arranged under various heads; as for instance, 'A Soldier must not do wickedly'; 'A Soldier must be valiant for God's cause'; 'A Soldier must love his enemies as they are his enemies, and hate them as they are God's enemies'; 'A Soldier must consider that sometimes God's people have the worst in battle as well as God's enemies'. There are eighteen heads in all.

It is often said that in Cromwell's army every man had a Bible in his knapsack, and some sceptical persons, struck by the inherent improbability of this statement, have asserted that what they carried was the little *Soldiers' Pocket Bible*. There is no evidence in favour of either statement, and much that contradicts both. If the soldiers habitually carried Bibles, the officers of the army in Ireland would not have made the following petition to Parliament in June 1651.

'And lastly, that in regard your poore souldiers there have few to instruct them in the feare of the Lord, who alone (not for your sakes, but for the iniquity of the inhabitants, and his owne free mercy to you) hath hitherto beene your strength in the three nations, this honourable councell would be pleased freely to bestowe upon them four thousand Bibles, or to every six men one, which would not cost above £500, to reade in their tents or quarters, which would probably prevent a greate deale of idlenesse, and, through the blessing of the Lord, might doe much good amongst the poore ignorant souldiers and natives; especially comeing from you, who I am sure, of any generation since the world beganne, have cause to sanctifie God as your strength and praise by all meanes possible.'[1]

The request was acceded to and some Bibles were sent. On 3rd August 1652 Bibles were ordered to be issued by the

[1] Nickolls, *Original Letters and Papers of State addressed to Cromwell*, p. 70.

commissary of stores to the several companies of foot and troops of horse within the precinct of Dublin, one Bible to every file. On the 17th of the same month a hundred Bibles were issued for the use of the forces in the precinct of Galway, for the propagation of the Gospel. The commissaries of musters were ordered to see that these books were periodically accounted for by the officers of the troops and companies.[1]

Bibles were also at different times supplied by the government to other forces in its pay. On 9th June 1655 the Council of State ordered that 2,000 Bibles of a pattern shown should be bought and sent to the soldiers in the West Indies.[2] Finally, on 29th June 1658, just after Cromwell's conquest of Dunkirk, the Council of State ordered that the garrison of Dunkirk should be provided with a Bible to each file of soldiers.[3]

Now in all these three cases the cause which led the government to make this issue of Bibles was that the soldiers had few or no chaplains to preach to them. We know that this was the case in Ireland, for it is expressly stated in the petition, and there is evidence of the same deficiency in Flanders and Jamaica. The Bibles were temporary substitutes for chaplains. Finally, it need scarcely be pointed out that if any large proportion of the soldiers had possessed Bibles already, the government, which was always in want of money, would scarcely have incurred the expense of providing them.

Much better founded is the popular view that the Parliamentary soldiers were great psalm singers. Sir Henry Slingsby describes how before the battle of Marston Moor began the Roundheads in Marston cornfield fell to singing Psalms, and Lord Saye mentions the 'psalm of praise sung to God after the victory'.[4]

Vicars in his *Parliamentary Chronicle* relates an incident which took place during the fight.

'In the rout of the enemy, and in their flying and scattering about, many of them ran most frightedly and amazedly to the place where some of the regiments of horse of the Parliament

[1] Prendergast, *The Cromwellian Settlement of Ireland*, p. 78, 2nd ed.

[2] *Cal. State Papers, Colonial*, 1574–1660, p. 426.

[3] *Cal. State Papers, Dom.*, 1658–9, p. 78.

[4] Slingsby, *Memoirs*, ed. Parsons, p. 112.

side were standing on their guard, and all or most of their riders
were religiously singing of Psalms, to whom as the aforesaid
runawayes of the enemy came near and by their singing of Psalms
perceiving who they were, they all most fiercely fled back again,
and cryed out, "God damn them, they had like to have been
taken by the Parliament Roundheades". For they only knew
them, I say, to be the Parliament soldiers by their singing of
Psalmes. A blessed badge and cognisance indeed.'[1]

To take another instance, a Royalist account of the second
battle of Newbury says, 'the rebels came singing of psalms'.[2]
Best known of all, thanks to Carlyle, is Captain Hodgson's story
how Cromwell, chasing the flying Scots after Dunbar, called a
halt and sang the hundred and seventeenth psalm.[3]

Equally well founded is the popular view that a good deal of
the preaching done in the Cromwellian army was done by the
soldiers themselves – the view which Scott illustrates in the
opening scene of *Woodstock*.

Such unauthorized preaching was prohibited by law when the
New Model was first established. On 25th April 1645 Parliament
passed an order that no person should be permitted to preach
who was not an ordained minister in this or some other reformed
Church, and sent the order to Fairfax with instructions to see it
strictly observed in the army and all transgressors properly
punished.[4]

The soldiers of the New Model, however, paid little attention
to this order. Edwards and Baxter are full of complaints of the

[1] Vicars, *Parliamentary Chronicle, God's Ark*, p. 281.

[2] Rushworth, v, 727; Sir Edward Walker, *Historical Discourses*, p. 113.

[3] *Memoirs of Capt. John Hodgson*, p. 148.

[4] *Commons' Journals*, iv, 123; Husbands, *Ordinances*, pt. ii, p. 645.
For a commentary, see *A Cleer and Just Vindication of the late Ordinance,
. . . from such malignant interpretations, as some ill-affected labour to fasten
on it*, 1645. It concludes with the following: 'You therefore, gentlemen of
the souldiery in the field, though (not intending the ministry) for reasons
best known to the State, you are forbidden to preach, as that in their judgment which belongs not to you; yet doubtless you may both pray and
speake too in the head of your companies, regiments, and armies, you may
deliver the piety of your souls, the well grounded confidence of your hearts,
the valour of your minds, in such orations, in such liberties of speech, as
may best enspirit the men that follow you with such a religious and
undaunted animation as may render them unconquerable to the proudest
enemy.'

manner in which they interrupted sermons, held public disputations with ministers on points of doctrine, and thrust themselves
into pulpits. Baxter records a dispute held in Chesham Church
between himself and the sectaries of the parish, in which the
local heretics were assisted by Captain Pitchford's troopers from
the gallery.[1] Edwards relates how Captain Pretty of Colonel
Ireton's regiment ordered a minister to come out of the pulpit,
alleging that he was drunk on Saturday night, and therefore
unfit to preach on Sunday morning.[2] A trooper of Cromwell's
regiment, when the minister had done preaching, stood up in
the church 'pretending to question something delivered, but
indeed fell upon venting to the people the doctrine of universal
grace, that no man was condemned for anything but unbelief'.[3]
At Bristol a lieutenant of horse preached publicly in his scarlet
coat laced with silver lace.[4] At Steeple Aston Lieutenant Webb
interrupted the sermon in the morning, and seized the pulpit
himself in the afternoon.[5] Next Sunday his colonel occupied the
pulpit both morning and afternoon, proving in his sermon the
lawful minister of the parish to be Antichrist by thirteen marks
of a false prophet.[6] One of the grievances of which Thomas
Edwards most complains is the conduct of the soldiers who
garrisoned Oxford after its surrender.

'Though the boldnesse and presumption of many of the souldiers, officers and common souldiers hath been very great, both
against the command of God, and the Parliament, to preach in
the open churches in all countries and places where they have
come putting by many godly and able ministers from their
office and invading their pulpits; yet their open and frequent
preaching in the University of Oxford, doth most of all declare
their imprudencie, that they should dare to do it in the midst
of so many learned men, and in a place so famous for learning;
and that in the public schools in Oxford to preach daily, and
that against humane learning as they did for some time; and after
complaint of it to the Generall as a thing so scandalous and
odious to all ingenuous men, and his forbidding their preaching

[1] *Reliquiæ Baxterianæ*, p. 56.   [2] Edwards, *Gangræna*, iii, 30.
[3] Ibid.   [4] Ibid., iii, 111.
[5] Ibid., iii, 251. Webb finally in a rage went out of the church calling Mr
Skinner, the preacher, 'the black frog of Revelation'.
[6] Colonel Hewson.

in the Schools; yet the souldiers continue still to preach in
Oxford daily in a great house where they meet for that end;
and I spak with one that came from Oxford in Aug. last who
told me they preach now daily in Christs Church (one of the
greatest colledges in Oxford) in a kind of gallery, where the souldier stands that preaches, many sitting on the stairs, others
standing below; and this young man heard one of them preach
there, discoursing on these words: God would require the life of
man at a beast; this souldier expounded that by beasts was
meant a wicked man.'[1]

Sometimes there was an effort made to stop officers from
preaching, but it was usually fruitless. Sir Samuel Luke, the
governor of Newport Pagnell, arrested in 1645 two of Fairfax's
captains, Hobson and Beaumont. They had not only refused to
take part in the public thanksgiving service for the victory at
Naseby, but set up a conventicle of their own. When the service
took place they withdrew themselves to a neighbouring village
'with a company of ignorant women, and a young boy, and
seven men more, where by the witness of a company of pots
and jugs they exercised their gifts.'[2]

Fairfax, however, was not inclined to lose the services of two
useful officers in the middle of a campaign, and obliged Luke at
once to release them. Though the Presbyterian divines clam-
oured loudly for the suppression of unlicensed preaching they
could not obtain their desire. On the other side the champions
of the army did not shrink from defending the practice in point.
Edmund Chillenden, a lieutenant in Whalley's regiment, who
subsequently became an Anabaptist minister, published in 1647
a tract called *Preaching without Ordination*.[3] Another writer, in
a tract called *Vox Militaris*,[4] carried the war into the enemy's
camp. 'We acknowledge,' said he, 'that through the want of
honest, able and godly ministers in our army, the soldiers have
endeavoured the mutual edification one of another, by exhorta-
tion on the Lord's days (without permission whereof we should
scarce have had so much as any solemn form of godliness found

[1] Edwards, *Gangræna*, pt. iii, p. 23.
[2] Ellis, *Original Letters Illustrative of English History* (Third Series), vol.
iv, pp. 254, 261–6.
[3] See Chillenden's *Life* in the *Dictionary of National Biography*.
[4] 1647.

amongst us).' If those who attacked the army on this ground, he continued, really cared about the propagation of truth and the prevention of error, why did they not take up the task of preaching to the soldiers themselves, or provide the army with better preachers than the soldiers they complained of? But the really effective argument against the suppression of unlicensed teaching was the practical one stated by Edwards:

'November last, the 18. day, so soon as I came out of the pulpit at Christ-Church, at the very foot of the pulpit stood a man, gentleman like all in scarlet, a young man, but being dusk-ish I could not perfectly discerne his countenance; he desired to speake a few words with me, so I stood still; and these were his words, "Sir, you speak against the preaching of souldiers in the army; but I assure you, if they have not leave to preach, they will not fight: and if they fight not, we must all fly the land and be gone: both you and I, must not stay here, for these men who are preachers, both of commanders and troopers, are the men whom God hath blessed so within this few months, to rout the enemy twice in the field, and to take in many garrisons of castles and townes, (as I remember he said to the number of 21) and I thought good to let you understand so much".'[1]

After 1648 less is heard of soldiers and officers usurping the pulpits, possibly because it was no longer a novelty and because the triumph of the army and the Independents made complaint somewhat useless. At the same time the increase in the number of army chaplains which took place about that date made amateur preachers less necessary.

Amongst themselves in their private gatherings the leaders of the army continued to preach with freedom. How naturally political meetings gave rise to prayer meetings and prayer meetings developed into discussions on practical politics is shown by the records of the debates of the Army Council in October 1647.[2] All important meetings of the General Council of the Army had the same religious character. At Windsor, for instance, in December 1647, after discussions on 'the present juncture of affairs' and on disciplinary questions:

'Wednesday, December 22, was according to appointment

[1] Edwards, *Gangræna*, pt. i, p. 111.
[2] *Clarke Papers*, i, 253, 280.

kept as a general fast by the General and officers; the duties of
the day were performed by divers of the officers, amongst whom
there was a sweet harmony, the Lieutenant-General, Commissary-General Ireton, Col. Tichborne, Col. Hewson, Mr Peters
and other officers prayed very fervently and pathetically; this
continued from nine in the morning till seven at night.'[1]

Sometimes ministers and officers amicably divided the duties
of the day. On 11th July 1649, when Cromwell set out for
Ireland, 'three ministers did pray and the Lord Lieutenant himself and Colonel Goffe and Colonel Harrison did expound some
places of Scripture excellently well and pertinent to the occasion'.[2]

Cromwell's invasion of Scotland and the English occupation
of Edinburgh brought out once more the opposition between the
Presbyterian and Independent views of the preaching function.
Nicoll notes in his *Diary* that Major-General Lambert demanded
in 1651 the use of the East Kirk at Edinburgh, 'being the special
kirk and the best in the town', for himself and his soldiers.
Sermons were preached there not only by Independent ministers,
but by captains, lieutenants, and even troopers of the army.
'When they entered the pulpits, they did not observe our Scottish forms, but when they ascended they entered the pulpits
with their swords hung at their sides, and some carrying pistols
up with them, and after their entry, laid aside within the pulpit
their swords till they ended their sermons.'[3]

This question of soldiers preaching was one of the subjects of
Cromwell's controversy with the Scottish clergy after the battle
of Dunbar. Cromwell invited the ministers who had taken refuge
in Edinburgh Castle to come down and preach freely in the
churches of the city. They declined, complaining that men of
mere civil place and employment should usurp the calling and
employment of the ministry to the scandal of the Reformed
Kirks, and particularly in Scotland.

'Are you troubled that Christ is preached,' replied Cromwell.
'Be not envious though Eldad and Medad prophesy. Where do
you find in the Scriptures a ground to warrant such an assertion

[1] Rushworth, vii, 943.

[2] Whitelocke, *Memorials*, iii, 66.

[3] Nicoll, *Diary*, pp. 68, 148.

that preaching is exclusively your function?' Ordination, in his view, was merely 'an act of conveniency in respect of order'.[1]

In the end both Cromwell himself and the majority of the leaders of the army seem to have come to the conclusion that some regulation of the right to preach was necessary in the interests of order and decency. On 17th July 1653, the Council of State which the army had established after the expulsion of the Long Parliament, passed an order which was almost equivalent to the ordination of five officers named. It declared that 'as the council is satisfied of the gifts and abilities of Major Packer, Captain Empson, etc., and that the public exercise thereof will be of great use in the Church, they being eminent for godliness' . . . therefore the said persons 'may have free use of any pulpit to preach in, as the Lord giveth opportunity', on the sole condition that the regular minister was not using it at the time.[2]

It was to meet the case of Packer and other officers in his position that the Protector in 1657 persuaded Parliament to insert an amendment in the constitution known as the Petition and Advice. A clause in the original draft incapacitated public preachers from sitting in Parliament. Cromwell urged that the House should make it plain that it meant to exclude professionals only, 'Such as have the pastoral function', for otherwise many excellent officers would be excluded from Parliament.

'For I must say to you on behalf of our Army – in the next place to their fighting they have been very good preachers, and I should be sorry they should be excluded from serving the Commonwealth, because they have been accustomed to preach to their troops, companies, and regiments – which I think has

[1] Carlyle, *Cromwell*, Letter cxlviii.

[2] *Cal. State Papers, Dom.*, 1653–4, p. 13. Empson was the officer referred to in Cromwell's letter to Colonel Hacker (Carlyle, *Cromwell*, Letter clxii). Hacker opposed his promotion to the command of a troop on the ground that he was a better preacher than fighter or soldier. Cromwell answered, 'Truly I think that he that prays and preaches best will fight best. . . . I dare assure you he is a good man and a good officer.'
The line between the minister by profession and the gifted officer with a taste for preaching was easily overpassed. Monck licensed one such officer to be the chaplain of a regiment. In Monck's *Order-Book* under 20th August 1655 is a note of a letter to Quartermaster Arthur Hebb of Colonel Pride's regiment, that the general had received his letter, dated 13th August, 'and in case he be to leave his quartermaster's place, and the regiment shall be well satisfied in choosing him to be their chaplain, the general will be well satisfied therewith'.

been one of the blessings upon them to the carrying on of the great work. There may be some of us, it may be, who have been a little guilty of that, who would be loath to be excluded "from sitting in Parliament".'[1]

All this freedom of preaching and discussion and speculation naturally produced in the army beliefs of every conceivable variety and of every possible degree of extravagance. Yet there was no period at which this freedom was absolutely unlimited. Throughout the whole time there were certain opinions which no man could publicly profess, without risking expulsion from the army. There were also certain religious sects whose members were gradually eliminated from the army, not so much, however, for religious as for political reasons. By the operation of these two processes the character and temper of the army was very sensibly modified during the later years of its existence. Religious enthusiasm still worked powerfully amongst the soldiers, but it had come to adopt less extravagant forms. A sober Congregationalism became the dominant form of religion.

The elimination of the more extravagant religious sects took place mainly during the Protectorate, though it began during the Commonwealth. The rising of the Levellers in 1649 was a purely political and social movement, but since extreme opinions in religion and politics were generally associated, the result of its suppression was that many of the wilder sectaries were driven out of the army.

It was to this no doubt that John Cotton referred when he congratulated Cromwell on 'cashiering sundry corrupt spirits out of the army', though his letter was written nearly a couple of years after the rising. 'Truly, Sir,' he added, 'better a few and faithful than many and unsound. The army on Christ's side (which he maketh victorious) are called chosen and faithful (Rev. xvii, 14), a verse worthy your Lordship's frequent and deep meditation. Go on therefore, good Sir, to overcome yourself (Prov. xvi, 32), to overcome your army (Deut. xxix, 9 with v 14), and to vindicate your orthodox integrity to the world.'[2]

The first important breach in the army which was primarily

[1] Carlyle, *Cromwell*, Speech xiii.

[2] *Hutchinson Papers*, published by the Prince Society, vol. i, pp. 262–5.

M

due to religious causes took place in 1654. The abdication of the
Little Parliament put an end to the hopes which the Fifth
Monarchy men had based upon its meeting, while the establishment of the Protectorate was a direct challenge to their most
cherished principles. They had dreamed of a theocratic republic; they saw in its place a government which seemed to be the
old monarchy in a new form. Cromwell, as they expressed it,
had taken the crown from the head of Christ and put it on his
own. From the moment of Cromwell's installation, therefore,
Feake and Simpson and Rogers and other Fifth Monarchy
preachers denounced the Protectorate and appealed to the army
to overthrow it. 'Lord,' cried Vavasour Powell, 'have our army
men all apostatized from their principles? What is become of all
their declarations, protestations, and professions? Are they
choked with lands, parks, and manors? Let us go home and
pray, and say, "Lord, wilt thou have Oliver Cromwell or Jesus
Christ to reign over us?" I know there are many gracious souls
in the army, and of good principles, but the greater they grow
the more they are corrupted with lands and honours.'[1]

The Protector regarded the 'Fifth Monarchy' as 'a mistaken
notion,' by which many honest and sincere people had unhappily
been misled. 'A notion I hope we all honour, and wait and hope
for: that Jesus Christ will have a time to set up his reign in our
hearts; by subduing those corruptions and lusts and evils that
are there; which now reign more in the world than, I hope, in
due time they shall do.' But this reign of Christ, he argued, must
be taken in a spiritual, not in a literal sense. 'Men could not be
permitted to betitle themselves that they are the only men to
rule kingdoms, govern nations, and give laws to people, and
determine of property and liberty and everything else, on such a
pretension as this is.' Yet, he concluded, as these misguided men
had many of them good intentions they should be treated with
lenity. But they must live peaceably and refrain from active
attempts to overthrow the government.[2]

Most of them were not disposed to remain passive. Major-
General Harrison, their leader, refusing to give an engagement
not to act against the government, was deprived of his com-

---

[1] *Cal. State Papers, Dom.*, 1653–4, p. 306.

[2] Carlyle, *Cromwell*, Speech ii.

mission and ordered to stay at his house in Staffordshire. Four times during the next five years he was arrested for complicity in revolutionary movements – at first only kept under restraint for a few days, afterwards imprisoned for some months in Carisbrooke Castle and the Tower.[1] Major-General Overton, whose views were less clearly defined than those of Harrison, was suspended from his government of Hull for some months, and then in the autumn of 1654 became second in command in Scotland. There he was implicated in a plot got up by officers under his command, for marching the Scottish army into England, and making himself its commander in place of Monck. Oates, the chaplain of Colonel Pride's regiment, was one of the chief contrivers of the design, and a major and several captains and lieutenants were cashiered for their part in it.[2] Overton, whose share in the matter is by no means clear, was imprisoned for the rest of the Protectorate in Jersey. Another member of what may be called the religious opposition in the army was Colonel Nathaniel Rich, who was deprived of the command of his regiment in 1655 and was for some time imprisoned.

Rich was rather an Anabaptist than a Fifth Monarchy man, but practically the views of the two sects did not differ much, however distinct they might be in theory.[3] Some, like Harrison, belonged to both sects, and the dividing line between the two was not clearly drawn either in politics or religion. Many Anabaptist officers, therefore, shared the fate of the Fifth Monarchy men, though others remained in the service. A pamphlet published in 1655 asserted that Cromwell had avowed his intention of turning all Anabaptists out of the army. *Queries for his Highness to answer to his own conscience* is its title. Its author addresses the Protector thus: 'The way you intend to take to bring about this design is twofold, (1) To purge the army of the Anabaptists. (2) To do it by degrees. But, O Oliver, is this thy design? And is this the way to be rid of the Anabaptists? And is

[1] See the life of Thomas Harrison in the *Dictionary of National Biography*, and that of Robert Overton in the same work.

[2] On Samuel Oates, see *Thurloe Papers*, iii, 29, and *Scotland and the Protectorate*, p. 241. Oates had been denounced to Parliament for his heresies in 1647 (*Old Parliamentary History*, xvi, 402), and is often also mentioned by Edwards in his *Gangræna*.

[3] A life of Rich is contained in the *Dictionary of National Biography*.

this the reason because they hinder the reforming the things
amiss in the Church? I confess, they have been enemies to the
Presbyterian Church; and so were you, when you were at Dunbar in Scotland, or at least you seemed to be so by your words
and actions; for you spake as pure Independency as any of us
all then, and made this an argument why we should fight stoutly,
because we had the prayers of the Independent and Baptist
Churches. So highly did you seem to love the Anabaptists then,
that you did not only invite them into the army but entertain
them in your family; but it seems the case is altered. But do
not deceive yourself nor let the priests deceive you; for the Anabaptists are men that will not be shuffled out of their birthrights
as freeborn people of England.'

A few queries followed:

'Whether the Anabaptists did not come more justly into
their employment in the army than you came into the seat of
government?

'Whether an hundred of the old Anabaptists such as marched
under your command in '48, '49, '50, etc., be not as good as 200
of your new courtiers, if you were in such a condition as you
were at Dunbar?'[1]

The report was not true. The Protector was more anxious to
keep the Anabaptists in the army than to turn them out.[2] Any
Anabaptist who was obedient to authority kept his commission
without difficulty. In Ireland, for instance, the Anabaptist section amongst the officers continually opposed and intrigued
against Henry Cromwell's government, but they were treated
with great tenderness by the Protector. Henry Cromwell continually complained that they found too much support from his
father. 'Time and patience,' said the Protector, 'may work
them to a better frame of spirit, and bring them to see that
which, for the present, seems to be hid from them; especially if
they see your moderation and love towards them. . . .' 'I think,'
he added in another letter, 'the Anabaptists are to blame in not

---

[1] *Thurloe Papers*, iii, 150.

[2] The pamphlet is also entitled *A Short Discovery of his Highness the Lord
Protector's Intentions touching the Anabaptists in the Army*. Cromwell was
alleged to have revealed his views in a conversation with Lord Tweeddale,
but that person denied that any such discourse took place, and his denial
was published in the newspapers (see *Mercurius Politicus*, 11th to 18th
October 1655).

being pleased with you. That's their fault. It will not reach you while you with singleness of heart make the glory of the Lord your aim. . . . Take heed of making it a business to be too hard for the men who contest with you.'[1] When Henry cashiered an Anabaptist, a lieutenant-colonel, for speaking words against his father, the Protector urged his son to 'let the poor man be handsomely restored'. He added, 'I would not believe two carnal men against one such protesting innocency, it being in a case concerning myself, where it is in my power to pardon without injustice.'[2]

Thus, though the number of Anabaptist officers was greatly diminished during the early part of the Protectorate, a considerable number still remained in the army.

In Scotland the progress of another sect caused Monck some alarm, namely, the Quakers. George Fox's account of his journey to Scotland says that he converted many officers and soldiers to his principles.[3] 'I think,' wrote Monck to the Protector, 'they will prove a very dangerous people should they increase in your army, and be neither fit to command nor obey, but ready to make a distraction in the army and a mutiny upon every slight occasion.' Monck's officers made similar complaints to their general. 'I fear,' wrote Major Richardson, 'these people's principle will not allow them to fight, if we stand in need, though it does to receive pay.'[4] Colonel Daniel represented that Quakerism was subversive of all discipline, and quoted the case of his own captain-lieutenant, Davenport:

'My Captain-Lieutenant is much confirmed in his principles of quakeing, makeing all the soldiers his equalls (according to the Levellers strayne) that I dare say in [a] short time his principles in the army shall be the root of disobedience. My Lord, the whole world is governed by superiority and distance in relations, and when that's taken away, unavoydably anarchy is ushered in. The man is growne soe besotted with his notions that one may as well speake to the walls as to him; and I speake it from

[1] Carlyle, *Cromwell*, Letters ccvii and ccviii.

[2] *English Historical Review*, April 1901, p. 345.

[3] *Journal of George Fox*, pp. 272, 276–9.

[4] *Scotland and the Protectorate*, pp. 350, 352; *Thurloe Papers*, vi, 136, 145, 162, 167, 208, 215, 241.

my heart, his present condition is the occasion of great trouble
to mee. Hee hath been under my command almost fowerteen
yeares, and hitherto demeaned himselfe in good order, and many
of these whimsyes I have kept him from, but now there's no
speakeing to him, and I doe professe I am affraid least by the
spreading of these humours the publique suffer, for they are a
very uncertayne generation to execute commaunds, and liberty
with equallity is so pleasing to ignorance that proselytes will be
dayly brought in, and any rationall person that speakes or acts
against it shall be censured as proud, or a disturber of liberty,
and when I thinke of the Levelling designe that had like to have
torne the army to pieces, it makes mee more bold to give my
opinion that these thinges be curbed in time; otherwise, wherever this principle remaynes there will bee great factions, which
I shall counterplot and discourage in my regiments, and will cast
all the water I can upon it. There was one example last day
when he came to St Johnston; hee came in a more then ordinary
manner to the soldiers of my company, and asking them how
they did, and the men doeing their duty by holding off their
hats, he bade them put them on, he expected no such thing from
them. My Lord, this may seeme to bee a small thing, but there
lyes more in the bosome of it then every one thinkes, and though
it's good to bee humble, yet humility would be known by the
demonstration thereof, and where all are equalls I expect little
obedience in government.'[1]

When Davenport was brought before Monck he refused to
take off his hat, and 'theed' and 'thoud' his commander.[2]
Not unnaturally he was sentenced to be cashiered. Half a
dozen other officers of the same sect shared his fate, and all the
regiments in Scotland were during the course of 1657 thoroughly
purged of Quakers.[3]

Another class of persons not permitted to remain in the army
– for they can hardly be called a sect – were the Antinomians.
According to Edwards in his *Gangræna*, speaking of 1645 and

[1] *Scotland and the Protectorate*, p. 362. The letter is dated 16th July 1657.

[2] *Clarke Papers*, iii, 122; *Journal of George Fox*, p. 279.

[3] There is a modern tract on soldiers who became Quakers. It gives an
account of eleven, but the number could be doubled. Its title is *The Changed
Warfare*, and it is number 226 of the publications of the *Friends' Tract Association*.

1646, the army was full of Antinomians of the worst type, and Baxter says much the same. 'You do them wrong: it is not so,' said Colonel Purefoy, when Baxter said something of this kind in his presence. 'If Noll Cromwell should hear any soldier speak but such a word he would cleave his crown.'[1] Though there were some Antinomians in the army then and afterwards, they were sooner or later expelled from its ranks. Many of them were obnoxious to military justice for their immorality, apart from their doctrinal views. Some were blasphemers, others evil speakers, others 'persons of loose conversation'. 'The discipline of the army was such,' asserted Cromwell, 'that a man would not be suffered to remain there, of whom we could take notice he was guilty of such practices as that.'[2]

There are several cases, however, in which officers were cashiered, not for acts, but for opinions, for holding religious views which were immoral or were judged to lead to immorality. In 1650 Fairfax issued a commission for the trial of Lieutenant Jackson, an officer of the garrison of Berwick, for holding divers dangerous and unsound opinions. The information begins by stating that Jackson had expressed himself in favour of communism, pantheism and other heresies, and concludes with the statement that he had asserted that he was as perfect now as ever he should be.[3]

A curious contrast to Jackson's case is that of Francis Freeman, the captain of dragoons, whom Colonel Okey drove out of his regiment because he disliked his theological views.[4] Freeman was not a vulgar atheist like Jackson, but a mystic. His creed eludes definition, though he sets it forth at length. He was neither Presbyterian nor Independent, Anabaptist nor Seeker. In the language of the time, he was one of those who had passed through all forms, and was above all forms, and above all ordinances; whose religion was not made up of laws and duties, but all exaltation and inward bliss. 'For such,' he said, 'all external forms of duties and performances are turned into praises and thanksgivings. Now there is nothing but mirth in them, there is a continual singing of birds in them, chirping

---

[1] *Reliquiæ Baxterianæ*, p. 52.   [2] Carlyle, *Cromwell*, Speech iv.

[3] See Appendix **K** for the text of the charge.   [4] See p. 304, *ante.*

sweetly, in a sweet harmony of soul-ravishing delightful
music.'[1]

Imagine such a man as this, called upon by an unsympathetic
colonel to explain his theological views, put through a series of
questions, asked his opinion on the value of ordinances and on
the authority of the Scriptures, answering his examiners lucidly
and patiently, but perfectly unintelligible all the time to the
orthodox every-day Puritan, until the exasperated colonel de-
nounces him as a dangerous man, swears to root him out of the
regiment, and finally succeeds in doing so!

Still more curious, however, is the account of the reasons
which led Cromwell to cashier a captain in his own regiment
during the campaign in Scotland. A news-letter, dated Glasgow,
12th October, 1650, narrates it thus:[2]

'This night his Excellency with the Major Generall, Lieut.
Generall, Commissary-Generall Whalley, Col. Thomlinson, Col.
Monck, Col. Twisleton, Col. Okey, Major Knight and some other
officers had a longe and serious discourse about the businesse of
cashiering Capt. Covell. His Excellency related how that hee
observed upon his coming into Scotland, that the said troope
was one of the worst in all that regiment, nay the thinnest in all
the army, that hee then feared there was some ill or miscarriage
in the captaine, that afterwards at Dunbarre uppon the day of
Humiliation Major Knight and some others were complayning of
the great profaneness and blasphemies that were in some troopes,
that Lieut. Empson did hint something in relation to Capt.
Covell, notwithstanding which hee tooke no notice of it, till
afterwards Capt. Packer came to him and told him of the desperate opinions broached by Capt. Covell, that thereupon his
Excellency sent for the said captaine and at Musleborough ad-
monished him to walke more cautiously, told him that hee was
sensible of his pride and his self-conceitednesse, which hee feared
did him much hurt. That Captain Covell denied all the said
tenents, and made a cleare confession of his faith, which gave
the Generall that satisfaction that hee bid him goe to his charge,
and that hee should bee willing to shew him any favour or res-

---

[1] *Light Vanquishing Darkness, or a Vindication of some truths formerly
declared. By Captain Francis Freeman, a late member of the army,* 1650, 4to.

[2] *Clarke MSS.,* in Worcester College Library.

pect that lay in his power. After this Capt. Packer acquainted his Excellency that the said Capt. Covell had asserted his vaine opinions to the troope with more confidence then before, and that openly, which was attested alsoe by Major Browne and others, whereupon hee told Capt. Covell that hee should not any longer command the troope; that notwithstanding hee found him at the last randezvous at the head of the troope, whereupon hee cashiered [him] himselfe for a terrour unto others from holding out blasphemous tenents. That hee would at any time have that liberty to cashier anyone out of his regiment as longe as hee was Generall, and that hee would make that condition with his officers. That hee had done it when hee was in lesse power. That hee would do it in opposition to the Levellers who complained that thinges were done arbitrarily, and that they should see hee had that power.'

The newspapers add further details on the nature of Covell's offences. He was a few days later tried by a court-martial and sentenced to be cashiered. The cause of his cashiering says one 'was his denying the divinity of Christ'. He had also said 'that sin was no sin, etc.,' which was sweeping, though somewhat vague. His sentence was based 'upon the general article [in the Articles of War] for speaking words tending to the dishonour of God, derogation of the Christian religion, to breach of civil society, and the scandal of the army'.[1]

It may be said, then, that absolute freedom of religion no more existed in the Puritan army than it did in the Puritan state. In each there were limits set to the propagation or the open profession of opinion, and a distinction was made between errors which were regarded as 'tolerable' and those regarded as 'intolerable'.

---

[1] *Mercurius Politicus*, 1650, pp. 337, 361, 375. Some of the papers give this officer's name as 'Cofield'.

CHAPTER XIV

Politics in the Army

IN DESCRIBING MOST armies it would hardly be necessary to
devote special chapters to their religion and their politics. The
Cromwellian army, however, was not an ordinary army. It was
a national army in so far as it represented England in its deal-
ings with foreign States and dependent communities. In another
sense it was not a national army, for it was not drawn indifferently from every party and every sect in the nation, but represented the particular sect and the particular party which had
gained the upper hand in the Civil Wars. It possessed in consequence a very definite set of opinions both in religion and
politics, and exerted a distinct and a continuous influence upon
the life of England from 1647 to 1660. The result of its intervention in domestic politics is part of the general history of the
country during that period. The nature and the source of the
ideas which inspired its action fall within the province of writers
on political theory rather than in that of the military historian.
What the latter has to consider is the method in which the
opinions of the army found public expression, and the development of the organs through which they were expressed. The history of the political organization of the army is therefore the
main subject of this chapter.

The political history of the army begins in 1647. Before that
date it made no attempt to influence the policy of the Parliament. The views of officers and men were those of the authority
whom they served, and if they petitioned it was only to ask that
their wants might be supplied and the war more vigorously
prosecuted. Yet temptations to intervention were not wanting.
In August 1643 the leaders of the House of Lords sought to enlist the support of Essex against the war party in the House of

Commons, and to secure by his aid the passing of peace-proposi-
tions which would have amounted to a capitulation on the part
of the Parliament. But Essex knew his duty too well to lend
himself and his army to the intrigues of one section of the Parliamentarians against another, and answered by a blunt refusal.
In June 1644, while the armies of Leven, Fairfax, and Manchester were besieging York, Sir Henry Vane tried to procure
the assent of the three generals to a scheme for deposing Charles
the First in favour of his nephew, the Elector Palatine, but all
three refused.

The risk of military interference in politics began when the
several armies in the pay of the Parliament began to represent
distinct creeds and different varieties of political opinion. About
the end of 1644 there were visible signs of that danger. The
Scottish Commissioners in England, and their friends in Parliament and the Westminster Assembly, looked upon the Scottish army under Leven as an instrument to be used for the
establishment of Presbyterianism in England and the suppression of schism. Robert Baillie in his letters avowed the hope that
it would 'ruin both the malignant party and the sectaries'. If
it was strong and victorious, it would 'keep all here in Church
and State right according to our mind'. . . . 'We would regain
this people's heart, and do with all sectaries and all things else
what we would.'[1] In like manner the rising Independent party
regarded the army of the Eastern Association as a weapon
providentially forged for the defence of liberty of conscience.
Cromwell boldly declared to the Earl of Manchester that seeing
the way the Scots behaved in pressing for the imposition of their
ecclesiastical discipline upon England, 'he could as soon draw
his sword against them as against any in the King's army'. He
confessed too that he desired to have none but Independents in
Manchester's army, so that 'in case there should be propositions
for peace, or any conclusion of peace, such as might not stand
with those ends honest men should aim at, this army might
prevent such a mischief'.[2]

The crisis passed away. Whilst the King was unconquered his
opponents could not afford to turn their arms against each other,

[1] Baillie, *Letters*, ed. Laing, ii, 268, 274, 293.
[2] *Camden Miscellany*, vol. viii.

whatever their mutual provocations might be. For the same reason the New Model army during the first two years or eighteen months of its life, abstained from any direct intervention in political questions. Besides this, at the beginning it was not the homogeneous army which it subsequently became.[1] Time and companionship in arms worked for unity and unanimity. As the adherents of independency were numerous, powerful, and zealous, the whole army became permeated with their ideas, and the majority of officers and men adopted their way of thinking. The progress of independency meant the spread of democratic principles, for 'Church-democracy' led by a natural sequence to 'State-democracy'. Thus agreement in politics accompanied agreement in religion, and by 1647 sufficient community of ideas existed to form a basis for joint action in public affairs. Moreover, in the minds of many members of the army, victory had fostered the belief that they had a mission to fulfil in the settlement which must follow the war. 'They plainly showed me,' says Baxter, 'that they thought God's providence would cast the trust of religion and the kingdom upon them as conquerors.'[2] The desire to intervene might never have ripened into action, the soldiers might have laid down their arms first and turned politicians afterwards, but for the unwisdom of the Parliamentary leaders. As it was, the unfairness of their scheme of disbanding the army roused an opposition which their persistence converted into a revolt. They supplied a grievance which touched every man in the ranks, and created unanimity; an opportunity which fired the hopes of the dreamer and woke the ambition of the self-seeker.

As soon as the revolt of the army took place its leaders were obliged to devise some machinery by means of which its opinion might be correctly ascertained and formally expressed. The elements of this machinery lay ready to hand. In the spring of 1647, when the Parliamentary leaders were endeavouring to persuade the army to disband and to take service for the reconquest of Ireland, their propositions were laid before gatherings of officers, and these gatherings claimed the right to speak for the army. These assemblages are indifferently described as 'a Con-

---

[1] See pp. 317–21.

[2] *Reliquiæ Baxterianæ*, p. 51.

vention of Officers' or 'a Council of War'.[1] The distinction between the two is not apparent. At both officers of all ranks down
to quartermasters and ensigns were present.[2] When the Commissioners of the Parliament came to the headquarters at Saffron
Walden on 15th April 1647 about two hundred officers were
collected to meet them. When Major-General Skippon and other
commissioners came a month later there were 'not above 30
officers of horse, and about 150 of foot'.[3] It is probable that these
'conventions' represented the old Council of War reinforced by
the addition of the subalterns, which would account for their
keeping the old name.

Meanwhile the private soldiers, thinking their officers slack in
representing their grievances, and determined to make their
views on the subject known, were meeting and choosing representatives. At the end of April 1647 eight regiments drew up a
letter to their generals. The troopers who presented it confessed
on examination that the letter 'was drawn up first at a rendezvous of several of those regiments and afterwards they had
meetings about it by agents from each regiment'.[4] Next month
the foot followed the example of the horse. 'The committee of
troopers met at St Edmundsbury, and the foot, who chose two
out of every company, sent them to confer with the troopers,
and every foot soldier gave fourpence apiece towards defraying
the charges of that meeting.'[5] The third step which followed
almost immediately was the election of a smaller body representing the privates of the whole army both horse and foot. In
the 'Solemn Engagement of the Army', of 5th June 1647, it is
declared that the soldiers finding their petition to their general
suppressed by Parliament, and their officers proceeded against
by it for taking their part, 'were enforced to an unusual (but in
that case necessary) way of correspondence and agreement
amongst themselves, to choose out of the several troops and
companies several men, and those out of the whole number, to
choose two or more for each regiment, to act in the name and
behalf of the whole soldiery of the respective troops and

---

[1] See the *Book of Army Declarations*, etc., published by Matthew Simmons in Sept. 1647 (164 pp., 4to), pp. 2, 17.

[2] Ibid., pp. 15, 20.   [3] *Clarke Papers*, i, 7, 29; cf. pp. 108, 111.

[4] *Clarke Papers*, i, 430; Rushworth, vi, 474.   [5] Rushworth, vi, 485.

companies'.[1] These representatives were the famous 'Agitators', which word meant simply agents, and had none of the sinister significance which modern usage has given it.

The final step was the fusion of the body representing the soldiers with the body representing the officers. The refusal of the army to disband, the seizure of the King by Cornet Joyce, and the decision of Fairfax and Cromwell to throw in their lot with the army against the Parliament, and to secure the redress of their grievances and the settlement of the nation by force, if force was needed, necessitated the establishment of some body qualified to direct the public action of the army. The result was the erection of the 'General Council of the Army'. This was defined in the 'Engagement' of 5th June as 'a Council to consist of those general officers of the army (who have concurred with the army in the premises) with two commission officers and two soldiers to be chosen for each regiment, who have concurred and shall concur with us in the premises and in this agreement'. They were to meet in council 'when they shall be thereunto called by the general'.[2] The army at the same time took a solemn pledge that it would not 'willingly disband or divide, or suffer itself to be disbanded or divided', until it obtained satisfaction for the past and security for the future. The Council was to determine on behalf of the army when these conditions were fulfilled.[3]

[1] Engagement of the Army, 5th June 1647; Simmons, *Book of Army Declarations*.

[2] Ibid.

[3] The advantages of this union were obvious. It secured a certain amount of unanimity in the army and put a stop to the separate and independent action of the Agitators. The following extract from a letter dated 17th July 1647 shows that these results were attained:

'Yesterday there was a great Councill of Warre call'd, it held till 12 a clock at night, consisted of above 100 Officers, besides Agitators, who now in prudence we admitt to debate; and it is not more than necessary they should be, considering the influence they have upon the souldiers, and the officer we hope hath such interest in them, as if any of more fierce disposition amongst them moderate not their reason, the officers can command it; and I assure you, it is the singularest part of wisdom in the General and the officers so to carry themselves considering the present temper of the Army, so as to be unanimous in Councills, including the new persons into their number. It keeps a good accord, and obtains ready obedience, for to this hour never any troop or company yet mutiny'd, and if a man consider the alterations of officers that are now admitted, and interests of officers that are gone, it is the greatest wonder, that there is unanimity still.' It was debated, the writer goes on to say, whether the army should not march nearer

The demand for security for the future necessarily led to direct interference in the political settlement of the kingdom. For the soldiers held that they could not be secure if the King was restored to his authority without proper restrictions, or the Parliament left in possession of the unlimited powers it had abused. 'All wise men may see,' declared the army, 'that Parliament privileges as well as royal prerogative may be perverted or abused to the destruction of those greater ends for whose protection and preservation they were intended, to wit, the rights and privileges of the people and the safety of the whole'.[1] This distrust of an unlimited Parliament, which is easily explained by the circumstances of the moment, is the key to the political history of the army.

To justify the claim to be heard in the settlement of the kingdom the army argued that it was not like other armies. 'We were not a mere mercenary army, hired to serve any arbitrary power of state, but called forth and conjured by the several declarations of Parliament, to the defence of our own and the people's just rights and liberties.'[2] 'As Englishmen,' added another of their manifestoes, 'and surely our being soldiers hath not stript us of that interest, though our malicious enemies would have it so, we desire a settlement of the peace of the kingdom and the liberties of the subject, according to the votes and declarations of Parliament; which, before we took up arms, were by the Parliament used as arguments and inducements to invite us and divers of our dear friends out; some of which have lost their lives in this war; which being by God's blessing finished, we think we have as much right to demand and desire to see a happy settlement, as we have to our money and the other common interest of soldiers, which we have insisted upon.'[3]

---

to London. 'Tho' this was much prest with reasons and earnestness by the Agitators, yet the Generall and the Officers after many hours debate so satisfyed them with arguments and reasons to the contrary, that they submitted it to the General and Officers, no man gainsaying it' (*Clarke Papers*, i, 215).

[1] Army Remonstrance of 23rd June 1647.

[2] A Representation of the Army, etc., *Old Parliamentary History*, xv, 459.

[3] Ibid., xv, 432. From the Letter to the City, 10th June 1647, which Carlyle, probably with justice, attributes to Cromwell.

The best justification of the conduct of the army, however, did not lie in these arguments and distinctions, but in the danger of a new Civil War in case the Presbyterian leaders in Parliament were allowed to carry out their plans.[1] As it was, after nearly two months spent in abortive negotiations between the army and the Parliament, the army occupied London and drove the Presbyterian leaders into exile. Just before it occupied London (1st August 1647) the army published its scheme for the settlement of the kingdom. The 'Heads of the Proposals of the Army', as the scheme was termed, was in the main the work of Commissary-General Ireton, but it had been revised by a committee of the Council of the Army, and accepted by the Council itself. As its title showed, it was not the draught of a new constitution to be imposed by the army upon the nation, but a series of propositions meant to serve as the basis of negotiations and to show the nation what kind of settlement the army desired. Its chief characteristic was that it aimed at permanently limiting not only the power of the King but also the power of the Parliament, and therefore it naturally failed to commend itself to either.[2]

During the autumn of 1647 a serious division of opinion began to reveal itself in the army. The Agitators, and many of the inferior officers, were far more democratic in their views than their leaders. The 'Heads of the Proposals' embodied a plan for making Parliament more truly representative by a moderate extension of the franchise and a redistribution of seats on a more equitable basis. The democratic party both within and without the army demanded manhood suffrage. At the same time there were loud complaints not only against the policy pursued by the military leaders in the negotiations with King and Parliament, but against the predominant influence they, and the superior officers in general, exercised in the deliberations of the army. The General's Council of War continued to exist side by side with the new Council of the Army, and was accused of usurping authority which properly belonged to the latter. John Lilburne, the leader of the democratic party outside the army, asserted that Cromwell, by his unjust 'subtlety and shifting tricks', had

---

[1] Cf. Gardiner, *Great Civil War*, iii, 259, 264.

[2] Ibid., 329–33; *Constitutional Documents*, p. 316.

robbed the honest Agitators of their power, 'and solely placed
it in a thing called a Council of War, or rather a Cabinet Junto
of seven or eight proud self-ended fellows'.[1] A second charge
was that the Council of the Army was not composed as according to the Engagement at Triploe Heath it should be. Cromwell
and Ireton, it was asserted, began 'to stomach the sitting of the
private soldiers in council with them . . . a council thus modelled
was not suitable to their wonted greatness and ambition; it was
somewhat of a scorn to them that a private soldier (though a
represener of a regiment) should sit cheek by jowl with them,
and have with an officer an equal vote in that council'. Accordingly, in order to promote their selfish ends, they had packed the
Council with officers, and it was 'over-swarmed with colonels,
lieut.-colonels, majors, captains, etc., contrary to and beyond
the tenour of the engagement'.[2] At the same time it was alleged
that the Agitators were systematically discouraged, with a view
to prevent them from exercising their rights as the political
representatives of their regiments.[3]

True or not, these charges would have had little effect but for
the discontent caused by the negotiations with the King, and

[1] Lilburne, *Jonah's Cry*, 1647, p. 9. Sir John Berkley noted as the result
of his observations: 'That the army was governed partly by a Council of
War, and partly by a Council of the Army, or Agitators, wherein the
General had but a single voice; that Fairfax the General had little power in
either; that Cromwell and his son Ireton, with their friends and partisans,
governed the Council of War absolutely, but not that of the Army, which
was the most powerful, though they had a strong party there also' (*Memoirs of Sir John Berkley*, ed. Maseres, i, 364). Clarendon speaks of 'The
General's Council of Officers' as forming something like a House of Lords,
and of an Assembly of Agitators which was like a House of Commons to the
Council of Officers, and says that the two bodies deliberated separately.
This is entirely erroneous if meant to describe the Council of the Army
(*Rebellion*, x, 83).

[2] *The Hunting of the Foxes*, 1649, *Somers' Tracts*, vi, 45; cf. *Clarke Papers*,
i, xlv. Though the tract quoted above was not printed till 1649, it expresses
the views which began to be circulated in the autumn of 1647.

[3] *The Case of the Army Stated* (p. 4, October 1647) asserts: 'In the prosecution of this breach there hath been many discouragements of the Adju-
tators of the regiments in consulting about the most effectual means for the
speedy redress of the people's grievances, and clearing and securing the
native rights of the army and all others the free Commons. It hath been
instilled into them that they ought not to meddle with those matters,
thereby to induce them to betray the trust the regiments reposed in them,
and for that purpose the endeavours of some hath been to pursuade the
soldiers that their Agitators have meddled with more than concerned
them.' It will be observed that 'Agitator' and 'Adjutator' are here used as
synonyms.

the fear of his restoration to power upon unsatisfactory terms. As it was, at the beginning of October 1647 the discontent of the democratic party amongst the soldiers became uncontrollable. Five regiments of horse, on the pretext that the Agitators who represented them were incapable or false to their trust, elected fresh representatives, known by the name of the 'New Agents'.[1] These Agents, in conjunction with the leaders of the democratic party outside the army, drew up a scheme of settlement called 'The Agreement of the People,' and published a manifesto called 'The Case of the Army Truly Stated'. In them they demanded manhood suffrage, equal electoral divisions, biennial Parliaments, and by implication the abolition of monarchy and the House of Lords. All authority was to be henceforth vested in the House of Commons, save that certain rights, such as freedom of conscience, freedom from impressment, and equality before the law, were declared to be the 'native rights' of all Englishmen which no Parliament could diminish or take away.[2]

This sketch of a constitution together with the accompanying manifesto was presented to the General and to the Council on 28th October 1647, with the request that it should be accepted by them and recommended to the nation for adoption. The debates which followed are fortunately very fully reported.[3]

[1] *A Declaration of the officers and soldiers of Col. Whalley's Troop against the New Agents,* published about the middle of November, says: 'Upon several informations that those formerly employed by us did more consult their own advancement than the publick settlement, we were induced, about the 19th of October last, to make choice of two new Agitators for a Regiment; not, in the least manner, intending that they should presume to usurp authority over the General, the Council of War, the old Agitators, or over the kingdom, or over us, so as to appoint conventions at their own pleasure, and then to compose, and publish in print to the world, strange and unheard-of Fancies, and frame Ideas of their own brain, and bring them to us to father. But the authority we derived upon them, was only to act according to our first-engaged Principles, with the Consent and Advice of the General, the Council of War, and the Agitators first elected – to clear those things that seemed dubious unto us; to prevent misinformations; to endeavour to facilitate things that appeared difficult; to make us intelligent subjects what progress had been made in order to our first engagement and representations to the Parliament, and to improve their best assistance to remove such obstructions as did any way impede the just and legal proceedings the Army' (Maseres, *Tracts,* lxv).

[2] See Gardiner, *Great Civil War,* iii, 378, 386; Borgeaud, *Rise of Modern Democracy,* p. 67.

[3] *Clarke Papers,* i, 226–418. For earlier debates, see pp. 176–214.

These reports, apart from their value as illustrations of the development of certain political ideas in England, supply the best evidence extant as to the usual procedure of the Council.

Its deliberations were not unfrequently preceded by a prayer-meeting in which officers themselves prayed and exhorted. A debate usually ended with the appointment of a committee to prepare business for the next meeting, and it is evident that a very large and important part of the business of the Council was transacted in these committees. When the General was present at the Council meetings he always presided, but Fairfax hardly ever spoke, and was apparently rather an inefficient chairman. The spokesmen of the superior officers were usually Lieut.-General Cromwell and Commissary-General Ireton, both of whom were able and effective debaters, but a large number of officers of all ranks habitually took part in the discussion. The 'Agitators', with the exception of two or three men of superior ability, such as Sexby and Allen, seem to have taken little part in debate, and probably confined themselves to voting.[1] There were, however, a number of inferior officers who represented the same shade of political opinion, and one at least amongst the superior officers. The latter, Colonel Rainborowe, was practically the leader of the Democratic party in the Council. Whilst the 'Agreement of the People' was before the Council one of the civilian allies of the 'New Agents', named John Wildman, was allowed to assist as their mouthpiece and representative.[2]

It is clear from the discussion about the 'Agreement of the People' that after the treaty with the King the question of manhood suffrage was the matter which the soldiers had most at heart. In theory they held that the suffrage was the right of every freeborn Englishman; in fact they regarded it as a right they had acquired by fighting for English freedom. Hence the indignation with which Sexby and others heard Ireton and Cromwell's arguments that the suffrage was a right attached

[1] The Agitators were generally sensible enough to be aware of their own deficiencies. 'I am but a poor man,' says one, 'and unacquainted with the affairs of the kingdom.' 'I suppose it is not unknowne to you,' says another, 'that wee are most of us but young statesmen, and not well able to judge how longe such things which wee heare now read to us may bee to the ends for which they are presented' (*Clarke Papers*, i, pp. 213, 286).

[2] Wildman was pretty certainly the author of *The Case of the Army Truly Stated*.

to the possession of property. 'We have engaged . . . and ventured our lives,' cried Sexby, 'and it was for all this; to recover our birthrights and privileges as Englishmen, and by the arguments urged there is none. There are many thousands of us soldiers that have ventured our lives; we have had little property in the kingdom as to our estates, yet we have had a birthright. But it seems now except a man hath a fixed estate in this kingdom he hath no right in this kingdom. I wonder we were so much deceived. If we had not a right in the kingdom we were mere mercenary soldiers. There are many in my condition, . . . it may be little estate they have at present, and yet they have as much a right as those two who are their law-givers,[1] or as any in this place.'[2]

Colonel Rainborowe backed up Sexby. 'I would fain know,' said he, 'what the soldier hath fought for all this while?' He went on to argue that unless the political rights of the soldier were recognized in the settlement, 'he hath fought to enslave himself, to give power to men of riches and men of estates to make him a perpetual slave'.[3]

After several days spent in excited debating a compromise was arrived at. Though the Council of the Army refused to adopt the 'Agreement' as the official programme of the army, it amended in a democratic direction the new proposals it was preparing to lay before Parliament, and introduced amongst them a request that the franchise should be given to all soldiers who had fought for the cause.[4] The compromise failed to satisfy the Levellers (as the advanced Democrats began to be called), and they resolved to appeal from the Council of the Army to the soldiers themselves. Under pretext that the pledge not to divide the army contained in the Triploe Heath Engagement had been broken by its separation into different quarters, they demanded that there should be a general rendezvous of the whole army.[5] At this rendezvous they hoped to get the 'Agreement' adopted by acclamation, and then to proceed to impose it upon Parliament and the nation. Ireton pointed out in reply that the real dividers of the army were those who were seeking to stir up a mutiny in

---

[1] Referring to Cromwell and Ireton.   [2] *Clarke Papers*, i, 323.

[3] Ibid., 325.   [4] Ibid., 366.   [5] Ibid., i, 346.

it. The real dividing, said he, is 'that dividing which makes no army'. The 'dissolving of that order and government which is as essential to an army as life is to a man—which if it be taken away such a company of men is no more an army than a rotten carcase is a man'.[1] Cromwell pointed out that the insubordination encouraged by the conduct of the 'New Agents' would be 'destructive to the army and to every particular man in the army'. The army therefore must 'conform to the rules of war' and be obedient to its general, and it must also conform itself to its proper sphere, leave Parliament to decide 'what is fit for the kingdom,' and content itself with requiring that Parliament should be properly composed. A few days later Cromwell proposed and carried a motion that the sittings of the Council should be temporarily suspended, and that the representative officers and the Agitators should be sent back to their regiments for the present (8th November 1647).[2]

A week later Fairfax held a rendezvous of the army, but not such an one as the Levellers demanded. It met in three divisions, on successive days, in three separate places. At each of these gatherings Fairfax published, on behalf of himself and the Army Council, an address declaring that he would lay down his command unless discipline were restored. He was willing to remain at his post, however, 'and to live and die with the army' in obtaining the redress of certain specified military grievances and the adoption of reforms which would make the House of Commons, 'as near as may be, an equal representative of the people that are to elect'. Other things must be left to the determination of Parliament, but the army might represent its desires and mediate for the redress of grievances. He concluded by requiring from the officers and soldiers of every regiment a signed engagement to accept these conditions. 'We shall,' it said, 'according to the General Engagement of the Army . . . acquiesce in what shall be agreed unto by the General Council of the Army' as to the military and political questions specified. 'And for the matter of ordering, conduct, and government of the army we shall be observant of and subject to his Excellency and his Council of War, and every one of us to our superior officers in

---

[1] *Clarke Papers*, i, 348.
[2] Ibid., i, 369–71, 412.

this regiment and the army, according to the discipline of
war.'[1]

This decisive action was immediately successful. The new engagement was accepted by the whole army. Only at the first
rendezvous, that which took place at Ware, was there any sign
of opposition. Two regiments appeared there unsummoned, with
copies of the Agreement of the People stuck in their hats. Cromwell made them tear the papers out of their hats, and had a
recalcitrant ringleader tried and shot upon the field. All the other
regiments present obediently submitted, and disavowed the
'New Agents' to whose proceedings these disturbances were due.[2]

When the General Council of the Army met at Windsor after
the adjournment, the restoration of discipline was followed by a
general reconciliation of opposing parties in the army. A certain
number of officers and men were tried for their share in the late
disorders, but as a rule 'upon their acknowledgment of their rash
and irregular proceedings, and promise to submit to the discipline of the army for the time to come,' they were pardoned and
dismissed.[3] For a time the Council refrained from political discussion. An address setting forth the grievances of the army with
reference to pay and disbanding was drawn up and presented
(7th December 1647).[4] When the House of Commons resolved
that no further addresses should be made to the King and undertook to settle the nation without him, the Council warmly approved its votes, and presented a declaration to that purpose.[5]
Thus, instead of seeking to dictate the policy to be adopted by
Parliament, it contented itself for the present with supporting
what Parliament determined. This declaration was the last public act of the General Council of the Army. 'To-morrow,' says a
news-letter, dated 3rd January 1648, 'all the council that met
this day are to dine with the General in Windsor Castle, to con-
gratulate the unity of the army, and to take their leaves of each
other before they be dispersed into the several garrisons and

[1] A Remonstrance from his Excellency Sir Thomas Fairfax and his
Council of War, etc., 14th November 1647, *Old Parliamentary History*,
xvi, 340.

[2] Maseres, *Select Tracts*, i, lv.

[3] Rushworth, vii, 922, 937, 940, 942–3.

[4] *Old Parliamentary History*, xvi, 370, 474.

[5] Ibid., xvi, 494–8.

great towns.'¹ So ended the attempt to introduce representative
government into the army. The experiment had been successful
in tiding over the crisis caused by the general military revolt of
May 1647. It answered so long as the representatives of the rank
and file were content to accept the political leadership of their
officers. But when a deep division of opinion revealed itself and
parties began to be formed in the army, the perils of the system
became manifest. For this reason the experiment was never tried
again, and all the assemblies which thereafter spoke in the name
of the army were entirely composed of officers.

In October 1648, after the conclusion of the second Civil
War, while the Commissioners of Parliament were treating with
Charles the First at Newport, political excitement again rose
high in the army. Regiment after regiment presented its petition
to the General, demanding justice against all responsible for the
war without respect of persons.² In November a General Council
of Officers met at St Albans and drew up a Remonstrance which
was presented to the House of Commons on 20th November.³
It demanded that the King should be brought to justice, and
his sons declared incapable of succeeding to the government. It
embodied also the old proposals for biennial Parliaments, equal
constituencies, and the speedy dissolution of the existing House
of Commons. As the House delayed its answer and proceeded
with the treaty, the army seized the King at Newport and
marched on London.⁴ The intention of the military leaders
originally was to dissolve by force the existing Parliament and
to call a new one as soon as possible. They were persuaded, however, by their friends in the House, to content themselves with
the exclusion of all Royalist members, or rather of all those who
had voted that the King's concessions during the treaty were a
satisfactory basis for a peace. The result was 'Pride's Purge', by
which about 140 members were either arrested or prevented
from sitting.⁵ The independent minority who remained behind
at the instigation of the army proceeded to establish a High

¹ Rushworth, vii, 959, 961.
² Cf. the petitions of the regiments of Ireton and Ingoldsby (Rushworth,
vii, 1297, 1311).
³ Ibid., 1318, 1320, 1324, 1330; cf. Gardiner, *Great Civil War*, iv, 236–45.
⁴ *Clarke Papers*, ii, 54, 58, 61, 67.
⁵ Gardiner, *Great Civil War*, iv, 263, 269.

Court of Justice for the trial of the King, and prepared to turn England into a republic.

Meanwhile the Council of Officers busied itself in discussing the constitution of the new State. For about a month these discussions continued, and on 20th January 1649 the result, embodied in a draft constitution bearing the familiar name of 'The Agreement of the People', was presented to Parliament.[1] This 'Agreement' was a far more detailed and more comprehensive scheme than that which the 'New Agents' and their allies had put forward in the autumn of 1647. On the other hand, instead of circulating the Agreement for signature amongst the people, and compelling Parliament to adopt it by force, as the Levellers both in 1647 and in 1649 had demanded, the Council limited itself to submitting the scheme to the Parliament with a request that it might be considered and, if the House thought fit, tendered to the nation. 'We desire,' said they, 'that with all the expedition which the immediate and pressing great affairs will admit, it may receive your most mature consideration and resolutions upon it; not that we desire either the whole, or what you shall like in it, should be by your authority imposed as a law upon the kingdom, for so it would lose the intended nature of an Agreement of the People, but that so far as it concurs with your own judgments, it may receive your seal of approbation only.'[2] In short, the form of government which the army had devised was to be established by the common consent of all supporters of the cause, not by military force.

Extremists both within and without the Council were dissatisfied with this result. The army, said some of the officers, ought to take in hand the settlement of the nation itself instead of leaving it to the Parliament. 'I must entreat your Excellency,' said one, 'whom the Lord hath clearly called unto the greatest work of righteousness that ever was amongst men, that your Excellency and the Council go not to shift of that work which the Lord hath called to you.' But with the majority of the officers the view that they were bound by their previous declarations not to seek power for themselves prevailed over this theory of their providential mission. They inserted in the Agreement a

[1] *Clarke Papers*, ii, xv–xxii.

[2] *Old Parliamentary History*, xv, 518.

provision that the present Parliament should be dissolved in April 1649, but when the time came they acquiesced in its continuance.[1]

A still larger party was dissatisfied with the substance of the Agreement, not merely with the method in which it was promulgated. The original draft had been the result of the deliberations of a joint committee representing all sections of the democratic party. Lilburne and other leaders of the Levellers had taken a very active and important part in drawing it up, and were angered by the refusal of the Council of Officers to adopt their scheme in its entirety, and still more by the alterations and amendments which the Council had introduced.[2] In printed pamphlets and petitions they attacked the composition of the Council of Officers, and denounced the exclusion of representatives of the soldiers from its deliberations. They denied its title to speak on behalf of the army, and contrasted it with the old 'General Council of the Army', whose revival they demanded. 'No transacting by Cromwell, Ireton and their officers,' said one of these pamphlets, 'though in the name of the General Council of the Army, will be accounted or imputed to the act of the army; for it is no general council, neither doth it represent the army, neither hath it the authority or commission of the army therein, for it is another council, differing from that of the Engagement of the Army. That was by election, this is by force and obtrusion; in that the soldiery were represented, in this only the officers; that is to consist of those general officers concurring with the Engagement, two commissioned officers and two soldiers chosen out of every regiment; this is only a Council of War whose power doth extend to no transaction in the name of the army as commoners, but only to matters of war as soldiers.'[3] As usual, Lilburne and his friends proceeded to incite the soldiers to mutiny, and urged them to present their petitions directly to Parliament instead of to their general. In answer to this the Council, on 22nd February 1649, imposed certain restrictions upon the right of petitioning in the army. The soldiers

---

[1] *Clarke Papers*, ii, 170, 181–6.

[2] Ibid., 254; see also Preface, pp. xv–xviii.

[3] *Somers' Tracts*, vi, 47, from *The Hunting of the Foxes from Newmarket and Triploe Heaths to Whitehall*; cf. also the first and second parts of *England's New Chains Discovered*, 1649, 4to.

of any troop or company might petition if they found themselves
in any way aggrieved, but each regiment must petition separately. Petitions must be 'first offered to the captain of the troop
or company and then to the chief officer in the regiment, and
from him to the general to be presented to the Parliament, and
in case the officers should refuse them, to present it to the general
themselves'.[1] On 1st March five troopers presented Fairfax and
the Council of Officers with a protest against these restrictions,
under the form of a petition. 'In the point of petitioning,' said
they, 'we expected your encouragement, and not to have man-
acles and fetters laid upon it; it is not the bare name or shadow
thereof will satisfy us, while we are gulled of the essence of
itself; it is a perfect freedom therein we desire, not therein to
be subjected under the gradual negative voices of a captain,
a colonel, your excellency, or this council; to pass the test from
one negative voice to another for its approvement we account
as the most vexatious labyrinth of thraldom that in this point
can be devised. . . . We had rather that in plain terms you would
deny us our right of petitioning, and pronounce and proclaim us
absolute slaves and vassals to our officers than secretly to rob
us of the right itself.'[2] The Council naturally declared the petition
seditious, and severely punished its promoters. Nevertheless the
result was the rising which took place in May 1649, and was
suppressed, at Burford. The demand for complete freedom of
petition and for the re-establishment of the General Council of
the Army formed part of the programme of the mutineers.

From the beginning of the Scottish war in the summer of 1650
to its conclusion in September 1651 the army was too busily
engaged in its proper business of fighting to have much time to
think of politics. When peace was restored they once more began
to intervene in the settlement of the nation. A Royalist writing
early in 1653 says: 'In regard that the whole army at present
have nothing to do . . . all the chief officers are at London who
meet in a grand council, called the Council of the Army, every
Tuesday and Thursday.'[3]

As usual the movement commenced with a petition. On 13th
August 1652 Commissary-General Whalley and five other

---

[1] *Clarke Papers*, ii, 191.

[2] *Somers' Tracts*, vi, 53.   [3] *English Historical Review*, 1893, p. 530.

officers appeared before Parliament with 'The humble Petition of the Officers of the Army,'[1] setting forth some dozen reforms which they desired the House to carry into effect with all possible speed. But for Cromwell's restraining influence they would probably have included in their list a demand for an immediate dissolution of Parliament.[2] The House, as usual, thanked the officers, but did little, and during the winter of 1652 and the spring of 1653 the impatience of the army increased and the movement for intervention grew stronger. There were all the usual signs which presaged a storm. There were frequent meetings of the Council, and long prayer-meetings in which, as the phrase ran, the officers 'waited upon God' and 'confessed their sins'. A news-letter in January 1653 significantly says: 'The officers have been seeking God two days: the Grandees fear a design in hand,'[3] Then came the despatch of a series of circular letters to the regiments stationed in Scotland, Ireland and remote parts of England, which were a necessary preliminary to concerted action. Cromwell endeavoured to check the movement, and sought to effect a compromise with Parliament. When the compromise failed, owing to what he considered the bad faith of some of the Parliamentary leaders, he too lost his patience, and putting himself at the head of the movement, called in a few files of musketeers and put a stop to the sittings of the House.

The revolution of 20th April 1653 made the army the government of England. Hitherto it had contented itself with influencing and at times dictating the votes of the House; now it exercised the supreme power directly instead of indirectly. But it had no intention of retaining this power, and claimed to be merely a provisional government. Before the Parliament was expelled the army had urged it to devolve the supreme authority upon some select number of 'men fearing God and of approved integrity', and to commit the government of the Commonwealth to them for a time. Since Parliament had refused to do this the army announced that it would carry out the scheme itself, and

[1] *Mercurius Politicus*, 12th–19th August 1652, p. 1803.

[2] Gardiner, *Commonwealth and Protectorate*, ii, 168.

[3] *English Historical Review*, 1893, pp. 527–8; Gardiner, *Commonwealth and Protectorate*, ii, 176, 178.

'call to the government persons of approved fidelity and honesty'.[1] Until such persons could be got together, 'for preventing the mischiefs and inconveniences which may arise in the meanwhile to the public affairs', a Council of State was appointed 'to take care of and intend the peace, safety, and present management of the affairs of this Commonwealth'.[2] The councillors so appointed were thirteen in number, and nine of them were officers. While these thirteen men, with the General at their head, carried on the daily business of administration, the Council of Officers debated the nature and the composition of the body to which their temporary authority was to be transferred. Some were for a small council of ten or twelve; some for a council of seventy persons, something like the Jewish Sanhedrim.[3] In the end it was resolved to select about 140 Puritan notables to represent the people of the three nations. Letters were sent to the Independent Churches in each county asking them to suggest the names of suitable men, and the names proposed were debated and voted upon. 'In the choice of which persons such indifference was used, and so equal liberty allowed to all then present with the General, that every officer enjoyed the same freedom of nomination and the majority of suffrages carried it for the election of each single member.'[4] They were then summoned by writs, which stated that they, being 'persons fearing God and of approved fidelity and honesty', had been nominated by Cromwell as commander-in-chief, with the advice and consent of his Council of Officers, to take upon themselves the trust of governing the State. With their meeting on 4th July, and the transference of authority to them by a signed indenture, the rule of the army ended. It had lasted rather more than ten weeks.

This assembly of nominees which assumed the style and claimed the rights of a Parliament failed to give satisfaction to the men who had called it into being. On 12th December 1653 a majority of their number were induced to abdicate their power. In the next three days the Council of Officers drew up

[1] Declaration of 22nd April 1653, *Old Parliamentary History*, xx, 140, 142.

[2] Declaration of 30th April, *The Perfect Politician*, p. 176.

[3] Ludlow, *Memoirs*, i, 358.

[4] Ibid., 359; Gardiner, *Commonwealth and Protectorate*, ii, 224, 230.

the constitution known as the 'Instrument of Government', and on 16th December the commander-in-chief, having accepted the limitations it imposed on his power, was installed as Protector. Thus within the short space of eight months the army had imposed upon England first a Council of State, next a Parliament, and lastly a new constitution.

While it retained power in its own hands it had ruled well, but the vice was in the origin of its power, not in the manner of its exercise. Recognizing the objections to military rule, and anxious to show what its general termed 'the integrity of divesting the sword of all power in the civil administration',[1] it had sought to establish a civil government. But it was all one to the nation whether the army governed directly or indirectly, whether the Council of Officers ruled England itself through a nominee or through an assembly of nominees. However it might be disguised by the forms and ceremonies of constitutionalism, the Protectorate rested almost entirely on the support of the army and represented military rule.[2] Hence it was never heartily accepted by more than a section of the nation, though there was an increasing tendency to acquiesce in its authority on the part of the rest.

As usual the army in general supported the policy of its leaders and expressed its support by addresses. It had hailed the expulsion of the Long Parliament by a unanimous chorus of approval and congratulation.[3] It approved the foundation of the Protectorate by similar addresses, but welcomed it with less enthusiasm and less spontaneity. The Council of Officers sitting at Whitehall sent out a circular letter to the regiments quartered in different parts of the kingdom and to the armies of Ireland and Scotland inviting their co-operation. 'Ourselves,' said they, 'and the officers and soldiers that now reside in and about the headquarters, have thought it our duty to strengthen the hands of his Highness, as much as in us lieth, and for that purpose have

[1] Carlyle, *Cromwell*, Speech i.

[2] Cf. Gardiner, *Commonwealth and Protectorate*, ii, 293.

[3] See the 'Humble Remonstrance of the General Council of Officers met at Dalkeith, 5 May 1653, on behalf of themselves and the Forces in Scotland', *Old Parliamentary History*, xx, 145; cf. *Scotland and the Commonwealth*, p. 129. Vol. xxv of the *Clarke MSS.* contains many addresses from individual regiments in Scotland, and the English newspapers testify to the approval of the regiments in England.

made our address in the form herewith sent unto you, which
we thought good to communicate to you, to the end you also
may join with us in so good and necessary a work.'[1] The army
in Scotland responded by signing the proposed address; that in
Ireland seems to have preferred a form of its own.[2]

But just as the expulsion of the Long Parliament had created
a breach between the civil and military elements of the Republican party,[3] so the institution of the Protectorate caused a
division in the army itself, and that division grew gradually
wider. Some officers, notably Major-General Harrison, refused
to serve under the new government. John Wigan, major of
Cromwell's own regiment of foot, declined to sign the address to
the Protector and lost his commission.[4] Others, while disapprov-

[1] See *A True Catalogue of the Several Places and Most Eminent Persons by
Whom Richard Cromwell was Proclaimed Protector*, 1657, 4to, p. 98. The
author gives the following account of the origin of this address in December
1653: 'The foresaid Address thus drawn up by the five or six persons, who
projected and design'd the Protectoral Government, being sent to the
several Regiments about the City, and Headquarters to be signed, as if it
had in the first place been drawn up, and signed freely by themselves,
undesired by any. The following Letter was likewise drawn up at *White
Hall*, and sent with the same Address inclosed in it to the several Regiments
in the Countreys, and also into *Scotland* and *Ireland* to be signed in like
manner, thereby to hold forth to the world, (and as an Example or Shooing-
horn to draw on others to do the like,) that the Armies desired him their
General, to take the Protectoral Government upon him; when as in truth
there was no such thing.'

[2] See *Scotland and the Protectorate*, p. 10. An address from the Irish army,
without a date, but probably belonging to this time, is printed in Nickolls's
Original Letters and Papers Addressed to Cromwell, p. 144.

[3] The most serious result of the conduct of the army in 1653, so far as the
prosperity of the common cause was concerned, was the lasting division it
created amongst the Republican party. Cromwell, declared John Lilburne
and his followers, had committed high treason against his lords the people
of England, 'being a hired servant to serve the lords the people of England
in the conduct of their the said lords the people of England's Army, against
the enemies of the said people's liberties, rights and privileges'. He ought to
have summoned a free Parliament after the expulsion of the old one, instead of an assembly of his nominees. He had committed the highest
treason possible, 'for that he the said Oliver did not intreat the lords the
people of England to elect their representative according to their indubit-
able rights, and that he would with their army stand by them as their
servants, as in duty he and they ought to have done'. Somewhat similar in
its nature was the objection of another Republican, Sir Henry Vane.
Sovereignty, according to him, resided 'in the whole body of the people that
have adhered to the cause', whereas the army and its rulers had assumed it
to themselves, 'setting and keeping up themselves in a divided interest
from the rest of the body of honest men' (*Somers' Tracts*, vi, 299, 310).

[4] *A True Catalogue*, p. 7; *Cal. State Papers, Dom.*, 1658–9, p. 45.

ing the late change, grumbled but remained in the army. In the autumn of 1654 the discontent amongst the officers found vent in what was known as 'the petition of the three colonels'. Beginning with a reference to the declarations of the army in 1647 and 1648, it proceeded to attack the 'Instrument of Government' as giving the Protector an absolute power which the King had never possessed. It expatiated on the dangerous consequences of granting him complete control of the military forces of the nation. In the hands of a corrupt ruler the army might become 'wholly mercenary, and be made use of to destroy the very being of Parliaments'. The reputation of the army was tarnished by what its leaders had done. 'Our ears,' said the three colonels, 'are filled daily with the taunts, reproaches, and scandals upon the profession of honesty, under colour that we have pretended the freedoms of our country and made large professions against seeking our private interests, while we intended only to set up ourselves.' They concluded by demanding that the nation should be left to decide what form of constitution it wanted 'in a full and free parliament'. The answer to the petition was the arrest of its promoters and their trial by court-martial. Colonel Alured was cashiered, Colonel Okey was allowed to resign, Colonel Saunders, who submitted, retained his command for a time but lost his commission later.[1]

A constitution drawn up by a Parliament instead of one imposed by the Council of Officers was exactly what the Republicans were always demanding,[2] and the leaders of the army could not grant it without undoing their own work. The vast majority of the army supported the Protectorate, and the Council of Officers faithfully reflected their views. During the government of Cromwell the Council of Officers appeared little in public affairs. Its meetings are rarely mentioned in the newspapers. Now that the commander-in-chief was head of the State, assisted by a council half of whom were soldiers, the influence of military opinion was so powerful that its formal manifestation was

[1] For the text of the petition, see *Cal. State Papers, Dom.*, 1653–4, p. 302, where its date is wrongly given. It was printed 18th October 1654. See Gardiner, *Commonwealth and Protectorate*, iii, 52–8. Lieut.-General Ludlow was also concerned in circulating the petition, and lost his command in Ireland in consequence (*Memoirs*, i, 406).

[2] Cf. p. 66, note 3.

scarcely needed. At any important crisis, however, the Council
of Officers made its voice heard. It came together at St James's
in the autumn of 1654, at the time of the petition of the three
colonels, when Cromwell's first Parliament was seeking to extend
its powers at the expense of the Protector's. The Council supported the Protector, declaring that they would 'live and die
with him', and presented a petition which demanded the regulation of the law, the maintenance of liberty of conscience, the
abolition of tithes and other radical reforms. Above all, they
would have no tampering with the constitution they had imposed upon England. 'There is no question,' wrote Thurloe,
'but they will live and die to maintain the government as it is
now settled, and possibly they may be too severe upon that
point, not being willing to part with any tittle of it.'[1]

In February 1657, when the proposal to make Cromwell King
was being discussed by his second Parliament, the Council of
Officers again emerged from its obscurity.[2] As soon as they met
they declared 'the fears and jealousies that lay upon them in
relation to the Protector's alteration of his title'.[3] On 27th
February 1657 a hundred officers presented an address to
Cromwell, begging that 'his Highness would not harken to the
title King, because it was not pleasing to his army, and was
matter of scandal to the people of God, and of great rejoicing to
the enemy; that it was hazardous to his own person and of great
danger to the three nations, such an assumption making way
for Charles Stuart to come in again'. In reply, Cromwell, while
protesting his indifference to the title, which he held of no importance one way or the other, pointed out the political blunders
which since 1653 had been caused by the pressure of the officers.
'They had made him their drudge upon all occasions.' First by
forcing on the expulsion of the Long Parliament, next by calling
an assembly of their own nominees in its place, then by calling
for the dissolution of the Parliament of 1654, and lastly by
setting up the rule of the major-generals and summoning the

[1] Vaughan, *Protectorate of Cromwell*, i, 85, 87; *Clarke Papers*, iii, 10, 11,
13; Gardiner, *Commonwealth and Protectorate*, iii, 59, 60, 63.

[2] There was also a meeting of the Council in September 1656 to consider
the military situation (*Clarke Papers*, iii, 71).

[3] *Clarke Papers*, iii, 92.

Parliament now sitting. They were responsible for these errors, not he. After all these failures it was 'time to come to a settlement and lay aside arbitrary proceedings so unacceptable to the nation'. He concluded by arguing that the constitution they had made needed mending, and that they had better allow Parliament to amend it by erecting a second chamber to balance the Commons, by altering the tenure of the supreme magistracy, and perhaps by altering its title.[1] Cromwell talked so persuasively that the 'fears and jealousies' of the officers were calmed. 'His Highness,' says a news-letter, 'having spoken to them at large the other night, this day they sent a committee to wait upon his Highness, and to assure him of their satisfaction in his Highness, and of their resolution to acquiesce in what he should think to be for the good of these nations.' 'Most of the officers here,' adds another letter, 'are not only come to a contented subjection to what is doing but to a liking thereof.'[2] The majority were willing to accept a House of Lords and an hereditary Protectorate, but there was a minority who had an insuperable objection to the restoration of kingship. When Parliament continued to press Cromwell to accept the crown in spite of his scruples, their patience gave way.[3] On 8th May Lieut.-Colonel Mason presented a petition to the House, signed by thirty-six officers, denouncing monarchy and urging them to press the Protector no more. Whether Cromwell knew of this petition beforehand or not is uncertain; it is certain that he knew how strong the hostility amongst the officers to this proposal was, and the same day he finally and definitely gave his refusal. Some of the opposition printed the petition, and circulated it with a postscript 'inviting two out of each regiment to own and subscribe it', but the presenters of the petition disclaimed its publication, and the Council of Officers condemned the attempted agitation.[4]

In the spring of 1658 the army once more declared its confidence in the Protector and its support of his government. The

[1] *Clarke Papers*, iii, 94; Burton, *Diary*, i, 382. This is a free paraphrase based on the two versions of Cromwell's speech.

[2] Ibid., ii, 94, 96, 98.   [3] Ludlow, *Memoirs*, ii, 26.

[4] *Clarke Papers*, iii, 109; *Scotland and the Protectorate*, p. 354; Thurloe, vi, 291, 310.

N

sudden dissolution of Cromwell's second Parliament on 4th
February 1658 had been mainly caused by the fact that the
Republican opposition were tampering with the discontented
section in the army. To secure their support a petition was to be
presented to the House, which included, besides a declaration
against the new constitution, a demand that no officer should be
cashiered but by court-martial. The Protector anticipated its
presentation by dissolving Parliament, harangued a gathering
of 200 officers 'in a large discourse of about two hours', and
cashiered Major Packer and five other officers of his own regiment of horse who declared their dissatisfaction.[1] Lieut.-General
Fleetwood called the Council of Officers together and proposed
an address to the Protector, which was unanimously signed.[2]
'Notwithstanding,' asserted the address, 'the base calumnies
and lies your and our enemies have cast upon us, that your army
is divided, and much of it from yourself, we do remain, through
the mercy of God, firmly united one to another and all of us to
your Highness as our General and Chief Magistrate.'[3] Scotland
had anticipated the movement by a series of addresses from
individual regiments and garrisons, and the Irish army imitated
the example of that of England. Nevertheless this appearance
of agreement was only superficial. The dominating influence of
Cromwell was the only thing that held the army together. Even
during his life the split which began to show itself in 1654 had
grown wider and wider; when his life ended it became a breach
which could not be bridged over, and the disruption of the army
began.

On the evening of the day on which his father died Richard
Cromwell was proclaimed his successor. The Council of State
officially communicated the news to the Council of Officers, as
if the latter was also one of the constitutional authorities of the
State. The new Protector was at once presented with loyal addresses of the usual type both from the army and from every
regiment in it. The army urged him to continue his father's work
in carrying on 'that good old Cause and Interest of God and

[1] *Clarke Papers*, iii, 139, 140.   [2] Ibid., 143.

[3] *Mercurius Politicus*, 27th March 1658. In the Irish army there were
some dozen dissentients, notably Major Low, who lost his commission by
opposing the address (Thurloe, vii, 21, 56, 71–3, 107, 115, 142).

his people'. 'We hope,' they continued, 'that God will assist
us to make it known to your Highness and all the world that
we aim at no private interest nor ends of our own, but that we
shall be heartily and faithfully with you as we have been with
your father, to adventure our lives and all that is dear to us to
stand by you.'[1] Already, however, a dangerous agitation was
spreading in the army. On 7th September, four days after the
new Protector's accession, Thurloe told Henry Cromwell that
there were 'some secret murmurings in the army, as if his Highness were not general of the army as his father was; and would
look upon the army and him as divided, and as if the conduct of
the army should be elsewhere and in other hands'.[2] There was a
general desire to shake off the control of the civil power and to
make the army an *imperium in imperio,* or rather a rival power.
It found vent in secret cabals amongst the superior officers; by
the inferior officers it was openly manifested. Early in October
a great meeting of officers took place, in which a petition was
brought forward asking the Protector to appoint Lieut.-General
Fleetwood commander-in-chief with power to grant commissions
to all but field-officers. The movement was premature. Fleetwood himself tried to check it, and ordered the meeting to break
up. A week later the Protector made a conciliatory speech to the
officers, declining, however, to comply with their demands. The
officers seemed to acquiesce in the refusal, but the insubordination to which their unauthorized meeting testified was a sign
of danger.[3] 'How came these two or three hundred officers together?' wrote Henry Cromwell to Fleetwood. 'If they came of
their own heads, the being absent from their charge without
licence should have flown in their face, when they petitioned for
a due observance of martial discipline. If they were called
together, were they not also taught what to say and do? If they
were called was it with his Highness's privity? If they met without leave in so great a number were they told their error? I wish
with all my heart you were commander-in-chief of all the forces
in three nations; but I had rather have it done by his Highness's

[1] Presented 18th September 1658; *Mercurius Politicus,* 16th–23rd September, p. 844; *Clarke Papers,* iii, 164.

[2] Thurloe, vii, 374.

[3] Ibid., 434, 437, 447, 452; *Clarke Papers,* iii, 165.

especial grace and mere motion, than put upon you in a tu-
multuary unsoldierly way.'[1]

Fleetwood made but a weak reply to these home-thrusts. He
allowed things to take their course, and the agitation recom-
menced. Toward the end of October the officers began a series
of weekly meetings, on Fridays, at St James's. At first they met
'to seek God for a blessing upon the affairs of the nation, and
a very eminent spirit of prayer appeared among the officers'.
They prayed and expounded and 'had several conferences upon
places of Scripture', and for a time kept off politics. Finally they
'began to break out, and to hint at some alterations made in the
army, as if good men were put out and worse put in'.[2] What
they wanted, in short, was a veto on the Protector's choice of
officers. The meetings were stopped, and the agitation again
temporarily allayed. But when Parliament met its proceedings
roused the officers once more to action. The Republican opposition attacked all the acts of the late Protector's government, and
assailed the Petition and Advice; the majority while it recognized
Richard as Protector and gave a general support to the government, showed marked hostility to the army. The new House of
Lords, established in 1657, in accordance with the provisions of
the Petition and Advice, was denounced as containing too large
a military element. It contained many officers. Its members,
somebody said, had the control of nineteen regiments of horse
and foot. Many garrisons, besides the Tower of London, were in
their hands. 'Men of great place in the army,' it was asserted,
'are not fit to give laws in Parliament.'[3] At the beginning of
April 1659 Richard allowed the Council of Officers to meet
again. On the sixth the army presented an address to the Protector, complaining of the great extremities they were under for
want of their pay, and requesting him to press Parliament to
vote supplies. They also complained of the increasing boldness
of the Royalist party, of the imminent danger of the 'Good Old
Cause,' and, without timely action, of its impending ruin. Not
obscurely they hinted at a new Pride's Purge, saying they were
ready to stand by and assist his Highness 'in the plucking the

[1] Thurloe, vii, 500.

[2] *Clarke Papers*, iii, 166-9.

[3] Burton, *Diary*, iii, 557; iv, 11, 31.

wicked out of their places, wheresoever they may be discovered'.[1] The House of Commons took the alarm, and after an
excited debate passed two drastic votes. The first was, that
during the sitting of Parliament there should be no General
Council or meeting of the officers of the army without the permission of the Protector and both Houses. The second was, that
no officer should henceforth have a command either in the army
or navy unless he signed an engagement that he would neither
disturb nor interrupt the meetings of Parliament or the freedom
of its debates.[2] On the same day the Protector sent for the leaders
of the officers to Whitehall, and ordered them to meet no more.
It soon became evident that they had no intention of obeying,
and the Commons prepared to back up the Protector by declaring him General, and by passing further votes against the
officers. On this the leaders of the officers demanded the dissolution of Parliament. It came to a trial of strength. At Fleetwood's
call all the forces in London gathered round him at St James's;
the few colonels who obeyed the Protector's summons to join
him at Whitehall found themselves deserted by their men, and
even his own regiment refused obedience. Richard was obliged
to yield to the inevitable, and on 22nd April he dissolved Parliament.[3]

For the next fortnight the government of England was in the
hands of the army. Again, as in 1653, the Council of Officers
plunged into the business of constitution-making. The day after
the dissolution it was engaged in 'debating what government
shall be settled, whether by the Petition and Advice, the Long

[1] *Old Parliamentary History*, xxi, 340. On 8th April Richard forwarded
this petition to the House of Commons (Burton, *Diary*, iv, 379). The Council
of Officers met first on 2nd April (*Clarke Papers*, iii, 187–8).

[2] Some very pertinent remarks were made during the debate. 'They are
no military council,' said Mr Swinfen. 'This is a council directly contrary
from a council of war. It is not known to the laws of war, nor to the laws of
the nation.' 'It does not appear,' said Colonel Terrill, 'that the army are
under any command. They are a loose army. They cannot be called to any
account as soldiers, but only as private persons. The great end of their
meeting is but to choose their masters.' Serjeant Maynard referred to the
threatening passage in the army's petition: 'Pluck the wicked out of their
places. It comes at last to you. Lord have mercy upon us if we cannot speak
to our army, to go to their stations and their charges, but we must discontent and disoblige them' (Burton, *Diary*, iv, 450, 452, 455).

[3] Ludlow, *Memoirs*, ii, 65–8; *Clarke Papers*, iii, 189, 191, 192.

Parliament to be recalled, or a new government to be constituted'.[1] Fleetwood and the superior officers wished to retain the Protectorate while limiting the power of the Protector, so as to make him, in the phrase of the day, 'a Doge of Venice'. Richard would reign and they would govern. 'I am sure,' says a well-informed witness, 'all endeavours were made by the principal officers in the army to piece and mend up that broken government.'[2] But the peculiarity of the military revolution of April 1659 was that the inferior officers, to whom the agitation in the army was mainly due, declined to follow the lead of their superiors. While the field-officers were assembling at Wallingford House, where Fleetwood lived, to draw up a new constitution, the captains assembled in the chapel of St James's and declared for the restoration of the Long Parliament. Petitions for its recall poured in from all quarters. 'All the inferior officers of the army, yea whole regiments of soldiers gave in their petitions for it, and almost all persons well affected centred (i.e. agreed) therein.'[3] Public opinion, so far as it found expression, was with 'the meaner sort of officers', and not with Fleetwood and the colonels. A negotiation began between the higher officers of the army and the leaders of the Long Parliament. Fleetwood and his associates wished to make terms with the Parliament before restoring it. They demanded indemnity for the past, and some security for the future. Constant in their distrust of the rule of a single chamber, they proposed the establishment of a select Senate to balance and limit it. The negotiation ended in smoke, for the Parliamentary leaders protested that they were only private men, and could make no binding engagements on behalf of Parliament. Vague promises were given to consider the views and the wishes of the army, but no definite agreement was arrived at.[4] Nevertheless, driven by the necessity of setting up some government, the Council of Officers issued a declaration inviting the members of the Long Parliament to return to the exercise and discharge of their trust, in which they admitted their own past backslidings and their 'wandering divers ways

[1] *Clarke Papers*, iii, 193.

[2] Ibid., iii, 213; cf. Baker, *Chronicle*, ed. Phillips, 1670, p. 659.

[3] *Clarke Papers*, iii, 214; *Thurloe Papers*, vii, 666.

[4] Ludlow, ii, 74; Baker, p. 661.

from righteous and equal paths' (6th May 1659).[1] Next day the
Long Parliament reassembled at Westminster.

There was great joy among the Republicans at the repentance
of the army. 'The Lord,' wrote one, 'is present eminently in the
army, with a sober, serious, yet warm and lively spirit of courage
for him and his cause; and if you had seen them in all these late
agitations, you would rather have judged them lambs than lions
by their deportment and carriage.'[2] Henry Cromwell in announcing his submission to the new government expressed a
pious hope that 'those worthy persons who have lately ack-
nowledged their interrupting you in the year 1653 to have been
their fault, will by that sense of their impatience be henceforth
engaged to do so no more, but be the instruments of your defence
whilst you quietly search out the ways of peace'.[3] But the
patience of the army did not last many months. On 13th May the
Council of Officers presented Parliament with a petition em-
bodying a summary of the principles they wished to see carried
out by the House, and received thanks for their pains.[4] But the
first measures taken by Parliament with reference to the army
sowed the seeds of discontent. It endeavoured, says Ludlow, 'to
bring the military sword under the power of the civil authority,
as it ought to be in a free nation'.[5] With this object, though it
appointed Fleetwood commander-in-chief, it limited his authority to the duration of the present Parliament, or till it should
take further order.[6] It also resolved that commissions should be
signed by the Speaker and delivered by him to their recipients.
The revision of the list of commissioned officers and the ejection
of many for purely political reasons added greatly to the rising
dissatisfaction amongst the soldiers.[7] At the same time the slow-
ness of Parliament to pass the promised Act of Indemnity, and
the restricted nature of the Act as it finally passed, excited the
fears of many officers who had supported the Protectorate.
Lambert said that the Act left him and others at mercy. 'You
are,' replied Sir Arthur Haslerig, 'at the mercy of the Parliament, who are your good friends.' 'I know not,' rejoined

[1] *Old Parliamentary History*, xxi, 367.

[2] *Clarke Papers*, iii, 215.   [3] Thurloe, vii, 684.

[4] *Old Parliamentary History* xxi, 399.   [5] Ludlow, ii, 88.

[6] Thurloe, vii, 679.   [7] See p. 53, *ante*.

Lambert, 'why they should not be at our mercy as well as we at theirs.'[1]

In August the Royalist rising under Sir George Booth put a stop for a moment to the dissension between army and Parliament. After its suppression by Lambert the officers who had served under his command seized the opportunity to draw up a petition to Parliament. They demanded the political reforms included in the petition of May, strong measures against the Royalists and their sympathizers, and added a request that Parliament should make Fleetwood permamently commander-in-chief and raise three other officers to the rank of general. The House answered by a vote that to have any more general officers was needless, chargeable, and dangerous to the Commonwealth. It declared that the petition was unseasonable and of dangerous consequence, and ordered Fleetwood to put a stop to it. Undeterred, the officers drew up a new petition, in which they vindicated their conduct, reiterated their request for the appointment of a commander-in-chief, and concluded by two new requests. One was that no officer might be dismissed except by a court-martial; the other, that no officer might be admitted to the army except by the choice of a Committee of Nomination appointed for the purpose. A few days later, while Parliament was considering the second petition, it discovered that the Council of Officers was sending it to all the forces in the three nations to procure signatures. It became manifest, as Ludlow observes, 'that they intended the petition to be the ground on which they designed to unite the army against the civil authority'.[2]

In this crisis Parliament acted with great vigour, but with little prudence. It promptly annulled Fleetwood's commission as commander-in-chief, vested the government of the army in seven commissioners, of whom he was one, cashiered Lambert and eight other officers responsible for the circular asking for subscriptions to the petition, and voted that anyone levying taxes save by the authority of Parliament should be guilty of high treason. Both parties appealed to force, but the soldiers who adhered to the Parliament were few in number. Lambert placed

[1] Ludlow, *Memoirs*, ii, 97, 100.

[2] Ibid., ii, 137; Baker, *Chronicle*, p. 677; *Old Parliamentary History*, xxi, 453, 460; Thurloe, vii, 766.

himself at the head of the regiments in London, set a guard about the doors of the House, and put an end to its sittings.

Public opinion, which had generally approved of the expulsion of the Parliament in 1653, pronounced this second expulsion to be dictated by purely selfish motives. 'It appears to us without doors,' wrote Milton, 'till better cause be declared . . . most illegal and scandalous, I fear me barbarous or rather scarce to be exampled among any barbarians, that a paid army should, for no other cause, thus subdue the supreme power that set them up. This, I say, other nations will judge to the sad dishonour of that army, lately so renowned for the civilest and best-ordered in the world, and by us here at home for the most conscientious.'[1]

The proceedings of the army after seizing power seemed to prove that, as Ludlow said, 'they would be content with nothing less than to have the government established in a court-martial'.[2] It declared Fleetwood commander-in-chief, appointed to command under him the general officers whom Parliament had refused to appoint, restored the officers Parliament had cashiered, and cashiered those who had been faithful to their paymasters. The commander-in-chief and five other officers were to nominate to all vacant commissions; no one was to be admitted to the army unless he signed an engagement to maintain the newly established order of things, and no one was to be dismissed save by a court-martial. Thus the army would become a close corporation, completely self-governing and completely independent of the civil authority. At the same time the Council of Officers took upon itself to settle how the nation should be governed. For the moment it established a Committee of Safety to whom the administration of civil affairs was to be entrusted, 'resolving to obey them so long as they would do what should be prescribed to them'.[3] As to the future, a new Parliament was to meet next February, under restrictions to be determined hereafter. A new constitution was to be imposed on the nation after it had been approved by a grand council representing the armies of the three nations. In that constitution there were to be 'seven principles and unalterable fundamentals to be perpetually kept and observed'.[4] There was to be no kingship and no government

[1] *Letter to a Friend Concerning the Ruptures of the Commonwealth.*
[2] Ludlow, *Memoirs*, ii, 130.   [3] Ibid., 131.   [4] Ibid., 159, 171, 173.

by a single person of any kind. There was to be no House of Lords, but instead of it a senate elected to keep the Commons within bounds. The legislative and executive powers were to be kept in different hands, and freedom of conscience was to be inviolably maintained.

Whatever the merits of the scheme might be, it had no chance of success. Apart from the general aversion of the country to the rule of the army, it had against it the fact that the army itself was not unanimous in supporting it. The Council of Officers which sought to impose it very imperfectly represented the army. When it resolved that a new Parliament should be called instead of restoring the old one, Ludlow pointed out that the deputies from the armies of Scotland and Ireland had not yet arrived, nor were there any from the army in the North of England. Moreover, at least a third of the officers present were against the resolution. 'It seemed to me,' he writes, 'to be an unaccountable presumption for two-thirds of about a fourth part of the army to put a period to the civil authority.'[1] There were many dissentients amongst the English officers, and those men of high ranks.[2] Five colonels and four other officers published a spirited protest against the acts of the army leaders.

[1] Ludlow, *Memoirs*, ii, 165.

[2] Captain Clement Needham, of Colonel Hacker's regiment of horse, wrote to Fleetwood pointing out the result of the army's proposals.

'My lord, to my understanding the designe of that proposeall is to create an interest in the army, distinct to that of parliament and nation; and this (says some) is our best security against the spirit of the nation, which may possibly bee introduced in parliament. My lord, I find many your officers, especially those of the Northerne brigades, much decry the constitutions of corporations, as emblems of Monarchy. It seems to me incongruous, that the same men should strive to bringe the army into a corporation. My lord, were it possible to forme an army of saints in reallity, such as would undoubtedly abide stedfast, and could this army support itself either by its owne interest and property, or by extraordinary food from heaven, I should not deny them a charter as the most renowned corporate body on the face of the earth. But, my lord, seeinge this army consists of men subject to infirmity; that seeinge this army was raised by authority of the people of England, called forth to defend the birthright and liberty of the meanest man in the nation, as well as their owne; that this army hath been paid and mainteyned out of the purses of the same people, and cannot in future stand but by the same meanes seeinge there remaines in this army but a handfull of those men that bare the burthen and heate of the warre, many beinge retired to private callinges, that have equally meritted with ourselves; that consideringe the distemper now on the spirit of the nation hath much of it arisen from the unstable spirit of the army, that had sett up what they had pulled downe, and pulled downe what they sett up; and now (that I mistake not) seeme to assert an interest of their owne, independent from that of the

'The Parliament of England,' said they, 'never raised or maintained soldiers to be law-makers, but to defend this nation against those who were law-breakers. . . . The English nation will be loth to lose their hereditary and birthright privilege of making their own laws. . . . But now we are told that as there is no authority in the nation, all authority is devolved upon and resides in the army, that is, in the officers; and our government must be a sword government. And shall this be spoken by any that shall presume to take the name of an holy and just God into his mouth? Is England's dear-bought freedom come to this?'[1]

Louder and more effective still, because it was backed by ten thousand men, was the protest of General Monck. Bred in the Dutch service, where, as he said, 'soldiers received and observed commands, but gave none', obedience to the civil power was his guiding principle. As soon as he received the news that Lambert and Fleetwood had expelled the Long Parliament he urged them to restore it at once. 'I am resolved,' said he, 'with the assistance of God, and that part of the army under my command, to stand by them, and assert their lawful authority. For, sir, this nation of England will not endure any arbitrary power, neither will any true Englishman in the army, so that such a design will be ruinous and destructive.'[2] For two months negotiations continued, while Monck organized his army to march into England. Envoys came to argue with him on behalf of the Council of Officers at London,[3] divines were sent to mediate and represent

nation, in which all the world will judge selfe to bee at the bottom; let us now thinke it our duty to settle on such a basis, as every man's interest may be involved, and all men see their owne property and right mainteyned.'

[1] Thurloe, vii, 771–4.

[2] Letter to Lambert, 20th October 1659.

[3] In declaring against the English army and in negotiating with its agents Monck took care to be supported by a council representing his own. 'We must needs begin in the old methods of government,' says Gumble, 'for the general had his Privy Council which was this committee, and his Great Council of all commission-officers in the army. It was a pleasant sight to see the general at the end of a table, in a room full of officers, putting the question ("As many as consent to this proposition, hold up your hands," which was their ceremony of assent), and then an ensigne to make a long speech to the contrary (who was but started from a corporal the other day), but all this he did suffer for the good of all and love to his country. . . . But though he submitted to these forms yet he kept an absolute authority by the prudence and artifice of those he trusted, but did it by the way of councel and perswasion' (Gumble, *Life of Monck*, p. 140).

the certain ruin which would fall upon the cause if he persisted.
But he remained firm to his principle. 'I am engaged,' he asserted, 'in conscience and honour to see my country freed from
that intolerable slavery of a sword government, and I know
England cannot, nay, will not endure it.[1]

Yet it was not Monck's arms but the disintegration of the
army itself which brought its government to an end. The popular
odium took the heart out of Lambert and Fleetwood's followers.
'The soldiers here,' said a letter from London on 6th December
1659, 'are so vilified, scorned, and hissed that they are ashamed
to march; and many officers when they go into the City dare
not even wear their swords for fear of affronts; and thus God
hath blasted them and they are become vile in the eyes of the
people.' The privates were not disposed to shed the blood of
their comrades in order to satisfy the ambition of their officers.
'The soldiers generally,' added another letter, 'say they will not
fight, but will make a ring for their officers to fight in.'[2] At the
beginning of December the garrison of Portsmouth declared for
the Parliament, and the regiments sent to besiege it went over
to the garrison. A few days later the fleet in the Downs followed
the example of Portsmouth. Finally the Irish army, hitherto
under the control of leaders acting in co-operation with Lambert
and Fleetwood, arrested its commanders, declared for the Parliament, and entered into communication with Monck. Stunned
by these successive blows Fleetwood and the troops in London
sullenly submitted, and restored the Long Parliament of their
own accord (26th December 1659).[3]

Thus the fabric of military rule fell without a blow. Monck
marched to London unopposed, became commander-in-chief by
the appointment of Parliament (25th February), and reduced the
army to complete submission by removing all officers whom he
could not trust to be obedient. 'There is not an officer in the
army,' Monck had written eighteen months earlier, 'that has
interest enough to draw two men after him, if he be out of
place,' and the failure of Lambert's attempted insurrection
proved the truth of his axiom (April 1660). The army in general
was bitterly hostile to the restoration of monarchy. It perceived
whither Monck's policy tended, but was too divided and too dis-

---

[1] *Clarke Papers*, iv, 153.   [2] Ibid., 166, 300.   [3] Thurloe, vii, 387.

heartened by failure to resist. At the beginning of March 1660 the Council of Officers met and urged Monck to declare for a Commonwealth, and to engage against all that should endeavour 'to set up a single person'. He refused to do so, saying 'that nothing was more injurious to discipline than their meeting in military councils to interpose in civil things'.[1] Not only did he forbid all similar meetings in the future, but he imposed on the whole army an engagement to acquiesce in whatever the next Parliament should do. 'We shall,' ran the Engagement, 'according to our duties, carry and behave ourselves as officers of an army instructed by your example and discipline to obey and not to dispute the orders of our superiors, and shall freely and readily observe such commands as we shall receive from your Excellency, or the Council of State, or the Parliament when assembled. And in particular, we shall, according to the late proclamation of the Council of State of the 17th of March, decline any meeting or meetings for the contriving or carrying on of any declaration or subscriptions concerning affairs of state or government, thereby avoiding those mischiefs which made many lately in arms so justly distasteful to the people, by making themselves a divided interest from the rest of them.'[2]

Thus ended the political activity of the Cromwellian Army. It had propagated democratic principles and imposed religious freedom with pike and musket; it had initiated many interesting political experiments and drawn up four constitutions. In time the aims which it had at heart were to be realized by other hands and by more appropriate methods. But for the present all that it bequeathed to English political life was a rooted aversion to standing armies and an abiding dread of military rule.

[1] Baker, *Chronicle*, p. 716.   [2] Ibid., p. 719.

Appendix: Table of Contents

Appendix

A. COMPANY DRILL

BECAUSE the Ambition of some doth strive to aime at higher things in their thoughts then what is practised abroad, I have thought good to set down the plain way of exercising a Company, as usually it is practised in the Army, our Companies consisting of one hundred men, two parts being Musketeers, and a third Pikes, the depth of our Files being alwayes six deep in the Armies of *England, Scotland and Ireland,* the Company being drawn up at Brest; the Exercise is as followeth, they standing in their closest Order in Rank and Files.

First, Command.   *Open Rancks backwards to* ⎫
Command.   *Files open to the Right to your* ⎭ *Order.*

Command.   *Rancks open backward to open* ⎫
Command.   *Files open to the left to open* ⎭ *Order.*

Command.   *Rancks open backward to double* ⎫
Command.   *Files open outward to double* ⎭ *Distance.*

Command.   *Rancks close forward to open* ⎫
Command.   *Files close inwards to open* ⎭ *Order.*

Command.   *Rancks close forward to your* ⎫
Command.   *Files close to the left to your* ⎭ *Order.*

Command.   *Face to the Right* ⎫
Command.   *Face to the Left* ⎪
Command.   *Face to the Rear* ⎬ *as you were.*
Command.   *Face to the Front* ⎭

Command.   *Face to the Center* ⎫
Command.   *Face to the Front and Rear* ⎪
Command.   *Face to the Right and Left outward* ⎬ *as you were.*
Command.   *Face to the Right and Left inward* ⎭

Rancks and   *Rancks to the Right Double.*
Files being   *Files to the Left Double.*
At open   *Rancks to the Left Double.*
Order   *Files to the Right Double.*

Command.   *Half Files Double your Front to the Right.*
Command.   *Files Double your Depth to the Left.*
Command.   *Half Files Double your Front to the Left.*
Command.   *Files Double your Depth to the Right.*
Command.   *Bringers up double your Front to the Right.*

Command.	*Files Double your Depth to the Left, every man falling behind his bringer up.*
Direction.	*Bringers up double your Front to the Left.*
	Files double your depth to the Right, every man placing himself behind his bringer up.
Command.	*Double your Rancks to the Right or Left intire* } *as you were.*
Command.	*Half Files Double your Front to the Right intire.*
Command.	*Right half Rancke double intire the depth of your left half Rancks.*
Command.	*Half Files double your Front to the Left intire.*
Command.	*Left half Rancks double intire the depth of your Right half Ranks.*
Direction.	*The same may be done to the Rear.*
Command.	*Files to the Right hand, Counter March and maintain ground.*
Direction.	*The same may be done in Rancks, as also both in Rancks and Files, either maintaining, gaining or losing ground; of these in the Army we use but little.*
Command.	*Wheel your Battle to the Right.*
Command.	*Wheel your Battle to the Left.*
Command.	*Wheel your Battle to the Right about.*
Command.	*Wheel your Battle to the Left about.*
Command.	*Files file to the Right or Left.*
Command.	*Rancks file to the Right and Left.*

1. The Musketeers being on both flancks, first firing let the first Ranck stand, and fire every Ranck, passing through before his Leader, after standing and fire, till all have fired over twice, or four times, the Pikes moving slowly in the mean time, they will upon a stand be reduced as at first.

Secondly, bring all the Musketeers before the Pikes, then let them fire in the Front, falling off, and flanck the Pikes upon the Right: Fire upon the right flanck, the body marching, and the Musketeers to passe on the left flanck; after the Pikes may charge to the right, the body moving againe: Let the Musketeers fire on the Left flanck, and fall in the Rear of the Pikes, who may after charge their Pikes on the Left: the body marching, the Musketeers may fire in the Rear, and fall off to the Right and Left, and flanck the Pikes as at the first, the body facing about the Pikes may charge to the Rear: We usually fire in the Front, sometimes two Rancks standing, the rest passing by turns, then standing after they have gained the ground, before their Leaders do fire, till all have fiered twice: other times three Rancks fire together, the first kneels down, the second stoops; the third stands upright, then falling down, the three last Rancks passe through: and

APPENDIX 385

do the like, this being done twice, reduces all as at first, the Pikes
moving slowly, this being the usual way of exercising our Companies
in the Army. (From *The Compleat Body of the Art Military*, by Richard Elton, London, 1659.)

B. SEVERAL REASONS WHY THE PIKE IS THE MORE HONOURABLE ARMS

First I shall begin to set down the postures of the Pike, before
the postures of the Musket, for these reasons following, as conceiv-
ing: First, they are the more honourable Arms, in respect the Colours
flying upon the head of them and vpon the drawing up of the Company there is the most properest place for the Captain to be, either
upon a Stand, or upon a March, provided he have ground sufficient to
March them all abrest. If upon a Stand the Captain shall have occasion to engage against an Enemy, thither his Officers may repair unto
him upon the head of the Pikes, there to receive directions. And if
the Captain shall cause the Serjeants to draw off part or all the
Musketiers from the Body of Pikes to fire against the Enemy, the
Gentlemen of the Pikes in the mean time stands undantedly to undergoe all the cruel shot of the Cannon from the contrary part for to preserve their Colours who are likewise a place of Rendezvous for the
Musketiers to repair unto when they shall retreat from fight. Farther,
it hath been the ambition of many Gentlemen, both in Holland,
France, and in these late vnhappy Wars in England, to trail Pikes
with severall Commanders whom they shall thinke fit. And lastly, to
conclude all, that the Pike is the more honourable Arms, it is so
in respect of its antiquity, for it hath been the use of the Pike and
Spear, many hundred years before there was any knowledge of the
Musket, as in many Histories you shall finde. And so for present, I wil
conclude this discourse of the Pike, desiring the Musketiers to have a
favourable censure of me: for I intend not by it to perswade all
Souldiers to the handling of the Pike, and none to be Musketiers, for
that cannot be, I should rather advise all Captains that have occasion
to raise their Companies to have two thirds of Musketiers, and but
one of Pikes: that is to say, if they should have 18 Files, to cause
twelve of them to carry Muskets, and the other six File Pikes. And
in my judgement they shall performe the better service unto any
Nation where they shall be employ'd; and I shall further desire the
Souldiers (especially those that be of low stature) to handle and take
delight in the use of the Musket; for it is an exceeding great honour to
him so to handle his Musket, as that he doth it with ease in a comely
manner, and he that shall become expert therein; I have often
observed this commendation to follow him, by the report of others;
Such a one is a good Muskettier, and an able Souldier; concluding

thereby, he that will take the pains to be a good Muskettier certainly
cannot be idle, but hath gained something more to make him capable
of such praise. To conclude, I shall desire the Gentlemen of the
Pikes, and the Gentlemen of the Muskettiers to goe hand in hand in
love like dear brothers, and neither of them to envie each other, and
in so doing, God will give a blessing to all their undertakings. (From
The Compleat Body of the Art Military, by Richard Elton.)

C. THE USE OF THE POSTURES OF THE PIKE

The use of Ordering the Pike. – The *Pike* being ordered is the proper
Posture of a Souldier upon a stand, which he ought ever to minde
upon any such occasion, so to make use of it. And I have likewise
seen in many places, in the daytime, this *Posture* to be used by the
Souldier standing *Sentinell*.

The use of advancing the Pike. – The *Pike advanced*, is usefull for
the Souldier upon a *Troop*, when they are to *march* swiftly, either for
the relieving of some *Court of Guard*, or to repair to their place of
Randezvous, or upon some sudden in approaching to an Enemy, to
make a *Charge:* for then he will be in a fit capacity to *clap* down
quickly his *Pike* upon the breast of the Enemy. It is likewise very
usefull in the time of exercise: to the *half-files*, and *bringers up*, upon
any *doubling* to the Front, for then they are alwayes to be *advanced*,
in respect of a longer *march* in their *doublings*, then those that
double Ranks and Files; but having *doubled*, they must always con-
forme in *Posture* to the part *doubled*.

The use of Porting. – The use of *Porting* was invented for the ease
of the *Reare half-Files*, upon a *Charge;* for the *Front half-Files* are
only for to *charge;* the *Rear half-Files* in the mean time are to *port*.
It is likewise very usefull at such times when the Souldiers are
marching through a *Gate*, or *Sally-Port;* from whence I conceive it
doth derive its name *porting*.

The use of Shouldering. – The use of *Shouldering* the *Pike*, is only
properest upon the *March*, and in some kinde very usefull upon a
Stand in time of Fight; provided they are at convenient *distance*
from the Enemy. For it much preserveth the *Pikes*, and *Pikemen*,
from the danger of the *shot*, the *bullets* then *gliding* off from their
Arms; which if they stood at such times, either *ordered*, or *advanced;*
the *bullets* would make such a *chattering* amongst the *Pikes*, that
what with breaking of them, and the *shivers* flying from them, may
much endanger the Souldiers which shall carry them.

The use of Comporting. – The *comporting* of the *Pike* is only usefull
to the Souldier marching up a *hill*, for if then he should be *Shouldered*,
the *But-End* of the *Pike* would always be touching the *ground*
to hinder him in his *March;* and much endanger his fellow-souldiers

that shall come after him. Neither can he *march advanced;* for if there should be any winde, it would be ready to blow him down. Therefore as above, that which is most commodious for the Souldiers marching up a *hill,* is to *comport his Pike.*

The use of Trailing. – The *trailing* of the *Pike* is seldome used, but when the Souldier shall *march* straight forward through a *Wood,* the *File-leader* before he enters in, *trails* his *Pike,* and consequently all the rest in his *File:* then *stooping down,* they take up the *But-end* of their *Leaders Pikes,* which they may easily gripe with their own in their right hands, and after *march* forward through the *busling leaves* in a straight *line,* every *file* single by himselfe, but as neare each other as possible they can *march* for more securitie sake; that when they are cleare, they may finde each other, and be in a condition to *rally* up againe, as occasion shall require. The *trailing* of the *Pike,* may also be of excellent use in a *Trench,* that at such time when they shall have intelligence, where the Enemy are preparing to make a *Breach,* they may then move forwards unto that place undiscovered, and may defend the same.

The use of Cheeking. – The *cheeking* of the *Pike,* is the proper *Sentinell posture,* and then to be used. (From *The Compleat Body of the Art Military,* by Richard Elton.)

D. EXAMPLES OF THE DEFECTS OF THE PIKE

Extracted from Donald Lupton's *Warre-like Treatise of the Pike,* London, 1642.

THE PIKE A POOR WEAPON

THERE is not one private Soldier of twenty shall by his utmost strength and skill together runne through a common Corslet, nay, nor through a Buffe-coat which is good, to wound mortally; and what wisedome or policy is it to have so many standing men in Armes, which are not able to kill the Invaders: Further, hath it not been seene that three or foure good resolute Soldiers with their swords and Buffe-coats only have cut off ten or twelve Pikeheads, and come off safe without wounds, and purchased to themselves honor and reward?

For an instance of this: The Prince of *Orange* his Leaguer lying before *Scenke-Sconse,* it so fell out, that there was a great uproare betwixt the *English* and *Switzers,* they being enquarter'd one next to the other; the occasion was small, being about a stiver or two lost at Cards; but the issue had likely to have produced wonder and amazement (if by faire perswasions and entreaties both parties had not been pacified) for the Tumult began to grow to an intestine Mutiny (many men being wounded on both sides) so that the *English* first, and *Switzers* at last call'd to Armes: whenas there stood one of the Divisions of the *Switzers* with pikes ready charg'd, did not then two Soldiers of Collonell *Burlacyes* Regiment with their swords only enter by force into that Body, and cut off divers Pike-heads, and came off againe with three or foure of them in their hands, which in fury and great derision they flung again amongst them, with this jeere to boote, *Oh doe us no harme, good men?* (P. 49.)

THE PIKE USELESS IN SIEGES

Whenas the Town of *Stoade* was beleaguer'd by the forces of Count *Tilly* and others, and defended by the *English*; for a good while we kept many Outworkes and Scoutes without the walls: It so fell out, that many Musquetiers being imployed in other services, and being, by reason of the perfidiousnesse of the Citizens, forced at all times to leave a sufficient number within, lest they should have betrayed the Towne; that there were an 100 or an 150 Pike-men, able, stout, expert, and well arm'd, appointed (with some few Musquetiers) to keepe a Scout not farre from the Towne: whereas 'twas thought there was little or no danger to be feared, came it not to passe, that the Enemy (roving about to spy all advantages) march'd that very night against that Scoute which was mann'd chiefly with Pikes; the Alarme was taken first by one of our Pike-men, by the sight of a Dogge, which (as he supposed, and so all the rest) came not alone; which proved true: for presently the Enemy gave fire, and hearing but one or two discharge from the Scout, supposed that we had either left the worke, or else were asleepe, and so unable to resist: 'twas true, that when the Enemy had twice or thrice furiously given fire, our men did retreate towards the towne, but upon notice given to our Generall, they were charg'd to maintaine and defend the worke, and to beat out the enemy againe: so they going on, did by their sudden returne, and the darknesse of the night, terrifie the Enemy so that they left their easie gotten purchase for a time (supposing that either we had increased our numbers, or else might have some plot to encompasse them in:) but hearing no further pursuit, made a stand; and upon advice set upon the Scoute the second time, wherein they made a fearfull slaughter, casting our men which were shot into the fire one upon another; kill'd and burn'd all that stood it out, shot divers of them who cast away their Armes to save themselves by swimming: so that we lost most, or almost all our men.

Now was not this an unequall fight, to set Pikes against Musquets? And had these men had Musquets, they would have defended that worke against double so many Musquetiers comming on. This was much lamented, but the losse was unrecoverable.

Nor yet will any impute any indiscretion to our Generall: for this Act could not at that time have been remedied; most of our Musquetiers doing daily service in all places, both within and without the

Towne, and halfe our forces almost (if not altogether) were Pikes; who, when they perceiv'd how that the heat of duties lay all upon the Musquet, did all of them very well like of their weapon, because it freed them from the most dangerous and forlorne places; which inconvenience as soone as it was so deerly understood, was remedied, and most of our Pike-men were urg'd to use the Musquet; and such as did not, were adjudged to be Cowards, as indeed they deserved. (P. 69.)

THE PIKE USELESS IN RETREATS

So that we (if we intend to get off fairely) must doe it by placing good stout Musquetiers in our Reare, who (like *Parthians*) can fighte and fly, or (as we say) can give fire and retreat: thus had our Army faine to doe when we came off from the *Long-line*, being followed close by the *Imperiall* Horse, each of them bringing a Musquetier with him, untill we enquarter'd at the *Berke* not far from *Breme:* which could not have been perform'd, had we not maintain'd our Reere not with Pikes but with stout shot.

And that was held the best Method in our marching from our Quarters at the *Berke* along to *Stoad;* for we left 150 or 200 resolute fire-men in a worke to finde the Enemy play, whilst the maine of our Army gain'd almost a whole dayes journey; neither was it a slow march to shew State, or refresh the Soldier, (for our safety lay in our speed;) but it was quick and hasty, so that those which were left behind were of most reputed for lost men, and all supposed that had not Captain *Hamonds* Company received the Enemy comming after us, though to the losse almost of all his Soldiers lives, that our men had been served with the same sauce, (the Enemy intending us for slaughter as well as his men) yet those few men taking the best opportunity in such a desperate straight, and having a good guide, recover'd our Troopes againe. Now what service did our Pikes doe all this while? did they not cause our march to be the slower? and in case the Enemy had overtaken us (as it was generally suspected he would) should not our Musquetiers then have been the best defence for our Pike-men? and was it not the wish of all, that all our Pikes had been Firemen? and had not that Order been observ'd, we might have all been cut off before we could have entred into *Stoad.* (P. 82.)

A DENIAL THAT THE PIKE IS EFFECTIVE AGAINST CAVALRY

This is surely grounded upon Tradition; and true it is, that in former times when the winged Cavalry were fenc'd with sword and lance onely, then the Pike had that virtue to keepe off their invading Horse, because the Lance was made 4 feet shorter then the Pike, the Pike being 16, and the Lance being but 12 foot long: So that of necessity, if the horsemen intended execution upon them, they could not choose but hazard themselves, or horses, or both. But now the Horse having left off the Lance, and using their Pistols and Carbines in place of it, which can kill and sinke 120 yards off, and above; I would desire to know, whether it be any wisedome or safety to stand charg'd with Pikes onely against Pistoll bullets? for now the Horse having that advantage, need not approach so neere, as to endanger their owne bodies, or their Horses: and therefore it is high time for the Pike-men to looke after another weapon, which can and will better defend themselves, and offend their Enemies, then their Pikes can doe. (P. 125.)

THE COWARDICE OF PIKEMEN

And it hath been seene, when young Striplinges have upon Commands gone resolutely forth by Sallies, in a dark, cold blustring, rainy, tempestuous night, whenas a lusty, tall Pike-man hath been glad that he hath had such Armes allotted him, which kept him from such dangerous onsets. Nay, upon suddaine Alarmes in the Night, when the Serjeants have come to fetch men out of all Companies to march out, with their usuall word, Up Musquetiers, up; 10 or more out of every Company: At these times the lusty and able Pike-man hath said, Well, I would not be a Musquetier, I am glad of my Corslet, I had rather lye still in my Quarters, let the Musquetiers get the honour, I desire it not at such times as this is: this hath been the language of the supposed valorous Pike-men; and I believe that they spake as they thought. (P. 130.)

E. A COMPARISON BETWEEN THE FIRELOCK AND THE MUSKET

I WOULD recommend the Fire-lock Musket above the Match-lock Musket, for several Reasons; some of which I shall mention.

First, It is exceedingly more ready; for with the Fire-lock you have only to Cock, and you are prepared to Shoot; but with your Match-lock, you have several motions, the least of which is as long a per-forming, as but that one of the other, and oftentimes much more hazardous; besides, if you Fire not the Match-lock Musket as soon as you have blown your Match, (which often, especially in Hedge-Fights and in Sieges, you cannot do) you must a second time blow your Match, or the Ashes it gathers hinders it from Firing.

Secondly, The Match is very dangerous, either where Bandeleers are used, or where Soldiers run hastily in Fight to the Budge-barrel, to refill their Bandeleers; I have often seen sad instances thereof.

Thirdly, Marching in the Nights, to avoid an Enemy, or to surprize one, or to assault a Fortress, the Matches often discover you, and informs the Enemy where you are; whereby you suffer much, and he obtains much.

Fourthly, In wet weather, the Pan of the Musket being made wide open for awhile, the Rain often deads the Powder, and the Match too; and in windy weather, blows away the Powder, ere the Match can touch the Pan: nay, often in very high Winds, I have seen the Sparks blown from the Match, Fire the Musket ere the Soldier meant it; and either thereby lose his Shot, or wound or kill some one before him. Whereas in the Fire-lock the motion is so sudden, that what makes the Cock fall on the Hammer, strikes the Fire, and opens the Pan at once.

Lastly, To omit many other Reasons, the quantity of Match used in an Army, does much add to the Baggage; and being of a very dry quality, naturally draws the moisture of the Air, which makes it relax, and consequently less fit, though carried in close Wagons: but if you march without Wagons, the Match is the more expos'd; and without being dried again in Ovens, is but of half the use which otherwise it would be of: And which is full as bad, the Skeans you give the Corporals, and the Links you give the private Soldiers, (of which near an Enemy, or on the ordinary Guard duty, they must never be unfurnished) if they Lodge in Hutts or Tents, or if they keep Guard in the open Field, (as most often it happens) all the Match for instant service is too often render'd uncertain or useless; nothing of all which can be said of the Flint, but much of it to the contrary.

And then the Soldiers generally wearing their Links of Match near the bottom of the Belt on which their Bandeleers are fastened, in wet weather, generally spoil the Match they have; and if they are to fight on a sudden, and in the Rain, you lose the use of your Small Shot, which is sometimes of irreparable prejudice. (From *A Treatise of the Art of War*, by Roger Earl of Orrery, 1677, p. 30.)

F. A SHAM FIGHT IN 1645

Friday, May the 9. – I shall this day in the first place present you with a May-game; but such a one as is not usuall, and deserves to be taken notice of, and it is an action of Warre too, and therefore the more sutable to the times.

In Kent the countrey people (no where more) love old customes, and to do every yeer what they have done in others before, and much pastimes, and drinking matches, and May-Poles, and dancing and idle wayes, and sin hath been acted on former May dayes.

Therefore Colonell *Blunt* considering what course might be taken to prevent so much sin this yeer, did wisely order them, the rather to keep them from giving the Malignants occasion to mutinie by such publique meetings, there having been so many warnings by severall insurrections, without such an opportunity.

Colonell *Blunt* summoned in two Regiments of his foot Souldiers to appear the last May-day, May the 1, at Blackheath, to be trained, and exercised that day, and the ground way raised, and places provided to pitch in, for the Souldiers to meet in two bodies, which promised the Countrey much content, in some pretty expressions, and accordingly their expectation were satisfied.

For on May day when they met, Colonell *Blunt* divided them into two parts, and the one was as Roundheads, and the other as Cavaliers, who did both of them act their parts exceeding well, and many people, men and women, young and old, were present to see the same.

The Roundheads they carried it on with care and love, temperance and order, and as much gravity as might be, every one party carefull in his action, which was so well performed, that it was much commended.

But the Cavaliers they minded drinking and roaring, and disorder, and would bee still playing with the women, and compasse them in, and quarrell, and were exceedingly disorderly.

And these had severall skirmishes one with the other, and took divers prisoners one from the other, and gave content to the Countrey people, and satisfied them as well as if they had gone a maying in another way, which might have occasioned much evill after many wayes as is before declared. (From *Perfect Occurrences of Parliament and Chief Collections of Letters from the Armie*, 9th to 16th May 1645).

G. THE DUTY OF OFFICERS IN A CAVALRY CHARGE

AMONGST Lord Orrery's *Particulars to be observed previously to a Battel* is an order against officers unduly and uselessly exposing themselves. He advises: 'That orders be given that no chief officer who commands a squadron, or commissioned officer who leads one with him, have that horse he charges on advanced above the length of his head beyond the front rank of troopers.

'My reason for it is this:

'Because if those who lead squadrons to the charge be before the front rank, they either without cause adventure to be shot by their own men behind them, or hinder some from firing, or which is far worse, when both bodies come to the shock, such as are out of the ranks and between both bodies are needlessly exposed, even when they are of most use to the men they command, and consequently the whole army. In answer to this, I know some have said, it does not a little animate the squadrons to see the officers which command them, lead them on 8 or 10 paces before the first rank, and then just when they are going to mingle to fall into it. But I must say, I believe good soldiers need not such airy animations, and the bad ones will not fight well even though they have more airy ones. Besides I believe it does rather disanimate than encourage soldiers, who have any consideration, when they see those officers whose conduct they relie upon, give them so ill an impression of it, as doing a vain thing, by which also they may too probably incapacitate themselves to command their men, when they are likely to have most need to be ordered to the best advantage, either as to their rallying if discomposed in the charge, or an orderly pursuit if successful.

'To which also may be added two other considerations; if the officers advancing some paces before their men be a great animating them, may it not be a greater disanimating of the soldiery, to see them when ready to charge put themselves in the first rank: for their going before their squadrons when there is no danger, and the returning when there is, will, in all likelihood, make the latter action dishearten more than the former can encourage, for all animations are more effectual when the danger is at hand, than when it is remote.

'When the squadrons advance to charge the troopers horses and their own knees are as close as they can well endure, so that it will be impossible for the officers to fall into the rank if it be well wedged up; or if it be not, thereby to give them admittance, it may leave such gaps in it as may hinder the close uniting of the rank, which is so necessary to make the charge effectual, and commonly the officers horses being of the best and of the highest mettle, when they come among strange horses, especially backwards, may by their fighting and kicking so disorder the rank, that the enemy is more likely to come in at the breach than they.' (Orrery, *Art of War*, pp. 198–9.)

H. THE DIFFERENT KINDS OF GUNS

ACCOUNTS of the artillery in use at the period of the Civil Wars are to be found in many military books of the time. Hexham devotes the third part of his *Principles of the Art Military* (2nd ed., 1643) entirely to artillery, describing the different varieties of guns in use in the Dutch service, and the method in which they were to be made and used. He also adds excellent diagrams and illustrations. Ward in his *Animadversions of War* (1639) devotes a section of his work, containing thirty-five pages, to 'The Use of Artillery in Forts', in the course of which he gives a comparative table showing the weight and range, etc., of all sorts of guns then in use.

Ward's account of the comparative weight of the shot of the various guns is as follows:

'Canon of Eight, 64 lbs; Canon serpentine, 52 lbs; French canon, 46¼ lbs; Demi-canon eldest, 36⅝ lbs; Demicanon ordinary, 32 lbs; Demicanon, 24½ lbs; Culverin, 19 lbs; ordinary Culverin, 16½ lbs; Demi-Culverin, 14⅔ lbs; Demi-Culverin less, 9 lbs; Saker ordinary, 5¼ lbs; Sakeret or Minion, 3¼ lbs; Fawcon, 2⅓ lbs; Fawconet, 1⅐ lbs; Rabinet, ¾ lb; Base, ⅓ lb.' (*Animadversions of War*, p. 109.)

Hexham does not describe so many different kinds of guns, but confines himself in the main to a description of those usually employed in the Dutch army. 'The greatest number of new pieces cast in the States Founderie at the Hagh every year, by the help of some 20 men, are six whole Canons, twelve half Canons, and sixe long Feildpeeces or demy Culverins, making in all the number of 24 peeces of ordnance. But of late years they cast diverse sorts of French short Demi-Canon and smaller Drakes as now the occasion of service requires.' He goes on to say that a whole cannon carries a ball of forty-eight pounds in weight, and a half-cannon one of twenty-four pounds, and that these two are 'pieces of battery used at sieges for to make a breach'. He speaks also of 'a fieldpiece or quarter cannon' carrying a twelve-pound ball, and of drakes carrying balls of six or eight pounds. (*Principles of the Art Military*, ed. 1643, pt. iii, p. 2.)

Sir James Turner after commenting on the difference in weight between French and German cannon and the disuse of the heavier varieties of the cannon, goes on to say that for the most part the Germans 'give the denomination of their guns from the weight of the bullet they shoot, as a four and twentieth pounder, a twelfth, a sixth, and a three pounder'.

'The Cannon, or battering ordnance, is divided by the English into Cannon Royal, whole Cannon, and Demi-Cannon. The first is likewise called the Double Cannon, she weighs eight thousand pound of metal, and shoots a bullet of 60, 62 or 63 pound weight. The whole Cannon weighs seven thousand pound of metal and shoots a bullet of 38, 39, or 40 pound. The Demi-Cannon weighs about six thousand pound and shoots a bullet of 28 or 30 pound. All of them will take the half of the weight of their bullet of fine, and two parts of ordinary powder, and may take much more if they be reinforced. These three several guns are called Cannons of eight, Cannons of seven, and Cannons of six; suppose inches, as being so many inches high of the diameter of their bores. For most part all Cannon, properly so called, are not above eighteen or nineteen diameters of their bores in length.'

A few pages later he speaks of a whole cannon of the lighter sort carrying a forty-pound ball, and of demicannons carrying balls of twenty-four pounds as employed in sieges by the Germans. Incidentally he speaks of the ordinary culverin as being a sixteen-pounder. (*Pallas Armata*, pp. 193–6.)

It is very difficult to determine with any certainty what variety of cannon or culverin was usually employed in England during the Civil Wars. Probably the lighter variety of each was used. In a survey of the arms and artillery stores in Edinburgh and Leith garrisons about 1653, taken by John Phipps, Controller of the Ordnance to the English Army in Scotland, it is noticeable that 1,200 shot for cannon of seven inches were then in store, and only thirty shot for cannon of eight inches. (*Clarke MSS.*, xliii, 9.) From this it may safely be inferred that the cannon of seven was the typical heavy siege-gun of the English army, which was what Turner calls a whole cannon and carried a ball of about forty pounds.

The kind of demicannon used in the English armies was probably the smallest variety of demicannon mentioned in Ward's list, and carried a ball of about twenty-four pounds, like the Dutch demicannon described by Hexham. At the siege of Newcastle in September, 1644, Leven wrote to London for a supply of shot, specifying balls of twenty-four, twelve, and nine pound weight. (Terry, *Life of Alexander Leslie*, p. 304). This means, I suppose, shot for demicannons, quarter-cannons, and demiculverins. The difficulty of ascertaining the weight of the ball carried by different pieces of artillery during the Civil Wars is largely due to the fact that bills and orders for the supply of ammunition usually specify the nature of the piece for which the shot is required, but not its weight.

I. REGULATIONS AS TO THE QUARTERING OF SOLDIERS

(a) Order issued by Sir Thomas Fairfax, May 22, 1646.

FORASMUCH as the Army under my command have for some time past for want of pay practis'd free quarter, to the great scandall thereof, and to the extream burthen of the Country, especially these parts which as yet do pay very great Contributions to many Garrisons, well nigh to the utter undoing of the Inhabitants. In consideration whereof, and confidence of due pay for the future, I do hereby strictly charge and order all officers and souldiers whatsoever, horse and foot, duely to discharge their quarters, according to the severall rates expressed in an Ordinance of Parliament, (viz.) 4.d. a night hay, 2.d. a night grasse, 4.d. a peck oates, 6.d. a peck pease and beanes, and also 8.d. a day for the dyet of every Trooper or Horseman, 7.d. a day for every Dragooner, and 6.d. a day for every foot souldier, pioneer, waggoner, or carter, that shall not be officers by Commission. Every Officer by Commission, or person of the Life-guard Troop, shall pay the full value for his provisions, both for horse and man. But if by want of pay, they be not able to satisfie to the full value, I do strictly require them from henceforth to give ticket both for what provision they have in these parts formerly had; And to order and command the severall Captaines and Quartermasters of Horse and Foote, upon paine of Cashiering, to give ticket under their, or one of their hands, expressing what provisions for Quarter or otherwise are, or have been had; in what time, by whom, wherein, and of what Regiment, Troope, and Company, from whom, and the vallue thereof: Being hereby also required to content themselves with such ordinary dyet for themselves and Servants as the parties with whom they Quarter are provided, without putting them to the trouble, or charge of seekeing abroade. I do also under the like penalty require all Quartermasters in every of their Tickets to set downe the names of every person within the severall tickets they or any by their Authority shall give out, expressing of what Regiment, Troope, or Company such person, or persons so quartered be; the number of Horse, or Foote there quartered, and at whose house, with the day of the moneth. And that thereunto the same Quartermaster, or Assistant subscribe his name, saving, that upon march where by reason of the great number of them, the names cannot be so sodainly incerted in the tickets as is requisite, the numbers so present shall be expressed in place of their names, and within one day after, or sooner if the same may conveniently, the names of the persons quartered shall by the quartermaster be written upon, or under such tickets; But if any Captaine, Quartermaster, or others whatsoever should contemptuously offend in any of the aforesaid perticulars conducing so much to the honour of the Army, the Kingdomes good, and peremptorie Commands of Parliament; They shall be severally proceeded against at a Councell of Warre where they are to expect no mercy, as I have accordingly acquainted the Country, and this I seriously recommend to the Majors of every Regiment, and require the Provost Martiall to see carefully proclaimed, and Copies fixed at or neare every Collonels Quarter, and Perados. Given under my hand and Seale at Heddington the head Quarter, the day and the yeere above written. – FAIRFAX. (From *Perfect Occurrences*, 22nd to 29th May 1646.)

(b) Orders and Rules by his Excellency the Lord Fairfax, For the taking off all Free-Quarter and Billet in this Nation, July 1649.

Whereas the Parliament hath made provision for the constant pay of the Army, and taking off all free-quarter, and Billet, and to that end have passed an Act with certain Rules and Instructions, intending the necessary provision for the souldiers most indifferently both to the Countrey and them, these are therefore in prosecution of the said Act to require all Colonels, Majors, Officers and Souldiers whatsoever to observe, and put in execution such Rules and Instructions in their respective commands and places, as hereafter followeth.

1. That no partie under the number of 25 upon a march quarter in private houses without the owners consent.

2. That whereas the Act allows the Souldier upon march to quarter in private houses two nights to the intent they may within that time provide for themselves, and divers Souldiers do take advantage thereby (contrary to the intent thereof) to remove quarters oftner then is necessary, and upon their remove march but two or three miles a day, or thereabouts. It is therefore ordered that the Lord General give order that no Troop march less then ten miles a day nor company of Foot then seven, except upon service or extraordinary occasions.

3. That upon settlement of quarters, the Officer in Chief of every Troop, Company, or commanded Party, make known to the respective Landlords within his respective quarters, that they are to discharge their Billet, and in case any Landlord shall complain to the Captain or Commander in Chief upon the place, that any of his souldiers have not paid their quarters, The said Captain or Commander in chief of the said Troop, Company or Party, to give satisfaction to every person out of the offendors pay within ten dayes after just complaint made, upon pain of cashiering, and if in case the Captain or Officer in Chief shall refuse, or neglect to give satisfaction as aforesaid, The Colonel or Major of the said Regiment to give satisfaction himself to the Landlord out of the said Officer or offenders pay next growing due, and to transmit the charge against the Officer so offending, with the examination, to the Judge Advocate at the Headquarters within ten dayes after he hath had full information thereof, etc.

4. That in regard the same care cannot be taken upon a March, it is ordered that the Quarter master, or any imployed to take up Quarters, do in their Tickets for Quarter express the names of the Souldier, or Souldiers to quarter there, and make known that they are to pay their Quarters, and in that case of neglect, upon complaint the next morning to the Commander in chief of the partie, Troop, or Company, they shall receive satisfaction; that if either the Quartermaster, or any imployed in that service, or the Commander in Chief, fail in the due observance thereof, that they incur the penalty of cashiering, giving satisfaction to the Complainers as before.

5. That this may be the better put in Execution, it is ordered that all Colonels and other Officers (but such as I shall appoint to attend the head-quarters) be resident with their respective Regiments, and not absent above fourteen days without special leave from my self, upon pain of forfeiting their pay during their absence: and that no Colonel do give leave to any of his Officers to be absent above fourteen days, without special leave from my self, the Officer so offending to loose his pay during that absence.

6. That the Deputy Commissaries of the Musters in their respective Circuits and Associations do certifie by name to the Commissary

Generall of the Musters, every Muster, what Officers of any Regiment, or belonging to any Garrison, they finde absent from their command, and upon what ground. And that the Commissary upon it do make certificate thereof upon every Muster, with all speed after Receipt thereof to the Major Generall, or those who give out Orders at the Head Quarter in his absence.

7. That by vertue of the Commissions formerly granted for the keeping of Courts of War in the respective Regiments, each Colonel or Major take care for the convening the Officers of his Regiment, as a Court Martial, once every moneth at the least, and examine what hath been done in the observing and executing the foregoing Orders, and the Articles of War; and to certifie to the Major Generall or Officer issuing out Orders in his absence at the Head Quarters, what Officers were absent then from their commands, and upon what grounds, as is exprest in the foregoing Article.

That all offences mentioned within these orders which have not a particular penalty appointed for them, be punished at the Judgment of the Regimentall Councel of War. Provided, it extend not to the loss of place of a Commission Officer, nor to taking away of life or limbe from any whatsoever. July 27. (From *The Moderate*, 24th to 31st July 1649.)

J. ORDER AS TO WILLS MADE BY SOLDIERS IN SCOTLAND

Tolebooth, Cannongate, Edinburgh.

At a Court Martiall held for the Head Quarters in Scotland the 12th day of February, 165$\frac{7}{8}$.

THIS Court taking into consideracion that souldiers of the army in Scotland when they are lying sick upon their death beds, doe for every inconsiderable reasons, and through the perswacions of their comrades make their last wills and testaments to their said comrades and others, many times to the prejudice [not only] of their neerest frinds and allies but [also] to their officers and others to whom they are indebted, thereby intending to put the afforesaid persons to troble in obtaining what is their proper right and due; Doth there-upon thinck fitt and order that all such wills and testaments which shall bee made (from and after intimacion hereof given) by any soul-dier or souldiers in the army in Scotland, lying sick upon his or their death bed or death beds as aforesaid and dying, bee not approved and allowed of by a Court Martiall except some comiscion officer of the companie, troope, or regiment be present at the making of the said will or testament, which said will is to bee attested by the officer soe present at the making thereof as aforesaid, unto which said will hee is to subscribe his name and quallitie, and iff any souldier or souldiers shall make any will and dye as aforesaid, quartered in any garrison or comanded forth with a partie upon service where noe comission officer is, that in such case the officer commanding in cheife of that said garrison or partie comanded forth upon service, is to bee present, which said will is to bee subscribed as aforesaid; and that the said souldiers may not pretend ignorance hereof, the said Court doth further order every Majour, or eldest Captain in every regiment where the Majour is absent, to cause publicacion hereof soe soone as the same shall come to his hands to bee made with all convenient speed by the Martiall of the said regiment at the head of every company being drawne upp.

Signed in the name and by the Order of the said Court

By THO: FOWLER,
Deputie Judge-Advocate.
(From the *Clarke MSS.*, vol. li, f. 39.)

K. TRIAL OF AN OFFICER FOR HERESY

INFORMATIONS given in by severall persons of divers dangerous and unsound opinions held out by Lt. William Jackson, vizt.

1. That Leiut Jackson hath often exprest his opinion for a community of all things, and that every man should share with his fellow creature, and further hath said that hee either did or should enjoy another man's wife as hee did, or otherwise the creature was kept in bondage.

2. That Lieut Jackson hath held forth that God is the Authour of much delusion, and that when wicked men act they doe as God would have them doe, and that Paul did as good a worke when hee persecuted the church as when hee preached, for when hee persecuted hee did act as it was revealed to him; and being asked if [when] a man did commit adultery or theft God was the authour of itt, hee said the creature can doe nothing otherwise then itt's moved and acted by God.

3. That there is noe God but what is in himself and whole creation, and that Hee is alike in beasts as in men.

4. That hee held forth that the Reviling Theife on the Crosse died as well as Stephen.

5. That hee is as perfect now as ever hee shall bee.

May 6, 1650.

Commission issued by the Lord Fairfax to Col. George Fenwick Governor of Berwick for the triall of the said Lt. Jackson. (From the *Clarke MSS.*)

L. THE ARTICLES OF WAR

[*Title*]. – Lawes and Ordinances of WARRE, Established for the better Conduct OF THE ARMY

London, Printed for *John Wright* at the *Kings-head* in the *Old-Bailey*.

[*Introductn*]. – *To all the Officers of the Army, Colonels, Lievtenant-Colonels, Serjeant Majors, Captaines, other Officers and Souldiers of Horse and Foot, and all others whom these Laws and Ordinances may concerne.*

Which Lawes *and* Ordinances *hereby Published to all the said Persons respectively and severally, are Required and Commanded to observe and keep, on the Pains and Penalties therein expressed.*

LAWES AND ORDINANCES OF WARRE,

Of Duties to GOD.

I

Blasphemy. – First, Let no man presume to Blaspheme the holy and blessed Trinity, God the Father, God the Sonne, and God the Holy Ghost; nor the knowne Articles of our Christian Faith, upon paine to have his Tongue bored with a red-hot Iron.

II

Cursing. – Unlawfull Oathes and Execrations, and scandalous acts in derogation of GODS Honour, shall be punished with losse of Pay, and other punishment at discretion.

III

Neglecting Divine Worship. – All those who often and wilfully absent themselves from Sermons, and Publike Prayer, shall be proceded against at discretion: And all such who shall violate Places of Publike worship, shall undergoe severe Censure.

Of Duties in Generall.

I

Intelligence with the Enemy. – All such as shall practice and entertaine Intelligence with the Enemy, by any manner of meanes or slights, and have any communication with them, without direction from the Lord Generall, shall be punished as Traytors and Rebels.

II

Releife of the Enemy. – No man shall relieve the Enemy, with Money, Victuals, Ammunition; neither harbour or receive any such, upon paine of death.

III

Yeelding up of Forts. – If a Towne, Castle, or Fort bee yeelded up without the utmost necessity, the Governour thereof shall be punished with death.[1]

IV

But if so it be, that the Officers and Souldiers of the Garrison, constrain the Governour to yeeld it up: In such a case shall all the Officers be punished with death, and the Common Souldiers who have been active, or have given their consent in constraining the Governour, shall cast lots for the hanging of the 10th man amongst them.

V

And withall to know in what case and circumstances a Governour, and the *militia* of the Garrison may be blamelesse, for the surrendring of a Town, Castle, or Fort, it is hereby expresly signified: That first they are to prove the extremity of want within the place, insomuch that no eatable provision was left them for the sustenance of their lives. Secondly, That no succour or relief in any probable wise could be hoped for. Thirdly, That nothing else could be expected, but that within a short time the Town, Castle, or Fort, with all the Garrison, and Arms, Ammunition, Magazine, and appurtenances in it, must of necessity, fall into the hands of the Enemy. Upon proof of which fore-mentioned circumstances, they may be acquainted in a Counsel of Warre, else to be lyable to the punishment above expressed.

VI

Carelesse Service. – Whosoever shall be convicted to doe his Duty negligently and carelesly, shall be punished at discretion.

VII

Violating of a Save-Guard. – Whosoever shall presume to violate a Save-guard, shall dye without mercy.

VIII

Whosoever shall come from the Enemy, without a Trumpet, or Drum, after the Custome of Warre, or without a Passe from *His Excellencie*, within the Quarters of the Army, or within a Garrison Town, shall be hanged up as a Spie.[2]

[1] Articles iii, iv and v differ considerably from the corresponding articles in the *Laws and Ordinances* issued by Essex.

[2] Not in the *Laws and Ordinances* issued by Essex.

O

Of Duties towards Superiours and Commanders.

I

Violating the Lord Generall. – Whosoever shall use any words tending to the death of the *Lord Generall*, shall be punished with death.

II

Quarrelling with Officers. – No man shall presume to quarrell with his superiour Officer, upon paine of Cashiering, and Arbitrary punishment, nor to strike any such upon paine of death.

III

Departing from Captains and Masters. – No Souldier shall depart from his Captaine, nor Servant from his Master, without license, though he serve still in the Army, upon pain of death.

IV

Silence in the Army. – Every private man or Souldier, upon pain of Imprisonment, shall keep silence when the Army is to take Lodging, or when it is Marching, or Imbattalio, so as the Officers may be heard, and their Commandments executed.

V

Resisting against correction. – No man shal, resist, draw, lift, or offer to draw, or lift his Weapon against any Officer, correcting him orderly, for his offence, upon pain of death.

VI

Unlawfull Assemblies. – No person shall make any mutenous assemblies, or be present or assisting thereunto, or in, or by them, demand their pay, upon pain of death.

VII

Resisting of the Provost Marshall. – No man shall resist the Provost-Marshall, or any other Officer, in the execution of his Office, or breake prison, upon pain of death.

VIII

Seditious words. – None shall utter any words of sedition and uproar, or muteny, upon pain of death.

IX

Concealing mutenous speeches. – A heavy punishment shall be inflicted upon them, who after they have heard mutenous speeches, acquaint not their Commanders with them.

X

Receiving of Injuries. – Whosoever shall receive any injury and shall take his own satisfaction, shall be punished by Imprisonment, and as it shall be thought fit by the Marshal-Court: But he that is injured shall be bound, if he doe not forgive the injury, to seek reparation by complaint to his Captain, or Colonel, or other superiour Officer, and it shall be given him in ample manner.

Of Duties Morrall.

I

Drunkennesse. – Drunkennesse in an Officer shall be punished with losse of Place; in a common Souldier, with such penalties as a Court-Marshal thinke fit.

II

Unnatural abuses. – Rapes, Ravishments, unnatural abuses, shall be punished with death.

III

Adultery. – Adultery, Fornication, and other dissolute lasciviousnesse, shall be punished with discretion, according to the quality of the Offence.

IV

Theft. – Theft and Robbery, exceeding the value of twelve pence, shal be punished with death.

V

Provocation. – No man shall use reproachful, nor provoking words, or act to any, upon pain of imprisonment, and further punishment as shall be thought fit to be inflicted upon enemies to Discipline and service.

VI

Seizing upon dead mens goods. – No man shall take or spoile the Goods of him that dyeth, or is killed in Service, upon pain of restoring double the value, and Arbitrary punishment.

VII

Murther. – Murther shall be expiated with the death of the Murtherer.

Of a Souldiers duty touching his Arms.

I

Full Armour. – All Souldiers coming to their Colours to watch or to be exercised, shall come fully armed, upon pain of severe correction.

II

Slovenly Armour. – None shall presume to appeare with their Armes unfixt, or undecently kept, upon pain of Arbitrary correction.

III

Loosing of Horses and Armes. – If a Trooper shal lose his Horse or Hackney, or Foot-man any part of his Armes, by negligence or lewdnesse, by Dice or Cards, he or they shall remaine in quality of Pioners, and Scavengers, til they be furnished with as good as were lost, at their own charge.

IV

Pawning or selling of Armour. – No Souldier shal give to pawne, or sell his Armour, upon paine of imprisonment, and punishment at discretion; and wheresoever any Armour shall be found so sold or pawned, they shall be brought againe into the Army.

V

Wilfull spoiling of Horses. – If a Trooper shall spoyl his Horse willingly, of purpose to be rid of the Service, he shall lose his Horse, and remain in the Camp for a Pioner.

VI

Borrowed Arms. – If one borrows Arms of another to passe the Muster withall, the borrower shall be rigorously punished, and the lender shall forfeit his Goods.

VII

Imbezelling of Ammunition. – None shall presume to spoyl, sel, or carry away any Ammunition delivered unto him upon pain of death.

Of Duty in Marching.

I

Waste and extortion. – None in their March thorow the Countries shall waste, spoile or extort any Victuals, Money, or pawne, from any subject, upon any pretence of want whatsoever, upon pain of death.

II

Taking of Horses out of the Plow. – No Souldier shall presume, upon no occasion whatsoever, to take a Horse out of the Plough, or to wrong the Husbandmen in their person or Cattel, or Goods, upon pain of death.

III

Stragling from the Colours. – No Souldiers, either Horse or Foot, shall presume in marching to straggle from his Troop or Company, or to Martch out of his ranck, upon pain of death.

IV

Spoyling of Trees. – No Souldier shall presume, in Martching or Lodging, to cut downe any fruit-trees, or to deface, or spoil Walks of trees, upon pain of severe punishment.

Of Duties in the Camp and Garrison.

I

Swerving from the Camp. – No man shall depart a mile out of the Army or Camp without licence, upon pain of death.

II

Going in or out by waies. – No man shall enter, or go out of the Army, but by ordinary wayes, upon pain of death.

III

Drawing of Swords after setting the Watch. – No man shall presume to draw his Sword without Order, after the Watch is set, upon pain of death.

IV

Giving a false Alarum. – No man shall give a false Alarum or discharge a Piece in the night, or make any noise without lawful cause, upon pain of death.

V

Drawing swords in a quarrell. – No man shall draw any Sword in a private quarrell within the Camp, upon pain of death.

VI

Revealing the Watch-word. – He that makes known the Watch-word without Order, or gives any other word but what is given by the Officers, shal dye for it.

VII

Offering violence to Victuallers. – No man shall do violence to any that brings Victuals to the Camp, upon pain of death.

VIII

Speaking with the Enemies Messengers. – None shal speak with a Drum or Trumpet, or any other sent by the Enemy, without Order, upon pain of punishment at discretion.

IX

A Sentinel asleep, or drunk. – A Sentinel or Perdue found asleep, or drunk, or forsaking their place before they be drawn off shall dye for the offence, without mercy.

X

Failing at the Rendezvous. – No man shall faile wilfully to come to the Rendezvouze or Garrison appointed him by the *Lord Generall*, upon paine of death.

XI

Remaining unrolled in the Army. – No man that carrieth Armes, and pretends to be a Souldier, shall remaine three dayes in the Army without being enrolled in some company, upon pain of death.

XII

Departing without leave. – No man that is enrolled, shall depart from the Army or Garrison, or from his Colours, without Licence, upon paine of death.

XIII

Outstaying a Passe. – No private Souldier shall out stay his Passe, without a Certificate of the occasion, under the hand of a Magistrate at the next Muster, upon pain of losing his Pay, during all the time of his absence.

XIV

Absenting from the Watch. – He that absents himselfe when the signe is given to set the Watch, shall be punished at discretion, either with Bread and Water in Prison, or with the Woodden Horse.

XV

Discontented with their Quarters. – Whosoever shall expresse his discontent with his Quarter given him in the Camp, or Garrison, shall be punished as a Mutineer.

XVI

Lying or Supping out of the Quarters. – No Officer, of what quality soever, shall go out of the Quarter to Dinner or Supper, or lye out all night, without making his superiour Officer acquainted, upon pain of cashiering.

XVII

Keeping of the Quarters clean. – All Officers whose charge it is, shall see the Quarters kept cleane and sweet, upon pain of severe punishment.

XVIII

Letting of Horses feed in sown grounds. – None shall presume to let their Horses feed in sown Grounds whatsoever, or to endamage the Husbandman any way, upon severest punishment.

XIX

Whosoever shall in his Quarter, abuse, beat, fright his Landlord, or any Person else in the Family, or shall extort Money or Victuals, by violence from them, shall be proceeded against as a Mutineer, and an enemy to Discipline.[1]

Of Duties in Action.

I

Repairing to the Colours upon an Alarum. – No man shall fail immediately to repair unto his Colours (except he be impotent by Lamenesse or Sicknesse) when an Alarum is given, upon pain of death.

II

Flying. – No man shall abandon his Colours, or flye away in Battail, upon pain of death.

III

Flinging away Arms. – If a Pike-man throw away his pike, or a Musketteer his Musket or Bandileer, he or they shall be punished with death.

IV

Burning and wasting. – No man shall burn any House or Barn, be it of friend or foe, or willfully spoil any Corne, Hay, or Straw, or Stacks in the fields, or any Ship, Boat, Carriage, or any thing that may serve for the Provision of the Army without Order, upon paine of death.

V

Killing an Enemy who yields. – None shall kill an Enemy who yeelds, and throws down his Armes.

VI

Saving of men armed with Offensive Arms. – None shall save a man who hath his offensive Armes in his hands, upon paine of losing his Prisoner.

VII

Flinging away powder. – Whosoever in skirmish shall fling away his Powder out of his Bandileers, that he may the sooner come off, shall be punished with death.

VIII

Imbezelling of the Prey. – No Souldier shall imbezzel any part of the prey, till it be disposed of by the *Lord Generall,* or others authorized, upon pain of death.

[1] Not in the *Laws and Ordinances* issued by Essex.

IX

Concealing of Prisoners. – No Officer or Souldier shall ransome, or conceal a Prisoner, but within twelve hours shall make the same known to the *Lord Generall*, or others authorized, upon pain of death.

X

Pillaging without licence. – No man upon any good Successe, shall fall a pilaging before license, or a sign given upon pain of death.

XI

Retreating before handy-blowes. – A Regiment or Company of Horse or Foot, that chargeth the Enemy, and retreats before they come to handy-strokes, shall answer it before a Councell of War; and if the fault be found in the Officers, they shall be banished the Camp; if in the Souldiers, than every tenth man shall be punished at discretion, and the rest serve for Pioners and Scavengers, till a worthy exploit take off that Blot.

Of the Duties of Commanders and Officers in particular.

I

Commanders must see God duly served. – All Commanders are straightly charged to see Almighty God reverently served, and Sermons and Prayers duely frequented.

II

Commanders must acquaint my Lord Generall with dangerous humours. – All Commanders and Officers that finde any of discontented humors, apt to mutenize, or any swerving from direction given, or from the policy of the Army set down, shall straightway acquaint the *Lord General* therewith, or others authorized, as they will answer their neglect.

III

Defraud of Souldiers pay. – Any Officer that dare presume to defraud the Souldiers of their pay, or any part of it, shall be cashiered.

IV

Stopping of Duellers. – No Corporal, or other Officer commanding the Watch, shall willingly suffer a Souldier to go forth to a Duel, or private Fight, upon paine of death.

V

Drunken and quarrelsome Officers. – What Officers soever shall come drunk to his Guard, or shall quarrel in the Quarter, or commit any disorder, shal be cahiered without mercy; and the next Officer under him shal have his place, which he may pretend to be his right, and it shal not be refused to him.

VI

Carelesse Captains. - A Captain that is carelesse in the Training and Governing of his Company, shal be displaced of his Charge.

VII

Officers outstaying their passe. - All Captains or Officers that shall outstay their Passe, shall be punished at the *Lord Generals* discretion.

VIII

All Officers bound to part quarrels. - All Officers, of what condition soever, shal have power to part quarrels and frays, or sudaine disorders betwixt the Souldiers, though it be in any other Regiment or Company, and to commmit the disordered to prison for the present until such Officers as they belong unto are acquainted with it: And what Souldier soever shal resist, disobey, or draw his Sword against such an Officer (although he be no Officer of his Regiment or Company) shall be punished with death.

Officers non-resident in Garrison. - IX. A Captain or Officer nonresident in the place assigned him for Garrison without License, shall have one monthes pay defaulted for the first offence, and two months for the second: upon the third Offence he shal be discharged of his Command.

Cashiering of Souldiers. - X. After the Army is come to the generall Rendevous, no Captain shal cashier any Souldier that is enrolled, without speciall Warrant of the *Lord Generall.*

Mustering of false and counterfeit troops. - XI. No Captain or Officer of a Troope or Company, shal present in Musters, any but reall Troopers and Souldiers, such as by their pay are bound to follow their Colours, upon paine of cashiering without mercy. And if any Victualler, Freebooter, Enterloper, or Souldier whatsoever, of any Troop or Company, shall present himselfe, or his Horse in the Muster, to mislead the Muster-Master, and to betray the Service, the same shall be punished with death.

Commissaries of Victuals and Ammunition must be true. - XII. No Provider, Keeper or Officer of Victuall or Ammunition, shall imbezell or spoyl any part thereof, or give any false account to the *Lord Generall,* upon paine of death.

The Duty of Muster-Masters.

Muster-Masters coniving at counterfeits. - I. No Muster-Master must wittingly let any passe in the Musters, but such as are really of the Troop or Company presented, upon pain of death.

Captains must send a Roll of their men to the Lord Generall. - II. All Captaines shall cause their Troops or Companies to be full and compleat; and two dayes after the Generall Mustering, they shall send to the *Lord Generall*, a perfect List or Roll of all the Officers of their Troopes and Companies, and likewise of all the Troopers and Souldiers that are in actuall Service, putting down distinctly on the head of each man his Monthly pay.

Every Pay-day. – III. The like Roll or List shall the Captains send to the *Lord Generall*, and to the Treasurer of the Army upon every Pay-day, during the Service, with a punctuall expression at the bottome of the said Roll, what new Troopers or Souldiers have been entertained since the last Pay-day, in lieu of such as are either deceased or cashiered, and likewise the day whereon they were so cashiered and entertained.

Subscribed by all the Officers of the Troop or company. – IV. Which said List or Roll shall be subscribed, not only by the Captain and his Lieutenant and Coronet or Ensigne, but also by the Serjeants and Corporals respectively, who shall declare upon their Oath, that the Troopers and Souldiers enrolled in the said List, are reall and actual Troopers and Souldiers of the respective Troops and Companies. And whosoever shall be convicted of falshood in any of the Premises, shall be cashiered.

Muster-Masters must use no other Rols. – V. No Muster-Master shall presume to receive or accept of any Roll to make the Musters by, but the forementioned Rols, upon pain of the losse of his place, and other punishment at discretion.

Counterfeit names in the Rols. – VI. No man shall presume to present himself to the Muster, or to be inrolled in the Muster-Rols by a counterfeit name, or surname, or place of birth, upon paine of death.

Of Victuallers.

Victuallers issuing naughty Victuals. – I. No Victuallers shall presume to issue or sell unto any of the Army, unsound, unsavoury, or unwholesome Victuals, upon pain of Imprisonment, and further Arbitrary punishment.

No Souldier must be a Victualler. – II. No Souldier shall be a Victualler without the consent of the *Lord Generall*, or others authorized, upon pain of punishment at discretion.

Unseasonable hours kept by Victuallers. – III. No Victualler shall entertain any Souldier in his House, Tent, or Hut, after the Warning-piece at night, or before the beating of the *Ravalee* in the morning.

IV. No Victualler shall forestal any Victuals, nor sell them before they be appraised by the Marshal Generall, upon severe punishment.

Of Administration of Justice.

Summary Proceedings. – I. All controversies between Souldiers and their Captains, and all others, shall be summarily heard and determined by the Councell of Warre, except the weightinesse of the cause require further deliberation.

The Provost Marshall must look to his Prisoner. – II. All Officers and others who shall send up any Prisoners unto the Marshall Generall of the Army; shall likewise deliver unto the Marshall, the cause and reason of the Imprisonment: And without such cause and reason shown, the Marshal is expresly forbid to take charge of the Prisoner.[1]

III. When a Prisoner is committed to the charge of the Marshall Generall, The information of the Crime which he standeth committed for, is to be given into the Advocate of the Army, within 48 hours, after the commitment; or else for default thereof, the Prisoner to be released, except good cause be shown wherefore the Information cannot be ready within that time.

Good of the destine [sic]. – IV. The Goods of such as dye in the Army or Garrison, or be slain in the service, if they make any Will by word or writing, shall be disposed of according to their Will. If they make no Will, then they shall goe to their Wives, or next Kin. If no Wife or Kindred appeare within a year after, shall be disposed of by the appointment of the *Lord Generall,* according to Laws Civil and Military.

Civil Magistrates imprisoning Souldiers. – V. No Magistrate of Towne or Countrey, shall without License imprison any Souldier, unlesse for Capital Offences.

For debts and other small offences. – VI. In matters of Debts or Trespasse, or other inferiour cases, the Magistrate shall acquaint his Captaine, or other cheife Officer therewith, who is to end the matter with the consent of the complainant, or to leave the party grieved to take his remedy by due course of Law: And if the Officer fail of his duty therein, the *Lord Generall* upon complaint of the party grieved, will not onely see him righted, but the Officer punished for his neglect in this behalfe.

Braving the Court of Justice. – VII. No man shall presume to use any braving or menacing words, Signs, or gestures, while the Court of Justice is sitting, upon pain of death.

Receiving of Run-awayes. – VIII. No inhabitant of City, Towne, or Countrey, shall presume to receive any Souldier into his Service, or conceal, or use means to convey such Run-awayes, but shall apprehend all such, and deliver them to the Provost Marshall.

Detecting of offenders. – IX. All Captains, Officers, and Souldiers shall doe their endeavours to detect, apprehend and bring to punishment all Offenders, and shall assist the Officers of the Army for that purpose, as they will answer their slacknesse in the Marshals Court.

X. If the Marshal shall dismisse without Authority, any Prisoner committed unto his charge, or suffer him to make an escape, he shall

---

[1] Clauses ii and iii are not in the *Laws and Ordinances* issued by Essex.

be lyable to the same punishment due unto the dismissed or escaped offendor.[1]

Offences whatsoever to be punished by the Laws of war. – XI. All other Faults, Disorders, and Offences not mentioned in these Articles, shall be punished according to the general Customs and Laws of War.

AND to the end that these Lawes and Ordinances be made more publike and knowne, as well to the Officers, as to the Common Souldiers, every Colonel and Captaine is to provide some of these Bookes, and to cause them to be forthwith distinctly and audibly read in every severall Regiment, by the respective Marshals in presence of all the Officers: In the Horse Quarters by sound of Trumpet; and amongst the Foot by beat of Drum. And weekly afterwards, upon the Pay-day, every Captain is to cause the same to be read to his owne Company, in presence of his Officers. And also upon every main-Guard, the Captaine is to do the like, that none may be ignorant of the Lawes and Duties required by them.

FINIS

—(From a copy in the Bodleian Library, *Godwin Pamphlets*, vol. cxvii, 14.)

M. ORDER ESTABLISHING REGIMENTAL COURTS-MARTIAL

FROM the Head Quarters at Putney we understand of a wholesome Order by the General to prevent Misdemeanors of Soldiers in their Quarters.

That his Excellency taking notice of the manifold Abuses and Injuries committed by the rude part of Soldiers (especially where they quarter) to the great Damage and Prejudice of the People, and to no less Dishonour and Scandal of the whole Army, notwithstanding the wholesome Laws and Ordinances to the contrary made and provided, and the severe Punishments inflicted upon the known Offenders. For Reformation whereof, and for the ease of Persons, that they may not be troubled to repair to the Head Quarters for Justice, hath therefore granted Commissions, thereby enabling the Commissioners of each Regiment to sit in a Council of War so often as need shall require, and to punish Offenders according to the Laws and Ordinances of War, in as large a Measure, to all Intents and Purposes, as if the Offenders were tryed before a Council of War at the Head Quarters, except in cases extending to Life or Limb, which are to be tryed at the Head Quarters only. (Rushworth, vii, 816.)

[1] Clause x is not in the *Laws and Ordinances* issued by Essex.

N. REASONS FOR THE CONTINUANCE OF CERTAIN OFFICERS

[THE following statement was drawn up by General Monck in 1657, when the Committee for the Army appointed by the Protector's Council wished to abolish certain of the officials named for the sake of economy. The original is amongst the *Clarke MSS.* in the library of Worcester College, Oxford (vol. li, f. 21).]

Reasons for the continuance of the officers undernamed that were not in the former Establishment, but afterwards continued by perticular order, being it was thought necessary to continue them.

COMMISSARY OF PROVISIONS

I must humbly desire hee may bee continued for these reasons, that hee keepes an account of all the garrisons and feild stores in Scotland, and charges the souldiers with any provisions they receive out of either of those stores, and soe gives a note to the Treasurer, and the Auditor Generall, is a check uppon the Commissarie, soe that if you doe not continue him I doe not see how the account of provisions can bee kept right, and the Commonwealth would bee greate loosers by it, being there is greate stocks of provisions in many of the garrisons and for the feild forces.

STORE KEEPERS AT ST JOHNSTON'S, INVERNES, AND AYRE

In the last Establishment these storekeepers were left out but after wards an order granted for their continuance, being there is a nessesity of having a storekeeper where there is a magazine of provisions, the cheese, corne, and biskett to bee turned, and as they begin to decay they may bee spent, or else there will bee a greate losse to the publique, soe I shall humbly desire those 3 storekeepers may bee continued till further order.

Officers and others who were ordered to bee disbanded by your Lord-shippes orders which it is humbly desired may bee continued.

ASSISTANT TO THE QUARTERMASTER GENERALL

I humbly desire hee may bee continued, in regaurd hee is healpfull every yeare in laying out the locallities of the severall troopes for straw in the country some times six or seaven parishes are to furnish straw for a troope, lickwise for grasse in the Summer, and for quartring of the regiments at Edenbourgh and neere the headquarters,

which cannot bee well done without some body bee imployed to see itt
done, for our quarters here are not as those in England, for wee
cannot gitt straw here at any resonable rattes, the people are soe
averce; they will not send in any for the horse unles it bee laid upon
every parish, for which the souldiers pay a reasonable rate as shall bee
agreed on betweene the country and souldiers, soe that I thinke there
is a nessesity to continue them.

A DEPUTY TO THE SCOUT MASTER GENERALL

Itt is humbly desired that hee may be continued. I must confes that
there has bin as much good service done for the publique by the
intelligence I have gotten by the helpe of a Deputy Scout Master
Generall, then hath bin done by the forces in preventing of rising of
parties, soe that I thinke his Highnes' affaires in these parts cannot
well bee carried on without the helpe of such a man.

PREACHER AT EDENBURGH CASTELL

It is likewise desired that hee may bee continued, there being but one
companie in the Castle and prisoners of conserment, and the
companie being not above 70, it will not bee safe for them to goe to
sermon into the towne on the Lord's day, besides there is but two
preachers allowed for Edenburgh and Leith, [and] this Gentillman
doth often assist in those places.

PREACHER TO INVERLOUGHEE

There is likewise 8 companies commanded out of severall regiments at
Inverloughee, and there are noe Scotch Ministers for that place,
being the place is uncomfortable, and if there should not bee a
Minister allowed for it, itt would make it much more uncomfortable
then it is, being a garrison wee must continue, else wee shall not bee
able to keepe this contry in peace.

GUNSMITH

A Gunsmith to each regiment of foote is desired to bee continued,
for truly they are very usefull to the regiments in mending of their
armes, besides where regiments have any companies that are in out
garrisons where there are none to mend their armes, the Gunsmith[s]
goe and mend them, and I thinke it will not be safe soe many armes
as wee shall have to bee mended should be in the hands of Scotchmen.
Besides if wee should come to march they would bee soe usefull to us
that halfe your armes and forces would bee to seeke if wee should
want them. Soe that I doe not see how the forces here can bee without
them.

APPENDIX

APPENDIX **415**

COMISSARY OF AMUNITION AND CLARKE

You are pleased to disband all the officers of the trayne, leaving none to take care of the amunicion, guns, and other provisions fitt for a trayne. I have made bould at present to continue the Coumptroller that was, as Comisarie to the trayne, and have given him an order to receive into his charge all the severall stores that belong unto the trayne, and lickwise I have afforded him a Clarke to assist him, which two officers I thinke of nessescity your Lordshippes should allow to looke after those stores, being it is of much concernment they being carefully look't after, besides what armes the souldiers have out of the stores (unles they bee broaken in service) the souldiers pay for them, and with the monies that is payd into the Treasurer for the armes wee supply the stores heere againe, soe that of nessesity you must have a Comisary to looke after these things with a Clarke, that hee may be a check upon the Treasurer what monnies hee does receive for armes, and the Auditour Generall having a list of all that is in the stores is a check upon the Comisarie.

TENTMAKER

It is humbly desired that a tentmaker may bee continued, for there are noe men in this country that have any skill in making or mending of tents as they should doe, and wee have continuall use of them, for when our horse goe to grasse in the Summer wee are faine to give orders for the horsemen to have tents to lye by their horses for a gaurd for them, and for their security that they may not bee suppriz'd, and besides wee have occation to send those companies that to goe to Loughaber through the hills, who make use of tents in their march, soe that these tents are every yeare to bee repaired and unles this man bee continued your tents heere will bee distroyed, which since I came into Scotland I made a shift to keepe in good condition by the helpe of this Tentmaker with a very little charge, and they will bee kept in very good condition a good while if you continue him.

TWO WAGGONS, 4 WAGGONEERS, AND 10 HORSES

It is humbly desired there may bee two waggons, 4 waggoners, and 10 horses for his Highnes' service in this nation, for wee know not how to furnish our garrison of Inverloughee without wee carry our amunition and other provisions by waggon to Dunbarton, and there a short way by water to Inverloughee, which if wee should not doe wee must bee forced to hire a ship at Leith to send them about, and a ship cannot goe safely about unles there bee a man of warr to attend it, which will bee a very greate charge, besides the other garrisons of Ayre, Glasgoe, and Dunbarton cannot be furnished with amunition and other things without the helpe of these waggons, besides they are usefull in remooving the stores either from Edenburgh Castle to Leith, or from Leith to Edinburgh, or from shipboard to the stores, and many other occations which would bee to long to troble your Lordshipes withall.

THE MATTROSSES FOR AMUNITION

It is humbly desired that their may bee two mattrosses belonging to the stores of the trayne to attend for drying of powder that is decayed in Summer, helping to remove the tents, collers, and cordage to keepe them in good condition, alsoe to helpe the Comisarie in delivering out amunition to the officers that come to receive it.

MASTER GUNNER

Your Lordshippes are pleased to allow but one Master Gunner for Edinburgh Castle and Leith. They are two considerable places and I cannot see how either of these places can bee without a Master Gunner, for without them the places will bee of little use if there should bee any rising in the country. Besides the two gunners I doe intend for those places have skill in fire works, and if there should be occacion to sett up a trayne you will not gitt such men againe, besides the use they will bee of at present in those places upon all occations, and if there should bee any breaking out, if any rouges should poses a castle and stand out, one of them must bee imployed for the feild service.

ENGINEERE

There were two Engineeres allowed by the Establishment, you pleas'd to disband one of them, though one of them is now looking after the cittadell at Leith, who cannot be spared from thence this yeare and halfe, and the other is at present imployed at Mardicke, being both an Ingineer, and has [s]kill in using the morter-peece, and skilfull in fortification, and [is] now in present imployment, and truly wee want him much at present in this country for looking after the rest of the workes, soe that of nessesity, being both in imployment, they must bee continued in pay.

The whole pay of those desired will come to monthly 129$^{li.}$ 6$^{s.}$: 6$^{d.}$

CONTINGENCIES

Whereas your Lordshipps are pleased by the Establishment to allow but 1000$^{li.}$ for paying of the gunners and mattrosses of the severall garrisons, and for the works at Invernes, St Johnstons, and Ayre, and repairing both the houses and works of all other garrisons in cittadells and Castles, and furnishing of them with beds, bedcloathes, and other nessisaries, and for rent for some of them, and for baggage horses for remooving provisions from St Johnstons, Aberdeene and Invernes to the other lesser garrisons, baggage horses for the companies that goe to Inverloughee (that one garrison of Inverloughee costs us a thousand pounds by the yeare for repairing the works, houses, bedding, and other nessisaries, alsoe there is a small man of warr in Loughnes which costs us in men [and in] repairing the shipp and tackle about 100$^{li.}$ a yeare, which must of nessessity be kept to keepe the country in order, and for carring of provisions for the forces uppon occation, being upon a Lough 24 miles long), alsoe for recruites of internall and externall medicaments for the Cherurgeons of horse and foote, paying for shipping of men to Orknay, Zetland, and Mull when they are releived, intelligence, and many other incident charges, that belong to an armey which cannot well bee reconed, I shall humbly desire your Lordshippes to consider of all these charges, and that there may bee 12000li. a moneth allowed for that porpose, which truly is as litle as I can possible doe it withall, if it could be done with les I should doe it, but I humbly conceave it cannot bee done under.

Index